BLACK POWER, WHITE HEAT

BLACK POWER, WHITE HEAT

FROM SOLIDARITY POLITICS TO RADICAL CHIC

ALICE ECHOLS

OXFORD
UNIVERSITY PRESS

Oxford University Press is a department of the University of Oxford.
It furthers the University's objective of excellence in research, scholarship,
and education by publishing worldwide. Oxford is a registered trade mark of
Oxford University Press in the UK and in certain other countries.

Published in the United States of America by Oxford University Press
198 Madison Avenue, New York, NY 10016, United States of America.

© Oxford University Press 2025

All rights reserved. No part of this publication may be reproduced, stored in a retrieval system, transmitted, used for text and data mining, or used for training artificial intelligence, in any form or by any means, without the prior permission in writing of Oxford University Press, or as expressly permitted by law, by license or under terms agreed with the appropriate reprographics rights organization. Inquiries concerning reproduction outside the scope of the above should be sent to the Rights Department, Oxford University Press, at the address above.

You must not circulate this work in any other form
and you must impose this same condition on any acquirer.

CIP data is on file at the Library of Congress.

ISBN 9780197789032

DOI: 10.1093/9780197789063.001.0001

Printed by Sheridan Books, Inc., United States of America

The manufacturer's authorized representative in the EU for product safety is
Oxford University Press España S.A. of Parque Empresarial San Fernando de Henares,
Avenida de Castilla, 2 – 28830 Madrid (www.oup.es/en or product.safety@oup.com).
OUP España S.A. also acts as importer into Spain of products made by the manufacturer.

For everyone who was a part of that great "surge of promise"
Inspired by Murray Kempton's Part of Our Time

Contents

Timeline		ix
Abbreviations		xiii
Introduction		xv

PART ONE. SNCC's "DREAM INSIDE A BUBBLE"

1.	"As If You Were Free"	7
2.	Parallel Institutions and Parallel Lines	31
3.	Atlantic City	59
4.	Black Power	81

PART TWO. AFTER BLACK POWER

5.	White Radicals Chart Their Own Course	115

PART THREE. THE BLACK PANTHER PARTY'S CROSS-RACIAL SOLIDARITY

6.	Making Each Other Up	141
7.	Working Across Difference and Paying a Price	163
8.	Repression's Repercussions	183

PART FOUR. RADICAL CHIC

9.	The Cause Party	217
10.	The Great Commotion	243
11.	Tom Wolfe	263

PART FIVE. THE CHANGING FORTUNES OF CROSS-RACIAL SOLIDARITY

12. "Allies Everywhere"	297
Conclusion	343
Afterword	353
Acknowledgments	355
Notes	359
Interviews	447
Index	449

Timeline

1954: The start of Joseph McCarthy's fall: Army-McCarthy hearings

1955: Montgomery Bus Boycott
Bayard Rustin, Ella Baker, and Stanley Levison form In Friendship to support boycott

1957: Formation of Dr. King's Southern Christian Leadership Conference

1960: Sit-ins at Woolworth's, Greensboro, NC
Founding of Student Nonviolent Coordinating Committee (SNCC)
Founding of Students for a Democratic Society (SDS)

1961: Congress of Racial Equality launches Freedom Rides

1962: SDS holds first national convention and issues the Port Huron Statement

1963: 250,000 take part in the March on Washington for Jobs and Freedom
President John F. Kennedy's assassination

1964: Civil rights protests: Sheraton-Palace Hotel and Auto Row, San Francisco
Mississippi Summer Project
Bodies of Chaney, Goodman, and Schwerner, murdered by KKK, found in Mississippi
SDS launches Economic and Research Action Project (ERAP)
Democratic National Convention in Atlantic City and battle over the seating of the Mississippi Freedom Democratic Party delegation
Congress passes the Gulf of Tonkin Resolution enabling escalation of war in Vietnam
Free Speech Movement at UC–Berkeley
President Johnson beats Barry Goldwater in landslide
Civil Rights Act of 1964 signed into law

1965: Draft calls increase dramatically
Assassination of Malcolm X
SDS organizes first national march against war in Vietnam
Voting Rights Act
Watts Rebellion

TIMELINE

1966: Stokely Carmichael and Willie Ricks introduce Black Power! on Meredith March
The Black Panther Party (BPP) forms and begins armed patrols of police
Eldridge Cleaver paroled
SNCC expels white staffers

1967: Armed Panthers protest gun control bill at California state assembly
Urban uprisings in Newark and Detroit
San Francisco's Summer of Love
Huey Newton arrested for murder, spurring Free Huey! campaign
FBI expands COINTELPRO to target "Black nationalist hate groups"
National Conference for New Politics

1968: Tet Offensive erodes support for war
Robert F. Kennedy enters presidential race and President Johnson withdraws
Assassinations of Dr. King and Robert F. Kennedy
Urban uprisings in more than 100 cities after killing of Dr. King
Gun battles between Panthers and police increase
Alliance of SNCC and BPP begins and ends
Richard Nixon elected president
Eldridge Cleaver flees the United States for Cuba
Women's liberation protests of the Miss America pageant

1969: NYPD announces charges against the Panther 21
Police murders of Panthers Fred Hampton and Mark Clark in Chicago
Panthers' United Front Against Fascism Conference
Massive moratoriums to protest the war in Vietnam
SNCC holds last staff meeting
James Forman delivers "Black Manifesto" for reparations at NY's Riverside Church
Stonewall uprising helps spark gay liberation
Woodstock music festival

1970: Benefit for the Panther 21 at the Bernsteins
Weatherman's Greenwich Village townhouse bombing
Tom Wolfe's "Radical Chic: That Party at Lenny's" published in *New York*
Nixon expands war into Cambodia
Massive antiwar protests: Students killed at Kent State and Jackson State
Chicano activists turn out 30,000 to protest war in Los Angeles
Hard Hat Riot in New York City
Huey Newton wins appeal and is bailed out to huge crowds

Revolutionary People's Constitutional Conventions
Trials of the Panther 21 and Ericka Huggins and Bobby Seale begin
Jonathan Jackson and others killed in armed attack at Marin County Civic Center
Angela Davis arrested

1971: East Coast/West Coast conflict, aided by the FBI, erupts within Black Panther Party
May Day protest in Washington, DC
Juries acquit the Panther 21 and Huggins and Seale
Leaking of the Pentagon Papers further damages U.S. case for war in Vietnam
Brutal attack on the Attica prison uprising
George Jackson killed

1972: Angela Davis is acquitted
Black Panthers pivot toward electoral politics in Oakland
Feminist Equal Rights Amendment approved by Congress
Watergate break-in to aid Nixon's re-election
Nixon defeats McGovern in landslide victory

1973: Paris Peace Accords signed ending U.S. involvement in war in Vietnam
American Indian Movement occupies Wounded Knee, South Dakota
U.S. Supreme Court establishes women's right to abortion in *Roe v. Wade*
OPEC's oil embargo against United States for supporting Israel in Arab-Israeli War

1974: Watergate scandal leads President Nixon to resign
Equal Educational Opportunities Act enacted
Anti-busing riot in Boston
Huey Newton flees America for Cuba to escape murder charge
Free Joan Little Campaign

Abbreviations

AAA	Afro-American Association
ACLU	American Civil Liberties Union
BAP-UD	Beverly Axelrod Papers, University of Delaware
BOSS	Bureau of Special Services
CDGM	Child Development Group of Mississippi
CIO	Congress of Industrial Organizations
COFO	Council of Federated Organizations
COINTELPRO	Counter Intelligence Program of the FBI
CORE	Congress for Racial Equality
CPJ	Committee for Public Justice
CUBPP	Columbia University Black Panther Project
ERAP	Economic and Research Action Project
FAF	Family Aid Fund
FBI	Federal Bureau of Investigation
FOS	Friends of SNCC
FSM	Free Speech Movement
HUAC	House Unamerican Activities Committee
HZP/WHS	Howard Zinn Papers/Wisconsin Historical Society
ICCASP	Independent Citizens Committee for the Arts, Sciences, and Professions
IPC	Indochinese Peace Campaign
IPS	Institute for Policy Studies
JSP/NYPL	Jean Stein Papers/New York Public Library
LAT	Los Angeles Times
LBC-LOC	Leonard Bernstein Collection, Library of Congress
LCFO	Lowndes County Freedom Organization
LNS	Liberation News Service
MAP	Mississippi Action for Progress
MCAR	Michigan Committee Against Repression
MFDP	Mississippi Freedom Democratic Party

NAACP	National Association for the Advancement of Colored People
NCASF	National Council of American-Soviet Friendship
NCCLU	North Carolina Civil Liberties Union
NCNP	National Conference for New Politics
NLG	National Lawyers Guild
NOI	Nation of Islam
NSA	National Student Association
NUCFAD	National United Committee to Free Angela Davis
N-VAC	Nonviolent Action Committee
NYPD	New York Police Department
NYRB	*New York Review of Books*
NYT	*New York Times*
OEO	Office of Economic Opportunity
PL	Progressive Labor Party
RAM	Revolutionary Action Committee
SAJGAP-UMSCRC	Stew Albert and Judy Gumbo Albert Papers, University of Michigan Special Collections Research Center
SBDC	Soledad Brothers Defense Committee
SCEF	Southern Conference Educational Fund
SCLC	Southern Christian Leadership Conference
SDS	Students for a Democratic Society
SIM	Student Interracial Ministry
SKP-UI	Seymour Krim Papers, Special Collections, University of Iowa
SLDC	Sleepy Lagoon Defense Committee
SNCC	Student Nonviolent Coordinating Committee
SSAC	Soul Students Advisory Council
SSOC	Southern Student Organizing Committee
TWP/NYPL	Tom Wolfe Papers, New York Public Library
UAW	United Auto Workers
UFW	United Farm Workers
WHS	Wisconsin Historical Society
YIP and YIPPIE	Youth International Party

Introduction

It felt like a turning point. Suddenly, masses of angry Americans were taking to the streets in protests that just exploded, seemingly out of nowhere. Making this all the more remarkable, the country was still in the depths of a pandemic lockdown, with no end in sight. That summer, the summer of 2020, between 15 and 26 million Americans participated in demonstrations, some of them day after day. It had the look of solidarity—that is, of unity across difference.

Igniting the protests was the May 25 murder of George Floyd, a Black resident of Minneapolis, Minnesota, whom police arrested for using a fake $20 bill to buy a pack of cigarettes. What made his murder so devastatingly incomprehensible was the sadistic casualness with which it was carried out. For nearly 10 minutes, the handcuffed Floyd was pinned to the ground, with the full weight of a white policeman's knee firmly planted on his neck. A bystander, 17-year-old Darnella Frazier, recorded Floyd's murder, including his choked cries. She posted the video to Facebook and Instagram, where it went viral instantly.

The reaction was immediate and fierce. More than 1,000 racial justice demonstrations occurred during the first two weeks. In a departure from previous antiracist protests, these were geographically widespread, breaking out in more than 40 percent of all counties in the United States. Something else setting them apart was the participation of whites. Nearly 95 percent of counties reporting protests were majority white. Many of the journalists providing commentary took note of the protests' size and intensity, but they were especially struck by their racial composition.[1]

Scholars knowledgeable about the Black freedom movement soon weighed in. Keeanga Yamahtta Taylor called the protests "stunning in their racial solidarity." She saw in them evidence of a movement with "firm political foundations," which she attributed to the work of Black Lives Matter (BLM).[2] Some scholars believed the protests vindicated Dr. Martin Luther King Jr.'s faith in the arc of the moral universe, that it was bending toward justice.[3] The journalist Nikole Hannah-Jones, the creator of the pioneering 1619 Project, was less certain about King's arc, but she nonetheless believed 2020 was a watershed moment. "Unlike so many times in the past, in which Black people mostly marched and protested alone," she wrote, "in 2020, a multiracial and multigenerational protest army braved a pandemic and took to the streets."[4]

Many Americans would have agreed with the sociologist Douglas McAdam, who ventured that the country seemed to be at "a social change tipping point."[5] Polls showing that 67 percent of Americans supported BLM suggested the country was experiencing a "racial reckoning," maybe even going "woke."[6] City councils and states acted, passing laws banning chokeholds, such as the one that killed Floyd. In New York, legislators repealed a law that kept police disciplinary records secret. In Minneapolis, city council members went further, pledging to develop an alternative public safety agency to replace its police department. Donations to BLM went through the roof, as the group took in $90 million in 2020 alone. A year after the protests started, 261 corporations had pledged more than $67 million to BLM. Throughout the corporate world and institutions of higher education, departments of diversity, equity, and inclusion (DEI) were launched or expanded.[7] The election of Joe Biden that November seemed to confirm that this was a true hinge moment. During the campaign, Biden admitted that he had wrongly assumed that in electing Barack Obama its president in 2008 the nation had shown that racism was a thing of the past. Now, he said, the scales were falling away from his eyes, just as they were for many other whites.[8]

But then, our national reckoning receded, before slowly disappearing, mirage-like. That one-time engine of protest, BLM, fractured, becoming a shadow of its former self.[9] Then came the 2024 election in which Republicans succeeded in peeling away millions of voters of color from the Democrats in a shift that aided Donald Trump's return to the White House. Our country's rightward lurch, whatever its specific causes, is part of a global phenomenon, which in time may reverse itself. But the hopefulness that progressives felt about racial solidarity just five short years ago is nowhere in sight. In retrospect, the odds of a durable multiracial movement taking hold in the wake of 2020 were slight because participation was both too easy and too hard. For performative allies interested in virtue signaling, taking part was a mere keystroke away. By contrast, committed allies were expected to abide by a set of rules so restrictive they amounted to what one critic called "a series of impossible tasks."[10]

I could catalog the explanations others have advanced for the great fizzle of 2020, but I prefer to focus instead on one understudied factor: the past. More specifically, I want to zero in on the collective fables that too often pass for the history of the freedom movement of the sixties.[11] Many readers will recall that BLM put itself forward as a determined break with the past, "not your grandfather's civil-rights movement."[12] As protests rocked the country in 2020, conservatives seized on this, assailing BLM for breaking with the gospel of colorblindness supposedly preached by Dr. Martin Luther King Jr.

Scholars quickly called out the right's distortion of King's actual record, which was one of solid support for race-conscious policies. Yet no one disputed the right's other line of attack, this one targeting BLM's allies. Senator Tom Cotton led the charge, claiming that they were part of a liberal elite who, "in the spirit of radical chic," turned a blind eye to the protestors' "orgy of violence."[13] Cotton was criticized for his characterization of the protests, but not for his description of BLM's supporters. Some readers would have known that "radical chic" was a phrase popularized by the journalist Tom Wolfe a half century earlier in his famous send-up of a 1970 benefit for the Black Panthers at the Manhattan penthouse of Leonard and Felicia Bernstein.

Before long, the problem wasn't racist policing, but the effort to change it, which the right framed as radical chic 2.0. Indeed, the phrase is there on page one of the foreword to the Heritage Foundation's *Project 2025*. Its author, Kevin D. Roberts, the foundation's president, opens with an attack on today's elites for having "repurposed the worst ingredients of the 1970s 'radical chic' to build a totalitarian cult known today as 'The Great Awokening.'" Roberts's solution was for conservatives to unite against wokeness as they had in the seventies against "radical chic," the shallow, but destructive trendiness of radical causes among the liberal elite.[14]

By the time Project 2025 was released in spring 2023, wokeness already had plenty of detractors, and from across the political spectrum. Even some leftish critics, while rejecting Roberts's critique, accepted the central presumptions in "Radical Chic"—the insincerity of liberal elites and the fraudulent, charade-like character of Black–white solidarity.[15] This idea has now become stubbornly attached, burr-like, to our collective memory of the sixties and 2020.

Black Power, White Heat: From Solidarity Politics to Radical Chic pushes back against this version of the past in the first substantive history of the interracial and cross-racial collaborations forged by Blacks and whites in the freedom movement of the sixties.[16] The people at the center of this book chose to work across difference in fighting racism, and in a way that acknowledged the significance of racial identity and the necessity of coming together around shared commitments and values.

I tell this story by focusing on two militant, Black-led organizations that bookend the sixties: the Student Nonviolent Coordinating Committee (SNCC, pronounced Snick) and the Black Panther Party for Self-Defense. Both groups worked with whites, but in distinct ways that reveal the shifting modes of solidarity as the sixties unfolded. They even joined forces briefly. *Black Power, White Heat* also pays careful attention to how solidarity lost credibility, with assistance from the Federal Bureau of Investigation (FBI) and the writer Tom Wolfe, who appropriated the leftish term "radical chic," remaking it into a tool that conservatives deployed against those to their left. Still, even as Black–white solidarity lost steam, it was not entirely played out. In some of the era's most high-profile political trials, juries, most of which were predominantly white, were educated by Black defendants and their lawyers about the workings of racism. Courtrooms became sites of solidarity as juries returned verdicts that suggested they trusted defendants such as Black Panther Afeni Shakur more than the district attorneys prosecuting them.

Black Power, White Heat is a people-centered history, though not everyone it features will be familiar to readers, even those well-versed in the literature on the freedom movement. In telling this story, I have cast the net widely to include self-declared radicals who put themselves directly in danger's way and liberals who were often ridiculed as nothing more than dabblers in radical chic.[17] Writing a check, penning a sympathetic article, even hosting a benefit may seem tame, but these were risky activities capable of triggering an FBI investigation or a raid on one's home by the local police. Even if some of the people in my book were "awkward allies," clueless "comrades," and even dilettantes, their contributions made a difference.[18] Admittedly, not everyone in the freedom struggle appreciated their participation, but one notable radical did. It was Ella Baker, mentor to the young radicals of SNCC, who advocated that they build a broad movement, one roomy enough for what she called the "matron in the fur coat."[19]

To be clear, I do not shy away from the complexity that marked partnerships between those who were racially privileged and those who were not. Solidarity was (and is) very tough going. The historian Robin D. G. Kelley supports solidarity, but he has emphasized its difficulties, calling it "not natural."[20] How could it feel otherwise when activists are shaped by the very asymmetries of power they are opposing? It is, as others have pointed out, the central paradox at the heart of solidarity. It is why so many of the questions that bedeviled activists in the sixties, beginning with the very meaning of solidarity, are still being debated today. Is it "the choice to bump up against other people . . . and allow oneself to be changed by the impact," as the scholar and activist Mie Inouye describes it? If it is, must both people be open to change? And what best serves solidarity, intimacy or distance, an identification with differently situated people or the recognition of our different locations?[21]

Whatever its current political relevance, *Black Power, White Heat* is first and foremost a scholarly study of solidarity that emphasizes its considerable consequences for the Black freedom movement and for the intersecting left-wing causes that made up what was called the "Movement."[22] Briefly, the interracialism that activists first championed set the freedom movement on a particular course, most decisively with 1964's Mississippi Summer Project. America's most ambitious experiment in solidarity, the Project, also known as "Freedom Summer," brought nearly 1,000 mostly white college students to Mississippi. There, they were meant to act as a shield for activists registering disenfranchised Black voters. One of its architects, SNCC leader Robert (Bob) Parris Moses, believed the Project would instigate what he called an "annealing process" that would generate a "white heat" capable of remolding Mississippi and the entire nation.[23]

That summer's white heat set in motion changes that eventually remade Mississippi. But more immediately, it reshaped SNCC, and in ways that altered the possibilities for solidarity down the line. As Black Power took shape, many of the group's Black staffers rejected the interracialism they had once believed was the truly radical solution to American racism. The shift toward Black nationalism, with its mandate that white activists organize their own communities, reverberated powerfully. It recalibrated the freedom movement and helped to build out what we think of as "the sixties," as other protest movements, from women's liberation to antiwar draft resistance, took off.

SNCC's nationalist turn and its expulsion of whites in late 1966 was transformative, but it was not the end of the road for Black–white collaborations in the Movement. By 1968, the Black Panther Party of Oakland, California, was advancing its own unique brand of "revolutionary nationalism," which advocated working with white supporters. Rejecting the prevailing separatist version of nationalism and working with white-majority groups such as Students for a Democratic Society (SDS) and the Communist Party (CP) made the Panthers a top priority of the FBI and antagonized rival nationalist groups, including SNCC. The party's outlier position helped to set it on a certain course, which, in turn, had ramifications for the broader Movement.

This is the briefest of outlines, but it suggests the broad narrative arc of how solidarity played out in the sixties. It hints at something else, too: that the interracial and cross-racial solidarity I foreground in these pages constitutes its own distinct history, one that goes some way toward rewriting the sixties.

There are no simple takeaways in *Black Power, White Heat*, which I would characterize as both sobering and exhilarating. Whether activists were fighting shoulder to shoulder and interracially, or, with the rise of Black Power, partnering at arm's length and cross-racially, their collaborations were thrilling *and* heartbreaking, effective *and* fraught.

****

Black Power, White Heat goes against the current in several ways. When it comes to the freedom movement of the sixties, there have been two broad waves of historical research. The earliest histories were groundbreaking. However, they often lavished attention on leaders, routinely shortchanging the everyday Black Americans, particularly the women, who were so essential to the movement's success.[24] In these accounts, America swiftly acknowledged the error of its ways, or at least the error of the South's ways, and victory was secured.[25] Some accounts made it seem as if the movement's complex history boiled down to "Rosa sat down, Martin stood up, and the white kids came down and saved the day," as one-time SNCC staffer Julian Bond jokingly put it.[26] Bond's satiric rendering of movement history could have also included a swipe at Black Power militants because that was also a pretty standard feature of much of this work. Nostalgic for interracialism and condemnatory of Black Power, this first wave helped to generate the idea that the period could usefully be divided into the "Good Sixties" and the "Bad Sixties."[27]

Over the past thirty-odd years, historians have produced a counternarrative.[28] What the work of this second wave shares, in a sharp break with older scholarship, is a deep appreciation of Black Power and its close cousin, Black nationalism.[29] It has revealed that SNCC, so often romanticized as an idealistic group enveloped in Christian love, was riven from early on. Yes, SNCC people sang "Kumbaya," and Bob Moses once discussed the workings of power using the example of Frodo in *The Lord of the Rings*.[30] Yet even before Freedom Summer, SNCC's dual commitments—to Black self-determination and interracialism—were sometimes at odds.[31] As for the Black Panther Party, newer histories have departed decisively from the older narrative that pathologized its members as "gun-toting thugs."[32] They have examined the party's community survival programs and its attempt to meld communism and nationalism. This new wave is concerned with solidarity, too, but among activists of color, often across the globe.[33]

This newer approach has remade the field, and my study builds on it.[34] Yet every revisioning necessarily creates new silences.[35] This newer body of scholarship, with some important exceptions, often frames SNCC's efforts at working interracially as naïve and futile and assumes, too readily, that once SNCC's white activists were definitively shown the door in late 1966, white activists' participation in the freedom movement—both as a reality and as a concern—became a nonissue.[36] What happened was more complicated.

Black Power, White Heat further reveals that one underappreciated virtue of solidarity was that in bringing together people from disparate backgrounds, it encouraged an openness to unconventional approaches. For example, SNCC's pioneering effort to sidestep the mainstream and create counter-institutions, including 1964's Mississippi Freedom Democratic Party (MFDP), was a collaborative effort that included a white Jewish sociologist. Ernst Borinski, a German Jew who fled Nazi Germany in 1938, taught in the United States at Tougaloo College, an historically Black college. It was in Borinski's class that Black students first learned about the concept of "parallel institutionalism" that would soon come to life during 1964's Freedom Summer.[37]

Even at the height of Black Power, the Black Panther Party built coalitions with white radicals. It also drew upon the skills of supportive professionals, most of them white sympathizers. There were movement attorneys, whose innovative and self-consciously radical lawyering resulted in numerous legal victories. Whether they were using the voir dire process, questioning jurors about their values and beliefs to minimize the racism of juries, providing friendship to their incarcerated clients, or acting illegally as couriers, these mostly white lawyers were highly effective. Aiding their efforts were the journalists who challenged the government's depiction of "the facts" in movement cases. Also crucial were book editors at some of America's biggest trade presses who made possible the publication of books by Stokely Carmichael (Kwame Ture), Angela Davis, and Huey Newton, among others. For the Panther leadership, making a buck or even a lot of bucks was not synonymous with selling out. It turned to a white radical and student of economic history, who served as the party's financial advisor, negotiating book contracts, managing the investment portfolio of the party's corporate spin-off, and forging connections between Panthers and radical activists and leaders at home and abroad.

My consideration of money, and the people contributing it, represents another way in which *Black Power, White Heat* breaks with most scholarly accounts of the freedom movement. Money and moneyed left-wingers have received little attention despite the fact that donors gave the Movement a much larger imprint than it otherwise would have had. Take the activist and donor Stanley Sheinbaum and his wife, Betty, daughter of Warner Brothers' Harry Warner. Their money propped up several left-wing periodicals, including *Ramparts*, the magazine whose coverage of the Vietnam War helped to turn Dr. King into a dove. Another key supporter was Bert Schneider, the white Hollywood producer behind *Easy Rider*, the *Monkees*, and the anti–Vietnam War documentary, *Hearts and Minds*. Schneider was an unapologetic hedonist, yet at points he almost singlehandedly bankrolled his good friend Huey Newton and the Panthers.

Most sixties histories typically sidestep the meaningfulness of money, preferring to emphasize theoretical and strategic breakthroughs and repositionings. Yet movements have bills to pay, and not just for bail, court costs, and lawyers' fees. There are staff salaries, demonstration permits, and communications operations, which can encompass everything from telephones and printing presses to automobiles. SNCC's field offices and projects ran on a shoestring, but they still required money ... and fast cars, 23 of which were provided at cost in 1964 by a Black United Auto Workers local in Detroit.[38] Curiously, money was a perennial problem for SNCC in a way that it was not for the Panthers, despite the latter's chants of "Off the pigs" and more. Inside both organizations, money could be controversial, as critics argued that even supposedly no-strings-attached donations might act as a brake on radicalism. Eventually, conservative opponents launched their own attack on this left-liberal network of financial support for the freedom movement.

Money is obviously central to the story of the 1970 fundraiser for New York's Panther 21, which the trendy "new journalist" Tom Wolfe crashed and famously skewered. Wolfe's "Radical Chic" is a brilliant piece of snark, whose accuracy has been assumed rather than proven.[39] Wolfe did justice to that evening's canapes, but little else. "Radical Chic" became a foundational text for the emergent political formation called neoconservatism. It was usefully deployed in Nixon's 1972 re-election campaign. Reprinted time and again, most recently in 2024, it is one of the most enduring pieces of writing from the sixties. *Black Power, White Heat* offers the first substantial analysis of the discourse of "radical chic" and reveals Wolfe's remarkable indifference to the factual as well as his long-standing, but then, little-known loathing of the left.[40] After its publication in 1970, deep-pocketed liberals were more likely to provoke cynicism, even contempt, and in a way that wealthy conservatives did not, and do not.

In delegitimizing liberalism, Wolfe's "Radical Chic" cast a long shadow over our understanding of liberalism. There is no denying that in the sixties liberals often were over-cautious. Liberal Democrats were complicit in the Cold War anticommunism that rationalized the escalation of the war in Vietnam. Moreover, their timid approach to civil rights led many of the people I study here—even moderates—to regard them as the mushy and unreliable middle of American politics. By 1966, when the left-wing folk singer Phil Ochs began performing his satirical song, "Love Me, I'm a Liberal," he captured the view of many of his audience members: Liberalism was synonymous with hypocrisy.[41] Their disdain only grew as the decade dragged on and as some liberals made themselves over into neoconservatives as they repositioned themselves as critics, even opponents of the Movement.

Recent historical scholarship on this period has also been sharply critical of liberalism, treating it as almost indistinguishable from conservatism, particularly in its approach to racism.[42] *Black Power, White Heat* confirms but also complicates this interpretation. First, liberalism was not monolithic. In the early sixties, radicals and liberals were not always at loggerheads. For a brief time, the relationship between young radicals and left-leaning liberals was sometimes "creative and energizing."[43] Even later in the decade, liberals did not move in lockstep. For example, Democratic President Lyndon Johnson, angry that 1968's Kerner Commission Report blamed white racism for urban rebellions or "riots," did his best to entirely ignore it. His vice-president, Hubert Humphrey, who headed up the Democratic ticket that year, also ignored the report, choosing instead to focus on fighting crime, not racism. Yet liberals outside the Johnson administration largely supported the report's findings. And as the decade progressed, some liberals moved to the left. After Richard Nixon won the presidential election of 1968, left-leaning liberals pushed harder against the war and came out against his administration's campaign to "doom" dissident domestic groups such as the Black Panthers.[44]

Finally, *Black Power, White Heat* aims to dispense with the usual victims and perpetrators, saints and villains who sometimes populate accounts of the sixties. All the people involved in the freedom movement—Black and non-Black, activists in the trenches, and those who supported them at a distance—are best seen as what the memory studies scholar Michael Rothberg calls "implicated subjects."⁴⁵ After all, no one moves through this world entirely outside power relations. Who doesn't wield power, even if only fleetingly or even habitually against those with fewer resources and less power?

Embracing the idea of the implicated subject can move us past the terrain of idealization and vilification. Much has been written about the inability of white activists to grasp their Black counterparts fully and on their own terms. In his first meaningful interaction with left-wing whites, the Black writer and SNCC staffer Julius Lester recalled feeling bewildered and troubled by their presumption of a shared history. Lester was still a teenager, and he found their company "flattering, yet disturbing, because they talked without any awareness that I had not spent summers on Martha's Vineyard." He wondered, "Why didn't I exist as vividly for them as they did for me?"⁴⁶

The obliviousness Lester described grows out of a kind of entitled incuriousness, but it is not uniquely white. Take the case of the Black Panthers who fled America for Algiers, where, as self-declared revolutionaries, they were welcomed and fully subsidized by the government. The struggle for Algerian independence had inspired them, but once in Algiers the Panthers reportedly acted as if they were "free agents, able to deploy the powers of protest and the media as they wished," with little concern for how it affected their hosts. In their obliviousness to the people around them, they behaved like many Americans abroad. Even after having spent some time in Algeria, their knowledge of the country was still largely based on what they had picked up from the film *The Battle of Algiers* and Frantz Fanon's *The Wretched of the Earth*.⁴⁷

✺✺✺✺

My decision to embark upon this project dates to 2018, when I was teaching an undergraduate course about the sixties and the discussion turned to the Panthers and their community survival programs. When asked how they funded these programs, I mentioned that they were partially funded by donations from liberals, including their Hollywood supporters. Later that day, one of my students emailed me, crestfallen, to say I had destroyed her image of the Panthers. How could they have taken money from *liberals*? Hers was a head-shaking email that left me wondering if she believed that it would have been better had the Panthers refused these donations, even if it meant that tens of thousands of Black schoolkids would have missed out on the group's free hot breakfasts.

It was this exchange that led me to think about the Panthers, money, liberals, and eventually, much more.

There is also a much longer backstory to *Black Power, White Heat*. In the summer of 1969, I lived a small piece of the story I tell in this book. Just before heading off to college, I was a part of a Quaker-sponsored project meant to fight racism in a white suburb of Washington, DC. The idea of tackling the problem of racism where it lived—in white communities—had been kicking around left-wing quarters for nearly a decade, not that I knew that. The five of us who volunteered were still teenagers and not well-versed in the volatile world of late-sixties radicalism. By contrast, the person directing our project was active in the leading new left group, SDS. I doubt that any of the five of us knew that just a couple of days before our project began SDS had imploded as rival factions battled each other.

This matters to the story I tell in this book because those factions—Weatherman and the Progressive Labor Party (PL)—had different views of solidarity. The militants of Weatherman fancied themselves the new John Browns, providing support troops for Black revolutionaries. PL, a youthful Maoist spin-off from the Communist Party, was convinced that the (mostly white) working class was America's revolutionary base, and it counted on the curative, antiracist effects of class struggle.[48] Our director appeared unable to make up her mind just which way the wind was blowing.

It played out strangely. You might have thought that we would try to connect with people at local churches and community centers. But for our first couple of weeks, we drove to nearby 7-11's and McDonald's, where we were on the lookout for white, working-class teenaged boys loitering outside. Once we spotted boys with a suitably delinquent look, we descended upon them with mimeographed flyers promising groovy films, soft drinks, and "rapping," as in "telling it like it is" at our house. The one night any kids ever showed up at our place, which was adjacent to the Friends meeting house, we were watching Emile de Antonio's anti–Vietnam War film, *In the Year of the Pig*. They left in short order, Cokes in hand.

The premise of our project, as I understood it, was that if we could stem the tide of racism growing in white working-class suburbs, we would be acting as an auxiliary to the Black freedom movement. It was the logic of solidarity. You might think that our whiteness provided some sort of entrée to the world of those teenaged boys, but whiteness created a bridge to nowhere. It wasn't only that our group was predominantly female, middle class, and decidedly hippieish; it was that we had nothing to offer them but stale rhetoric. What was in it for them? It was not as if our project was connected to, say, a local unionization drive meant to bring together workers over the racial divide. I later learned that the Weatherman faction had their sights on white, working-class teenaged boys (they called them "the grease") because they believed they harbored antigovernment feelings that could be harnessed for the group's revolutionary ends.[49]

After our 7–11 outreach campaign failed, we went to nearby College Park, Maryland, where we tried to talk skeptical university administrators in the admissions office into letting us lead antiracist workshops during their orientation sessions for incoming freshmen. When they nixed our plans, we pivoted to the city. We tagged along as our director, increasingly weary of her teenage charges, made the rounds of familiar DC haunts, mostly the SDS house and its printshop. One evening a visiting Weatherman dignitary—if memory serves, Bill Ayers—lectured a group of us about next steps for the Movement. If you're serious about supporting the Panthers, he sneered, his head slightly cocked, it's time to pick up the gun.[50]

Our plans did shift, but not in accordance with Weatherman's strategy. Instead, we walked picket lines, first at Union Station, where the city's cab-drivers were conducting a one-day strike, and then at Anacostia's Curtis Brothers Furniture Store, where Black truck drivers were on strike. We spent a few weeks at Curtis Brothers, where an enormous 4,600-pound mahogany chair, designed a decade earlier to attract shoppers, loomed over the parking lot and us.[51]

It turned out that in joining these picket lines at Curtis Brothers we were a part of PL's campaign to build a "worker–student alliance." I only discovered this recently through an article in DC's radical or "underground" newspaper. I also learned that union truck drivers honored the strike and that the number of shoppers had sharply declined.[52] Typically, PL emphasized how solidarity of this sort usefully broke down barriers.[53] The experience of connecting across difference was undeniably powerful, although not so powerful that I swore off college that fall. When our project ended, did PL supply replacements or were strikers left to walk the picket line alone?

That summer was a dizzying, directionless blur. What had happened to our original plan of fighting racism in the nearby white communities? I don't recall ever discussing it. Talk now centered on Weatherman's upcoming Days of Rage action, which promised battling it out with the police in the streets of Chicago, in part to prove to white working-class kids that these white radicals were scrappy streetfighters, not wimpy students. Weatherman could say that this was an action taken in solidarity with the Panthers, but the Illinois Panthers repudiated it. Nor was there much enthusiasm among young white radicals for this action, which is doubtless why I found myself buttonholed by a Weatherman eager to recruit me.

I realized then that if the next step in my radicalism required that I shed my supposedly white, middle-class inhibitions about violence, I would steer clear of Weatherman. This was less a question of principle than it was a matter of self-preservation. In the years (and decades) to come, I participated in plenty of progressive marches, protests, and projects, but I did not become a revolutionary or even a full-time, dedicated activist.

My memories of that summer—walking those hot picket lines, visiting SDS's house with its ironic "Eat Shit, 10 Million Flies Can't Be Wrong!" graffiti, driving around in search of the so-called grease, learning up close what counted as radical—have never gone away. The experience left me with a lifetime of wondering how this thing—social change—*ever* happens. Deepening my bemusement was the way the Movement continued falling apart as the government cracked down on dissent and some radicals gave up entirely on movement building. Why bother with winning people over or taking part in coalitions of the not-quite-like-minded when you and your tiny group could claim yourselves the vanguard that would ignite the revolution? For people in this camp—and they were a minority, though a headline-grabbing one—the immediate task became manifesto writing and target practice.

Many Movement people came to regret the fantasy of revolutionary armed struggle, including the one-time Panther firebrand Eldridge Cleaver. It was 1976, and Cleaver, once the most militant of all the Panthers, had returned to America after eight long years in exile. Cleaver had rocketed to fame as the author of the 1968 memoir, *Soul on Ice*, in which he wrote about politics, his life behind bars and, more controversially, his past as a rapist. After returning to the States, he mentioned to journalists that he had read and been deeply affected by the feminist Susan Brownmiller's recent book, *Against Our Will: Men, Women, and Rape*. *The Phil Donahue Show* promptly booked the two for a joint segment.

As the two walked onto the set together, Cleaver muttered to Brownmiller, "Uh-oh, white women in polyester, they're your people." Yet once Cleaver turned on his outsized charm, they were his people, and Brownmiller, who came across as uncompromising and arrogant, was toast. "Have *you* been raped?" someone shouted at her. In the green room later, Brownmiller reports that everyone, even Cleaver, felt devastated by the audience's treatment of her. "He looked at me gravely," Brownmiller recalled. "'Don't make the mistake I made,'" he warned her. "'Don't get too far ahead of your people.'"[54]

By this point, Cleaver was already backing away from the left, but there is no reason to think he was being disingenuous. He knew from experience how difficult it is to find that sweet spot, between leaving people behind and being left behind. Panther cofounder Huey Newton had already conceded several years earlier that the party, in conceiving of itself as a revolutionary vanguard, had likely gotten ahead of itself, with the assistance of white radicals.[55]

Getting ahead of "your people" was not just a problem for the Black radicals of SNCC and the Black Panther Party. Dr. King lost support as he moved to the left, organizing a multiracial movement of poor people, and coming out against the war in Vietnam. As for the white radicals in and around SNCC and the Panthers, many of whom grew up middle class, their alienation from their roots ensured that many of them operated at a remove from their origins. In the late sixties when multiracial crowds of progressives shouted "power to the people" the people they hoped to mobilize were the marginalized and downtrodden. In time, the ranks of the oppressed would expand to include women and sexual minorities, but they would constrict when it came to members of the white working class, some of whom were already rightward bound. It is not too surprising, then, that many Americans felt little if any affinity with the Movement.

It is sobering from the vantage point of 2025 to consider how little progress left-liberal activists have made in figuring out how to reach American voters who see the world differently than they do.[56] Reversing this situation requires knowing something about what happened when activists tried uniting across difference six decades ago. As the scholars Karen E. Fields and Barbara J. Fields have pointed out, in a useful tweak of a famous saying, "those who do not learn from history will have no idea what they are repeating."[57]

PART ONE

SNCC's "Dream Inside a Bubble"

Part One: Introduction

The new decade was only a month old when a group of Black students took a stab at cracking the South's "wall of Never."[1] On February 1, 1960, four freshmen at North Carolina's Agricultural and Technical State University, an historic Black university in Greensboro, sat down at their local Woolworth's lunch counter and ordered coffee. They behaved as though this was customary, an everyday occurrence. The students did not declare it a sit-in; they just placed their order and did not budge after the staff refused to serve them. Their action built on decades of activism that historians call the "long civil rights movement."[2] Nearly 20 years earlier, civil rights activists pioneered this effective "stool-sitting technique," which reliably brought business to an unprofitable halt.[3] The four Black students did not know this history, but they did know that segregation was evil. It had to end right now, "not in a minute, not after this one more committee meets, not after we have the legal defense and the court costs promised."[4]

By the end of that first week, more than 400 students, almost all of them Black, had participated in the sit-in.[5] By year's end, nearly 70,000 students had taken part in a sit-in or marched in support, with the result that parts of the upper South took important steps toward desegregation. Something else happened. Just two months after that first sit-in, during Easter weekend 1960, those sit-in students formed a loosely knit organization, the Student Nonviolent Coordinating Committee (SNCC).

SNCC was the taproot of sixties radicalism, pushed forward by an audacity that attracted sharecroppers and college students alike. Building parallel or alternative institutions, putting your body on the line, and engaging in personal politics—what was called "living in the solution"—were first practiced in SNCC, even if they were popularized by other sixties' movements.[6] Much of what gave SNCC its aura of newness was its interracialism. The students of SNCC often spoke of the "beloved community," the integrationist ideal of Black and white together.⁷ They chose as their logo one Black hand and one white hand clasped in a handshake.

Yet during those first months as SNCC was taking shape, its interracialism was largely theoretical. Its members had virtually no experience collaborating across the color line. They also had little experience working across intraracial divides, including those rooted in region, education, and class. One sees this in their response to newcomer Robert (Bob) Parris Moses, who would soon loom large in SNCC. Moses had little firsthand knowledge of the South, except for the time when his involvement in an Alan Freed rock'n'roll concert tour (as the tutor of teenaged R&B star Frankie Lymon) took him there. When SNCC people first met Moses in 1960, they found him odd, and not just because he suggested SNCC work with a white couple suspected of being communists. What most perplexed them was why this bespectacled, "hyperintellectual Yankee" wanted to attach himself to *their* struggle. The 26-year-old set off a kind of cognitive dissonance. "We knew why we were doing these things," recalled Julian Bond. "We lived in the part of the country where segregation was rampant." But Bob Moses? He was a Harvard-educated Northern Black who taught at New York's elite Horace Mann School. "So why would he care?"⁸

Over the years, many more "outsiders," some Black and some not, made their way to SNCC. Although the group's apprehensions about outsiders receded at points, they never entirely went away. Are they really one of us? Are they as invested as us, and how might their participation alter SNCC's alchemy and goals? Those questions were never too far from the surface, even as the categories of "us" and "them" shifted.

Nonetheless, during SNCC's early years, people managed to keep their anxieties about outsiders mainly at bay. Working across difference and working interracially prevailed. Given the profound separateness of Black and white America at mid-century, it is remarkable that SNCC succeeded in transforming itself into an interracial community. SNCC's beloved community grew into far more than a rhetorical gesture. If integration was a key goal, then you lived together, thought together, slept together, and battled racism together. Staff meetings could not begin until people greeted each other in what white worker Mary King calls "emphatic rocking embraces, wrapping our arms around each other in bear hugs." In those years, there were "never any wan handshakes or limp greetings at SNCC meetings."[9]

SNCC was a contentious group in which everything was up for debate. Meetings went on forever, sometimes for days, but in the process, barriers often melted away. To Black staffer Stokely Carmichael, SNCC felt "like a dream inside a bubble," one in which "race, class, and indeed even gender did not really matter."[10] White staffer Bob Zellner was transformed by his years in the group, which led him, he said, to see the world through Black eyes. His experience was not unique. "There were people who came South to work in the movement who were not Black," remembers Black staffer Bernice Johnson Reagon. "Most of them were white when they came. Before it was over, that category broke up."[11]

How did SNCC pull this off when virtually nothing in the background of these young people prepared them for bridging such deep differences? And how sustainable was its interracialism?

ONE

"As If You Were Free"

Frequently called the "shock troops" of the Black freedom movement, the Student Nonviolent Coordinating Committee (SNCC) nonviolently "softened up" and pried open the South.¹ Its members developed a reputation for their willingness to go to the brink, as they did during 1961's Freedom Rides. The Congress for Racial Equality (CORE) first organized racially mixed groups to travel on buses to the South to challenge the nonenforcement of the recent Supreme Court ruling declaring segregated facilities for interstate passengers illegal. After horrific violence led CORE to call them off, SNCC workers kept the Freedom Rides alive. Over a three-month period, more than 300 student activists were jailed for participating. In November 1961, the Interstate Commerce Commission issued new rules that desegregated Southern transportation facilities. Although compliance remained uneven, many regarded it as a victory for the movement.² The Freedom Rides did more than just dismantle a key part of Jim Crow; they shifted consciousness within Black America. "Little kids would just look up at me and say, 'There's goes a Freedom Rider,'" recalled Bob Moses of his experience in the South. To locals, *any* civil rights worker was now a "freedom rider."³

SNCC became best known for the community-based projects it initiated in the Deep South. Activists sometimes called this region the "Cotton Curtain," calling attention to its similarity to the "Iron Curtain" hemming in Soviet bloc countries. In choosing to go where resistance would be fiercest, the students were taking on work that the bigger and more established civil rights organizations mostly backed away from.⁴ Although they were careful to not get ahead of the communities they were organizing, SNCC people also had little patience for those counseling "all deliberate speed," as the Supreme Court had in its 1954 *Brown* decision.⁵ By the spring of 1962, it had 41 full-time staff members.⁶ A year later it had the largest staff of full-time voter registration workers of any civil rights organization.[7] In spring 1965, SNCC had the largest staff of any civil rights group in the South.[8] How did SNCC manage to organize Southern Black communities considered too difficult to tackle?

Politics and Religion

SNCC developed distinctive approaches and strategies, some of which were learned on the job. Take Bob Moses's voter registration efforts in Amite County, Mississippi, in the summer of 1961.[9] Almost as soon as Moses arrived in Amite County in July 1961, the authorities pegged him as an "outside agitator" and arrested him for assisting Blacks as they tried to register at the courthouse. After his release, he returned to the courthouse. This time, the cousin of the local sheriff went after him, beating him brutally. The next day Moses pressed charges against his assailant. Locals said it was the first time in the history of Amite County that a Black person had filed charges against a white person. Moses was sending a message to both the Black and the white community: He would not be intimidated. He made a point of behaving as if Blacks enjoyed the same rights as whites. Moses's bravery was unprecedented. "From that day on," said one Black resident, "Well, I can stand for myself."[10]

Charles Sherrod, a divinity school student from Virginia, also understood the importance of grappling with your own fears and walking through the world "as if you were free to act." You had to get local people over their fear of that "giant in the canyon," by which he meant the local sheriff.[11] Sherrod was SNCC's first "field secretary," a term to describe staffers based in local communities. He succeeded in getting many Black people in Albany, Georgia, over their fear of the local sheriff. SNCC organizers did this time and again, using their physical presence in a community to help check locals' understandable fears about racist retaliation.

SNCC's "as if" philosophy reflected the group's view that the battle they were waging was in many ways psychological.[12] Through her participation in SNCC, Bernice Johnson Reagon came to feel that "if something puts you down, you have to fight against it."[13] Moses once characterized the group as a "small, striking force," whose members delved deep into themselves and into the community to "wage psychological warfare."[14]

Still, SNCC activists had to gain the trust of communities. Their ability to win people over owed a lot to how they moved into a community, first gaining

Image 1.1 Cambridge, Maryland, was SNCC's northernmost base of operations. In spring 1964, SNCC-led protests there brought the Maryland National Guard to town. Guardsmen found their effort to arrest SNCC staffer Clifford Vaughs complicated by Stokely Carmichael, who held onto his comrade's foot.
Danny Lyon/Magnum Photos

the respect of local leaders, often National Association for the Advancement of Colored People (NAACP) leaders such as Mississippian Amzie Moore, whom Moses called his "movement father." These were the people "whose word meant something in the community."[15] If they accepted you as Moore did Moses, it provided you (and SNCC) entrée to the wider community. Charles Sherrod did likewise in the small city of Albany. This was a key part of the group's organizing playbook, and it complicates the usual understanding of SNCC as an exemplar of "bottom-up" organizing.[16]

SNCC organizers also emphasized their long-term commitment to communities. In contrast to the preacher-dominated Southern Christian Leadership Conference (SCLC) of Martin Luther King Jr, which favored short-term campaigns, SNCC embedded itself within a community. SNCC put it this way: "SCLC mobilized, but SNCC organized."[17] The students focused much of their work on poor communities. Crucially, in those early years, they listened to people rather than telling them what to do. "Talk to people, laugh with them, joke with them; do most anything that gets some kind of conversation," advised one talented SNCC organizer. "It is very important to learn what bugs them."[18] Some of the people they approached were high-school kids, some barely younger than themselves. It made sense to work with kids because, as Charles Sherrod pointed out, they were not yet fearful. Moreover, nothing brought the adults to a demonstration like their children getting arrested.[19]

SNCC's audaciousness was risky. It provoked uneasiness among many liberals and more moderate civil rights groups. Were the SNCC kids moving too fast? Would they put Black communities at risk? Could they provoke a backlash? Yes, they could. Particularly risky was Charles Sherrod's insistence on using interracial teams of organizers. Sherrod believed organizers had to "strike at the very root of segregation . . . the idea that white is superior." He believed the only way to "break this image" was to have Black and white people working together.[20] By the spring of 1963, five of the eleven staffers on his team were Northern white college students.

More seasoned activists often questioned working interracially in the Deep South. One such activist thought those who did had to be "a little bit wacky" or be "gripped by a vision of a whole new world."[21] A *New York Times* account of a voter registration rally that Sherrod presided over at a church in Sasser, Georgia, shows how far he was willing to go. There were 38 local Black people at the Mount Olive Baptist Church, and a thuggish contingent of white law enforcement officers and their buddies, who showed up to harass them. Among the six SNCC people there, three were white or so light-skinned they appeared white. After the rally ended, a white female staffer got into a car with young Black staffers, which caused great consternation. It's quite possible that the presence of reporters acted as a deterrent, keeping the sheriffs and their posse from turning violent. Perhaps this was the event that persuaded Sherrod to institute what he called the "lynch prevention code," exercising extreme caution lest they run afoul of Southern paranoia about racial "mixing."

Despite its riskiness, in some communities the bravery and commitment of the SNCC "kids" won the locals over. "They loved us before they ever saw us," recalled Howard University student Jean Wheeler Smith of the local Black people she encountered in southwest Georgia. "They would do for you like you were their own children."[22] Locals' affection often extended to white students.

Charles Sherrod and Bob Moses both believed in interracial organizing and nonviolence, but they moved through the world and thought about that world differently. Sherrod was deeply religious, while Moses, who had been

Image 1.2 SNCC staffers Charles Sherrod, standing at right, and Randy Battle, seated, visit a supporter in the countryside of southwest Georgia.
Danny Lyon/Magnum Photos

a graduate student in philosophy at Harvard, was secular. Sherrod's reference point was the Bible. Moses's intellectual lodestar was the French existentialist Albert Camus.

The lanky Sherrod smiled boyishly when he talked, and he talked a lot. He was smart and he looked it in his thick glasses. An inspirational preacher, "the wild man of nonviolence," who could stir people to action, Sherrod was comfortable in the limelight.[23] The cerebral Moses was as quiet as Sherrod was garrulous. He spoke softly, and he listened to others . . . very intently. He was known to pose difficult questions in meetings, sometimes drawing upon his knowledge of philosophy. Moses also had the ability to "help people come up with what they really felt and wanted."[24] That talent meant he was "always working himself out of a job, turning power over."[25] Kind and incisive, self-composed *and* self-effacing, Moses drew people to him, despite himself.[26] He kept his chest and shoulders open to the world.[27] He was a bit of an enigma to others. Even physical descriptions of him vary widely. Was he "a little bitty fella," as one Black local described him, or was he built "a little like a boxer," as coworker Bob Zellner claimed?[28]

Image 1.3 From left to right, Martha Prescod Norman, Mike Miller, and Bob Moses ask about the whereabouts of neighbors whose home had been shot up the previous day because of their movement activism.
Danny Lyon/Magnum Photos

SNCC accommodated their different styles and philosophies because the group was shaped by two overlapping streams of mid-century protest: the political left that helped to shape Moses and radical Christianity that so influenced Sherrod. As historians have shown, although SNCC seemed entirely new and of the moment, it was deeply indebted to an older, iconoclastic generation of Black and white activists, many of whom had worked together for some time.

No one was more influential in advancing radical Christianity than the Reverend James Lawson. Many of SNCC's first members attended Lawson's Nashville workshops on nonviolence, which he began in March 1958. Lawson's activist Christianity, with its focus on nonviolence and integration, shared common ground with left-wing politics. For example, Lawson was a fierce critic of the NAACP's legalistic approach, calling the group out as a "black bourgeois club" to the *New York Times*.[29] Instead, Lawson argued for direct action, using the Gandhian tool of civil disobedience.[30] Lawson, whose faith in nonviolence was unwavering, maintained it was not a tactic of weakness, as its critics argued. It was an empowering tactic because, he argued, "you never let any outside force, nothing outside yourself, control what you do."[31]

Lawson challenged the assumption that racist whites were powerful. If these people were "truly powerful or confident or well loved," Lawson pointed out, they wouldn't be assaulting you. He believed in nonviolence as a tactic and a philosophy that offered activists the possibility of nudging their adversaries out of a space of fear, opening them up to nonhateful possibilities.

So many early SNCC people were religious, including many whose fathers were ministers, that it enabled them to reach out to Black ministers in the communities they were organizing.[32] The majority of ministers, fearing racist retaliation if they worked with SNCC, kept their distance from the movement. But in many communities SNCC people found at least one minister willing to affiliate. Their risk taking made an enormous difference as churches became hubs of movement activity. "Any time you heard the words *mass meeting*," said one Albany local, "you would know that meeting would be held at one of these churches."[33] A volunteer who worked with Sherrod recalled spending a lot of time in church during the summer of 1962. "A great deal of movement teaching and learning took place in churches." They were the usual site for voter registration classes and courses in literacy.[34] Mass meetings created what Moses called a veritable "energy machine" of testimony and analysis that enabled people to develop "collective self-respect."[35] Pivotal were those moments when individuals literally stood up or spoke up for the movement. In doing so, they "created a public face for themselves, which they then had to live up to."[36] Because they were the site of these transformative meetings, Black churches were targeted time and again by opponents of the movement.

SNCC was equally shaped by a group of left-wing mentors. They included Anne and Carl Braden, the married white couple that early SNCC people feared were communists.[37] They directed the Southern Conference Educational Fund (SCEF) and were very much part of the mix. So were Myles Horton, the white director of the Highlander School, a training site for unionists and civil rights workers, and the white historian Howard Zinn, who taught at Spelman College, an historically Black college in Atlanta, Georgia. Most influential of all were Bayard Rustin, cofounder of CORE and advisor to Dr. King, and the veteran civil rights activist and SCLC staffer Ella Jo Baker. The founding mother of SNCC, Baker was the one who encouraged the sit-in students to form an autonomous organization and resist the efforts of King's SCLC to annex the new group as its youth wing.

Baker was perhaps the most ecumenical of this group, bringing together "the Black Baptist missionary values of charity, humility, and service with the

Image 1.4 Called by many the mother of SNCC, Ella Baker was a brilliant organizer who generated a "whirlwind" of activist energy.
Danny Lyon/Magnum Photos

economic theories of Marxists and socialists of various stripes."[38] Baker was a 57-year-old dynamo when SNCC was taking shape. A petite and elegant woman, she was always put together. She usually showed up in a classic ensemble, which she often topped off with a fashionable pillbox hat. She cut a striking figure. More than anyone else, it was Baker who enabled the students to think of themselves as "full-time freedom fighters," operating independently of other groups.[39] Her approach to organizing, rooted in her conviction that "strong people don't need strong leaders," made sense to the young people of SNCC.[40] She spoke her mind, and often, after "nailing someone's foibles, she'd chuckle." She wasn't mean-spirited; she just "found humanity humorous."[41]

Baker's levity, rationality, and emotional generosity informed her political organizing. When she was working for SCLC, she pushed for the group to start a literacy project that would give people tools that would enable them to be effective activists. Such a project would function as a "respectable" vehicle for movement participation for people made uneasy by any signs of militance. She insisted the movement needed to make space for a variety of people, not all of whom would share your worldview. Growing the movement mattered to

Image 1.5 SNCC's first office secretary was the white Southerner Jane Stembridge. In SNCC's earliest days, the people most often in the group's tiny Atlanta office were Ella Baker, Bob Moses, and Stembridge, who was a theology student and a poet.
Danny Lyon/Magnum Photos

Baker, which is why she argued that organizers should even struggle to bring onboard the "matron in the fur coat." That could be a hard sell in SNCC.[42]

Baker believed SNCC should be Black led *and* interracial. She hired SNCC's first paid staffer, someone to manage its tiny office in the corner of SCLC's Atlanta office, a space she gave to the students. Baker chose Jane Stembridge, a white theology student and a poet. The daughter of a white Baptist minister, Stembridge was a Southerner from Virginia. Only there on an interim basis, Stembridge made the most of her time. SNCC historian Clayborne Carson has wagered that the group would probably have collapsed that first summer had it not been for the energy and skills that Baker and Stembridge brought to their work.

Baker's choice of Stembridge illustrates a truth about her: The struggle for civil rights was essential but was also part of something bigger—a larger struggle "for the freedom of the human spirit, a larger freedom that encompasses all of mankind."[43] "We can only create a new world," she argued, "out of a commonness of purpose and a decent respect for all the people who are helping to contribute to it." This meant understanding that "human beings are human beings worthy of respect and dignity wherever they are, irrespective of who they are." To SNCC staffer Charles McDew, Miss Baker, as she was called, was a movement titan, a woman who "made us in her image."[44]

Ella Baker influenced the students, but Bayard Rustin held considerable sway, too. A powerful orator, Rustin was politically shrewd, charismatic, and good looking. Stokely Carmichael was a student at the Bronx High School of Science when he attended one of Rustin's lectures. "That's what I'm gonna be when I grow up" was his reaction. Everything about Rustin, especially his Blackness, Carmichael found thrilling.[45] Like his friend Ella Baker, Bayard Rustin was not a famous movement leader. He tended to operate behind the scenes, and very many scenes at that. He was already working for the Fellowship of Reconciliation, an international pacifist group, when, in 1942, he helped to form a new group, CORE, which promoted the Gandhian tactic of nonviolent resistance. During World War II, he served a two-year prison term as a conscientious objector. He is best known for his role in organizing 1963's galvanizing March on Washington for Jobs and Freedom. Rustin's distance from the limelight was not of his own choosing. It was forced on him by his prior involvement in the Young Communist League from 1938 until 1941, and by his homosexuality, both of which were serious liabilities in Cold War America.[46] A pacifist and a Quaker, Rustin worked closely with King...when King's other advisors permitted it.

Rustin proved hard to sideline entirely because he was brilliant and had played such a central role in King's activism. Rustin, Baker, and their friend Stanley Levison, a white Jewish attorney and businessman (and one-time communist), were living in New York City, but intensely interested in the growing Southern struggle. During 1955's Montgomery Bus Boycott, they formed a group, In Friendship, to support the struggle. The threesome came to believe that King and his associates should form a new organization. Their discussion with King and other allied ministers was pivotal in the formation of SCLC.[47] By the sixties, Rustin was vehemently anticommunist, but he considered himself part of an interracial left that in New York City included many Jews and Blacks.

Collaborations between progressive Jews and Blacks were not new. In the early twentieth century, W. E. B. Du Bois called Jews "our best friends."[48] For a time, the Holocaust would deepen the Jewish–Black connection. It was a partnership marked by mutual self-interest. Rustin's mentor was A. Philip Randolph, a civil rights activist and the head of the Brotherhood of Sleeping

"AS IF YOU WERE FREE" 17

Image 1.6 Civil rights activist Bayard Rustin, left, receives help from the writer James Baldwin in securing his armband. Rustin and Baldwin participated in the National Day of Mourning in New York City for the four Black girls killed in September 1963 in the KKK's horrific bombing of the 16th Street Baptist Church in Birmingham, Alabama.
New York Daily News/Getty Images

Car Porters, a Black-led labor union. This is the way that Randolph reportedly discussed their bond: "Negroes have large numbers and small money; Jews have small numbers and large money. Together, the two have large numbers and large money."[49] Partly opportunistic, partly idealistic, this was a left-wing partnership rooted in the belief that joining together in solidarity was the most effective way to challenge anti-Semitism and anti-Black racism.

Rustin was a role model to many of the young people in SNCC. And his enmeshment in this network left its mark on SNCC. In the case of Bob Moses and Stokely Carmichael, it consolidated their connection to the Jewish left. Rustin sent Bob Moses to Atlanta to work with Ella Baker, but as a child Moses had attended Camp Wo-Chi-Ca, a Jewish socialist camp.[50] Rustin was also a key mentor to a group of Howard University students—Courtland Cox, Ivanhoe Donaldson, and Stokely Carmichael—who went on to play important leadership roles in SNCC.[51] Like Moses, Carmichael had connections to New York's left. His best friend was the son of Eugene and Peggy Dennis. Both were Communist Party stalwarts, and Eugene Dennis headed up the Party from 1959 until his death in 1961. The first demonstration Carmichael attended was organized by the Young Socialist League, and in support of Israel. The college Carmichael had his eye on was Brandeis, where so many of his Jewish classmates at the prestigious Bronx School of Science were headed.[52] Although in its early years white Southern Christians outnumbered white Jewish members in SNCC, the latter enjoyed an outsized influence because of their unapologetic militance.[53] Historian Clayborne Carson contends that a feeling of affinity developed among SNCC's left-wing Jews and Blacks, one that was rooted in a shared alienation from the dominant culture.[54]

Consolidating this Black–Jewish connection were the ties between SNCC and their left-wing Jewish allies in the North, which deepened when the group turned for legal representation to the National Lawyers Guild (NLG), a left-wing group that did not exclude communists.[55] Carson believes a "symbiotic relationship" grew up between SNCC, which was in need of money, but refused to compromise its politics, and "a radical minority of leftist Jews," who were attracted to SNCC's militance.[56] This would change, but for a short but critical period this Black–Jewish constellation helped to define SNCC's politics.

These left-wing and religious strands eventually diverged, but in SNCC's early years they meshed fairly well. The more religiously and spiritually inclined—say John Lewis, Diane Nash, Casey Hayden (née Sandra Cason), and Bob Zellner—were not actively at odds with Bob Moses, Courtland Cox, and Stokely Carmichael, whose orientation was more explicitly left-wing. In its early years, what most divided SNCC was whether it should remain focused on direct action or should move into voter registration—a division Ella Baker helped to resolve. Staffers also disagreed about whether nonviolence was a matter of principle or simply strategic, but they agreed that nonviolence enabled substantial numbers of Black people to participate in the movement.[57]

Interracialism

SNCC staffers' views of interracialism also differed. Some were skeptical of Sherrod's interracial organizing, but nonetheless saw themselves fighting for integration. Bob Moses spoke for many when he contended that the one thing SNCC "can do for the country that no one else can do is to be above the race issue." He saw a strategic advantage in an integrated movement because he doubted that Black people could end white supremacy by themselves. Moreover, he thought working interracially changed "the whole complexion of what you're doing so it isn't any longer Negro fighting white, it's a question of rational people against irrational people."[58]

SNCC's commitment to integration was, of course, one of its attractions for many left-wing whites. Take the historian and activist Howard Zinn, who, with Ella Baker and several others, served as one of SNCC's official advisors. He believed that SNCC's commitment to interracialism "pointed the way to a race-less society," which he favored.[59] Had Zinn been a SNCC field secretary, however, he likely would have seen that while SNCC people worked to rid themselves of the habit of racial categorization, they were also highly aware of the workings of race. How could they not be, given the depth of the white terror they encountered? If racelessness was ever their aim, it wasn't for long.

Moreover, even though SNCC was integrated, it was Black led, which set it apart from most integrated groups and spaces in America, which remained white dominated.[60] In SNCC's offices and projects, Black staffers did not have to struggle to first figure out and then adjust to whites' cultural referents, customs, and idioms. Instead, whites bore the burden of assimilation. To veteran civil rights activist Anne Braden, SNCC's freshness derived precisely from its Black centeredness and its rejection of the white dominance that too often undergirded liberal interracial organizations.[61]

Integration on Black terms required whites to accept Black leadership. Those who could not or who were uncomfortable working with Black people as equals did not stay on. Those who did and also proved their mettle were accepted into the group's "circle of trust." Their white privilege did not make them forever suspect, perennially on probation. One reason SNCC accepted them was that in the South they were considered "race traitors" for having taken up the fight for Black freedom.

Stokely Carmichael, best known as the SNCC leader who steered the group toward Black Power, was adamant that the white activists of SNCC were not actually "white." They may have been white when they joined, but he believed that through working in SNCC they ceased being "'white' in most conventional American terms."[62] Some of them, including Michael Schwerner, the Northern Jewish activist in CORE who died in Mississippi, stopped identifying as white.[63] In those early years, they often felt as Casey Hayden did, "like we were the beloved community, harassed and happy just like we'd died and gone to heaven and it was integrated there."[64]

SNCC was also a place of hard struggle. According to Jane Stembridge, staffers would "fight each other, love each other, talk till three or four o'clock in the morning, work through the stuff as best we could, get out the next day and talk to people about why they should vote." She contends that a lot of their energy was taken up in dealing with "all or own anger, our own woundedness, our own racism. That was the real fight."[65] Staffers' ability to wage this fight within the broader struggle owed a lot to the group's small size.

The experience of being part of a tight-knit interracial community rooted in love and respect was intoxicating, but integration had pragmatic virtues as well. SNCC staffers came to understand early on that they were waging war in the South. To wage that war, SNCC needed office staffers working behind the lines to get out the word, conduct research, fundraise, arrange bail, and communicate with the media, the Justice Department, and the group's far-flung supporters. Black staffers' greater enthusiasm for field work was one reason the office staff leaned white. With the appointment of James Forman as its executive secretary in 1961, SNCC began to develop an infrastructure, as it shifted from being loosely connected clusters of organizers—or as one critic put it, "an amorphous collection of people"—to a functioning organization.[66] Forman, "big shaggy, importable, bearlike," was "always scrambling to keep the organization afloat to keep cars running, the rent paid."[67] With Forman presiding over the office, there was always office work that needed doing.

SNCC also needed money to do battle. In its early years, SNCC relied upon donations from church congregations, individual ministers and rabbis, the National Council of Churches, labor unions, wealthy individuals, activists, the National Student Association, and perhaps most crucially, Dr. King's SCLC. Shortly after coming onboard, Forman pushed SNCC to set up its own fundraising division to target left liberals. It is undeniable that SNCC's interracialism made it attractive to church groups and leftists alike.[68]

The range of work SNCC's white staffers performed can be seen by focusing on three key people: Casey Hayden, Jack Minnis, and Bob Zellner. Sandra

Image 1.7 James Forman, SNCC's executive secretary, hard at work in the group's Greenwood, Mississippi office, fall 1963.
Danny Lyon/Magnum Photos

"Casey" Cason Hayden was one of those who worked behind the lines in SNCC. Hayden, a student at the University of Texas in Austin, was a part of the university's integrated interfaith community and was active in the YWCA. When the sit-ins came to Austin in the spring of 1960, she was on the picket line in her yellow dress and high-heeled white pumps. With her blonde hair, Hayden was conventionally pretty. She dressed stylishly, but in a good-girlish way, which had its strategic uses. She was also deeply serious. When Constance Curry, a white Southerner who headed up the Southern Project of the National Student Association (NSA), came to Austin, she met with Hayden and told her about the sit-ins. Their conversation marked the start of a new life for Hayden.[69] Curry, with Ella Baker, was an adult advisor to SNCC, and she talked at length with Hayden about the new group.[70] Theirs was a fateful meeting, which led to Hayden speaking at the NSA convention. She urged NSA to support the student sit-ins, civil disobedience, and the freedom movement, and it did. NSA would provide crucial support to SNCC in the years ahead.

Through Curry and Ella Baker, for whom Hayden worked on the National Student YWCA project, she made connections with SNCC. In fall 1962,

Image 1.8 Casey Hayden, one of several white Southerners in SNCC, in the group's Freedom House in Savannah, Georgia, 1963.
Danny Lyon/Magnum Photos

Hayden's brief marriage to Tom Hayden, a founder of Students for a Democratic Society, fell apart. She moved to Atlanta, where she became a SNCC worker. Hayden was not usually on the front lines of the movement, but she was no stranger to racist violence. Over the course of several years, she was pursued by white men at gunpoint in Tennessee, dragged by white police from the Black section of a Georgia courtroom, and rear-ended and forced off the road by whites in Mississippi.[71]

Casey Hayden had contacts in the emerging Northern student movement, partly through Tom Hayden, and Forman appointed her SNCC's first Northern coordinator. Casey Hayden traveled to university campuses and gained crucial support for SNCC. Afterward, most of her time was spent in SNCC offices, whether it was in SNCC's national office in Atlanta or during Freedom Summer on the Literacy Project in Tougaloo, Mississippi, just outside of Jackson. Some might have seen her in a SNCC office and thought she was "just a secretary," but that's not how Hayden saw herself. Working in a SNCC office was nothing like being a secretary in a traditional setting. Hayden consulted with others, but she was largely "self-directing." She handled everything—"the headwork of research and strategizing as well as the footwork, the physical work." Years later, she claimed that she and others in SNCC "stood the [gendered] division of labor on its head."[72]

The work that Casey Hayden and others did was crucial, and at its core much of it was relational. Take one especially time-consuming task: coordinating bail money for arrested workers. SNCC had favored a "jail-no bail" approach to arrests from direct action, but early on concluded that few students were willing to make that sacrifice.[73] Handling bail meant building relationships with local Black lawyers and ministers, as well as Northern donors and a smaller number of white lawyers. Hayden and others in the office were "building relationships with everyone external to SNCC," and that included "the campuses, the donors, local people, the shopkeepers, and media people."[74] Staff made sure that the media knew about SNCC's planned actions so they would get covered by the press. They also stayed in contact with the staff in the field. During the summer of 1964, another white office worker, Betty Garman, began every morning with check-in calls to every project in Mississippi using SNCC's all-important, flat-rate Wide Area Telephone Service (WATS) telephone line.[75] They also built relationships with Burke Marshall and John Doar, sympathetic Justice Department officials. Local Blacks protected their families and civil rights workers with fully loaded shotguns. SNCC office workers tried to keep them safe using fully loaded Rolodexes.[76]

Much of their outreach was to Friends of SNCC (FOS), the group's nationwide network of support. In the case of arrests or worse, the Atlanta staff would contact FOS chapters and be able to "mount a national response basically overnight."[77] FOS chapters raised money through parties, concerts, art shows, and special mailings. They organized food and clothing drives, especially for Black communities in the Deep South that were suffering economic reprisals for their activism. These drives enabled SNCC to show local people that the organization could actually "set up its own welfare system" for them. FOS chapters also pressured the press to cover what was happening in the South, and they sent people South to discover firsthand the conditions and publicize their findings.[78] Hayden described this Northern network as "our only protection," as they were "the source of calls to northern liberal politicians, and a lifeline to local press who could then ask the Associated Press for stories."[79]

Another essential part of SNCC was its research department, whose white director, Jack Minnis, was a trained lawyer and a very able researcher. "He

Image 1.9 James Forman with Bob and Dottie Zellner, June 1963, in Danville, Virginia, the site of some of the most brutal police attacks on movement protestors.
Danny Lyon/Magnum Photos

was this crusty older white guy who smoked like a fiend, looked generally unkempt, and could get research from a turnip," is how Black staffer Judy Richardson remembered him. By comparison to most others in SNCC, Minnis was older, but he was only in his mid-30s when Forman hired him in 1962. Enterprising and indefatigable in hunting down information, he spent much of his time in public libraries where he turned up voter registration data that proved crucial to field organizers trying to organize local Black communities.[80] He also devoted considerable time to studying the white power structure in the places where SNCC was organizing. His research department managed to figure out the complicated and tangled network of ownership of plantations in the Deep South. Black staffer Courtland Cox considered Minnis, who popularized the term the "power structure," among the smartest people in SNCC.[81]

Whites, and in particular white women, provided much of the labor in SNCC's offices. This made sense, given that many of the people that the office staff were dealing with were whites, whether journalists, government officials, or Northern supporters. However, this isn't the whole story. As pioneering as SNCC was, its members nevertheless were shaped by the period's gender conventions. When Dorothy Zellner first went into SNCC's Atlanta office, the first question James Forman asked her was "Can you type?" He was right in thinking she could, which she emphasized later had not offended her. That was the way the world worked back then.[82]

The much bigger problem was that the South was SNCC's theater of operations, and nowhere did categories of gender, race, and everything else carry the psychic weight that they did there, which meant that working interracially was a very risky business. If a white and a Black person were together, and not in an obviously hierarchical relationship to one another, it was a dead giveaway: They were civil rights workers. In such circumstances, "both of their lives were in jeopardy," observes Black staffer Muriel Tillinghast.[83] And no matter how much people were committed to working across race, they were usually more committed to staying alive and keeping those around them alive. "Being a white woman meant that wherever I was, the Movement was visible, and where there was visibility there was danger," Hayden explained. Nothing put activists at greater risk than the presence of a white *woman* and a Black *man* together, which is why Black male staffers sometimes posed as chauffeurs when in a car with a white woman. Often white SNCC workers would hide under blankets to avoid being seen traveling with their Black comrades. The Southern paranoia about interracial sex meant that white women were much more likely to be working in a SNCC office than in the field.

Office work was essential to SNCC's survival in all sorts of ways, but it was not the work that was most valued. Working at your desk for hours on end in an office that was tiny and boiling hot was not considered heroic. Within SNCC, it was the risky world of activism, the dangerous work of being out in the field, risking a beating, arrest, and death, that was most admired. This devaluing of working behind the lines followed in large part from SNCC's culture of self-sacrifice and rejection of all things middle class. SNCC workers struggled to live like the sharecroppers they were organizing, going so far as to dress in jeans, bib overalls, work shirts, and tee-shirts. To a sympathetic white reporter, James Forman admitted, "Maybe we've overdone it; it's almost a uniform now." But it stuck for a while.[84] Eventually, staffers would wield what historian Charles Payne called the "stick of Selfless Dedication" against each other, particularly against those deemed more privileged.[85]

This hierarchy of work was unfortunate because working in a SNCC office was hardly stress-free. Often, office workers ended up having to make consequential decisions on the spot about who to try to mobilize when SNCC people were arrested or were not accounted for. To Hayden, the "worst stress was knowing that only I and a few others at the phones in the offices, with the contacts to the press and federal agencies and our far-flung supporters, stood between the people we loved in the field and their injury or death."[86] And then there was the stress of knowing that some questioned the value of your work or your courage. The fact that working behind a desk carried less respect than taking part in demonstrations and being out in the field did not go unnoticed

Image 1.10 From left to right: Dorie and Joyce Ladner, wearing denim overall dresses—the "SNCC uniform" for women—at the March on Washington for Jobs and Freedom in August 1963. Behind them is the SNCC staffer Mildred Forman, who was then married to James Forman.
Danny Lyon/Magnum Photos

by those laboring in those offices. Cathy Cade, another white woman who worked in the Atlanta office in 1963, believed that doing office work rather than being in the field and risking arrest or worse posed a real conundrum for serious activists. To her, there was "a built-in contradiction, stress, and marginalization in doing office work" when you were a part of SNCC.[87]

This was not a problem for white men such as Bob Zellner. A native of Alabama, Zellner came from a Ku Klux Klan (KKK) family. His father was a Methodist preacher who left the KKK. He came to SNCC through SCEF, which gave SNCC a grant of $5,000 a year for Zellner to engage in political outreach to bring other Southern white students into the movement.[88] Zellner's baptismal movement experience came at an October 1961 protest in McComb, Mississippi, where he had just arrived. The only white person in a group of 114 peaceful protestors, Zellner was singled out by a vicious mob of white counterprotestors who kicked and punched him and gouged his eyes until he was unconscious. Joining the movement made you a pariah in the white world, but it enabled your entry into a community of love. What Zellner most remembered about the experience was the protectiveness SNCC workers showed him as they tried to shield him from the mob. That experience led him to feel "welded" to the movement "by a feeling so deep it was akin to a religious experience."[89] That SNCC people took so many risks owes a lot to their self-sacrifice and what Casey Hayden characterized, positively, as their "armor of righteousness."[90]

Struggle and Terror

The presence of whites such as Zellner jolted some Black people who had never witnessed a white person stand up for racial justice, but it also inflamed white locals. Moreover, the payoff, especially as SNCC pivoted away from direct action and toward electoral politics, was miniscule. Almost every Black person who tried to register to vote was thwarted.[91] Even worse, their efforts frequently opened them up to retaliation because local newspapers printed the names of these potential registrants.[92] Other civil rights organizations were distressed, particularly by what was happening in Mississippi. NAACP officials came to regard Moses as an "amateur" with a very dismal track record. He "produced deplorable net results" was their verdict.[93] And SNCC did provoke a backlash. Between 1961 and early 1964, the organization recorded over 150 incidents of intimidation and violence against civil rights workers and Black residents in the state of Mississippi alone.[94]

Yet stories of white terror rarely found their way into the national news. Their invisibility meant that both the Kennedy and Johnson administrations could backburner civil rights, thereby ensuring the continued loyalty of Southern whites to the Democratic Party, then the party of the segregationist South.[95]

There was a war happening in the South, but the country didn't know it. Just as crucially, it was becoming increasingly clear to SNCC workers that if the federal government refused to protect them against white terrorists, no amount of organizing would persuade Black residents to go to the courthouse to exercise their democratic rights.

Two acts of white terror in Amite County, Mississippi, catalyzed Bob Moses and SNCC. Amite was Klan-dominated, and in September 1961, a white state legislator, E. H. Hurst, killed Herbert Lee, a Black farmer and local NAACP leader who had tried to register to vote. Hurst murdered Lee,

Image 1.11 In Atlanta, a white bystander upbraids racists attacking SNCC protestors. When one of the counter-protestors said to her, "If you feel that way, why don't you marry one of them?" she joined the demonstrators. This act of solidarity on the part of a white Southern woman was rare. SNCC photographer Danny Lyon said that until that day he had never witnessed such a thing.
Danny Lyon/Magnum Photos

who had been a childhood playmate, in broad daylight and in front of others. Lee was the first person to lose his life because of his association with SNCC. His murder underscored SNCC's inability to protect the people they were organizing. Locals grew warier. At the funeral, Lee's widow confronted Moses. "*You* killed my husband!" she said to an already devastated Moses.[96]

Among those who witnessed Lee's murder was Louis Allen, who ran a small timber business in Liberty. In contrast to Lee, Allen was not a Movement man. In fact, under pressure from local law enforcement, he initially lied about the circumstances of Lee's murder. That lie ate away at him, and eventually he agreed to speak to the grand jury if the Justice Department could promise him protection. When Justice Department officials declined his request, Allen chose to stay silent. But by that juncture local law enforcement officials had learned that Allen had very nearly testified. What followed was more than two years of harassment, arrests, and beatings. Finally, Allen decided to sell his

Image 1.12 Maryland was not a Southern state, but the resistance SNCC faced there suggested that white racism was not a Southern problem. During a spring 1964 protest in the Chesapeake Bay community of Cambridge, the National Guard used pepper spray on protestors, and in the case of Stokely Carmichael, sprayed it directly into his face.

Danny Lyon/Magnum Photos

house and move North. On January 31, 1964, the night before he was due to leave Mississippi, Allen was gunned down in his driveway. Allen's teenaged son discovered his father's body. The whole left side of his face had been blown away and lay in pieces several feet away from the rest of him.

The murders of Lee and Allen and the absence of justice was having the desired effect.[97] Moses and some of his comrades knew they needed a different strategy to break open Mississippi, where the culture of white supremacy seemed ineradicable. "There had to be a response . . . a major gesture," Moses believed.[98] A "blitzkrieg" is what Casey Hayden called it.[99] As the next chapter details, SNCC's response involved looking beyond the South and turning instead to some of America's most elite colleges and universities to staff what came to be known by many as Freedom Summer.

TWO

Parallel Institutions and Parallel Lines

The Student Nonviolent Coordinating Committee (SNCC)'s plans to take on Mississippi in the summer of 1964 built on the "Freedom Vote," an experimental initiative begun in fall 1963. It also rode the wave of optimism engendered by the massive March on Washington that August in Washington, DC.[1] The Freedom Vote began the long process whereby SNCC, working with other civil rights organizations, "took the regular Democratic Party and turned it on its head."[2] The Council of Federated Organizations (COFO) was a collaborative venture, though some called it a mere "shell" of an organization.[3] Movement lawyer Len Holt put it this way: "SNCC, for all practical purposes, is COFO."[4] Largely under SNCC's direction, the Freedom Vote project crossed boundaries of race, generation, and power in surprising ways.

The Freedom Vote

The idea that SNCC should focus on registering Black voters was suggested to Bob Moses by local National Association for the Advancement of Colored People (NAACP) leader Amzie Moore of Cleveland, Mississippi. Moore told Moses in 1960 that the lunch counter sit-ins would not defeat the racial caste system. Not in the Delta. "Not enough food on the table," Moore said.[5] The shift to voter registration had another advocate—Attorney General Robert F. Kennedy, who advanced it at a June 1961 meeting with civil rights leaders. CORE's James Farmer suspected that Kennedy just wanted "to get CORE and SNCC off the streets with their highly visible demonstrations."[6] It seems likely that Kennedy aimed to refocus the movement away from the confrontational methods of direct action to what he imagined was the less incendiary terrain of voter registration. Such a move would quell the fierce white backlash generated by the lunch counter sit-ins and Freedom Rides, thereby shoring up the Democrats' increasingly fragile coalition and improving his brother's chances of re-election.[7]

The meetings between Justice Department officials and civil rights leaders led SNCC's representatives to believe that Washington would have their back if they conducted voter registration drives in Mississippi. Officials made promises about federal marshals protecting activists and about making money available to the movement.[8] During this period, a small delegation from SNCC, which included Charles Jones and Yale University law student Timothy Jenkins, also met with the entertainer and civil rights activist, Harry Belafonte, who was a friend of the Kennedys. They talked about the need for a massive voter registration effort, and about the people and money required for such a campaign. Jones ventured that the movement would need to expand and deploy as many as 100,000 students to help with the effort. Jenkins and Jones left the meeting believing that Belafonte, who was a substantial donor (the movement's "Daddy Warbucks," as he put it), would play a role in raising the necessary funds.[9]

Although some SNCC people, such as Jenkins and Jones, were onboard with this reorientation, many felt that if they acceded to the wishes of the administration, they were being "bought off" by the liberals. It was Ella Baker who kept peace when she proposed that the group maintain two wings—one devoted to direct action and the other to voter registration. By August 1961, when SNCC endorsed her compromise, voter registration also began to seem like less of a sellout. After all, this was when Bob Moses was trying to register voters in Amite County and discovering that it was plenty controversial and dangerous, not at all what Kennedy imagined.[10]

Still, the resistance to registering Afro-Mississippians required original thinking and innovative tactics. The person who reportedly provided the "theory" for the Freedom Vote was none other than an émigré, a German Jew who in 1938 fled Nazi Germany and came to America. Ernst Borinski had enlisted in the U.S. Army and served for four years before entering graduate school and earning his doctorate in sociology. For several decades Borinski taught at Tougaloo in Jackson, Mississippi. He was one of about 50 German Jewish émigrés who taught at historically Black colleges in this period. Borinski was among the college's most vociferously antisegregationist faculty members.

The local paper attacked him as a communist, and state legislators called him "that white radical professor."[11] His classes attracted activist students, including Joyce Ladner and Lawrence Guyot of SNCC. In his classes he introduced students to the idea of developing parallel institutions as pathways to change. For example, Black Americans who were prevented from participating in the existing political structure could create a parallel political party.[12]

Theory became praxis when Timothy Jenkins arrived in Mississippi in the summer of 1963. By this point, Jenkins was a student at Yale Law School and a member of the Law Students' Civil Rights Research Council. The Council's research was funded by the long-standing group Women's International League for Peace and Freedom. Jenkins and his Council compatriots discovered a state statute permitting residents to cast protest votes in party primaries.[13] Black people were prevented from participating in the regular political system, but this statute suggested there was nothing to stop them from registering in a parallel political party and casting their "freedom ballots" in a mock election. It was agreed that COFO would run a mock election in which Blacks (and sympathetic whites) would vote for their slate of candidates in November's gubernatorial race. A strong turnout was crucial. It would prove that Black people were not content with the status quo and wanted the franchise, contrary to what segregationists self-servingly claimed.[14]

Bob Moses had already concluded that activists needed to shine a "spotlight" on Mississippi, and he was considering using whites to do so. SNCC had some success with this in Greenwood, Mississippi.[15] Someone eager to promote this was Allard Lowenstein, a Northern white liberal and Democratic Party activist involved in the fight for civil rights.[16] Lowenstein believed in Blacks casting "protest votes," and he met on multiple occasions with Bob Moses and others in SNCC. He cut a curious figure, "part big shot and part itinerant waif," as he moved comfortably, and somewhat mysteriously, between Democratic Party bigwigs in Washington and movement activists in Mississippi.[17] Lowenstein was a staunch Cold War liberal, and that, before long, put him at odds with SNCC, which early on shifted on the matter of accepting help from those in and around the Communist Party. Lowenstein advocated using white college students from outside the South as volunteers for the campaign, a strategy that made some COFO staffers bristle. An Ivy Leaguer, he planned to use his connections at Yale and Stanford, where he briefly held positions, to help bring onboard volunteers, possibly as many as 100.[18]

The response from students outside the South was encouraging, and it showed that for young people committed to racial equality SNCC was emerging as *the* engine of change in America. By this point, some people in SNCC were in regular dialogue with activists in the Northern Student Movement, Students for a Democratic Society (SDS), and Friends of SNCC (FOS) chapters.[19] The white-majority New Left's enthusiasm for SNCC was increasingly evident. In September 1963—just days after the March on Washington—at a meeting of the National Student Association, Stokely Carmichael challenged SDS members to move into America's cities and organize the poor, particularly whites. Such was SNCC's moral authority and cachet with New Leftists that SDS took up his challenge. Some maintain that Carmichael's counsel was the "direct impetus" that put in motion the creation of a pilot program to kick off SDS's Economic Research and Action Project (ERAP) with bases in several Northern cities.[20]

Carmichael's call was soon amplified. At SNCC's November 1963 conference in Washington, DC, where whites outnumbered Blacks, the group's chairman, John Lewis, gave a speech in which he argued that Northern students—Black and white alike—needed to "go into the ghettoes of Harlem, into the ghettoes of Chicago and Detroit, and organize a mass movement similar to what we have in the South." Bayard Rustin also called on white student activists to organize the "white unemployed to join us in struggle." Such an effort might nudge the liberal labor establishment to the left. Advocates also believed that a class-based approach might diminish what felt like the coming backlash of poor and working-class whites.

To white New Leftists, a lot of what made SNCC so attractive was that its people were *doing* something, and they were doing it beyond the campus. By contrast, SDS seemed like "this bullshit talk organization," as SDS leader Todd Gitlin put it. It may have generated "a lot of smart working papers and talked a lot," Gitlin recalled, but the feeling was that it "didn't do anything." Or as Paul Potter, another early SDS leader put it, SDS was considered "high on analysis, low on action."[21] The yearning to act characterized many white New Leftists. The Freedom Vote tapped into their desire to move beyond intellectual discussion, beyond the campus. That fall, and on very short notice, about 80 students, most of them from Stanford and Yale, left mid-semester to work for two weeks on the Freedom Vote campaign in Mississippi.[22]

When November 2 came, Black Mississippians went to their churches, beauty parlors, and pool halls, and they voted over a three-day period. Mike

Miller, a white field secretary in the Delta that fall, said that "everybody realized it was a test of whether we can really get people to put their bodies on the line for the right to vote, because they would have to show up in a public space and check a ballot."[23] Eighty-three thousand Afro-Mississippians did just that, casting their freedom ballots. Digging into the vote tallies revealed that two-thirds of the total vote came from only eight counties and that 25 of Mississippi's 82 counties produced less than 100 votes each. Disappointingly, less than one-fifth of the vote came from counties where SNCC and CORE were operating projects.[24] These were the areas of greatest resistance to the movement. Still, exercising their right to vote, even unofficially, got many Afro-Mississippians thinking of themselves as citizens. Voting was no longer understood as "white folks' business," observed Ivanhoe Donaldson.[25] It was in those pool halls, beauty parlors, and churches, claims the historian Wesley Hogan, that "people learned how to act as if they were free to act as full citizens."[26]

Some SNCC staffers attributed the success of the Freedom Vote, at least in part, to the presence of white volunteers.[27] Donaldson was not the only one who felt the mock election showed that whites (or white men) could work effectively in Mississippi.[28] People started to discuss the possibility of repeating the effort, but on a much larger scale.[29] To Bob Moses, the election results suggested that winning the vote there would take "the equivalent of an army" coming into Mississippi.[30] It proved something else as well—that the presence of well-heeled white volunteers led the Federal Bureau of Investigation (FBI) to reverse itself when it came to civil rights activism. After years of saying their hands were tied, agents were there and observing across the state.[31]

To be sure, everyone was offended by the underlying logic of the FBI's shift—white lives mattered—and it really was that obvious and "just that gross," recalled Black SNCC staffer Lawrence Guyot. But some staffers decided to see if they could exploit the FBI's racism and make it work for the movement. Maybe involving white volunteers finally would force the federal government to intervene on the side of civil rights.[32] Local Afro-Mississippian leaders favored an expanded Freedom Vote. They wanted "exposure," Moses recalled, anything that would open the state's "closed society."[33]

The Summer Project provided a potential path toward achieving Black voting rights. It did something else equally revolutionary: It forged an entirely original approach to dismantling Jim Crow. "It didn't matter if white Mississippians refused to integrate," observed Moses. Black communities would do the integrating because they would have "whites living in their homes, going to their churches, eating at their tables." In creating "a parallel social arrangement," the Project executed an ingenious end run around segregation.[34] Moses saw it as their best chance for cracking Mississippi open, and eventually he did something he rarely did, which was to throw his weight behind it.[35]

Soon the word went out to college campuses, and journalists began writing about their audacious plan. To the press, Moses pitched it this way: "These students bring the rest of the country with them. They're from good schools and their parents are influential. The interest of the country is awakened and when that happens, the Government responds to that interest."[36] To a smaller audience, Moses employed a metallurgical analogy, as he argued that the Summer Project would bring about an "annealing process." Just as metal can be "shaped and molded" once it's been brought to "white heat," so could the South and the nation.[37]

Moses's strategy depended upon young Northern whites providing the all-important "white heat."[38] Yet these were not metals that SNCC was messing with. This became apparent when the state of Mississippi declared its intention to fight back against what white Mississippians routinely called the "invasion."[39] It would be purchasing armored cars and tanks and hiring an additional 200 men to work as state police officers. One leader of a White Citizens' Council in the state roused his troops by telling them, "They don't want something *like* what you got, they want *what* you got—your women!"[40]

Interracialism and Its Discontents

Within SNCC people were divided about the Summer Project. Dorie Ladner, an Afro-Mississippian who became involved with SNCC during her first year at Tougaloo College, favored it. She believed from the start that when the summer was over, "Mississippi would never be the same."[41] But the Project generated more opposition than support. Some felt uneasy about bringing so many white students into the state. SNCC had always been a Black-led organization, and the recent uptick in the number of white staffers made many people uncomfortable. At the end of 1963, whites constituted about 20 percent of SNCC's staff of nearly 100.[42]

Skeptics were especially critical of putting whites in the field, particularly because of the racial dynamics between veteran Black staff and white volunteers that sometimes emerged during the Freedom Vote.[43] Even slotting whites into office work, especially in the Jackson headquarters, irritated some Black staffers, who complained about the officiousness of male volunteers for whom taking over was second nature. Staffers were still shaking their heads about volunteers who arrived in Mississippi in their sports cars, or as one put it, "Yalies running around in their Triumphs."[44]

Also troubling were the interactions between local Blacks and white volunteers. That fall, Black staffers looked on, incredulous, as Afro-Mississippians who earlier had brushed off their appeals that they get involved, turned instantly compliant with white male volunteers. Even Charles Sherrod, an advocate of interracial organizing, had second thoughts about the project. Sherrod had successfully put together interracial teams in southwest Georgia, but he always emphasized sharing uncomfortable feelings, which likely enabled real bonding across the color line. Still, he noted that local Blacks who repeatedly brushed aside the entreaties of veteran Black organizers, sometimes paid attention to a white student who had only just arrived in the South. How radical was interracial organizing if whites were unintentionally reinforcing the very patterns of racial deference that SNCC was committed to eradicating? Some staffers contended that interracialism was undermining SNCC's ability to develop local Black leadership.[45] It was dispiriting for SNCC staffers when older locals would ask, "when are those *white* civil rights workers coming so that we can do something?"[46]

Early in the planning of the Summer Project, these critics of interracialism proposed establishing limits on the kind of work that whites could do.[47] At a November 1963 meeting of Mississippi staffers, it was proposed that directing projects, writing platforms, or operating the Wide Area Telephone Service (WATS) would be off-limits.[48] They stressed that every effort should be made to screen whites and to funnel them into projects working in white communities. Some staffers apparently thought that whites had no place in the movement.[49] "All we have to do," said Dona Richards, "is tell the whites your function is to be seen but not heard."

Bob Moses usually had about him a "quality of serenity that made him a rock of steadfastness," but not that day.[50] Even though his critics included Richards, the woman he was currently dating and would soon marry, he grew impatient. "People say if Negroes and whites work in the field, they're more articulate and they're going to do the talking. And then if you say put them in the office, they're better typists [and] they get into leadership positions [so] you don't want them *there* ... then there's no place for them." When his Black coworkers complained about the whites taking over the WATS line in SNCC's Greenwood office, Moses seemed angry. "Just the reverse had been happening," he argued. Mike Miller and Dick Frey, who ran the Greenwood office that summer, were relegated to performing "dirty work," such as wiping desks and sweeping floors. Meanwhile, the Black staff put severe limitations on what they could do. "They had to stay in the office—they couldn't go out in the street, they couldn't go to dances, they couldn't go to this café or that café."

Moses bristled further when someone complained about Mendy Samstein working the WATS line. He argued there was "a big difference between saying, a white man's on the WATS line and *Mendy's* on the WATS line." He labeled this sort of generalizing "dehumanizing" and maintained that it fallaciously suggested that "any Negro can talk to any other Negro because he is a Negro." Moses knew from his own experience that it wasn't so. "If you want to run that kind of an organization—a racist organization—then you can count me out," he said.

Yet there were Black staffers who were uneasy about working with white staffers, even Mendy Samstein. Ivanhoe Donaldson was troubled by the growing presence of whites. He worried that "we're losing the one thing where the Negro can stand first." Moses seemed unable to cope with the feelings of his Black coworkers. He later admitted that he generally discouraged the kind of "soul-sharing" that Charles Sherrod encouraged in the Southwest Georgia project.[51] "The one thing we can do for the country," he said, "which no one else can do, is to be above the race issue." Moses came close to reprimanding his colleagues, who responded by admitting that they knew their feelings were irrational. The discussion concluded at midnight when Moses called it to a close. Everyone stood up and, locking hands, sang what Howard Zinn thought was an especially heartfelt and impassioned version of "We Shall Overcome."

Minutes of a mid-January 1964 COFO staff meeting reveal that skepticism about the Project continued to run deep among both white and Black activists. Moses may have felt frustrated by this, but he nevertheless argued for an honest airing of differences. He warned that the group would find itself in a "great mess ... if we superficially agree to the program, allow the North to mobilize and not prepare for them because of internal division and lack of enthusiasm." Supporters carried the vote, but a quarter opposed it, and several more expressed strong reservations, particularly about whether the "COFO machinery can handle it," as Casey Hayden put it.[52] She advised scaling down the project and so did Maria Varela, who, with Elizabeth "Betita" Sutherland Martínez, was one of two Latinas on staff. To Varela, bringing 1,000 students into Mississippi seemed "like chaos looking for a place to self-destruct."[53] Moses observed that to "think about 1000 college students, mostly white, in Mississippi for the summer was overwhelming. The staff needed time to bat it around, shape it up, sink it in."[54]

Bat it around they did, with debate continuing until February 1, when an urgent phone call interrupted a COFO staff meeting in Hattiesburg. The caller relayed the terrible news of Louis Allen's death. Literally mid-debate, the staffers committed themselves to the Project.[55] Still, agreement within SNCC hinged on the recruitment of a much more manageable number of volunteers. COFO was a coalition effort, or what Mary King called "an ersatz coalition." SNCC was very much the junior partner, providing most of the personnel and resources, but having to defer to the other more established organizations. All parties had to be onboard with policy changes, and SNCC's effort to limit the number of volunteers to 100 failed.[56] Once again, the talk turned to bringing in 1,000 students. The COFO staff did try to rein in the tendency of white male students to take over by mandating that all project directors be Black.[57]

Meanwhile, by this point some SNCC staffers had been working for nearly a year to involve Afro-Mississippian college students in voter registration work. Bob Moses, Dona Richards, and Jane Stembridge were all part of this effort. They knew that some of these students wanted to participate in the movement but were worried about how it might interfere with their studies. They devised an innovative work-study project that enabled college-age Blacks in the state to attend Tougaloo College on scholarship during the 1965–66 academic year if they had spent the previous year working in the voter registration effort. By the summer of 1963, they had secured a $40,000 grant from the Field Foundation, which was enough to fund 30 students. The application for the project indicated applicants would be notified of their status by the end of July. That August, having attracted not even one applicant, Richards circulated a memo to SNCC's Mississippi field staff in the hope of stirring some interest. The project, she said, would enable SNCC to realize one of its "main objectives: that of affording potential indigenous leadership the opportunity to develop itself." She emphasized just how crucial this was to next year's plans—presumably the Summer Project.[58] Eventually, 20 Black students took advantage of the Work-Study Project that year.[59]

Years later, James Forman said that he and other SNCC staffers had tried their best to recruit Black people for the Summer Project so it would not come off like a white invasion. In the end, they came up short, with Blacks making up less than 10 percent of the applicants.[60] Parental resistance may account for why the turnout was not more robust. There is some evidence that quite a few of the Black students who volunteered for the Summer Project pulled out upon realizing they would be so outnumbered by white students.[61] And not just ordinary white students. Forman later said that the planners "made a conscious attempt . . . to recruit from some of the Ivy League schools." Forman maintained that he and others who backed the Summer Project "knew what we were up against," which is why "we were, in fact, trying to consciously recruit a counter power-elite."[62] Involving students whose parents were well-to-do and well-connected could only improve the odds that they might succeed in making a crack in Mississippi's wall of never that summer.

There was another reason they focused their recruiting efforts on such students: They had money. This was a real consideration because SNCC's coffers were so bare that spring that workers went three times without paychecks.[63] As a consequence, SNCC selected only those students who could pony up $150, the sum necessary for covering living expenses and posting bond in case of arrest. This was a lot of money, in today's dollars just shy of $1,500.[64] Back in June 1961, SNCC believed their voter registration effort would be funded. Hadn't Kennedy and other Justice Department officials promised this? The attorney general had recruited philanthropists Stephen and Audrey Currier of the Taconic Foundation, which began to funnel money to the movement through the Southern Regional Council and COFO.

The Taconic Foundation enabled civil rights workers to spread out across the Delta in 1962–63.[65] However, in a curious twist, the great bulk of that money went to other civil rights groups, even though SNCC was providing the bulk of the full-time voter registration workers.[66] At the time, Forman claimed that one reason SNCC's finances were so dire was that the financial support promised by prominent people and by institutions had not materialized. This is reportedly why Forman initiated SNCC's fundraising arm, the FOS, in 1962.[67] Although FOS chapters brought in a lot of money through direct mail campaigns and benefits, they could not meet SNCC's growing financial obligations. The result was that the spring of 1964 began "in typical SNCC fashion—moneyless."[68] SNCC's lack of money was a daunting obstacle in recruiting Black students, few of whom came from families with

Image 2.1 From left, Bob Moses, Minister Bruce Hanson of the National Council of Churches, and James Forman discuss with other SNCC staffers on June 18, 1964, the training sessions for Freedom Summer volunteers in Oxford, Ohio.
Gene Smith/AP

the financial resources that would permit them to underwrite their children's activism. Still, some Black college students arrived unfinanced. Ruth Howard (later Ruth Howard Chambers) was part of a contingent of Black volunteers from Howard University and described herself and quite a few of the others as "un-financed."[69]

If the volunteers were overwhelmingly white and economically privileged, it was crucial that their aims be compatible with those of the Project, that they be what Moses called "the right type of persons."[70] SNCC leaders made it clear to the FOS people choosing the volunteers that they should look for people who could take orders from Black staffers, and who were motivated neither by thrill seeking nor by liberal paternalism. White staffer

Mike Miller supervised this work in the Bay Area and says that he weeded out such people. So did Dottie Zellner, a white SNCC stalwart and the wife of Bob Zellner. Along with Katie Clark, the daughter of Black psychologists Kenneth and Mamie Clark, she interviewed applicants from colleges in the Northeast.[71] Black activist William Strickland, who headed up the Northern Student Movement, was also involved in the recruitment process.[72]

Redefining Solidarity

SNCC was not only culling applicants. It began doing something more ambitious: redefining the very terms of solidarity. It was no longer acceptable for outsiders to see themselves as "helping" Black Southerners. Your involvement, they told volunteers, needs to be rooted in an understanding of your own personal investment in changing the system. This was a substantial shift, and it's evident in a spring 1964 speech that a SNCC field secretary made to Stanford students. "When you come," he advised, "come to help yourself, not the Negro."[73]

Most Stanford students were likely puzzled by the notion that they were helping *themselves* by heading off to Mississippi. But what this field secretary was trying to get across was an alternative to what he and others in SNCC considered the liberal paternalism involved in aiding others. After all, the idea that Blacks needed help could have undertones of pity that rendered invisible their bravery, tenacity, and ingenuity in the long battle to win their freedom.[74] Volunteers needed to understand that the system oppressed them, too, and to fight it. Take Hayden, whose participation in the struggle stemmed in large part from her desire to live an integrated life.

Impressing upon white volunteers that they should consider themselves stakeholders in change would be a refrain that summer. It was a refrain at the training session for volunteers in Oxford, Ohio, in June. SNCC advisor Vincent Harding asked volunteers there, "Are you going as 'In' members of the society to pull the 'Outs' in with you? Or are we all 'Outs'?" Bob Moses spoke at the training sessions, too. "Don't come to Mississippi this summer to save the Mississippi Negro," he urged them. "Only come if you understand, really understand, that his freedom and yours are one."[75]

Embedded in this mandate was SNCC's growing skepticism about liberalism. They were not alone in this. In the winter of 1963, the Black writer Amiri Baraka (né LeRoi Jones) described liberals as "people with extremely heavy consciences and almost nonexistent courage. Too little is always enough."[76] In any case, when Vincent Harding asked trainees in Ohio whether they were trying "to make liberal readjustments or basic change," it was clear which side he was on. The SNCC field secretary who addressed Stanford students came right out and said, "SNCC has no place for white liberals."[77] The idea that white liberals weren't welcome in a civil rights organization would have seemed odd to the audience, most of whom identified as liberal. However, SNCC workers' impatience with liberals was turning into out-and-out antagonism. If liberals were content to "go slow" on civil rights, then liberalism be damned.

Nonetheless, those choosing who would go to Mississippi did not disqualify applicants for being liberal. Paternalism was a different matter. Yet efforts to eliminate applicants motivated by feelings of noblesse oblige were not totally successful.[78] According to Doug McAdam, the leading scholar of the Project, the journals and letters of Northern white volunteers reveal that a good number of them "brought a kind of 'missionary' attitude to the project."[79] One piece of proof comes from Dennis Sweeney, a Stanford undergraduate whose blue-collar roots made him a rarity at the Palo Alto campus.[80] Recruited by Allard Lowenstein, Sweeney had gone to Mississippi in the fall of 1963 for the Freedom Vote. In his recruitment pitch to his fellow students for the Summer Project, Sweeney said that "any white Northerner" with even an average education was "so much more talented than the Negro leadership in the movement in the South, that in *one day*, he can make a significant contribution."[81] Sweeney would change, but his casual racism, even after being in Mississippi, reveals the mismatch between longtime SNCC staffers, who dominated COFO, and some newcomers and volunteers.[82]

Envisioning yourself as having a stake in the freedom movement was perhaps easier for Jewish volunteers, though the attraction of helping was not foreign to them. It is likely that between 20 and 30 percent of the volunteers that summer were Jewish, a high number given that Jews comprised less than 3 percent of the total U.S. population.[83] In the aftermath of World War II, anti-Semitism was still a reality, which is one reason Jewish émigrés often taught at historically Black colleges and universities. American Jews faced educational quotas, restrictive housing covenants, job discrimination, religious bigotry, and ugly stereotyping. Because anti-Semitic and anti-Black discrimination overlapped, activists often spoke of the parallel experiences that marked the lives of Jewish Americans and Black Americans.[84]

The growing consciousness in the United States about the Holocaust solidified this feeling of parallelism, particularly among left-wing Jews and some Black activists. In fact, the Nazi analogy became a staple of 1960s left liberalism, which likened the American South to Nazi Germany and chastised as "good Germans" white Americans who turned a blind eye to racism in the South.[85] Martin Luther King Jr., speaking to the American Jewish Congress in 1958, reminded his audience that racists "make no fine distinctions between the Negro and the Jew." When Rabbi Joachim Prinz, then the president of the American Jewish Congress, spoke at 1963's March on Washington, he claimed Jews understood "neighbor" as a "moral concept," and that their own painful history enabled their "complete identification and solidarity" with Black people.[86]

Rabbi Prinz's views notwithstanding, Jews' history of oppression and genocide did not always generate an identification with Black people. Indeed, those whose liberalism was more cautious grew increasingly critical of Jews such as Rabbi Prinz for prioritizing anti-Black racism rather than anti-Semitism. Moreover, by mid-century, Jewish people, regardless of their politics, were becoming more integrated into the American mainstream and becoming more unambiguously "white" as they did. This was particularly true in the South, where anti-Semitism made many Jewish communities keep their distance from the movement. When one Jewish SNCC worker went to a synagogue in Albany, Georgia, looking for support, a man by the name of Stonewall Cohen told him Jews needed to be as white as possible and to keep quiet about segregation. Cohen then kicked him out.[87]

Some summer volunteers had a consciousness of parallelism, which was transmitted by their left-wing parents or acquired through their repudiation of assimilationist parents. For others, such as Mendy Samstein, a white Jewish left-winger with working-class roots, this consciousness developed independent of his relationship to his parents. Samstein, who became involved in late 1963, did so to prevent the "destruction of a race" from happening again.[88] That summer, participants often advanced this analogy between the American South and Nazi Germany.[89]

The connections between anti-Semitism and anti-Black racism were brought home for some in the third week of June. The second group of volunteers had barely arrived in Ohio when a worried call came in from Hayden in Jackson, Mississippi, to Bob Moses in Ohio. Three civil rights workers in Neshoba County were missing, she said. James Chaney, an Afro-Mississippian, and Michael Schwerner, a white Jewish New Yorker, were CORE workers. Andrew Goodman, who was also white and Jewish and from New York, was a summer volunteer who had literally just set foot in Mississippi. Before the call ended, Hayden told Moses, "You have to tell people to be very careful." No sooner had she spoken than she realized the uselessness of her advice. Caution was no shield in Mississippi.[90]

Veterans of the struggle expected the worst. They knew Schwerner and Chaney had been working in the town of Meridian for several months. It was their partnership that led the Ku Klux Klan (KKK) to target them. "Goatee" was the KKK's nickname for Schwerner, who did look like a beatnik.[91] The three men had been arrested on trumped-up charges after driving to the small town of Philadelphia to investigate the burning of a Black church with ties to the Project. They disappeared after being released from jail in the middle of the night. Six weeks later, FBI agents exhumed their bodies, which had been dumped by their killers in a fresh earthen dam.[92]

It might be tempting to say that their murders, a coordinated effort carried out by the KKK and one of its members, the deputy sheriff, was a case of parallel lives. The Imperial Wizard of the KKK who masterminded it boasted that it was "the first time that Christians had planned and carried out the execution of Jews."[93] But Chaney died differently from Schwerner and Goodman. He was savagely beaten before being shot, whereas each of them was shot once in the chest. Still, the most troubling difference was the nation's response to their murders. President Lyndon Baines Johnson, who became president after Kennedy's assassination in late November 1963, personally reached out to the families of the two white men, but not to the family of James Chaney. SNCC Chairman John Lewis declared it "a shame that national concern is aroused only after two white boys are missing."[94] Of course, this was the logic of the Summer Project, making the national response completely expectable, but no less infuriating. The press remained focused on the white volunteers, not the Black veterans who had been putting their lives on the line for some time.[95] Just how parallel were their lives? Someone might have pointed out that "parallels are two lines that run side by side and never meet except in infinity."[96]

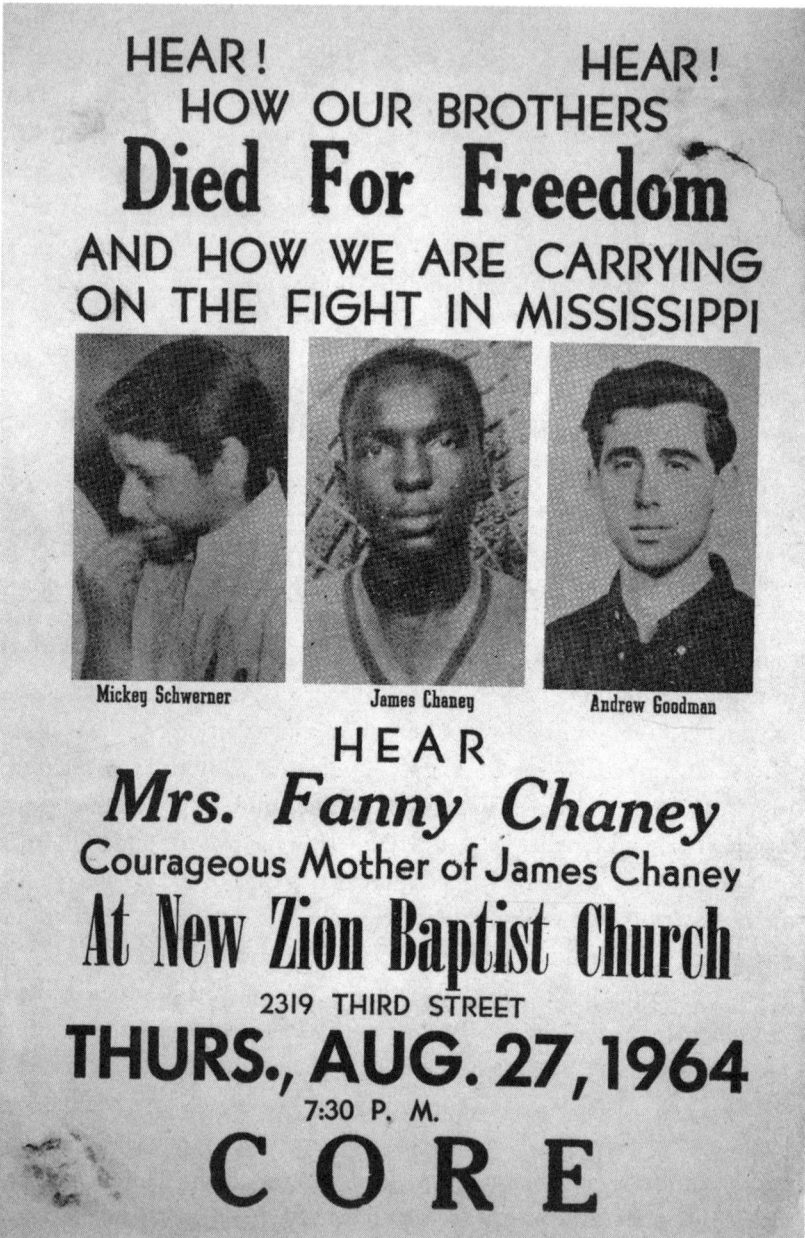

Image 2.2 Poster for a CORE-sponsored event, three weeks after the discovery of the bodies of civil rights workers James Chaney, Andrew Goodman, and Mickey Schwerner.

Danny Lyon/Magnum Photos

Image 2.3 In December 1964, Dr. Martin Luther King Jr. commended the federal government for arresting the killers of Chaney, Goodman, and Schwerner. Andrew Young is to his left.

George Brich/AP Photo

Freedom Summer

But to return to the start of the summer, to the period when the disappearance of Chaney, Schwerner, and Goodman weighed on everyone. It was a tense and tough beginning. The volunteers had only one week of training on the campus of the Western College for Women in Oxford, Ohio, before arriving in Mississippi.[97] The training they received there could not begin to prepare them for what they would confront in "The Hospitality State," as Mississippi called itself. One speaker who addressed them tried to prepare them for what lay ahead. "There's not even a sharp line between living and dying," he said wearily, "it is just a thin fuzz."[98] Once in Mississippi, so much about it was disorienting, particularly the extreme poverty of rural Black communities. A woman volunteer from an upper-middle-class Jewish family in New York remembers "seeing too much, feeling too much. Things weren't supposed to be like this."[99]

The people who helped orient the volunteers were their Afro-Mississippian hosts. Taking in white guests made you vulnerable to retaliation—losing your job and/or losing your home, sometimes through a bombing. Despite the risks involved in housing people whom most white Mississippians regarded as "outside agitators"—beatniks and communists—their hosts treated the volunteers with warmth and generosity.[100] Not all Afro-Mississippians approved of the volunteers, and some allege that the class divide within Black communities widened that summer.[101] However, those who hosted volunteers showed generosity and courage. One woman wrote her mother to say of the family with whom she was boarding, "such love oozes from this house I can't begin to explain."[102] And then there were the churches. Of a powerful mass meeting in a church, one volunteer wrote, "It was just so different from the way I had been raised; you know, to be proper and demure and all that." The release she experienced in a Black church "was just a great feeling."[103]

If Afro-Mississippian locals expressed gratitude, SNCC workers often seemed to be waging a gratitude boycott. Moses later acknowledged that the staff's response to the volunteers was mixed. Some wondered why it was incumbent upon them to be grateful when the volunteers had yet to do anything but perhaps sacrifice a laid-back summer at the beach. If they were truly *in* the struggle, they shouldn't need validation. White volunteer Sally Belfrage was a red-diaper baby from New York City and no stranger to politics. Staffers' resentment felt palpable to her. "This was as difficult for some volunteers to assimilate as it was understandable: the volunteers wanted gratitude . . . and couldn't understand why there was a tendency to use them simply as the most accessible objects of Negro anger." The staff's response "acted to diminish any self-important, bloated white pride," which she thought was no bad thing. Still, the feeling of many newcomers was wounded frustration at being rejected. "*I want to be your friend, you black idiot*, was the contradiction everywhere," Belfrage wrote.[104]

The truth was that SNCC staffers neither needed nor wanted new friends. They were already enveloped in a circle of trust. "They were *SNCC people*," explained Cleveland Sellers, a Black student from Howard, new to Mississippi. "They had a definable lifestyle" that included reading the same books and dressing in much the same way—blue-jean overalls, work shirts, and tees. "They worked, ate, socialized and slept together." The vibe they gave off, he recalled, was that they "considered themselves different from those who had not shared their unique experience."¹⁰⁵ SNCC workers may have labored out of the spotlight with little if any recognition, but they saw themselves as "a band of brothers and sisters" who understood and sustained each other.¹⁰⁶

For movement veterans, SNCC was their home, where they truly belonged. Now they had to contend with all these strangers. There were only 136 SNCC people and as many as 800 volunteers, cycling in and out of SNCC-controlled projects over the course of the summer.¹⁰⁷ Who were these volunteers, and how could they be certain of their motivations? That old question—Why would they care?—resurfaced. Then, veterans would remind themselves that the volunteers were coming despite the very real risks. White veteran staffers were no less ambivalent. Mary King observed that some felt threatened by the newcomers who threatened their sense of "specialness." Hayden said it was "weird" being around so many white people. "I felt exposed," she later admitted, "like I'd been passing before and now was found out."¹⁰⁸ Perhaps white veterans also worried about the volunteers embarrassing them and reinforcing their Black comrades' skepticism about interracialism.

What we do know is that the volunteers craved approval. Quite a few tried to copy the dress and style of the SNCC veterans. Off came their preppie clothes and on came the SNCC uniform of denim. Soon some volunteers were using Black slang and trying to sound "Black."¹⁰⁹ No one in SNCC was more copied than the COFO director Bob Moses. White volunteer and future student activist Mario Savio later wrote of wanting "to be Bob Moses."¹¹⁰ Sellers admits that almost everyone, Black and white alike, shared that fantasy. Moses had a habit of rolling his hand as he spoke, and others copied him. "We thought we were smarter if we did that," recalled Julian Bond with a smile. However, for whites, Moses became a full-blown "*culture hero.*" In only a matter of days some of the volunteers started to appropriate Bob Moses's "slow, thoughtful manner of speaking," an affectation that did not endear them to Black veterans. They wanted to belong, but they were ignorant about so much: Mississippi, racism, the SNCC art of organizing, and just who they were and could possibly be.¹¹¹

So how did solidarity politics play out during the summer? Did all that white heat have the effect that Moses promised?

Voter registration was what ignited the Project, and it remained central to the whole effort, whether it involved trying to get Afro-Mississippians officially registered, which was close to impossible, or registered in the parallel party, which became known as the Mississippi Freedom Democratic Party (MFDP). Within the world of Freedom Summer, canvassing and voter registration were clearly "where it was at." "There was a feeling in the air," recalls Staughton Lynd, the white academic and activist who initially directed the Freedom Schools, "that the voter registration folks were, so to speak, the 'elite' troops."[112] Local customs and the "macho adventurism" of many of the white male volunteers meant that the ranks of this elite featured Black staffers—both women and men—and white male volunteers. A few white women wrangled their way onto interracial teams with Black women. But for the most part, the Project's goal was, as it had always been in SNCC, to keep white women out of view. "Hiding" them in offices, schools, and community centers was their aim, as Stokely Carmichael later admitted.[113]

Canvassing and voter registration were exceedingly tough. "We drive from farmhouse to farmhouse," recalled one young white man who averaged up to 200 miles a day in the Project's car.[114] Sometimes they got lucky and their talks with individuals succeeded in getting them to show up to a meeting. However, people often greeted them with a ready list of excuses for staying away. Muriel Tillinghast, a Northern-born Black SNCC project director, recalls she and her team began their days at 4:30 a.m. to be able to talk to the cotton and day workers without jeopardizing them or their livelihoods. "We worked, family by family, person by person," she recalled. "As a rule, we did not talk to anybody unless someone we knew said it was okay." Wherever you were, you had to know "its roads and every possible means out of town . . . like the back of your hand." Tillinghast emphasized, "your life depended on it."[115]

Less prestigious but vitally important was the Project's work in community centers and freedom schools. Community centers took on a wide range of services that included everything from daycare and youth recreation to adult education, job training, and assistance with Social Security. The centers spawned groups focused on everything from health care to the election of local Black farmers to county committees of the U.S. Department of Agriculture's Agricultural Stabilization and Conservation Service. As for the Freedom Schools, like the MFDP, they were part of SNCC's strategy of establishing parallel institutions. It was Black SNCC staffer Charles Cobb who argued for Freedom Schools as a component of the Summer Project.[116] They seemed necessary in a state determined to provide Black children with a "mis-education" rather than a real education.[117] (Mississippi allocated $81.66 to each white student and $21.77 to each Black student.) Demand was so overwhelming that organizers who had expected a turnout of 1,000 students attracted nearly three times that number in the 41 schools they operated.[118] Indeed, overcrowding was often a problem.[119] Local and state officials tried whatever they could to shut down the schools. Terrorist tactics were deployed, too. Take Hattiesburg, where the three churches that had agreed to host Freedom Schools were burned down. When the school finally opened there, teachers worried that the attacks might dampen the children's attendance, but over 600 students, over six times the number they had expected, showed up.[120]

The Freedom Schools did not operate out of public school classrooms, to which they had no access. They were held in church basements. The schools were supposed to enhance students' literacy and understanding of civics, particularly the Constitution, so they could pass the qualifying test and vote. But organizers also had much bigger aims: to undo the damage done by the state's public schools. If the goal of Mississippi schools was to teach Black students to "stay in your place ... and be satisfied—a 'good n****r,'" as Charles Cobb put it, then Freedom Schools were designed to get students "to articulate their own desires, demands and questions." It was the first time that most Black schoolchildren had the experience of being taken seriously by a schoolteacher. Engaging students was hard work, not made any easier by the fact that the children were raised to distrust whites. "There is a lot of 'Yes Ma'am' and constant agreement with what you say," noted one frustrated teacher.[121]

There were many success stories, too. Years later, Stokely Carmichael ventured that the Freedom Schools, with their curricular and pedagogical innovations, were "probably the most unambiguous successes" of that summer.[122] White volunteer Pam (Chude) Parker Allen said her students "know they have been cheated and they want anything and everything that we can give them." If local Afro-Mississippians wanted exposure to the wider world, their children got it in the schools. The schools provided the state's earliest instruction in Black history and French language instruction. The curriculum also reflected SNCC's political leanings. The dominant view in both SNCC and SDS was that the movement should commit itself to building an interracial movement of the poor. This view was reflected in the curriculum, which emphasized the commonalities between the South's poor whites and poor Blacks.[123] The schools also made a point of making analogies between Mississippi's anti-Black racism and Nazi Germany's anti-Semitism. Students were given mimeographed pamphlets detailing Hitler's rise to power and the "oppression of Jews as they sought to accommodate themselves to terror." The point was to probe the parallels between how power operated in Nazi Germany and Mississippi.[124]

Was this controversial? There is some evidence that Black teachers at one school substituted their own more Afrocentric curriculum. Moses and his wife, Dona Richards, reportedly criticized these particular instructors for teaching propaganda rather than history.[125]

Skilled support staff, composed mostly of white professionals, played a consequential role, too. Nearly 150 lawyers and law students, affiliated with a range of groups, came to Mississippi to represent activists arrested by the authorities. Some 300 ministers who were a part of the National Council of Churches, an organization that provided material support to the Project, offered their services as well. Roughly 100 physicians, nurses, and psychologists tended to movement workers. They formed the foundation of what became the Medical Committee for Human Rights, a post–Summer Project organization that provided health care to poor Mississippians.[126]

The Summer Project's Tensions and Accomplishments

What were the effects of all this activity? Some were felt right away. Black students who attended a freedom school in Philadelphia, the town where Chaney, Schwerner, and Goodman were killed, returned to their public school that fall wearing buttons that read "SNCC" and "One Man One Vote." School officials sent them home, but the federal court upheld their right, under the First Amendment, to wear those buttons.[127] The historian John Dittmer saw the longer-term effects of a Freedom School education. Dittmer taught for years at Tougaloo College, where Ernst Borinski taught. He says he always knew which of his students had attended Freedom Schools. They spoke up freely and easily, and they had no compunction about challenging their professors, including their white ones.[128]

The disappearance of Chaney, Schwerner, and Goodman and the efforts by FOS chapters to publicize it, made a difference. The tragedy exposed conditions in Mississippi, which, in turn, galvanized a wider base of support, particularly outside the South. This had a knock-on effect, which helped to "stimulate a recalcitrant Congress" to pass the Civil Rights Act of 1964, which was signed into law by President Johnson on July 2.[129] And three years after the murders of Chaney, Schwerner, and Goodman, justice of some sort was finally meted out to seven of the white terrorists in Mississippi.

The Project's voter registration campaign, hair-raisingly dangerous though it was, also paid off. By the end of July, another 50,000 Afro-Mississippians were registered in the MFDP. Remarkably, 17,000 Black Mississippians made the trip to the courthouse to register. Even though the registrars accepted only 1,600 registrants, their courage in making the trip was noteworthy. Moreover, their efforts to officially register turned up overwhelming evidence of racial inequities. That evidence, and the brutal police attack on nonviolent marchers on the Pettis Bridge in Selma, helped to create the necessary momentum for the Voting Rights Act, which was signed into law on August 6, 1965.[130]

Central to Moses's plan was putting a spotlight on Mississippi, with the assistance of the national media. The media showed up in full force. Contrary to what Moses had hoped, though, the spotlight did not shield civil rights workers from violence, though likely it would have been worse without the media attention. Another problem was that over the course of the summer, journalistic coverage shifted from sympathetic to skeptical. Reporters began to ask questions about why SNCC chose to be represented by the left-wing National Lawyers Guild, a group with known "red" connections. Soon rumors began to circulate that SNCC had been infiltrated by communists. It had not, but the effort to label civil rights "communistic" was a tried-and-true tactic to defeat civil rights, one that was very effective in the Cold War years after World War II.[131]

The "red" angle was worrying, and so was an apparent shift in some national journalists' views of the volunteers.[132] Once praised for their courage and selflessness, they were now criticized as "spoiled, overindulged, rich white kids looking for a 'black experience.'" Journalists were especially tough on female volunteers whom they depicted as thrill-seeking sexual tourists. To Dottie Zellner, the idea was ludicrous. "I mean, let's face it, if sex is your motivation, why get killed?" Carmichael asked, "Why would any affluent, young, white college woman, intent on a summer of sexual adventure across the color line choose a destination with a violent history, hostile natives, high risk, constant tension, and a nervous host community vigilant for and intolerant of any sign of sexual impropriety?"[133] But precisely this trope of the white woman as false ally, nothing more than a sexual tourist, would be amplified six years later by Tom Wolfe when he satirized a "radical chic" white woman swooning over macho Black Panthers.[134]

Complicating any assessment of the Project at summer's end was that many of its successes would only become known years later. But certainly, if one measured the Summer Project's success through the violence of the backlash it generated, it was wildly successful. The tally stood as follows: 4 project workers killed; 4 people critically wounded; 80 workers beaten; 1,000 arrests; 37 churches bombed or burned; 30 Black homes or businesses bombed or burned. These were only the most glaring acts of terror. COFO compiled a chronological list of "hostile incidents" during Freedom Summer. It ran 25 pages.[135] "Hate and viciousness seemed to be everywhere," recalled Sellers.[136] People were exhausted and traumatized. "Fear can't become a habit," one volunteer had written to a friend that summer.[137]

Exhaustion made intragroup tensions loom large, overshadowing what the Summer Project had accomplished. The number of Northern Black staffers had been increasing since 1961, and from the beginning there was friction. SNCC's first chairman, Marion Barry, felt the Northern Black staffers behaved as though "they were there to teach us everything." He discerned "a barely concealed contempt and condescension on their part in the way they treated local people, as if they saw themselves as liberators." Gwen Patton believed some of the Northern Blacks, particularly the men, harbored stereotypical views of their Southern counterparts, assuming they could not be "deep thinkers, let alone [be able to] make analysis." Many Southern Black staffers seem to have considered their Northern colleagues "arrogant and pushy, too prone to seeing themselves as saviors."[138]

African Americans from the North often were better educated and more likely to be middle-class than their Southern counterparts. They began to take over the leadership. They started to dominate SNCC headquarters, reportedly because James Forman, the powerful executive secretary and more Northern than Southern, assigned them there. In one revealing passage in his memoir, Forman praises John Lewis's bravery, but admits that he sidelined SNCC's then-chairman from one especially important meeting with established civil rights leaders. Why had he done this? Forman judged Lewis "young, inexperienced, from a small Southern town" and likely to be "lost among those overpowering, tricky infighters."[139]

Forman was not the only one who seemed to favor Northerners. Even in the heart of the Mississippi Delta, where you would have expected Bob Moses to put a native Mississippian in charge, he chose Stokely Carmichael, a fellow New Yorker. Carmichael had "a feel for the common person," Moses thought, and "the ability to work with the white Northerners, all these sophisticated students, and command their respect."[140] Carmichael was many things—brilliant, fiery, and wickedly funny—and one can understand Moses's choice. Still, this shift in leadership was troubling to Southern staffers, who, like Joyce Ladner, believed that they "had much more of a stake in what happened in the South, in Mississippi than Northern Blacks."[141] But it seems that few Black Northerners did what Martha Prescod Norman Noonan did, which was to assign herself an "auxiliary and supportive" role.[142]

SNCC might have usefully tackled its intraracial differences, whether rooted in region, education, class, or gender.[143] But what felt more pressing and problematic was the very fact of the group's interracialism. This was clearly an effect of the Summer Project. Never had there been so many whites, and so many Blacks who wanted them gone. Some resented having to devote any amount of time to educating white volunteers, some of whom were badly in need of education.[144] "Too many people are naïve!" was the reaction of one white staffer.[145] Black staffer Prathia Hall Wynn worked closely with Charles Sherrod in the interracial Southwest Georgia project. She felt that white volunteers "never had to not speak their mind. They never had to not do whatever they felt like doing."[146]

However, it is also true that in some projects white volunteers were forced to lead very circumscribed lives that felt totally at odds with what they imagined participating in a freedom movement would be. For them, Mississippi was the land of rules. Worse, the rules that white volunteers were meant to obey were ones that veteran SNCC workers frequently flouted.[147] Confrontations became common in projects where white staffers questioned the authority of Black directors. To the white students, authority resided in the collective, not the project director. However, for many Black directors, heading up a project was the one area where they had authority. In the Canton COFO project, one white volunteer, angry at the inflexibility and hostility of the Black director, called him a "little Caesar" whose authoritarian methods were at odds with the ideals of the freedom movement. Fighting authoritarianism was why he was in the movement, he said indignantly.[148]

Even more destabilizing was the propensity of some white male volunteers to sideline local Black leaders because they considered themselves more competent or just took over because it was second nature. In some projects the effort to build indigenous leaders was set back that summer. Years later, one white volunteer talked about how ashamed he subsequently felt about how he had just taken over, effectively displacing the Black project director, who gradually withdrew. "I had absolutely no sensitivity to what might have been going on," he admitted.[149] Then there were those volunteers who made a point of impressing everyone with how enlightened and politically active they were. Their "500 causes," groaned one volunteer who was critical of this sort of showboating.[150]

Anger about the white volunteers could not help but affect relationships between longtime white and Black staffers, even those who were friends. Many SNCC people—Black and white—would have agreed with one white activist who came to feel, "White people were hopeless."[151] Whites' feeling of shame about their whiteness was another complicating factor. Black staffers likely didn't want to spend time around guilt-ridden whites. Provoking Black anger and white guilt was SNCC's long-standing practice of funneling whites into office work. Black staffers preferred staying in the field, but that had the unintended effect of giving whites a fair amount of power, which will be discussed in greater depth later.[152] The offices where whites predominated were also the ones where "the money went in and out."[153] Moreover, office work was seen as the least courageous and therefore least important work. At least one Black SNCC worker contends that he and other Blacks in the field resented the way that most of the whites in SNCC's offices spent their time "coffee clatching and talking with their friends on the WATS line all around the country" while they were risking their lives.[154]

Add sex into this mix, and it's no surprise that by summer's end, relations between Blacks and whites were frayed. Over the years, accounts of Freedom Summer have emphasized this part of the story, sometimes to the anger or bemusement of SNCC veterans. John Lewis, for one, maintained that way too much is made of '64 as the Summer of Sex. "When you're facing the razor-edge intensity of true life-and-death situations, the last thing on your mind is having sex with someone."[155] Others remember it differently. "There *was* a lot of sex in SNCC," says Jean Wheeler Smith, a Black staffer. "We were 20 years old!" As this suggests, accounts vary. However, people agree that white men's long-standing exploitation of Black women was a barrier to relationships between Black women and white men, although they did happen.[156] Sexual intimacy was more common between Black men and white women, though project directors strongly discouraged it because of the likelihood it would cause racist retaliation.[157]

Sometimes sex across the color line was a revelation. To one white volunteer the extent of heterosexual experimentation was "not so much license as one more small expression of a liberation that was taking place on all fronts."[158]

That said, individuals seem to have sometimes felt unseen, even exploited. White women sometimes felt that for some Black men sex was more about "hostility masquerading as normal sexual attraction." Black men have said little about this, but likely they sometimes felt unsure about the motives of the white women who slept with them. One thing for sure, the indiscretion of some white women in the company of Black men left Fannie Lou Hamer dismayed and "worried sick."[159] Experiences ran the gamut, but what happened that summer created further tensions between white and Black women, and that would have consequences down the line.[160]

How sex registered during the summer is not something we are likely to ever understand fully, if only because so much ink has already been spilled on it. Who could blame participants for steering the conversation elsewhere? Take the case of Bernice Johnson Reagon. She readily admitted there was "partnering going every way you can imagine between people who were risking their lives every day." Reagon's comment raises the possibility that not all the hooking up that summer was heterosexual, but whether heterosexual or not, this was not a topic she wanted to pursue.[161] It is reasonable to think that sex ramped up the tensions between Blacks and whites that summer, but it did not singlehandedly cause the emotional tumult that lay ahead for SNCC.

The Summer Project devised multiple ways of breaking through the "iceberg" of hate and fear that was white Mississippi.[162] Founded on the idea of parallelism, the project created freedom schools, alternatives to the substandard official schools that Black children attended, and community centers for the larger Black community. Through the voter registration campaign, they built an alternative political party. Whites either lived with Black families or they lived communally and interracially in freedom houses. But Moses's parallel world was an explicitly interracial world, and for some within SNCC, the events of that summer called into question the wisdom of working interracially. Amplifying Black staffers' doubts about integration—inside SNCC and in the larger world—was what happened immediately after the Project ended when the MFDP tried to displace the all-white Mississippi delegation in Atlantic City at the Democratic National Convention.

THREE
Atlantic City

Histories of the sixties often repeat the same story about the Democratic National Convention of 1964. It was there that the liberals of the Democratic Party crushed young activists' faith in liberalism, the political system, even America. Both for the left-wing activists of the sixties and for many of the scholars writing about them, "Atlantic City" became shorthand for liberal duplicity.[1] But was the rupture at the Democratic Convention the inevitable result of liberalism's moral bankruptcy?[2] Were the activists of SNCC correct in their post-Convention assessment of those they now dismissed as "allies" and "friends"—always with scare quotes? Were these "friends" sellouts intent upon cozying up to the Democratic Party establishment, or did they have legitimate reasons for advocating compromise? And what were the aims of the Student Nonviolent Coordinating Committee (SNCC) in this? It was in SNCC that the idea for an alternative political party that would challenge the all-white Mississippi delegation at the Democratic Convention in Atlantic City first took root. Did SNCC people imagine they would prevail at the convention? Were they united in thinking that an integrated Democratic Party was worth the fight?

Complicating the Story of Atlantic City

Answering these questions requires returning to late 1963, when Bob Moses first raised the idea of the Mississippi Freedom Democratic Party (MFDP) challenging the Mississippi regulars at the Democratic National Convention. Stokely Carmichael recalled that "folks thought he was nuts. Or fantasizing."[3] SNCC researcher Jack Minnis took part in the earliest discussions of a convention challenge in the final weeks of 1963. He had zero expectation that the Democratic Party would seat the delegation. Civil rights attorney Len Holt, who worked closely with SNCC that spring and summer, was there in late April 1964, at the launching of the MFDP at the cavernous Masonic Temple in Jackson, Mississippi. SNCC had expected hundreds to show up, but response was limp, with only 85 people turning up. "The scene bordered on the ridiculous," wrote Holt.[4] Four months later, at the party's state convention, the same Masonic Temple would be packed with 2,500 MFDP supporters. But for most of the spring and summer, the notion that the MFDP had a chance of unseating the Mississippi regulars in Atlantic City was a pipe dream.

Remember that the original reason for organizing the MFDP was symbolic: to demonstrate the deep desire of Afro-Mississippians to exercise their constitutional right to vote. Challenging the Mississippi regulars at the convention was not a part of the plan. Minnis, for one, pushed for the MFDP to go the convention, but not because he believed the delegation would be seated. He appreciated it as a tactic. Then, beginning in late February 1964, the goalposts started to move. It started at a meeting of the left-leaning California Democratic Council. There, the labor organizer and photographer George Ballis, the San Francisco civil rights attorney Beverly Axelrod, and Claude Hurst of Fresno introduced a resolution calling for the seating of the MFDP, which was unanimously adopted. In fact, it was Ballis, who had photographed the Southern movement, who came up with the name, the Mississippi Freedom Democratic Party. More than anyone, though, it was Ella Baker who built momentum for the challenge. Baker relentlessly lobbied Democratic members of Congress and the leadership of the United Auto Workers. On June 13, Americans for Democratic Action (ADA) came onboard, and eventually, so did nine state Democratic Party delegations.[5]

The support that the MFDP was garnering that spring and summer reinforced the conviction of some SNCC staffers that the MFDP might act as an opening wedge in a realignment of the nation's two political parties. The dream of "party realignment," whereby progressives were housed in the Democratic Party and conservatives in the Republican Party, stretched back to the 1930s. However, realignment required dislodging white supremacist Southerners from the Democratic Party, which hadn't happened 30 years earlier. It was aided in a curious way by the Cold War, in which American racism became a weapon used by the Soviet Union in its effort to win over the "Third World."[6] Democratic President Harry Truman's civil rights reforms were meant to undercut the Soviet Union's campaign to publicize the chasm separating America's democratic ideals and the reality.

Yet anyone dreaming of realignment had to acknowledge that on the cusp of the sixties the GOP was still the party of Lincoln. All its senators voted in favor of the 1957 Civil Rights Act, whereas only 11 of the Democrats' 29 senators did.[7] As the historian Steven F. Lawson has shown, the Black vote was critical to John Kennedy's victory three years later in the 1960 presidential race. The problem was that the votes of Southern whites were, too. Indeed, while the New Deal coalition was still capable of achieving landmark reforms, it was also increasingly fragile, on the verge of coming apart, and those "cross-pressures" put Kennedy in a "serious strategic straitjacket."[8]

Despite the strength of the white Southern Democratic wing, party realignment was the aim of left liberals such as Rustin; Walter Reuther, president of the United Auto Workers (UAW); Michael Harrington, author of the bestselling book about poverty, *The Other America*; and some people in SNCC and Students for a Democratic Society.[9] The way they saw it, with left liberals in control, no longer hamstrung by the party's reactionary Southern wing, Democrats could be unapologetically progressive, as long as unionists, Black Americans, and students provided crucial support. However, in contrast to SNCC activists, they prioritized the election of Lyndon Johnson in November over the seating of the MFDP at the convention.[10] At this point, Johnson was not yet the loathed warmonger he would become to many leftists. He began down that disastrous path in Vietnam just three weeks before the convention in Atlantic City.

Bob Moses and Cleveland Sellers of SNCC believed that the MFDP challenge at Atlantic City might kickstart party realignment. For a time, they believed they had the support of Bayard Rustin.[11] If they succeeded in getting the MFDP seated in Atlantic City, they intended to deploy similar tactics in other Southern states. Theirs was a long-game strategy. "Our ultimate goal," Sellers said, "was the destruction of the awesome power of the Dixiecrats," whose longevity in Congress meant that they headed up many important committees. With the Dixiecrats out of the way, Democrats could pursue "a wide-ranging redistribution of wealth, power and priorities throughout the nation."[12]

Nonetheless, there were some Black staffers—Southerners and Northerners alike—who strongly disagreed with the plan. At an early June meeting, they questioned why their colleagues were even bothering with the Democratic Party. Ruby Doris Smith Robinson asked what the challenge would accomplish besides "having Negroes in the National Democratic Party." Charles

Cobb saw "negligible value" in Black Americans being part of the Democratic Party. He also worried Black people might be "manipulated" by the parties, which he believed were "decadent." Ivanhoe Donaldson favored using the more "radical tool" of creating a "parallel structure." Even the more moderate John Lewis questioned whether they could achieve what they wanted from "liberal politics."[13]

On a trip to Mississippi in July, Rustin got a whiff of this sentiment. The SNCC people are "going to try and accuse everybody of selling them out," he complained to Martin Luther King Jr. He worried that their behavior at the convention would come across like "an assault on our friends."[14] By this point, Rustin had taken to calling himself "the Lone Wolf of Civil Rights."[15] A subsequent visit a few weeks later to the MFDP's headquarters in Washington, DC, did nothing to allay Rustin's fears. He worried that people in SNCC, who had only limited experience with the politics of compromise, would be unwilling to work cooperatively with those whose politics differed from their own.[16]

The point is that within certain quarters of SNCC, skepticism about the MFDP's prospects and the advisability of the whole exercise predated the convention. "I never thought we'd be seated," recalled Casey Hayden. "It was more a question of ethical necessity than winning."[17] But even the doubters began to feel that seating the MFDP delegation would be a way of honoring and making worthwhile the sacrifice paid by James Chaney, Andrew Goodman, and Michael Schwerner.[18] Once in Atlantic City, they gave it their all. On the boardwalk, right outside the hall, they displayed the burned-out shell of the blue Ford station wagon in which the three had been traveling, and large photographs of them.[19] Nonetheless, one white summer volunteer noted that when it came to the likelihood of the MFDP delegation being seated, "'optimism' among Mississippi veterans is a quality so muted as to be barely discernible."[20]

The Democratic Party, the Mississippi Challenge, and Backlash Fears

If some SNCC staffers were already cynical about the whole affair, what about the Democrats? Were the Democratic heavyweights the duplicitous sellouts of legend? There is no doubt that the leaders of the Democratic Party and their labor allies wanted to derail the challenge, which they believed would further

Image 3.1 Members of the Mississippi Freedom Democratic Party jam an entrance to Atlantic City's Convention Hall, the site of 1964's Democratic National Convention. Police barred them from entering because they lacked the proper credentials.
AP Photo

alienate working-class white Democratic voters. They pulled out all the stops. President Johnson's "remote control mistreatment" and his allies' strong-arm tactics were real and deplorable.[21] When MFDP delegate Fannie Lou Hamer appeared on national TV, detailing to the Credentials Committee the terrible violence she had endured in Mississippi when she tried to register to vote, President Johnson hastily called a news conference, to knock her off the cameras. He put vice-presidential hopeful Hubert Humphrey on notice that if he failed to manage the MFDP crisis he was off the national ticket. He also used J. Edgar Hoover in ways that so blatantly violated Federal Bureau of Investigation (FBI) procedures that it made even Hoover uneasy. Johnson ordered the FBI to put both the SNCC and MFDP people at the convention under surveillance. Hoover went so far as to tap the phones of SNCC headquarters in Atlanta.[22]

Johnson's ally Walter Reuther, erstwhile labor leader, was also ruthless. Through his powerful union, the UAW, Reuther had provided key support and funding for the freedom movement. Earlier that summer when SNCC

Image 3.2 Mississippi Freedom Democratic Party delegate Fannie Lou Hamer details the abuses she suffered trying to exercise her right to vote in testimony before the credentials committee of the Democratic Party on August 22, 1964.
AP Photo/File

telegrammed Reuther asking him to pressure Johnson and his Attorney General Bobby Kennedy to send the FBI agents to Mississippi to investigate the disappearance of Chaney, Goodman, and Schwerner, he got right on the phone. However, his priority in 1964 was a victory that November for the Democratic ticket. Reuther went on the warpath, threatening and bullying everyone from Dr. King to Joseph Rauh, who was simultaneously the legal counsel for MFDP and the UAW in Washington. Rustin likely faced intense pressure, too. Reuther made it clear that heads would roll, and funding would evaporate, if the convention descended into chaos around the Mississippi challenge. Rustin, King, Allard Lowenstein, and others were dispatched to preach the virtues of compromise to the MFDP and its allies.

Johnson and company went very low, and the SNCC people at the convention were repelled by their hardball politics and their undisguised contempt for poor Black Mississippians such as Fannie Lou Hamer. At a meeting with Johnson's delegation, they exploded at the unfairness of it all. Why should the MFDP compromise? And why should they listen to these liberals as though they were the movement's friends when they so clearly prioritized Johnson's election over the rights of Afro-Mississippians? Rustin had supported the challenge and his turn against it puzzled and stung those SNCC people who had looked up to him as a true radical. Amid the tumult, white SNCC staffer Mendy Samstein bolted from his seat. "You're a traitor, Bayard, a traitor!" he shouted.[23] Rustin, a man whose politics SNCC had judged too left-wing just four years earlier, was now considered a pariah by many in that same organization.[24]

To many Blacks and whites in SNCC, the convention revealed Johnson's obscene grandiosity. Carmichael sized up the situation as "King Johnson" trying to turn a political convention into his "coronation."[25] What they did not know was that Johnson was not coolly orchestrating his nomination. LBJ was beside himself, convinced that the convention would spiral out of control, and that his political rival, Robert Kennedy, whom he suspected had concocted the idea of the convention challenge, would opportunistically seize the reins of the party if conflict erupted on the convention floor. Those in Johnson's inner circle knew the truth: He was so distraught that he threatened to withdraw his name from nomination.[26]

Ultimately, a deal was hammered out, largely through the efforts of Reuther, but without the blessing of the MFDP. The regulars would not be ejected; the MFDP would have two at-large, nonvoting delegates, not of their choosing, on the floor. "We didn't come all this way for no two seats," was Hamer's response. Those lousy two seats overshadowed the party's most significant concession to them: the outlawing of segregated delegations after 1964.[27] This was an undeniable victory, and it represented the fruit of Freedom Summer.

The deal also left the white segregationists furious. It prompted Southern delegations to threaten a "wholesale walk-out" to protest the compromise. That news so exasperated Johnson that he threatened to walk right onto the stage of the convention and quit. "Fuck 'em all," Johnson told his press secretary.[28] Johnson was a wheeler-dealer politician, but he did support change. Privately, in a phone conversation with a Southern governor, he argued that the MFDP deserved representation. "Only pistols kept 'em out" of the political process, he contended, and things had to change, and change now.[29] Of course, Johnson did not refuse the nomination, but he knew that the Democratic Party had lost the South. On Election Day, Johnson crushed Goldwater everywhere, except for the South and Goldwater's own state of Arizona.

How do we understand the desperation and cold ruthlessness of these liberals? We could do worse than to start with some context. In America, liberals were both haunted by memories of what had not happened and what might happen. What had not happened was the social-democratic turn that characterized most Western European democracies in the aftermath of World War II. The white segregationist South tugged on American liberalism, making it "limited and distorted," not at all like the robust social-democratic governments of the United States' former allies. Liberal Democrats had been appeasing the Southern wing of their party for decades. Further distorting liberalism was the Cold War. SNCC had already run afoul of Cold War liberals by working with leftists with ties to the Communist Party. Democrats, whom Republicans had blamed for "losing" China to the communists, often went out of their way to be as aggressively anticommunist as their Republican counterparts.[30]

And then there was what might happen. Could America backslide on its tentative moves toward racial equality, as it did a century earlier? Both Democratic politicians and people in the civil rights establishment saw signs that the country might be doing just that. As early as December 1963, Bayard Rustin said that white Americans were growing weary of the civil rights movement. "They wish we would get lost." By the spring of 1964, their worries were growing, with the ascent of George Wallace and Barry Goldwater, and the losses the Democratic Party might sustain because of Johnson's Civil Rights Act of 1964 and July's uprising in Harlem. Johnson was worried that if the MFDP was seated, all the Southern delegations would stage a walkout, which would deliver the South, and maybe more, to his Republican rival, Goldwater. He and other liberals worried about what it meant, going forward, that an extremist like Goldwater had captured the nomination of the Republican Party. After all, of the two parties, the GOP had always been more supportive of Black civil rights. That year's Republican Convention held some disturbing clues. Baseball legend Jackie Robinson, a lifelong Republican, said of the convention, "I now believe I know how it felt to be a Jew in Hitler's Germany."[31]

The white supremacist campaign of George Wallace was also a huge worry. Wallace withdrew from the presidential campaign three days after Goldwater's nomination, thus signaling to his supporters whom they should vote for in the general election.[32] To Reuther, Rustin, Johnson, and other liberals, Wallace's campaign was perhaps the most troubling curveball of all. Wallace's shocking performance in the North—grabbing 30 percent of the vote in primaries in Indiana, and Wisconsin, and doing even better in Maryland—revealed that what had started as a Southern segregationist movement to counter the civil rights movement was evolving into a "more generalized nationwide 'white backlash.'"[33] Wallace embedded his anti-integrationist politics in a larger attack on big government, and it was resonating with many white voters north of the Mason-Dixon line.[34] Johnson's signing of the Civil Rights Act earlier that summer made the Democrats the party of civil rights—for the first time—and at the very moment when support for racial equality was weakening, a development they feared might have been accelerated by the riot in Harlem that July.

For left liberals who believed in party realignment, these developments pointed to a nightmarish version of realignment. The Democratic Party could rid itself of the Dixiecrats but find itself without a crucial part of its base: the blue-collar workers who had voted Democratic for three decades. Is it any wonder the party turned wobbly in the moment? Labor historian Nelson Lichtenstein believes that Johnson "may well have understood the centrifugal forces set in motion by the civil rights movement better than many liberals."[35] If the backlash gained traction, it would unravel the New Deal coalition that Johnson needed to enact his Great Society programs. For civil rights veterans such as Rustin, the fight for racial equality required holding this coalition together no matter what. LBJ was the movement's best hope for change, not, as many in SNCC contended, the movement's "main enemy."[36]

As they surveyed the political landscape, they saw an unforgiving white backlash. They were stunned that MFPD delegates and SNCC workers failed to see that the Democratic Party's promise to outlaw segregated delegations in the future was a huge victory. Rustin understood the disappointment felt by younger activists, "but to understand them," he wrote, "is not to say that they are right."[37] To him, opponents of the compromise were "trying to pluck defeat out of the jaws of victory."[38]

Rustin's view is not the one that has prevailed in the history books, which often chastise Northern white liberals for trying to bring the Black movement into line with the liberal orthodoxy. Yet this view fails to acknowledge that support for the compromise included leftists not known for toadying up to the liberal establishment. Consider the independent leftist journalist I. F. Stone. He kowtowed to no one. In the fifties, he criticized Democrat presidential candidate Adlai Stevenson's "nervous sidestep on civil rights." His coverage of Emmett Till's lynching emphasized the pervasiveness of white supremacy, North and South. Stone was also the only American journalist to challenge the Johnson administration's account of North Vietnamese aggression against the

United States in the Gulf of Tonkin earlier that August. Its story of "unprovoked attacks" against the United States was the basis for a congressional resolution that gave LBJ a "blank check" to prosecute the war. Yet when it came to the compromise at Atlantic City, Stone, who remained a stalwart supporter of the MFDP and SNCC, favored it.[39]

Tellingly, Arthur Waskow, who, with Marcus Raskin, was a mainstay at DC's left-wing Institute for Policy Studies (IPS), charted an intriguing third way. Waskow wrote to Bob Moses in early September about what he saw as a "crisis of sorts" in the way that the liberal establishment and the larger country understood "the whole Mississippi effort." He emphasized that it would have been a "disaster" for the MFDP to accept the compromise. But Waskow wanted Moses to know that within his political orbit he was in the minority. Even the very "best of the liberals," including "my good pro-SNCC friends," were dismayed by the MFDP's rejection of the compromise. People who had always stood with SNCC, including those at the National Council of Churches, which had generously funded SNCC from the start, felt wounded, he reported.

Waskow acknowledged that some people might believe that the compromise proved that "white liberals always were bound to crump out." However, he saw things differently. "I think we are all partly at fault for not immediately getting across to the country with perfect clarity what the reasons for rejection were." Waskow suggested that Moses write an article for a big national magazine that explained the MFDP's decision. Most of all, he advised SNCC to heal the emerging generation gap by re-establishing its relationship to the liberal-labor-church leadership.[40] The point is that left-wing people outside the liberal establishment believed the compromise represented real progress.

One crucial difference separating left liberals such as Waskow, Stone, and Rustin from many young activists in SNCC and SDS was their keen awareness of the fragility of America's liberal center. Stone, for example, took umbrage at folk singer Phil Ochs's song "Love Me, I'm a Liberal," his snide putdown of liberals. Indeed, for Stone, Rustin, and Waskow, while LBJ was not their friend, neither was he their enemy. This stance characterized many leftists, including those in the Communist Party. In a debate with the leftist journalist Robert Scheer, who in 1966 ran for Congress against the Democratic incumbent representing Berkeley and northern Oakland, Dorothy Healey of the Communist Party warned against "the mistaken optimism so prevalent on the New Left that the country's ruling circles had made a permanent decision to rule through the cooptive politics of liberalism rather than the coercive politics of reaction."[41] Years later, Scheer admitted that the New Left's big error was "exaggerating the strength of the liberal center."[42]

SNCC Turns Away from Coalitions with Liberals

Yet Moses and others in SNCC were not inclined to wrestle with the precariousness of liberalism or with why some on the left also supported the compromise. Moses did meet with people in the National Council of Churches, but there is no evidence that he was persuaded by Waskow or anyone else trying to get SNCC back into the civil rights fold.[43] When it came to the white backlash, SNCC people may have been paying less attention to what was happening in the North, but in the South they were certainly living in the belly of that beast. In the aftermath of Freedom Summer, Charles Sherrod noted the growth of right-wing white citizens councils across the United States.[44] Still SNCC saw things very differently from many people in the left-liberal orbit. Where was the evidence that the Democratic Party would combat the ongoing white backlash in the South? Despite Bob Moses's hopes, the federal government had done little to protect civil rights workers during Freedom Summer. Yes, the FBI devoted a lot of man hours (and money) to locating the bodies of Chaney, Goodman, and Schwerner, but that summer its agents were unwilling to pressure local officials about the violence against them, with the result that there was little meaningful protection to living, breathing civil rights workers.[45]

In fact, conditions on the ground in Mississippi were depressingly the same, and sometimes worse. The town of McComb is a prime example. Over a nearly three-week period in September 1964, white supremacists bombed at least 10 Black-owned businesses and homes. Nine local whites were convicted in connection with those bombings, but the judge suspended their sentences, arguing that they "came from good families," and only resorted to violence because they were "unduly provoked by outside agitators, some of whom are of low moral character, some of whom are unhygienic."[46] Mendy Samstein had been in McComb and described what went through your head at the sound of a bomb blast. You wondered, he said, "Whose house, who is dead? It's not mine. Then who? My neighbor, my friend—my mother, my father, my son, or maybe SNCC again?"[47]

There was also the retaliation against Black parents who tried to enroll their children in white schools following the federal government's April 1965 issuance of guidelines for the implementation of Title VI. Public schools were now able to offer a "freedom of choice" plan that would allow Black parents to send their children to the school of their choice. However, choosing a white school was usually met with white terror. In Mississippi's Issaquena County, the 37 families who believed they truly had freedom of choice and opted to send their kids to white schools faced intense retaliation, including being fired from their jobs and removed from Social Security, welfare, or veterans' pensions. Sometimes their homes were fired upon, their crops turned over, their barns (with animals inside) torched, and their credit at local stores terminated. Most gave up. White ally Constance Curry, who worked closely with SNCC as an adult advisor, saw this up close. Curry worked for the Quakers, whose American Friends Field Service organized the Family Aid Fund (FAF) in Mississippi to assist families whose efforts to desegregate schools resulted in retaliation.

The terror visited upon these parents left Curry "wanting to strangle HEW, the Justice Department, and all the people who passed the Civil Rights Bill and everybody else who had allowed this kind of hope to be followed by such wondering kind of disappointment."[48] Again, the racist blowback against progress and the inadequacy of the federal response were depressingly the same. Nevertheless, it would be a mistake to imagine that Northern liberals, including those in the Johnson administration, moved in lockstep away from civil rights.[49]

Accounts often stress that after the convention a malaise set in within SNCC. Given this backdrop, it's hardly surprising that it did.[50] Carmichael claimed that when he returned to Mississippi, he felt a "limpness," not in the Black community, but inside SNCC. To him, it was "like a taut bowstring suddenly going slack, or a balloon collapsing as air escaped."[51] Burned out and traumatized, some people were said to have turned to alcohol and drugs. Even the Black psychiatrist Alvin Poussaint, who had spent the summer in Mississippi treating the traumatized, returned home needing therapy. Casey Hayden likened SNCC to "a nation after a war." Her description seems apt. "Staff had no marching orders; volunteers were everywhere, like refugees; projects were operating without funds, in essence outposts whose supply lines had been cut."[52]

Contributing to SNCC's lack of focus was the group's decision to accept Harry Belafonte's invitation to travel to Africa. Belafonte was aware of the extent of staff burnout, and in the end, 11 SNCC people traveled to the newly independent African nation of Guinea. The three-week trip proved restorative, and it enabled them to experience a newly decolonized country and to be in dialogue with its leaders, including its president, Sékou Touré. Still, it left the organization in a holding pattern.[53]

If there was ever a time SNCC could not afford to be in limbo, this was it. That fall, SNCC would confront its many problems, most of which were related to the Summer Project. SNCC's chronic lack of money was a case in point. That summer, Friends of SNCC chapters had succeeded in filling SNCC's coffers, reportedly with as much as $250,000. That was a welcome reprieve, but SNCC was flush for only a "hot minute," as Carmichael put it.[54] During those few months in which it was operating in the black, SNCC had incurred substantial expenses. It had committed to buying a church, listed at $125,000, in downtown Atlanta to serve as its national headquarters. It had already spent $18,000 on the 23 new tan Plymouths that were the core of its essential Sojourner Motor Fleet.[55]

Providing bail money—a constant that summer, and beyond—was costly, too. Sometimes headquarters said it couldn't pay. The trip to Africa also seems to have cost $10,000.[56] But by the fall of 1964, with the group's coffers nearly empty, projects began to close, and plans for continuing community centers and freedom schools were shelved. In some places, including Jackson, this happened before the year was out. Cleveland Sellers alerted Jim Forman to the closing of the Hollis Springs project by early December 1964 because their allotted $200 from Atlanta did not come anywhere close to paying their expenses, particularly for bail and for automobile repair and maintenance. Gas alone for the project's eight cars was, he claimed, an astounding $600 a month, and yet the project received only $200 a month from Atlanta headquarters.[57] Moreover, Sellers complained that the staff had not received any checks since late August.

SNCC's ballooning payroll costs were also financially burdensome. Many staffers received only a subsistence stipend of $10 a week (before taxes) and not always that, still, payroll costs were substantial.[58] By some estimates, the staff had numbered only 20 in 1962, but by the end of 1963 had grown to 100, before swelling to 170 by the fall of 1964.[59] Some of that swelling was caused by how many volunteers elected to stay on: 200. Some accounts suggest that SNCC added to its staff 85 of those summer volunteers so that its payroll obligations increased significantly.[60] That so many volunteers wanted to join the staff testifies to the Project's life-changing quality. However, no one had expected it or planned for it. Financially, it was a burden the group could not bear, even in the short term.[61] What all of this meant was that SNCC's annual budget, which in early 1963 was $75,000, had grown to more than $200,000 in 1964. By November 1964, no one had been paid since Atlantic City.[62]

The Summer Project's culmination in the MFDP's challenge in Atlantic City affected the way participants and observers alike assessed the Project. Afterward, many SNCC staffers were eager to embark on a course starkly different from that of the civil rights establishment, which was planning to launch its own Summer Project, deliberately without SNCC, for the summer of 1965.[63] SNCC was going to set upon a road very different from the one it had so recently traveled. What they had fought for, whether it was integrating public accommodations or voting rights, seemed woefully inadequate, not the systemic radical change they now believed necessary. "After Atlantic City," Cleveland Sellers declared, the struggle was no longer "for civil rights, but for liberation."[64] Voting rights seemed largely irrelevant. Some began saying, "the best way to keep someone a slave is to give him the vote and call him free."[65]

Rejecting electoral politics and building on the strategy of parallelism, Bob Moses suggested SNCC try to build a shadow government in Mississippi, one that Black people would recognize as their own. Setting up radical alternatives was one way of ensuring that the most disenfranchised would not be shoved aside by more middle-class Blacks, which was a fear among many SNCC workers, post–Atlantic City. At the organization's first gathering after the Democratic National Convention, the political programs workshop reported that its participants focused on what would happen "after we built a power base, the kind of Negro leaders who will sell out will take over."[66] It was a reasonable worry. Yet SNCC's tendency to castigate the middle class ignored the fact that it was sometimes middle-class Blacks who provided SNCC an entrée into their communities. They were people like Carolyn Daniels, who owned a beauty shop in Albany, and whose support of the movement led racists to shoot up and bomb her house.[67]

Perhaps not surprisingly, in the years ahead SNCC's assumptions about class—that the middle-class was corruptible, and the poor "pure and uncorrupted"—would be tested.[68] It was these folks, the most disenfranchised, whom SNCC staffers had in mind when they said, "Let the people decide." Yet even the poor people many SNCC workers idealized found that their own views diverged from those of many SNCC people. Certainly, SNCC's cynicism about electoral politics was not embraced wholeheartedly by the

MFDP.[69] Instead, a divide opened between SNCC and the MFDP, in large part because the latter favored the politics of pragmatism. Many SNCC staffers were troubled that fall when the MFDP campaigned for the national Johnson-Humphrey ticket as well as their own slate of local candidates.

The divide deepened with the arrival of LBJ's Great Society programs in Mississippi. Many locals, including the most impoverished, were "overjoyed" about them. SNCC people, by contrast, felt "very bitter" about the Great Society programs, which over time supplanted their own programs. For some, MFDP's receptivity to the Democratic Party proved that Black people could be "manipulated" by America's political parties, a fear Charles Cobb had articulated well in advance of Freedom Summer.[70] Yet, as historian Charles Payne has shown, in going its own way, the MFDP was fulfilling SNCC's hopes for it. Nevertheless, not all SNCC workers approved of the path the MFDP was taking.[71] In the view of Black staffer Ed Brown, their disappointed response demonstrated that some within SNCC were only interested in letting the people decide when the people agreed with them. Locals who "deviated" from SNCC's line were "ostracized," says Brown.[72]

Some think that as the movement became more successful, the disenfranchised began to move to the political middle and those who previously had spurned activism became involved in the movement's more mainstream manifestations. "Success breeds moderation" is how Ed Brown explained it. Certainly, many in SNCC were cynical about what locals considered genuine victories. To SNCC people, these so-called victories would do little more than enable the Black elite, who had sat out the struggle, to try to profit from newly won reforms. The way that SNCC people—Black and white, veterans and newcomers—increasingly imagined themselves a "band of revolutionaries" banged up against the much more modest aspirations of most locals. Some SNCC people questioned the group's recent focus on creating freedom schools and community centers. "Too damn many nursery schools," grumbled one such organizer.[73]

SNCC's cynicism was a measure of how much had changed. As Payne points out, what was attacked as selling out in 1965 "would have been called progress in 1963." Why shouldn't people be able to take advantage of new opportunities with the arrival of poverty programs and Head Start? Why shouldn't they run as a Democrat for political office?[74] Another dynamic may help to explain the growing divergence between local Black communities and SNCC people. From the beginning, the people in SNCC and the people they were trying to organize were inventing each other, making each other up. This often worked to the advantage of both groups.[75] SNCC workers' idealization of local people, their conviction that oppression guaranteed political and moral incorruptibility, likely kept them going. But over time, some locals' willingness to pursue a pragmatic agenda eroded SNCC's faith in their purity.

As for the locals, they began to have doubts about SNCC. Their decision to get involved in the movement had required a leap of faith about these "freedom riders." Some staffers succeeded in getting locals onboard by emphasizing their ties to powerful people at the Justice Department. Because SNCC people usually were outsiders to whatever community they were organizing, local people had no way of knowing if this was true or not. There is some evidence that SNCC staffers, at least in the early years, were open to locals defining them as they wished. "I was who they wanted me to be," admitted Ivanhoe Donaldson years later. "However they saw me," he said, "I would try to build on that." Some locals may have imagined that the preaching skills of some SNCC organizers meant they were, in fact, ministers, which likely helped in getting locals (and their ministers) onboard.[76] But by 1965, all the denim overalls in the world could not overcome the growing divide that separated the two groups. SNCC staffers' explicit disdain for the Democratic Party and the federal government, and their diminishment of movement gains flew in the face of the optimism many locals felt.

Coalitions were, as noted, a victim of this shift, which accelerated with Atlantic City. In the aftermath of the Democratic Convention, many in SNCC—no matter their racial identification—came to view coalitions as a naïve relic of the group's past.[77] With this turn, SNCC disowned key allies such as Bayard Rustin. Carmichael had once idolized Rustin, a man who, in his youth, had looked remarkably like Carmichael. As for Rustin, he admired Carmichael, judging him, despite their differences, "essentially a humanist, terribly bright, and always willing to put his body on the line." However, the political gulf dividing them was widening. Rustin held onto his dream of keeping alive the civil rights–labor coalition that would ensure further Democratic success, while Carmichael was engrossed by his own dream of moving past that coalition and forging a pathway toward Black liberation.[78]

Some have claimed that Rustin was "tactically sharp," as opposed to young dreamers like Carmichael.[79] But how sharp were Rustin's calculations? From the start, unionized white Southern workers were antagonistic to the freedom movement, as evidenced by how many joined their local White

Citizens Council.⁸⁰ Even without more inner-city conflagrations, even without SNCC's growing militance, growing numbers of white people were starting to move . . . out of the Democratic Party and into the welcoming arms of the GOP. White unionized workers of the North were well represented in this migration.

It is impossible to know if the civil rights–labor coalition could have remained intact with so many factors working against it.⁸¹ One thing is for sure. SNCC would keep its distance from any such coalition and their former "friends" who made it up. In 1966, Rustin and his mentor, A. Philip Randolph, began promoting a decidedly left-leaning Freedom Budget designed to wipe out poverty in America. It called for universal health insurance, full employment, a basic income for all, a massive public housing initiative, and major investments in job training. SNCC should have been on board, but the differences between left liberals and SNCC were no longer easily bridgeable.⁸²

Bayard Rustin's reputation among his former admirers in SNCC plummeted further when he refused to come out against the war in Vietnam even after Johnson reneged on his campaign promise not to send American troops there. To Rustin's critics, it was further proof that he had become a liberal insider, willing to do the bidding of the American Federation of Labor and Congress of Industrial Organizations (AFL-CIO) and the Democratic Party establishment. His attacks on Black Power, arguing that its aim, perhaps unconscious, was "the creation of a new black establishment," consolidated his status as a sellout. Rustin's motives may have had something to do with pleasing the AFL-CIO, which effectively paid his salary, but it also stemmed from his genuine commitment to working across difference to build politically efficacious coalitions that addressed economic inequality. Rustin had begun describing himself as the lone wolf of civil rights before Atlantic City, but it was a painful reality by 1966.

A Left-Liberal Divide Deepens

From the distance of 60 years, there is little doubt that the Mississippi Summer Project resulted in real, demonstrable change. By Bob Moses's inspired design, the Project began the process of cracking Mississippi open. Even though the MFDP delegation came away without the victory it sought in Atlantic City, the long view suggests it was not the defeat many imagined. Writing about it many years later, Carmichael admitted that the MFDP laid the groundwork for what happened when Congress reconvened in January 1965. One hundred and forty-nine members of the House challenged the seating of the all-white Mississippi delegation, which prevented its seating. The whole process that ensued, in which each side gathered evidence, and white racist Mississippi politicians had to go to the Black community to have their depositions taken, "really turned things upside down," recalled MFDP leader Victoria Gray. It was the Congressional Challenge that she believes led some of the moderates in the regular Democratic Party to "take courage and reach out to us through whatever channels they thought they had."[83]

Even though the MFDP eventually lost its challenge, it helped to build support for the Voting Rights Act of 1965. In some places, the effects of that bill were felt immediately. Federal examiners were in place in Alabama, Louisiana, and Mississippi four days after President Johnson signed it into law. It "transformed the color of American politics," and it did so in a strikingly short period of time, as the federal government got involved and the Justice Department pushed back against racist electoral practices.[84]

In Mississippi, more than 300,000 Blacks were registered to vote a decade after the passage of that 1965 act. Some would say that the Summer Project was a key factor in why Mississippi soon led all the states in the number of Black Americans it elected to public office.[85] Nationally, the results of the Voting Rights Act were also stunning. The Act increased the percentage of Black registrants to 59 percent in just three years.[86] The election of Blacks to political office had consequences far afield from America, too. As Forman later argued, "How could we have passed sanctions on South Africa without having black officials?"[87]

However, making this new federal legislation stick on the ground required that local people once again organize and protest. And they did, restarting groups and forming new ones. This is where the most impressive growth happened as a movement culture took root, encouraging local people to see themselves as agents of change and "to take ownership over what they are doing," in Moses's words. How that culture happened is still a matter of contention. Some staffers feel that the crucial factor in precipitating change was the Summer Project's reversal of the usual flow of integration, with Northern whites integrating the homes and churches of Afro-Mississippians. For Moses, local people were transformed, in large part, by "all the different kinds of people who were coming in and out of Mississippi."[88] Emmie Schrader Adams, a white volunteer, maintains that it was "exactly SNCC's black-led 'black and white together' organizing period that was a critical ingredient in the dynamite that blew apart the old southern 'way of life.'"[89]

Yet many Black SNCC staffers believe that the presence of hyperefficient white volunteers impeded their ongoing efforts to cultivate indigenous leadership. And the testimony of some local people corroborates these claims. Mary Lane, for one, recalled working with white volunteers and making the uncomfortable discovery that "they can do a better job of it than you could." She felt diminished, and she witnessed this happening to other locals, too.[90] Complicating this narrative is Ruth Howard's account of that summer. She remembers the performance of Northern Black staffers like herself producing feelings of diminishment in Lane and other local Blacks.[91]

Some local people, feeling edged out or just uncomfortable, drifted away from activism. Still, there is considerable evidence suggesting that by summer's end many Black communities where SNCC and COFO had operated were fired-up, ready to take on the white power structure. Take Greenwood, Mississippi, where local African Americans revived the National Association for the Advancement of Colored People (NAACP), remained active in the MFDP, kept the Freedom Schools going, and began the Voters League.[92] White volunteer Elaine DeLott Baker argues that you can measure how profoundly Afro-Mississippian communities were affected by the events of that summer by their refusal to abide by the old rules and customs. She confirms what others have said: that locals were energized after the events of the summer. In the late fall and winter of 1964, they inundated SNCC with requests for help.

Elaine Baker became involved with a group of farmers and sharecroppers in Panola County, Mississippi, who took it upon themselves to challenge the powers that be. Rather than accept the local white agent's demand for a price cut on their okra crop, they formed an okra marketing cooperative. Baker proved useful in that endeavor, particularly in setting up meetings between them and federal officials. Even if Afro-Mississippians did not always succeed in getting all they asked for—and in Panola County they *did* obtain a $78,000 War on Poverty loan to buy farm equipment—their interactions with officials profoundly altered the traditional power dynamics of the region.[93]

And then there were the Freedom Schools, which laid the foundation for the Child Development Group of Mississippi (CDGM). In the summer of 1965,

Freedom School veterans launched the CDGM, which became a part of the new statewide Head Start Program, which was put into place by the new federal agency, the Office of Economic Opportunity (OEO). It was a blow when Mississippi's white establishment, particularly its two determined segregationist senators—James Eastland and John Stennis—went on the warpath against the CDGM. Attacks on progressive initiatives were not limited to Mississippi. Longtime Southern Progressive Virginia Durr was disgusted by how the staff at the Atlanta OEO folded in the face of conservative opponents. They "are so frightened of attack by right wingers that they let them take over the program."[94] In Mississippi, CDGM fought back against attacks on it as subversive, but finally folded in 1967, when Head Start funded a less politically restive group, Mississippi Action for Progress (MAP). In Moses's view, if the right had not gone after the CDGM from the start, it could have helped to restore unity in the movement. Yet SNCC did not endorse the proposal for the CDGM.[95] There were already staffers for whom "nursery schools" seemed insufficiently revolutionary, and quite possibly a government plot to buy off movement workers with the offer of stable employment. In the end, the CDGM did briefly meet a need, serving 5,600 kids in the summer of 1965 through 84 centers in 24 counties across Mississippi.[96]

As for the volunteers, for now it is enough to say that despite their shortcomings, they mostly performed ably. Although movement veterans sometimes grumbled that this was just a two-month respite from their privileged lives, that is too cynical an assessment. Pam (Chude) Parker Allen admits that, at the Project's end, the volunteers could have left it all behind. "But could we go home and be able to go back and integrate into what we'd come from?" she asked. Answering her own question, she said, "I don't know if anyone could do that."[97] Indeed, many of the volunteers remained politically active in the sixties.

Stokely Carmichael and John Lewis traveled very different political paths, but they both came to feel that the volunteers of 1964 acquitted themselves admirably. Decades later, Carmichael observed that what made Freedom Summer so unique was its "bringing together two strata of the society that were never supposed to meet in friendship and equality ... and that never did again in quite the same way."[98] Bob Moses agreed. "It is to their everlasting credit," he said, that the volunteers "had within them, individually and collectively, some kind of moral toughness" to deal with the hostility they faced, both from white Mississippians and sometimes from within the Project.[99]

Yet in that moment, it felt as if the white heat generated by the Summer Project had done more to reshape SNCC than Mississippi. SNCC only briefly entertained the possibility of participating in a second summer of voter registration in Mississippi. Instead, SCLC ran a program in Alabama during the summer of 1965, which was modeled on the Mississippi Summer Project.[100] Atlantic City set in motion intense organizational soul searching, particularly about the wisdom of working interracially, once so central to the group's identity. SNCC had advanced the idea that summer volunteers needed to understand their own personal stake in the movement. "Come to help yourself," SNCC people told them. It was intended as a prophylactic against paternalism, but it implied that this was their movement, too. However, by the fall of 1964, there were some staffers who wanted to put behind them all of that and a lot more.

FOUR

Black Power

It was early November 1964 by the time people in the Student Nonviolent Coordinating Committee (SNCC) came together after Atlantic City. They gathered in Waveland, Mississippi, right on the Gulf of Mexico for a weeklong retreat meant to get them grappling with where SNCC had been and where it needed to go.[1] Driving the discussion was a stack of 40 position papers generated from within their ranks. Papers mostly focused on SNCC's aims and internal structure, its relationship to local communities and other organizations, and its future direction. For the first time, gender inequality was raised, uncomfortably, but then, much of the talk that weekend was unsettling. Most of it ended up circling back to race. Waveland revealed that what SNCC had stood for was now squarely in the crosshairs of some staffers.

Life After Wartime

If race dominated the discussion, it had a lot to do with the composition of the attendees. Judy Richardson, a veteran Black staffer looking forward to seeing old friends, felt uneasy as soon as she walked into the meeting room. "For the first time since joining SNCC, I was in a meeting that was majority white, and many were total strangers to me—college students who had come down for the summer project." Richardson felt bonded to longtime white staffers, but they were so unlike these newcomers, with whom she felt no connection.[2] For veterans, that crucial feeling of being "home" was gone.

Doubtless Richardson was not the only staffer thinking: Why are they still here? Why haven't they gone home? It's not clear that most veterans knew about the decision to put 85 volunteers on the payroll. Casey Hayden remembered that a memo at the time of the convention in Atlantic City mentioned that staff and volunteers were "staying in the state." She recalled wondering if

Image 4.1 Jean Wheeler Smith, standing, addresses people at SNCC's Waveland conference in November 1964. Seated on the far right is SNCC's white researcher, Jack Minnis.
Danny Lyon/Magnum Photos

the staff had decided they could stay or if it had just happened.³ Throughout the retreat, people returned to the question of who could rightfully claim to be a part of SNCC and what that meant.

Most accounts of Waveland focus on the destabilizing effects of all those unwanted white volunteers, but they weren't the only newcomers whose presence changed the group's chemistry and perhaps its politics. At the start of the summer, SNCC recruited a much smaller group of Black college students to serve as staffers. Cleveland Sellers of Howard University was presumably a part of this group. The new staffers were, as Casey Hayden later observed, an entire college generation away from the sit-ins and nonviolence that had shaped SNCC veterans. They were more likely to be skeptical of interracialism as the cutting edge of change. Strife was also more likely because, as Hayden noted, the summer's frenetic pace meant "we hadn't really even all been introduced."⁴

SNCC lacked the cohesion of its early period, and given all that had gone down that summer, people were unsure about how best to proceed. Should SNCC continue to embrace consensus decision-making and allow its staffers to move around as they saw fit from project to project? Or should SNCC be a disciplined revolutionary organization whose top-down leadership determined its direction, including who worked where? "Do we build a SNCC machine," Bob Moses asked, "or do we organize people?" Moses favored returning to the days when SNCC was a decentralized and highly democratic group of organizers. He didn't see the point of nailing in place the structural parameters of SNCC, or the Council of Federated Organizations (COFO) for that matter. "Now suppose," he observed, "a person can tell you exactly what COFO is but can't run one little freedom day. What does he know?"[5]

However, at Waveland, Moses, convinced that SNCC had grown too reliant on his leadership, stepped back from the fray. He did circulate a paper which, like all the papers, was anonymous. Moses wanted SNCC to abandon its hang-ups about who was authorized to be SNCC staff and who held decision-making power. "*We do not have to be hung up over this question. Instead, we could just do the work.*"[6] For Moses, that included strengthening SNCC's ties to Southern Black colleges and continuing that summer's freedom schools. In this same paper, Moses also likened SNCC's precarious situation to that of a leaky boat in the middle of the ocean. "It has to be rebuilt in order to stay afloat," but it "also has to stay afloat in order to be rebuilt."[7] Moses's metaphor was secondhand, taken from the work of another philosopher, but many people would have assumed Moses was its author. "No one could tell me," Howard Zinn later said, "that when Jim Forman came across that metaphor, he didn't know who wrote it."[8]

In Forman's opening speech—the first time a SNCC executive secretary made such a speech—he went after the idea that SNCC was a leaky boat adrift in the ocean. He put the boat on a river, a "river of no return."[9] Forman never spelled out what he meant by a river of no return. However, he used the phrase to emphasize the importance of SNCC committing itself to "programs and to people in the bayous and in the Deltas, in the back woods, in the Black Belt, in Northern cities and Southern hamlets." He favored a more robust and hierarchical leadership structure.

In the end, nothing was resolved at the retreat, but before long people were characterizing the conflict as one between "hard-liners" and "floaters" on a "freedom high." Originally, the term "floater" was used to describe a Black project director whose exhaustion led him to abandon his project, but soon its meaning shifted. Floaters did not just move around as they wished; critics

Image 4.2 Bob Moses determinedly on the sidelines at the Waveland conference. Danny Lyon/Magnum Photos

said that they also had a penchant for philosophizing, for taking "a small but significant incident" and riffing about it at such length that meetings would come to a "screeching halt."[10]

One paper that circulated that weekend satirized this style.[11] Reportedly written by the Black staffer Michael Thelwell, "Mississippi's Metaphysical Mystics: A Sect Wrapped Up in a Clique Within a Cult," described the style as trafficking in the formlessness of the Beats, the exhibitionism of the literary avant-garde, with the patina of "proletarian populism." Thelwell did not name anyone, but he seemed to be attacking Bob Moses's many imitators, all the wannabe-Bobs that now populated SNCC. "To the accompaniment of the index finger moving in ever-narrowing circles, the anguished brow, and in a tone so soft as to be inaudible I am treated to what can only be a distortion of the newest Dogma." These are pretenders, Thelwell argued, self-involved people intent on cultivating their uniqueness to underscore just how unlike their middle-class parents they are.[12]

Thelwell does not categorize these people as white, but his caricature helped to establish the freedom-high style as a "white" style. After all, many of Moses's most ardent admirers were Northern white students who strained to emulate him. One can imagine how irritating it must have been to many Black staffers that of all the styles within SNCC to choose from that most whites seemed drawn to the cerebral Moses, a man whose thinking was shaped by the French existentialist Camus and whose idea of a good time was folk dancing. No one could get angry at Moses himself, however. His sacrifices were undeniable, and his sensitivity was well known.[13] It was far easier to express exasperation with the whites who idolized Moses and his preference for a democratic, decentralized SNCC.

Hard-liners frequently characterized the freedom-high contingent as whites who were intellectually inclined and work-averse, or at least "not doing a specific job."[14] It did not matter that "letting the people decide" and consensus decision-making were pioneered by Black staffers, now that these styles of organizing were being categorized and disparaged as white and middle class. Over time, some of the hard-liners who were Black claimed that their stance was connected to their shift toward Black nationalism.[15] Yet many whites supported Forman's push for a more top-down structure, and the ranks of the so-called floaters included many Blacks. Race and class did not determine how people situated themselves in this debate, but within SNCC some staffers came to believe that they did.[16]

Then another fissure emerged, this one around the question of whether the people who ran the Friends of SNCC (FOS) chapters, 24 of whom were designated "Northern staff," should play a more meaningful role in SNCC. One FOS leader complained that the national office seemed indifferent to FOS, citing all the phone calls to Atlanta that went unanswered for days. It hampered their effectiveness. "To carry on fund-raising activities in the North, there must be some kind of response to our desperate cries for help." Moreover, when FOS people spoke to the media, they often did so without knowing where the organization stood on particular issues. Atlanta staff responded by sometimes reprimanding FOS people for putting out misinformation, but the staff did little to keep the FOS chapters up to date.

Exasperated, one FOS leader pointed out that chapters across the country included committed movement veterans (as opposed to naïve do-gooders) who could be more effective if they were just allowed to participate more fully.[17] This was the feeling of Dottie Zellner when she and her husband, Bob, moved to the Boston area. In the spring of 1964, she complained to the Atlanta office about being left out of the loop. She asked the Atlanta staff to tell her what SNCC thought of Malcolm X. She was going on the radio and needed to know if SNCC agreed with her that he wasn't any more "radical" than Roy Wilkins, except that he advocated Black self-defense.[18]

In advance of the Waveland meeting, a memo was circulated to the Southern staff encouraging them to treat their Northern counterparts respectfully, and as staff.[19] Forman acknowledged the hard work of FOS people and supported giving them a real voice, but that view was controversial. Forman also laid out SNCC's salary structure, which dismayed some. Why was SNCC paying money to people in its FOS chapters? The discussion turned to Elizabeth Betita Sutherland Martínez. Martínez grew up in the 1920s and '30s in Chevy Chase, Maryland, a tony, all-white suburb of Washington, DC.[20] After graduating from Swarthmore College in 1946, she held a series of jobs before moving into publishing, first at Simon & Schuster and then at the liberal *Nation* magazine. Older than most SNCC staffers, Martínez was a professional woman who was increasingly drawn to radical politics. Capable of moving comfortably between New York's artistic fringe of "Beat poets, junkie painters and LSD experiments" and the chic world of Fifth Avenue social events, she was a logical person to run SNCC's major fundraising office. However, she needed to be paid substantially more than the stipend provided to Southern rural staffers. Forman spent some time explaining that Martínez was leaving a good-paying job to work for SNCC.[21]

Nevertheless, the salaries of Northern staff provoked incredulity and anger from some quarters, including from the unnamed author(s) of a short story called "The Fairy Tale." One of the retreat's many papers, it mocked Northern "helpers" whose "expensive apartments" required that SNCC pay them inflated salaries. "All the time, their every thought was on the poor civil rights worker who was sleeping on the floor and eating bean soup."[22] It was not the first time, and it wouldn't be the last that SNCC people would use the "stick of Selfless Dedication" against one another. The fact that white people (this included Martínez, who looked "Mexican," but was not seen as non-white and did not yet identify as such) were disproportionately engaged in office work, so-called soft work, gave such discussions a racial cast.

Waveland is said to be the last time SNCC veterans, Black and white, were able to come together with each other un-self-consciously and have fun. It was there that a small group, mostly of veterans, hung out together one night, drinking and mellowing out, away from others. Stokely Carmichael, riffing on a position paper about sex roles that had generated derision in the meeting, cracked a joke, which several years later, with the growth of women's liberation, became the joke heard around the world.

Image 4.3 Former SNCC staffer Elizabeth Betita Sutherland Martínez, undated, Bob Fitch Photography Archive, Department of Special Collections, Stanford University Library.

Mary King recalled Carmichael being on a comic tear that evening. An attention-getter, Carmichael loved to regale crowds with his humor. That night he made fun of himself, his fellow Trinidadians, and Afro-Mississippians, before turning to the position paper. Its authors were no longer anonymous, and Carmichael, staring straight at King, "grinned broadly and shouted, 'What is the position of women in SNCC?'" He quickly answered his own question: "'The position of women in SNCC is prone!'" King remembered he then "threw back his head and roared outrageously with laughter." Curious as it might seem today, the paper's lead authors, Mary King and Casey Hayden, laughed as hard as everyone else. Both subsequently maintained that Carmichael was poking fun at himself. But this anecdote came to stand as damning proof of SNCC's (and Carmichael's) sexism, a verdict that many of the women of SNCC, Hayden and King included, have contested.[23] "The real question," observed white SNCC activist Emmie Schrader Adams, "is which organization in the world before 1965 did not manifest male chauvinism?" Moreover, compared to the larger world, and even other Movement organizations, SNCC was substantially better.[24]

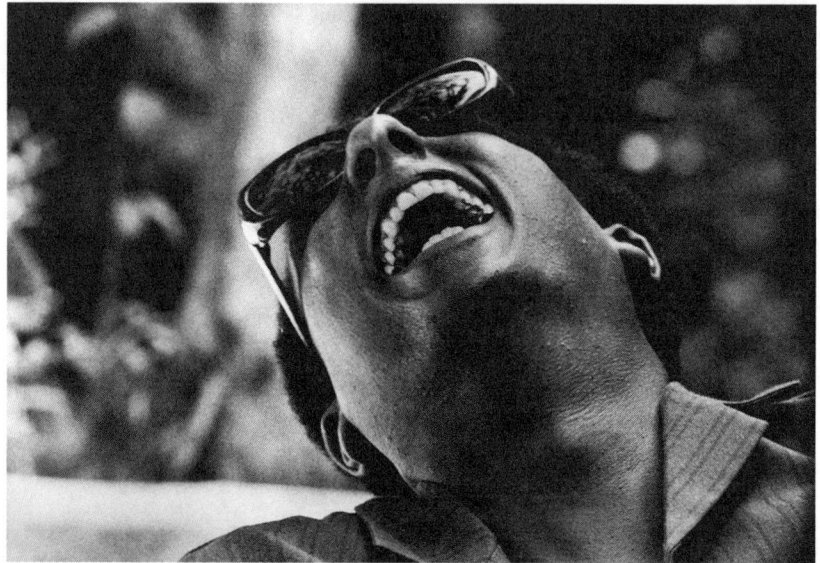

Image 4.4 Few people laughed as heartily as Stokely Carmichael, shown here in 1969 at the Pan African Festival in Algiers.
Bruno Barbey/Magnum Photos

In any case, the kind of lightheartedness on display that evening was not in great evidence that week. Something had shifted in SNCC, and it was partly captured in a searching position paper written by the thoughtful Southwest Georgia field secretary, Charles Sherrod. After acknowledging that all SNCC people, irrespective of race, were "prejudiced and insecure," Sherrod went deeper. "In fact, we are more prejudiced and bitter, frustrated and impatient and hateful than our parents because we have had more and seen more and *think we can get more* than they did and *we think we can get it now* because we have done miracles."²⁵

What Sherrod was describing was the moving of SNCC's goalposts, now defined not as one man, one vote but as nothing short of liberation. Of course, from the time students "sat-in" in Greensboro or Bob Moses pressed charges against his attacker in Amite County, SNCC was about more than gaining access to a lunch counter or ballot box. Still, there was a new consciousness taking root in SNCC as people absorbed the enormity of what they were up against, that they might end segregation and disfranchisement, but still be up against white supremacy and capitalism. Years later, Betita Martínez identified what she saw as the problem facing SNCC: "How in hell to make revolution in these United States."[26] Increasingly, talk of revolution signaled something more concrete than it had in the past, possibly even the actual overturning of the government.[27]

The Ubiquity of Race

At Waveland, people struggled to come up with something commensurate with the immensity of the problem. Moses and Forman were on opposing sides of the debate about the structure of SNCC, but they agreed the group needed to tackle economic issues. They understood that doing so in a way that acknowledged the racial dimensions of capitalist exploitation would exacerbate SNCC's already strained relationship with many liberals. "We are raising fundamental questions about how the poor sharecropper can achieve the Good Life," Moses wrote. He had concluded that looking to liberalism for answers was hopeless.[28] Moses once again suggested establishing parallel structures, and people would continue to pursue change in this fashion, whether through alternative political parties or economic cooperatives.[29] More people were willing to consider socialism, especially given its traction in parts of the Third World. But new ideas sometimes butted up against older practices. If SNCC was part of a pan-African struggle, why was it trying to make common cause with poor whites?

During the retreat, it was hard to escape the ubiquity of race. Forman had opened the meeting calling for SNCC to develop "a spirit that transcends black and white." However, powerful crosscurrents were present at Waveland. Charles Sherrod spoke out against race hatred but admitted he hated white people. For him, the solution required that SNCC people "curse and swear and fight and tear away at the masks that each of us wears."[30] For the most part, however, those masks stayed on during the retreat. Even though many whites were themselves cynical about liberalism and increasingly saw themselves as radicals, their relationships with Black staffers were fraying.

Years later, Mary King and Casey Hayden admitted that though their position paper was informed by reading Simone de Beauvoir's *The Second Sex*, it also grew out of what was happening to their friendships with Black women in SNCC. They hoped their paper might help repair those once-close friendships. Hayden also wanted to preserve what she later called "the radical nonviolent core of SNCC, our old womanist, integrationist ways," which she believed Ella Baker had modeled.[31]

It is not entirely clear why these discussions did not result in their hoped-for rapprochement and why talk about women's situation came to be seen as a white woman's issue. After all, several Black women were part of the discussions that summer that informed King and Hayden's paper. For that matter, several male stafffers were receptive to talking about what came to be called sexism.[32] However, it seems likely that one key factor impeding Hayden and King's desired sisterhood was the fact that, organizationally, Black women were differently situated than white women in SNCC. Racism required that white women work in offices and schools and keep a low profile. Moreover, in contrast to white women, more than a handful of Black women held positions of authority in SNCC, including Ruby Doris Smith Robinson, who eventually succeeded Forman as SNCC's executive secretary. But the position paper also illustrates what Bernice Johnson Reagon said about SNCC, that the group taught people that "if something puts you down, you have to fight against it."[33]

If people arrived in Waveland unaware of the depth of intragroup divides, they could not remain oblivious. Mendy Samstein summed it up when he said of their differences, "We are not brothers just because we've been put on payroll," a comment that may have been directed to those volunteers who had stayed on.[34] But his comment must have made some wonder what it would take to be included in SNCC's circle of trust. From very early on, SNCC people regarded themselves as the most righteous and least compromised activists. Mary King felt this way, too, but she later came to believe that, strategically, SNCC needed to question its investment in its own specialness and open itself up to more people, not tighten the rules for belonging.[35]

Twenty-five years later, Moses admitted that most SNCC veterans wanted the white volunteers gone and therefore gave no real thought to using them "as an organized force." He expressed contrition about this and attributed it to the fact that "there wasn't enough in the black community to hold the whole." He explained that everyone "couldn't all be in that one little space," not in a way that would permit SNCC to continue to practice consensus, not without it "tear[ing] people apart."[36] But at the time, Moses seems to have felt conflicted. He understood Black activists' desire to own the movement they had themselves made, and to meet by themselves, but he also deplored the racial tensions that were "welling out like poison" and "don't seem to be exhaustible."[37]

The conflicts between Black and whites in SNCC were inexhaustible and in large part because of the emergence of what came to be called Black Power. Admittedly, no one was yet using this term, though its origins stretched back to Black novelist Richard Wright's 1954 nonfiction book of that title. But the belief that Black Americans needed to discover and celebrate their own unique consciousness, reject liberalism and nonviolence, and pursue Black self-determination rather than integration, captures much of its reach. The turn to Black Power reflected a growing awareness of the freedom movement as part of a global struggle of decolonization. As early as the spring of 1964, John Lewis had noted that Black activists in the south were "identifying with people of color" and becoming aware of "things that happen in Cuba, in Latin America, and in Africa."[38]

Black Power was a labile idea that was either a close cousin to or inseparable from Black nationalism. Although it seemed completely of the moment, the kinds of Black nationalism that informed Black Power were not brand new. In Black Power there were echoes of the nationalism advanced by the Garveyites, Black Belt communists, and the Nation of Islam (NOI), where Malcolm X rose to prominence.[39] In the sixties, one of the earliest public affirmations of growing Black militance emerged from within the National Association for the Advancement of Colored People (NAACP). In the fall of 1962, the pioneering Black attorney and ex-communist Loren Miller, writing in the *Nation*, bid white liberals "a fond farewell, with thanks for services rendered." Miller clarified he was calling for their withdrawal "until you are ready to re-enlist as foot soldiers and subordinates in a Negro-led, Negro-officered army under the banner of Freedom Now."[40]

Black Power: Watts and Lowndes County, Alabama

By the mid-sixties, this view had gained a foothold within SNCC, which was becoming one of the defining epicenters of Black Power. The turn to Black Power would remake the Congress for Racial Equality (CORE), too, but that happened more slowly in CORE's Southern operations. From the beginning, there was an elasticity to Black Power that allowed all kinds of people, including conventional politicians, and eventually even corporations to hitch their wagon to it.[41]

By February 1965, even John Lewis, a voice of moderation in SNCC, declared his openness to charting a new course. As SNCC's chairman, Lewis had spent much of his time fundraising on the liberal cocktail party circuit, and he was fed up. One Black staffer, an Afro-Mississippian, was so traumatized by speaking at fundraisers in private homes that he sometimes retreated to the host's bathroom to throw up.[42] Lewis was more seasoned, but he was frustrated by the dynamics of these parties, where he found himself time and again "telling white people that we are ready to be integrated into their society." The real question, Lewis said, was whether whites, in an interracial movement with Blacks, would consent to having Blacks "run their own revolution."[43] Lewis had not given up on working interracially, but he now believed the movement needed to build "Black centers of power."

With the rise of Black Power, much of the focus shifted to Black consciousness, in what was undeniably a world-changing move. Everything shifted, from music, literature, and the arts to politics and standards of beauty. Consider the trailblazing musician James Brown. The soul singer seemed utterly oblivious to the expectations of white America, even when he performed on schlocky Middle American TV programs like *The Ed Sullivan Show*.[44] Black Power changed it all—culturally and politically—in ways that were revelatory. But it also raised a new set of questions. Were those Black "firsts" in the entertainment world, people such as Lena Horne and Sammy Davis Jr., nothing more than "sops, tokens, buy-offs for the white race's conscience," as Black radicals now contended?[45] Did certain groups of Black Americans have a more legitimate claim to Black consciousness? Did it reside in a particular class or region of Afro-America? What were the determinants of authentic Blackness? Was educational attainment, particularly at an elite institution such as Harvard, disqualifying? This wasn't abstract. In February 1965, a proposal was advanced to exclude people who had attended college from serving on SNCC's executive committee.[46]

To be clear, Black Power did not just emerge from the ashes of the Summer Project and Atlantic City. It was a Southerner, Robert F. Williams, the president of the Monroe, North Carolina, chapter of the NAACP, who in 1959 formed an NAACP rifle club to defend the Black community, and would later, in exile, write the book *Negroes with Guns*.[47] There was the fact that some Afro-Mississippian customs, particularly armed self-defense, were rubbing off on SNCC people, leading them to question the wisdom of nonviolence.[48] How could they not have second thoughts about nonviolence as they came to comprehend how routine (and necessary) gun ownership was in rural Black communities? "We were nonviolent," Moses remembers, "but we were in the houses of people with rifles."[49] A rifle was a multipurpose weapon, necessary not just for hunting but also for defending one's family. Over time, as they grappled with the extent of white terror, civil rights activists learned to live with weapons. This was true even of Martin Luther King, who remained a believer in nonviolence, but whose home reportedly became "an arsenal" after it was bombed.[50] Over time, most SNCC workers came to question even the tactical value of nonviolence.[51]

There was also the trip to Africa, which deepened the SNCC delegation's appreciation of their movement as part of a global anticolonial struggle, and the inextricability of racism and empire. Something else figured in this shift: an unexpected encounter in Nairobi that fall between Malcolm X, who had left the Nation of Islam, and SNCC's John Lewis and Donald Harris, who had continued to travel after the rest of the SNCC delegation returned home. Malcolm X reached out to people in SNCC. He spoke at a Mississippi Freedom Democratic Party (MFDP) rally in Harlem and invited Fannie Lou Hamer and the SNCC Freedom Singers to come to a meeting of his new organization, the Organization of Afro-American Unity (OAAU). At SNCC's invitation, Malcolm X went to Selma in February 1965, just weeks before his assassination, to speak to Black demonstrators in the voting rights struggle there. Just days before his assassination, he told a reporter that he now believed that militant whites were possible allies in a Black-led movement.[52]

By this juncture, Malcolm X's pan-Africanist approach and his cynicism about liberalism no longer seemed off base. Many in SNCC now agreed with him that integrating America was tantamount to integrating a "sinking ship."[53] After all, what had the focus on integration achieved? Some of the most egregious examples of Jim Crow had been vanquished, but an awful lot remained unchanged. A full decade after the Supreme Court's *Brown* decision, schools were still mostly segregated and Black schools underfunded. Had the single-minded emphasis on integration worsened the neglect of Black institutions? It was a legitimate question.[54] Another factor was the 1963 publication, in English, of Frantz Fanon's *Wretched of the Earth*, which argued for the therapeutic effects of violence. The book was gaining a following among SNCC staffers.

Then, less than a year later, in August 1965, a blast of violence hit Los Angeles when the Watts neighborhood of South Central exploded. Many in SNCC saw the uprising as evidence that the struggle had moved from the rural South to America's cities where fed-up, but largely unorganized Black Americans seemed poised to ignite a real civil rights revolution, and not through nonviolence. Clayborne Carson was an activist in the Los Angeles chapter of the Nonviolent Action Committee (N-VAC), a SNCC affiliate located in South Central. Carson felt that Watts "made our nonviolent, interracial militancy seem so insignificant and so inadequate." Carson was a relative newcomer to the group, but he felt the Black community supported this insurgency in a way it never had N-VAC.[55] However, just 15 months earlier, residents of Watts actively supported N-VAC activists as they picketed a popular burger joint in Watts. They treated the interracial team of N-VAC picketers as their "freedom fighters."[56] Still, it was undeniable that feelings had shifted.

Northern Black communities had long concerned SNCC, which decided in a June 1962 meeting to send field secretaries to Chicago, New York, Philadelphia, Detroit, and Cleveland. SNCC's aim was to use these five offices as a "propaganda base" that would also help fundraise.[57] But by November 1964, Bob Moses was suggesting a more central role for America's cities, that they were the freedom movement's "jungles," and were ripe for guerrilla warfare. When Watts blew up, nine months later, some in SNCC worried that they might be outflanked on their left. James Forman predicted that if SNCC didn't get itself together, "the revolution was going to leave it behind."[58]

One place where SNCC seemed to be making progress in 1965 was far away from Los Angeles, in Lowndes County, Alabama. Stokely Carmichael decamped there that spring, with little more than a sleeping bag. Lowndes County was over 80 percent Black. It was also legendarily racist. Carmichael believed SNCC could develop an alternative Black political party there, one that would not waste its time trying take over the Democratic Party but would dedicate itself to wiping it out. Carmichael and his comrades thought they had found what Cleveland Sellers called "*The* Lever" of change in the Black Belt. Because Blacks so outnumbered whites, using that lever would enable disenfranchised Black people to bypass the traditional political parties and enact Black Power on the ground.[59]

Carmichael followed Bob Moses's patient style of organizing there, but he and his SNCC comrades were also boldly militant as they formed the Lowndes County Freedom Organization (LCFO). In Alabama, every party had to have an emblem, and the regular Democratic Party was represented by a white cock or rooster. Courtland Cox asked SNCC staff member Ruth Howard to come up with an emblem for the LCFO. She chose a white dove, which everyone rejected. "No, this won't do," declared Jack Minnis. Mary King remembers people asking, "What might eat a white cock?"[60] Minnis suggested she go to Atlanta's Clark College, another historically Black university, because he remembered it boasted a black panther as its mascot. As historian Hasan Jeffries points out, "everyone knew that cats preyed on roosters." Howard did look at Clark's cat before producing her black panther sketch. Years later, she said that for her Jim Forman was the "original Black Panther." Almost immediately, the LCFO became known as the Black Panther Party.[61]

The very first Black Panther Party is rightfully seen as an outgrowth of SNCC's turn toward what became known as Black Power. However, its success in bringing out the Black vote owed a lot to the federal registrars who arrived in August 1965, soon after passage of the Voting Right Act.[62] Although the LCFO initiative was all-Black, it came to be through a collaboration of Black and white SNCC staffers committed to Black Power. LCFO might never have happened without Jack Minnis, who discovered an obscure Reconstruction-era state law designed by ex-Confederates. The law gave aggrieved Alabamians the right, at the county level, to form an independent political party, and Minnis understood how Black Alabamians could deploy it.[63] He was not the only white involved in the LCFO. Carmichael handed Dorothy Zellner the initial sketch of the panther that Ruth Howard had drawn and asked her "to fix it up." Years later, she remembered that she "made the panther's whiskers fuller and straighter and inked in his body, making him black." The collaborative drawing, which appeared on LCFO pamphlets and billboards, became the basis for the panther that soon appeared on the literature and buttons of the Oakland-based Black Panther Party, and that, in short order, became an instantly recognizable symbol around the world.[64]

The origins of the LCFO underscore the fact that some white staffers were pivoting to Black Power. But could they do so within SNCC? If whites impeded Black leadership, whether in offices or in the field, what work could they do? Making this question even more pressing for whites was that Black staffers were starting to "close the door and meet in their own group," as Bob Moses later put it. Black Power was many things, but it commonly involved a kind of internal decolonization process that could only be pursued in Black spaces. It presumed that Black people needed to "close ranks" to achieve group solidarity.[65] Separate meetings threatened some white staffers.[66] Being snubbed by your friends was worse, and that became a feature of life in SNCC. Bob and Dottie Zellner were rarely given the cold shoulder, but it made them uncomfortable when long-term Black friends assured them, "When we're talking about white people, we're not talking about you."[67]

Many white staffers did bristle at being treated as politically irrelevant. One white SNCC staffer was blunt, and in a way that suggested the upending of the usual power dynamics between Blacks and whites. Within SNCC, whites had been reduced to "useful maids and servants of the black man's revolution, nice and maybe even necessary to have around, but obviously incapable of assessing the real situation."[68] News about SNCC becoming an unbeloved community traveled. Betita Martínez was so bothered by it she wrote to Jim Forman. "I don't think that whites should be forced out by being made so miserable that they resign or hang on unable to function." To her, the conflicts over whites veiled larger problems about how SNCC should move forward. About white activists, she insisted, "they aren't colonial powers, they're Movement people."[69]

For white Southerner staffers, being treated as oppressors had to be especially galling. After all, they (and their families) were paying a greater price than Northern whites for their movement participation. Consider Doy Gorton, who became involved in SNCC before the Summer Project. His mother's house was destroyed in an explosion that left her with a lifelong physical injury. Destroyed as well were his relations with extended kin and with many of his childhood friends. "Those were the real costs" of civil rights activism "in 1960s Mississippi," he wrote.[70]

The effort to create a new Black identity sometimes made life difficult for Black staffers, too. It's ironic, of course, since the promise of Black Power was that it would unite Black people. But even in SNCC, this proved largely chimerical. Not everyone could measure up to some abstract ideal of Blackness. In any case, who would be the arbiter of what constituted an authentic Black identity?[71] With the parameters of acceptable behavior narrowing, SNCC people, who had always taken seriously the imperative of "living in the solution," could easily find themselves hoist by their own petard as politics turned intensely personal. Historian Clayborne Carson writes that "Black SNCC workers who had white friends or were too light-skinned or too imbued with 'white' cultural values became targets for criticism from other blacks."[72] SNCC people in interracial relationships were sometimes treated like pariahs, race traitors for talking Black and sleeping white.[73] "In the name of radicalism people started destroying their friends," observed the historian Charles Payne.[74]

Publicly, SNCC Chairman John Lewis tried to reconcile the new with the old. Exploring Black consciousness was not, he said, at odds with the effort to integrate America.[75] However, in his memoir, Lewis made it clear he was exasperated by all the talk about Blackness and getting rid of whites. He found it ironic that "some of the people who were most outspoken in asserting their black identity and disassociating themselves from whites were the ones who had grown up among and been very close to whites and who had, in many cases, disowned their own backgrounds." Lewis singled out Carmichael as an example of someone who must have felt compromised by the deep connections he had once enjoyed with white people. Carmichael is often characterized as a hardcore Black separatist, but while he was happy to be inflammatory when the cameras were rolling, he leaned toward political pragmatism in SNCC meetings. Still, the left-wing interracial politics that helped to form him and some other SNCC leaders made them easy targets for separatists. Proving oneself required disaffiliation from the old, as it seemed to for Carmichael. Lewis was not alone in his skepticism about the focus on "Blackness." One staffer argued Southern Blacks "don't need to wear Afros to show we are black. We *know* we are black."[76]

The Mandate to Organize White Communities

However, over time fewer Black staffers were expressing skepticism about Black separatism. Most preferred moving white activists into antiracist activism in white communities.[77] The idea that whites should address racism where it thrived was not a new idea. Recall that back in 1961 Bob Zellner's assignment when he joined SNCC had been to help build a base of support for civil rights among Southern white college students. Two years later, Bayard Rustin advised young white activists to "stop putting on blue jeans and going to Mississippi." He urged them instead to "do something that is harder and much less glamorous: stay home, go into white communities . . . to convince the white people to support this movement." Rustin's suggestion was not an early stirring of Black Power.[78] He was advocating white-on-white organizing because he believed that if the movement were to prevail it had to expand its base to include large numbers of whites.

By the spring of 1964, as Freedom Summer was taking shape, small groups of white activists were taking up this less glamorous work. SDS'ers were launching ERAP initiatives in 13 Northern and Midwestern cities, the first step in their effort to build an interracial movement of the poor. Also in the mix was a group of Southern white college students whom SNCC staffer Sam Shirah brought together in a new group, the Southern Student Organizing

Committee (SSOC) in April 1964. SSOC was meant to expand the reach of the freedom movement to predominantly white college campuses in the South. SNCC acted, too, by founding the White Folks Project, which was initially meant to organize liberal white Southerners who might counter the influence of the Ku Klux Klan (KKK) and the White Citizens' Councils.[79]

Originally, all this white-on-white organizing presumed that the movement would remain interracial. However, the argument for racially segmented organizing efforts shifted as Black Power began to take shape within SNCC. This was well before the May 1966 staff meeting where Stokely Carmichael unseated John Lewis as the group's chairman in a very dodgy maneuver engineered by white staffer Jack Minnis.[80] "But he's not even a Southerner," a stunned Lewis said.[81] Lewis's ouster happened before the June 1966 Meredith March, where Willie Ricks and Carmichael used the term "Black Power" to such great effect. Increasingly, those arguing that whites should go into their *own* communities did so because they believed Black separatism was the way forward, the logical next step, their river of no return.

Over time, Carmichael stopped emphasizing the benefits of white-on-white organizing as a prophylactic against backlash. Instead, he stressed the psychological harm that interracial organizing inflicted on Black people. He took to arguing that "all black people question whether or not they are equal to whites," a self-doubt, which was then unintentionally reinforced by working with white organizers.[82] Soon Carmichael went further and accused whites of supporting integration as "an insidious subterfuge for white supremacy."[83] He chided them for living vicariously, for behaving like a member of "the Pepsi generation who comes alive in the black community."[84] Now that Black Power was making white liberals expendable, Carmichael complained that all they did was whine about it. "'What about me?' they ask, rather than saying: 'Tell me what you want me to do and I'll see if I can do it.'"[85] The Black writer and former SNCC worker Julius Lester echoed him, arguing that most white liberals "simpered and moaned" about SNCC's shift because the group had been "a kind of teddy bear they could cuddle."[86]

It's hard to imagine a time when white staffers experienced SNCC as a cuddly teddy bear. Yes, for some white people in SNCC, particularly the volunteers, being in the Southern struggle offered them their first experience of feeling really loved, mostly by local people. Black staffer Jimmy Garrett heard more than one white activist say that "the first time they'd ever been embraced, hugged physically was by some Black woman or person in whose house they stayed."[87] In Black people's homes and churches, whites often felt connected, physically connected, and in ways that were new and profound. However, SNCC was a much less forgiving environment; its emotional economy was not fully reciprocal. Whites and Blacks forged intense bonds in SNCC. But the need for affection and approval characterized whites' relationships with Blacks more than Blacks' relations with whites, and in ways that felt oppressive to some Blacks.

Carmichael and Lester's characterization of white activists as moved more by self-interest than by the struggle for racial justice might be a fair description of some. However, it did not characterize the behavior of SNCC's veteran white staff or that of some of the newcomers.[88] It also misrepresented white-on-white antiracist organizing as easily achievable in the American South, something that civil rights activists knew was untrue. Bob Zellner's experience of trying to organize whites in 1961 led him to ask if it was possible to work with white Southerners "without them stringing you up?"[89]

Despite the odds they faced, some whites in SNCC kept trying, at least for a while. The White Folks Project, initiated in 1964, quickly abandoned its original goal of mobilizing moderate white liberals to counteract the influence of the KKK and the White Citizens' Councils. Instead, it turned its attention to trying to reach the white working class. The Project put 25 people to work in Biloxi, Mississippi, where they hoped to establish a "beachhead" for the movement among whites.[90] What little headway they made was undone by a malicious rumor that the group was there to help Blacks, not whites, get jobs. Evicted from their office, the staffers were forced to leave town. White SNCC worker Emmie Schrader Adams spent part of the summer of 1964 in a more rural part of the state trying to organize poor whites. Any progress the staffers made came to an abrupt halt when locals discovered they were civil rights workers, "race mixers." They felt the young activists had hoodwinked them. "They hated us, they felt angry and betrayed," and they refused to open their doors. In some cases, "they went for their guns or the telephone."[91]

Organizing poor white people, especially to forestall a backlash against the civil rights movement made sense . . . in theory. However, as Bob Moses had argued in that contentious November 1963 meeting, "It's not true that whites can go into the white community."[92] As soon as white organizers tipped their hand and "broke the rules of the racial caste system," they became the enemy.[93] In 1963, Carmichael laughed with white SNCC staffer Theresa Del Pozzo about the "clear absurdity" that she could "organize" the white toughs in her Atlanta neighborhood who were attacking Black people.[94] Luke (Bob) Block, a white activist involved in SCLC's voter registration project of 1965, tried working with Anne and Carl Braden to organize poor whites in Louisville, Kentucky. "It was like beating your head on a rock," he said. Acquaintances in SNCC had urged Block to do this, but everyone in SNCC should have understood the near impossibility of winning poor white Southerners over.[95] In one 1966 speech, even Carmichael admitted that for antiracist whites "to go into a poor white community in Mississippi or Alabama and talk about integration is to invite suicide upon oneself."[96]

Yet time and again in SNCC white-on-white organizing was advocated as though it was the litmus test for white activists' seriousness. At the May 1966 staff meeting in Kingston Springs, Tennessee, longtime SNCC staffer Ivanhoe Donaldson argued that white activists should "organize the white community around black needs, around black history, the relative importance of black history in the world today." Bob Zellner tried to find a way they could do so inside SNCC. James Forman pushed for passage of a resolution mandating that white staffers organize white communities, leaving Black organizers to organize in their own communities. Jack Minnis drew up the resolution, which passed with the support of the Blacks and whites present.

Despite what looked like consensus, the discussion caused some staffers considerable pain and a growing uneasiness about SNCC's direction. "That hurt a lot of people, white and black alike," John Lewis recalled. "It hurt me terribly." Cleveland Sellers fully supported the motion, but it was not lost on him that some members left the meeting with "furrowed brows and tears welling in their eyes." Word of the shift traveled to Betita Martínez in New York's SNCC office. She doubted the seriousness of those advocating that whites organize white communities. And she had a point. After all, how were white organizers meant to organize whites around *Blacks'* needs, as Donaldson had suggested? In Martínez's view, what SNCC was clearly signaling to whites was "Get out." Emmie Schrader Adams was on the ground and agreed. In her view, the injunction to "'go work in the white community' was often a smokescreen for 'Get lost!'"[97]

The Nationalist Minority

"Get lost" was the explicit message from a determined nationalist minority, though its most vociferous member, Bill Ware, had not attended the Kingston Springs meeting. Ware and other separatists, working within SNCC, established what became known as SNCC's "Atlanta Project" or the "Vine City Project." When SNCC funded the project in February 1966, it was meant to organize support for Julian Bond, who, having won a seat in the Georgia state legislature, was barred from serving because of his public opposition to the Vietnam War. However, the project soon became a pilot for SNCC's possible transition to Black-on-Black urban organizing.[98]

What people in the broader SNCC community apparently learned only years later was that the Atlanta Project's core members belonged to a small, clandestine Northern-based group of Marxist Black nationalists called the Revolutionary Action Movement (RAM). Most of them were relative newcomers to SNCC.[99] RAM's cofounder Maxwell Stanford (later Akbar Muhammad Ahmad) was not a newcomer, though he barely registers in SNCC's records. In one June 1964 meeting, just prior to the start of the Summer Project, Lawrence Guyot brought him up. Guyot said he was "disgusted with nationalists who planted themselves in staff, i.e. Max Stanford" and then proceeded to oppose SNCC's commitment to nonviolence. Fellow Black staffer Willie Peacock felt differently. "I like what Max preaches," he said.[100]

The RAM contingent did not announce its intentions to SNCC people, but its aim was to infiltrate it, radicalize it, and remake it into a Black nationalist organization. RAM did so on the grounds that SNCC "lacked the correct ideological orientation."[101] The Atlanta Project pushed for more than just the expulsion of all whites from SNCC. It did its best to permanently sever SNCC's ties to its past and to any remaining liberal supporters and donors. In August 1966, someone leaked to the *New York Times* a ten-page document purporting to be SNCC's position paper on Black Power. It was just two months after the Meredith March, where Black Power had landed with such a wallop. The *Times* devoted a whole page to Black Power, with excerpts of SNCC's so-called position paper and a long profile of Carmichael, who it claimed had played "a leading role" in its preparation.

In fact, the position paper did not represent the views of SNCC, nor did Carmichael have a hand in its writing. Indeed, SNCC staffers had voted against the position paper at a March 1966 staff meeting when the Atlanta Project put it forward for a vote. Some people privately fumed about the appearance of the Atlanta Project's paper in the *Times*. Carmichael was apparently "furious" about it. Some SNCC people believe it was leaked by a disgruntled former staffer. The journalist Mark Whitaker has speculated that in printing excerpts of the paper, the *Times* may have fallen for a "government-supported gambit," which was enabled either by disaffected former SNCC officials or by the separatist Atlanta Project faction. It was their intent, he argues, to undermine and embarrass SNCC's new chairman Carmichael.[102]

Readers of the *Times* would have learned from those two articles that the central proposition of Black Power was Black separatism. As the Atlanta Project's statement made clear, Black Power meant Black people cutting themselves off from white people. For SNCC, the paper argued it meant breaking off ties with whites, whether they were radical SNCC staffers or liberals whose donations had helped to keep the group going. Years later, Black staffer Michael Thelwell criticized the statement's facile "pop psychological stereotyping" of whites and Blacks, which he believed betrayed "a near complete ignorance of SNCC history, culture and experience." How could anyone who had been a part of SNCC contend that Blacks, across the board, felt intimidated by whites? To Thelwell, it read like a "parody of what we used to derisively call 'bone in the nose' nationalism." No matter, the paper was widely circulated and cited, and it had an outsized influence on how people understood SNCC and Black Power. Crucially, SNCC's fundraising efforts plummeted in the wake of the *Times* articles. If SNCC was meant to be "black-financed," as the paper proclaimed, most of its donors probably saw little reason to continue offering financial support.[103]

When the issue of expelling whites was raised again, just four months later, only seven whites remained. This was SNCC's December 1966 staff meeting, which was held at the Peg Leg Bates resort in the Catskill Mountains. Many Black staffers, including Stokely Carmichael, had little stomach for forcing out the handful of whites who remained. After all, they pointed out, the original purpose of the meeting was to hash out SNCC's next steps. However, the separatists had already determined what the next step should be. For three days they focused all discussion on what they called the "fundamental" question: Would SNCC pledge its loyalty to Blackness by expelling its remaining white staffers? Carmichael opposed this, explaining the knock-on effects of such a decision. SNCC, he argued, needed white financial support and a "buffer zone" to forestall repression. Unmoved, the separatists declared "the whites had to go."[104]

Fannie Lou Hamer was by this juncture a believer in Black Power, but not *this* kind of Black Power. A devout Christian, Hamer objected to what she saw as a racist move. The separatists responded by calling her politically underdeveloped, and, worse, "no longer relevant."[105] Judy Richardson counted herself among those who had grown steadily more nationalist, but she was alarmed by what she felt was a new "current of viciousness and hostility." Some members of the Atlanta Project were "kicking in doors with such rage," she says, "I was actually afraid—for myself and for the organization."[106]

"Exhausting," "painful," "pitiful," and "horrendous" were some of the words used to describe what transpired.[107] It was well after midnight at the end of the third day, when the matter finally came to a vote. By that point, as many as 40 people had departed the meeting.[108] After the meeting, people tried not to look at Bob Zellner, who had been there longer and taken more beatings than almost everyone there.[109] Years later, long after he had repudiated nationalism, Julius Lester wrote about that vote. He recalled sitting there with his friend, Maria Varela, the daughter of a Mexican father and an Irish mother. They agreed SNCC should be exclusively Black, but as he later wrote, "the heart has its own kinds of knowledge, which the correct 'political line' cannot reorder."[110]

The separatists carried the day, but just barely. The vote could easily have gone the other way. Nineteen people voted for the motion to "expel," 18 opposed it, and 24 abstained. Every white staffer abstained.[111] The vote reflected genuine ambivalence rather than consensus.[112] Moreover, as SNCC's white staff photographer Danny Lyon observed, the meeting was "so chaotic that it was not completely clear to many people who were present what had actually been decided there."[113] Some people erroneously thought whites could be nonvoting members, while others wanted to revisit the vote. Black staffer Bill Hall agreed with the expulsion but admitted that he and some other staffers were close to whites and had "tremendous problems . . . separating from them."[114] A few months later, in May 1967, after SNCC had fired the leader of the separatist faction for reasons unrelated to his politics, Dottie and Bob Zellner asked the Central Committee of SNCC to allow them to work in white communities in and around New Haven, Connecticut, and as voting SNCC members. Their request was turned down.

Years later, Carmichael called the separatists of the Atlanta Project "opportunists," who had latched onto the issue of white participation to make themselves seem "Blacker than thou." It was nothing short of a power play, he said, to control the group.[115] Michael Thelwell later wrote that kicking out white staffers was unnecessary. SNCC had always been Black led, and by this juncture it was a "nationalist movement of black and white people." He believes the vote would have turned out differently had more Black veterans who had worked with Casey Hayden, Dottie and Bob Zellner, and Mendy Samstein been present.[116]

Decades later, Thelwell was still puzzled by how the separatists held the meeting "hostage." The whole episode remains for him "an abiding mystery on which it is tempting to speculate."[117] It is indeed tempting to speculate, and some veterans have wondered if RAM might have unwittingly aided and abetted the Federal Bureau of Investigation (FBI)'s effort to neutralize SNCC.[118] They may have. But surely the separatists prevailed because veteran Black staffers let them, perhaps because they anticipated a fierce backlash from the nationalists, not just from those in their midst, if they didn't expel whites. The Atlanta separatists threatened to tell the world that SNCC was anti-Black if the vote didn't go their way.

Forcing out white staffers did not have all its hoped-for effects.[119] Yes, interracial tensions no longer plagued SNCC. But the unity that staffers desired largely eluded them as they often found themselves ensnared in what Charles Cobb called tribalism.[120] This was no longer the SNCC of big bear hugs. Charles Sherrod was SNCC's very first field secretary, but he had been on the outs with headquarters for some time. The Atlanta staff came to regard him as a kind of rogue field secretary—insubordinate and badly out of step with SNCC's separatist direction.

In fall 1964, Sherrod took a "sabbatical" from SNCC to attend Union Theological in New York City. He did so in part to convince people in the Student Interracial Ministry (SIM) at Union to commit funds and seminarians as interns for the Southwest Georgia Project he led. When he succeeded in gaining SIM's support in spring 1965, he tried to win SNCC's approval. SNCC's leadership in Atlanta balked. More than anything the sticking point was Sherrod's proposed use of white seminarians. Atlanta headquarters reportedly directed "considerable antipathy" Sherrod's way. Sherrod persevered with his plans, and from 1965 to 1968, SIM volunteers provided the Southwest Georgia Project with a "tremendous boost" in energy. There was a steep cost, though: Sherrod's broken relationship with SNCC.[121] "I didn't leave SNCC," he made a point of saying, "SNCC left me."[122]

Sherrod was hardly the only one to part ways with SNCC. Betita Martínez, who headed up the group's New York office, publicly supported the group's move to Black Power. Privately, she "seethed." Particularly difficult was the discovery that because she was "white," she was unable to vote. "It's a time for tough people and opportunists; few others survive. Lord have mercy," she wrote in her diary. Before long, Martínez moved West and became involved in the emerging Chicano movement, first in New Mexico.[123] Julian Bond was also disenchanted with the group's direction, including its separatist turn. He resigned from SNCC in September 1966. John Lewis claims Bond told him, "The crazies are taking over."[124]

Bob Moses had many qualms about SNCC's makeover, but he understood why interracialism had fallen out of favor. For a time, he stopped speaking to white people, including several close friends. Although Moses did not officially resign from SNCC, he did drift away.[125] As the next chapter explains, he became involved in the antiwar movement, which may explain why, at age 31, five years past the legal draft age, he was told to report to his draft board in New York.[126]

Like Bob Moses, Ella Baker never repudiated Black Power or the organization that for a few years in the sixties had been her lifeblood. Those years had been the best of her life, she said. But she was an advocate of interracial organizing and coalitional politics. She began to make herself scarce. Although she lived in New York City, she rarely stopped by SNCC's office there. She remained a part of Anne and Carl Bradens's organization, the Southern Conference Educational Fund. She believed that when SNCC turned its back on the "nonviolent, Christian tradition," it lost the regulator curbing the group's disputatiousness.[127]

Black Power, as it developed within SNCC, took aim at that very regulator, and with broad consequences. Its sidelining of Christianity affected its relationship to churchgoing Black Americans. "Once Black Power became anti-white," Lawrence Guyot says, "you couldn't sell it to Miss Jones, who's a Baptist lady, and believes the Bible, which states everybody should be treated equally." Guyot, the SNCC person who continued working with the MFDP, was emphatic about not being able to "sell an anti-white thing in the churches."[128] It wasn't just Miss Jones who wasn't buying this version of Black Power.

Within the Black intellectual community, there were dissenting voices, too. Harold Cruse believed that Black Power left unanswered just "which class is going to wield this power." Years later, the philosopher Cornel West echoed Cruse. "Beneath the rhetoric of Black Power, black control and black self-determination," argued West, "was a budding 'new' black middle class hungry for power and starving for status."[129]

Meanwhile, Carmichael had become the public face of Black Power, and he often seemed determined to operate without any regulator whatsoever. One white SNCC staffer observed that as long as Carmichael leaned into his "power to shock and intimidate whites," both his own and others' "quieter concerns for a coalition of the poor will remain unconvincing."[130] Liberal supporters grew alarmed by how Carmichael's incendiary speeches were landing, and they were not the only ones. SNCC's new executive secretary, Ruby Doris Smith Robinson, supported Black Power and much of what the charismatic and brilliant Carmichael said. But the media lavished attention on Carmichael (or "Starmichael," as some SNCC staffers called him), which seemed to encourage his rhetorical excesses—part of his penchant perhaps for playing to the crowd. When he claimed to reporters that the goal of Black Power was nothing less than the destruction of Western civilization, Robinson was furious. In an internal memo from October 1966, she observed that talk of this sort might go down well in Chicago, but not in Alabama.[131] "Cliché after cliché has filled his orations," she wrote, "things that many like to hear but few understand . . . things that feed those who want to destroy us . . . things that hurt us even in the black communities where we organize . . ." Carmichael promised to dial it down, but soon reverted to his most fearsome self. By June 1967, he was done with all the blandishments about Black Power as Black pride. "If Black power means violence to you," Carmichael said, "that is your problem."[132]

The Fallout from Black Power

The fallout from SNCC's separatist version of Black Power was substantial. As Carmichael himself had predicted, the expulsion of white staffers had financial repercussions, too. But even before Black Power took hold as a slogan, SNCC was in financial straits. The Watts uprising in August 1965 made a big dent in SNCC's successful fundraising operation in Hollywood. "There was fear," recalled James Garrett who headed up SNCC's Los Angeles office, and it "paralyzed whole sectors of people." Not everyone, for sure. But once Los Angeles's police chief, William Parker, blamed the violence on activists, some of the celebrities with whom Garrett was friendly made themselves very scarce. "All the energy that was building in Hollywood almost totally disappeared," he said.[133]

SNCC took another hit when in January 1966 it came out against the war in Vietnam.[134] In 1965, draft calls had grown to such an extent that Vietnam was no longer a remote conflict that young men could ignore. Between 1964 and the end of 1965, the number of U.S. troops in Vietnam increased from 15,000 to 184,000. Despite the massive and rapid escalation of the war, antiwar activists were few and widely disparaged as a fringe element. When Dr. King criticized the war, a full 15 months later, in April 1967, he, too, faced intense criticism. Most Democrats loyally supported President Johnson even as troop numbers mushroomed.[135]

Eight months after the by-now infamous staff meeting in the Catskill Mountains, SNCC's donor base shrunk further when it declared its support for Palestine in its conflict with Israel. Rumors of SNCC's anti-Semitism had been circulating for some time, and the group's official statement, issued in mid-August 1967, seemed to offer irrefutable evidence to the group's critics. SNCC's repudiation of Israel was a nose thumb to many of its Jewish supporters whose loyalty to Israel was still strong. It was also a signal to nationalists that SNCC had fully broken with its "civil rights past," a past that had included close ties between Blacks and Jews.[136] Just weeks later, at the National Conference for New Politics in Chicago, a failed effort to build an interracial left, James Forman denounced Israel and any coalition in which Black people were not in control, no matter how slender their numbers.[137] For some SNCC people, the fundraising drought proved what they'd been saying about the pervasiveness of anti-Black racism. We speak our minds and look at what happens: Whites can't take it![138]

Money was always a conundrum for SNCC, which had looked to its FOS chapters and liberal foundations to scrape by financially. Bob Moses later said that "one way of thinking about the movement is that it's an alliance of the bottom and the top. At the top there's the Justice Dept, the civil rights division, and there's a philanthropic arm."[139] Yet Black staffer Michael Thelwell spent a lot of his time in the "corridors of power" trying to wrangle funding from liberal foundations and institutions. In his view, SNCC "brought very little power to the equation. We had no cards to play."[140]

SNCC could boast of its fiery spokesmen, such as Carmichael, James Forman, and H. Rap Brown. The success with which they were landing in the headlines and on the nightly news may have led them to imagine, as Charles Payne argues, "that they were getting things done, they were shaking the world." But their world shaking was not translating into new organizational initiatives within SNCC. Moreover, their incendiary speeches and the group's outreach to other radicals of color put SNCC on the government's radar. It was the *Times*' early August 1966 coverage of Black Power that prompted President Johnson to demand that the FBI provide him with updates about the activities of Carmichael. Within a year, the FBI added SNCC to the list of groups targeted by its illegal counterintelligence program, COINTELPRO. Hoover created COINTELPRO in 1956 as a way of circumventing Supreme Court rulings that constrained the ability of the FBI to gather intelligence on dissidents, especially communists. A Senate committee later called it "a sophisticated vigilante operation against domestic enemies." By August 1967, some SNCC leaders found themselves surveilled, harassed, and locked up on one cooked-up charge after another.[141]

In that same October 1966 memo, Ruby Doris Smith Robinson warned staff against judging their success by the group's exclusivity or the extremism of its radicalism. In her view, SNCC was already too isolated. No matter what she said, SNCC grew less flexible and more isolated. The group continued to operate a few projects, but with the steady departure of field staff and donors, the organization lacked the resources to keep them afloat.[142] Shortly after the Black Panther Party was defeated at the polls in November 1966, SNCC even left its Black Power pilot program in Lowndes County. Within two years, the LCFO dropped its Black Panther emblem.[143] Impeding SNCC's organizing efforts was its shift away from starting from where people are—the approach that Ella Baker had long preached.[144] "Ideological agitation increasingly obscured community organizing," according to Clayborne Carson, as "'the people' were no longer the sources of innovative ideas, but targets of consciousness-raising."[145] To make matters worse, most local people had no intention of enlisting in any revolution. They wanted to move against the local white power structure to get their fair share of the pie.

It's shocking how quickly some SNCC/COFO projects collapsed or limped along. The combination of disorganization, political disappointment, exhaustion, and lack of money was overwhelming. "I won't even speak about SNCC here," wrote one SNCC worker about Albany, Georgia, to an ex-Snicker. He did mention two problems—the arrival of heroin and political corruption—but did not linger on the difficulties there. "It will just make you all depressed like it does me." This was December 1964, in the aftermath of the Waveland retreat.[146]

Without money to keep very many projects running, SNCC people—Black and white—began to move away, mostly to the North. By late 1966, two-thirds of SNCC's staff either worked in Atlanta or in Northern cities.[147] Ruth

Howard was one of the Black volunteers from Howard University who arrived in the summer of 1964. Eventually, she moved to New York City, but not without guilt about having "walked away" from the movement of the South. As a Northerner who saw herself as an "outsider," she felt "guilt that you could leave the situation . . . and pick up your life when other people could not."[148]

What did not limp along were those local people whom SNCC workers and those summer volunteers had energized. People accustomed to being deferential no longer bowed their heads. They had "developed another image of themselves." Some of them were ready to fight, particularly in places where the movement, in the form of SNCC and COFO, had taken root. Over time, all their efforts—the CDGM, okra cooperatives, low-income housing, and electoral politics—changed the balance of power.[149]

Decades later, the historian Darlene Clark Hine and the writer Kathleen Thompson shrewdly observed of these pivotal years, and especially of the dramatic increase in registered Afro-Mississippian voters, that one could find countries where "armed revolutions have taken place that made less of a difference than that."[150] Yet at that moment what many young Black activists yearned for was a whole new movement, not more of the same voter registration drives or freedom schools or Black and white together.

PART TWO

After Black Power

White Radicals Chart a Course

Part Two: Introduction

What now? This was the predicament for all those edged out of the Student Nonviolent Coordinating Committee (SNCC). For whites, the experience of going from comrade to oppressor was often devastating. SNCC had been Casey Hayden's "home and family, food and work, love and a reason to live." When she had moved to the Deep South, she crossed over from white America to what she called the "blackside." Now she felt like she was on the edge of the world. Years later, she said that she "wouldn't have missed it for the world," but she admitted it had been "an expensive ride."[1] For Dorothy Zellner, losing the "most creative, funny, innovative, daring, fearless group of people I ever met" was among her life's biggest hurts.[2] Even at the distance of half a century, Mike Miller still felt "the pain of SNCC's disintegration, and of black people deciding they would no longer talk with former white colleagues."[3]

They shared nothing with the journalists who were "aggressively clamoring" for stories about SNCC's alleged racism. They had no wish to damage SNCC's reputation.[4] They all remained activists. SNCC paid Hayden's salary while she worked in Chicago trying to build an interracial movement of the poor in that city's Economic Research and Action Project (ERAP).[5] Miller joined the legendary organizer Saul Alinsky's Industrial Areas Foundation, and Dorothy Zellner, with her husband, Bob, moved to New Orleans, where they tried to organize working-class whites around economic issues. In all their endeavors, they were, as they had been in SNCC, organizers from the outside working on behalf of others.

Over the next few years, other white leftists took a different tack. What if they explored their own unfreedom and built radical movements based on their discoveries? They grappled with how *they* felt oppressed, and persuaded themselves that what they had been doing, particularly in the freedom movement, was little more than liberal do-gooding, a kind of altruism that was, as one put it, "transparently self-deceptive."⁶ They now believed that the path to genuine radicalism entailed struggling against one's own oppression. The idea that the activism of white middle-class people fighting their own oppression was legitimately radical was an exciting breakthrough. One could come from a privileged background and still be radical. In Part Two, I examine how this idea took shape, the headwinds it encountered, its advantages and shortcomings, and its durability.

FIVE

White Radicals Chart Their Own Course

The New Left: Rejecting the "Unassailable Logic of the Next Step"

How did white activists come to see working on their own behalf as uniquely radical? Just two years earlier their fellow activists would have considered such a view heretical. Imagine his coworkers' reaction if Bob Zellner had decided in the fall of 1962 that he needed to attend to his own oppression! Yet two years later, the ground beneath the movement was shifting. Still, the roots of this idea were present in the period's new social movements, and from their very beginning. The New Left aimed to move past what much of the Old Left regarded as settled knowledge. In the words of Norman Mailer, the New Left, at least at first, "had no respect whatsoever for the unassailable logic of the next step" that characterized much of the Old Left.[1] No one was more important in helping these young leftists make their own way than the radical sociologist C. Wright Mills. It was the motorcycle-riding Mills who urged them to ditch the Old Left's economistic understanding of the world and its faith in the revolutionary potential of the working class.[2]

Most members of Students for a Democratic Society (SDS) followed Mills's advice. Like Richard Flacks, a founding member of the group, they believed what mattered were "social movements, coalitions and alignments, not classes." Accordingly, they focused on students, intellectuals, and Black Americans. SDS'ers diplomatically muted their skepticism of the Old Left in their founding document, the *Port Huron Statement,* but some of their elders took note of the differences, particularly that their targets were bigger and considerably vaguer than capitalism.[3] The group's manifesto emphasized personal politics, uncovering the "political, social, and economic sources of [people's] private troubles."[4] Student Nonviolent Coordinating Committee (SNCC) organizers were already doing this, encouraging locals to identify what "bugged" them. Here's another key element: SNCC's critique of paternalism and its understanding of unfreedom as a shared predicament, albeit one experienced more intensely by Black people than most other Americans.

This framing of unfreedom reached its apex in SNCC during the summer of 1964. Most white volunteers likely heard this message more than once during their stay in Mississippi. Some students absorbed this bit of wisdom and carried it back to their college campuses. For example, just weeks after leaving Mississippi, New York native Mario Savio took what he had learned there and deployed it at the University of California–Berkeley, where he was a scholarship student.[5] What led Savio to take up the freedom struggle at Berkeley was the decision of university administrators to enforce a campus rule restricting political leafleting, petitioning, speechmaking, and fundraising on campus.[6] Berkeley's activist students were convinced that in doing so the administration was caving in to the Bay Area's establishment, which had been infuriated by students' participation in a successful campaign, begun a year earlier, to end racially discriminatory employment practices at local businesses. The administration's efforts in the fall of 1964 to inoculate the university against activism, even preventing students from collecting money for the southern freedom movement, was the trigger that sent students, especially the more than 100 Freedom Summer veterans, into action.[7]

No one was more outraged by the administration's move than Savio, the wiry, six-foot-tall undergraduate who became the spokesperson of Berkeley's Free Speech Movement (FSM). Shy and intense, Savio was a stirring orator for whom a speech was what Tom Hayden calls "an exercise in reasoning out loud, essentially unrehearsed, yet perfectly clear in the end." He spoke with a fluency that was remarkable given his long-standing stutter, which magically disappeared in front of FSM crowds.[8]

For Savio, the FSM was about carrying on the work of the movement in Mississippi. Are we simply going to "forget the sharecroppers whom we worked with just a few weeks before" now that we're back in "the comfort and security of Berkeley?" he asked. He emphasized the interconnectedness of oppression, as Bob Moses typically did. Just as Southern Blacks were denied their democratic rights, Savio maintained that university students were denied a voice in the governance of their campus. He likened the campus to a factory—a "knowledge factory."[9] Even as he analogized the campus to the factory, Savio

Image 5.1 Mario Savio of the Free Speech Movement being dragged offstage by the police in front of 16,000 students, faculty, and staff at the Greek Theatre at the University of California, Berkeley, December 7, 1964.
Robert W. Klein File/AP Photo

was not a Marxist. Although his views were anticapitalist, he believed that what most ailed America was a "depersonalized, unresponsive bureaucracy," which had the effect of making inquisitive, searching college students feel like nothing so much as "strangers in their own lives."[10]

In part, FSM's success at mobilizing a wide swath of the campus, including conservative students, was the newness of Savio's analysis, that it was not "vintage 1930."[11] Savio wasn't looking to the working class to lead the revolution. Rather, it was his hope that the freedom Berkeley students were demanding would be what "the rest of an oppressed white middle class will some day demand." As he provocatively put it, this was "freedom for all Americans, not just for Negroes!"[12] How this would happen, and without losing sight of the fight against racism, went unexplained. About the same time, in the spring of 1965, Bob Moses was trying to persuade SNCC to join him in the still-tiny antiwar movement. It was an opportunity for SNCC to move away from its "isolation," he argued, and begin working in a movement committed to organizing the "entire American public" rather than focusing on "the Negro ghetto."[13]

Savio and Moses's enthusiasm for expanding the movement's reach into the middle class would have appealed to some in SDS, but more of its members were excited by the Economic and Research Action Project (ERAP), and its aim of building an interracial movement of the poor. To be clear, ERAP provoked skepticism. It is unlikely that ERAP would have happened without Tom Hayden, yet at the ERAP summer institute, which offered seminars on organizing, he turned to his friend Richard Flacks and asked, "Dick, are we creating a 'Frankenstein?'"[14] One of SDS's most incisive thinkers, Paul Potter, was himself part of Cleveland's ERAP, but he, too, harbored serious reservations about the whole undertaking. At SDS's June 1964 convention, just as the projects were launching, he voiced them. Did ERAP mean SDS was writing off the middle class? That would be a problem, he said, because a successful revolution required a "radical coalition" that included the middle class. In his view, SDS's vision of participatory democracy could only be realized "through the experience of the middle class and the anesthetic of bureaucracy and mass society."[15] Potter was subsequently elected SDS's new president, but probably not because he was championing the radical potential of the middle class. What members were most jazzed about was organizing the downtrodden, not people like themselves.

ERAP was very much of the moment. It reflected Americans' growing awareness about poverty, largely because of left-winger Michael Harrington's surprise bestseller, *The Other America*. It was also a response to the alarming predictions of experts who claimed that automation threatened to throw millions of workers out of work. Fearing such a cataclysm would provoke a racist backlash from poor whites, ERAP's advocates saw themselves bringing around poor whites and poor Blacks to a shared class-based analysis of their economic precarity.[16] Underscoring the importance of interracial unity among the poor was the undeniable popularity of reactionary white politicians in the North. If white supremacist politicians, such as Goldwater and Wallace, were successful on the national stage, they could crush the freedom movement.[17] Tom Hayden later admitted that he had prioritized class because he wanted to "prove in action that an integrationist perspective stressing common economic interests could still work."[18]

It was quite a mission they were on, but ERAP was predicated on the idea that the urban poor were so consistently getting "creamed" by the system that they were ripe for conversion. The ERAP initiative was SDS's opportunity to go "directly for the jugular vein of the system," thereby sparking a radical insurgency.[19] It also presumed that the poor's marginalization conferred on them an authentic radicalism, immunizing them against corruption and co-optation. SDS'er Todd Gitlin spoke for many when he asserted that the poor were "less tied to dominant values."[20]

In this, as in so many ways, SDS was following SNCC.[21] The corollary was that middle-class people, by virtue of their comfortable embeddedness in the system, could be counted on to sell out the movement. How ERAP activists, who were themselves overwhelmingly white and mostly middle class, could be trusted to guide the supposedly more revolutionary poor, was a paradox that organizers tried to make go away, either by mimicking the habits and mannerisms of the locals or by "letting the people decide." Of course, if the locals were meant to chart their own course, "What did they need us for?" as one project organizer put it. Or, as Paul Potter later said, "if poor people were going to make the revolution, then who were the middle-class people who came to work with them?"[22]

It did not take long for ERAP activists to discover that all their theorizing about the poor as a powder keg of revolutionary anger and fortitude was just that: theoretical. The "discrepancy between the metatheory and what you did every day" proved daunting.[23] First, those "armies of white unemployed" never materialized. It turned out the experts were wrong about automation triggering a serious economic downturn.[24] And then there was the organizing itself, which was occasionally inspirational, but mostly discouraging. On those rare occasions when their efforts resulted in, say, better garbage pickup, the locals, believing the battle had been won, showed little interest in further activist forays. When their efforts fell short, which was the more typical outcome, locals often grew disenchanted and dropped away. There were real successes, including the efforts of ERAP women in organizing female welfare recipients, but there were many more defeats.

Part of the problem was that some organizers came to feel that there was a fundamental dishonesty in how they went about organizing. Writing in the summer of 1965, Peter Countryman of New Haven ERAP articulated what was on the minds of more than a few organizers. Were they "using people to gain ends that [the poor] do not (now at least) understand and accept"?[25] Wasn't it straight-out "manipulation" for them to mobilize locals around limited goals without revealing their own much larger radical agenda?[26] The problem was that when organizers did come clean, as when they tried, for example, to push back against racism, white locals grew suspicious of them.[27] Redbaiting was not uncommon.[28]

At its height, ERAP boasted 13 projects, with Newark, Chicago, Cleveland, and Boston the most successful. Perhaps the projects sometimes proved that, as Tom Hayden argued in early 1966, "students and poor people make each other feel real." Even if they did generate feelings of authenticity, they never produced what Hayden had hoped for: a "revolutionary trajectory" in which "day-to-day reforms can lead to revolution." There was no evidence they were succeeding in building "a base of mass radical insurgency."[29] The mismatch between their expectations of mass mobilization (their models ran the gamut from the Southern civil rights movement to the Russian Revolution) and the persistent feeling of "not knowing if we are getting anywhere" exhausted them.[30] So did their inexperience, the opposition they faced, and the punishingly spartan lives they led.

Then there was the obstacle of the poor themselves. How could you possibly organize a group as heterogeneous as the poor?[31] The most motivated locals often regarded ERAP as "an opportunity for social mobility and uplift," not a radical insurgency.[32] However, many others led lives that put them "in such distress they were almost too poor to organize."[33] Finally, contrary to all that SDS'ers imagined about the poor, it turned out that the brutal conditions of poverty were no guarantee of integrity and political purity. Instead, as Paul Potter discovered, being poor required "an unending reserve of energy and courage to do anything *but* sell out."[34] A few projects kept going until 1968, but many folded after just two years, and some even more quickly.[35]

SDS had tried to emulate SNCC, an organization that Casey Hayden knew better than anyone else in ERAP. However, six months of working in Chicago ERAP in the spring and summer of 1965 was enough to convince her she "didn't have the heart" to spend the five years it would take to build a solid project there. She also doubted that SDS could pull off what SNCC had accomplished in the South. For one, the poor and working-class whites she met in Chicago lacked the collective orientation that made the freedom movement tick in the South.[36]

Your Own Revolution, Not Stokely's

By spring 1967, SDS was internally riven. Going up against powerful Democratic machines in cities such as Chicago made ERAP organizers more cynical than ever about liberalism. "Most of us became Communists, Socialists, something to the left of where we were," recalled one ERAP participant.[37] If they became communists, very few joined the Communist Party. Even the youth wing of the Communist Party, the Du Bois Clubs, never exceeded more than 1,000 members, and collapsed by 1969. Some joined the Progressive Labor (PL) Party, a Maoist spinoff from the Communist Party, that was burrowing into SDS, with the aim of taking it over. PL supported moving SDS off campus, but not as ERAP had tried it. PL envisioned students going "straight," cutting their hair, which was not especially long by this point, ditching the love beads and any other hippie affectations, taking factory jobs, self-proletarianizing, and organizing the working class.[38]

At the same time, a different strand began to take shape within the New Left. Paul Potter pointed out that although SDS'ers took onboard C. Wright Mills's dictum about making "the connection between personal troubles and public issues," they behaved as if it applied to everybody but themselves.[39] He asked: What if we take ourselves seriously as legitimate radical actors? Instead of organizing other people, Potter and some others argued, New Leftists needed to acknowledge their own "unfreedom" and come together in a radical movement with those like themselves. They went even further, arguing that if New Leftists wanted to be authentically radical, they had to recalibrate and fight "for their own liberation."[40] In a March 1967 speech, Greg Calvert, SDS's national secretary, exhorted the group to "develop an image of its own revolution, its own struggle, instead of believing that you're revolutionary because you're related to Fidel's struggle, Stokely's struggle, always somebody else's struggle."[41]

How did New Leftists arrive at this position? Typically, they traced its origins to SNCC. In a February 1967 speech, Calvert argued that SNCC "slapped us brutally in the face with the slogan of black power." According to Calvert, Black Power "said to white radicals, 'Go home and organize in white America which is *your* reality and which only you are equipped to change.'"[42] SNCC staffers had indeed been urging white activists to do antiracist work in white communities since 1963. Likewise, the refrain about whites' unfreedom was already well established in SNCC. But as Calvert and his collaborators in SDS were developing this idea, they emphasized the importance of the white student movement developing its own identity—"what we call 'that white middle class thing.'"[43] Yes, it was vital to be in solidarity with the Black freedom movement, but they emphasized liberating *themselves*. Calvert and those in his camp did not spell out what this "white middle-class thing" was, but their aim was to affirm the radical legitimacy of white middle-class New Leftists.[44]

Black Power provided the ideological ammunition for people of color to organize autonomously, but had its architects imagined that it would empower radical whites, too? Black Power's primary message to white activists often was

"Get lost!" But sometimes its spokesmen gestured toward whites fighting their own battles. One-time SNCC staffer Julius Lester came close to endorsing this when he maintained that any coalition Blacks might form with white radicals required that they acknowledge their own oppression and disavow their whiteness. In Lester's view, whiteness, which he called "a condition of the mind," not the skin, was white supremacist. White radicals could disavow it by yelling "'honky' as loud as a black radical." Yelling that slur was like "throwing mud on a sheet," and white radicals needed to feel its liberatory power.[45]

For white male radicals, exploring their unfreedom led instead to organizing against the war in Vietnam. Several SNCC members came out against the war early on. They also endorsed white radicals' efforts to build an antidraft movement in their own communities.[46] President Johnson's rapid escalation of the war made the draft a burning issue. Between September 1965 and January 1966, a staggering number of men—170,000—were drafted and another 180,000 enlisted after being classified 1-A.[47] Stokely Carmichael called on white radicals to leave the campus behind, to go into "white ghettos" and organize against the draft.[48] After the March 1967 antiwar march on the Pentagon, H. Rap Brown, who succeeded Carmichael as SNCC's chairman, was uncharacteristically supportive of white radicals, calling them "brothers in the vanguard of revolution."[49]

Bob Moses engaged in a more complicated maneuver around the war, one that may help us to understand how the imperative to fight one's own oppression took hold among white radicals. To be clear, Moses was sincerely opposed to the war in Vietnam. As early as August 1964, he signaled his skepticism of the war. He spoke at SDS's first antiwar protest, which was held in April 1965 in Washington, DC. In the months that followed, he worked with the white activists David Dellinger, A. J. Muste, and his friend Staughton Lynd on another antiwar protest in Washington, DC, the Assembly of Unrepresented People.[50] Moses was perhaps the best-known Black activist involved in the fledgling antiwar movement. Years later he said he had joined the peace movement as a "way of helping the white students get out of the civil rights movement," presumably to end the racial acrimony tearing SNCC apart. According to James Forman, SNCC's Executive Committee suggested that Moses and Courtland Cox develop a peace project that would include white volunteers. Within a year of pressing hard for the deployment of white volunteers in the Summer Project, Moses was now struggling to find a way to offload them to the antiwar movement.[51]

Image 5.2 Two Black protestors in the Yippie encampment across the street from the Conrad Hilton, hotel to the delegates of the tumultuous Democratic National Convention, burn a draft card in front of National Guardsmen, August 1968.
New York Daily News via Getty

Whether Bob Moses privately suggested to his former white colleagues that they focus on their *own* oppression we will likely never know. What we do know is that the white activists to first articulate this shift were a part of Moses's circle of friends and comrades.[52] In the spring of 1965, former SNCC volunteer Dennis Sweeney, now back in Palo Alto, California, advocated that whites fight their own oppression. Sweeney seems to have not had any concrete ideas, but a year later Mendy Samstein did. For Samstein, and for many other New Leftists, Johnson's escalation of the war in Vietnam was an outrage . . . and an opportunity. In an April 1966 visit to Palo Alto, Samstein shared his thoughts with Sweeney and his fiancée, Mary King. Starting a draft resistance movement would enable them, he said, to do what Black SNCC staffers had asked of them, that is, to go into their own communities to "organize against their own oppression."[53] He made the same pitch at SDS's annual convention in the summer of 1966, advocating that SDS'ers put their bodies on the line, just as SNCC members had, but this time to stop the war.[54]

The Movement Explodes: Draft Resistance, Women's Liberation, and Yippie

Samstein and his friends hatched a plan to mobilize white middle-class students with the goal of throwing a monkey wrench in America's war machine. If students refused their deferments and the government drafted them, they could refuse induction, which would clog the whole machinery of war. Staughton Lynd worked closely with Samstein, and they convinced themselves that this was a game-changer, a genuine strategic breakthrough. It would take only 10,000–20,000 draft resisters to stymie the federal courts and the prison system.[55] Think of how unpopular the government would be if it imprisoned thousands of draft resisters.

For Lynd and Samstein, draft resistance was also the way to build a "new 'white SNCC.'" Lynd believed this intense kind of antiwar activism should have "the same spirit, ask as much of us, and challenge the system as fundamentally as had our work in Mississippi." It could provide New Leftists with "a politics of daring," without participants falling into the familiar role of "auxiliary" to someone else's radicalism.[56] By the fall of 1967, the Resistance had grown to nearly 36 chapters because the draft was the issue that "really touches people personally and desperately."[57] Even though SDS had backed away from leading the antiwar movement, in part to prioritize ERAP, sentiment against the war led many college students to join the organization.[58]

Redefining radicalism as the fight for one's own liberation found some support in SDS, where it was bolstered by a new theoretical turn that claimed to elucidate how class worked in postindustrial societies.[59] The "new working-class theory" was first advanced by young French intellectuals who argued for expanding the theoretical parameters of the working class to include the college-educated professionals necessary for the functioning of advanced capitalist economies. These workers may be educated—indeed, the very people we think of as middle class—but they were stuck in "stifling careers."[60] The idea struck a chord with a small group of SDS'ers in New York City who penned the "Port Authority Statement," a rebuttal of sorts to SDS's founding statement. Its title was meant to be humorous, but it also suggested that New York City's gritty, behemoth bus station was more relevant than a predominantly white town in rural Michigan.[61]

The idea that people should organize around their own oppression had real appeal and quickly traveled. It's not surprising that it so quickly found its way into the hippie counterculture, which valorized personal freedom. Abbie Hoffman, a self-dramatizing white activist on the far fringes of SNCC, was its emissary. Hoffman may have picked up the idea from his college friend Mendy Samstein. Most politicos regarded hippies as politically naïve or indifferent, not a serious force for change. Hoffman had been known to deride hippies as "glassy-eyed zombies," yet in the summer of 1967, during the "summer of love," Hoffman turned himself into a hippie.

Going hippie, with the possibility of all that sex, drugs, and rock'n'roll, was hardly a hardship for Hoffman, who was an unabashed hedonist. But he reportedly chose to become a "freak" to politicize hippies, a move he attributed to SNCC's directive to whites to organize their own communities. His community, he declared, was the counterculture, and its territory the Lower East Side.[62] Maybe Hoffman felt this connection sincerely, or maybe he was invoking SNCC to immunize himself from attacks.[63] After all, such was the power of SNCC that invoking it conferred legitimacy on white activists. It's worth noting that SNCC's marching orders to white radicals—antiracist organizing in white communities—was turning into something else: organizing hip white youth around their own freedom. Although he called hippies America's "new n*****s," he did not seem centrally interested in challenging racism. At one point, he said, "We can't say, 'Get Whitey.' We're white."[64]

No group embraced the idea of fighting your own oppression more enthusiastically than the young white women of the Movement. Women active in the Resistance and in ERAP projects were especially receptive. ERAP projects varied, but the assumption often was that of the locals, the men were the ones worth cultivating, the ones who mattered. Vivian Rothstein worked with girls in Chicago and recalls one male colleague asking her why she believed "teenaged girls had anything to with the revolution." Then there was the time a male organizer ordered all the women to leave a meeting because they were too distracting. "We got serious things to talk about here and we can't have women with all their legs all hanging out all over the place." Although women were often more effective community organizers than their male counterparts, their work was consistently devalued because they focused on women.[65] ERAP staffer Jean Tepperman had plenty of company in feeling about women's liberation, that at long last here was a movement encouraging one to "accept one's own needs as legitimate."[66]

Women's experience in draft resistance organizations was also galling. Because women couldn't be drafted, there was little they could do in this new movement besides being endlessly supportive to male resisters; that is, they were an auxiliary to someone else's struggle once again. Mimi Feingold, who had been involved in the Freedom Rides, felt that "women were playing this most unbelievably subservient role" in draft resistance.[67] Moreover, because of the "pervasive view of draft resisters as cowardly 'draft dodgers,'" the movement emphasized that resistance was about manhood, "not emasculation."[68] The sexism that undergirded draft resistance led some disgruntled women to put their energy instead into feminism, where they came to see that they mattered in their own right.

Fighting your own oppression became a feminist mantra, and it provided young white Movement women with a political and psychological reset. Crucial to this recalibration was the article "Sex and Caste" by Casey Hayden and Mary King. Published in November 1965 in the pacifist magazine *Liberation*, it was not a call to arms, but it did get radical women thinking about what would come to be called gender. Within a few years' time, young radical white women would stop saying yes to everyone but themselves. Enabling this shift was the focus on fighting one's own oppression.[69] One measure of its popularity is that in the spring of 1969, the New York journalist Gloria Steinem, in a feature article about the sixties' newest movement, observed that women's liberationists had reached the same conclusion that Black militants before them had: "You don't get radicalized fighting other people's battles."[70] This idea became a bedrock principle of women's liberation.

Recasting white, middle-class women and men as legitimately radical was consequential. For one, it emptied SNCC of whites, thereby enabling it to move past the dynamic of Black anger and white guilt that had proven so debilitating. It pointed to a more realistic idea about how to build the Movement. As Marge Piercy and Bob Gottlieb argued in March 1968, "we cannot build a Left in America simply on identification with peasants and guerrillas in the Third World."[71] In doing so, it usefully pushed back against the hierarchizing of oppression, whereby only the most downtrodden enjoyed political legitimacy. Whether the idea originated with Black Power or was a creative reinterpretation of it, white radical movements mushroomed. To Todd Gitlin, it felt as if SNCC's makeover "threw off centrifugal energies like a dying star."[72] With their proliferation came a groundswell of protest bigger and more consequential than Bob Moses or Casey Hayden could have imagined in 1964.

The antiwar movement, which in its early years was widely viewed as fringe, was attracting a wider swath of the American public by decade's end. The first Moratorium to End the War in Vietnam, in mid-October 1969, brought one-quarter million protestors to Washington, DC. A month later, a half million came to the nation's capital for the second Moratorium, where speakers included politicians and artists, including the composer and conductor Leonard Bernstein.[73] Antiwar activists knew that the opposition to the war played a role in Johnson's decision to not run for re-election. They did not know that they were affecting his successor, Richard Nixon. Only White House insiders knew those fall Moratoriums helped deter Nixon from dramatically escalating the war.[74]

Draft resistance was the radical center of the antiwar struggle. Turning in or burning one's draft card never achieved mass appeal, and why would it when prosecutors could (and sometimes did) push for a full five-year prison sentence. Yet it did jam the offices of prosecutors and it constrained the ways the government could maneuver.[75] The Johnson administration chose to retain the 2-S deferment for college students because it believed one-quarter of all students would refuse induction if it was abolished.[76] The Nixon administration instituted the lottery system at the end of 1969 to "lessen the steam behind student protests." It then ended the draft entirely and pivoted to an all-volunteer army.[77]

Fed in large measure by the war, movements for student power also flourished. It is hard to know whether their growth was in any way attributable to Greg Calvert's efforts as SDS national secretary. He was insistent that white radicals "must stop apologizing for being students and for organizing students."[78] He made that case in a spring 1967 speech and a subsequent SDS pamphlet. In any case, by 1969, SDS, a group that two years earlier had only 15,000 members, had 100,000. Student mobilizations fundamentally changed college campuses, which dismantled the restrictive rules and regulations that constituted the entire *in loco parentis* (in the place of a parent) apparatus. As students moved off campus, dorms turned co-ed, and as the birth control pill became increasingly available, heterosexual cohabitation became commonplace.[79] Then there was the college curriculum, a target of student radicals, which became more relevant, particularly with the emergence of Ethnic Studies and Women's Studies, often taught by young radicals who were beginning to join the ranks of faculty.

Image 5.3 Vernon Grizzard, Anne Weills Scheer, Tom Hayden, and Stewart Meacham, left to right, at Orly Airport near Paris, on July 10, 1968. The antiwar activists (minus Hayden) were on their way to Hanoi, where they facilitated the release of three captured American pilots by the North Vietnamese.
AP Photo

Meanwhile radicals organized teach-ins about the Vietnam War in which experts disputed the government's many misrepresentations of the war and exposed universities' complicity in the "war machine." Students, in turn, pushed to get the military and military research off campus. They staged protests, most famously in 1968 at Columbia University in New York, to prevent their institutions from expanding further into poorer neighborhoods of color. Following the model of Mississippi, they created free universities. Indeed, just as early New Leftists had hoped, universities became sites of dissent and opposition, proving the prescience of C. Wright Mills, who had noted in

1960 that it was youthful members of the intelligentsia who were "getting fed up, and all over the world."[80]

As for the counterculture, six months after Abbie Hoffman joined it, he came together with other white radicals to form the Youth International Party. Yippie, as it was known, was meant to nudge the counterculture toward political radicalism and the New Left toward cultural radicalism. It started out as a "paper party." It was "a put-on and a prank."[81] For, as Yippie Judith (Gumbo) Albert explains, they wanted to "*have* a party not *be* one."[82] However, their pranking style of radicalism encouraged some hippies, persecuted for their long hair, drug use, and antiauthoritarianism, to take up protest. It also led to the prosecutions of Yippie leaders, and to a surprising partnership with Black radicals, which Part Three chronicles.

The most successful of all the movements that took shape in the wake of Black Power was feminism. Employment and educational discrimination, restrictive abortion laws, sterilization abuse, ineffective rape laws that punished women, domestic violence, incest, and what was called "sex-role socialization" were in its sights. The changes were massive and nowhere greater than in the realm of personal politics. Women renegotiated their relationships with men, opened themselves up to same-sex intimacy, and chose single lives. It was a tidal wave of change, yet many New Leftists initially responded by attacking women's liberation as diversionary, bourgeois, and frivolous. Over time, deploying the logic of Black Power to legitimate feminism enabled women's liberationists to blunt the worst of the attacks. Soon the strategy would be used by gays and lesbians, too.

There is one intriguing sidenote about women's liberation. Casey Hayden and Mary King helped to launch the new movement with their piece "Sex and Caste." Yet they both kept their distance from the new movement as it was taking shape. Hayden later said she was alienated by the way women's liberation "emulated black nationalism." She longed for a more humanistic movement committed to "a compassionate concern for others." All four white women who worked on that first fall 1964 position paper felt that their primary loyalty was to the freedom movement.[83] Sociologist Wini Breines astutely observed that this group of white SNCC veterans "felt closer to SNCC than they did to white women in other movements, including the white feminist movement."[84]

Although the ranks of radical dissenters were growing, the reality of each group fighting for its own liberation threatened to render the "Movement," the constellation of sixties protest movements, so unwieldy that referring to it as the Movement seemed aspirational. After all, Chicanos, Asian Americans, and Native Americans were also hijacking the logic of Black Power to forge their own autonomous movements. Was it possible to rein in the Movement's centrifugal tendencies? Was there really even a "Movement"?

The idea of organizing around your own oppression also had unintended consequences. How could activists develop what today is called an intersectional analysis or achieve diversity in conditions of balkanization? This became a point of contention in the women's liberation movement, whose mostly white participants assumed, at least in the early days of movement building, that women of color preferred organizing separately from white women. Over time, the logic of separatism allowed white women to grow comfortable in a movement composed of people like themselves. It would prove difficult diversifying a movement that had developed along such highly segmented racial lines. When it came to the New Left, Greg Calvert assumed that white activists' recognition of themselves as "one of the un-free" would draw them into solidarity with a broader struggle. Radicals of different stripes, particularly radical activists of color, did come together, but it was tough going breeching the color line, working cross-racially, when whites were involved.

But if there were pitfalls in white middle-class radicals fighting their own oppression, it is important to not lose sight of its significance. Setting out on their own, claiming themselves legitimately radical was a bold move that might have been the foundation on which the New Left built a broader movement.

Two Movements: One Black and One White

Militating against this outcome were the escalating war in Vietnam, further urban rebellions, and political assassinations. Increasingly, people on the right and the left persuaded themselves that America was on the brink of revolution. If an actual revolution was coming, what role could middle-class whites play? The leftist journalist Andrew Kopkind articulated the "impotence" that many white radicals felt by the summer of 1967, the summer America's cities burned. To be white and radical, he argued, "is to watch the war grow and know no way to stop it, to understand the black rebellion and find no way to join it." It meant admitting that the "politics of a generation has failed and the institutions of reform are bankrupt." Finally, it meant having "neither ideology, programs, nor the power to reconstruct them."[85]

Kopkind's was an apocalyptic stance that ignored the draft resistance movement and any other hopeful manifestation of white radicalism. Certainly, there remained a lot of energy in parts of the Movement. Nevertheless, anyone looking for evidence of white radical impotence could have found it at the National Conference for New Politics (NCNP), a gathering of between 2,000 and 3,000 people during 1967's Labor Day weekend in Chicago. NCNP's organizers aimed to unite a broad swath of progressives—"electoral reformers, radical organizers and Black militants"—into a single, interracial movement that could be the basis of a radical third party.[86] It was America's biggest-ever meeting of progressives to date.

However, for many Black radicals the idea of unity seemed like a red flag, a provocation. Even before the proceedings began, they formed a caucus. Only eight months had passed since SNCC had slammed the door on working with whites, and those SNCC people who participated made it clear they were inclined to keep the door shut. The planners' failure to reach out to Black activists, and then their mad scramble to include them when they realized Black representation would be meager, understandably annoyed many Black activists. Yet many young Black radicals—those in and around SNCC, certain Congress for Racial Equality (CORE) chapters and freelancers—had already given up on working with white radicals. In a spring 1967 article that appeared several months before the conference, Clayborne Carson opined that the "cold, hard reality is that white radicals without much power would not be considered a worthwhile ally and may be a detriment to the goals of the black radical." It made more sense, he argued, for Black radicals to seek ties with "other non-white people in the world." Indeed, it was already happening, he noted optimistically.[87]

To many of the Blacks (and a minority of the whites) in attendance, the NCNP seemed an effort to resurrect liberal paternalism, with whites setting the terms of the conference, as though Black Power had never happened.[88] The conference began with the Black caucus threatening to pull out entirely unless delegates accepted all of 13 demands. Although Blacks constituted somewhere between 15 and 20 percent of all delegates, the caucus demanded that they be given 50-percent representation on all NCNP committees, and that delegates condemn as an "imperialist Zionist war" the Six-Day War between Israel and a coalition of Arab states. Despite whites deferring to Blacks, a chasm separated them. Some participants believed that government informants and agents provocateurs disrupted the event. A month after Chicago,

Roy Innis of CORE noted the presence of hypermilitant Blacks at several recent gatherings, including the NCNP. Innis believed the "psychotic trend," which he thought might be the work of agents, could result in the "destruction of the whole black revolution."[89]

Several accounts of the NCNP stress the damaging role played by infiltrators, but by this juncture Black Power was ascendant and talk of armed struggle was becoming standard fare, particularly among SNCC's leaders. James Forman was something of a moderating force in Chicago, but he insisted Black people should be the ones leading the next American revolution. Anyone who disagreed could "go to hell," he said. H. Rap Brown was among the Black activists at the conference who refused to talk to whites. Roy Innis, echoing Carson, questioned why he should negotiate with the whites at the NCNP when "they've got nothing to deliver." He preferred to "bargain with the power structure." As he moved rightward, Innis did exactly that, endorsing Republican Richard Nixon in 1968's presidential race.[90] The power structure held no allure for SNCC's leaders, but they emphasized they would only work with white radicals once they had succeeded in building a base of support in white communities. "We now know that there is not thunder, but only static on the left" was the verdict of one leftist journalist about the debacle in Chicago.[91] His was not an entirely fair judgment because, despite the rancorousness of Chicago, California's Peace and Freedom Party grew out of the NCNP.

Nevertheless, for many white leftists eager to develop working coalitions with Black radicals, Chicago was a sobering event. Following the conference, Arthur Waskow, an Institute for Policy Studies fellow and a key NCNP organizer, said that the Blacks who threw up roadblocks that weekend had been right in refusing to "bow to any majority but their own."[92] However, he also opined that the conference proved there was "not one movement but two: one Black and one white."[93] And if African Americans were the revolutionary vanguard, were white radicals meant to return to their role as auxiliary to someone else's struggle? One white liberal attendee declared himself ready to be "a little tail on the end of a very powerful black panther."[94]

The left-wing journalist and activist Robert Scheer had a different takeaway from Chicago. Scheer was a writer and editor at *Ramparts*, a magazine at once radical and slick, where David Horowitz also worked. To Scheer, white activists' disdain of the middle class stemmed from self-contempt and was utterly self-defeating. Until white radicals could reach "normal America," he observed, "we're not going to develop a base and we're going to be useless."[95]

The White New Left Remakes Itself into an Adjunct

By this point, advocates of white middle-class radicals fighting their own oppression faced intense headwinds. In the years ahead, women's liberationists and gay and lesbian activists were among those who pressed on. There were some New Leftists, such as the radical philosopher Marshall Berman, who continued to call upon white radicals to "affirm" themselves. "We have demanded 'Power to the people!' and we've identified with any and every people in the world—except our people," Berman pointed out. While he supported "getting into other people, identifying ourselves with them," he maintained it "is not enough for radicalism."[96]

Nevertheless, many on the left had never bought the idea that the dissatisfactions of the middle class amounted to oppression. Take the case of Martin Kenner. A Berkeley undergraduate before the FSM, Kenner became friendly with leftists in and around the campus, including Robert Scheer, Maurice Zeitlin, David Horowitz, and Franz Schurmann. Kenner had taken part in the anti-HUAC hearings in Berkeley in May 1960. Academically peripatetic, his next stop was Columbia University, where he became active in its CORE chapter. Kenner spent much of the sixties in graduate school, at Rutgers and the New School, but he remained an activist. By the late sixties, he had been a member of Fair Play for Cuba, M2M, an anarchist group called the Motherfuckers, and Weatherman. One group he did not join was SDS, whose politics he found "wimpy." As for all the talk about organizing around one's own oppression, he was skeptical. He resented the way that its advocates looked down upon the political work he favored—radical organizing on behalf of others—as little more than "charity work." He felt they were making the revolution about themselves, and it struck him as way too "touchy-feely."[97]

Kenner wasn't the only one who felt this way. Among young leftists there were endless disagreements about which groups constituted America's true revolutionary vanguard. But for a determined minority of SDS'ers the only white middle-class young people who might be considered true revolutionaries were those who had renounced their white-skin privilege and declared their willingness to pick up the gun. The working class won't take students seriously, wrote one SDS member, until we prove we're "willing to kill and die" for freedom—ours and "the people's."[98] Within SDS, members were succumbing to what felt like the inexorable pull of Marxism, Leninism, or Maoism, all competing for dominance, as they paid rapt attention to whatever fiery pronouncements Stokely Carmichael and H. Rap Brown were making.

Greg Calvert came to believe that the new working-class theory, which he had helped to popularize, ended up paving the way for orthodox Marxism, which he had always opposed. Marxism had the advantage of offering a blueprint for change, which in and of itself was appealing. Doubtless, PL's efforts to take over SDS also played a role in the group's Marxist turn. As a consequence, base building and working in broad-based coalitions fell by the wayside. Carl Oglesby, who had been SDS president from 1965 to 1966, wanted the organization to do what it did best: build campus chapters, and, in league with liberals and libertarian conservatives, oppose the war. To his comrades in SDS who worried over liberal co-optation, he advised, "Stop being scared of being reformed out of things to do."[99] As we have seen, these same fears of selling out, going soft, and opting for reform had already knotted up SNCC.

What happened next was in some ways predictable, but in other ways not. By the end of 1967, a group of Black radical activists in Oakland were shaking things up, including what Black Power might look like, and who might be allowed along for the ride. It's to these new-style radicals, California's Black Panthers, that we now turn.

PART THREE

The Black Panther Party's Cross-Racial Solidarity

Part Three: Introduction

Less than a year after Stokely Carmichael led crowds in chants of "Black Power" in Alabama, a group of Black Americans carrying loaded firearms paid a visit to the California State Assembly in Sacramento. What they were doing—openly bearing arms—was not illegal in California. However, it would be if the assembly voted that day to toughen the state's gun laws. And that was why 26 members of the Black Panther Party for Self-Defense showed up at the Assembly on May 2, 1967. The group, which was only six months old, had made a name for itself, at least locally, with its provocative armed observations of the Oakland police. If the legislature passed the Mulford Act, which banned the public carrying of loaded weapons, it would criminalize the party's sole claim to fame: "policing the police" while armed, and not just with law books.[1]

The protest "threw the building into a turmoil," much of it caused by the cameramen, who in their frenzy to capture the event, rushed onto the assembly floor in front of the protestors as they snapped away.[2] The Panthers' plan had been to occupy the spectator gallery, but they found themselves following the photographers onto the assembly floor. After escorting the Panthers back to the hallway, the police briefly seized their weapons. Once the Panthers had spoken to the press and were again in possession of their firearms, they headed for their cars. At first, it seemed as if they might get off scot-free, but after one of their cars broke down, they pulled over into a nearby gas station. That's when the state police descended upon them. The police struggled to come up with a justification for arresting them but settled on charging them with violating an obscure provision of the state's fish-and-game laws. By the next morning the district attorney dropped those charges and instead levied two other charges. One of them, disrupting the state legislature, was only a misdemeanor, but the other, conspiracy to disrupt the legislature, was a felony.[3]

News of a radical Black group that wasn't just talking Black Power but was doing it, "invading" California's state capitol, quickly traveled. In parts of Black America, the Panthers' action generated pride that at long last some Black people were ditching nonviolence and embracing Malcolm X's directive: by any means necessary. "It's beautiful that we finally got an organization that don't walk around singing," said one Bay Area Black man.[4] But the Panthers were not beautiful to most whites whose long-standing fear that Black America would seek violent retribution seemed to have come true.[5] Reflecting upon the Sacramento action years later, Black Panther Party cofounder Bobby Seale summed up white Americans' stunned reaction: "'N*****s with guns.' It's like a fear. I mean they don't even have to say it. Their faces said it."[6]

As for the local press, it was both "excited and repulsed" by the Panthers, a reaction that came to characterize the response of the national media in the months and years ahead.[7] White journalists took one look at the Panthers' guns, and their sartorial style, which included black leather jackets and berets, and assumed that they were part of an anti-white hate group. The very first sentence of the *New York Times*' coverage of the Panthers' action described them as "antiwhite." Yet the party's statement to the press, which Bobby Seale read aloud several times that day, was not explicitly anti-white. It focused on anti-Black racism, but it acknowledged that Native Americans, the Japanese, and Vietnamese experienced racism, too. Nevertheless, when Huey P. Newton, the other founder of the party, met with reporters the next day, they peppered him with questions about his position on white people. Their presumption was that he and the party were anti-white.[8] This became (and often remained) the mainstream media's take on the party.[9]

Yet evidence of the Panthers' cross-racial collaborations, many of them with whites, was not difficult to find. Video footage of the aftermath of the Sacramento protest provides ample evidence of this as a professionally dressed white woman, briefcase in hand, comes into view.[10] We see her in the lobby and in the courtroom, where she consults comfortably with party members. Instantly recognizable to most local activists, Beverly Axelrod was a Bay Area Movement lawyer. She had been one of the members of the California Democratic Council, the group that provided the early push for the MFDP in 1964. Axelrod was not the Panthers' only white collaborator.

The Black Panther Party was always determinedly pro-Black. However, early on, it developed an approach to Black Power at odds with the versions being promulgated by most other Black radicals, including its leading architect and spokesman, Stokely Carmichael. What most set the Panther Party apart was that it sought alliances and collaborations with people outside their world, often with white radicals.[11] It did so during the high tide of Black Power. How did the Panthers manage to remake Black Power so that there was room for non-Black supporters committed to furthering the party's aims? How did they pull this off without losing all credibility with other Black radicals? And the most challenging question of all: Why did they even try? In the pages that follow, I examine how cross-racial solidarity played out, and what its payoffs and costs were for the Panthers and for the larger Movement.

First, some preliminaries. The Black Panther Party presents considerable challenges to any researcher. For one, not all the party's activities were documented. There are many rich Panther memoirs and autobiographies, and its party newspaper is a useful source. However, the party was a far cry from SNCC, whose executive secretary James Forman exhorted coworkers to "write it down!"[12] SNCC's commitment to democratic methods also led to robust debate and its documentation, whereas the Black Panther Party's often clandestine workings encouraged opacity.[13] As a result, it is sometimes hard to know just what was going on in the party. This is especially true of the Panthers' cross-racial collaborations, the full extent of which were not widely broadcast. Where these partnerships were best known and longest lasting was in Oakland among the Panther leadership, which is why this part of my book is more top-down than bottom-up. It is also detail laden, but there is no way to tell my story without the considerable backfilling that allows us to understand the Panthers.

Another challenge is that the Panthers polarize their chroniclers, who often feel compelled to either heroize or condemn them. Because there was a "certain, intractable duality" to the party, as the scholar Ernest Allen Jr. put it, a case can be made for its revolutionary righteousness or its criminality.[14] If the party led a double life, so did many of its leaders, including the telegenic Huey Newton. James Baldwin saw something of his duality early on. "Huey looks like the cleanest, most scrubbed, most well-bred of adolescents—everybody's favorite baby-sitter." However, Baldwin also noted how Newton's "eyes take in everything." And "behind the juvenile smile," Baldwin wrote, "he keeps a complicated scoreboard."[15] Angela Davis was only briefly a part of the Panthers, and was never a part of Newton's orbit, but she came to think that some of the "danger and chaos" surrounding the Panthers came from within. She decided to "remain uninformed about the organization's inner operations."[16]

Historians, of course, cannot take Davis's position, but my goal in Part Three is not to sit in judgment. Two things seem true to me. The Panthers "demanded too much of themselves," as the white left-wing journalist Murray Kempton put it. And perhaps because of this, there also came a time later in the seventies when, as the historian Clayborne Carson contends, the leaders of the Black Panther Party were no longer "worthy of the dedication of their followers."[17]

SIX

Making Each Other Up

Accounts of Black Power often associate its rise with Northern cities, not with the rural South. But, of course, the first Black Panther Party was in Lowndes County, Alabama. Also worth a mention is the Black North Carolinian Robert F. Williams, who in advocating meeting violence with violence, anticipated the Student Nonviolent Coordinating Committee (SNCC) by several years. His 1962 book, *Negroes with Guns*, was one of the texts that most influenced Huey Newton.[1] This is to say that when it comes to the movement's turn to Black Power, the South played a significant role. Yet it was mostly in American cities that Black organizations began to articulate and proselytize Black nationalism.

"Bay Area Exceptionalism"

Oakland was one such city, a true hothouse of Black Power, and Huey Newton and Bobby Seale were part of the mix. They took classes at their local community college, Merritt College, where Black nationalism began taking shape in the early sixties.[2] There, they were involved in organizations that exposed them to the work of Frantz Fanon, Malcolm X, and Karl Marx. The Afro-American Association (AAA), formed in 1962 on the University of California–Berkeley campus, was one such group. In its promotion of Black pride and self-reliance and its emphasis upon the entrepreneurial, the AAA announced its ideological indebtedness to the Nation of Islam (NOI). Among those active in the AAA were future Democratic Party politicians Ron Dellums and Willie Brown, the couple Donald Harris and Shyamala Gopalan (who became the parents of Vice President Kamala Harris), Cedric Robinson and Ron Everett, who became better known as Maulana Karenga, the founder of the nationalist group US (as in "Us" Blacks versus "them" whites).³ Founded in Berkeley, the AAA shifted its focus to neighboring Oakland, and Merritt College, which is how Seale and Newton came to be involved.

Newton and Seale were also involved in the college's Soul Students Advisory Council (SSAC), which had ties to the local chapter of the Revolutionary Action Movement (RAM), the same group whose members had infiltrated SNCC.⁴ The two men eventually fell out with both SSAC and the AAA, which they characterized as insufficiently activist, but they learned from them. "Revolutionary black nationalism," which reframed Black America as a colony and its freedom struggle as part of a global, anti-imperialist movement, came to them via Malcolm X and RAM. In writing the Panthers' 10-point program, the two men drew upon the 10-point program Malcolm X had devised for the NOI in 1963, as well as the U.S. Constitution and Bill of Rights.⁵ Rooted in Black self-determination, the Panthers' program called for an end to police brutality, white men's exploitation of the Black community, and Black men's incarceration. It also demanded that Black men be exempted from military service, and it called for positive rights such as full employment, education, and decent housing.

Newton and Seale always described themselves as having begun their political journey as Black nationalists.⁶ Not all nationalists were separatists opposed to working with whites, but they likely leaned that way for a while. After all, Seale and Newton founded the party in late October 1966, the year of Black Power, so it is not surprising that nationalism spoke to them. They did so in the wake of an all-day conference on Black Power organized by UC–Berkeley's SDS chapter. The headliner at the October 29 conference was Stokely Carmichael, the unofficial emissary of Black Power. Local Black activists had requested that Carmichael not talk about Black Power to a largely white audience. Gubernatorial candidate Ronald Reagan sent a telegram asking Carmichael to cancel his talk.⁷

Carmichael did not accede to the wishes of others, telling the press that SNCC was "not a tool of the radical left or right."⁸ He appeared at the university's Greek Theater, where he spoke about Black Power to an oversized crowd of more than 10,000, most of them white students. Carmichael emphasized that the people who needed to dedicate themselves to nonviolence were not Black people, but the primary perpetrators of violence: white people. He issued a warning to the Oakland police department: "If you play like Nazis, we playing back wit' you this time around—get hip to that." He called on white activists to organize against the draft and, predictably, to fight racism in the white community. The SNCC leader ended his speech with a stark declaration. If whites do not struggle against their own racism, he declared, "we have no choice but to say very clearly: Move over, or we're going to move on over you."[9]

Carmichael spent much of 1966 on the road, trying to help Black activists in several cities set up Black Power organizations. He and his friend Max Stanford of RAM hoped these groups would provide the foundation for a national Black Panther Party.[10] He may have met with Seale and Newton on this October trip. If he did not manage to squeeze them into his schedule on this trip, he soon did. Carmichael later said that his encounter with the two men left him wondering if they represented anyone other than themselves. To him "the party seemed to spring full-grown out of the fertile political imagination of Huey P. Newton."[11] In truth, quite a lot about the Black Panther Party was hijacked from other Black activist groups, including the black panther logo of the Lowndes County Freedom Organization, which appeared on the program of the Berkeley conference. Community activists in Watts, following the 1965 rebellion, came up with the idea of monitoring police activity in their neighborhood. They wore armbands and carried law books and tape recorders. Newton's innovation was to have the Panthers conduct patrols while armed with law books *and* guns.[12]

Newton and Seale's emphasis on being armed extended to their dealings with other Black activists in the Bay Area where the competition for the title of the Black Panther Party was fierce. Some say that the two succeeded in laying claim to the Panther name by threatening their competitors with physical violence. Those with more activist experience opted to back off.[13] The Panthers' emphasis upon guns had an undeniable appeal to Newton's target audience of "brothers on the block." Ever since the summer before, when Watts erupted, Black radicals, including those in SNCC, had dreamed of mobilizing the kinds of people who were out on the streets during the uprising. Poor and working-class Black Americans, many of whom had spent time in gangs and in prisons, were precisely the people that the civil rights establishment had kept their distance from.

Given how much traction separatist renderings of Black Power had in the Bay Area, Newton and Seale might have figured that the best way forward for their Black Panther Party was to embrace separatism. Certainly, their intended recruits—those brothers on the block—were more excited by nationalism than socialism, more Malcolm X than Chairman Mao. But from early on, Newton and Seale did things their way. This was particularly true when it came to two essentials in the Black Panther Party arsenal: guns and books. Take the guns. They turned to a Merritt College friend, Richard Aoki, whom Seale judged "a Japanese radical cat." Aoki supplied them with serious weapons, not the less lethal shotguns that had been the party's staple.[14]

When Seale and Newton resolved to buy more guns, they did something most Black nationalists would not have done. They went across the bay to China Books, which sold books and periodicals from the People's Republic of China and bought copies of *Quotations from Chairman Mao Zedong*. They did not try to sell the Little Red Book, as it was called, in their own neighborhood. Instead, they went to the UC–Berkeley campus.[15] Years later, Seale laughed about how they had "sold them motherfuckers at Cal campus some Red Books." They were shocked at how quickly they sold, even with their mark-up: from twenty cents to a dollar. Mind you, Seale and Newton did not read the Little Red Book . . . yet.[16] But the fact that they were peddling it to white students was not typical in the world of Black Power. Neither was their musical taste. The album that they listened to, on repeat, as they put together an early issue of *The Black Panther* newspaper was Bob Dylan's *Highway 61 Revisited*. One track in particular, "Ballad of a Thin Man," spoke to Newton, who believed it illuminated the dynamic of racial othering.[17]

If Newton showed signs of ideological nonconformity from early on, this owed something to the place he came from. The Bay Area had boasted bohemian enclaves for some time. And by 1966, the Beats' successors, the hippies, were making their presence felt. Dances featuring psychedelic rock were happening in city parks and in electric ballrooms such as the Avalon and the Fillmore. A new organization fighting for greater sexual expressiveness, the Sexual Freedom League (SFL), set up shop in the Bay Area in 1965. The SFL was opposed to censorship and restrictive abortion laws. It also sponsored nude parties that reportedly became sexual free-for-alls. Richard Thorne, the man who briefly led the SFL, knew Newton from their time together in the AAA. Newton spent a lot of time with him and tried practicing the "nonpossessive" heterosexual love that Thorne preached.[18]

Arguably, the left had an even greater influence on Newton and other Panthers. In the cities of Oakland, San Francisco, and Berkeley, there was a continuous left-wing tradition, much of it organized around the Communist Party. "Bay Area exceptionalism" is what the one-time radical and writer Steve Wasserman calls it. Even during the darkest days of McCarthyism, the Bay Area left was not cowed. Fortifying it were these almost dynastic left-wing families. Particularly prominent were the Proctors, the Prices, and the Hallinans. These families acted as "magnetic poles," Wasserman argues, "around which the left was created and populated."[19]

Something else made the Bay Area unusual: a "distinct laborite culture" that melded union politics and civil rights. It was a culture made by local Blacks in the Brotherhood of Sleeping Car Porters and in the left wing of the International Longshoremen's and Warehousemen's Union (ILWU), which operated on the docks, and the Marine Cooks and Stewards Union (MCSU), whose members worked on the ships. Black longshoremen, some of whom had been active as far back as the 1930s, gave voice to an internationalism that historian Robert Self argues was sufficiently influential for it to have affected Seale and Newton some three decades later.[20] It is true that a surprising number of the area's Black residents, particularly in Oakland, were part of the Communist Party orbit. Some were influential. Dr. Carlton Benjamin Goodlett, the editor and publisher of the *Sun-Reporter* newspaper, which served the Bay Area's Black community, had close ties to the Communist Party.[21]

The upshot is that Bay Area progressives, who often worked within the Communist Party and on its periphery as fellow travelers, were accustomed to collaborating across difference in that multiracial and multiethnic region. One organization that modeled interracialism from the mid-forties through the mid-fifties—when McCarthyism finally did it in—was the East Bay branch of the Civil Rights Congress (CRC).[22] The CRC was on the frontlines of the fight for racial equality, often focusing on police brutality and the racist justice system. At its height, this Black-led organization had as many as 500 dues-paying, mostly Black members, although few were aware of the group's ties to the Communist Party.[23] Huey Newton reportedly said that he and his friends considered the CRC's white lawyer, Robert Treuhaft, a hero because of his spirited defense of a Black teenager, Jerry Newson, who was falsely accused of murder. Treuhaft, who was the husband of the muckraking journalist (and fellow CRC member) Jessica Mitford, became well known in the Black community for defending Newson in a long, drawn-out case that featured many appeals and made headlines locally.[24]

When progressive politics came to life again in the Bay Area, energized by the emergence of an emboldened civil rights movement and a fledgling New Left, it bore the influence of this decades-long left-wing interracialism. The protests that began in late 1963 against racist employment practices at several San Francisco businesses—Mel's Drive-in, the Sheraton-Palace Hotel, and the car dealerships on Auto Row—employed civil disobedience and were racially mixed. The Du Bois Club, the Communist Party's national youth group, played a key role in those pivotal protests. One of its members, Tracy Sims (now known as Taman Tracy Moncur), a charismatic 18-year-old Black woman, became the unofficial spokesperson for the protests.[25] The lawyers representing the hundreds of protestors who were arrested were left-wing whites, including Bob Treuhaft, Vincent Hallinan, and Beverly Axelrod.

As we have seen, those protests propelled some students to Mississippi, where their involvement in the Summer Project set in motion the first substantial wave of campus-based student activism during the sixties: the free speech movement at UC–Berkeley. From the start, the Bay Area civil rights and student movements were connected by a core group of activist students.

Even if civil rights and the left had long been conjoined in the Bay Area, by 1966, when Seale and Newton were trying to make theirs the area's sole Black Panther Party, separatist versions of Black Nationalism were in ascendance. Their interaction with a prominent left-wing writer and activist suggests how little interest the two men had in making common cause with white leftists. In spring 1966, several months before they founded the party, when the duo was heading up Merritt College's SSAC, they were approached by Robert Scheer, an editor at the left-wing magazine *Ramparts*. Scheer was running as an antiwar, left-wing candidate for Congress. He was taking on the Democratic Party establishment in the primary and needed all the support he could garner. Scheer came to a meeting of the Soul Students' Advisory Council at Merritt to ask for the group's endorsement. Newton and Seale barred him from even making his pitch because, they said, his candidacy didn't matter to Black people. They also hit up Scheer for a $100 donation, and he obliged.

The Convict and the Lawyer

The paths of these three men would cross again after the writer Eldridge Cleaver entered their lives in the spring of 1967. It is conceivable that Newton and Seale would have developed ties to the Bay Area left even if Cleaver had never joined their fledging party. After all, the Black Panther Party was only about six months old when the 31-year-old Cleaver signed up. At this stage, the party was, as Bobby Seale later observed, "a broke little organization with a number of shotguns, a very weak treasury, and worried about how to pay the rent."[26] Although the Sacramento action garnered the party headlines, it seems to have barely increased its numbers. As late as October 1967, its membership likely was between 10 and 20.[27] According to one source, the party consisted of a handful of people and was falling apart.[28] In its crucial first year, the Black Panther Party was a work in progress, and Cleaver's presence was a crucial factor in nudging it toward the organized Bay Area left.

Why would Cleaver, who himself had earlier leaned toward nationalism, steer the Black Panthers toward the white-majority left and to Bob Scheer, the very person the Panther cofounders had rebuffed? Answering this question requires digging into his past. By the time Cleaver was 30 years old, in 1965, he had spent most of his adult life in prison. He landed in San Quentin in early 1958. It was his second prison stint, after being convicted of two counts of assault with a deadly weapon and three counts of assault with intent to commit murder. He wasn't charged with the crime at the center of the case: the attempted rape of a white female college student who was in a parked car with a white male student. Cleaver argued he was innocent, but he later revealed that in this period he believed it was an "insurrectionary" act, a blow against white men and white supremacy, for a Black man to rape a white woman.

Moreover, before targeting white women, he chose to first "refine my technique and modus operandi" by raping "black girls."[29] In San Quentin, Cleaver joined the NOI. When Malcolm X left the NOI and embraced secular nationalism, Cleaver followed suit. To win parole, he took part in the prison's educational programs and made himself over into a writer.[30] He was influenced by fellow prisoner and writer Caryl Chessman. On death row, Chessman wrote bestselling books, though they did not spare him death by execution. Cleaver read widely, but he was especially keen on reading the work of left-wing writers. *The Communist Manifesto* was among his favorites.

Cleaver's aspirations as a writer led him to seek legal counsel. Stymied by prison administrators, who considered his work dangerous and racist, he was unable to get it out into the world. Cleaver had been searching, without success, for a lawyer to represent him. Then he heard about Beverley Axelrod, a Movement fixture and a 1948 graduate of Brooklyn Law School. He first learned of Axelrod in a newspaper article about the trials of protestors involved in the Sheraton-Palace and Auto Row demonstrations. Accompanying that spring 1965 article in the *Sun-Reporter* was a photograph of the lawyer with a group of Black men. Cleaver was struck by how comfortable Axelrod seemed in their company. Fellow prisoners told Cleaver she was dating a Black man.[31]

Axelrod was indeed dating a Black man. She often dated Black men. The attractive, sexy 41-year-old was drawn to Black men who were part of the freedom movement. One recent lover was the Black journalist Reggie Majors.[32] In the summer of 1965, she traveled to Jakarta, Indonesia, as part of a 10-member delegation of Women Strike for Peace who opposed the war in Vietnam.[33] Her curious travel route home, via Washington, DC, was noted by a journalist for *Jet* magazine who reported that she had taken the detour to dine in the nation's capital with the recently elected Black Congressman from Detroit, John Conyers. Herb Caen, columnist for the *San Francisco Chronicle*, reported that the two were engaged to be married. Whatever happened between Axelrod and Conyers, they did not marry. She had an extensive friendship network that included Dick Gregory, the civil rights lawyer Len Holt, New Leftists such as Jerry Rubin, and Old Leftists such as Jessica Mitford and her husband, Bob Treuhaft.[34]

Image 6.1 Attorney Beverly Axelrod exits the hearing room at the Cannon Office Building at the HUAC inquiry into New Left activism, following the unwarranted arrest of fellow lawyer Arthur Kinoy, August 17, 1966. Axelrod was representing the Berkeley activist Jerry Rubin.

Rowland Scherman, photographer. Courtesy of the Rowland Scherman Collection, Robert S. Cox Special Collections and University Archives Research Center, UMass Amherst Libraries

Twice divorced and raising two sons on her own, Axelrod had a busy, but hardly lucrative law practice focused on housing and employment discrimination in San Francisco.[35] She found it difficult juggling parenting, her activist commitments, and her law practice. She gave her legal services freely, to the National Association for the Advancement of Colored People (NAACP), Congress for Racial Equality (CORE), and the United Farm Workers. She represented people arrested during the Auto Row and Sheraton-Palace protests and the Free Speech Movement. Before moving to San Francisco in 1954, she had lived in Modesto, California, where she headed up its NAACP chapter. She volunteered for an intense six-month stint in 1963 in Louisiana as a lawyer. On her return from the South, she told a reporter, "For six weeks I carried a toothbrush wherever I went." This was the drill in Louisiana. "It was the accepted thing. You just didn't know when you might be thrown in jail."[36]

The Federal Bureau of Investigation (FBI) routinely linked civil rights activism with subversion, so it's not surprising that the agency believed she was a member of the Communist Party, a charge she denied. She may have once been a fellow traveler, but the reminiscences of a friend who had been a member suggest that Axelrod had considerable reservations about the Communist Party. According to another friend, Frank Browning, Axelrod insisted that "a revolution without humor was no revolution at all, that any proper study of Marx had also to include Chico and Groucho."[37] Still, Axelrod's left-wing connections extended into the Communist Party. Upon arriving in San Francisco, she had turned to Charles Garry, who helped to mentor her as a lawyer. She was on the executive board of the San Francisco chapter of the National Lawyers Guild and was friendly with people in the local Du Bois Club. Younger movement lawyers, particularly women, admired her passionate activism.[38]

However, by the time she began representing Cleaver, in the fall of 1965, Axelrod was no longer prepared to give up everything, including her personal life, for the Cause. She was happy to partner politically with communists and socialists, but she confessed that their style turned her off. She seems to have been drawn instead to younger New Left activists, people like Jerry Rubin and Stew Albert. Anne Weills recalled seeing Axelrod cutting loose on the dancefloor at a party sponsored by the Du Bois Club. Like most other partygoers there, Weills was in her early 20s. She remembered thinking that Axelrod "had a kind of edgy way of being," particularly for someone whom she considered middle-aged, even old.[39]

Maybe Axelrod was feeling especially edgy that night. The evidence shows that she was ambivalent about her struggling law practice. She complained of "the pain" that her law practice caused her. She dreamed of a very different kind of life, getting into what she called a "rock&roll bag." Maybe living in the neighborhood of Haight-Ashbury, ground zero for the emerging hippie scene, led her to think about leading a more bohemian life.[40] Her tenant Wes Wilson was a poster artist for the electric ballrooms and part of this scene. Despite all the demands on her time, Axelrod was known for her great parties, many of them fundraisers that were interracial, left-wing, and queer friendly. At some point she found herself at an event with Senator Hubert Humphrey, presumably well before the summer of '64, and taught him how to do the popular rock'n'roll dance, the Twist, a dance that Cleaver would soon be writing about.[41]

Curiously, given her ties to New Leftists, she seems to have been untouched by the mid-sixties view that radicalism required organizing around your *own* oppression. For her, working on behalf of others did not make you a liberal, which, in any case, was not how she saw herself. Like the New Leftists to whom she was drawn, she identified as a radical. But she was also weary and yearned for a less stressful life, without the pressure of people, including prisoners, seeking her aid. Sometimes, days went by when all she could do was sit at home and play solitaire. So why on earth did Axelrod take the time to write back to a convict at Folsom Prison, someone to whom she owed nothing? The other lawyers he had contacted, including Charles Garry, the man who had mentored Axelrod, had not bothered to respond. Maybe it was Axelrod's long-standing proclivity for risk taking. As a shy young girl, she became addicted to the scariest rides on the boardwalk in Atlantic City, where her family lived for a time. The barker for one ride let her on for free to induce anxious people to get on. "This little girl is not afraid to ride," he would yell, shaming them into climbing onboard.[42]

All those years later, the grown-up Axelrod was still intrepid. She appears to have exhibited no fear or apprehension about Cleaver, who wrote to her in May 1965. She was drawn to his "extreme intelligence." He wasn't just literate; he was literary. Cleaver's repudiation of his former self, a Black Muslim who had subscribed to what he called the NOI's "racist doctrine," likely made him especially attractive to her.[43] From his very first letter to her, he was signaling his specialness. He was writing about race relations, but in a way that foregrounded sexual "deviance" or at least the sexually problematical—homosexuality in men and women, female frigidity, and male impotence. His book's provocative working title was *Black Man/White Woman*. Axelrod agreed to meet with Cleaver, who was the victim of Folsom's censorial overreach. At their first meeting, he hugged her and slyly slid his manuscript into her briefcase. Thus began a pattern in which she smuggled his writing out of Folsom and put her considerable energy and talent into getting it out into the world.

Axelrod was convinced that Cleaver's writing was his ticket out of prison, and within a few short weeks his freedom became her project. Their epistolary dialogue was feverish, much of it about his writing, which she set about editing. Cleaver wrote obsessively to her. The typed and transcribed copy of their correspondence numbers nearly 2,000 double-spaced pages, most of them his letters. Soon, she was editing his pages-long letters into essays. In her letters, Axelrod sometimes challenged him or suggested relevant writers or different angles of vision. She was an able interlocutor.

Axelrod knew that winning parole for Cleaver required circulating his work to people who could get it published. Soon she was wearing another hat as well: business agent. She worked tirelessly, contacting important left-wing writers and critics whom she believed might appreciate his writing. Her first stop was to friends at the left-wing *Ramparts* magazine, who needed little convincing. A radical Black convict who could write! Through its publisher Edward Keating and editor Warren Hinckle, Axelrod extracted their promise to employ Cleaver as a contributing editor after he was released from prison. This would meet one of the parole board's biggest concerns: that a parolee had secured stable employment. She negotiated his book deal and hired a legitimate literary agent to place his articles. Axelrod's secretary even typed his final manuscript. She sent him books and magazines. Although she did not have a lot of money, she also provided him with material comforts: a sleek portable typewriter, a new record player, and the latest jazz records.

She also wrote to hundreds of prominent people, mostly men, whom she hoped would be willing to write in support of Cleaver's parole plea. Many did because Cleaver was undeniably talented. He was also very well read. He had devoured books in prison, books by the existentialists, Norman Mailer (his "idol"), Thomas Merton, Karl Marx, Sylvia Plath, Frantz Fanon, and Khalil Gibran, as well as Bay Area writers Lenore Kandel and Tillie Olsen. He had dreams of opening a bookstore/community center, but his biggest dream was that he could "write forever more."[44] In any case, Axelrod succeeded in garnering letters from literary titans such as Norman Mailer, Norman Podhoretz, Thomas Merton, and Alex Haley, as well as the *Ramparts* people. She obtained letters from the politicians Willie Brown and Phil Burton, and from Cecil Williams of the progressive Glide Memorial Church in San Francisco.

Although the parole process moved with glacial speed, the relationship between Cleaver and Axelrod quickly shifted into high gear. From the beginning, Cleaver's letters to Axelrod bristled with his restless intelligence and his seductiveness. Some of his letters may have troubled her, as when he wrote, "I assault you with my words" or "I fuck the paper with my typewriter!" He later apologized, characterizing those words as "an act of Rape." Toggling between the brazenly inappropriate and the politely respectful, he probed her willingness to ignore the normal attorney–client boundaries. It aroused her suspicions, and she made it clear she had zero tolerance for "being manipulated or used, or lied to."

Axelrod's apprehensions soon evaporated as Cleaver waged a full-throttle charm offensive. Quite likely, she had never met a man so flattering, so eager to glue himself to her. Cleaver made himself irresistible as he embraced the righteousness of their relationship and of interracial political alliances. "Even if Beverly had not fallen in love with him," observed her daughter-in-law Melanie Kask, "she was already in love with the *idea* of him." Cleaver was both the man she needed and the man the movement needed. She believed he was a Black messiah. He wrote of her as a "rebel, a revolutionary."[45]

Not everyone who was a part of Axelrod's circle of friends and acquaintances approved of her willingness to flout lawyerly conventions. Sheila O'Donnell, a left-wing private detective who worked with Axelrod, was reportedly shocked when "Beverly crossed that line" and became lovers with Cleaver.[46] However, to some young left-wing lawyers and antiracist activists, she was a trailblazer. Her relationship with Cleaver became the template for left-wing white female lawyers and prisoner rights advocates and their Black male convict clients. Fay Stender, who was part of Garry's legal team and worked on the cases of two high-profile Panthers, Huey Newton and George Jackson, modeled herself on Axelrod, who had shared with her details of her relationship with Cleaver.[47]

The prisoners' rights movement that took shape in these years featured many such relationships between (mostly) white women and the (mostly) Black convicts seeking counsel. Eve Pell, a white journalist, and part of the progressive Prison Law Project, explains how she fell for George Jackson, one of the most famous incarcerated Black writers of the era. You were led into a meeting room for visitations that was "horrible, with guards and officials who don't want you there." But then sitting across from you is this prisoner, and he is "focusing on you with a quality of attention I don't think you'll ever get anywhere again." Pell believes "half the reason almost every woman I know in the project fell in love with some prisoner" was the attention they lavished on their visitors.[48]

White women were by no means the only ones who fell in love with prisoners. Charles Garry, the Armenian lawyer who represented virtually all the Oakland-based Panther leaders, "just fell hook, line and sinker" for Huey Newton.[49] Black women, even veteran Panthers such as the New York Panther Afeni Shakur, found themselves played. For Black women, Shakur pointed out, "there aren't that many men, and the ones in prison say the right things." About the letters they wrote, Shakur learned that they had "nothing to do with normal relationships, love and all that ... and everything to do with survival."[50]

Axelrod had her suspicions, but she still fell hard for Cleaver, just as he intended. He wrote her the tenderest of love letters and proved himself the most attentive boyfriend. After one of their earliest meetings, he wrote about the image in his head: the "swirling, dazzling image of your pink dress and the matching ribbon in your hair." Later, he wrote to her of the "polysyllabic burden of your name pounding in my head BEVERLY AXELROD." He often called her his wife, and they went so far as to stage a nonbinding, private marriage ceremony in prison.[51] The changing nature of their relationship presented a conundrum for prison authorities who permitted Axelrod to change hats during her visits. In the first part of her meeting with Cleaver, she acted as his attorney in a room designated for lawyers. After they had conducted business, they were each allowed to move to the room in which prisoners met with friends and family. They sometimes were quite physical with each other.

In some respects, their backgrounds were not so dissimilar. They grew up in poverty in families abandoned by their fathers, and with relatives who had passed as white rather than Black or, in Axelrod's case, Jewish.[52] Yet the asymmetry in their relationship, perhaps inevitably, gave rise to his anger and her guilt. Axelrod's solution to her freedom and Cleaver's continued incarceration (and her attendant guilt) was to shrink her very big life to create some sort of equivalence. Nevertheless, as he took to reminding her, it was she who had the power to get his manuscript in shape, obtain a book deal, and locate famous writers to support his parole effort. She also had the power to walk away from him, although one imagines not without some anxiety about the consequences. Yet, as time passed and his articles began appearing in *Ramparts* and even in mainstream magazines, Cleaver became less dependent on her. As he developed a name, he grew impatient about his continued imprisonment and the hurry-up-and-wait nature of publishing, especially as writers like LeRoi Jones (soon to be Amiri Baraka) threatened to outstrip him ideologically. By the time his book hit the bookstore shelves, would his faith in interracialism be antiquated, perhaps even to himself?

Recalibrating their relationship was Black Power, which began to be felt by the spring of 1966. Axelrod identified primarily as a civil rights activist and wondered if there was any longer room for her in that struggle. The organization with which she was most closely affiliated, San Francisco CORE, was growing less hospitable to whites. This was happening across the country in the spring of 1966 as CORE embraced separatism. Even in Utica, New York, where relations between white and Black CORE members had been very positive, whites were asked to leave.[53] Axelrod was hurt when the chairman of CORE's San Francisco chapter told her that, as a white woman, she no longer had any role in the movement. She felt frustrated by the fragmented state of the larger Movement, and the unwillingness of some Black organizations to work in coalition with left-wing white groups.[54]

What made Black separatism especially awkward and painful for Axelrod was that for some time and in many contexts, she had passed as Black. People often thought she was Black because she was olive-skinned, her law partner John Bussey was Black, and their office was in a Black neighborhood. Given that combination of factors, it seems likely that many people did assume she was Black. For her part, Axelrod "loved it" when people thought she was Black. Axelrod counted Black people among her friends, including Laverne Williams, who was then Huey Newton's fiancée. "I have lived so long in a black or integrated world," she wrote Cleaver, "that I really had ceased to think of myself as black or white." As someone who had a great appreciation of the Black world, she was proud she could "pass in it and be accepted."[55] Black Power jeopardized that.

Axelrod and Cleaver corresponded about separatism, but not very deeply. She assured Cleaver that at least her ability to pass would make their life together easier once he was free. He surely knew better. Any serious reckoning with separatism was pushed aside by the "grandiose" way that they saw themselves as "a symbolic political force," at least for a while.[56] Cleaver described himself as a "Pan-Humanitarian" opposed to tribalism. As for Axelrod, she declared, "Either of us, alone, can be quite formidable. Together, we will be invincible."[57] Their epistolary agreement was that their relationship modeled interracial intimacy.

Cleaver and Axelrod and the Black Panther Party

By the time Cleaver walked out of prison on December 12, 1966, and drove to San Francisco with Axelrod in her MG, the militant wing of the Black freedom movement had moved on from where it had been 18 months earlier when he first reached out to her. December was the month that SNCC decided, if ambivalently, to become exclusively Black. Did Cleaver still see his relationship with Axelrod as a grand experiment in interracialism? He knew that he still needed her in some ways, but not to the degree that he had in prison. He was paroled, employed, and becoming known. A handsome man with green eyes "as cool and impervious . . . as the steel bars of a prison," Cleaver aimed to be inscrutable.[58] Early on in their correspondence, he had bragged to Axelrod that when it came to other people he had developed "an elaborate system of 'games' going on at all times." These games, he wrote, were "designed to suit my purposes and achieve my ends."[59] Was she too infatuated to notice? Six months later, Axelrod felt him pulling away and grew afraid that she was no different from everyone else he had played.

That December day as they drove to San Francisco, Axelrod may have thought back to an earlier moment in their torrid epistolary relationship. Back then, when the outsized avowals of love came fast and furious, she summoned the courage to ask a sobering question. "Are we making each other up?" How do we know we aren't simply fantasizing when we have "no way of testing the reality?" Axelrod meant that each of them harbored fantasies of the other, but, of course, each of them was also presenting a curated version of themselves to the other. This drama of making each other up marked not just their relationship, but, as subsequent chapters show, relations between the Black Panther Party and many of its white allies as well. However, in Cleaver's case, he did not have to indulge in fantasies about what Axelrod might do for him. He emerged from prison with a healthy respect for what the seduction of a white female left-wing lawyer might yield: freedom, money, contacts, and perhaps even fame.

During the Black Panther Party's first six months many of the people who joined up were teenaged or unemployed, and sometimes both.[60] They were what Seale and Newton called the "lumpenproletariat," the very people the two men had dreamed of organizing. Yet the party's numbers were small as the two struggled to gain some traction over their more conventionally nationalist rivals. Despite the bravado of Newton, whose willingness to confront, belittle,

Image 6.2 Free Huey! Rally, DeFremery Park, Oakland, California, in 1968, where Black Panther Party minister of communication Eldridge Cleaver is speaking. Fellow Panther Bill Brent is at his side, and Field Marshal Don Cox, in black, at right, is looking on.

Bob Fitch Photography Archive, Department of Special Collections, Stanford University Library

and threaten the police made him a mythic figure, the Panthers grew slowly. Of all their recruits none was more prized than Eldridge Cleaver. After all, he had attended what Newton called "graduate school," that is, prison.[61] Not surprisingly, he had the respect of the Panthers' "lumpen" recruits.

By the time Cleaver joined the party in mid-April 1967, he had been hanging out with Axelrod's friends and acquaintances for a full four months.[62] She introduced her fiancé to all her lefty friends, which included people in and around the Communist Party as well as the young white radicals of Berkeley. It was the younger radicals, including Jerry Rubin, Stew Alpert, and Jack Weinberg, whom Cleaver was most drawn to.[63] He was also becoming friendly with some of his coworkers at *Ramparts*, particularly Robert Scheer. To left-wing whites, he was the real deal: an ex-con and organic intellectual. Many found him irresistibly appealing.

Cleaver had been in prison as Black Power was taking hold, which may explain why he was so receptive to young white lefties. During his time in prison, he had followed the exploits—writerly and otherwise—of Berkeley's young white radicals.[64] By the time of his release in December 1966, he understood that "the black movement and the white movement were not speaking to each other," as he later put it. But that wasn't where he was at. Cleaver wrote to Axelrod in April 1966 that the Movement needed more coalitions, especially in this "age of rampant Nationalism."

When he met them, he felt a kinship with these young white radicals, which informed the stance he took toward the white-dominated left while in the Panthers.[65] Thinking back on his first visit to Stew Albert's Berkeley "pad," he recalled fondly how they had "turned on and talked about the future." His feeling was reciprocated. "The possibility of building a relationship with a hot Black organization, in the new era of Black Power and separatism was delicious," recalled Albert. He acknowledged that "we wouldn't exactly be joining hands in a loving community." Still, he felt the Black Panthers "represented the best news white radicals had heard from Black America in quite some time."[66]

However, by the spring of 1967, with separatist versions of Black Power in ascendance, Cleaver began spending more time at the Black House, a Black arts center in which Amiri Baraka, Marvin X, and Ed Bullins were also involved.[67] At a February meeting to plan for a visit from Betty Shabazz, the widow of Malcolm X, Cleaver witnessed the Panthers up close. For him, they were "the most beautiful sight I had ever seen: four black men wearing black berets, powder blue shirts, black leather jackets, black trousers, shiny black shoes—and each with a gun!"[68] Days later, when he saw Newton, who was part of Shabazz's security detail, challenge a white cop, Cleaver decided to join up and become a Black Panther.

Cleaver quickly became part of the Panthers' orbit that spring, but so did Beverly Axelrod. She believed in the Panthers, and some of them believed in her, too. "Most of the time I have never thought of her as a white person," Newton later wrote.[69] He trusted her totally. Alex (Sascha) Hoffmann, a white left-wing lawyer who would work closely with Newton, recalled the time that the Panther leader shared with him an incriminating detail about his life. This was early on in their relationship, probably 1967. "I said to him," recalls Hoffmann, "Huey, why do you trust me?" And Newton responded, "Oh, I don't know. Beverly said you were okay."[70]

The relationship between the Panthers and Axelrod barely registers in histories of the Black Panther Party, perhaps because interracialism of this sort seems like a throwback, so at odds with the party's image of Black pride, beauty, and self-love. Axelrod is "the inconvenient white woman in a story about Black Power," as the scholar Jo-Ann Morgan observes of Axelrod's invisibility in most histories."[71] Yet Axelrod was there, representing Panthers in the Sacramento action, typing the first issues of the *Black Panther* newspaper, which were written and put together at her home. Initially, the Panthers used the mimeograph machine at one of the white alternative presses.

Axelrod's Carmel Street home was also the site of the photo shoot that produced the iconic image of Newton in the rattan chair. Perhaps the first widely available poster of a Black radical, it was taped to walls across America, from Panther offices to college dorms. Reprinted in the underground and mainstream press and slapped onto protest signs, the photo became the dominant image of Newton and the Panthers. The photograph of the gorgeous and implacable Newton in that rattan chair is firmly enough lodged in our cultural memory that some 40 years later the creative team for Marvel's 2018 action film, *Black Panther*, featured a futuristic Wakandan throne that cleverly referenced it.

It was Cleaver who came up with its mash-up of styles—slick urban and faux African—cannily designed to appeal to a very broad spectrum of radicals and rebels. However, the African-looking spear and shields, which were purchased at the import store Cost Plus, belonged to Axelrod's teenaged sons. The rattan chair was donated by Axelrod's white gay male hairdresser. And the man snapping the pictures was Blair Stapp, a white photographer. The photo shoot could not have happened at the Black House, not with this crew. Yet Newton's admirers likely imagined it had been staged at just such a space, not at the home of Cleaver's white girlfriend, with help from her sons and white friends.[72]

Over time, Cleaver's relationship with Axelrod, forged in the fall of 1965 when interracialism was just barely still alive, came to feel like a burden to him.[73] Axelrod recalled Cleaver telling her that if he wanted to be the new Malcom X, which he very much did, he would have to leave her.[74] He said he was taking flak at the Black House for not ending their relationship.[75] Amiri Baraka later confirmed this, reporting that "the sisters" there were very critical of Cleaver for still "tipping around seeing his lawyer and old love, Beverly Axelrod."[76] Two years earlier, in 1965, Baraka publicly left his first wife, Hettie (and less decisively their two daughters). He did so, even though their marriage had been rooted in "exercising their bigger and better selves," not in proving the righteousness of interracial marriage.[77] If Baraka and Jones had not survived the Black Power turn, there was no way that the bond between Cleaver and Axelrod, which was rooted in politics, could last. He knew he would have to leave Axelrod if he were to have any credibility with many of his Black admirers.

Then, in April 1967, Cleaver's head was turned by a young and beautiful SNCC volunteer whom he met a conference in Nashville, Tennessee. How did Cleaver describe Kathleen Neal to the white lawyer Alex Hoffmann? He bragged that he had found himself "a Black Beverly Axelrod."[78] Even after falling in love with Neal, Cleaver maintained an on-again, off-again relationship with Axelrod. As late as October 28, 1967, the night of Huey Newton's deadly shoot-out with the Oakland police, Axelrod and Cleaver were out of town trying to "take some space" to talk about their relationship. No sooner had the couple arrived at the Highlands Hotel in Carmel than they heard about the deadly police stop that left policeman John Frey dead, his partner Herbert Heanes badly wounded, and Newton with a bullet in his abdomen. The couple drove straight back to Oakland. By the time Axelrod and another attorney, John George, arrived at the hospital, they found Newton shackled to a gurney surrounded by police. The cops hated Axelrod because of her role in freeing Cleaver, and, according to Newton, they "viciously ridiculed her and mocked George."[79]

Axelrod initially served as Newton's legal co-counsel, but her deteriorating relationship with Cleaver led her to withdraw from his case.[80] Even after she had stopped formally representing Newton, she continued to visit him, acting as an intermediary between him and Cleaver. When Axelrod explained to Newton why Cleaver had ended their relationship, Newton came up with the bright idea of issuing what David Hilliard called "Proclamation Number One." In a letter to his girlfriend Laverne Williams, Newton explained that when Axelrod had visited him in prison, everyone, including other Black prisoners, assumed she was Black. Newton declared that the party was now to regard Axelrod as a Black woman, a status that he pointed out came with privileges.[81] Three weeks later, Cleaver married Neal.

Axelrod was shattered when Cleaver walked away from her. "She couldn't let go of the dream," recalled Kask. "That became her only reality and she was really out of touch with everything else."[82] Even after Cleaver dumped her, she worked in support of the Panthers. She signed onto a scheme, devised by Panther leader Don Cox, to spring Newton from the Alameda County jail. According to Cox, Axelrod was the one person who had consistent contact with Newton. She was the "linchpin" of the breakout plot, which, in the end, was never attempted.[83]

In the spring of 1968, the publicity machine for Cleaver's book *Soul on Ice* revved up. The book bore the dedication, "To Beverly with whom I share the ultimate love." It also included two love letters from him to her, and the one from her in which she ventures that the greatest danger they faced as a couple was that they had made each other up. By the time the book was in stores, they likely felt exposed and embarrassed, she about having been dumped, and he about having expressed love for a white woman. But Cleaver had a full plate that spring, plotting armed insurrection and flogging his book, while Axelrod sunk into a deep depression.

Rather than stay in the Bay Area, where she would be constantly reminded of Cleaver, she moved to Northern New Mexico, where the Chicano activist Reies Tijerina and the Alianza Federal de Mercedes land reform movement were shaking up things. There, she collaborated on a new project with Betita Martínez, who had moved there after leaving SNCC. Perhaps someone in Axelrod's circle of friends knew Martínez and thought their recent histories and similar political stance would make a good match. In the small town of Española, the two women began publishing a bilingual Chicano newspaper, *El Grito del Norte*. Axelrod also represented Tijerina and the Alianza.

One item that Axelrod took with her to New Mexico was the famous high-backed rattan chair in which Newton was photographed. In 1973, after Cleaver reneged on paying Axelrod the 25 percent of the royalties they had contractually agreed to (initially, he had offered to pay her 50 percent, which she declined), she sued him.[84] That same year, Axelrod became one of the left-wing lawyers assisting the American Indian Movement (AIM) during the

Wounded Knee Occupation and founded its Legal Defense/Offense Committee. By 1975, she was back in California, where she served as the administrative law judge for the California Agricultural Labor Relations Board, a post that required she travel the state to hear cases that were usually brought against growers by workers.[85]

Axelrod remained politically active in the Movement, and she had many friends and lovers, but Cleaver was hard to forget. Perhaps he harbored fond feelings for Axelrod, too, but the way he spoke of her once *Soul on Ice* was published suggests she had become an embarrassment. In July 1968, about nine months after their relationship ended, the Black writer Cecil Brown interviewed him for the *Evergreen Review*. Brown criticized the loving way he had written about his relationship with his white lawyer. Cleaver explained that as a prisoner asking for help, he believed that "any reluctance to relate to her would be very unbecoming to me in the condition I was in." Lest the readers fail to appreciate the pragmatic calculus at work here, Cleaver said, "from the moment I wrote her my first letter . . . I wanted to attract her . . . I only had words, and I used those words . . . and I got out of the penitentiary."[86] Of course, this was the era, as the historian Donna Murch argues, when "the confession and repudiation of desire for white women became an important proving ground for Black nationalist identity." Maybe he did love her? When asked that question years later, Cleaver responded somewhat evasively. "Who wouldn't love Beverly?"[87]

Indeed, genuinely affectionate relationships sometimes developed between Panther leaders and their white collaborators and supporters. Take the one that existed between Cleaver and Yippie Jerry Rubin. They had been Bay Area co-conspirators during the late sixties, but their post-sixties trajectories swung rightward. In 1994, when Cleaver heard the news that Rubin had been hit by a car and was in critical condition at a Los Angeles hospital, the 60-year-old Cleaver, poor and in bad health, hitchhiked from the Bay Area to see him. When informed that only family members could visit Rubin, Cleaver told the hospital staff, "He's my brother." When they didn't budge, the ever-resourceful Cleaver added, "We're half-brothers . . . same mother, different father." That did the trick.[88]

It is a sweet story, and there are others, but Stew Albert was right that even those Panthers actively seeking the assistance of white radicals were not interested in creating a "loving community" with them. Black Power had changed the emotional economy of relationships across the color line. If their white collaborators made demands on the Panthers, either individually or collectively, if they proved too needy or too pushy, the Panthers walked away. The kind of drama that had for a time so absorbed SNCC, they avoided. Did the Panthers sometimes use white people? Yes, but they used Black people, too. However, the role that the Panthers permitted whites was a largely backward move, one in which they would once again be an auxiliary to the Black struggle. Only this time, no one imagined they were part of a beloved community.

SEVEN

Working Across Difference and Paying a Price

Even after walking away from Axelrod, Cleaver maintained his friendships with the white radicals to whom she had introduced him. They enjoyed getting together, smoking dope, listening to music, especially Bob Dylan, and talking politics. Hanging out with Cleaver gave Berkeley's white radicals cachet. Cleaver had all the cachet in the world at that point. He also had money, though not enough to maintain the under-resourced and struggling Black Panther Party. This need became especially acute after Newton's arrest. By that juncture Cleaver already had helped to put together a legal defense committee for those arrested in Sacramento. Cleaver understood just how useful Scheer, Rubin, and his other white New Left friends might be with the prodigious fundraising challenge that lay ahead. If Axelrod, drawing on her legal expertise and her connections to the predominantly white left, succeeded in both springing him and setting him up in his new life, couldn't Cleaver mobilize those same connections to raise the money to meet Newton's legal fees?[1]

Making Moves to the Left

When Axelrod backed away from Newton's case, she steered the Panthers to the white, left-wing lawyer Charles Garry. Nearly sixty years old, Garry was something of an eccentric, a yoga enthusiast who dressed like a gangster, and relished his reputation as a scrappy streetfighter in the courtroom. Garry was Armenian, and had been raised by his parents, who had emigrated to America from Turkey, on a farm in California's San Joaquin Valley. It was the discrimination he suffered there that shaped his political consciousness. Axelrod knew Garry because he had lent her a helping hand years earlier when she first arrived in San Francisco as an unemployed lawyer.[2]

Image 7.1 In fall 1968, Eldridge Cleaver vowed to give 20 speeches across the many campuses of the University of California, defying the decision of the UC Board of Regents that he be allowed to deliver precisely one speech. Here, at the University of California, Irvine, on September 26, 1968, *Ramparts* editor Robert Scheer, seated and on the left, looks on as his friend and colleague Eldridge Cleaver speaks.
George Brich, AP Photo

Garry may have been a member of the Communist Party. The Federal Bureau of Investigation (FBI) believed he still was, and over time Hoover became obsessed with uncovering his connections to the Communist Party.[3] Whatever the case, Garry had been a part of the Communist Party's Civil Rights Congress (CRC), which understood defense committees as a key component of movement building. People involved in a defense committee often became more involved in activism.[4] Garry counted among his friends William Patterson, one of the most influential African American members of the Communist Party. Oakland-born Patterson was a lawyer and an activist whose civil rights work went back decades to the CRC, which is how he had first met Garry. The Communist Party now had a way into the Black Panther Party.

Garry met with Eldridge Cleaver, Kathleen Neal, and Huey Newton's brother and sister. The state threw the book at Newton, charging him with first-degree murder, assault, and kidnapping. Garry was frank about the time

Image 7.2 From left to right, lawyer Charles Garry, in a wheelchair and wearing a hospital bracelet, Bobby Seale and Kathleen Cleaver hold a press conference in Mount Zion Hospital on April 29, 1969, about a police action against the Panthers in San Francisco's Fillmore district.

Ernest Bennett, AP Photo

and cost involved in the legal battle. It would take at least three years, he warned them, and it would cost $100,000. "Kathleen Cleaver kind of laughed," Melvin Newton recalled, "and we said, we don't have any money, but we'll raise the money."[5]

Axelrod was friendly with people in both the New and Old Left.[6] At the same time that Garry (and the Communist Party) had the ear of Newton, there were Bay Area New Leftists who had Cleaver's ear. Most New Leftists regarded the Communist Party as a bunch of "stodgy reformist sell-outs" while the leadership of the Communist Party considered the rhetoric, and increasingly the behavior, of the New Left dangerously inflammatory.[7] Over the next few years, the Panthers would allow themselves to be courted by people in each broad formation. But at this moment, with Newton in jail awaiting trial for murder and Seale still in prison for the Sacramento action, the charismatic and quotable Cleaver found himself in a position to play a pivotal role in the party. He steered the Panthers toward the white New Left.

Any other party newcomer advocating closer connections to white radicals might have been challenged. But as an ex-convict, Cleaver had substantial credibility. Exuding coolness even at his fieriest, he acquired the party nickname "El Rage" or just "Rage." Moreover, earlier that summer Cleaver set out the terms of cross-racial engagement. That July in the Panther paper, he lambasted whites in the Socialist Workers Party and the Communist Party for their racially patronizing behavior. In a blistering critique, Cleaver established the parameters of white support. White allies could give money, raise money, and share their skills and knowledge. Within the party that article may have inoculated Cleaver against the accusation that his pursuit of cross-racial collaborations contravened the basic principles of Black Power.[8] A shrewd operator, Cleaver may have written the piece to outflank his nationalist critics. But that fall, Cleaver quickly proceeded to hook up the Panthers with Berkeley's white-majority New Left. He resolved to turn the party's loss—Newton's incarceration—into an opportunity by spearheading a national "Free Huey!" campaign, which succeeded in capturing the imagination of many young radicals.

Newton's all-white defense team played a role in capturing their imagination, too. The defense advanced by Newton's lawyers was that he had passed out after being shot; if he did shoot Officer Frey, he did so while unconscious. The ambiguity built into Newton's defense made the Panther cofounder an irresistible symbol, and one who embodied the party's aforementioned duality. As the journalist Murray Kempton noted, the response to Newton after the shooting "could encompass two quite contradictory reasons for admiring his character." It was possible to celebrate how "bad" Huey was because he had killed a cop and equally possible to praise how "good" Huey was because he had not meant to kill a cop.

Within months, Newton's case became a cause célèbre. That was precisely the plan that Communist Party leader William Patterson had laid out to Huey Newton's brother Melvin with whom he met at the time of the shooting. Patterson happened to be in Oakland just then and shared his thoughts with Melvin Newton. He emphasized the importance of establishing a defense committee—an entity apart from the Black Panther Party—that could both propagandize and raise funds for the trial. "He wanted my mother to go on a world tour" as part of the propaganda effort, Newton recalled. The Communist Party often relied on mothers, such as Mamie Till-Mobley, in their defense committee work. Apparently, the communists would have foot the bill.[9]

The world tour did not happen, but a lot did happen to spread the word about the injustice done the Panthers and Huey P. Newton. One reason the defense committee worked so well was that Eldridge Cleaver was a consummate hustler. He had no compunction about pressuring sympathetic whites for money. Many of his white radical friends were part of the newly formed antiwar political party, the Peace and Freedom Party (PFP), and Cleaver proposed a trade-off. If the PFP, which had barely reached out to Black communities, donated its sound truck and $3,000 to the Panthers to pay for the Free Huey! campaign, the Panthers would work to get out the Black vote to aid the PFP's faltering effort to get the signatures required to qualify for the California ballot.[10]

This quid pro quo would grow into an alliance, albeit an uneasy one, between the two organizations. Kathleen Cleaver, Bobby Seale, and the imprisoned Huey Newton were chosen as PFP candidates for state or local offices, and Eldridge Cleaver as the presidential candidate.[11] According to an FBI memo, the PFP also leased a building for the Panthers in Los Angeles, which served as the chapter's headquarters.[12] In a fall 1968 interview with the white jazz writer Nat Hentoff in *Playboy* magazine, Cleaver said he was running for political office "to create a radical political machinery in coalition with whites." He was looking to upend the old society and "build a structure fit to exist on a civilized planet inhabited by *humanized* beings.'"[13]

Cleaver was an early adopter of alliances, but Newton, Seale, and Hilliard were onboard, too, though by this point they were perhaps more influenced by discussions with Black members of the local Communist Party chapter. Black freedom, Newton argued, would remain unattainable unless Black radicals formed "as many alliances as possible of people that are equally dissatisfied with the system."[14] Hilliard later wrote that the partnership between the Panthers and the PFP was "the first functional black-white alliance since the civil rights mobilizations in the early sixties."[15] Ericka Huggins has argued that the Black Panther Party may have been conceived as a Black nationalist organization, but pivoted away from that position. The party, she notes, "didn't even continually call itself a Black Power organization ... Remember our slogan was All Power to the People."[16]

The Panthers' openness to working with the PFP alienated some Bay Area Black radicals, who worried the Panthers "were being used by whites for the whites' own purposes."[17] Cleaver later described their partnership as "narrow, limited, tentative and viewed with mutual suspicion."[18] The tensions were undeniable. Hilliard recalls the reaction of a new party member to working with a long-haired white PFP worker. "Man, what is that?" he asked. Hilliard said that the hippie driving the wildly colored psychedelic bus, which was plastered with Free Huey! signs, was an ally. Equipped with a sound system, the bus enabled the Panthers to spread the word about Newton's case in Oakland's Black neighborhoods. "We're gonna go out with him," Hilliard explained to the member, who replied, "I ain't working with that motherfucker."[19] Sartorially, the Panthers tended to be very put together, so perhaps his reaction stemmed from the white activist's hippie-like appearance, but he may not have wanted to work with any white person. Other Panthers, however, appreciated the willingness of PFP people to work for Newton's freedom.

In the end, working together had an undeniable upside for both parties. The PFP got the signatures it needed to qualify for the ballot, and support for it grew. Assistance from the PFP proved crucial to the Panthers in the staging of impressive Free Huey! rallies and benefits that attracted large multiracial crowds.[20] A donation from the PFP allowed the Panthers to open a new office in North Oakland.[21] There was even a white radical group in Berkeley calling itself "Honkies for Huey."[22] Within six months the Huey Newton Defense Fund had raised $10,000.[23] New chapters of the Black Panther Party began cropping up all over. By the end of 1968, there were Panther offices in 20 cities.[24]

Attempted Merger with the Student Nonviolent Coordinating Committee

While the Panthers were partnering with the predominantly white PFP, they were also looking to merge with the Student Nonviolent Coordinating Committee (SNCC). After some arm twisting, Seale and Cleaver persuaded the PFP to pay for them to travel to Washington, DC, to meet with Carmichael to firm up plans for an upcoming Oakland rally to support Newton. The rally would feature Carmichael and other SNCC people.[25]

By this point, SNCC was, organizationally, a shadow of its former self.[26] Moreover, in the year since SNCC had expelled its white members, its stance had not really softened. SNCC leaders continued to reject cross-racial collaborations, and even a request for support from the PFP, which made talk of a merger somewhat bewildering.[27] However, in this period, positions were somewhat fluid. After the October 1967 march on the Pentagon, H. Rap Brown described white demonstrators who took militant action as "brothers in the vanguard of revolution," though he was soon denouncing white radicals.[28] Just as surprising was James Forman's claim that in February 1968 when he met with Newton in jail, he told him how much he had liked Forman's separatist speech, "Revolution Will Come from a Black Thing."[29]

In any case, positions quickly hardened. By the spring of 1968 Brown and other SNCC leaders opposed working with whites ... the very people that the Panthers were increasingly relying upon for money and resources. Speaking in spring 1968 to a newly formed radical Black group focused on fighting the draft and the war, Carmichael returned to criticizing the white left. In contrast to Black people, white leftists were not fighting for their very survival. That supposed difference meant that white leftists were trying to save America, whereas Black radicals recognized that "we have to burn America down."[30] Black Power elder Robert Williams, who was then living in exile in Cuba, denounced white leftists as the "Trojan Horse of counterrevolution."[31]

Given their differences, why did the two organizations even try to merge? For Carmichael and others in SNCC, the hope was that the Panthers "could be our channel into the Northern urban struggle."[32] Carmichael reasoned that for the Panthers the draw was the valuable "six years' experience on the front lines" that SNCC workers had accumulated.[33] Cleveland Sellers of SNCC believes that the Panthers also hoped that with the famous Carmichael, Brown, and Forman onboard, their campaign to free Newton would gain more traction.[34] According to Newton, however, the Panthers pursued the merger to fix the Panthers' lack of administrative expertise. In a characteristic dig at a rival organization, Newton later explained that SNCC people had the "bourgeois skills" that most of the party members lacked.[35]

Even had theirs been a purely transactional arrangement, these were two fundamentally different kinds of organizations. For SNCC, organizing involved face-to-face conversations, whereas for the Panthers it was often symbolic, confronting the cops or dropping new revolutionary slogans like "Off the pigs," when possible, on television. In contrast to SNCC, where organizing involved penetrating "*deep inside* the day-to-day fabric" of a community, the Panthers organized its members and recruits through directives and political education classes.[36] These were classes where members were tested on their memorization of passages from *The Little Red Book* and suffered physical punishment if they fell short.³⁷ Although SNCC no longer scorned hierarchy, it was a model of democracy compared to the Black Panther Party.

Even sartorial style became contested. SNCC staffers were famous for dressing down in jeans and overalls, while the Panthers favored slick black leather jackets, shades, and berets. Cleaver was especially eager to establish the Panther style or brand, which contributed to the outsized media attention the group was attracting. At one tense meeting, he stared at a group of SNCC leaders sitting across from him, one of whom was wearing a leather jacket, and said, "Oh, you're trying to look like us now?" In the mid-1990s, when he was living again in the Bay Area, Cleaver would sometimes deck himself out in red corduroy overalls and an old straw hat and "laughingly call himself a 'Snicker.'" But in 1968, when the Panthers were enjoying the hot glare of media attention, he didn't want old-school SNCC people copping *their* look.³⁸

Despite their differences, the leadership of each group decided to go public with their partnership on February 17, 1968, at a much-anticipated rally and birthday party for the Panthers' imprisoned leader Huey Newton. Well in advance of the rally, SNCC leaders were complaining about the Panthers' willingness to work with white people. Hiring a white lawyer, taking money from white donors, and allowing white people onstage (and giving one a speaker's slot) offended them. Nonetheless the Free Huey! rally at the Oakland Auditorium was a success, drawing somewhere between 5,000 and 7,000 people—Black and white—who seemed blissfully unaware of the tensions between the two organizations.

The program featured Panther and SNCC leaders, and singer Curtis Mayfield of the popular R&B group, the Impressions. The night was electric with possibility as the crowd roared its approval of just about everything shouted from the stage. It was Cleaver who announced they were merging, a pronouncement that SNCC's James Forman walked back, clarifying that they were forming an alliance, not merging. There were other off-key moments. Bobby Seale emphasized that the Panthers were not anti-white, but the SNCC speakers went out of their way to show that they were.

Carmichael was on a mission to create "black unity," which is why he refrained from explicitly attacking the Panthers. Still, anyone conversant with Black radical politics knew he was underlining the different versions of Black Power alive in SNCC and the Panther Party. He denounced communism and socialism as ideologies unsuited to Black people—an obvious dig at the Panthers. So was his declaration that "the honky" was the "major enemy" of Black people and should be in their crosshairs. He extended the olive branch to the Black bourgeoisie and the "Uncle Toms" but also promised that if they crossed Black radicals, "we gonna off them." Then there was H. Rap Brown, who provocatively asked the crowd, "How many white folks you kill today?"[39]

Despite SNCC's provocations, the crowd seemed oblivious, tuned into Jim Forman's chant, "Free Huey or the sky's the limit." After two years in which it felt as though splintering was what the Movement did best, unity seemed tantalizingly within reach.

By summer, that dream lay in tatters. Negotiations had grown fraught, in no small measure because of the supersize egos involved. Both Carmichael and Cleaver were celebrities, sought out by the media. Carmichael had been in the spotlight for two years by this point; Cleaver, basking in the success of *Soul on Ice*, had become reporters' new favorite. He could be hostile to Black activists whom he regarded as competition, especially if they were not a part of his orbit. When Amiri Baraka first met Cleaver at the Black House, a place the poet had helped to found, he said Cleaver approached him with "absolute hatred," even though Baraka had "never even talked to the dude."[40]

Personalities aside, the talk of a merger also raised anxieties that one group might end up dominating the other. Some members of SNCC also felt that the Panthers were intent upon "badding [them] out." Ethel Minor of SNCC witnessed some contentious conversations between the Panthers and Carmichael. In her view, the Panther leaders "could see that even though they were trying to use Stokely, Stokely was also trying to use them, and Eldridge was not going to stand for anyone trying to use him." Cleaver made a point of dissing SNCC, telling a group of white radicals that the group was just a bunch of middle-class, college-educated "black hippies," disconnected from the streets that the Panthers were trying to organize.[41]

One decisive moment in the deteriorating relationship between the two groups happened in the summer of 1968. Jim Forman had agreed to handle arrangements for a joint Panther-SNCC press conference at the United Nations about a Black plebiscite in which Black Americans would vote on forming their own nation. When Forman, who was in a psychologically fragile state, dropped the ball, a group of West Coast Panthers reportedly confronted him physically.[42] That was the end of any alliance between the two groups. Stokely Carmichael allowed the Panthers to call him their Honorary Prime Minister for nearly a year, but his involvement was very limited. The sticking point, Carmichael explained, was the Panthers' willingness to work with white radicals. It was later revealed that the friction between the two groups was amplified by FBI agents.[43]

There are many reasons the SNCC–Panther Party partnership failed, but the latter's advocacy of cross-racial solidarity was a crucial obstacle. In 1968, the most vocal leaders in SNCC advocated a separatist version of Black nationalism wherein white support inevitably translated into white control. By contrast, the Panthers were promoting what they called "revolutionary nationalism," which Newton distinguished from the "cultural nationalism" that prevailed in SNCC. The Panthers' version of nationalism was explicitly socialist and favored joining forces with white radicals. In their view, separatism reinforced "the power structure's game of divide and conquer."[44] Newton even attributed the failed merger to the fact that SNCC, unlike the Panthers, had been under the thumb of whites, which was why the group was so wary of cross-racial coalitions.[45] Obviously, Newton's characterization of SNCC was off the mark, but what is true is that the Panthers never had to renounce interracialism. This is one reason that the Panthers could be antagonistic toward "cultural nationalism," going so far as to label it "reverse racism," a charge considered wrongheaded by many Black Power militants.[46]

Had the two groups brokered a working alliance, the political landscape might have shifted. For one, Black radicals would have been in dialogue with each other rather than taking each other down a peg. Perhaps SNCC could have taught the Panthers something about organizing, and just possibly the Panthers could have mitigated SNCC's go-it-alone separatism. It was a lost opportunity.

White Allies: The Benefits and the Backlash

Working with non-Black radicals for a socialist future set the Panthers further apart from many other Black Power groups. The Black journalist Reginald Major, who wrote an early book about the Panthers, observed that the party's willingness to work with white radicals led "quite a few revolutionary blacks to dismiss the party as being run by white people."[47] This criticism appeared in the mainstream publication *Negro Digest*, which in December 1969 published an attack on the Panthers, though not by name. The fact that condemnations of "cultural nationalism" were emanating from "the ramparts of slick, white-controlled 'leftist' magazines (of ambiguous financial backing)" suggested to the writer that "the revolution . . . will revolve around a *white*, western-oriented cultural matrix."[48] Reportedly, Black nationalists even staged anti-Panther protests at the offices of *Ramparts* magazine. Panther member Earl Anthony later said that the white radical press's praise of the Panthers made them "the enemy of other black organizations."[49]

One group that viewed the Panthers as the enemy was Maulana Karenga's US. Karenga's group dominated Black activism in Los Angeles, so much so that the February 1968 Free Huey! rally at the L.A. Coliseum had a decidedly nationalist cast.[50] Tensions between the two groups, which were magnified by the FBI, remained high that year, with the Panthers deriding US as "pork-chop nationalists."[51] The conflict turned deadly on January 17, 1969, when members of US killed two prominent Panthers, John Huggins and Bunchy Carter, in Los Angeles. The fatal shoot-out occurred in a classroom building on the UCLA campus where the rival groups were fighting for control of UCLA's Black Studies program.[52]

Although college campuses tended to be sympathetic to the Panthers, that was not always the case with Black college students. "Everywhere I went in 1967," Newton said, "I was vehemently attacked by Black students" because he argued forcefully for "strong and meaningful alliances with white youth."[53] It did not matter to more nationalist Black students that the party was all-Black and that it emphasized the importance of Black control. In the students' view, working with whites was counterrevolutionary. Nevertheless, the Panthers continued to speak up for such alliances. In a December 1969 issue of the *Black Panther*, David Hilliard urged Black student unions to expand their membership to include other groups so that students could become "a more formidable force so that we can withstand the repression that's being meted out against us."[54] The Panther leadership was confident about its position on working cross-racially with white radicals.[55]

As the historian Robyn C. Spencer has argued, some members, who entered the Panthers believing that whites were the enemy, had their heads turned around. Learning about and having contact with the Panthers' dense network of white supporters changed their understanding of how change might be made. Take Panther Janice Garrett-Forte, who knew that money was coming from "whites . . . movie stars . . . doctors." She realized that when a Panther was shot but could not go to a hospital for fear of being arrested, it was usually a white ally—a nurse or doctor—who would tend to their wound. When

Panthers were on the lam, "wealthy white contacts" enabled them to "get lost in the United States." Garrett-Fort ended up making a "big leap from . . . you know, kill all white people, to understanding that it is a class struggle." A class struggle in which one's allies were, improbably, sometimes rich.⁵⁶

But even within the party not everyone was committed to solidarity politics. In March 1968, Black Panther leaders (most likely Cleaver) wrote an editorial for the party newspaper acknowledging that the party's coalition with the PFP had "freaked out a lot of people."⁵⁷ This became a more pressing matter by the fall of 1968 when branches of the party started cropping up across the country, often without any meaningful connection to headquarters. The ties between local chapters and national headquarters were "tenuous, often contentious, and sometimes purely notional," as the historian James T. Campbell has noted. "People were coming together under the name of the Black Panther Party," recalled Panther Field Marshal Don Cox, "but they had no idea what we stood for."⁵⁸

One reason so many recruits to the party were so clueless was that the Panthers' attempts to deploy the media in a kind of stealth recruitment of young Blacks had backfired. Years later Kathleen Cleaver admitted that what came across Americans' TV screens was not the substance of the Panthers' program, but rather their "flamboyant tactics."⁵⁹ Making the Panthers especially irresistible was their style, their swagger, and their firepower. Collaborating with white radicals was rarely a part of what the media communicated. Working with long-haired white radicals was a turnoff to many recruits. The leadership's contention that authentic Black radicalism meant working with white radicals was a hard sell.

In New York City, for example, some Panther leaders may have attended hippie dances, but they leaned toward cultural nationalism and, at least early on, showed little interest in working with white radicals. According to onetime Panther Mumia Abu-Jamal, many of the young people joining the party there were Black Muslims who had been influenced by Malcolm X. Panther Don Cox contends that by the late sixties among many young Black New Yorkers "black nationalism was practically in their genes."⁶⁰ New York Panthers' brand of cultural nationalism—their African-inspired names and the cowrie shells they sewed into their Panther uniforms—made the Panthers back at party headquarters in Oakland uneasy. "What is this stuff?" was Hilliard's response on his 1968 trip to the Brooklyn chapter. Some of them had taken African names, which he admitted "none of us . . . could pronounce." And they were more militaristic "with walrus or elephant teeth on rawhide loops, and big, sleek, copper .45-caliber cartridges hung around their necks."[61]

There was something else that David Hilliard found disconcerting about the New York Panthers. "They treat us as equals, as though their opinions bear the same weight as ours."[62] However, there was no setting the New York Panthers straight. Even years later Dhoruba bin Wahad was still putting down the Oakland Panthers. "All them country boys from Oakland were intimidated by New York."[63] Eventually, derision became the leadership's default response. Riffing on Chairman Mao's saying, "Political power grows out of the barrel of a gun," Seale declared, "Power for the people doesn't grow out of the sleeve of a dashiki."[64]

Despite the Panther leaders' outlier position on solidarity politics, however, the group retained its credibility among a good number of Black activists. How was this possible? According to Panther leaders, the reason they were not "getting shot down with the charge of selling out" by other Black militants was that their politics were absolutely "uncompromising" in their opposition to white racism.[65] What they likely meant was that they were not armchair revolutionaries, but the real thing, committed to armed self-defense. In fact, by late 1967, some Panthers, particularly Eldridge Cleaver, were advocating armed insurrection.

Stokely Carmichael believed there was a connection between the Panthers' violence and their willingness to work with radical whites, both of which he condemned. Carmichael was the Panthers' Honorary Prime Minister, but from the very start, he was at odds with the leadership in Oakland. In his view, the party styled itself a revolutionary vanguard because its leaders were pandering to white leftists' fantasies of the Panthers as "the black shock troops" of the Movement. Curiously, a few years earlier Carmichael had not seemed bothered when SNCC workers were called the "shock troops" of the civil rights movement. But this became one of his differences with the Panthers. Carmichael thought the results of the Panthers' shoot-outs with the cops had proven catastrophic, with so many young Black freedom fighters needlessly gunned down or imprisoned.

Carmichael was onto something when he connected the Panthers' advocacy of armed insurrection to their commitment to partnering with whites, but the evidence points to a different conclusion. First, there were many reasons the Panthers fashioned themselves as urban guerrillas at war with the police, not the least of which was the thrill of fighting back. Many Black

Power activists, including Carmichael in his fall 1966 speech at UC–Berkeley, advocated such fighting back. And in the immediate aftermath of King's assassination, Carmichael reportedly took the streets of Washington, DC, where he waved a pistol in the air and told Black people to arm themselves.[66]

Panther fantasies of armed insurrection also predated their partnership with the left. In fact, the Panthers' decision to pursue collaborations with Bay Area radicals happened largely because of Newton's arrest for the murder of Oakland police officer John Frey in fall 1967. Pragmatism played a significant role in the decision by Cleaver and other Panthers to work with white radicals. Whites proved useful when it came to fundraising, organizing rallies, and publicizing the case. But that doesn't mean the party was without reservations about this collaboration. Dan Siegel was among the 12 or so Berkeley white radicals who were friendly with a few of the Oakland Panthers. "The Panthers were not at all eager to sort of parade us at rallies," Siegel recalls, "and present us as 'these are our white radical friends.'" Panther leaders worked with whites, but they did so with a greater or lesser degree of ambivalence, depending on which Panthers were in the mix.[67]

The evidence suggests that the Panthers' off-the-pigs stance was not about currying favor with white radicals but rather their way of countering attacks from rival Black activists, particularly cultural nationalists. What better way to disprove nationalists' portrait of the Panthers as dependent upon whites than going up against the cops? One crucial bit of evidence is the little-known back story to the New York Panthers' January 1969 skirmish with the police. The New York Panthers leaned in the direction of cultural nationalism, but they were eager to elevate themselves in New York, where rival kinds of nationalism were in the mix. They were not trying to impress white radicals, with whom they had virtually no contact. The January gun fight amplified Panther–NYPD tensions and was a pivotal part of the charges brought against the Panther 21 less than three months later.

A cadre of New York Panthers, headed by Lumumba Shakur, planned to set off bombs at several police stations, including one in the Bronx. As police fled the bombed station in the Bronx, two Panther snipers, situated on a slope across the Harlem River from Manhattan, were meant to take aim at the fleeing cops. It was always an improbable plan—using a rifle without a telescope aimed at too far a distance—that went badly wrong when two police officers turned up as the Panthers were beginning to set up their sniper station. One of the Panthers apparently fired, allowing them both to escape, but leaving their fellow Panther, a female driver, in the car.

Although neither cop was injured, offing some pigs was what they intended to do that evening. The reason the Panthers planned their attack for that evening was that its architect, Lumumba Shakur, wanted to upstage Maulana Karenga of US, who was speaking that night at a Black cultural festival at Harlem's Rockland Palace. Shakur and other New York Panthers were not as hostile to Karenga's nationalism as the Panther leadership in Oakland, but they opposed his armchair approach to revolution. Shakur figured that once news of their action circulated among the crowd, "it would be universally understood that the Panthers had acted while Ron Karenga was only jiving." Although the two events were not connected, January 17 was the same day US members gunned down Panthers Carter and Huggins in Los Angeles.[68]

The point is that the Panthers hardly needed to talk about killing the police (or for that matter engage in gun battles with the police) to win the support of the left, much of which was already infatuated with them. The Panthers' "off-the-pig" philosophy was largely about proving they were the genuine article, the real revolutionaries, not the pawns of white radicals that the nationalists charged they were. But within the world of Black radicalism, the Panthers' ceaseless attacks on Karenga and other cultural nationalists, and their openness to working with white radicals, intensified the bad feelings between them and their political rivals.

What Can You Do for Me?

Given how negatively cultural nationalists viewed the Panthers' partnerships with white leftists, what did the Panthers get out of it? More than anything, they got much-needed support from individuals who believed in the Panthers. Their aid was especially useful in the party's first few years, when many in the Black community withheld their support. Photographs of Free Huey! rallies or other Panther demos and events reveal multiracial gatherings. Were it not for the bell bottoms and long hair of their supporters you might think it was the summer of 2020.

Sometimes white radicals did more, putting themselves between the Panthers and the police. In the fall of 1968, when the Panthers believed the police might stage a raid on the Cleavers' home on Pine Street, 100 mostly white Panther supporters, carrying antipolice signs, formed a protective shield around their home and spent the night there.[69] Meanwhile the Cleavers were holed up elsewhere, at the homes of left-wing whites, including the couple Anne

Weills and Bob Scheer. Dan Siegel, who was the president of UC–Berkeley's student body in 1970, recalls that when the situation felt especially tense, he and other student activists organized all-night vigils at the Panther headquarters on Shattuck Avenue.[70] Jim Berland, a young white Communist Angeleno, recalls getting a phone call from Panther headquarters in Los Angeles on one of the occasions it was under police attack. "All you white people come down and be present," the Panther on the other end commanded him. "So we went. There were bullets whizzing by."[71]

The left-wing and countercultural media also provided critical support by pushing back against the mainstream media's largely hostile coverage of the Panthers. *Ramparts*, which employed Cleaver, was the first to publish favorable articles about the party. Before long, it was joined by "underground" newspapers that catered to young white politicos and hippies in big cities and college towns across America. The first radio journalist to give Cleaver airtime was Elsa Knight Thompson, the news director of the left-wing KPFA.[72] After the runaway success of Cleaver's *Soul on Ice*, editors at several big publishing houses were eager to publish books by party leaders, about 10 of which appeared between 1968 and 1975. Several became bestsellers, which provided around $250,000, from their advances alone. Publishers assumed that the core demographic for these books was young, white, and countercultural.[73]

Although most accounts of the Panthers stress their reliance on guns, symbolically and literally, the party, from its earliest days, also relied on books. Huey Newton carried a law book when patrolling the police, members peddled *The Little Red Book* in Berkeley, and eventually its leaders turned out their own books, which challenged the standard narrative of the party as violent and anti-white. Writers and editors sympathetic to the Panthers facilitated this. Toni Morrison, who early in her writing career worked as an editor at Random House, was responsible for bringing out books by Black activists such as Carmichael, Newton, and Angela Davis. "I wanted to give back something," Morrison later said. "I wasn't marching. I didn't go to anything. I didn't join anything. But I could make sure there was a published record of those who did march and put themselves on the line."[74] The publishing industry in that period consisted almost entirely of white editors, and one such editor, John Simon at Random House, brought out quite a few Movement books.[75]

Solidarity politics brought another dividend: sympathetic, white left-wing lawyers, most of whom were associated with the National Lawyers Guild. Some of these lawyers provided considerably more than legal representation. Take two Movement lawyers who worked alongside Charles Garry: Alex Hoffmann and Fay Stender. Some of the time that Newton was at the Alameda County jail, he was in isolation under harrowing conditions, which was only broken by visits with lawyers. Hoffmann and Stender made a point of visiting him often and regularly. That continued, albeit to a lesser degree, after he was sentenced and went to prison. They discussed trial preparations related to his appeal, but they also provided emotional support. "Huey was totally isolated," recalled Hoffmann. "It was important that he be allowed to express himself and interact instead of going crazy in jail with nobody to talk to."[76] Both attorneys also acted as messengers between Newton and the Panther leadership. They smuggled into the jail tape-recorded messages from Panther leaders and smuggled out back to them Newton's tape-recorded instructions. Had this been discovered, they would have faced penalties, even disbarment.[77]

A small group of white doctors and nurses also did what they could to assist the Panthers. When a Panther was shot, the party could call on a medical professional, usually a white ally, who would treat the wound and stitch them up. That way wounded Panthers could avoid the hospital, where medical personnel were required to report guns wounds to law enforcement.[78]

The Panthers were the beneficiaries of another kind of support, too. Money . . . all kinds of money and from all kinds of places. Most histories of the Panthers have given little consideration to how finances helped to shape the Black Panther Party, despite its substantial financial needs.[79] Income from the sale of the *Black Panther* was substantial, between $20,000 to $40,000 a month. But even when supplemented by leaders' hefty lecture fees on college campuses, that sum fell short of meeting the party's needs.[80] Much of the money flowing into the party was in the form of $5 and $10 donations, which supporters mailed to defense fund committees during high-profile prosecutions such as Newton's.

However, sometimes the Panthers were the beneficiaries of larger donations, such as the one made by a group of liberal Episcopalian ministers who mailed a check to Panther lawyer Charles Garry after King's assassination.[81] Sometimes money just landed in the Panthers' laps, as when two hippies hailed a small group of Panthers, as they walked across campus at UC–Berkeley. "We love what the party's doing," they yelled. "We want to contribute." Bobby Seale was there and reportedly replied, in a pleasant but perfunctory way, "Yeah, write us a check," and kept walking. But the couple was insistent. "No, we're good for much more money." They went to a nearby café, and there Seale learned that the brother and sister sitting across from him were trust-fund babies. They made a million-dollar donation on the spot.[82] But all this white heat around the Panthers, including that produced by their deep-pocketed donors, made them easy targets for other more orthodox nationalists.

Although the generosity of donors increasingly meant that the Panthers had the money to rent (or, in time, even buy) space, they were often stymied, both by their militant reputation and by racism. As they expanded their social welfare services, this became a greater issue. Sympathetic pastors and ministers often provided space for the Panthers' Breakfast for Children Program, but they sometimes found themselves targeted by FBI agents who staged letter-writing campaigns, posing as parishioners angry about the Panthers' use of church space.[83] As for landlords, they needed no encouragement from the FBI to not rent to Panthers. The party found a way around the situation in the Bay Area through the realtor Arlene Slaughter, a longtime fair-housing activist. Slaughter, who was white, obtained her real estate license after she and her husband, who was African American, came up against racist real estate practices. Slaughter served as the "white front" for people of color and interracial couples, a practice she deployed on behalf of the Panthers.[84]

Both rival Black militants and the U.S. government were curious about how the Panthers kept themselves afloat. FBI Director J. Edgar Hoover believed that much of the Party's income came from what he called the "artistic crowd." He was right. Hollywood's white left liberals were especially generous. Black artists were more precariously situated, and many kept their distance from the Panthers, although Aretha Franklin, Sammy Davis Jr., and Godfrey Cambridge were among those who contributed money.[85] Hollywood people lent their homes for fundraisers that netted the party thousands of dollars.

One of the Panthers' earliest supporters was the Hollywood star Marlon Brando. A month after the assassination of King, Brando appeared on Johnny Carson's popular *Tonight Show* and explained he was tithing—that is, contributing 10 percent of his salary—to civil rights organizations. He urged white viewers to give 1 percent of their salary. Carson responded by not only pledging to do so but also by giving Brando a check on air that night. In addition, Brando gave Bobby Seale a significant sum of money so that he and a group of Panthers could attend Martin Luther King's funeral, and he gave a eulogy at the funeral of a fallen Panther.[86]

Other reliable Hollywood allies included the movie stars Jane Seberg and Jane Fonda. Playwright Donald Freed and the Canadian actor Shirley Douglas, who was married to the movie star Donald Sutherland, were the major organizers behind a Friends of the Panthers chapter in Hollywood. A distant connection, but a meaningful one involved Irving G. Thalberg Jr. The son of Hollywood royalty—producer Irving Thalberg and actor Norma Shearer—Thalberg Jr. was a philosophy professor at the University of Illinois–Chicago. He donated a bus to the local Panther chapter, which made it a mobile People's Health Clinic.[87]

By 1970, the Panthers would attract even broader support from Hollywood people and a variety of white radicals and leftists. Understanding why and how that happened requires first chronicling the party's history from the time that its proposed merger with SNCC hit its first roadblocks in February 1968 to the end of 1969. During this nearly two-year period, a fault line developed within the party about its direction. What was the Black Panther Party's mission? What was its message and where should it direct its energies?

EIGHT
Repression's Repercussions

At the time of its birth in late 1966, the year of Black Power, parts of the broader Movement had signed onto the proposition that the worse things got, the better they really were. There were activists who challenged this view. In the fall of 1966, Dorothy Healey, the iconoclastic leader of the Southern California Communist Party (CP), challenged the "theory of 'the-worse-the-better,'" calling it "political LSD—hallucinatory politics." But Healey's critique convinced few radicals.[1] Certainly not Huey Newton. Less than a year later, in the summer of 1967, the Panther leader explicitly endorsed bringing on repression. Challenging those who argued that the party's aggressive stance toward law enforcement carried the risk of violent retribution, Newton countered that "when the man becomes more oppressive, this only heightens the [people's] revolutionary fervor."[2]

Panthers Answer King's Assassination by "Vamping on the Pigs"

But as Huey Newton sat in jail, it seems that he came to believe that the party needed to acknowledge the losses it was sustaining. Newton had plenty of time to ponder the fate of the party from his jail cell. According to his close friend David Hilliard, by 1968 Newton was coming to terms with the way in which the party's militarism alienated much of the Black community. He came to question the wisdom of guerrilla warfare and all the loose talk in the party about offing the pigs. Newton continued to view the Panthers as a vanguard, but he now claimed that the party was never meant to be primarily a military organization. A vanguard party, he argued, was meant to raise the consciousness of the masses, primarily through education.[3]

Eldridge Cleaver and many others in the party saw the matter differently. They persuaded themselves that conditions in America were sufficiently ripe for revolution to make armed struggle viable. Cleaver had used his royalties from *Soul on Ice* to buy what Hilliard called a small arsenal, and he and others were itching to use it against the cops.[4] The opportunity came in the aftermath of Martin Luther King Jr.'s assassination on April 4, 1968. Newton, however, was arguing against urban rebellions, which he maintained were hardening the white backlash against the Panthers and other radicals. Look at how 1965's Watts uprising had played out in California: the election of right-wing Republican Ronald Reagan.

Hilliard knew of Newton's growing wariness about shoot-outs with the police and tried to talk Cleaver out of taking retaliatory action. Cleaver insisted the Panthers had to "prove we're the vanguard." It was "time to intensify the struggle," he argued. Otherwise, the party would look soft. After all, what had immunized the Panthers against attacks from cultural nationalists was their willingness to fight back. Cleaver's plan was to draw the Oakland police into an ambush, what he called a "pre-emptive strike" against the cops.[5] Cleaver believed the Panther ambush would model taking revolutionary action for radicals and spark a coordinated series of attacks on the police, which would, in turn, ignite rebellions across America's inner cities.[6] Cleaver's plan was popular among plenty of Panthers, but not with everyone in the party's leadership. Nonetheless, with Bobby Seale sitting out this argument, and David Hilliard unable to stop Cleaver, plans went ahead.

On the night of April 6, 1968, the Panthers drew a group of Oakland cops into a prolonged gun battle. Two police officers were wounded, but the Panthers' losses were far worse. The party's first recruit, Bobby Hutton, was dead, and Cleaver was wounded.[7] Moreover, the police arrested nine Panthers, including Hilliard and Cleaver, whose parole was revoked. Cleaver spent two months in prison until a judge restored his probationary status for roughly six months. He was told to surrender to the authorities in late November for his role in the ambush. After the charges against Hilliard were initially dismissed, they were pressed again. He stood trial and was sentenced in July 1971 to a one-to-ten-year prison sentence for his involvement in a gun battle he had opposed.[8]

The attack further hobbled the Oakland leadership. It left Newton feeling very depressed about Hutton's murder and about Cleaver's unchecked power in the party.⁹ But for many Panthers, April 6 did not stand as a cautionary tale. Instead, it consolidated the Panthers' revolutionary bona fides. And because the Panthers lied about who did the ambushing, and because Hutton was gunned down with his arms in the air, Movement people saw it as another case of the state's murderousness toward the Panthers. Then there was the thrill of the violence itself. Cleaver later said that shooting it out against the cops for over an hour was his "first experience of freedom."¹⁰

The Panthers could see how gun battles with the police, while organizationally destructive, grew the party. New chapters formed, and donations flowed into Panther coffers. Movement support for the Panthers further antagonized law enforcement, fueling the cycle of violence. In Los Angeles, an early August confrontation between Panthers and the police left three party members dead.¹¹ In Seattle, a group of Panthers tried, unsuccessfully, to ambush the police.¹² Then, in early September, in response to an unexpected verdict in Newton's trial, two members of the Oakland police force shot up Panther headquarters, taking care to target the iconic poster of Newton taped to the storefront's window.

Cleaver's response to the September 1968 attack was to tell the press that "we have to get our black army together and drive these dogs [police] out of the community."¹³ By the summer of 1968, Cleaver's charisma—rooted in his verbal agility and his street-tough coolness—and his rhetorical flamboyance made him the public face of the party. Newton, speaking from jail with Charles Garry at his side, gave a conspicuously measured response. The Panthers' losses seem to have further convinced him that they needed to change course. Maybe his shift in thinking stemmed from his own experience. While all the Free Huey! rallies were the catalyst that sparked the party's growth and support for the party, Newton's incarceration marginalized him. He communicated with party leaders through his lawyers, but he was unable to engage in face-to-face encounters with them. Possibly Newton's contact with people who were a part of a broader CP orbit also affected his political analysis. In this period, he moved away from the rhetoric of violence and emphasized the importance of building a durable and substantial base of support, a position promoted by the CP.

Party leaders, however, kept up their talk of offing the pigs. After his release from prison in early June, Cleaver gave fiery speeches as he barnstormed

Image 8.1 In September 1968, two Oakland policemen, angry about the manslaughter verdict in the Huey Newton case, shot up the party's headquarters, making sure to hit the iconic poster of Newton.

Bob Fitch Photography Archive, Department of Special Collections, Stanford University Library across parts of California as the Peace and Freedom Party's presidential candidate. Asked what whites could do to support the Panthers, he said, "Kill some other white people."[14] In August 1968, Bobby Seale, speaking at a Chicago rally of mostly white antiwar activists protesting the Democratic National Convention, offered advice on how they might best handle police aggression. "If a pig comes up to us and starts swinging a billy club," he shouted, "and you check around and you got your piece, you gotta down that pig in defense of yourself."[15] That speech figured in the federal government's indictment of Seale on charges of conspiracy with intent to cause a riot.[16] Seale's arrest a year later as one of the Chicago 8 marked the beginning of the government's nearly two-year neutralizing of the Panther leader. Several months later, in November 1969, Hilliard delivered an incendiary speech that led to his being charged with threatening the life of President Nixon.[17]

Just about the only hope that the Panther leadership would not be entirely wiped out or sidelined was the jury's decision in the trial of Huey Newton for first-degree murder, in the fall of 1968. In a surprise verdict, the jury found Newton guilty of the lesser charge of manslaughter in the death of Officer Frey, and not guilty of the other charges, including the wounding of the other officer. Avoiding the death penalty was a victory, albeit a partial one. Charles Garry immediately appealed, and Fay Stender and Alex Hoffmann got to work on the appeal. Newton was relieved but also apprehensive about an acquittal. First, he would have to live up to people's expectations that he was that tough guy in the poster. Secondly, he would have to confront Eldridge Cleaver, whose fantasies of guerrilla combat had not abated.[18]

But then, less than three months later, Cleaver chose to flee the country rather than surrender to the authorities on the agreed-upon date, November 27, 1968. The Yippie couple, Stew Albert and Judy Gumbo Albert, were among the white radicals that Cleaver turned to for assistance. They never knew if they were aiding and abetting a fugitive from justice or just serving as a decoy, but they were eager to help.[19] His decision to dodge his parole hearing and jump a $50,000 bail was a leading news story.[20] Cleaver would show up in Cuba, and after his relations with the authorities there soured, in Algeria. Newton may have breathed a bit easier knowing that Cleaver was now a world away.

The Party Pivots to Serving the People

Proving himself politically nimble, Newton executed a more emphatic about-face for the party. In December 1968, just weeks after Cleaver's disappearance and Richard Nixon's election, he announced a new direction for the party: serving the people. To reach those people, Newton advised his Panther comrades to tone down their overheated rhetoric about "vamping on the pigs." The Panthers "survival programs" were intended as an organizing tool, enabling them to achieve a meaningful foothold in Black communities and get some much-needed good publicity.[21]

The first program the party unveiled was its Free Breakfast for School Children Program. People's memories of the program's origins differ, but David Hilliard says the Panthers were inspired by the free-food efforts pioneered by the San Francisco anarchist group, the Diggers. Emmett Grogan was a hip, straight-shooting Digger who often came by the Panther office to deliver bags of beans and rice for distribution in the Black community. He was refreshing, Hilliard remembered. "Nothing of the eager-to-please liberal" about him.[22] One day, Seale said of those bags, "Damn this is a good idea . . . Help people survive."[23] If the Panthers were inspired by the Diggers, the Diggers' focus on creating a counterculture was prefigured by the Student Nonviolent Coordinating Committee (SNCC) with its alternative institutions.

The Oakland Panthers announced plans for a Free Breakfast for School Children Program in fall 1968. When it began that September, it proved so popular that Seale ordered all chapters to follow suit.[24] By the summer of 1969, it is estimated that 10,000 African American children across the country were eating breakfast at one of the Panthers' spaces.[25] The party soon expanded into health care, legal services, clothing, and transportation to visit incarcerated friends and relatives—all of it free.[26] By early 1970, the popular magazine *Newsweek* observed that the Panthers had "softened" their image. To visiting journalists, Seale claimed "the Panther program is 'not too different from the things Martin Luther King advocated. We've just moved to a higher level of tactics.'"[27] In the fall of 1969, Newton predicted that the Panthers would soon have millions of members.[28]

However, for many Panthers this tactical shift to community survival programs was a betrayal of the party's militance. Cleaver, who was in exile but still very involved in the party's newspaper, strongly opposed the party's about-face.

One especially telling detail illustrates how differently Cleaver and Newton were envisioning the party. While Newton was in prison reading Isaac Deutcher's anti-Stalinist biography of Leon Trotsky, Cleaver was maneuvering to put Stalin on the cover of *The Black Panther* newspaper. "No, you should not put Stalin on the cover," was Newton's irritated response.[29] Eventually, Cleaver publicly denounced the survival programs as "right wing." Privately, he complained that the Panthers of Oakland were "acting like a bunch of sissies."[30] Years later Kathleen Cleaver explained that she and her husband simply "couldn't get excited about survival."[31]

If the Panthers hoped their survival programs would de-escalate tensions with law enforcement and provide the party with some breathing room, they were wrong. J. Edgar Hoover, who was anxious that the Panthers' social welfare programs might shift public opinion in their favor, made sure that the Panthers were squarely in COINTELPRO's crosshairs. By early 1969, Hoover was urging agents "to disrupt the BPP," particularly its free breakfast program, pretty much by any means necessary.[32] That summer, Hoover labeled the Black Panther Party the "greatest threat to the internal security of the country."[33] COINTELPRO tried its best to disable the party by harassing and arresting its members, often as they sold the *Black Panther* newspaper on the street. The FBI knew that the *Black Panther*, which had a worldwide weekly circulation exceeding 139,000 in 1970, was a vital source of revenue for the party, so it did what it could to disrupt its distribution.[34]

The FBI also used disinformation to sour the Panthers' relations with Black businesses, churches, and other political groups. Earlier, in fall 1968, the Los Angeles FBI office proposed amplifying tensions with the nationalist group US and the Peace and Freedom Party (PFP). The FBI planned to send an anonymous letter to PFP leaders alleging that in closed meetings, Panthers had said that when the time comes, they would "line up the Caucasians in the PFP against the wall with the rest of the whites." To maximize the damage the agency could inflict on the Panthers, Hoover demanded that FBI agents become literate in Black English (and the Black lingo of the day) and use it in their forged letters and anonymous messages to sow as much paranoia as possible.[35]

Hoover's suspicions that the Panthers' community programs were masking what the Panthers were up to was not entirely wrong. The shift to "serving the people," while crucial to the party's survival, did not signal an end to the group's militarism. The party, building on the dualism that had always characterized it, worked simultaneously on two levels—one aboveground, the other underground. The same party that served breakfast to schoolkids maintained a "military arm" or "security detail." The people on that detail were the ones who shook down recalcitrant shop owners who refused to donate money or goods to the Panthers. Before long, they also demanded that pimps, drug dealers, and the managers of after-hours clubs pay them off to stay in business.[36]

This dualism did not characterize the lives of all Panthers, but for some it did and was continuous with their earlier lives.[37] Many of these members were from the so-called lumpenproletariat whom Newton and Seale had targeted as ideal recruits back in 1966. Many had been in gangs. For example, Bunchy Carter, who headed up the Los Angeles chapter, had been the head of the notorious Slauson gang, from which he recruited Masai Hewitt and others. Carter and Hewitt and many such party members were committed to the cause. But local police and the FBI sometimes turned less committed members facing criminal charges into informants and agents provocateurs. Prison was the alternative. Under these conditions, paranoia was unavoidable. Members whom the leadership found suspicious or who committed some disciplinary infraction could find themselves the victims of beatings.[38] The party even established a Board of Methods and Corrections, and beginning in the fall of 1968, the purges began.[39]

The Party's Growth and Law Enforcement's Campaign of Repression

The party was Janus faced and it was riven, but the Panthers could take pride in the fact that by the end of 1968 the party could boast of its twenty chapters and 5,000 members.[40] The Chicago-based Illinois chapter had especially strong leadership, with Fred Hampton at its helm. A one-time National Association for the Advancement of Colored People (NAACP) youth leader with ties to the church, Hampton was trying to forge an ambitious multiracial "Rainbow Coalition" of poor and working-class people that, remarkably, included working-class whites. Realizing this vision meant resisting the allure of the tribal, or at least the comforts of the familiar, and this proved hard work. Especially controversial was his partnership with the white group, the Young Patriots, who flew the Confederate flag. "Many of the Panthers left the group

Image 8.2 In this 1969 photograph, the chairman of the Illinois chapter of the Black Panther Party, Fred Hampton, is speaking. In the center of the frame is FBI informant William O'Neal, who was acting as Hampton's bodyguard.
Hiroji Kubota/Magnum Photos

when we built alliances," recalled Panther Bobby Lee. "Some didn't like the Patriots, some just didn't like white people in general. They were heavy into nationalism." For Lee and Hampton, Rainbow Coalition was a "code word for class struggle."[41] Hampton was a charismatic leader, so perhaps he could have pulled this off. He was reportedly on track to move into national leadership, which did not escape the notice of the Chicago police or the FBI. Might he be a new Black messiah, they wondered?[42]

The Panthers and their allies anticipated that Nixon's election would bring an uptick in police violence. During his 1968 campaign, Nixon practically ran against the Movement. Just days after the election, J. Edgar Hoover declared "justice is incidental to law and order."[43] In New York City, law enforcement officials needed no encouragement from Nixon's Justice Department to go after the Panthers. Tensions between New York's Black Panther Party, which officially formed in June 1968, and the New York Police Department (NYPD) had been growing all summer. On August 1, 1968, two Panthers were arrested on charges of assaulting a policeman. The next day, two fake phone calls for help from the Crowns Heights section of Brooklyn resulted in the ambushing of two patrolmen. The two cops were seriously wounded, and the assistant District Attorney blamed the Panthers.

On August 21, three more Panthers were arrested, allegedly for assaulting a policeman. Then, on September 4, two weeks later, 150 white policeman, off-duty and out-of-uniform, showed up for a bail hearing involving three Panthers at a Brooklyn courthouse. After the judge announced a change in room, the cops attacked the Panthers, their lawyers, and their supporters. At a meeting later that night called by the NYPD to calm things down, Panther leaders stunned the NYPD brass by calling the police "pigs" right to their faces.[44]

At a press conference a week later, Panther leader Joudon Ford denied the party had anything to do with the early August ambush in Brooklyn. "It should be clear to all that the Black Panther party was not involved because if we had been . . . the pigs [police] would be dead."[45] Then there was that January 17, 1969, shoot-out when two would-be Panther snipers shot at the two police officers who had stopped to check their car, which was parked off the highway. The Panthers, whose bullets missed the police, fled the area. At roughly the same time, there were minor explosions at two police stations and a Board of Education building.

The next two and a half months brought relative quiet. But on April 2, 1969, just days before Easter, the New York City police department made a series of dramatic predawn arrests to thwart what Manhattan's District Attorney characterized as a diabolical plot that posed a catastrophic danger to the city. Two hundred detectives wearing bulletproof vests arrested 12 members of the New York Black Panther Party. The thirteenth was seized at a veterans' hospital, where he was undergoing treatment for epilepsy.

The plot, District Attorney Frank Hogan explained, was part of the Panthers' effort to "destroy the power structure." He outlined to the media the details of a vast and terrifying conspiracy, which came to be known as the Easter Plot. These were homegrown terrorists, Hogan argued, using guerilla warfare. Had it not been stopped by the NYPD, the city "that very day" would have experienced massive bombings and the indiscriminate killing of its citizens.[46] Twenty-one New York City Panthers were charged with conspiring to both kill policemen and dynamite popular Midtown department stores, a police station, a commuter railroad's right-of-way, and the Bronx Botanical Gardens. According to Hogan, had the plot gone as planned, innocent people doing their Easter shopping in those crowded stores would have been blown to bits as they looked over merchandise such as ladies' purses that the Panthers had packed with bombs.[47]

To reporters from the left-wing media, it seemed like a preposterous plot. One such skeptical reporter called the so-called plot "splendidly baroque." But the mainstream media seemed to trust Hogan, who had a reputation for incorruptibility. Accounts emphasized that one of the men arrested had been convicted of trying to blow up the Statue of Liberty four years earlier—information that a jury would have been barred from hearing. The *New York Daily News* reported that the police had warned airlines of possible hijackings by Panthers seeking to go to Cuba, and that evidence had emerged suggesting Cuba was funding the Panthers. The *New York Post* revealed that the District Attorney thought there might be a link between the Panthers and the theft of $2.7 million from the Neighborhood Youth Corps.[48] It was enough to frighten even hardboiled locals. The story of the Panther 21 is consequential, and we will return to how it played out in Part Four.

New York City was part of a larger pattern of state repression. By late October 1969, according to the Panthers' tallies, party members had been targeted and arrested in 88 separate incidents over the previous two-and-a-half years.[49] Then, in early December 1969, the attacks suddenly escalated. In a predawn raid on December 4, the Chicago police assaulted a Panther house. Aiding the police that night was information the FBI had gleaned from William O'Neal, a petty criminal whom the Bureau had successfully turned, and who was serving as Fred Hampton's bodyguard. The police department claimed that they were the victims of a Panther assault as they tried to peacefully enter the apartment, but the 82 or so bullet holes, all but one of which were facing into the apartment, revealed that for the lie it was. Panther Mark Clark was not targeted for death, as Hampton was, but he was killed by the gunfire. Several Panthers were badly wounded.

The cops' brazen assassination of Hampton, one of the party's most promising young leaders, suggested the government was ratcheting up its war against the Panthers. It wasn't as though the police killed Hampton because he had offered any resistance. Someone reportedly drugged Hampton before he went to bed. When the police broke in, he was very soundly asleep next to his fiancée, who was nine months pregnant with their child.[50]

Just four days later, in another predawn raid, the Los Angeles Police Department attacked the Panther headquarters at 41st and Central Avenue in South Central Los Angeles. This was an entirely new kind of police offensive.

It marked the first time that a police force anywhere in the world had deployed a Special Weapons and Tactics (SWAT) Team in a major raid. The 13 Panthers inside the building found themselves up against not only 350 cops, who the Los Angeles Police Department said were there to execute arrest warrants, but also an array of military-grade equipment. The police used major explosives and deployed their armored tank against the 13 Panthers who fired back. In the end, the police and the Panthers used more than 5,000 rounds of ammunition. Somehow no one was killed, although four policemen and six Panthers were wounded.[51]

However, it was not just through violent repression that law enforcement tore apart the Panthers. As Kathleen Cleaver later observed, "We thought that the FBI wanted to kill us. I don't think we understood how insidious their plan actually was."[52] Why have local police or the FBI pull the trigger when Black police informants and agents provocateurs could do the dirty work of "neutralizing" the Panthers? NYPD agents were essential to the government's case against the Panther 21. And in many other places, local police red squads worked in coordination with the FBI. Often the government achieved its greatest success through the paranoia and distrust it sowed within the party.

The leadership of the Black Panther Party, hyperaware of the informants and agents provocateurs in their midst, took to disciplining members, sometimes violently, often purging them from their ranks. Panther memoirs reveal how routine such violence became. Still, consider this: Of COINTELPRO's 295 officially authorized actions against Black nationalist groups, 233 targeted the Panthers.[53] The FBI moved quickly to use the Panther purges to destabilize the party further. In a late November 1968 memorandum to all resident agencies, J. Edgar Hoover highlighted the new purge policy for the Panthers. He pointed out that it "presents an opportunity to further plant the seeds of suspicion concerning disloyalty among ranking officials in order to disrupt and exploit BPP fears."[54] In many places it was the local police, often internal Red Squads, who planted those seeds.

One such troubling instance involved the May 1969 torture and killing of Panther member and suspected agent Alex Rackley, which was carried out by a group of Panthers in New Haven, Connecticut. Rackley was a neophyte Panther active in New York who was wrongly suspected of having supplied information to the police that led to the April 1969 arrest of suspects in the Panther 21 case. His torture was brutal and drawn out. Thirty-four arrests, including those of Oakland Panthers Bobby Seale and Ericka

Huggins, were made possible, either directly or indirectly, by the investigation of Rackley's murder. The New Haven chapter, which had fostered what one member called a "whole family cohesiveness-camaraderie," was destroyed by the paranoia generated within Panther ranks by the FBI and the local police.[55]

One key figure in the destruction of the New Haven chapter was Stokely Carmichael's former bodyguard, George Sams, who was among several Panthers involved in Rackley's murder. Several months before leaving the party himself, Carmichael persuaded its leaders to reinstate Sams, whose violence and volatility had led to his expulsion. Upon his arrest in the Rackley murder, Sams turned state's evidence and declared he "had every intention of destroying the party." He fingered Bobby Seale as the one who ordered the hit on Rackley. Whether or not Sams was an agent, and many Movement people assumed he was, his testimony on the stand was maximally damaging to the Panthers. When a defense lawyer asked Sams if he had engineered Rackley's murder to aid Carmichael in taking over the Black Panther Party, he denied the charge.[56] Carmichael denounced the Panthers for working with left-wing whites, but would he have tried to take over the party by setting up Seale on a capital offense? Six weeks after Rackley's murder, on July 6, 1969, Carmichael formally announced his resignation from the Panthers.[57]

Meanwhile, the FBI worked behind the scenes to influence press coverage of the Panthers. The FBI both fed negative stories to Bureau-friendly journalists and sometimes tried to coerce Panther-friendly reporters into divulging what they had learned about the Panthers. Hoover was particularly angry about the stories filed by the *New York Times* reporter Earl Caldwell. A Black reporter who enjoyed unusually good access to the Panthers, Caldwell wrote balanced accounts of the group, and at a time when the *Times*' coverage of the Panthers increased dramatically.[58] Caldwell was served a subpoena in February 1970 requiring his testimony before a federal grand jury investigating the Panthers. He was ordered to surrender his research notes and tape recordings of interviews with the Panthers. Some people knowledgeable about the case believe that the reason Caldwell was targeted was his failure to toe the government's line about the group. And calling him before the grand jury was also a way to drive a wedge between Caldwell and the Panthers, effectively ending their relationship.[59] Caldwell was not the only one. He refused to comply, but CBS reporter Mike Wallace did talk to a grand jury when subpoenaed.[60]

By the fall of 1969, it seemed clearer than ever that America's courts were also part of the problem, not at all the citadels of judicial neutrality that most white Americans imagined. Judge Julius Hoffman, who presided over the Chicago 8 trial in an imperious and idiosyncratic fashion, took extraordinary measures to silence one especially obstreperous defendant, Bobby Seale. On October 29, Hoffman ordered him gagged and bound and chained to his chair. Courtroom drawings of Seale, shackled and gagged, appeared in the *New York Times* and circulated widely. About a week later, Hoffman separated Seale's case and sentenced him to four years in prison for 16 counts of contempt.[61] The government's war against the Panthers led the group to pursue more alliances and partnerships with the left and to try to establish meaningful connections with anti-imperialist Third World governments.

Growing Close to the Communist Party

The Black Panthers had garnered aid and assistance from individual whites, and without any risk to the autonomy or integrity of their party. There is no evidence that Marlon Brando, Stew Albert, or Alex Hoffmann tried to influence party policy. However, the same cannot be said of all the organizations with which the Panthers partnered from 1967 through 1969. It is to this part of the story that we now turn.

As we have seen, through Cleaver (by way of Axelrod), the Panthers were introduced to a variety of left-wing activists. They included people in the PFP whose partnership with the Panthers was in some respects mutually beneficial, though it also provoked opposition in both camps. The people with whom Cleaver felt some sort of kinship were Bay Area radicals, many of whom went on to form the nucleus of Yippie. Cleaver spent time with Jerry Rubin, Stew Albert, and Stew's partner, Judy Gumbo. The Yippie leadership believed that the mostly white counterculture could become politically radicalized, and Cleaver promoted that idea among the Panthers.

They fantasized about making a revolution. Cleaver decided the Panthers should "seize Merritt College," according to David Hilliard, "take on the pigs and hold out until the community rallies to our defense." He tried to enlist the aid of his friend, Yippie Stew Albert, so that "white mother country radicals" would turn out in numbers and support their action. It would be just like the movie *The Battle of Algiers*, Cleaver promised Albert.[62] Cleaver never pulled off the Merritt College action, but he stayed in contact with his Yippie friends.

In October 1968, the *Berkeley Barb*, the city's leading underground paper, proclaimed a whole new day with the news that there was now a "Yipanther pact." Yippies took stabs at solidarity, perhaps most usefully when Abbie Hoffman handed over his entire book advance for *Revolution for the Hell of It* to help cover the bail costs of the 13 Panthers incarcerated in New York.[63] Berkeley's Yippies also assisted Eldridge and Kathleen Cleaver in various ways.

There was some shared ground between the two groups, particularly their flamboyance, which they hoped, when captured by television cameras and broadcast into American homes, would radicalize the country's young people. Beyond that, what brought them temporarily together was their penchant for misrecognizing each other. As Judy Gumbo later pointed out, the Yippie idea of revolution was a "nonviolent, guerrilla theater—of bringing our Yippie revolution to Washington armed with thousands of kazoos."[64] Going into battle with kazoos was a far cry from what the Panthers had in mind for white mother country radicals. Cleaver continued to have hopes for hippies' revolutionary potential. However, David Hilliard claims that by the time of the Democratic National Convention in August 1968 he was hardly the only Panther who had concluded that Yippie was made up of pranksters, not serious revolutionaries.

If the partnership between Yippies and Panthers never really materialized, at least Jerry Rubin and the other Yippies had no designs upon the Panthers. There were other white-majority left-wing groups that did. The same time that Cleaver met Berkeley's Yippies, he had his first contacts with members of the CP's Bay Area community, which was one in which Black members played a prominent role. Roscoe Proctor reportedly first approached the Panthers in early 1967 with an offer to fund their efforts to organize Black communities. Reportedly, the major catch was that the Panthers would have to disband and join the CP, and that proved to be a deal-breaker.[65]

The CP continued to make overtures to the Panthers, likely through its local Black leaders, including Roscoe Proctor, and William Patterson, now living in New York.[66] Patterson was a legendary figure on the Black left. In the 1930s, he had been crucial to the defense of the Scottsboro Nine, and in 1951 he had written a landmark book-sized petition from the Civil Rights

Congress to the United Nations, entitled "We Charge Genocide: The Crime of Government Against the Negro People." With Paul Robeson, he had presented it to the United Nations. In the fall of 1967, Patterson was among those advising the Panthers to retain Charles Garry as legal counsel in Newton's murder case. Patterson claimed he helped structure the Oakland-based fundraising committee. Did Patterson push for Garry solely because he was an aggressive lawyer? Possibly, but perhaps he did so with the expectation that Garry and his assistants could move Newton in a political direction in line with that of the CP. Doing so would involve abandoning the Panthers' vision of armed insurrection and instead pursuing cross-racial working-class unity.[67]

Whatever the reason for Garry's selection, once installed as Newton's lawyer, he seemed to sometimes exceed his remit as a lawyer. For example, Newton gave a taped interview to a select group of journalists, one of whom was Joan Didion. Garry was also present. Didion was struck by Newton's "rapid-fire" speechifying. Full of stock phrases such as "the American capitalistic-materialistic system," Newton's speechifying was like encountering a "wall of rhetoric." Newton was so accustomed to delivering these rhetorical blasts that his words began to run together. Then a curious thing happened; Newton went off script. He started talking about the colonization of Africa and ventured that "the European started to be sick when he denied his sexual nature." Before Newton went much further down that unauthorized psychological path, Garry interrupted him. Didion thought Garry was carefully redirecting Newton to what she called "first principles," presumably the first principles of Marxism.

Listening today to this bit of the interview corroborates her view. After Newton had raised the issue of white sexual repression, Garry redirected his client. "It's true, isn't it, Huey," Garry asked, that "racism got its birth through *economic* reasons?"[68] It sounds a lot like the "friendly reminder" that Didion considered it, as though Garry was his political tutor as well as his lawyer. Newton agreed with Garry but, tellingly, went right on emphasizing the psychological roots of white supremacy. Stokely Carmichael later observed how curious it was that the Panthers seemed to take instructions from their lawyers, not the other way around.[69] What happened that day suggests that while Garry may have tried to mold the political views of his Panther clients, he did not always succeed. Newton was listening to a variety of people.

Image 8.3 Huey Newton exhales as he listens to his lawyer Charles Garry during a July 18, 1968, jail cell news conference from the Alameda County Courthouse in Oakland, California. Newton accused his jailers of trying to break his spirit.
AP Photo

Still, the CP clearly influenced Panther leaders. Certainly, William Patterson believed that the Panthers were listening to him. By mid-1968 he was in "more or less regular correspondence" with Panther leaders. Contact with the CP also came through longtime Black members of the Bay Area party such as Proctor. In Los Angeles, Angela Davis and Jimmy Garrett were among those briefly connected to both the CP and the Panthers.

The growing connections between the two parties did meet with some resistance from some leaders within each group. The national leadership of the CPUSA, particularly its general secretary Gus Hall, neither understood nor approved of the Panthers. Dorothy Healey, the unorthodox head of the Southern California branch of the CP, recalls that it drove older CP members crazy when some of the party's younger Black members who were also part of the Panthers bought guns and practiced with them. Healey herself considered the Panthers brave but politically wrong-headed. For that matter, within the Panthers, Cleaver expressed his doubts about Old Left groups to a Seattle Panther leader. "You have to be careful of those Socialists," he cautioned. "They like to use shit for their own purposes." Cleaver believed that defense committees were one effective way that socialists and communists penetrated the Panthers. "Just don't let them use you," he warned of the Old Left.[70]

Were the Panthers being used? This is hard to gauge, in part because they had already been exposed to the multiracial solidarity politics of the Bay Area CP. Moreover, Cleaver came to the Panthers believing in the necessity of coalitions with white people. In early 1967, as he tried to find his bearings in San Francisco, he observed, "whether they know it or not, whether they like it or not, neither white radicals nor black radicals are going to get very far by themselves, one without the other."[71]

But the Panthers did make adjustments that suggest the influence of the CP. Party leaders began to echo the CP's emphasis upon building a multiracial working class. In his memoir, *Seize the Time*, which was put together in 1969, Bobby Seale repeatedly stressed the importance of working across lines of race and the necessity of addressing class. *Seize the Time* reminds readers time and again that the Black Panther Party was not racist, and that it opposed cultural nationalists.[72]

Readers of the party's newspaper also began to see different faces and different political lines in its pages. The paper praised William Patterson. It also offered a new rationale for its popular Free Breakfast for School Children program. Its new selling point was that it enabled people to experience "a concrete act of socialism."[73] By August 1969, Newton, in an article praising the peace movement, argued that the power and reach of corporate America had led him to conclude that the "whole American people have been colonized," not just Black people.[74]

In the pages of the CP's organ, the *Daily Worker*, Patterson likened Bobby Seale's bravery in the Chicago 8 trial to that of a once-famous and now-obscure Bulgarian communist, Georgi Dimitrov, who had faced down Nazis in a courtroom. Soon, the Panther paper began to tout the decades-old work of Georgi

Dimitrov on the importance of left-wing unity in the face of fascism. The party also adopted the top-down model of governance used by the CP: democratic centralism.

The *Black Panther* also took to praising North Korea's communist leader, Kim Il Sung. This was the work of expatriate Cleaver, now in Algiers, who was actively seeking support from any communist strongman willing to give it. But with Cleaver in exile, the CPUSA was exerting a strong influence on the Panthers.

In the spring of 1969, the Panthers and the CP collaborated in planning a conference about how best to fight what many left-of-center people considered the rise of fascism in America.[75] Other groups were involved, including Los Siete de la Raza, Students for a Democratic Society (SDS), the Young Lords, and the Young Patriots. However, this was fundamentally a CP-Panther co-production. Right before their July 1969 United Front Against Fascism (UFAF) conference, the party altered number three of its Ten Point Program, to reflect that it now blamed the "CAPITALIST" rather than the "white man" for "the robbery of the Black Community."[76]

The conference, which was held in Oakland, featured a variety of left-wing speakers, with communists prominent among them. Its planners had hoped it would be the launching pad for a new multiracial initiative to push for community control of America's police. Each community, according to this plan, would make decisions about their local police. It was an unwieldy and perhaps poorly thought-out plan, given the racial and ethnic heterogeneity of many communities, and it faced opposition, particularly from SDS. Nonetheless, the organizers went ahead with their plan to set up local chapters of what were called National Committees to Combat Fascism (NCCFs) in quite a few communities. The NCCFs were intended as multiracial organizations in contrast to Black-only Panther chapters.

Troubling to many Panthers involved in the UFAF conference was who showed up. Only 20 percent of the 3,000 people who attended were Black.[77] The racially lopsided figures suggested the thinness of the Panthers' support in Black communities. Perhaps one reason few Black people attended the conference was the way in which it was promoted. In the run-up to the conference, its organizers arranged for showings of *Z*, director Costa-Gavras's powerful movie about a right-wing coup in Greece. The film was apparently meant to get radicals excited about fighting fascism, but it's not obvious that a foreign film would have had much appeal in Black neighborhoods. In any case, Black people seem to have not been the target audience, since the organizers held screenings in largely white neighborhoods of Los Angeles and the Bay Area.[78]

The Panthers' collaboration with the CP was sufficiently controversial that Bobby Seale felt compelled to push back against rumors that the Panthers were dominated by the CP. However, he clarified that the party was not anticommunist. "We dig Communism." After all, Seale notes, it was the CP that had offered support for the Panthers when others backed away.[79] The CP had proven to be a stalwart supporter, but it did more than offer support. Patterson tried to mold the Panthers ideologically. After meeting with a group of Oakland Panthers in 1969, Patterson expressed his admiration of Bobby Seale, who admitted that he had once had a "mistaken attitude towards some whites."

Patterson credited communists like himself who had "started [the Panthers] thinking of the principles," presumably of Marxism. However, over time he grew concerned that Charles Garry's "confidence in Bobby and David [Hilliard] as to loyalty to Huey and devotion to Marxism-Leninism" might be premature. On one trip to Oakland, Patterson spent two hours with his friend Garry before they met with Seale, with whom they spoke for a few more hours. That was followed by another hours-long meeting with more Panther leaders who wanted to tape the meeting for instructional purposes within the party. The meeting left Patterson feeling that the Panthers' "degree of dependence" on the CP was "very great," particularly in three areas—developing their own variant of Marxism, strategizing about combatting government harassment, and organizing a "mass defense" for Panthers who were facing prosecution.[80]

The Panthers' partnership with the CP was consequential in ways that they could not have foreseen. For one, it further inflamed Hoover and the FBI. At least this was Patterson's worried assessment. The FBI believed it had defeated Patterson once and for all in the 1950s, and now he was "influencing and directing a new generation of activists bent on bringing socialism to North America."[81] Then there were cultural nationalists who saw the relationship as evidence that the Panthers were controlled by white people, even if their contacts were mostly with Black members. The Panther–CP connection also affected the way that a small but influential band of white radicals who called themselves Weatherman viewed the Panthers.

Weatherman as the Panthers' White Heat

The people who formed Weatherman (aka Weathermen, Weather Underground, or simply Weather) did so as SDS was coming apart in the summer of 1969. By this point, all the factions within SDS had repudiated the New Left's focus on white students organizing around their own oppression. They had reversed course and had returned to an earlier position, serving as an adjunct to the truly oppressed. "Since black revolutionaries are already engaging in armed struggle, whites should support them," was their reasoning, claimed Weatherman Mark Rudd. Rudd recalls Weather leaders Terry Robbins and John Jacobs always saying things like "White people are pigs. This whole society has to be brought down. We have got to defeat white-skin privilege; we can't let the Panthers and the Vietnamese bear all the costs."[82]

At SDS's June 1969 convention, with rival factions shouting over each other, the people who would head up Weather purged their rivals in the Progressive Labor (PL) faction, reportedly with a covert assist from the FBI. Figuring that that the proto-Weather faction was less formidable an enemy than the highly organized PL, the FBI did what it could to ensure the expulsion of PL. What most distinguished Weatherman from other white radicals in SDS was its commitment to "bringing the war home" to America. They envisioned a violent campaign in which they, with legions of white working-class kids, acted on behalf of Vietnamese people and Black Americans. They were happy to kill off SDS, which was perhaps the most promising mass radical organization in American history. "Boy, this is a great organization to destroy," said Weather leader Jeff Jones.[83]

In the run-up to that conference, most of the people who became leaders within Weather had nothing but praise for the Black Panther Party. On some occasions, they argued that Black Americans, led by the Panthers, could pull off the revolution by themselves. Other times, they presented themselves as "white mother country radicals" whose intrepid acts of violence would force law enforcement to deal with them, thereby diverting the cops' attention from repressing the Panthers. White radicals could give the Panthers some much-needed breathing room. They only had to train themselves out of their white, middle-class uptightness about violence.

Their goal was to prove themselves tough enough to win the Panthers' respect. But deep down, what many of them really wanted, as Cathy Wilkerson of Weatherman later admitted, was to *be* Black Panthers.[84] Despite their best

Image 8.4 Ken Love, outside the Chicago Coliseum where SDS was holding its June 1969 convention, burns both his draft card and his SDS membership card to protest his "deepest disgust for the violent ways of both SDS and the U.S.A."
AP Photo

efforts to emulate or outdo the Panthers, members of Weatherman did not have a warm relationship with them. "I very much doubt," says Weatherman insider Mark Rudd, "you'd find any Weather people at any level, top or bottom, who partied with the Panthers." He figures it was the CP people who got to hang out and drink with the Panthers.⁸⁵

Weatherman did not reach this position entirely on its own. For some time, the Panthers had been asking for precisely this kind of unquestioning support from white radicals. In an interview that appeared in early June 1968 in the left-wing New York newspaper, *The National Guardian*, Seale declared, "If any white person wants to act in the manner of a John Brown and in accordance with the needs of black people, then we can work with him."[86] About the same time, after his arrest in April 1968, Cleaver went even further. He predicted that America was on the brink of guerrilla war, and this time, he said, "thousands of white new-John-Browns" would support Black revolutionaries.[87] A year later the two organizations were starting to collaborate. A group of Panthers attended SDS's June 1969 convention and backed the faction that became Weather. Decades later, Bill Ayers likely spoke for many Weathermen when he described the group's relationship to the Panthers as one of dedicated comrades, not allies.[88]

Yet if there ever was any reciprocal feeling of comradeship, it was fleeting. Just weeks after the SDS conference, at the July UFAF conference in Oakland, all kinds of white radicals showed up. At first, it seemed that the Panthers and Weatherman were in sync, with the Panthers roughing up Weather's rivals in PL and ejecting them from the hall.[89] But when Weatherman opposed the conference's push for community control of the police, the Panthers were furious.[90] Weatherman likely defied the Panthers because at the UFAF conference they picked up on the ubiquitous presence of the CP, an organization that Weatherman considered so lamely reformist it was counterrevolutionary. According to one underground paper, many white radicals there feared that "the Panthers' UF tactic was attempting to enlist liberal support at the expense of revolutionary militancy" and suspected that the CP might be behind this shift.[91]

The Panthers' attack did not rattle Weatherman, which was focused on its upcoming October 1969 Days of Rage action in Chicago. Young white radicals had spent years analyzing how to organize white people. In the Economic and Research Action Project, some had tried to radicalize poor and working-class white people. Weatherman envisioned a different future, one in which they would pick up the gun, hopefully with white working-class youth—"the grease"—by their side to do battle against white people and the U.S. government. "Fight the People" was the battle cry in Chicago because, as some Weathermen argued, "white people are pigs."[92]

As it happened, Weatherman came into its own at the very moment that the Panthers were turning to survival programs, which Bill Ayers of Weatherman derided as "gun-toting liberalism."[93] Publicly, Weatherman pledged its undying faith in the Panthers as America's revolutionary vanguard. But as they gathered in Chicago to plan their action, Weatherman refused to listen to Fred Hampton, who told them it was crazy to battle cops on the streets of Chicago. Steve Tappis, a white radical with the white working-class group Rising Up

Angry, worked with the Illinois Panthers in this period. "It's kind of ironic" that Weather paid no attention to Hampton, he said. After all, "the whole ideology of Weatherman was that Fred *was* the vanguard." Hampton thought so, too. "They come into town," Hampton complained of Weatherman, "you'd think they'd stop in and say 'hi' to the vanguard?"[94]

Eventually, the two groups did meet, but their meetings degenerated into shouting matches between Hampton and Weatherman leader Bernardine Dohrn.[95] Hampton told Dohrn that the Days of Rage action risked further provoking the cops, whom he fully expected would take out their anger on the Black community and the Panthers. The best way forward, he argued, was through aboveground organizing, starting a breakfast program, and mounting big demonstrations. But Weatherman's leaders were determined to prove they weren't middle-class kids afraid of fighting the cops.

Weatherman no longer cared what the Panthers' thought because they believed the CP had turned them into "revisionists" and robbed them of their revolutionary edge.[96] The group's leaders ignored all criticism. When a Weather delegation met in Havana with representatives of the Cuban government and the Provisional Revolutionary Government of South Vietnam (the Vietcong), they, too, cautioned Weatherman against the Days of Rage action. Mount big antiwar demonstrations instead, they advised. But after the delegation of Weathermen returned to the States, and debated this among themselves, the message came out differently. They claimed that the Vietnamese and Cubans supported the Days of Rage.[97] Weather had its supporters on the left, including Yippies such as Stew Albert, but even if everyone else had opposed them, Weatherman would have gone to Chicago. It knew the best way forward: small guerrilla bands ("focos") that would jump-start the revolution . . . by any means necessary. After all, Castro had pulled it off in Cuba.[98]

The leaders of Weatherman predicted thousands coming to Chicago, but only a few hundred hardcore cadre showed up to tear up Chicago's affluent Gold Coast section. On the second day of action, Hampton publicly condemned their action as "Custeristic."[99] The Days of Rage resulted in $100,000 damage to the city, injuries to several dozen policemen, and the arrest of nearly 300 Weatherman, many of whom sustained injuries and faced exorbitant bail costs.[100] Moreover, as Hampton had feared, the police intensified their war against the Panthers.[101] Weatherman convinced itself the action had been a success.

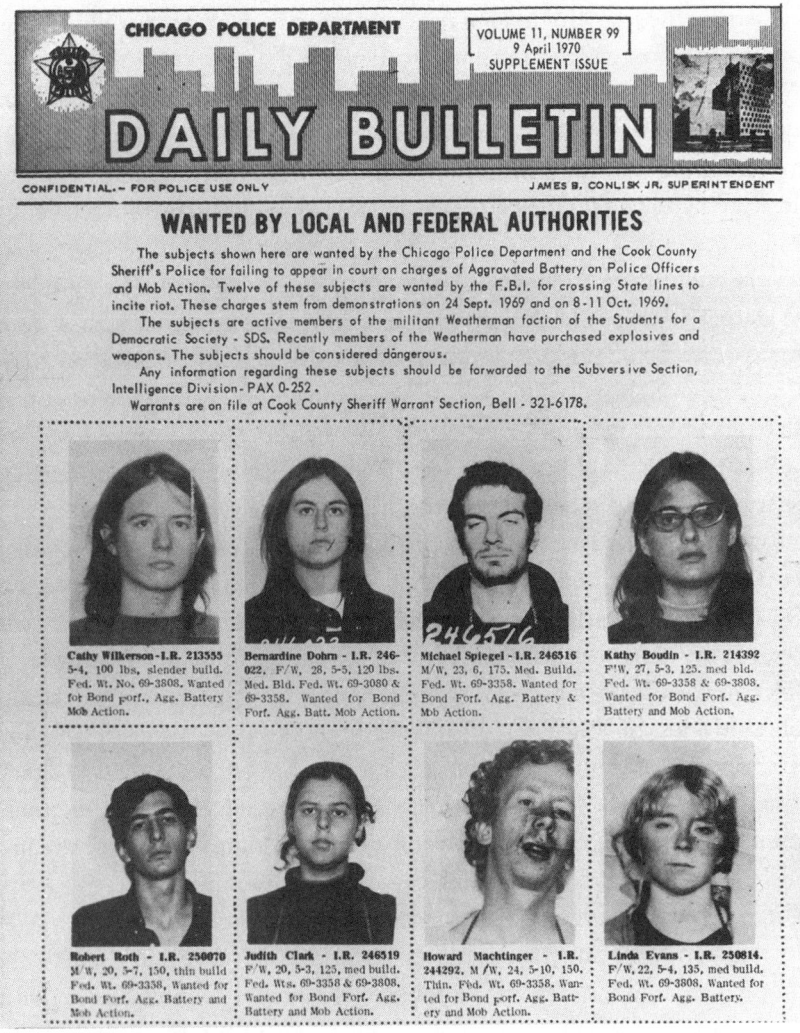

Image 8.5 The front page of the Chicago Police Department Daily Bulletin, issued April 9, 1970, showing eight members of Weatherman sought on warrants related to the group's November 1969 Days of Rage. Top row, left to right: Cathy Wilkerson, Bernardine Dohrn, Michael Spiegel, Kathy Boudin. Bottom row, left to right: Robert Roth, Judith Clark, Howard Machtinger, Linda Evans.

AP Photo/Chicago Police Department

Weatherman angered Hampton, but Eldridge Cleaver penned a glowing review of Weatherman (and Stalin). "In order to stop the slaughter of the people we must accelerate the slaughter of the pig," he wrote from Algiers. About

Weatherman, he said, "In times of revolution, just wars, and wars of liberation, I love the angels of destruction and disorder."[102]

When the police assassinated Fred Hampton less than two months after the Days of Rage, any misgivings that Weatherman had privately entertained about him were apparently forgotten. Weather declared themselves the "americong" who would avenge Hampton's death by unleashing a torrent of violence on "honky America."[103]

In the months that followed, Weatherman hoped to pull off a "modern-day Harper's Ferry." Their referencing of the famous abolitionist—"John Brown—Live Like Him"—was not frivolous. To them, Brown was an exemplary freedom fighter, willing to use lethal violence to ignite a rebellion of enslaved people. The group's leaders, or Weather Bureau, reportedly believed that Weatherman should carry out acts of violence that would inspire Blacks to take armed struggle "to a higher level," presumably outdoing the Panthers.[104] To that end, a Weathermen collective firebombed empty squad cars of Chicago cops. The Detroit collective tried to set off a powerful bomb at a police precinct house in Detroit after the acquittal of three cops on trial for killing three Blacks at the Algiers Motel. In Berkeley, Weather set off dynamite-filled pipe bombs besides the squad cars of Berkeley police. They did so at a shift change to ensure a substantial loss of "pig" life. Luckily, their bomb was largely ineffective, but even so one policeman suffered serious injuries to his arm, and others had their eardrums broken.[105] Then on February 21, 1970, the New York City townhouse collective set off three gasoline bombs at the home of the judge presiding over the Panther 21 trial. The bombs outside Judge John J. Murtagh's home might have caused more damage had a neighbor not taken action.

In this period, Weatherman neither phoned in advance warnings to the authorities, nor did they "claim" responsibility for them. Consequently, police had no way of knowing who was responsible for these bombs, and very likely blamed Black radicals. Their failure to set this straight was especially unconscionable in the bombing of Judge Murtagh's home. "If whites did that act," wrote the radical white journalist Andrew Kopkind, "they should have made it their own responsibility—and they should have set its political meaning straight." The defendants in the Panther 21 case had to go into the courtroom and deny that the Panthers had anything to do with what looked like an effort to kill the judge and his family.[106]

The collective's bombing at Murtagh's home and its failure to take responsibility for it was indefensible. What was the group thinking? Could its members actually have wanted people to assume that Black radicals carried out the bombing? Incredible though it seems, it seems that this is possible.[107] According to one FBI informant who had infiltrated Cleveland's Weather collective, its leadership was doing its best to kickstart the revolution by "provoking incidents between the black community and the police." They planned to do this by targeting cops and police facilities.[108] A Bay Area activist even claims that a Weatherwoman seriously suggested that the Black community, which she believed was in the doldrums after Hampton's murder, might be revitalized if Weatherman cadre, in blackface, assassinated a well-known enemy of Black people. The community would feel rejuvenated because "it would appear to have been done by one of 'their own.'"[109]

The Panthers' leadership, its Central Committee, wanted nothing to do with Weatherman, which increasingly behaved as if it was the vanguard, not subordinate to the Panthers. Eldridge Cleaver was another matter entirely. He continued to push for armed struggle, arguing during the summer of 1970 that he was "drafting Whitey to take the first heat." By "Whitey" he seems to have mostly meant Weatherman.[110] By 1970, Weatherman and Cleaver and his partisans in the party were locked in a dance of mutual misrecognition.

****

Five years earlier in 1965, SNCC's John Lewis posed this question: Could Blacks and whites together embark upon an unprecedented "political experiment . . . in which the first condition would be that whites consented to let Negroes run their own revolution?" In certain respects, the Panthers had been even more successful than SNCC in reversing the usual racial dynamics that had obtained in the left-wing world. In contrast to SNCC, militance did not impede the Panthers' ability to hold onto donors and attract new ones. But in other ways, the record seems mixed. When it came to the Panthers and the CP, who was using whom? Or was this just a mutually beneficial partnership . . . until it wasn't? Tellingly, by late 1970, the Panthers distanced themselves from the CP, albeit quietly.[111]

Panther headquarters (though not all Panthers) eventually cut its ties with Weatherman, too. Weatherman's behavior stands as a cautionary tale about cross-racial solidarity. The usual critique of allies, particularly white allies, is that they fall short in their revolutionary dedication. With Weatherman, there was another dynamic at work. Here, one sees white radicals whose faith in themselves as "moral giants," as Mark Rudd later put it, permitted them to put others at risk, even their one-time heroes.[112]

Weatherman's example raises the intriguing possibility that the people most vital to the Panthers' survival were not those fighting the police on the streets or planting bombs in federal office buildings and corporate headquarters. Rather, it suggests that those whom history has judged most harshly might have provided the most meaningful support. These were the people who harbored no illusions about being street-fighting revolutionaries. They had no desire to compete with the Panthers over who was most militant. They knew that answer. Instead, they helped to keep the party going through their donations and fundraising efforts. To understand why we have come to so ridicule these kinds of allies requires moving across the country to New York, where their efforts at cross-racial solidarity in support of the Panther 21 met an unexpected curveball: the accusation of radical chic.

PART FOUR

Radical Chic

Part Four: Introduction

At the start of the new decade, the Black Panther Party was besieged. Beleaguerment had often worked to the Panthers' benefit. One Black writer familiar with the Panthers said that the group had almost folded twice, and only came back from the brink because clashes with police mobilized support.[1] That January it looked again as though it might see a resurgence. Multiple law enforcement agencies were having a crippling effect on the Panthers, but they were also making "heroes out of those they would demolish."[2] This happened in many Black communities when the police went after the Panthers. For example, the tiny Panther chapter in Santa Ana, California, had little support until the police targeted its leaders. One Black moderate there observed that law enforcement's actions against the Panthers brought the group "a whole lot of support."[3]

Significantly, support for the Panthers was growing throughout Black America. According to the *Wall Street Journal*'s sampling, a clear majority of Black Americans in four metropolitan areas strongly endorsed both the goals and the methods of the Panthers. A larger majority believed the police were out to "crush the party" by arresting or killing its key leaders.[4]

Even established civil rights leaders who had criticized the Panthers or at least kept their distance from them now attacked the government's war against them. "One must protest vigorously against what the police have done," declared Bayard Rustin, "and one should also support the right of black people to defend themselves." Harlem assemblyman Charles Rangel denounced as "vicious" any suggestion that "responsible Blacks were unwilling to associate with the Panther cause." When Cecil F. Poole, the nation's only African American District Attorney, announced his retirement, he said it looked to him like the Justice Department was "out to get the Black Panthers." Congresswoman

Shirley Chisholm spoke at a pro-Panther benefit, where she likened the government's campaign against them to what the Nazis had done to the Jews. Moderate civil rights leader Roy Wilkins, executive director of the National Association for the Advancement of Colored People, together with Ramsey Clark, the former U.S. Attorney General, led a citizen's committee to investigate the government's war on the Panthers.[5]

With so much outrage about the government's treatment of the Party, the Panther leadership in Oakland, in concert with an as-yet-untested group of allies, made plans for benefits in and around New York City for the Panther 21. Over the years, the Bay Area and Los Angeles had seen their fair share of Panther cause parties. New York was a riskier gambit. The people planning Bay Area benefits knew individual Panthers, sometimes quite well.[6] They shared the Panthers' politics. Even in Los Angeles, there were people who somewhat bridged the world of the Panthers and that of liberals and leftists hosting benefits. However, in New York, where Panthers advanced the sort of cultural nationalism that Oakland's leaders joked about, such connections were slender to nonexistent. New York City was also the country's media capital, home to journalists happy to take down anyone or anything they considered overhyped.

Part Four tells the story of what happened when the Panthers expanded their fundraising efforts to New York's Upper East Side, specifically to the Park Avenue penthouse of Felicia and Leonard Bernstein. It was there in mid-January 1970 that nearly 90 people gathered at the invitation of Felicia Bernstein to meet and hear from the Panthers and the lawyers representing the Panther 21. For now, it is enough to say that the initial coverage of the event was mixed, but not sufficient to make it a touchstone event of the sixties. What made that happen was an uninvited journalist who showed up with the Bernsteins and their guests already in his crosshairs. Five months later, party-crasher Tom Wolfe let it rip, lampooning it all in "Radical Chic: That Party at Lenny's." Wolfe's skewering of the benefit—jet-set liberals mingling with Black radicals in the penthouse of America's most famous conductor—landed "like an earthquake."[7]

Few journalistic articles from that period have proven as enduringly impactful as Wolfe's "Radical Chic." One reason is that chroniclers of the sixties take Wolfe's account at face value. His essay also lines up well with a popular view of the Movement—that by 1970 it had lost its way; it had jumped the shark. Rather than treat "Radical Chic" as a reliable account of an embarrassingly cringe-making event, in Part Four I suggest that Wolfe's essay is best understood as a shot across the bow to liberal supporters of radical causes, and to the idea of solidarity politics more generally. "Radical Chic" aimed to make campaigns for social justice, particularly multiracial ones, seem chimerical, wrongheaded, *and* ridiculous. Conservatives were quick to understand its significance. *Commentary*'s Joseph Epstein was not the only one who believed that the essay put a "serious dent" in the Movement. At a moment when cross-racial solidarity was on the ropes, "Radical Chic" delivered the coup de grace. And in a fascinating twist, it did so with few objections from progressives, many of whom laughed along with Wolfe or kept quiet about all the opprobrium being heaped upon the disgraced "partygoers."[8]

Part Four covers a lot of ground, including the place of cause parties in the twentieth-century American left, a topic Tom Wolfe studied as a PhD student at Yale. Radical chic—both as a phrase and a concept—is essential to this part of the story, and my discussion of its little-known leftist origins helps to explain how it came to have such traction. Making sense of radical chic requires renarrating the benefit itself. Here, I emphasize the cross-generational left-wing collaboration behind it, the Bernsteins' political commitments, and the press's response, from the *New York Times*' curiously vacillating stance to Wolfe's gleefully malicious coverage. The aftermath of the brouhaha begins with the Federal Bureau of Investigation's harassment of the Bernsteins, which was aided by the Jewish Defense League, and seemingly calculated to further damage relations between Black radicals and Jewish progressives. It concludes with the profitable deployment of the phrase "radical chic" by Nixon's 1972 re-election campaign and by neoconservatives. Throughout, I keep track of the Panther 21, without whom there would be no story. How did the case against the 13 Panthers awaiting trial, the benefit for them, and the fallout from the benefit affect the Black Panther Party and the prospects for cross-racial solidarity?

NINE

The Cause Party

Felicia Montealegre Cohn Bernstein's benefit for the Panther 21 stands as a quintessentially sixties event. For conservatives, no event so embodied the era's "crazy scramble of values" than "the rich, the famous, and the brainy kowtowing to a band of black radicals," as Tom Wolfe later described it.[1] Yet cause parties, even those in which the rich rubbed elbows with anarchists and communists, were not a brand-new feature of American politics.

The Cause Party

The roots of what came to be called "radical chic" stretch back at least to the early twentieth century when modernity took hold in America, most definitively in New York City. Young bohemian rebels embraced all that was "modern" and "new," those "big, blowsy words" of those changing times. Transgressing the boundaries of class and gender (much less so race) was fundamental. In their hands, modernism was syncretic, encouraging coalitions and collaborations of disparate people.[2] This was the moment when prestige, heretofore defined and monopolized by the elite, began to reverse course. Going forward, those without "class" began to determine what was cutting edge and fashionable.[3]

Take the case of Mabel Dodge, a writer and wealthy art patron who became an impresario of the new and the modern. Famous for her legendary Greenwich Village salon of the 1910s, Dodge brought together in her elegant apartment an eclectic "collage of types." There were artists, anarchists, socialists, women's rights activists, journalists, and lawyers. What gave her salon its frisson were people like the anarchist Emma Goldman and Big Bill Haywood of the Industrial Workers of the World (IWW). Dodge's weekly conversations, which were followed by a lavish meal, were meant to narrow "the separations between different kinds of people," thereby undermining entrenched power differentials.[4]

Dodge understood that these separations could not be fully breached. Although Goldman and her friends appeared to be focused on publishing their anarchist magazine, Dodge noticed that there was about them "a great busy humming complex of Planning." She was sure she overheard talk about "blood flowing in the streets of New York." The historian Christine Stansell observed that Emma Goldman and her patron Mabel Dodge shared a well-developed theatricality, which complicates efforts to get at their dynamics and intentions. However, it's worth noting that what apparently mattered most to Dodge was that Goldman and her co-conspirators "think well of me." After all, she explained, "they were the kind of people that *counted*. They had *authority*."[5]

Among radical bohemians, opinion about Dodge was mixed. The socialist and birth control activist Margaret Sanger loved Dodge's salon, but her husband dismissed it as so much fakery: "Parlor Discussion, Parlor Artists, Parlor Socialists, Parlor Revolutionists, Parlor Anarchists." Dodge *was* a self-aggrandizing poseur, but she did embrace the left and feminism, and not entirely for show. She wrote for the socialist magazine *The Masses*, and she belonged to the Heterodoxy Club of "tabooless" feminist women. Dodge also funded a variety of left-wing and feminist causes, including Margaret Sanger's journal, *Woman Rebel*. During the 1913 silk-workers' strike in Paterson, New Jersey, she showed up with her car, which transported striking workers to and from the picket line. She was an organizer of a citizens' group formed to make sure labor's side of things would be represented on the Commission on Industrial Relations, a presidential commission set up in 1912 to determine the causes of workplace militance.[6]

Dodge was not alone. There were the wealthy women of the Women's Trade Union League (WTUL). Founded in 1903 to bring together the labor movement and the women's movement, the WTUL was meant to assist the stalled unionization efforts of American working women. The WTUL's leisure-class women called themselves "allies" to signify their commitment to aiding working women rather than calling the shots for them. The WTUL provided crucial support for an eight-hour workday, the minimum wage, workplace safety regulations, and the abolition of child labor.[7]

Allyship of this sort could be vexed, particularly for the workers themselves. Nonetheless, some radicals saw substantial benefits in these cross-class relationships. Emma Goldman, for one, had few reservations about turning to the well-intentioned rich to finance the revolution. She advocated working in cross-class coalitions. After the success of the 1912 strike in the textile mills of Lawrence, Massachusetts, even the radicals of the IWW began to appreciate the advantages of working with middle-class supporters.[8]

This vibrant, heterogeneous left of the 1910s did not survive America's first Red Scare, which followed on the heels of World War I and the Russian Revolution. When the left revived during the Depression years, it was dominated by the Communist Party, which was intellectually less rambunctious than many of the radical organizations of the 1910s.[9] Nonetheless, the CP and other leftist groups attracted their share of rich radicals. No one sent them up more brilliantly than one of their own: the 29-year-old writer Tess Slesinger. Her 1934 novel *The Unpossessed* satirizes a group of parlor radicals too tied up in knots to even launch a little magazine, much less start a revolution. At the novel's center is a swanky cause party, the Hunger March Party. Life-sized banners, depicting hunger marchers, hang right above a buffet table creaking underneath the weight of "six whole Virginia hams, two sliced turkeys, six platters of devilled eggs, sturgeon and salmon, and a tray designed in canapés of caviar, cheese and anchovies," and more. One discerning partygoer, the hostesses' shrink, notes the complicated dynamics at play that evening, "*they* want to blow us up; but they come here and enjoy our company. Also, we *know* they want to blow us up; yet we enjoy theirs."[10]

Slesinger was there before Wolfe, just as Dostoevsky was there before Slesinger with *The Possessed*, his 1872 novel about Russian revolutionaries. However, she approached the subject differently from either Wolfe or the Russian novelist. Slesinger wrote from inside the left, which she never repudiated, even if it did amuse her. After she and her husband, Herbert Solow, an editor at a left-wing magazine, divorced, she moved to Hollywood, where she became a screenwriter.[11] She married another screenwriter, Frank Davis, and became a part of Hollywood's CP scene, which cynics sometimes sneered at for offering nothing more than "Hollywood cocktail party communism."[12]

The poet and writer Archibald MacLeish was a fellow traveler in the period when Slesinger was active. The sincerity of the radical rich he encountered surprised him. "They *meant* it all," MacLeish told Tom Wolfe, then a Yale graduate student researching left-wing American writers from the late twenties through the forties.[13] Many of them did indeed mean it all and offered crucial support to the striking workers of Gastonia, North Carolina, the Scottsboro

Boys of Alabama, and Los Angeles' Sleepy Lagoon defendants.[14] The Sleepy Lagoon Defense Committee (SLDC) sought and received the support of influential liberals, including Hollywood celebrities such as Rita Hayworth, Orson Welles, and Anthony Quinn. CP member Alice McGrath, a Jewish working-class immigrant involved in the SLDC, was not unusual in favoring political groups and movements with space for the privileged and the exploited.[15]

While the left accepted wealthy radicals and liberals, albeit somewhat grudgingly, conservatives went on the attack. During the New Deal, tarring left liberalism with the brush of elitism became a reliable weapon in the conservative arsenal.[16] With World War II winding down and a second Red Scare winding up, the already divided left further fractured as anticommunism became bipartisan and virtually compulsory. Investigated by the House Un-American Activities Committee (HUAC) and attacked by red-baiting Senator Joseph McCarthy, left liberalism ruptured. The National Association for the Advancement of Colored People (NAACP), for example, shifted gears as it became an exemplar of liberal anticommunism. Its publication *The Crisis* attacked the Black communist Paul Robeson for his extravagant lifestyle, claiming that it proved he was a phony. Of Robeson's relationship to Blacks, it declared, "He is of them, but not with them."[17]

Relations between communists and other leftists and liberals were so riven that people accused of being communists received little support. Those who appeared before HUAC and pleaded the Fifth Amendment usually lost their jobs and their reputations. As I. F. Stone noted, "This satisfies the committees, for their purpose is nothing less than an ideological purge of radicals and liberals from all positions of influence in American life and the demonstration to others that nonconformity is dangerous." In a national survey, 78 percent of Americans said they thought it was a good idea to report relatives or acquaintances suspected of being communists.[18] These were not advantageous times for cause parties, though there were people such as the family of Andrew Goodman (of Goodman, Chaney, and Schwerner) who held fundraising parties for professors being persecuted for their connections to the CP.[19]

It took more than a decade for the most extreme versions of anticommunism to be repudiated. It was not until 1959 that ex-President Harry Truman declared HUAC the "most un-American thing in the country today." With the surge of civil rights activism, and the slow revival of the left, the cause party returned.[20] For most of the sixties, these benefits garnered no headlines. Student Nonviolent Coordinating Committee (SNCC) benefits, for example, which were crucial to keeping the organization alive, were sometimes in the homes of ex-communists or fellow travelers. These were often where parties to support civil liberties were held, too. Yet in 1963, when Joan Baez took Bob Dylan to the home of the rich activist Corliss Lamont for a fundraising event to benefit an anti–Cold War organization, the Emergency Civil Liberties Committee, it went unmentioned in the press.[21] Nor was it a news item when Leonard Bernstein opened his home to jazz-in-the-afternoon benefits, with proceeds going to civil rights organizations.[22]

It was not until the late sixties that these benefits or cause parties began to be featured in the press. What seems to have piqued the interest of journalists was that the people hosting them tended to be younger and hipper, and able to attract popular actors, artists, writers, musicians, and politicians as their guests. These were not the kind of cause party hosted by well-meaning but poorly paid junior faculty in unprepossessing spaces with cheap wine, Kraft cheese, and Ritz crackers.[23]

A prime example of the new cause party was a mid-April 1969 benefit for the United Farm Workers (UFW), hosted by the couple George and Freddie Plimpton in their Manhattan duplex. George Plimpton was a well-known writer in his early forties, but his wife, Freddie, an artist and designer, was still in her twenties. The Plimptons' party was the last part of a $25-a-person benefit ($250 in today's terms) that began with the premiere of Albert and David Maysles's latest documentary, so it would have drawn an arty crowd. The *New York Times* reporter detailed the unlikely mix of people gathered there: "tieless grape pickers," filmmakers such as Melvin Van Peebles; Alan Jay Lerner, the celebrated lyricist of many Broadway musicals; actors Rip Torn and Geraldine Page; and Norman Mailer, with his entourage in tow.[24]

The *Times* reporter covering the Plimptons' benefit noted its fashionableness, but without snark, though it did provoke grumblings in some journalistic quarters. Six weeks later when the New York City politician Andrew Stein opened his Long Island home to another benefit for the UFW, the coverage was more skeptical. Even before it had happened, the journalist Gloria Steinem heard rumors that it might be criticized in the press. An ally of the UFW, Steinem had a close working relationship with the UFW's president, César Chávez. She explained to him her concerns and advised calling it off. "César just laughed," she recalled. This was a no-brainer to him. He would risk the bad press because even if they raised only $500 it would enable a hundred strikers to keep at it for another week.[25]

As it happened, Steinem was right about the press. Conservative columnist William F. Buckley used the occasion to chastise the event's Honorary Chairman, Ethel Kennedy, whose husband Robert F. Kennedy had been assassinated a year earlier during his presidential campaign. Listening to these liberal do-gooders, Buckley scolded her, made as much sense as asking "Zsa-Zsa Gabor to rewrite the Constitution."[26]

The *New York Times* reporter Charlotte Curtis was also critical of the Steins' benefit, but her views were very different from those of the conservative Buckley. Curtis, despite her position as the editor of the style section (formerly the society section), was a quiet sort of renegade. *Time* magazine observed that she brought to her work "the detachment of a professional sociologist," though it was hard to miss her irreverence toward the society people she covered. Curtis was "the tiny lady who went to all those chic, elegant dinner parties with a firecracker in her purse."[27] Tellingly, *The Rich and Other Atrocities* was the title she chose for her collected essays, published in 1975. About the Steins' benefit, she noted that many of the attendees seemed more upset by the way that the damp sea air was wrecking their hairdos than by what the speakers were saying about the exploitation of farmworkers. She was attentive to what she imagined was the social discomfort felt by some of the farmworkers attending the event.[28]

Limousine Liberals, Linoleum Liberals, and Radical Chic

So why was newspaper coverage becoming less sympathetic and more pointed? Perhaps because 1969 was the year that "limousine liberal" entered our vocabulary. It was the coinage of Mario Procaccino, the Democratic mayoral candidate in New York City. Procaccino was facing off against the liberal incumbent, John Lindsay. A patrician do-gooder, Lindsay was an ex-Republican running on the Liberal Party ticket. Procaccino hoped that the label would appeal to white, ethnic working-class voters of the outer boroughs who increasingly resented well-to-do liberal politicians. It is true that many of these people considered Lindsay the typical liberal, indifferent to their concerns, and, worse, making their lives harder with tax-and-spend policies designed to help Blacks, not them. By 1970 they were also growing alarmed by the support some liberals were giving to feminists and gays. In tarring liberalism with the brush of elitism, Procaccino was taking a page from the GOP's playbook. Procaccino's supporters took to calling his opponent "Lefty Lindsay" and "faggot." Lindsay

Image 9.1 Charlotte Curtis, seated left, *New York Times* society page editor, taking notes during an August 20, 1964, interview with Mrs. T. Robinson. Curtis was a quiet supporter of the Black Panthers, but her sardonic coverage of Felicia Bernstein's benefit hindered fundraising efforts for the Panther 21's legal defense.
Ben Martin/Getty Images

narrowly won the race, but Procaccino won the white ethnic working-class vote in a sign of things to come.[29]

It is conceivable that the talk of limousine liberals made some journalists more aware of what the historian Steve Fraser calls America's ever-growing "grand canyon of class and cultural division."[30] But the journalists covering Procaccino did not usually find common ground with him. Usually, they made fun of him, as they joked about what to call his brand of liberalism. If Lindsay was a limousine liberal, someone suggested Procaccino was a linoleum liberal. Linoleum, one imagines, because of its popularity among nonelite white voters of the outer boroughs.[31] Whatever the cause of journalists' increasingly skeptical treatment of cause parties, it probably was not fed by the white anger nourishing Procaccino's campaign. One clue is that "limousine liberal" was not the term of derision that journalists typically deployed against the Bernsteins and their guests. Their preferred phrase of choice, "radical chic," emerged from an entirely different milieu, one very different from the outer borough world of Procaccino.

Radical chic was the brainchild of the little-known writer Seymour Krim. In the heyday of marquee journalists such as Hunter Thompson, Joan Didion, and Tom Wolfe, Krim worked on journalism's margins. An uncompromising outsider, Krim may have been only a "semi-name," but he had his admirers.[32] The memoirist and essayist Vivian Gornick called him "a Jewish Joan Didion."[33] Fellow journalist Dan Wakefield considered him "the unsung father of what was later called the New Journalism." Wakefield argued that Krim paved the way for others by using "his personal experience as material—often like raw wounds" to grapple with the literature, culture, and politics of the day.[34] "Hot mortal telegrams from writer to reader" was how Krim described his articles.[35] His telegrams were controversial, especially his articles chastising white hipsters for their objectifying romanticization of Black people.[36]

Krim was a contrarian who was ideologically nonaligned. Mostly, his left-leaning politics came through his writing, as in 1962, when he put himself on journalism's barricades in an essay about *The New Yorker*.[37] "Who's Afraid of the *New Yorker* Now?" appeared that year in a November issue of the *Village Voice*, the irreverent granddaddy of "alternative" journalism in America. To Krim, *The New Yorker* had once published work that "any selfrespecting intellectual or chic-ster had to take a stand in relation to." But now, the magazine was, he said, "middleaged, safe and increasingly divorced from the action." As a cultural force, Krim thought it was spent, done.[38]

What Krim did not know was that *The New Yorker* was gearing up to publish an uncompromising essay by James Baldwin that had been in the works for many months. Baldwin's "Letter from a Region in My Mind" dropped two weeks after Krim's "obituary" of the magazine.[39] Baldwin's essay took aim at white liberal sensibilities, and in the very magazine that Krim had excoriated as a "castrated and even reactionary publication."[40] The timing of it all must have embarrassed Krim, who doubled down with another piece calling *The New Yorker* "a cover-to-cover tranquilizer" for the "little old lady from Dubuque."[41]

What seemed to bother Krim most about the magazine was its "buttery liberalism." It was content to sit out what was happening—politically, culturally, in all ways. Its editorial voice emanated a "liberal kindness" that had "all the power of a canary used to its cage." Krim admired Baldwin's essay, which he considered bracingly honest. But it was one solitary piece in a magazine that remained otherwise unchanged. Krim contended there was no better example than *The New Yorker* of how "the liberal conscience is fast becoming the compromised conscience." In closing, he argued that in publishing

Baldwin's "Letter," the magazine demonstrated only that it was "stretching its now rubber conscience to include tokens of radical chic and impressiveness at the top but not the bottom where it counts."[42]

In the nearly eight years it took for the phrase "radical chic" to become the term du jour, it had lost all connection to the man responsible for its coinage. In large part, Krim's erasure stemmed from the *Voice*'s decision to pass on his follow-up essay, in which he further eviscerated *The New Yorker*. Krim's addendum to "Who's Afraid" did not appear until January 1970, when a volume of his collected essays was published. The *Voice*'s decision was another gut punch in Krim's hard-luck life, which included being dumped by Lynn Nesbit, who, before she was famous, was his literary agent and, it seems, lover.[43] (Nesbit would represent Wolfe.) In his best-known essay, "For My Brothers and Sisters in the Failure Business," Krim memorialized falling short.[44]

Wolfe may have encountered the phrase for the first time in Krim's 1970 collection, when he was writing about the Bernstein benefit, which took place that same January. It is equally possible that Wolfe read Krim's unpublished piece years earlier when he was writing his own takedown of *The New Yorker*, 1965's "Tiny Mummies!" Certainly, the two men knew each other from having both worked at the *New York Herald Tribune*. It's possible Wolfe heard or read the phrase earlier because "radical chic" was out in the world by the fall of 1967, if not earlier.[45] Krim hung out with other writers in the bars and cafes of the Village, so maybe that's how "radical chic" got out into the world.[46]

When the term entered the vocabulary, it had no fixed meaning. Krim had used the phrase, almost in passing, and he hadn't explained what it meant. He used it to call out liberals' timid gesturing toward radicalism. If *The New Yorker* was serious about embodying what he called "the stinging voice of the accelerated present," it would not have turned to James Baldwin, who was already an established writer, but to lesser-known ones.[47] For him, radical chic amounted to liberal tokenism. Krim's cynicism about liberalism was not common in 1962, even in SNCC and Students for a Democratic Society (SDS). But, as we have seen, within two years it was much more so, and by 1970, it had become the gospel truth among many in the Movement.

Krim's aim in coining the phrase was not shared by everyone who appropriated it. Krim spoke as a radical taunting the milquetoast liberalism of the early sixties. This would be the way that the Black writer Ishmael Reed used it, too. Reed claimed that Krim had coined the expression to characterize Baldwin's decision to publish his piece in *The New Yorker*, "the epitome of uptown pretensions and snobbery." Reed seems to have misidentified the target of Krim's attack, but he had a firmer grasp than many about what Krim meant by radical chic.[48]

Others, usually veterans of the internecine wars of the Old Left, understood the phrase not as a call for greater radicalism, but, rather, as a way to mock what they saw as the phoniness of so much that passed as radical. Irving Howe, an ex-Trotskyist and now a staunch social democrat, was critical of this new radicalism, which he saw as something very different from "the radicalism of desperate Negroes and disaffected youth which, for all its political failings, is at least grounded in urgent experience." Howe argued that "the radicalism now arising in the intellectual world is in quality and content as rude, fashion-driven, smugly moralistic, and supremely verbal as was the turn to conservatism in the Fifties. It is a 'radicalism' of posture, gesture, *frisson*." To Howe, young radicals and the intellectuals supporting them were only performatively radical. Pull back from your fantasies of revolution and turn your attention to building effective coalitions, he argued. Work with liberals; don't fight a war against them.[49]

Howe's suggestion had merit. While it is true that most Democratic politicians remained hawkish on the war, partly out of loyalty to Johnson, on economic issues the party was moving to the left. In fact, the platform the party put forward at its tumultuous 1968 convention was remarkably left-wing. It wholeheartedly endorsed its liberal achievements, including the War on Poverty, Medicare, and Medicaid. It also held out the promise of universal health care, full employment, and an increase in public housing. It was, as the historian Michael Kazin argued, nearly indistinguishable from the agenda of Britain's Labour Party. But, by this point the Vietnam War had become *the* issue to such extent that the Democrats' economic platform barely registered on the campaign trail.[50]

When Tom Wolfe appropriated the phrase "radical chic" later, claiming it as his own, he was not interested in pushing liberalism to the left or in pulling the left back from the precipice of "revolution for the hell of it."[51] Wolfe wanted America to be done with exploring its social conscience, perhaps especially at the expense of his South. This is another key difference. Here, it is worth noting that even Progressive white Southerners sometimes found Northern liberals patronizing. In June 1965, Virginia Durr, a true civil rights pioneer, wrote to her good friend Jessica Mitford to complain about the "missionary attitudes" she detected in two groups of Northern liberals—the "rich Harvard boys" launching the *Southern Courier*, a pro–civil rights newspaper, and the "rich Wednesdays in Mississippi ladies" who opened dialogues with white Southern ladies. She understood they meant well but she also resented how the Movement had become a "fashionable cause, as you can still be 'in' and live on Park Avenue and make a big splash by spending a few weeks in the South, when the people in Harlem also need help very badly."[52]

The Politics of Leonard and Felicia Montealegre Bernstein

If one were to apply the "radical chic" as Krim intended it, the Bernsteins' Panther benefit did not fit the bill. First, the Panthers were not analogous to James Baldwin. White left-wing journalist Robert Scheer worked closely with Eldridge Cleaver and emphasizes how far from the realm of anything approaching radical chic the Panthers were. "They were radical, much more radical, with the guns and everything."[53] Here's the other thing, hosting a benefit for the Panther 21 was an easy path to one thing only: harassment by the Federal Bureau of Investigation (FBI). Nor did the Bernsteins represent wishy-washy liberalism. By 1970, Leonard Bernstein's FBI file was already several hundred pages long.

Bernstein's involvement with the left—he was a fellow traveler, not a CP member—went back to his college years at Harvard. In 1939, more than 30 years before his wife hosted the Panther benefit, Bernstein staged Marc Blitzstein's 1937 agitprop musical, *The Cradle Will Rock*, with the result that he landed on the FBI's radar. Bernstein was not shy about his political commitments, which included racial equality. In 1944, he and his collaborators created *On the Town*, a musical that took on the racist taboos of the day in many ways. First, they cast Sono Osato as Ivy Smith, a major role. Osato's father was Japanese, making her an edgy choice while the United States was still at war with Japan. Bernstein and his partners also included Black performers as dancers and cast members. On stage, Black men and white women held hands, and Black and white soldiers mingled, unlike the country's segregated military. Nine months in, they chose the show's concert master, a Black man, as its conductor. It was likely the first time that a Black man conducted a mixed-race Broadway show. In November 1947, Bernstein published a piece in the *New*

York Times about the National Negro Congress's efforts to overcome racial discrimination in the music industry.[54]

Leonard Bernstein's politics were shaped by the Old Left, and as the second Red Scare took hold, Bernstein initially stood his ground, supporting the Hollywood Ten, and defending Paul Robeson.[55] He helped form the Progressive Party, which ran Henry Wallace for president in 1948. That year he opposed the repressive Mundt-Nixon Communist Control bill. All around Bernstein, friends and associates who were CP members or who had signed petitions circulated by the CP, one of its fronts, or some other left-wing group came under attack. Having once hosted a cause party for what now seemed the wrong cause could land one in big trouble. All those early left-wing opponents of fascism were now labeled and condemned as "premature anti-fascists." Anyone who moved in that world was liable to be exposed and denounced as a communist by red-hunting publications such as *Red Channels* and *Counterattack*, or by a gossip columnist like Ed Sullivan.

That is what happened to Bernstein's frequent collaborator, the dancer and choreographer Jerome Robbins. A former CP member, Robbins had hosted a party for the Soviet Friendship League. Sullivan, who would later become famous for his TV variety show, promised to expose Robbins's homosexuality if he did not reveal who had attended that party. "Robbins knows and can name Communists," Sullivan alleged, particularly those "who are prominent as conductors and arrangers in concert music."[56] He called on HUAC to investigate the choreographer, which it did.[57] Among the Bernsteins' closest friends was the famous and famously controversial left-wing writer Lillian Hellman, whom they would choose as godmother of their youngest child. Hellman was blacklisted in Hollywood, and in 1952 she was called before HUAC. Even the film director Sidney Lumet, who was a left-wing Democrat, not a CP member, recalled that "when the whole blacklist thing came [it] not only affected me but certainly everybody I knew was in great trouble."[58]

As for Leonard Bernstein, his political activities, and his sexual activities, which included homosexual liaisons, ensured J. Edgar Hoover's interest in him. Up until 1949, Bernstein's career had soared. He was the musical director of the New York City Symphony Orchestra, a frequent guest director of the New York Philharmonic, and had a lucrative recording contract with RCA. Then in 1950, both *Counterattack* and *Red Channels* named him a dangerous subversive. CBS put him off limits, and Hollywood considered him beyond the pale. He was banned from performing at official State Department events overseas.

In April 1951, the FBI placed his name on the Security Index that came into being with 1950's antisubversive McCarran Act.[59] It meant that were there to be a national emergency, Bernstein would be among those arrested and incarcerated in a detention camp.[60]

In July 1953, Bernstein's situation grew more dire when the State Department refused to renew his passport, grounding him in America when much of his growing fame as a conductor stemmed from his work in Europe. Only after he signed an obsequious affidavit of contrition, composed by his lawyer, did his career revive. Signing the groveling affidavit in which he recanted his past, which he attributed to his political naivete, was a "ghastly and humiliating experience."[61] Some of his friends who appeared before HUAC, including Jerome Robbins, named names. Bernstein never found himself in Robbins's position; he never had to make a decision about actually naming names. But nor was it the end of his travails. Getting hired onto projects required that his affidavit be sent to the very archconservatives he despised. As his biographer Barry Seldes points out, the affidavit "was a mark on him—if not as an informer upon others, as an informer upon himself."[62]

Bernstein's passport was reinstated a month later, but problems arose again when he applied for its extension. His passport situation was not fully resolved until May 1954. Then, nearly two years later, he learned he was about to be investigated by a Congressional committee concerned with communist subversion. Bernstein's recently formed friendship with John F. Kennedy, the junior senator from Massachusetts and a fellow Harvard graduate, may have played a role in making this problem go away. In 1954, Bernstein's career started to revive. But from 1949, when *Life* magazine named him among the country's 50 most prominent "Reds," to 1956, Bernstein worried about what new investigation might be mounted.[63]

By 1956 he was serving as a guest conductor for the New York Philharmonic. What lay ahead of him—particularly *West Side Story* and his popular TV show, *Young People's Concerts*, which began in 1958 and ran for 14 seasons—all contributed to his growing fame. The State Department (and covertly the Central Intelligence Agency [CIA]) made use of Bernstein and other prominent artists to contrast the artistic freedom enjoyed by American artists to the censorship faced by Soviet artists. It was part of the effort to win over nonaligned nations in the cultural Cold War. However, the FBI saw the matter very differently. The FBI maintained its dossier on Bernstein and was still trying to dig up evidence he had been a CP member so he could be prosecuted for perjury.[64]

Once dissent gathered steam in the sixties, Bernstein took part. He joined 1965's Selma march, walking the final miles to the state capital in Montgomery. Increasingly, his was not a quiet or discreet dissent. In August 1968, he addressed a sold-out campaign benefit at Madison Square Garden for antiwar Democratic candidate Eugene McCarthy, organized by Hannah Weinstein.[65] On November 15, 1969, just two months before the Panther benefit, he was a featured speaker at the Washington, DC, demonstration of the Moratorium to End the War in Vietnam, which drew a half-million protesters. Bernstein also operated at local, lower-wattage events, as when he served as the emcee for the Theatre Community for Peace rally held in Times Square just two days before the Moratorium in DC. While the Bernsteins marched together in antiwar demonstrations, Felicia became involved in human rights activism, from Mothers for Peace to the American Civil Liberties Union. In the months leading up to the benefit, she led the effort to form the women's division of the New York Civil Liberties Union. As her career as a stage and television actor wound down, she increasingly put her energy into human rights.[66]

The Bernsteins' political activism, past and present, suggests the couple would have understood that hosting a benefit for the Black Panthers carried risks. Everyone knew that the Black Panther Party was not the UFW or the Moratorium to End the War in Vietnam. The Panthers advocated armed self-defense, chanted "off the pigs," and more. Just six months earlier, FBI director Hoover had declared the party "the greatest threat to the internal security of the country."[67] Sometimes the police targeted their supporters as well. In Chicago, the police raided the home of one Panther supporter as he was hosting a cocktail party for their defense. The police beat him up for good measure.[68] As Robert Scheer observes, "You're supporting the Panthers, well, you're going to pay a price."[69]

Panther 21

The possibility that the people hosting these events might pay a price was not uppermost in the minds of those planning the New York benefits. What most mattered to them was the situation of the Panther 21, 13 of whom had been sitting in jail for eight months. This was the group of Panthers who stood accused of a labyrinthine conspiracy to shoot police officers and carry out the bombing of police stations, Manhattan department stores, and the city's beloved

Botanical Gardens.[70] The prosecutors were cocky because they had mounds of evidence, most of it accumulated through paid informants. Moreover, among the 13 who had been apprehended, few showed any inclination to turn on the charm, to come across like "everybody's favorite baby-sitter," as Huey Newton did. About Dhoruba bin Wahad, the journalist Murray Kempton observed that the defendant would find in the lead prosecutor "someone who believed that he was as bad as he wanted to think himself."[71]

The outrageousness of the alleged Easter Day plot (bombs in handbags on sale at Macy's) led many radicals to assume that the charges were completely cooked up. Yet the New York Panthers were more hooked on fantasies of armed struggle than the Oakland leadership. "They wanted to create a war!" remarked Bobby Seale's brother, John.[72] Years later, Afeni Shakur admitted that when the police arrested her in April 1969, she assumed it was for her attempted hold-up of a parkway tollkeeper. When the tollkeeper refused to hand over his money to her, and instead slammed his window shut, she shot at him anyway. Luckily, the bullet ricocheted off the glass, which meant the only real injuries from her attack that day were the powder burns on Shakur's neck. "I wanted to rob something to show I'm big and bad," she admitted.[73] Her attitude was fairly typical among the New York Panthers.

During that first week of April 1969, following their arrests, several hundred people, mostly white and Black radicals, demonstrated at the criminal courthouse and the Women's House of Detention. The following week, after considerable publicity and organizing, much of it by SDS, 2,000 people—many of them white—rallied outside the courthouse in Lower Manhattan, also the site of the Manhattan Detention Complex, better known as the Tombs. They were joined by 250 uniformed Panthers. However, few ordinary Black New Yorkers showed up to these protests. "There were many demonstrations," recalled Mark Rudd, though "made up mostly of white radicals, many of whom, like myself, wanted to get it on with the police." Indeed, when protestors heard that the presiding judge in the Panther 21 case refused to lower their bail and cited their lawyers for contempt, they "went wild" and headed toward Wall Street where they rampaged, smashing the windows of shops and limousines. There were few non-Panther Black protestors at these rallies. "Black people were way too smart," says Rudd. "They didn't want to die."[74]

However, with preparations for the trial moving at glacial speed, and with SDS, which initially mobilized support, in collapse, the story of the Panther 21 faded from the news. The lack of money and awareness mattered because the conduct of New York State regarding the Panther 21 case revealed the racism of the American justice system. For starters, the 13 defendants in custody were slapped with bail of $100,000. The Panthers' lawyers pointed to another recent case involving four white non-Weatherman radicals who set off bombs rather than merely conspiring to do so, which was the charge against the 21. In that case, the judge agreed to lower bail from $500,000 to between $20,000 and $50,000. Lawyers for the 21, citing that case as precedent, argued for bail reduction, but Judge Murtagh was unmoved.[75]

Also troubling was the way the state scattered the defendants across the city in six different jails, making it impossible for their lawyers to prepare their defense. This only changed a month before the start of the trial in early February, when most of the male prisoners were put into their own separate unit. The defense attorneys also attacked as prejudicial the city's standard policy of denying media access to prisoners awaiting trial. When a reporter for the *Washington Post* requested an interview with three of the defendants, New York's Corrections Commissioner denied it. The lawyers also alleged their clients' mistreatment at the hands of prison officials.[76]

The unfairness of it all was felt most keenly by the defendants, but their lawyers felt it, too. In the fall of 1969, one of them, Gerald Lefcourt, decided to look beyond the courtroom for help. Scrappy and brash, the 27-year-old white lawyer, who sported a formidable Afro-like hairdo, had already begun to make a name for himself as part of the legal team for the Chicago 7. Lefcourt was now working in tandem with several other leftist lawyers on the Panther 21 case. Most of them were part of a newly formed legal group, one with countercultural aspirations that they called the Law Commune.[77]

The Committee to Defend the Panther 21: Martin Kenner and Hannah Weinstein

Lefcourt was filled with revolutionary righteousness, and he turned to one of his clients, someone who was also filled with that kind of righteousness, to see if he would help to generate support for the Panther 21. The client was Martin Kenner, the previously mentioned white radical who had spent most of the sixties as a peripatetic graduate student looking to hook up with the right revolutionary group. Kenner had taken part in 1968's occupation of Columbia University and was facing the stiffest charge levied against any

Image 9.2 Yippie leader Abbie Hoffman smiles broadly as he is escorted by police after his arrest at O'Hare Airport on September 17, 1968. At his side, also grinning, is his attorney Gerald Lefcourt, one of the lawyers for the Panther 21.
AP Photo

protestor. Kenner wasn't even a Columbia student; he was a graduate student about eight miles due south at the New School for Social Research, where he studied economic history. He was charged, unfairly, with conspiring to murder a police officer. If convicted, he was looking at a 15-to-20-year prison sentence. In the meantime, he was free on bail and remained politically active.

Kenner was not a paying client, and when Lefcourt asked for his help in lieu of payment, he was more than happy to oblige. It wasn't as though Kenner was a high-profile radical like Abbie Hoffman, a client who would help Lefcourt's career. Lefcourt was vague about what he needed. "Raise a little money or bring a little attention" were the words that stayed with Kenner. Lefcourt conveyed the urgency of the case, that, in his view, the authorities planned to "smear the whole movement" by accusing the Panthers of scheming to commit such heinous crimes.[78]

Kenner traveled a circuitous route to Panther defense work. Older than most other New Leftists, he felt part of an "in-between generation," situated between the Old and the New Left. He had been active in the Progressive Labor outfit, M2M, an anarchist group called the Motherfuckers, SDS, and Weatherman. Although he had always dreamed of being a professor, after the siege of Columbia he dropped out of graduate school and became a full-time activist. He helped deserters from the American military who had fought in Vietnam and were living in Europe. After returning to the states, he was briefly involved with a Weatherman collective in Chicago.[79]

In August 1969, Kenner returned to New York. He and some friends organized an anti-imperialist group called Mad Dogs, but it never went anywhere.[80] Organizationally adrift, he agreed to help with the Panther 21 case and placed small notices about the Panther Defense Fund in left-wing and underground newspapers. Money trickled in that fall but began to pick up in late October as images of Bobby Seale, bound and gagged, were all over the newspapers and TV news. Still, Kenner did not see himself opening envelopes for very long. He had plans to return to Chicago to organize white working-class kids with another ex-Weatherman.

Kenner likely would have headed off to Chicago had it not been for the mother of Paula Weinstein, a student radical he knew. Sometime that November, perhaps it was when Judge Hoffman sentenced Seale to four years in prison for contempt, Hannah Weinstein rang up Kenner at his office at the Law Commune. They had already met, so he may have known about her Old Left background. It's very unlikely that he grasped the serendipity of Hannah Weinstein, once the foremost publicist and organizer of left-wing events in New York, calling him up with an offer to help. Weinstein wanted to introduce him to some people she thought might be helpful to his defense work. Referring to what was happening to Bobby Seale, she said Panther supporters had to do more.

It was hardly the first time that Hannah Weinstein, faced with an injustice, took this position.[81] Born Hannah Dorner in New York City in 1911, she was raised in an upwardly mobile immigrant family. She studied journalism for four years at New York University, while also moonlighting for much of that time at the New York *Herald Tribune*. She left journalism to work as a speechwriter for the mayoral campaign of Fiorello La Guardia. After marrying a fellow speechwriter on the campaign and starting a family, she worked for a public relations company. By 1941, she was handling major

Image 9.3 Martin Kenner of the Committee to Defend the Panther 21, looking slightly out of place at a Yippie meeting at the Underground Press Syndicate loft in New York City, possibly 1970. Front row, left to right: Jerry Rubin, Abe Peck, David Fenton, Abbie Hoffman, and Jim Retherford. Back row, left to right: Ed Sanders, Super Joel, Martin Kenner, Nancy Kurshan, Anita Hoffman, and Tom Forcade.
Leni Sinclair (Michael Ochs Archives), Getty Images

accounts, including a new one for the National Council of American–Soviet Friendship (NCASF).

NCASF was comprised of Communist Party (CP) members and fellow travelers, and Weinstein's relationship to it went way beyond handling its account. Although she never joined the CPUSA, she was suspected of being a "concealed Communist." It's true that her best friends were CP members and fellow travelers who believed that a more progressive world required an American–Soviet partnership. Among her closest friends was the writer Lillian Hellman, who for two years was a CP member, and whose view of the Soviet Union struck many liberals and leftists as too rosy. Yet Hellman was hardly alone in thinking that over time the Soviet Union would democratize and that it was needed as a counterbalance to American power. Time would erode that optimism.

Weinstein brought her public relations canniness to left-wing politics. To publicize the work of the NCASF, she organized an event in fall 1942 to commemorate the 25th anniversary of the October Revolution in Russia. The event she organized at Madison Square Garden was a sold-out affair where Soviet diplomats and businessmen mixed with left-wing Americans, some in evening clothes, others in bohemian denim. In February 1944, Weinstein organized a celebration of the Red Army at the Garden that included praise for the Soviet Army from America's military leaders, including General Dwight D. Eisenhower. Throughout she was learning how to fundraise, as she did for the Joint Anti-Fascist Refugee Committee, bringing in $75,000 to aid refugees of the Spanish Civil War.

Weinstein organized Garden rallies for Roosevelt's re-election, and after this, she organized more to urge him to expand the New Deal. These rallies were sponsored by leftist groups with bland-sounding names such as the Independent Voters Committee of the Arts and Sciences for Roosevelt, and Independent Citizens Committee for the Arts, Sciences and Professions (ICCASP). Although the leadership of these groups included many communists, the membership itself was more far-ranging politically. Weinstein was careful to bring in celebrities in the entertainment industry—Frank Sinatra, Ethel Merman, the playwright Robert Sherwood—as well as scientists such as Albert Einstein and Robert Oppenheimer. She largely operated behind the scenes, though she was featured in *Mademoiselle* magazine as the "spark plug" of ICCASP. Blacklisted screenwriter Ring Lardner Jr. noted that Weinstein's response to troubling events was to stage counter-events. He emphasized they were always "bigger and broader than anyone else thought they could be."[82]

Enlisting celebrity sponsors and speakers made leftist politics respectable for a time. But as relations between the United States and the Soviet Union soured and as Republicans blamed Democrats for enabling Soviet aggression in Eastern Europe, the political sands shifted. They shifted further after Truman became president following Roosevelt's death and positioned himself to the right of his predecessor. By the end of 1946, ICCASP responded by launching a new organization with the leftist Congress of Industrial Organizations (CIO). Soon that group had morphed into the Progressive Party, which, in 1948, unsuccessfully ran Henry Wallace as its presidential candidate in a campaign marked by redbaiting.[83]

After that loss, Weinstein joined with others in organizing the March 1949 Cultural and Scientific Conference for World Peace at the Waldorf-Astoria Hotel. Meaning to foster world peace and peaceful coexistence between the United States and the Soviet Union, the organizers succeeded in getting 600 people to sponsor the Waldorf conference. Lillian Hellman, Arthur Miller, Leonard Bernstein, and many more famous people were involved. The scripted quality of the affair and the counterconference its opponents staged earned it negative coverage.[84] In its wake, anticommunist liberals formed the American Committee for Cultural Freedom, and the CIA funded the International Congress for Cultural Freedom and *Encounter* magazine. Weinstein's participation in the Waldorf conference amplified the FBI's interest in her, and in the summer of 1950, an ex-CP member claimed she was a party member. In December, she and her three daughters left the United States and resettled in Paris to wait out the Red Scare.

Weinstein had succeeded in getting favorable publicity for the left through the deployment of famous artists, writers, and scientists. With the Cold War intensifying, some of those people now faced the consequences. When the scientist Robert Oppenheimer, who had agreed to serve in a titular fashion as the chair of the ICCASP committee on nuclear power, tried to resign because of its pro-Soviet tilt, Weinstein resisted, claiming that the committee's position in no way signaled a departure from that of Roosevelt. She suggested that since he was often in New York City, perhaps a time could be found for Oppenheimer to meet in person with the committee. Oppenheimer resigned from the ICCASP, but the committee kept using the same letterhead, one that included his name, which was embarrassing. Oppenheimer had many bigger worries, but his association with ICCASP was yet another damning bit of evidence against him.[85] His case suggests that Weinstein's strategy of tying famous people to causes, while great for these causes, could damage people. Still, there's no denying her skill at fighting the powers that be, at least until 1949.

After living in Paris among other leftist ex-pats and learning the ropes of moviemaking, she moved to England, where she became a television producer of several historical costume adventure shows. In the fall of 1955, her most popular show, *The Adventures of Robin Hood*, debuted in Canada, England, and America. Most of the screenwriters whom she hired were blacklisted Americans, and in need of the work she made a point of providing. Although this never caused serious problems, it attracted the attention of at least one employee at a British spy agency, who noted that Weinstein's company, Sapphire Films, was a "nest for 'un-Americans'/or Communist Americans."[86] Doubtless, making a TV series about a bandit who stole from the rich to give to the poor, thereby encouraging viewers to "identify with outlaws," offered these blacklisted leftists a sweet revenge. Perhaps it also lodged somewhere in the brains and the hearts of baby boomers. One of its writers, Ring Lardner Jr., wondered if the show may have helped in "setting the stage for the 1960s, by subverting a whole new generation of young Americans." Indeed, *Robin Hood* may have been Weinstein's most successful counter-event of all.[87]

By 1964, bad choices—in marriage and in work—led to the end of Weinstein's production company, Sapphire Films, and her return to America. By 1968, she was putting on rallies again at Madison Square Garden, this time for the antiwar candidate Eugene McCarthy, and featuring some of the same celebrities—Leonard Bernstein, for one—whom she had linked to earlier causes.

Party Planning

Hannah Weinstein's daughters, at least two of whom were politically involved, acted as a bridge to activists such as Kenner. As for Kenner, he felt suspended between generations, which likely made it easier for him to begin "working Park Avenue," as he later put it.[88] Further enabling this move was his frustration with Weatherman, which focused so intently on members' own revolutionary transformation, making themselves the center of the revolutionary project. Take the group's obsession with "smashing monogamy"—to him it seemed both beside the point and wrongheaded.

Still, when Kenner had his first meeting with Hannah Weinstein and her collaborators, it marked a real shift for him. "It was 1969, and my former friends from Columbia University were now Weathermen, planning on blowing things up," he recalled, "and here I was with these very elegant ladies." In contrast to younger white radicals, Weinstein and her collaborators were not tripped up by the seeming contradiction of living well, even being rich, and working for radical change. Consider Lillian Hellman, who was highly critical of capitalism but never stopped enjoying the benefits it bestowed on her. Hellman was not present at that first meeting, but the women who were there left Kenner feeling rather stunned.[89]

It was a stylish group at that first meeting that included Iris Moore, the wife of defendant Dhoruba bin Wahad (Richard Moore), the actress Judith Braun Bernstein, wife of the blacklisted screenwriter Walter Bernstein, and Gail Lumet, the daughter of the singer Lena Horne and the wife of film director

Sidney Lumet. At first, Kenner assumed that the glamorous Moore was either the wife of a movie star or one herself. How Weinstein chose that group is unclear, although she knew Walter Bernstein (no relationship to Leonard) because he had written for her while he was blacklisted. (Decades later, he recalled that his name had appeared in the anticommunist tract *Red Channels*, right after Leonard's.)[90] The heavy concentration of wives is striking and characterized the benefit at the Bernsteins, too. Either the men were too busy to participate, or Weinstein calculated that any conservative counterattacks that might ensue would prove less damaging to wives than to husbands.[91]

Weinstein came to the meeting with a battle plan. Even more than raising money, the point of the benefits, she said, was to persuade influential people, the "opinion-makers," that the repression of the Panthers was vitally important. "The first thing we're gonna do since Gail Lumet is here, we're gonna have a little party at Gail's," Weinstein said. "We're gonna have some Panthers speak." Key to Weinstein's plan was to get Felicia Bernstein, who was in her friendship circle, to attend the party. "The goal of this party is very simply just to get Felicia Bernstein . . . to agree to have another party."[92]

Why did Weinstein believe that they needed Felicia Bernstein to host a party? She was married to classical music's only true star, and he commanded tremendous respect as a composer, conductor, and teacher. Musically, he went everywhere, an "amalgam of high-brow, low-brow and every brow." His televised Young People's Concerts made him a familiar figure to many Americans. Handsome, magnetic, and verbally agile, Bernstein was also a musical genius. According to one of their friends, there was a lot of cachet around the Bernsteins. "Everyone wanted to be with them."[93]

Overshadowed by her husband, Felicia Montealegre Bernstein was not well known outside of New York, but she was beloved by those who knew her. "I always thought she should have been a queen," said the civil rights lawyer and journalist Roger Wilkins. "Delicate, intelligent and beautiful" was how he described her.[94] To Weinstein, the Bernsteins had the cultural capital that would lead opinion makers, people like the *New York Times* reporter Tom Wicker, to attend.[95] Wicker and Leonard Bernstein did not know this, but they shared something: Richard Nixon's hate. Each man would land on Nixon's Enemies List of 10.[96]

With the recent murders of Hampton and Clark, this seemed the time to reframe the Panthers, particularly the Panther 21, and in a way that emphasized the government's denial of their civil liberties. The Panthers' defense fund had already seen an enormous uptick in donations, more than had been made after the shackling and gagging of Seale. Money was pouring into the defense committee's office. Between November 1969 and January 1970, donations came to at least $100,000. Again, what drove those donations were the murders of Hampton and Clark, not the plight of the Panther 21. However, at first the beneficiaries were the 13 arrested New York Panthers and their lawyers—and not those Panthers who had been arrested elsewhere. Kenner's original arrangement with Lefcourt was to raise money for the Panthers sitting in jails throughout New York.[97]

So, the parties began, with John Simon, the editor at Random House who brought out Bobby Seale's 1968 memoir, *Seize the Time*, hosting the first. Then there was the one at the home of Gail Lumet. The Panther defense committee pulled out all the stops for the gathering at the Lumets' home, going so far as to fly in from Los Angeles the Black Panther Party's charismatic Minister of Education, Ray "Masai" Hewitt. Hewitt explained the Panthers' ideology to the assembled. Masai was a hit that day. But the speaker who moved Felicia Bernstein was Marva Berry, the wife of Panther Lee Berry, the Vietnam veteran who suffered from epilepsy. Berry was being treated at a VA hospital on April 2, 1969, the day the police carried out their arrests. He wasn't spared. The police arrested him there and threw him into solitary confinement in the Tombs, without his medicine or proper medical attention. Felicia Bernstein was so upset about Berry that she added her name to the sign-up sheet for hosting a benefit.

Weinstein succeeded in snagging Felicia Bernstein as a host, but it seems that they may have had somewhat different ideas about how this would play out. For one, Weinstein wanted publicity, which meant attracting the press, whereas the host believed she was having a closed-door affair, with only a select few journalists invited.[98] Moreover, Weinstein and Kenner believed in the Panthers, whereas Felicia and Leonard Bernstein were more ambivalent, claiming they were supporting the Panthers' civil liberties. When people in and around the CP were red-baited, others supported them under the banner of civil liberties, and so it was with the Panthers. In fact, in mid-December 1969, Congressman Edward I. Koch made this distinction when speaking to an antiwar rally. "I don't agree with the goals or the methods of the Black Panthers, but civil liberties transcend the issue of the Panthers' goals."[99]

Felicia Bernstein understood how best to frame the benefit, but did she grasp the risks posed by the press? Did she understand the political crossfire that her benefit might provoke among New York City's quarrelsome intellectuals? Probably not. Always a hothouse of contention, by 1970, the world of intellectuals there was more riven than ever, particularly when race was concerned.

If some believed that the repression of the Panthers and the Chicago 8 proved that America was on the road to fascism, others maintained that the real problem was the anti-Americanism and revolutionary enthusiasms of these groups. The decision to invite Robert Silver, the editor of *The New York Review of Books*, who published some of the more apocalyptic New Left writing, signaled to some that the Bernsteins were supporting the Panthers, not just their civil liberties. Dubbed by some the *New York Review of Each Other's Books* because of its ingrown culture, it already had run afoul of many, including some leftists, by putting on its cover a how-to diagram of a Molotov cocktail in August 1967.[100] Silver had okayed the cover, which accompanied a piece by Tom Hayden about the recent uprising in Newark, New Jersey. James Wolcott pointed out that the cover was obviously "a symbolic gesture and not an actual incitement—no one expected assistant professors of English to start hurling firebombs at the Good Humor truck." Nevertheless, it helped to further fracture New York's intellectual scene.[101]

It wasn't just political pundits such as Norman Podhoretz at *Commentary* who, as they tracked ever rightward, were critical of their former allies at *The New York Review*. Veteran leftist Michael Harrington thought the New Left's descent into militance amounted to nothing more than "pseudo-radicalism." Even more antagonistic was Harrington's friend, the veteran leftist Irving Howe. In this period, he assailed the *Review*'s support of young militants, particularly their faith in a coming apocalypse (the-worse-the-better syndrome) that a vanguard party could then exploit, thereby igniting the revolution! Howe, like Harrington and their one-time Trotskyist comrade Bayard Rustin, embraced a more modest goal: working through coalitions to expand the welfare state. Howe believed Silver and others at the *Review* seemed to just rush after the latest thing.[102]

Moreover, Bernstein's benefit for the Panthers would likely not succeed in sidestepping the growing rift between white Jewish liberals, on the one hand, and advocates of Black Power, on the other. From 1967's Six-Day War (the third of the Arab-Israeli wars), 1968's Ocean Hill-Brownsville dispute about community control of the public schools in Brooklyn, to affirmative action, the two groups found themselves increasingly at odds. The result was that the coalition of Jewish progressives and Black radicals that had done so much to power the civil rights movement was unraveling. 1970 certainly was a different world from 1963 when a core group of Jews and Blacks were united in militance in SNCC. As for the Panthers, they were not monolithically anti-Semitic as some Black Power groups were. Like SNCC in its early years, the Panthers sometimes told the story of Black Americans using the analogy to Jews' experience in Nazi Germany. Even the Panthers' early fondness for the beret was inspired by the French resistance. Finally, the Panthers' closest white allies were Jewish. Still, it was not difficult to come across outrageous examples of anti-Semitism in the pages of the *Black Panther*

Even had Felicia Bernstein fully grasped the difficulty of the undertaking, she might have gone ahead. Certainly, something that she shared with her husband was a desire to be on the right side of history. "Who are we anyway," one imagines Felicia Bernstein asking her husband, "if we can't even host a benefit?"

TEN

The Great Commotion

On the evening of the benefit, January 14, 1970, there were no intimations of any trouble. Felicia Bernstein, looking elegant in an understated black dress, greeted guests in the hallway of their duplex. Members of the Panther 21's legal and fundraising teams were already there: Hannah Weinstein and her daughter Lisa, Martin Kenner, as well as lawyers Gerald Lefcourt, Sanford M. Katz, William Crain, and Leon Quat. They were joined by a handful of Panthers and their kin, including the Party's Field Marshal Don Cox, local Panther Henry Mitchell, and two women, Marva Kirton Berry, who was married to defendant Lee Berry, and Iris Moore, the wife of Richard Moore, who was then going by the name Dhoruba bin-Wahad.

There was a lot of buzz around the Bernsteins, which is doubtless why so many people turned out for the benefit.[1] Still, accounts of the fundraiser frequently overstate the celebrity wattage on display that evening. It seems that Jason Roberts, Lauren Bacall, Lillian Hellman, Sidney Lumet, Richard Avedon, Jerome Robbins, Mike Nichols, Aaron Copeland, Larry Rivers, Steven Sondheim, and Mrs. Vincent Astor did not attend. The *wives* of Richard Avedon, Sidney Lumet, Harry Belafonte, filmmaker Arthur Penn, and Walter Bernstein did show up, and so did several other wives, unaccompanied by their better-known husbands. One presumes that many husbands, seeing little advantage, and possibility quite a lot of harm in showing up, stayed away that night.[2]

The most recognizable celebrities were *Today Show* host Barbara Walters, film director Otto Preminger, opera star Leontyne Price, and the bandleader Peter Duchin, one of the few famous men to appear with his wife. However, many influential New Yorkers who were not household names did show up. They included *New York Review* editor Robert Silver; civil rights lawyer and journalist Roger Wilkins; composer and lyricist Burton Lane; Broadway lyricist Sheldon Harnick, who cowrote the songs for *Fiddler on the Roof*; the philanthropist, writer, and scenester Jean Stein; the playwright Peter Stone; gallerist Richard Feigen; and, as hoped, *New York Times* columnist Tom Wicker.[3]

First-time visitors were perhaps struck by the scale of the Bernsteins' 13-room penthouse. The living room was big enough to hold the composer's twin grand pianos and nearly everyone there that night, but it was a tight fit. The Bernsteins' penthouse was an imposing space, with tall windows set off by heavy ceiling-to-floor curtains, views of Central Park, and bookcases filled with not-for-show books, eye-catching flower arrangements, family photographs, and artwork.

The first hour of the fundraiser featured socializing—some of it rather stiff—as nearly 90 people, many of them strangers to each other, tried to behave as though what was happening was perfectly normal, as though Black Americans *without* money ever found themselves mingling with white Americans *with* money, and on something like equal footing.[4] No one tried harder than the benefit's host to put everyone, particularly the Panthers, at ease. Staff circulated among guests with cocktails and canapés on silver trays, and people did not hesitate to grab some food or take a drink.

Felicia Bernstein, whom Kenner described as "this unbelievably attractive and wonderful Chilean actress," organized the event to break down the divides separating her guests. You can see this in the famous photograph of the Bernsteins sitting together, with Don Cox standing beside them.[5] Look carefully and you will see that Felicia had discretely reached behind her husband to rest her hand on Cox's wrist. She could not be everywhere that evening, and it is fair to say that some interactions went better than others. For Cox the one encounter that stayed with him years later involved the pioneering African American opera star Leontyne Price. There he was, enjoying talking to Price when she spotted a photographer headed toward them. She fled to avoid being photographed with him.[6] Still, nothing went badly wrong.

The second half of the evening—the meeting part—was meant to feature the lawyers and Black Panther Party's representative, Don Cox. Felicia began by introducing Leon Quat, a middle-aged Old Left lawyer who specialized in real estate law, which he practiced from a Manhattan office. Quat, who functioned as a kind of emcee, tried to warm up the crowd with some jokes about Vice President Spiro Agnew.

Next up was 33-year-old Cox in a black turtleneck sweater and gray pants. "It was a curious evening to say the least," recalled Cox, whose mood that evening seemed to toggle between amusement and exasperation.[7] The Panther Field Marshal was a cool character, with an impressive glower. Cox, who had lived in San Francisco since 1953, was cosmopolitan. Before joining the Panthers, he was a part of an interracial crowd of artists and musicians that included the jazz saxophonist John Handy. He dated both Black and white women. Like most of his fellow Oakland Panthers, Cox was not a cultural nationalist for whom the problem was reducible to whites. His grandmother was white and white friends had been the ones who, at first, furthered his political education. Cox had been active in Congress for Racial Equality (CORE) in 1964 and 1965, but after the murder of Malcolm X in February 1965, he left CORE behind to become involved in a more militant group. While a part of this new group, Cox claimed to have carried out an action entirely on his own. Using a high-powered rifle, he shot and wounded a policeman. The incident made the headlines locally, but he was never identified as the sniper. By 1967, Cox threw in his lot with the fledgling Black Panther Party.[8]

By January 1970, Cox had been with the Panthers for two-and-a-half years. There was a lot about the Panthers, including their growing reliance on Stalin's teachings, that gave him pause. He kept his misgivings to himself because he could see that "only 'yes people' were kept at headquarters," and people who fell out of favor found themselves often denounced and expelled.[9] People at the benefit would never have known that he no longer believed in the Panthers as he once had.

Cox's emotional steadiness and his familiarity with Panther ideology made him a plausible choice to speak at Felicia Bernstein's benefit. He was also already in New York City, trying to reorganize the decimated Panther chapters there. However, Cox had very limited experience as a public speaker, and he was not charismatic. That evening his explanation of the Panthers' philosophy did not sound entirely coherent. One minute, he was coming out with standard-issue Marxist calls for the redistribution of wealth; the next, he sounded as if he would settle for full employment. Then, he claimed that the Panthers wanted what the people at the gathering had—that is, a "good life." Later that evening, he shifted gears again and declared that real change required violence of some sort. To be fair to Cox, in this period his toggling between reform and revolution typified Panthers who were part of the Oakland leadership.

Cox was followed by the Panther 21 lawyer Gerald Lefcourt, who was a recent convert to radicalism. Back in late August 1968, in his first appearance representing members of the Black Panther Party, Lefcourt began to grasp the racist nature of the justice system. It was there as the judge slapped the defendants with an exorbitantly high bail that Lefcourt learned about, "Panther Bail," which amounted to preventive detention. Just weeks later at another bail hearing for the Panthers, Lefcourt was with the famous left-wing lawyer William Kunstler at the Brooklyn Criminal Court. That day, the courtroom was unusually crowded, its seats filled with as many as 150 white men, many of whom were wearing large Hawaiian shirts, some with "George Wallace for President" buttons pinned to them. They were off-duty and out-of-uniform policemen, though neither lawyer yet knew that.

Faced with an overcrowded courtroom, the judge abruptly announced they would be moving to a larger room. As Lefcourt and Kunstler, following the judge's order, began to exit the room, they were set upon by these Hawaiian-shirt-clad cops who kicked and punched them, screamed "n****r lover" at them, and chanted "White tigers eat Black Panthers." Lefcourt found it "incredible to see such a thing in a courtroom."[10] The *New York Times* reporter David Bright Burnham was there that day, too, and captured the mayhem in a front-page, above-the-fold story. The violence spilled over into the hallway, where the cops, now using blackjacks hidden beneath their oversized shirts, bloodied a small group of Panthers and their white sympathizers.[11] The cops' lawlessness, which prefigured the notorious spring 1970 Hard Hat Riot, was a key moment in Lefcourt's radical transformation. Like many others committed to solidarity politics, Lefcourt was a believer in the righteousness of the revolution and in the Panthers' ability to lead it. "We were so wild then, such believers," he recalled, "and we had no cynicism."[12]

Lefcourt did not talk about revolution at the Bernsteins' duplex that night. Instead, he laid out the systemic injustice of America's justice system, particularly the unfairness of the state's case against the Panther 21. He described their prohibitively high bail, and he mocked the idea that any American courtroom would provide Panthers with a jury of their peers. The government's vicious repression of the Black Panther Party proved, he argued, that America was quite possibly on the road to fascism, following some 40 years later in the footsteps of Germany.

There were no fireworks. No one seems to have objected to the Nazi analogy, or to anything. But then the Maestro, who had earlier slipped in, made his presence felt. According to both Kenner and Curtis, no one expected he would be there, and he showed up late, just before the talks.[13] Among his friends and associates, Leonard Bernstein had a well-deserved reputation for showboating. As a conductor, he was tasked with changing the temperature of every hall he was working. The problem was that he had grown accustomed to "changing the climate," no matter where he was.[14] Bernstein was wearing black watch pants, a double-breasted navy-blue jacket, and under that, a black turtleneck, topped off with a pendant hanging from a thin chain. By the time Bernstein arrived, lawyer Quat was already asking for donations. Quat's call for donations prompted a guest to ask about the Panthers' community service projects. In answering, Cox noted that the Panthers sometimes found it difficult locating sympathetic church leaders willing to donate space to the party's Breakfast for School Children Program.

Cox's admission of the Panthers' often tense relationship with Black ministers was all that Leonard Bernstein needed. He pounced on Cox. Suddenly, he was demanding that Cox explain why Black ministers would be wary of the Panthers. This prompted a larger question from the conductor: What was the relationship between the Panthers and the civil rights establishment and, for that matter, the larger Black community? How popular was the party among Black Americans, Bernstein asked? A cascade of questions, courtesy of the Maestro.

Cox tried to respond, but Leonard Bernstein was "on," revved up from that afternoon's rehearsals of Beethoven's opera *Fidelio*, which he was due to conduct at the Metropolitan Opera.[15] Unwilling or unable to shake his inner conductor, Bernstein was incorrigible. His friends had come to expect such behavior. Ned Rorem admitted that he could be "socially exasperating." Frank Stanton was traveling that night, but his wife, Domna Stanton, went to the fundraiser and found Bernstein's interaction with Don Cox embarrassing. But then, "Lenny was always slightly embarrassing," she says. "What I mean by that is that he was a very self-dramatizing man. He had to dominate a room."[16] Kenner only knew Leonard Bernstein from his Young People's Concerts, which he had loved. Seeing him take over the room that night left him and his fellow organizers feeling bad for his wife. Kenner believed she was "ashamed of her husband."[17] Jamie Bernstein was not there, but she was familiar with her father's knack for making himself the center of attention. Faced with her husband at such "cringe-worthy" moments, Felicia Bernstein was known to mutter under her breath, "Tierra, trágame." "Earth, swallow me" was probably about right.[18]

Accounts of that evening often present it as a case of the Panthers alternately guilt-tripping and terrorizing the Bernsteins and their guests. They mau-maued, and the guests, most of whom were white liberals, masochistically kowtowed. The night featured some noteworthy moments, as when Barbara Walters confessed her fear that a Black revolution led by the Panthers would be a death knell for rich white people like herself. Marva Berry assured Walters it wouldn't. Indeed, *Washington Post* reporter Karl Meyer discerned no such mau-mauing or kowtowing. What he witnessed that evening was an "evident wariness about a movement that has violent overtones."[19] The film director Otto Preminger, for example, challenged Cox's indictment of America as the most oppressive country in the world. Then he began grilling Cox about Israel. Preminger was not someone who backed down. He had helped to shatter the Hollywood blacklist by openly hiring the blacklisted writer Dalton Trumbo to write *Exodus* in 1960.[20] Wolfe noted that he was going toe to toe with Cox, but Wolfe was more interested in mocking Preminger's heavily accented English. Tom Wolfe was intent on indicting guilt-ridden white liberals, but his own detailed account of the meeting suggests that the person most guilty of badgering was not Don Cox, but Leonard Bernstein, with Preminger a close second.

The Maestro would not shut up, as he interrogated Cox, particularly about the Panthers' advocacy of violence. Wasn't it true that the group had threatened their critics in the civil rights movement, including Bayard Rustin, the man behind 1963's famous March on Washington? He claimed that Rustin, who had been invited to the benefit, stayed away because the Panthers had threatened him. He attacked the Panthers' strategy as incoherent, a charge that Rustin himself had made in the pages of that week's *Amsterdam News*, New York City's Black newspaper.[21] Leonard Bernstein later claimed that his inquisition of Cox was meant to be deliberately provocative to "achieve clarity in the room."[22]

Bernstein often took on the role of the teacher, even in conversations. On more than one occasion he described himself as a "closet rabbi."[23] His intention that night, he later said, was that Cox, in answering his fusillade of questions, would reveal what he called the Panthers' "Marxist or Maoist or anti-Israeli position so that those in attendance could then rebut his position."

These were not the words of a man engaged in kowtowing.[24] In fact, it suggests that he was operating at cross-purposes to the defense committee that had organized the benefit.

Felicia Bernstein had invited people to hear from the Panthers and their lawyers, not from her husband, whose plan for exposing the Panthers as both hapless and dangerous was likely news to her. She offered an answer to her husband's insistent question about what Black people felt. "I'll tell you," she reportedly said, and then read from a *New Yorker* article that included a letter written by civil rights leader Roger Wilkins, the nephew of the National Association for the Advancement of Colored People (NAACP) leader Roy Wilkins. In his letter, the younger Wilkins, who was there, warned of more violence if America did not take meaningful action to fight racism. As soon as she finished, her husband resumed talking, although in a more psychological register. Bernstein's friend Ned Rorem once said the composer had a penchant for "simultaneously focusing on his navel and on the universe," and the assembled witnessed it that evening.[25] Maestro shared his revelation: Everyone in the room suffered from feeling unwanted. Leonard Bernstein managed to steer a discussion of systemic racism to a monologue about the universality of rejection.

What fireworks there had been, and there were some, had not dampened anyone's spirits. Cox went off to have dinner with Preminger, who, by evening's end, claimed that as a refugee he identified with the Panthers. At the end of the meeting, the two men hugged each other.[26] Cox thought the meeting had gone well, and not just because the Panthers' defense committee had netted nearly $10,000. He believed that his remarks that evening might have led some people to question the fairness of the American judicial system. For his part, Lefcourt likely felt lucky to have raised a decent sum and to have dodged all those bullets about anti-Semitism, Black preachers, and Bayard Rustin.

Marva Kirton Berry, married to the epileptic defendant whose situation so upset Felicia Bernstein, felt it was a good thing that people were talking to one another. She found it "a very welcoming event."[27] However, the benefit also deepened her dismay about America, a country where "one segment of the population has so much while others don't have water and heat." Iris Moore agreed that it had gone well, but she was struck by how ignorant most of the guests were about the case. "It's like nobody's heard of us."[28]

The *New York Times*' Coverage of the Bernstein Benefit

After their guests had finally departed at 10 p.m., the Bernsteins escaped their apartment for a "solitary meal at the Chinese restaurant down the block."[29] On their return they may have picked up the 10:30 edition of the *New York Times*. If they did, they would have felt relieved because that edition's account of the benefit was about as positive as one could hope for from the *Times*' society page editor Charlotte Curtis. Leonard probably thought he had managed to support the Panthers' civil liberties while distancing himself from their aims or methods. If Felicia was irritated with her husband for hijacking her event, there is no record of it. Their daughter Jamie reports seeing her parents later that night and noticed that her mother was uncharacteristically sitting in her father's lap. They seemed, she wrote, "united, aligned, purposeful, loving."[30] Likely they went to bed thinking that they had struck a blow for justice at an especially dire moment.

If the point of the Bernsteins' benefit was ending the invisibility of the Panther 21, it was a huge success. Not incidentally, the nearly $10,000 raised that night would help to meet the state's exorbitant bail demands, and, the host hoped, help to meet the survival needs of the families of the jailed Panthers.[31] That night the fundraiser seemed like a success. Domna Stanton, a Columbia University graduate student just embarking on a long and successful academic career, left the party that night and "never thought there would be a backlash."[32]

So how did the benefit come to be known as "the social disaster of the century" or worse?[33] Just as Felicia Bernstein apparently feared, the press played an outsized role in creating this legend. It wasn't as though the journalists reporting on the fundraiser disguised themselves. Tom Wolfe wore an uncharacteristically sober gray suit, but he spent his time there scribbling away in his notebook, which now resides—in an undecipherable variant of Gregg shorthand—in his archive. Charlotte Curtis of the *New York Times* was photographed taking notes, and not surreptitiously, at the benefit. Roger Wilkins did not know who she was, but he saw a tiny woman with a notebook perk up when a guest said something stupid. Wilkins heard someone nearby mutter, "Uh-oh, he's in trouble. That's Charlotte Curtis."[34]

Why didn't anyone ask the working reporters to leave? Wolfe speculated the organizers simply assumed that the journalists and everyone else there were sympathetic to the Movement. He was likely right. Hannah Weinstein and Martin Kenner may have also figured that any publicity was bound to help. That may be why Barbara Walters was invited. Perhaps they hoped that they could win over this most mainstream of reporters, who might then use her platform, the *Today Show*, to publicize the case. According to Wolfe, Felicia Bernstein greeted him warmly when he arrived. She also welcomed a man who turned up without an invitation but with his cameras and umbrella light in tow. Steve Salmieri told her he was the photographer, and she ushered him right in and offered him a drink. In fact, Salmieri only showed up because Wolfe crept into a room and phoned him during the benefit and told him to head right over. It was Salmieri who took the famous shot of the Bernsteins with Don Cox. He later recalled that when he came into the room where the three of them were talking, they seemed "like old friends happily discussing what a breakthrough the event was whilst also planning for their next event."[35]

Although reports of the benefit appeared in the *New York Post* and the *Daily News*, Charlotte Curtis insisted that those papers' stories were based on her reporting in the *Times*. In any case, Doug Ireland, of the still-liberal *New York Post*, took a cynical left-wing view of the fundraiser. It was too great a paradox, he claimed, that Cox was trying to persuade the city's "beautiful and bejeweled capitalist elite to break out their checkbooks" when the Panthers were "dedicated to the elimination of the very system that provided the cocktails and canapés last night."[36] It is very unlikely that either the Bernsteins or the organizers cared very much about the *Post*'s coverage. They cared about what the *New York Times* had to say, and they probably hoped that Tom Wicker would devote a column to it.

But Wicker never wrote about the evening, so they had to content themselves with Charlotte Curtis's article.[37] Curtis began by noting Felicia Bernstein's impressive history of raising money for a variety of respectable causes, perhaps to underscore the edginess of this benefit. She quoted Gail Lumet, who motioned to the eclectic crowd and said, "This isn't exactly your regular charity ball set." Curtis reported that the event's host was especially keen on getting the facts out about the inhumane treatment of the Panthers. But Curtis offered few facts, nor did she report on what the speakers said. She did quote the "rich wife" of the bandleader Peter Duchin, who told Curtis of her excitement about meeting a Panther, a first for her, she said. Still, Curtis, whose original account ran just hours after the event, was more generous than she often was.

Image 10.1 Black Panther Party Field Marshal Don Cox with Felicia and Leonard Bernstein at the Panther 21 benefit, January 14, 1970. "They seemed like old friends," recalled the photographer Stephen Salmieri of Cox and the Bernsteins.
Photo: Stephen Salmieri

Typically, Curtis's article would have run, unchanged, in the morning edition of the *Times,* too. However, the article that ran in the January 15 edition bore little resemblance to Curtis's first take. After filing her initial copy, Curtis wrote a much more substantial article, "The Black Panther Philosophy Debated at the Bernsteins," which took a mean-spirited swipe at the Bernsteins and their guests.[38] Although Curtis's story appeared on page 48 of the *Times,* it was front-page news in much of the world because it went out on the *Times'* international wire, perhaps because Bernstein's celebrity was global. In the days after the benefit, this would be the story people remembered. It established the template for all that followed.

In her second version, Curtis focused laser-like on Leonard Bernstein and his often-testy exchanges with Don Cox, noting, "there were even moments when both men were not talking at the same time." Curtis's nimble edit of their dialogue made the conductor look like a suck-up, as she focused on those moments when he appeared to agree with, or kowtow to Cox. According to Curtis, when Cox ventured that if "business won't give us full employment," Black people would have to "take the means of production and put them into the hands of the people," Bernstein replied, "I dig absolutely." But Curtis reportedly edited a key moment of this exchange. Bernstein's use of hip jargon followed Cox having first asked him, "You dig?" Picking up on someone else's language and throwing it back at them was something he habitually did. But the way Curtis told the story, he came off "like a pathetic, middle-aged guy trying to act groovy."[39]

The Maestro was in Curtis's crosshairs that evening, but she had others in her sights as well. She gave ample space to an awkward exchange between a local Panther, Henry Mitchell, and Cynthia Phipps. Young and pretty, Phipps was a member of one of the city's most prominent families, which, as Curtis pointed out, Mitchell had no way of knowing. At some point in their conversation, he complained to her about the Federal Bureau of Investigation (FBI)'s bugging of the Panthers' phone. Mitchell joked that the FBI would probably pay their phone bill to ensure that they'd know what the Panthers were talking about. "Sometimes," Mitchell added, "we have to wait six or seven minutes for a dial tone" because of the tap. Phipps replied, "I have the same problem. They really ought to do something about it." The effort of the rich to find common ground with the oppressed, Curtis seemed to be saying, amounted to a charade, an artificial leveling of an exceedingly slanted playing field.

Curtis ended her piece with one final jab, this one about the cheapness of one of the wealthiest guests, Mrs. August Heckscher, wife of New York City's powerful administrator of parks, recreation, and cultural affairs. Many New Yorkers had at least some vague awareness of her family because a Central Park playground as well as a parkway, a museum, and a state park on Long Island bore the Heckscher name. After quoting Mrs. Heckscher on the importance of supporting justice—a value she claimed to have developed growing up in France during the years of Nazism's ascent—Curtis noted, in her usual deadpan style, the underwhelming amount of Mrs. Heckscher's donation: $100. Yet what Curtis did not mention was that on the very day of the Panthers' arrest in April 1969, it was none other than Mr. August Heckscher who told the press he was standing by Robert Collier, one of the 21. It was a gutsy move on his part to defend Collier, whom he emphasized had been recommended by both the police and religious leaders for a post within his department.[40]

Martin Kenner recalled feeling "punched in the stomach" as he read Curtis's piece the next morning. "It couldn't have been more devastating." Kenner regarded her as a "committed anti-racist." Curtis and a *Times* colleague had donated a mimeograph to the defense committee, whose meetings she attended. He remembers her showing up to meetings of the Panther defense committee impeccably dressed, wearing white gloves, and with her mother in tow. She may not have dressed like the Panthers and their young white allies, but he felt her support was genuine. How could Curtis, who had helped Kenner "work Park Avenue," using her connections to convince people to come to these benefits, have written such a damning piece?[41]

Making matters worse was the decision of the *Times* editorial board to take a stand against the benefit. The cumulative effect of her story and the appearance the very next day of the *Times* editorial attacking the fundraiser was a bruising one-two punch. Cleverly entitled "False Note on Black Panthers," the editorial denounced the fundraiser as "elegant slumming that degrades patrons and patronized alike." As for the Black Panther Party, the *Times* disparaged its "confusion of Mao-Marxist ideology and Fascist para-militarism." The editorial invoked the tried-and-true trope of "responsible black leadership," which it claimed, incorrectly, opposed the Panthers. The *Times* pulled out all the stops, claiming the benefit "mocked the memory of Martin Luther King, Jr." This was the same paper that in April 1967 blasted Dr. King when he came out against the War in Vietnam.[42]

So why did Curtis file the second story? Had one of her bosses suggested a rewrite? *Times* editors read the late-night edition and sometimes mandated changes for the morning edition. David Bright Burnham, the *Times* reporter who broke the Serpico story of police corruption, says that a revision of this sort, while not unheard of, was "pretty unusual."[43] Making this less likely was Curtis's status at the paper. She was a powerful insider whose stories could be "killed but never cut." She would soon be appointed editor of the op-ed page. Curtis had her critics at the *Times*, including those who believed she was too cozy with management. *Times* reporter Nan Robertson thought Curtis behaved like "the little woman of the Great Man."[44] She would have known that the *Times* management took a very dim view of the Black Panther Party.

Politically, Curtis's own views were to the left of those of her employers, and this sometimes came through in her coverage. For example, her article on the women's liberation demonstration at 1968's Miss America contest was respectful, unlike so much of the coverage, which was openly derisive. This was the first protest of the fledgling movement to gain the attention of the mainstream media, and Curtis spent the whole hot day on the boardwalk in Atlantic City with the demonstrators. She even bailed out several women who were arrested for disrupting the contest later that night. When feminist Robin Morgan called to thank her, Curtis asked that it be kept secret. If it became known that she had provided their bail, it could cause problems for her with the "dreary grey guys running the *Times*," as she put it.[45]

Curtis may have done the *Times*' bidding, but she was a journalist who prioritized getting the story "right," no matter the damage.[46] Several months later, on the *David Susskind Show*, she said that she believed it was her job to tell readers what had happened "as coldly, as objectively, and as dispassionately as possible."[47] What she did not say was that she also enjoyed mocking the rich. One additional reason that her article may have seemed "merciless," as Susskind put it, was that she felt confronted at the Bernstein party by a fake version of her own allyship. Allies turning on other allies as deficient was already a recognizable dynamic, and one that became more so after the publication of Wolfe's "Radical Chic" essay. One other possibility is that Curtis and Wolfe, who were seen together at the Bernsteins, may have spoken to each other later that night. Wolfe may have read Curtis's tame first take in that evening's paper, or she may have shared it with him. Perhaps Wolfe chided her for not going after what he regarded as the phoniness of the event. Maybe their conversation left her feeling she hadn't been tough enough.[48]

What we do know is that almost as soon as her second article appeared Curtis regretted having written it. The *Times* editorial made her second piece land differently. In that same appearance on the *Susskind Show*, she said she "violently disagreed" with it.[49] In the immediate aftermath of the *Times*' pillorying of the Bernsteins, she did her best to undo the damage. This was typical of Curtis, who "was always trying to figure out ways of bending things to her will."[50] She spoke at some length to Felicia Bernstein and 10 days after the benefit, the *Times* printed Curtis's corrective, "The Bernsteins' Party for Black Panther Legal Defense Stirs Talk and More Parties." This piece indirectly took issue with the *Times* editorial. Curtis claimed that few people at the benefit truly belonged to the "jet set."[51] Moreover, she said, no one associated with the fundraiser was backing down. Despite the backlash, she claimed that planning in New York was underway for nearly a dozen parties, with more meetings and fundraisers in the works. In truth, there were no more such parties, at least with that set. Curtis and the *Times* had managed to kill what momentum the defense committee built on Park Avenue.[52]

Of all the articles Curtis penned in her long career, it was her takedown of the Bernstein fundraiser that seems to have most troubled her. She confided to her mother that she regretted all the grief that it caused the Bernsteins, and she lamented the *Times*' antagonism toward the Panthers. Six years later Curtis admitted that in bringing together people from vastly different worlds, Felicia Bernstein "should have been a heroine."[53] Of course, the fact that she felt instead like a fool was largely the doing of Curtis and the *Times*. Pained by the paper's coverage, Felicia wrote a letter to the editor, objecting to the "frivolous way in which [the benefit] was reported as a 'fashionable event.'" It was "unworthy of the *Times*," she argued, "and offensive to all people who are committed to humanitarian principles of justice." The *Times* sat on her letter for five long days before publishing it, a move that diminished whatever impact it might have had.[54]

The Blowback from the Benefit

The *New York Times*' hostility to the Panthers was typical of the mainstream media. The management of the *Washington Post* also took a dim view of the Panthers and the benefit. Journalist Karl Meyer of the *Post* filed a detailed and sympathetic article about the Panther 21 and Felicia Bernstein's benefit, which he had attended. As he explained in a letter to the Bernsteins, his piece never saw the light of day, presumably because it was too sympathetic to the Panthers and the Bernsteins. His thoughtful piece was entirely rewritten by his editors, who claimed, disingenuously, he thought, that time constraints prevented them from consulting him about their cuts. "My editors anticipated my indignation [about their bowdlerizing] by removing my name from a piece cut without any consultation from me."[55]

Time magazine, which weighed in with an upbeat appraisal of the benefit, was the most notable outlier. But that was largely attributable to Kenner and Cox who set up a meeting with an editor there. The Bernsteins and their guests "came not to gabble, not to glitter," said *Time*, "but to listen." The magazine noted that Otto Preminger not only defended the benefit but also criticized the *New York Times* as "very old-fashioned." Preminger emphasized that the reporter could quote him.[56] *Newsweek*, in this period the most reliably liberal newsmagazine, provided even-handed treatment as well.[57] Longtime left-leaning journalist James Weschler offered the most discerning coverage in his *New York Post* column. Weschler cautioned against romanticizing the Panthers, but he also offered support for the Bernsteins. "If that party on Park Av. gave [some of] the Panthers a sense that we are not all participants in a massive search-and-destroy operation, it was not a frivolous exercise, regardless of who said what to whom." Weschler closed by noting, dryly, that the benefit might just have had "some connection with the Bill of Rights."[58]

The Bernsteins received supportive letters from Coretta Scott King, Gloria Steinem, and Jacqueline Onassis. Steinem mentioned that she and others intended to contact established civil rights leaders known to be privately supportive of the Panthers to see if they might be persuaded to write a letter rebutting the *Times* editorial. But from the civil rights establishment the only person offering public support was Andrew Young, SCLC's executive vice president. Roger Wilkins and Jean Stein, who had been at the benefit, prevailed upon Young to do something. He wrote a letter to the Overseas Press Club in which he assailed the government's persecution of the Panther 21, who "faced 150 years in prison for crimes that allegedly took place only in their heads." He made a point of supporting those people who had gone out on a limb to stand up for the Panthers' civil liberties.[59]

But for the most part, the Bernsteins had to face the attacks alone. Jamie Bernstein remembers her parents becoming the laughingstock of New York. In the days after the *Times* blasted their "elegant slumming," her father wrote several drafts of an intemperate press release. He got in a dig at Charlotte Curtis, complaining that the *Times* had assigned the editor of the "woman's page," whose expertise was limited to flower arranging, fashion, and party-going, not politics. He emphasized that no one at the meeting supported the anti-Zionist Panthers; they supported Americans' civil liberties. As for their alleged jet-set social life, he improbably claimed that it had been years since they had thrown a party and a very rare occasion when they attended one. A less defensive version appeared in the *Jewish Ledger*, Connecticut's only Jewish newspaper. The *New York Post* carried an article about Bernstein's response.[60]

But by the time the press covered Bernstein's response, Rabbi Meir Kahane, national chairman of the Zionist organization, the Jewish Defense League (JDL), had gone on the offensive. At a news conference a week after the benefit, Kahane blasted Bernstein for being part of the recent "trend in liberal and intellectual circles to lionize the Black Panthers," whom he considered vicious racists.[61] The attacks from other Jews pained him. In 1979, Bernstein and other prominent Jewish artists, writers, and scholars were to object to Israel's decision to expand settlements into the densely populated areas in the West Bank, but in 1970 Bernstein was solidly behind Israel.[62] The tensions between Jewish progressives and Black radicals dated back several years, but the FBI worked overtime to amplify them.[63]

The New York FBI office may have already been involved in the harassment of the Bernsteins by this juncture, but in February, J. Edgar Hoover formally authorized agents there to send letters to the Bernsteins' guests exposing the anti-Semitism of the Panther Party. The Bernsteins found themselves deluged by a flood of hate mail and by vicious and threatening telephone calls. At the same time, Hoover directed agents to comb the social columns for the names of benefit attendees, and open files on them ... those the agency wasn't already surveiling. The harassment did not let up. In October 1970, the JDL set up a noisy picket outside the Bernstein apartment building, which reportedly included FBI agents posing as JDL members. It was not until the mid-1980s that a lawsuit revealed that the FBI and the JDL had together staged the campaign of harassment and intimidation against the Bernsteins. The FBI also tried to plant stories in the press about Bernstein's homosexuality to "neutralize" him, but because he had no arrest record the effort failed.[64] Even so, he was firmly on Nixon's Enemies list. Bernstein told his longtime publicist Margaret Carson, "Between the C.I.A. and the F.B.I., I'm keeping at least a few people busy."[65]

Making matters worse for everyone associated with the benefit was the knowledge that one reporter had not yet weighed in. Even the gossip columnist for *Women's Wear Daily* considered Leonard Bernstein's worry about Wolfe's impending article newsworthy. "Lenny's in a state, waiting for the other shoe to drop."[66] Likely ratcheting up the Bernsteins' nervousness was their suspicion that certain friends were talking to Wolfe or his research assistant. Doubtless friends of theirs were also passing onto the Bernsteins what they knew about Wolfe's dirt-digging efforts. Domna Stanton recalls hearing from Barbara Goldsmith, a founding editor at *New York*. Goldsmith called to say she had read a draft of Wolfe's article in which he claimed Stanton was wearing a "cult necklace."[67] The necklace she wore read, "war is not healthy for children and other living things," which by 1970 had become an almost anodyne sentiment, at least among liberals.

In any case, Leonard Bernstein's long-scheduled travel plans meant that he escaped the crisis a month into it, leaving his wife to deal with the fallout. Part of the fallout for Felicia Bernstein was personal. In his public pronouncements, her husband was generally supportive, but privately he apparently believed that the benefit had been a mistake. Given his often-hostile questioning of Cox, he may have thought so the night of the benefit. With her husband gone, Felicia Bernstein turned to friends but felt little support. Exceptions included the couple Arthur Gold and Robert Fizdale, who wrote to offer their sympathies about the "Great Commotion."[68] Gail Lumet spoke to Wolfe's research assistant and told her that Felicia felt abandoned, as though "her friends have gone underground."[69] Lumet admitted she felt like backing away, too. Within the Bernstein family, Felicia Bernstein's decision to hold the benefit was controversial. Her brother-in-law Burton Bernstein, *The New Yorker* writer, was furious with her and refused to speak to her for months. How could she have not anticipated the harm this would cause Israel and Jewish people, he demanded? Their relationship reportedly never fully healed.[70]

Leonard Bernstein briefly complicated matters by appearing to backpedal. Cornered by journalists in England, he disassociated himself from the fundraiser and declared the Panthers a "bad lot." News of his apparent reversal traveled quickly. The very next day with the press hounding him, he denied that his views about the Panthers had shifted. His good friend and traveling companion, the "patriarch of arts in New York," Schuyler Chapin, emphasized that the Bernsteins were "absolutely unchanged in their views, despite the shooting gallery they've been in," Chapin added. "He is certainly not refuting anything he has done."[71]

Meanwhile, Kenner and Cox set up a meeting with Felicia Bernstein to apologize for the way that the fundraiser had blown up in her face. They met in her painting studio, where she described the hell that life had become, with the hate mail and threatening phone calls. Could they do anything to help, she asked them. They didn't know how they could. But given that it was the Panthers' antipathy to Israel and support for Al Fatah that was fueling much of the backlash, she may have hoped that the Panthers could reaffirm their opposition to anti-Semitism. This was not Kenner's last conversation with her.[72]

The Bernsteins felt the blowback more personally than anyone else. And their feeling of being besieged and unsupported continued through the year because of the publication of Tom Wolfe's "That Party at Lenny's" in *New York* magazine in June and its publication in book form (with another of Wolfe's essays) as "Radical Chic" that fall. We will delve into Wolfe's essay in the next chapter, but for now it is sufficient to say that the Bernsteins felt humiliated. Their friend John Gruen, who worked at *New York*, recalls both of them forcing the issue of loyalty, with Leonard threatening to end their friendship unless Gruen quit his job in protest.[73]

The collateral damage was substantial, beginning with the canceled benefits. Whether it was the Chicago 7 or the Panther 21 or any other case involving Movement people, an adequate defense cost money. None of the large legal defense agencies, including the American Civil Liberties Union (ACLU), could handle the Panther 21 case, because of the nature of the charges. That left the job of defense to those few, struggling private attorneys willing to take political cases. If wealthy progressives stopped offering financial support because of the heat they were taking, radicals would find it impossible to get a fair trial. In a lengthy press release, Aryeh Neier of the New York branch of the ACLU pointed out that the U.S. Attorney in New York was trying to force attorneys defending political dissidents to reveal the names of people who had contributed bail anonymously. It was a maneuver designed to ensure public attacks like those directed at the Bernsteins.[74]

Writing to the *New York Times*, Leon Quat emphasized just how costly trials can be, even when attorneys are serving without compensation. Engaging professional ballistics and electronic experts and interviewing witnesses were expensive. He pointed out that transcripts of testimony, which are essential, could run as much as $300 a day (nearly $3,000 in today's dollars). And then there was the cost of bail, often prohibitively high for political radicals. Quat's point was that for people without financial resources constitutional rights are meaningless unless those with money subsidize their defense. As with several other letters supportive of the Bernsteins, the *Times* chose not to print his letter to the editor.[75]

The benefit reverberated far beyond Manhattan. Daniel Patrick Moynihan, who served as presidential counselor to Richard Nixon in a cabinet-level position, made sure that his boss knew about the Bernsteins' "star-studded" benefit. In a controversial memo that advised Nixon to adopt a stance of "benign neglect" toward Black Americans, he singled out the benefit as proof that the country was paying too much attention to "extremist" groups such as the Panthers. Nixon was appalled by the benefit, and in a handwritten note on that memo described Bernstein as the embodiment of the "'the complete decadence of the American "upper class" intellectual elite.'"[76]

The event intensified the Nixon administration's interest in uncovering just who was funding the Movement. On March 2, 1970, less than two months after the Bernstein benefit, Nixon wrote to White House Chief of Staff, H. R. Haldeman to reiterate his support for reactivating the then-dormant Subversive Activities Control Board. Nixon wanted the board to investigate the donors funding the country's subversive groups. Two days later, Haldeman wrote to Egil Krogh about getting to the bottom of the matter. Krogh became one of the leaders of the secret "Plumbers" group that broke into the office of Daniel Ellsberg's psychiatrist, an act that established the precedent for the Watergate break-in that brought down Nixon.[77]

Don Cox believed that the outrage about the Bernsteins' benefit marked a turning point in the history of the Black Panther Party. Just as well-respected, influential people like the Bernsteins were beginning to shift their view of the Panthers, and at least support their rights as American citizens, the reaction from the authorities was "immediate and fierce."[78] There is a reason for this. It has become dogma on the left that power is consolidated through the targeting of the most oppressed. We all know that line, "First they came for . . ." followed by socialists, trade unionists, Jews, and then, you! It was Leon Quat who had said at the benefit, "fascism always begins by persecuting the least powerful and least popular movement."[79]

But hegemony requires the consent of the privileged, too. What the Bernstein benefit signaled in that volatile moment was that powerful and influential people were questioning the demonization of the Panthers. It was a remarkable change. In June 1971, left-wing journalist Murray Kempton wrote about the Panther 21 trial in the *New York Review of Books*. Kempton was in the courtroom day in and day out. After it was over, he wrote that the state's prosecution of the case was marked by a "fixed conviction that, while there might be somewhere an excuse for the Panthers, there could be no excuse for anyone who *liked* them." Kempton's criticism extended to the *New York Times*. "In all those two years, the only event that stirred the editorial pages of the *New York Times* to really *felt* indignation had been the support Mr. and Mrs. Leonard Bernstein had given the efforts to raise funds for the trial expenses of the New York Panthers."[80] Within just a few months it would become clear that it was Tom Wolfe's unmatched talent as a satirist, not the felt indignation of the *Times*, that caused the most damage to solidarity and allyship.

ELEVEN
Tom Wolfe

It was one thing for a newspaper as establishment as the *New York Times* to condemn Felicia Bernstein's benefit.[1] It was quite another matter for Tom Wolfe, whose public persona was decidedly antiestablishment, to go after it. Wolfe relished his reputation as one of the enfants terribles of the "new journalism." What could be more fun than taking a wrecking ball to old-school journalism with its stodgy insistence on objectivity and its fusty fidelity to facts? To hell with being like the newspaper reporters of old, those boring "clerks of fact."[2] Wolfe was also confounding the boundaries between high and low culture as he explored the hip and odd fringes of American society. In 1963, what caught his imagination were hot-rod designers; a few years later it was the psychedelic subculture of the novelist Ken Kesey and the Merry Pranksters. His prose had the same manic, souped-up quality found in so much pop art. Wolfe published in *Esquire*, *Rolling Stone*, and other magazines, but he was most identified with *New York* magazine, which was launched as the Sunday magazine of the New York *Herald Tribune*. His fellow journalists included people like Gloria Steinem who were integral to the city's left-liberal orbit. Wolfe's dandified look—he favored suits that were either modish or high-end Colonel Sanders—cemented his hip image. It was easy enough to imagine that Wolfe might be a Movement sympathizer.

Tom Wolfe and the Left

Wolfe bears some responsibility for this misrecognition. In contrast to new journalists such as Joan Didion, Hunter Thompson, or Seymour Krim, Wolfe typically revealed little about himself, including his political leanings. The problem, as his friend Thompson saw it, was that Wolfe was "too crusty to participate in his stories."³ Whatever the reason for his reticence, it's fair to say that his preference for cream-colored suits, which were evocative of the Southern plantation class, signaled more about Wolfe's Richmond, Virginia, roots than did much of what he wrote in those early years.⁴ Wolfe was the son of a professor of agronomy who also edited the *Southern Planter*, an influential agricultural journal. Watching his father edit the magazine was, Wolfe said, what awakened his interest in journalism.⁵

If Wolfe mostly kept his distance from the Movement, it was not because he was politically neutral or indifferent.⁶ As far back as the mid-fifties, when he was a graduate student in American Studies at Yale, Wolfe had an aversion to the left.⁷ Wolfe's dissertation focused on the communist front organization, the League of American Writers, which was active from the mid-thirties through the early forties.⁸ Many famous and "prestigeful" writers were members. Wolfe's aim in writing about the League was to show how communists succeeded in turning writers into a "manipulable mass." What made them join the League was not so much its ideological attraction as it was communists' "organizational devices," the most subtle of which was the organized cocktail party or cause party. There, hosts plied guests with food and liquor to achieve maximum malleability. For a time, he argued, the League functioned like a "literary agency of unprecedented proportions." In a prefiguring of Wolfe's fascination with status (he took to calling his journalistic beat the "American statusphere"⁹), he emphasized that it was writers' obsession with status that led them to join. Had history played out differently, had there been no Nazi–Soviet Pact, Wolfe argued that the League could have "established hegemony over the content of several media."¹⁰

The faculty members evaluating Wolfe's dissertation were somewhere between appalled and astonished by his chutzpah and incompetence. Wolfe claimed that his professors objected to his anticommunism, but they agreed with him that the writers in question had been manipulated by the Communist Party.¹¹ It's hardly surprising they did. After all, anticommunism remained a real force, even if Joseph McCarthy had been defeated. In fact, Yale's American Studies Program was intimately connected to America's Cold War mission. In 1950, it was the beneficiary of a $500,000 gift ($650 million in today's dollars) from a donor who expected the program to advance the "fundamental principles of American freedom" against the "menace of foreign philosophies."¹² No, what disappointed and confounded his Yale examiners was Wolfe's aggressive flouting of scholarly norms. Mocking and disparaging one's subjects—even left-wing writers—was at odds with the conventions of scholarly objectivity. It was "polemical journalism," not scholarship, judged one faculty member.[13]

Particularly concerning was Wolfe's way of making a case. It was not just that he leaned heavily on testimony given at House Unamerican Activities Committee (HUAC) hearings, and his own interviews with apostate leftists. More disturbing was how little he apparently cared about distorting the evidence at hand. His readers were also concerned by his reliance on a "one-factor explanation" that had not persuaded them and likely could not be proven. Here, they were referring to his preoccupation with status. As program chair, it fell to the historian David Potter, a fellow Southerner, to write Wolfe about his dissertation's many deficiencies. What Potter singled out as the most damaging criticism was the careless way Wolfe "misused [his] sources, giving incorrect quotations, misstating evidence, etc." Wolfe was provided a list, a partial list, of some of his more egregious errors. Potter informed Wolfe that the program's executive committee would not recommend him for the degree. Wolfe would have to revise it to conform to scholarly conventions.

"I am sure this will be a blow," Potter wrote. Quite a blow, one would imagine, coming a mere two weeks before graduation.[14] Yet nothing in Wolfe's archive suggests that he took any of the faculty members' criticisms to heart. Instead, in a June 1956 letter to a friend, Wolfe complained about the "stupid fucks" at Yale who had turned down his dissertation. "They called my brilliant manuscript 'journalistic' and 'reactionary,'" which meant, he said, that he would have to "strike out all the laughs and anti-Redpassages [sic] and slip in a little liberal merde, so to speak, just to sweeten it."[15] To "help get him over the finish line," Wolfe replaced his thesis advisor Ralph Gabriel with the more politically sympathetic Norman Holmes Pearson. It was under Pearson's guidance that the American Studies Association became an instrument of American government influence during the Cold War.[16] Eventually, his revised dissertation was deemed acceptable, and he was awarded a doctorate in 1957. Wolfe left Yale with a well-developed antipathy toward what he regarded as the East Coast liberal elite.

Did he develop this animosity over the course of his time at Yale? Might it explain how he came to flunk the required dissertation assignment for the PhD? Did he not share chapters with his committee members because he was already disaffected? One curious bit of evidence that survives is a letter to his undergraduate advisor at Washington and Lee University. In this letter, Wolfe describes his topic as a "great pot boiler."[17] It seems that somehow Wolfe either never took on board or chose to ignore what is common knowledge in Humanities graduate programs: The dissertation and the pot boiler are two distinct genres, with no shared borders. Wolfe's PhD conferred the expectation that he knew something about conducting research. *New York* magazine emphasized Wolfe's academic pedigree in its promotion of 1970's "Radical Chic." Academia was spared any more low-bar performances when Wolfe fled its precincts, but the journalistic world was not. One imagines that Wolfe's Ivy League credentials were enough to shut up any newsroom skeptics who believed a degree in journalism was a prerequisite.

After earning his doctorate, Wolfe seems to have put his dissertation very firmly behind him, though he could be said to have repurposed it 14 years later in "Radical Chic." What he did not leave behind in New Haven were his methods and his prejudices. Lack of evidence, even contrary evidence, rarely deterred Wolfe from making an argument he was determined to make. If he was going for the jugular, as he sometimes did, facts were optional.

"Tiny Mummies" and *Acid Test*

Facts were certainly optional in Wolfe's putdown of *The New Yorker* magazine. Wolfe was writing for *New York*, the struggling Sunday supplement of the storied New York *Herald Tribune*. Wolfe and his colleagues at *New York*, including his editor Clay Felker, had little use for their rival, which they regarded as "unbearably dull" and self-regarding.[18] He leapt at the opportunity to take the esteemed magazine down a peg or four in their upstart magazine. Wolfe's two-part series opened with "Tiny Mummies! The True Story of the Ruler of 42nd Street's Land of the Walking Dead!" which appeared on April 11, 1965.[19]

Complicating Wolfe's assignment was the nearly solid wall of noncooperation that he encountered from the magazine's staff.[20] He tried to solve that problem by crashing *The New Yorker*'s 40th-anniversary party. Staying on the edges of the party—it was by invitation only—Wolfe spent his time observing the magazine's idiosyncratic editor, William Shawn. This proved to be some aid to him. Still, unable to get to longtime insiders, he chose to rely on rumor, unattributed sources, and secondhand and thirdhand gossip. As Ben Yagoda pointed out, Wolfe often boasted about his journalistic chops, yet "almost every time he attempted to state a fact about the workings of the magazine, he got it wrong."[21]

For Wolfe, "blowing up" *The New Yorker* meant launching an attack on Shawn, the mummifier-in-chief. In trying to preserve what the magazine had been under Harold Ross, his illustrious predecessor, Wolfe argued that Shawn had turned himself into the "smiling embalmer" of what had become a dead institution.[22] Wolfe also criticized Shawn's publication of Baldwin's "Letter from a Region of [sic] My Mind," which he called "the favorite bogey-whip for white liberal masochists all over the country."[23]

Wolfe was not content to limit his criticisms to Shawn's supposed editorial missteps. He mocked his physical appearance, his clothing, and his obvious discomfort in even casual social interactions. Just as Wolfe had violated scholarly norms with his dissertation, he now crossed a journalistic line, and the reaction was immediate and fierce. J. D. Salinger, the famously reclusive author of *The Catcher in the Rye*, denounced Wolfe's piece as "inaccurate and sub-collegiate and gleeful and unrelievedly poisonous."[24]

Rebutting Wolfe was easy because "Tiny Mummies" was littered with factual errors. When *New Yorker* contributor Gerald Jonas took it upon himself to fact-check "Tiny Mummies," he discovered a staggering number of factual errors. His colleague Renata Adler dug up more damning evidence. "The piece dissolved," Adler wrote, "down to the smallest, apparently most knowing detail."[25]

Wolfe and his editor Felker tried to shut down the controversy about "Tiny Mummies" by threatening to sue anyone who exposed Wolfe's lax reporting.[26] Their threatened libel suit delayed the publication of Leonard C. Lewin's article, "Is Fact Necessary?" in the *Columbia Journalism Review*.[27] Lewin's even-handed piece emphasized the necessity of distinguishing between fact and fiction. "Even when it spoils the fun, it's one of the entrance requirements of the trade." That applied to Felker, too. Indeed, Lewin ended his piece with this question: "But where was the editor?"[28]

The left-liberal cultural critic Dwight Macdonald produced the most penetrating attack on Wolfe's reporting. A longtime staff writer at *The New Yorker*, Macdonald penned two articles in *The New York Review of Books* about Wolfe's journalistic malpractice.[29] What Wolfe was producing was "parajournalism . . . a bastard form, having it both ways, exploiting the factual authority of journalism and the atmospheric license of fiction."[30] Macdonald analyzed the way Wolfe made his case, persuading the reader with all his "'knowing' factual touches," crude but powerful devices of suggestion ("one can imagine . . ."), and bold assertions masquerading as evidence, which were made possible by his "habit of deducing his facts from his assumptions."[31]

Macdonald was not even the worst of it. An avalanche of criticism—everyone from the legendary political columnist Walter Lippmann to Murray Kempton—hit them.[32] However, all the brouhaha, as well as the publicity arising from the publication of *The Kandy-Kolored Tangerine-Flake Streamline Baby* that same year, made Wolfe newsworthy. Wolfe had longed for that sort of attention. When he was still a junior reporter in Springfield, Massachusetts, he wrote his parents about his "hankering for more status and for bylines."[33] Now he had it, with profiles about him turning up in *Time* and *Newsweek*. "Tiny Mummies" also helped to make *New York* magazine, as ad revenue doubled, enabling it to become a freestanding magazine a year later when the *Tribune* went belly up.[34]

As with his dissertation, Wolfe showed no sign of remorse or shame about "Tiny Mummies." In his history of the *Tribune*, Richard Kluger maintains that Wolfe and Felker regretted the essay's many factual errors, but still thought his takedown had "captured the figurative truth" about *The New Yorker*.[35] Publicly, however, Wolfe treated the attacks as absurd. It was his long-held belief that when one's character was impugned the best strategy was to "attack the attacker!"[36] He brushed off his critics for wasting their time writing up "lists of [his] 'errors,'" which he ridiculed as "marvelous lists as arcane and mysterious as a bill from the body shop."[37] Wolfe did not forget these attacks or that the most devastating one appeared in the pages of the *New York Review of Books*. But perhaps as an acknowledgment of the trouble its publication had caused, he refrained from including the 1965 essay in his 1968 or 1976 essay collections. It did not see the light of day until 2000, when Farrar, Straus, and Giroux brought out his collection, *Hooking Up*.

Wolfe's 1968 book, *The Electric Kool-Aid Acid Test*, with its admiring account of Ken Kesey and the emerging counterculture, further enhanced Wolfe's reputation as a radical disrupter. Yet political activists might have noticed that Wolfe's radicalism did not extend to politics. Neither did Kesey's, which is probably one reason why Wolfe wrote so sympathetically of him. One can see it in how Wolfe wrote about Kesey's dismissive stance toward antiwar protestors. Addressing marchers in Berkeley in 1965, Kesey told them to forget about fighting the system, advising instead that they "turn away from

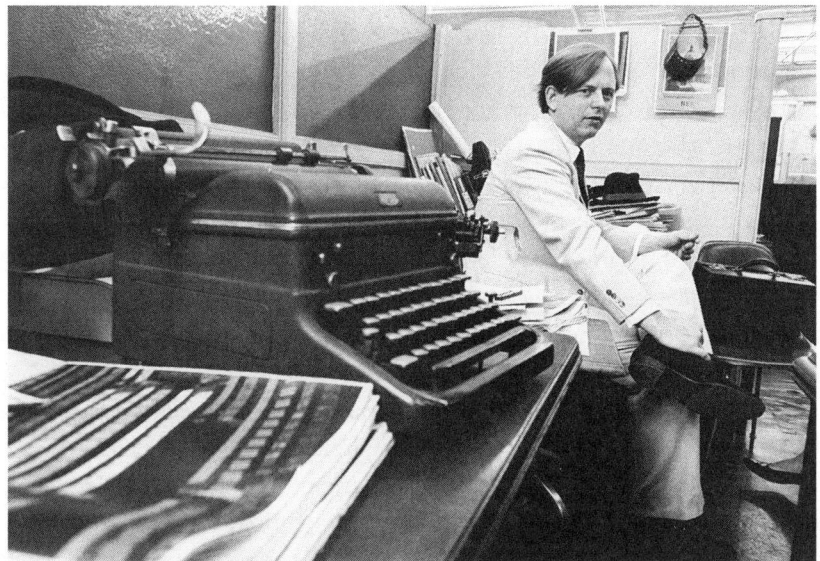

Image 11.1 The writer Tom Wolfe, wearing a cream-colored suit in the dead of winter, at his desk at the New York *Herald Tribune*, in late 1965.
Jack Robinson/Hulton Archive/Getty Images

it and say, 'fuck it.'"³⁸ Writing about the apolitical hippie scene of Haight-Ashbury that the Pranksters had helped to spawn, Wolfe observed that Kesey had "prophesized" the "new withering attitude toward all those who are still struggling in the old activist political ways for civil rights, against Vietnam, against poverty."³⁹ Wolfe also seemed taken by the way the new bohemia was redefining the racial dimension of hip masculinity. "For twenty years in the hip life," Wolfe claimed, "Negroes never even *looked* square." Now, white LSD freaks were, as Kesey put it, "outni**erring" the men they had emulated, rendering Black men's "hip spade soul authority" passé.⁴⁰

To be sure, in *Acid Test*, Wolfe was touting Kesey and company, not Ronald Reagan. Yet the correspondence in Wolfe's archive reveals him to have been surprisingly conservative, more so than his father. He shared with his parents his dismay about the "communist takeover in Cuba." In October 1961, he complained to his parents about all the "bleeding heart stories on the poor and downtrodden" that appeared in the *Washington Post* where he then worked as a city desk reporter. Writing about a female friend in San Francisco who had managed to get her daughter into a good but inexpensive private school, he noted, it was "fortunate in view of the school row going on out there over segregation."⁴¹

Wolfe's letters to his parents are straightforward in a way that suggests they may be a reliable guide to his politics. His archive also contains several mock insulting letters to male friends, written while he was at Yale. In two such letters, he disparaged Jews, South Asians, and Blacks. In one, he alerted a prep school friend to his imminent return home, "at which time I'll rouse all the slumbering ni**ers and challenge you to an afternoon of tennis." In another letter to a Yale friend, he complained of the "black slimy hair" left by a Ceylonese student, a floormate, in their shared bathroom basin. Wolfe noted that some people considered the student white, but that he believed he was a "fucking A-Rab and a ni**er to boot."⁴² One might imagine that his racist remarks were part of the abusive persona he was taking on in these letters. However, Wolfe complained about this same student in an entirely different kind of letter to a female friend, which suggests he really was repelled by living in such close proximity to someone who was not white, not like him.⁴³

Pure Gold

Within minutes of entering the Bernsteins' penthouse and surveying the crowd, Tom Wolfe felt he had hit pay dirt. There were Black Panthers in black leather, tweedy intellectuals, a couple of gray-suited Old Lefties, and an assortment of well-turned-out people, including socialites and a few recognizable celebrities. And there were Roquefort cheese morsels covered in crushed nuts that Wolfe thought an amusing juxtaposition with Black Panthers. Years later, Wolfe sometimes described the evening as a farce of rich contradictions; on other occasions, he claimed it marked the beginning of political correctness. The two may have been one and the same for him. His first thought, however, was "pure gold."

He walked into the penthouse, took in the scene, and felt he grasped the essence of it all. After all, it was a version of the cause party he had written about in his dissertation. Wolfe did not ask himself, "Might something be going on here other than status-seeking Park Avenue types adopting this year's fashion of radical chic?" Instead, his first account of the evening, "Radical Chic: That Party at Lenny's," found Wolfe doing what Dwight Macdonald criticized him for—working from a set of cherished assumptions that drove his facts.

The *New York Times* writer Christopher Lehmann-Haupt knew Wolfe's work rather well. In *Acid Test*, Wolfe had written about his brother Sandy, who had been a mostly un-merry Prankster. Lehmann-Haupt thought "Radical Chic" provoked "the usual Tom Wolfe questions" about his journalistic reliability. "At exactly what points did Wolfe's imagination impinge on his inferences, and his inferences on his facts?"[44]

In the case of "Radical Chic" the slippage is evident on page one. Or it would have been if critics had perused Wolfe's source material. However, Wolfe habitually avoided citing sources in the body of his work. Many journalists emphasized their sources, but not Wolfe, who tended to ditch the evidentiary scaffolding of his work. Citing sources involved moving away from the action, which interfered with what mattered most to him: telling a compelling story.

Wolfe opened the essay with what he described as one of Leonard Bernstein's late-night insomniac hallucinations. Sleeping through the night was a struggle for Bernstein. On the night of his 48th birthday in August 1966, Wolfe said, Bernstein awoke in a "state of wild alarm." He had a vision of himself, the "egregio maestro," onstage in his concert in white tie and tails. But rather than walking to the podium, he takes a seat, picks up a guitar, and declares, "I love" . . . to "mortifying" effect. At that point, a Black man stands up from the curve of the piano and begins to articulate the audience's annoyed reactions to Bernstein's dismaying performance. After giving a "heartfelt antiwar speech," Bernstein exits the stage. Bernstein liked this idea, Wolfe says, and at first imagined the admiring newspaper headlines it would garner. But then he started to ponder the Black man. "Who the hell was this Negro . . . informing the world what an ass Leonard Bernstein was making of himself?"[45]

In Wolfe's telling, the Black man is censorious while Bernstein is preoccupied with himself, one minute on a grandiose high (headlines!), and the next in despair about the ridicule he has suffered at the hands of this mysterious Black man. Wolfe opens "Radical Chic" in this way because it foreshadows the derision that he believed Bernstein brought on himself in his dialogues with Don Cox, who did indeed stand by one of Bernstein's pianos. Wolfe closes "Radical Chic" with Bernstein asking himself, "Would that black apparition, that damnable Negro by the piano, be rising up from the belly of a concert grand for the rest of his natural life?"[46]

Yet there is no evidence that Bernstein felt about any of it the way that Wolfe imagined. For example, it was not the benefit that Bernstein found shattering, but rather its coverage in the *New York Times*. Nor was Bernstein's so-called vision troubling in the way Wolfe imagined. In fact, examining Wolfe's lone source for this vivid opening demonstrates how determinedly Wolfe bent the facts to fit his story. Wolfe learned about the composer's supposed vision from a curious 1968 coffee-table book, *The Private World of Leonard Bernstein*.[47] Its author, John Gruen, was part of the Bernsteins' extended circle of friends. To assist Gruen in writing his book, Bernstein gave him a sheaf of notes he had written on sleepless nights. Gruen found himself taken with the idea that had absorbed Bernstein on that August night a year earlier. What Bernstein described was not some nightmarish hallucination, but rather his idea for an experimental antiwar concert piece he called *Prelude*. Bernstein's notes for *Prelude* were not the mad scribblings of a tortured man; they were written in very neat, coherent paragraphs. According to Bernsteins' insomniac note, the piece does not go down well with the audience, which thinks various things, including "Why does [Bernstein] stoop to this East Village crap?" The Black man, who entered with the orchestra and remains sitting throughout in a chair within the curve of the piano, occasionally expresses the audience's dismayed reactions.

Bernstein's note indicates that he didn't think this "germ" of an idea worked. He never imagined the "Bernstein Electrifies Concert Audience" headlines in Wolfe's account. Yes, he was troubled, but not by the mocking Black man that Wolfe imagined was permanently lodged in his consciousness. He was bothered by his inability to think his way through the piece. "Who is the Negro" Bernstein wonders, "sitting there, saying practically nothing?" It was an intellectual question more than an emotional quandary.

Bernstein had long been an admirer of African American music. His senior thesis at Harvard, which was entitled "The Absorption of Race Elements into American Music," argued for the centrality of Black music to American music.[48] As a composer, he often incorporated what most characterized Black music, especially its syncopation, into his compositions. As early as 1940, his political affiliations led to his involvement in the National Negro Congress, a communist front group. Through that connection, Bernstein was approached about organizing and conducting an all-Negro Symphony Orchestra. It was an idea, he wrote his piano teacher, Helen Coates, that he said, "excites me [to] no end." Bernstein believed that if it succeeded, it would be a "great social triumph" because it would conquer Blacks' understandable suspicion of whites.[49]

It could be that "the Negro" in *Prelude* reflected Bernstein's uncertainty about what the newly ascendant Black Power movement meant for him as a longtime believer in integration. It was the summer of 1966, the summer of Black Power. One clue that this might have been the case is that Gruen segues from this insomniac note into another "impossible challenge" that Bernstein was taking on in fall 1967 with his frequent collaborator Jerome Robbins. They wanted to stage a revival of Berthold Brecht's play *The Exception and the Rule*, this time foregrounding racism in America. The plan was to transform it into a contemporary satire, using an almost entirely Black cast, with Zero Mostel, the white actor, cast as a storeowner in a Black neighborhood. After working on it for more than a year, Bernstein abandoned the project because he believed that he and his collaborators lacked clarity. "Who are we to write about Negroes, anyway?"[50] How best to address racism, how to represent Black lives and culture, when he and his collaborators were outsiders, were intellectual questions with which he was grappling.

Racism, including possibly Bernstein's own, became an issue in 1969 when two Black musicians alleged racial discrimination at the New York Philharmonic. In a complaint filed with the City Commission on Human Rights, the musicians claimed that Bernstein and the Philharmonic discriminated against Black musicians. Ultimately, the musicians lost their case, but Bernstein said their case would have been "farcical had it not been heartbreakingly bad." After all, stretching back to the forties, Bernstein had advocated for Black orchestral musicians, and he routinely hired Black soloists.[51]

None of this helpful context found its way into "Radical Chic." In any case, it was not accidental that Wolfe opened and closed with Bernstein feeling ridiculed by Black men. Depicting one of the most accomplished and celebrated members of the culturati fretting over how Black men viewed him was apparently absurd in a way that encapsulated what Wolfe believed was the ludicrousness of the entire evening. Framed in this fashion, these two stories also hint at the masochistic feelings that Wolfe believed undergird radical chic. He doesn't make that accusation explicitly in "Radical Chic," though he had five years earlier about white liberal admirers of Baldwin's "A Letter."[52] Here, he lets others make it. Wolfe tells us that the blowback against the benefit included "cultivated people, intellectuals [who] were characterizing Bernstein as 'a masochist.'" He quotes William F. Buckley, who had observed that the white liberal seems beset by a "weird masochism."[53] Years later, Wolfe said it out loud when he described the benefit as the rich and famous "baring their soft white backs the more poignantly to feel the Panthers' vengeful lash."[54]

In presenting Bernstein as the ultimate masochist, Wolfe was adding his voice to the national chorus of those who were either turning rightward or were already there. Just that May, Vice President Spiro Agnew had assailed the prevailing "spirit of national masochism," which was, he argued, "encouraged by an effete corps of impudent snobs who characterize themselves as intellectuals." For Agnew, the Bernsteins and their guests would have been exhibit number one. Well before Agnew began attacking liberals in this fashion, Jewish intellectuals, such as Nathan Glazer and Norman Podhoretz, were calling out Jewish supporters of Black Power as self-hating masochists. In his history of neoconservatism, Justin Vaisse notes the striking similarity between Nathan Glazer's "ad-hominem attacks on Jewish intellectuals who agreed to support black radicals calling for war on Israel" and Tom Wolfe's satire of "radical chic."[55] In writing off the Bernstein benefit as an exercise in white liberal masochism, Wolfe was repeating what was, by 1970, a common trope.[56]

There were likely more than a few masochistically inclined white liberals in Manhattan, but it is not obvious from "Radical Chic" nor other sources that Leonard Bernstein was one of them. Nor do Wolfe's research notes indicate that he knew about Bernstein's long history of involvement in left-liberal causes, stretching into the present. Had Wolfe even dipped into a recent clipping file about him, he would have found evidence of Bernstein's growing willingness to take a stand, from showing up at the end of the Selma march to speaking at rallies for the antiwar candidate Eugene McCarthy. Bernstein made his dissenting voice heard. It likely came as a surprise to the sales representatives at a Columbia Records sales convention in April 1967 when Bernstein explained that the composer Gustav Mahler prophesied the catastrophes of the twentieth century. His list of catastrophes, which covered the full political spectrum, included "the smoking ovens of Auschwitz," "frantically bombed out jungles of Vietnam," "the arrogance of South Africa," "Trotskyist purges," and "Black Power."[57] Of course, providing Bernstein's political backstory would have undermined Wolfe's depiction of him as a dilettante.[58]

In his conversations with John Gruen, in the summer of 1967, Bernstein emphasized that he primarily identified as an artist, not an activist. Yet he made it clear that he still believed in politically engaged art. It bothered him that after World War II most artists were disconnected from politics, as if political work was doomed to be some kind of "Soviet tractor-art." It disappointed him how few contemporary artists engaged with the big problems of the days—war, civil rights, and global human rights. Bernstein also admitted to Gruen that he no longer felt he knew how to bring about change. "I've gotten to the point where I feel I know nothing," he said.[59]

Two-and-a-half years later, listening to Don Cox recite Panther rhetoric about, for example, putting the means of production into the hands of "the people," was doubtless very familiar. And yes, Bernstein "dug it," as in, he understood it. Here was Bernstein, now a doubter about some of what he once believed in, listening to a leader of a revolutionary organization that was "certain about almost everything."[60] When Cox admitted that the Panthers doubted that the current system would permit real change, Bernstein responded, "So you're going to start a revolution from a Park Avenue apartment!" It was one of several times that evening that he criticized the Panthers, and in a way that undermined the efforts of Weinstein, Kenner, his wife, and the Panthers. Yet Wolfe depicted Bernstein as pathetically needing to be right-on and relevant, "this little man" with his "Groovy gear and love beads," though Wolfe likely intended that putdown to be a thought bubble emanating from Don Cox's head.[61]

Wolfe also gave his imagination free rein when it came to the so-called servant crisis on Park Avenue. Wolfe's assumption was that radical chic, like pretty much everything in life, was about status. At that moment, status among the radically chic required the appearance of being attentive to people on society's margins. If this was very 1970, Wolfe argued that it was also a case of *nostalgie de la boue*, which he defined as the "romanticizing of primitive souls," a phenomenon stretching back to the eighteenth century.[62] In its current incarnation, it was, he claimed, upending life among affluent white liberals who believed that employing Black servants would reflect poorly on them. Imagine the embarrassment of hosting a Panther benefit with your own Black servants! The point of this digression was that it allowed Wolfe to mock the Bernsteins' "genius" work-around: employing South American servants. According to the couple's friends, the Bernsteins proved so helpful in their own hunt for non-Black servants that they had taken to calling them "the Spic and Span Employment Agency."[63]

Wolfe's notes indicate that someone did tell him this. However, the Bernsteins' employment of South Americans as housekeepers and nannies was not a radical chic affectation, "the cutting edge in Radical Chic," as he put it.

From the early fifties onward, their staff had been South American. Felicia Bernstein, who had been raised in Chile, determined that all household matters would be conducted in Spanish. Her daughter, Jamie, believes that the staff gave her mother "a comforting balance in that Bernstein-heavy universe." It also meant that their children were bilingual.[64] Julia Vega, the family's Chilean housekeeper and nanny, was much beloved. Jamie Bernstein includes in her memoir a photograph of herself and her brother Alexander hugging her. In Wolfe's account, though, the Bernsteins' staff stood as further proof of the performative calculation animating radical chic.

The "General Mindset"

There are many more "Tom Wolfe problems" in "Radical Chic"—too many to enumerate here.[65] Many of them arise from Wolfe's use of what he called either the offstage narrator or the downstage voice. Bored by the understated voice, the "pale beige tone" assumed by most nonfiction writers, Wolfe was determined to jazz things up by handing over much of the narration to the character(s) who might be downstage from the protagonist, or by appearing to go directly inside the protagonist's mind. In "Radical Chic" he did both, but he claimed much of it is narrated by an offstage narrator whose "mind is the general mindset of the people through whose eyes you begin to see."[66]

Yet in "Radical Chic" it is sometimes impossible to know just who the narrator is. Who is it that calls out Bernstein on his "groovy gear?" Who is it that refers to "the huge Panther" with the "Fuzzy-Wuzzy-scale" Afro? And who utters these memorable words about the Panthers: "These are *no civil rights* Negroes *wearing gray suits three sizes too big ... these are* real men." Questioned decades later by a journalist who notes that such a statement might have made an editor uncomfortable, Wolfe responds that "things were less PC" then. But he also explains that "the passage is *mocking* the attitudes of the people at the party."[67] Yet in "Radical Chic" the phrase appears three times—twice when it is unhinged from any narrator and is presumably the utterance of the offstage narrator and the next time when it is noted that the words were first articulated by a Park Avenue matron who goes unnamed.[68] (Earlier drafts have those words spoken by someone else, A Miss Wonderful, who uses the n-word rather than the term "Negroes."[69]) One advantage to such fuzziness is that it enabled

Wolfe to dodge blame for any of the politically incorrect bits of "Radical Chic." It wasn't *his* view.

There is also the problem of determining what the "general mindset" *was*. If Wolfe is talking about the liberal elite, that group included people as different from each other as Otto Preminger, who successfully challenged the racism of Hollywood, and the socialite Cheray Duchin, wife of the prominent orchestra leader. What enabled him to see into this so-called mindset, to write as if he knew exactly what was going on in people's minds? Asked this and other pointed questions during his December 1970 appearance on William F. Buckley's television show, *Firing Line*, Wolfe was adamant that work like his within the genre of new journalism was a "prodigious exercise in sheer fact." He went still further, arguing that his work was "totally dependent on reporting of a depth that I don't think anyone else has ever done."[70]

Wolfe often said that the way new journalists like himself were able to get into other people's heads was by interviewing them. However, his research notes do not suggest that extensive interviewing went into this essay.[71] His notes and his correspondence with his research assistant reveal a journalist more interested in situating people in Manhattan's statusphere than in understanding their mindset. Had he interviewed people in their circle he would have learned that fashionableness was not what moved the couple.[72] He would have learned that Felicia Bernstein was publicity-shy and *hated* attending openings, surrounded by photographers snapping pictures.[73] A less socially ambitious person than Felicia Bernstein would have been hard to find. As for Lenny, music critic Alex Ross's description of him as "a man genetically incapable of saying anything but what he really meant" jibes with the views of his friends.[74]

But the truth was never an impediment to Wolfe. Because Bernstein contested the *Times*' characterization of the benefit as a party of "politico-cultural jet set" and claimed that he and his wife never had parties, Wolfe was determined to disprove him. He put his researcher on the case, and after she failed to produce the desired evidence, she eventually explained why. "FLASH!" she wrote Wolfe, "they rarely entertain."[75] John Gruen told her this, but had she and Wolfe read Gruen's book, they might have come across this gem: "The Bernsteins are not part of the jet set, and 'society' leaves them cold."[76] Nevertheless, five pages into "Radical Chic," Wolfe writes at length about the Bernsteins' star-studded "après-concert suppers" in which all sorts of high-wattage celebrities mingled.[77]

Most of Wolfe's research notes suggest a journalist focused on pinning down who certain people are, to whom they are married, and where they live. Julie Robinson Belafonte is a person of interest, but his researcher hits a brick wall because her husband Harry's public relations man is "very curt and non-obliging." Ellie Guggenheimer often appears in Wolfe's notes as Guggenheim. His researcher noted a recently published book of interest, *The Guggenheims and the American Dream*. At some point, however, either Wolfe or his researcher cottons onto the fact that the Bernsteins' guest was not a member of the illustrious Guggenheim family.[78]

Someone else who figures in these notes is Frank Stanton, presumably because Wolfe wondered if he might be the famous CBS executive. Even though he was not *that* Frank Stanton, his lifestyle made him a valuable quarry. Wolfe or his assistant learned, presumably from someone in the couple's orbit, about the duplex in which Frank Stanton and his "new wife," Domna lived.[79] With its "apricot velvet walls" and the "trompe l'oeil murals" in its dining room, their place "made Lenny's look like a fourth-floor walk-up." Wolfe used these details, many of which he got wrong, to explain how the Stantons allegedly got cold feet about hosting a benefit. After the blowback from the Bernsteins' event, Wolfe claims the Stantons chose to host a benefit for antigovernment Buddhists from South Vietnam rather than the Panthers. It struck the couple, Wolfe says, that a "few photos of the Panthers in this backdrop—well, you could write the story yourself." Domna Stanton maintains that she and her husband never had plans to host a Panther benefit, nor did they ever hold one for Vietnamese Buddhists. Wolfe, she said, "would just invent anything."[80]

Some people did back out of Panther benefits, however, and Wolfe argued that by doing so they revealed who they really were: Park Avenue dilettantes whose participation in radical chic had always been about being chic, not radical. They were never going to put their "whole status on the line for *nostalgie de la boue*" because their only true commitment was to their own fashionableness. To prove his point, he depicted the Bernsteins and their friends desperately scrambling to deal with the fallout from the January 14 benefit. Wolfe claimed that in a meeting to discuss their next steps—a meeting Stanton says never happened—they denounced the "witchhunt" being waged against them by the press. Wringing their hands, they complained about being "too exposed" to offer any more aid to the Panthers. They made plans instead to hold fundraisers for the National Association for the Advancement of Colored

People (NAACP)'s Legal Defense Fund or the newly formed Friends of the Earth or the Buddhists of Vietnam—anyone but the Panthers.[81]

Wolfe made light of their concerns. Presumably he did not know that the Bernsteins and many of their friends had been concerned about what they saw as the growing threat of fascism in America. Nor does it seem that he knew about how the blacklist had affected Bernstein and some of the others in their circle. In "Radical Chic," Wolfe downplayed the blowback that they were facing. Yes, he acknowledged there was some hate mail from "Jews of the Queens-Brooklyn Jewish Defense League variety," but that was about it. He makes fun of the idea that they were being attacked in the press, but they were. So was the Black Panther Party.

To better understand the "strategic withdrawal" of the radically chic, Wolfe might have considered the mainstream media's coverage of the party at the center of the party. On January 14, the very day of the benefit, the widely syndicated conservative columnists Rowland Evans and Robert Novak claimed that overseas communist parties were funding the Black Panther Party. They also claimed that donations from well-meaning people to the Panthers might be intended for its breakfast for schoolchildren programs but were being used for entirely different purposes. They never cited the Bernstein benefit, but they observed the emergence of a new and dangerous alliance between liberals and the Panthers. Liberals believed that the Panther party was "really nothing more than a small, badly divided civil rights group under constant police harassment." In fact, it was a "well-disciplined and centrally directed party with potential for growth and . . . with a criminal record much longer and stronger than any civil rights record."[82]

Evans and Novak were conservative columnists, so liberals may have shrugged their shoulders at their "Red Panthers" column. However, three days after the benefit at the Bernsteins, there was a story in the *New York Times* that might have landed more effectively. The article, entitled "A Panther Admits He Killed Another," was about the unfolding case in New Haven, Connecticut, involving the murder by the Panthers of a fellow Panther suspected of being an informant. It appeared below the fold, and took up little space, but it was nonetheless a first-page story.[83] That same month CBS correspondent Richard Hottelet broke the news that Eldridge Cleaver had reached an agreement with Al Fatah, which agreed to train Panthers during actual battles against Israel. Al Fatah would also allow Panthers to take part in Fatah operations in the Middle East so that they could learn "combat and sabotage." Trained by Al

Fatah, Panthers could then carry out with "quick and deep strikes in the United States."[84] It would be surprising if such stories did not undermine support for the Panthers among liberals, particularly liberal Jews.[85] That is what the Federal Bureau of Investigation (FBI) hoped to accomplish.

There were no extenuating circumstances in Wolfe's account of liberals' withdrawal from the fray. The Bernsteins and their friends simply copped out. Wolfe does not stop there, though. He goes on to argue that had the radically chic stood firm, they "might well have struck an extraordinary counterblow in behalf of the Movement."[86] Here, Wolfe was writing unambiguously in his own voice. Yet he did so in the service of an argument curiously at odds with his own private views. Why would Wolfe criticize the Park Avenue set for letting down a Movement he loathed? Perhaps because he hated the Bernsteins and people like them more than even young radicals? Or maybe Wolfe figured that such an argument counterbalanced some of the dodgier bits of "Radical Chic"—think of the fuzzy-wuzzy scale Afros—rendering him less politically legible. In this scenario, attacking radical chic in a predictably left-wing way— using "radical chic" as Seymour Krim intended—had the advantage of muddying the waters, making him appear neutral or disinterested, which is how he typically presented himself in this period.[87] As Christopher Lehmann-Haupt observed, Wolfe was "a complete chameleon, capable of turning any color."[88]

The same slipperiness characterized his portrait of the Panthers. Wolfe spared the Panthers the unrelieved hostility that he directed at the radically chic. Sometimes he captured the annoyance that he believed Don Cox, the Panther with the "Plexiglas gaze," felt toward Mr. Maestro. But mostly what interested him about the Panthers, though perhaps it was his offstage narrator, was their hip style and the men's unapologetic masculinity. He is silent on whether their claims of government harassment and violence have any merit. He could have indicated what journalists had already turned up about the disinformation the Chicago police put out about the December 1969 murders of Hampton and Clark. Instead, he introduces readers to Oakland Panther Robert Bay by noting he had been arrested in a skirmish with the police just 41 hours before meeting Felicia Bernstein.[89] Years later Wolfe likened the Panthers to the Hell's Angels in their "willingness to be violent at any moment."[90] In 1987, Wolfe was asked if he thought AIDS fundraising was a case of radical chic redux. There was nothing funny about saving lives, he bristled, because there was nothing radical about trying to save lives.[91] Many AIDS activists would have taken issue with the idea that their activism was not radical. One wonders if it was the Panthers' radicalism, their violence, their theatricality, or perhaps their Blackness that made the effort to save their lives something deserving of ridicule?

In any case, Wolfe's decision to remain in the closet about his conservatism was likely a professional calculation. Wolfe suspected that his aloofness from The Cause hurt him. It may be that this was why the *National Observer* killed Hunter Thompson's positive review of *Tangerine*. Thompson, who was one of Wolfe's friends, filled him in on the backstory. Thompson's glowing review was nixed by an editor at the newspaper who knew Wolfe from their time together at the *Washington Post* and "hated the air he breathed." Given Wolfe's feelings about the *Post*'s liberalism, the two men may have been at political loggerheads.[92] However, the review of *Tangerine* that seems to have most annoyed Wolfe appeared in "Book Week," a Sunday supplement included in the *Herald Tribune*, which Wolfe probably assumed was friendly territory. But no, *Tangerine* was assigned to Wallace Markfield, who produced a cool review, which then prompted Wolfe's book editor to complain to the "Book Week" editor about his choice of reviewer. Markfield, he argued, was a lefty, or as he put it, "an old-line *Partisan Review* type [who] would have been unlikely to be 'well-disposed' to Tom's talent."[93]

Wolfe had reason to be cagey about his conservatism, and not just because of liberal editors and fellow writers. There were his young fans to consider, too. By 1970, Wolfe was supplementing his writing income with speaking fees on college campuses. He was in correspondence with Jann Wenner of *Rolling Stone*, a lucrative outlet for his articles. Why would he write honestly about his political views when doing so could alienate the young, hip people who constituted much of his readership?

The Impact of "Radical Chic"

New York magazine devoted virtually its entire June 8 issue to "Radical Chic," which it aggressively promoted in advance of its publication. With its accompanying 14 pages of photographs, half of them of the benefit at the Bernsteins' penthouse, the issue landed as it was meant to—like a sledgehammer. It helped that it sported a provocative cover of three chic but determined-looking women—one elderly, one middle-aged, and the third a twentysomething—each of them with her right fist in a black leather glove and raised to the sky in a Black Power salute. Above their heads were the words "Free Leonard

Bernstein!" Its publication marked the second time that an article by Wolfe changed the fortunes of the magazine, and for the better. After that summer, *New York* reportedly stopped being a "shoestring operation."[94]

Soon, the radical chic trope became ubiquitous. Later that summer, the *Los Angeles Times* gossip columnist Joyce Haber deployed it when describing a fundraiser for the Los Angeles 18, a group of Panthers arrested in that brutal December 1969 raid. Haber was no friend of the Movement. In a late August 1970 column, she wrote of a benefit to aid the Committee United for Political Prisoners hosted by the film director Abby Mann at his Santa Monica beach house. She opened with "talking about radical chic" and went on to identify the "two kinds of BPs there: Black Panthers and Beautiful People." The invitation listed as hosts Jane Fonda, her brother Peter, Don Sutherland, Dennis Hopper, Sydney Pollack, Mary Rydell, Joe Hyams, and Benjamin Spock. Attendees included Fonda's husband, Roger Vadim; Charlotte Rampling; and Seymour Cassell.[95]

"Radical Chic" was such a sensation that Farrar, Straus and Giroux, Wolfe's publisher, released "Radical Chic" in book form, paired with his essay "Mau-Mauing the Flak Catchers." The same dynamic of Black rage and white masochism that Wolfe believed characterized the Bernstein benefit he found in the relations between Black community activists (the mau-mau'ers) and white antipoverty bureaucrats (the flak catchers). Wolfe found that, as with the Park Avenue set, status made the ghetto go round. Becoming a community activist, intimidating welfare workers, and getting a piece of the action was how one made it. As with "Radical Chic," Wolfe made a lot of the hypermasculinity of Black men and the emasculation of white men. Wolfe's research notes reveal that he was thinking about undertaking a new project on America's "virility gap."[96] In any case, the book offered readers two case studies of the same phenomenon. Sales "are jumping out there," his editor wrote him at the end of December. It was also widely and positively reviewed. Within one year, the book, in its various editions, including one by the Book-of-the-Month Club, was in its sixth printing. Wolfe received admiring letters from others in publishing and journalism—Gay Talese; Norman Podhoretz; Joan Didion's husband, John Dunne; William F. Buckley; Katherine Graham of the *Washington Post*; the gossip columnist Liz Smith; San Francisco columnist Herb Caen; and Daniel Boorstin, who requested an in-person meeting.

Unsurprisingly, he received negative letters, too. Leonard Bernstein's sister, Shirley, castigated him for distorting the truth and "for the meanest of self-serving interests." She also accused him of writing "as if on order from Messrs. Agnew and Hoover." In the end, she said, his message was that people should stay clear of radical causes; if you don't "you'll be maligned, mocked and humiliated." One of the guests whom Wolfe had ridiculed—his name for her in the essay was "Ash Blond"—argued for the importance of keeping "all channels of communication open" and making sure that "the wealthy and influential" were a part of the conversation. She included a postscript pointing out that his description of the Radical Chic crowd as preoccupied with "causes exotic and far away" did not explain that evening's event. The Panther 21, she pointed out, "are right here in New York!" Someone, perhaps an academic, criticized what he believed was Wolfe's badly mangled explanation of nostalgie de la boue, especially how it supposedly operated in Regency England.

Wolfe faced some public pushback, but not a lot because his writing in "Radical Chic" is so sharp, so "on." Wolfe largely absented himself from the narrative, but as the writer Michael Lewis observes, there was still this "boom—this personality coming off the page."[97] Wolfe's delight in presenting the liberal elite as doing themselves in is palpable. Likely another reason Wolfe faced very light headwinds is that he was operating in an entirely different register than that of the Nixon White House whose condemnations of the Bernsteins and their guests were righteously indignant.

Satirizing the Park Avenue set from an apparently disinterested position won Wolfe fans from across the ideological spectrum. Irving Howe criticized Wolfe's snobbism, but otherwise seemed unbothered by "Radical Chic," claiming that no one had come forth to challenge Wolfe's accuracy. Howe had written dismissively of radical chic three years earlier, and he remained a critic. "I can't tell the differences between the revolutionaries and the counter-revolutionaries," he said. Michael Harrington, echoing his friend Howe, put down today's radicalism as "pseudo-radicalism." Philip Rahv opined that "revolution is a process, not a happening."

By and large it appeared that those who had been active in the Old Left shared Wolfe's contempt for radical chic.[98] The same could be said of many New Leftists, although at the time "Radical Chic" seemed to barely register among most of them. Of course, "Radical Chic" had a lot of competition for their attention—the Greenwich Village townhouse explosion; Nixon's Cambodian Invasion; the student strikes engulfing college campuses, 500 of which were shut down or closing less than a week after Nixon's announcement; the shootings of students at Kent State and Jackson State; and the Hard Hat Riot.[99]

If Wolfe's essay affected young radicals in the immediate aftermath of its publication, it was by reinforcing their conviction that what they were doing was authentic activism. Take white radical Jane Alpert, who was part of that non-Weatherman group that in 1969 bombed eight government or corporate offices in Manhattan. Whether she felt this way at the time likely cannot be known, but in her 1981 memoir she dismissed the support she and her co-conspirators received as indicative of "a certain avant-garde chic among well-placed liberals."[100] True radicals weren't hosting benefits and writing checks; they were putting their bodies on the line. To the extent that young radicals absorbed "Radical Chic," it would only have hardened their conviction that anyone whose politics weren't explicitly revolutionary was part of the problem.

Some Panthers probably savored Wolfe's disparagement of the liberal elite and the "paper Panthers" who mingled with them at cocktail parties. But other Panthers, including those who advocated armed insurrection, agreed with Don Cox about the significance of liberal support and the backlash it provoked. Jamal Joseph (formerly Eddie Joseph) noted that while Wolfe called it "radical chic," the "Panthers called it fund-raising and consciousness-raising."[101]

One robust left-wing dissent that appeared that year was penned by Jason Epstein of the *New York Review of Books*. Epstein was not a New Leftist, but he was sympathetic to it and published work by its young radicals. Epstein's piece was distinctive in its full-throated defense of the Bernsteins and their guests. If they could be said to have sinned, Epstein wrote, their only sin was their optimism. "What [Wolfe] calls radical chic is, in fact, only the unhappy residue of the broken promises and defeated politics of the Kennedys, the still flickering desire of an impotent and aristocratic liberalism . . . to engage the poor as citizens in the life of the country."[102]

This was not, however, how conservatives, particularly neoconservatives, saw it. The one-time liberals who came to be labeled conservatives attributed their rightward turn to having been "mugged by reality," as Irving Kristol, the most prominent of them, tellingly put it.[103] Many of them felt about Wolfe's essay the way that Wolfe felt about the benefit at the Bernsteins—pure gold! James Q. Wilson was among them. Wilson is best known as an architect of the broken windows theory of crime, which called for the aggressive policing of even small infractions such as panhandling. In New York City, where theory became practice, some critics have argued that the broken windows approach played a key role in the development of the carceral state.[104] In 1970, when he was a professor in Harvard's Department of Government, Wilson wrote Wolfe to say, "Don't be worried about having been discovered by William Buckley." Wilson joked that it had happened to Daniel Moynihan, and he was pretty sure he had survived.

Buckley did reach out to Wolfe, who was quite open to being courted. Someone else who wrote to congratulate him was Raymond K. Price, who knew Wolfe knew from his days at the *New York Herald Tribune*, where Price was the editorial page writer. When Richard Nixon won the election in 1968, he hired Price, a moderate Republican, to be his "principal idea man," that is, his speechwriter.[105] Price considered Wolfe's essay "one of the deftest bits of literary dissection I've ever seen."[106]

Some believed that its publication in the reliably liberal *New York*, its rapid repackaging in book form, and the book's strong sales and reviews signaled a shift in the country's political currents. Writing as 1970 was coming to a close, the journalist Nathan Miller maintained that, at least within the world of New York intellectuals, "something strange" was afoot. Suddenly, some of them were joining Tom Wolfe in attacking what Miller characterized as "the radical chic that pervades some intellectual salons." However, most of Miller's examples were pundits who regularly wrote for Norman Podhoretz's *Commentary*, the journal where neoconservatism was taking shape. In its pages, Joseph Epstein (not to be confused with Jason Epstein of the *New York Review*) lavished praise on Wolfe. Epstein called "Radical Chic" a "minor comic masterpiece." That same year Nathan Glazer declared himself, unsurprisingly in the pages of *Commentary*, "deradicalized."[107]

Inside the Nixon White House, Wolfe's work registered beyond the office of Raymond Price. Plans were made to weaponize "Radical Chic" in the upcoming 1972 presidential election. In a secret June 8, 1972, memo, Patrick Buchanan and Ken Khachigian spelled out how they planned to do this. Called "Assault Strategy," the memo laid out a campaign plan whereby Nixon could vanquish the Democrats' candidate, South Dakota's liberal senator George McGovern. "As the campaign progresses, we should increasingly portray McGovern as the pet radical of Eastern Liberalism, the darling of the *New York Times*, the hero of the Berkeley Jet Set, Mr. Radical Chic." While they plotted about marginalizing McGovern as an elitist radical, they strategized about how best to present Nixon as "the Candidate of the Common Man."[108]

Conservative intellectuals were quick to claim Wolfe's "Radical Chic" as a transformative text. In May 1971, *Commentary* writer Dorothy Rabinowitz declared that Wolfe had "achieved what almost no imaginative writer can realistically hope for in a lifetime; he had effected 'social change.'" To Rabinowitz, it seemed that virtually overnight his essay had "put an end to the phenomenon to which he had given a name—radical chic."

Could Wolfe's "Radical Chic" really have had such an outsized impact? Among those already on the right or moving in that direction, it did not so much effect social change as validate their dissatisfaction with the Movement and the liberals supporting it. They may also have felt emboldened by where "Radical Chic" was published. *New York* magazine had a reputation as "pretty much the house organ of radical chic," as Raymond Price put it. There is some evidence that even among conservatives who were more heartland than coastal the essay was influential. One such conservative, the syndicated columnist and talk-radio host Reverend Lester Kinsolving, proclaimed that *Radical Chic and Mau-Mauing the Flak-Catchers* should be required reading for denominational officials who had unwisely funded an array of dubious initiatives and leaders to fight racial injustice. In his view, "few churchgoers are any longer able or willing to continue subsidizing ecclesiastical masochism."[109]

And how did it land among those on the periphery of the Movement, those who signed an occasional letter of protest or turned up at the big antiwar marches? For some, Movement fatigue had set in several years before 1970, and for those pulling away after 1970, there were likely multiple causes for their alienation. Take the case of Christopher Lehmann-Haupt, who was the senior Daily Book Reviewer for the *New York Times* from 1969 until 1995. With James Baldwin, Elizabeth "Betita" Sutherland Martínez, Gloria Steinem, and others, he had been among the signatories to the pro-Panther letter "Violence in Oakland." A response to the clash between Panthers and the police, following the murder of King in April 1968, it appeared in the *New York Review of Books*. Yet in May 1971, six months after writing a mixed review of *Radical Chic and Mau-Mauing the Flak Catchers*, Lehmann-Haupt admitted that the whole subject of the Black Panthers "has become a little tiresome." It wasn't just that the Party was riven or that its rhetoric seemed "screechier" now, it was also that Leonard Bernstein had dumped the Panthers for the antiwar Catholic priests, Philip and Daniel Berrigan. Lehmann-Haupt was joking about Bernstein, but his weariness seems genuine, and it presumably stemmed from multiple sources.[110]

Felicia and Leonard Bernstein remained politically engaged, though not as supporters of the Black Panther Party. This was despite having been in what their friend Schuyler Chapin called a "shooting gallery."[111] Their daughter Jamie said years later that her mother "never recovered from the heartbreak and shame of this incident." Martin Kenner recalled that every so often after the benefit, Felicia Bernstein would ring him up to say he had ruined her life. But it was not just Felicia Bernstein who was damaged. "No one was all the way to happy again," Jamie Bernstein said of her family.[112]

Nonetheless, the couple attended demonstrations where they risked arrest, and on at least one occasion, they were arrested. On May 12, 1971, they held a fundraiser for the antiwar group the "Harrisburg Seven," which included the Catholic priest Philip E. Berrigan. The government unsuccessfully prosecuted the Seven with charges ranging from conspiracy to kidnap Nixon's national security advisor, Henry Kissinger, to blowing up heating systems in federal office buildings in Washington, DC. The Bernsteins' guests, some of whom had attended the Panther benefit, contributed $35,000 for the group's defense. Leonard Bernstein also signed onto a new group that Lillian Hellman and Hannah Weinstein formed called the Committee for Public Justice. Intended as a counter force to President Nixon's attacks on sixties movements, it played a critical role throughout the seventies in resisting state secrecy and the creeping spread of surveillance.[113] Felicia Bernstein became less active after being diagnosed with breast cancer in the summer of 1974. Four years later, at age 56, she died of lung cancer.

For his part, Leonard Bernstein did not let up, despite never succeeding in setting the record straight about "his party for the Panthers." It did not matter how many times Bernstein said, "It *wasn't* a party and *I* didn't give it."[114] His name was forever linked to the Panthers. In the eighties, Bernstein, whose homosexual discretion ended in the early seventies, was the first celebrity to become involved in the fight against AIDS. Bernstein conducted 1987's "Music for Life" benefit concert, which raised $1.7 million to fund AIDS research, and he gave money to the cause. Two years later, he refused the prestigious National Medal of Arts from George H. W. Bush to protest the revocation of a grant from the National Endowment for the Arts that had helped to fund an exhibit of artwork related to AIDS.[115]

Bernstein was bothered by the way conservatives mocked him. In the last substantial interview before his death, Bernstein said they regarded him as "silly Lenny . . . what does he know, poor soft-hearted asshole musician, talking 'liberal shit' and 'soft talk.'" Nonetheless, Bernstein remained adamantly progressive. "Basically a liberal is a progressive who wants to see the world change and not just remain stuck in the status quo."[116] It is worth noting that well into the seventies, the FBI tracked his activities, proving that second Red Scare was still playing out much later than usually assumed.[117]

As for Tom Wolfe, eventually he made his ideological leanings more legible. In the eighties, he accepted invitations to go to the Reagan White House, and he appeared at gatherings of conservatives. In 1983, he told an interviewer that "socialism, when put into effect by experts, leads only to extermination camps."[118] In 1985, speaking to a conservative group, he launched into an attack on those whom he said really had power in America. These were the Marxist intellectuals who were part of what he called the "New Class." Wolfe opined that there was in Marxism an "implicit secret promise... of handing power over to the intellectuals,'" which was why, he argued, intellectuals gravitated toward it.[119] He also voiced his admiration for hard-right figures such as Taki Theodoracopulos, who, with Pat Buchanan and Scott McConnell, founded the *American Conservative* magazine.[120]

In the end, what is most troubling about "Radical Chic" is Wolfe's mocking characterization of efforts to cross the color line. Discussing the benefit years later, he opined of the Panthers and the Park Avenue set that you could not find "a starker contrast between... two sensibilities."[121] To Wolfe (and the Panthers' Black Nationalist rivals) these were unbridgeable differences. Wolfe's success in rendering the project of cross-racial solidarity nothing more than a ludicrous charade has shaped our historical memory of the Black Panther Party and the whites who supported them and altered the conversation about racism and white efforts to challenge it.[122] Wolfe's work obscured the significance of Panthers courting liberals and of liberals questioning the dominant narratives about the Panthers. This is no small thing, yet it is largely missing from histories of the period.[123]

What is not missing from histories of that era is "Radical Chic." In contrast to so many other influential texts of the period, Wolfe's essay has remained a cultural touchstone, seemingly more relevant than the timeliest and most urgent writing of the sixties. Bestsellers from that period such as Eldridge Cleaver's *Soul on Ice*, Charles Reich's *The Greening of America*, and Kate Millett's *Sexual Politics*, are long gone from bookstores, college syllabi, and commentary of the pundit class. By contrast, Wolfe's slim volume, *Radical

Chic and Mau-Mauing the Flak Catchers, has had a very different fate. Ironically, the book that skewered the sixties is the one sixties text that has attained the status of a relevant classic.

One would be hard pressed to find a single other piece of writing from that era which has so shaped how people understand the Movement and cross-racial efforts to fight racism. Andrew Ferguson, writing in a 2012 issue of *Commentary*, declared "Radical Chic" as "funny and germane today as it was in 1970."[124] *Commentary*'s Joseph Epstein, writing at the time of Wolfe's death in 2018, maintained that "Radical Chic" succeeding in putting "a serious dent in the movement that was then sweeping America." It helped to sharply narrow the Movement's impact, consigning it, he said, to "the much shabbier surroundings of university humanities and social-science departments."[125]

For conservatives, "Radical Chic" has been pure gold. Their own considerable financing of think-tanks and foundations to roll back the sixties—to make what the historian Alice O'Connor calls a "counterrevolution"—was overshadowed by the preoccupation with the Movement's "radical chic" donors. Through new foundations, such as the Heritage Foundation, which was formed in 1973, conservatives pushed for free enterprise, law and order, low taxes, and the inviolability of property as well as the traditional nuclear family. Like so many conservative efforts of the seventies, they adopted the "playbook" of their liberal adversaries, in this case, the Ford Foundation, which had advanced racial equality, feminism, and environmentalism.[126]

Conservative donors have faced criticism for funding right-wing initiatives, but not because there's anything amusing about their support. One telling example is what happened when the former Black Panther Eldridge Cleaver returned to America in 1975 and made himself over into a Christian conservative. The press paid little attention to the fact that it was Norman Podhoretz of *Commentary* who hosted a fundraising party for the former Black Panther leader.[127] Indeed, the financial support that rich conservatives provided their favorite causes did not prompt talk of conservative chic, and why would it when their giving usually aligns so closely with their financial self-interest? It was easy to send up champagne socialism, but not so champagne conservatives, whose political contributions were entirely predictable, devoid of what Wolfe called "double-track thinking." In 1973, Lewis Lapham of *Harper's Magazine* tried to interest Wolfe in writing a piece about "California, the Western Establishment, USC and Nixon's supporters in Orange County." He promised Wolfe "long space, reasonable expenses and lavish praise." Unsurprisingly, Wolfe did not take him up on it.[128]

To many young radicals, double-track thinking was the very definition of American liberalism. It is not surprising that older liberals who felt connected to the Movement were among those who eventually challenged the simplicity of Wolfe's binary. Gail Lumet was among those who had felt burned by Wolfe.[129] Five years later, in 1975, when she was approached by the United Farm Workers (UFW) about holding a benefit, she hesitated, before agreeing to host. The *Washington Post* headline read "Viva La Causa! Radical Chic Revisited," but Lumet was unapologetic. "I'm a radical and I'm chic," she told the reporter. "I also know I am committed, but I'm not a worker in the fields." She had no intention of being scared off any longer by the fear of being ridiculed. "I've got the time and the money and the only way I can help is to do what I do." As for the UFW feeling patronized or used by Lumet and other donors (who included the Bernsteins), Delores Huerta, UFW vice president, told the *Post*, "I certainly don't feel used by them. On the contrary, I'm using them." Both Lumet and Huerta acknowledged something that those to the left of them had difficulty acknowledging—that there was a place in the Movement for Ella Baker's lady in the fur coat.[130]

There are many reasons that "Radical Chic" has enjoyed such staying power, but one of them is that New Leftists' disdain of liberalism led them to view radical chic as nothing more than a kerfuffle among liberals, certainly not their battle. In "Radical Chic," few characters were more ludicrous than the young woman Wolfe derisively called Ash Blond. It was she who asked the Panthers, "What can we do?" By 1970, it was no longer politically acceptable for white people to ask Black people helplessly what they could do to further the cause. "Educate yourself" was a typical response. In Wolfe's account, her question provoked one of the Black guests to respond with such sarcasm— "If sarcasm could reach 550 degrees, she would shrivel up like a slice of Oscar Meyer bacon."[131] Yet, the ridiculed woman did not shrivel up, she did not slink away from the benefit. And after Wolfe's essay hit the newsstands, she wrote him a chastising letter that shows that the benefit affected her. Nothing in her letter suggests she resented being mocked by a Black guest. And what was her closing salutation to Wolfe? "Power to the People!"[132]

Indeed, her letter suggests that even clueless white liberals are redeemable. This is a point that the actress and activist Jane Fonda made in her 2005 memoir. Reflecting some 40 years later about her very first fundraiser, she recalled feeling not exactly guilt-tripped, but very much like "an outsider." Nevertheless, at the end of the benefit, which was for the Student Nonviolent Coordinating Committee, she volunteered and became involved in writing letters and asking others for money. Reflecting on the start of her activism, she admitted she was politically naïve, but she emphasized that she was "indefatigable." For Fonda, what happened at that benefit demonstrates that organizers should "never underestimate what might be lying dormant beneath the surface of a back-combed blonde wearing false eyelashes. All she might need is to be asked."[133]

Yet the accusation of radical chic leveled at privileged people seems to have affected Fonda, too. In a 2018 documentary about her life, Fonda made a point of distinguishing herself from the radical chic elite. "I wasn't some privileged person kind of doling out money and then going about my life," she said of herself in the late sixties and seventies. What she was doing was nothing less than "full-time activism."[134] More work needs to be done on the reception of "Radical Chic" in left-wing quarters. For now, it seems fair to say that New Leftists' failure to contest Wolfe's characterizations of the Movement and its supporters enabled his critique to sink deeper roots into American politics and culture.

****

Perhaps one reason that radicals did not push back against Wolfe's "Radical Chic" is that the New Left was much less forgiving than the Old Left of moneyed radicals. And there was no shortage of deep-pocketed sixties radicals. One-time sixties radical Steve Wasserman is no stranger to such people. In the early 1980s, he drew up a list of all the left-wing people he knew who had money... substantial money. These were people who could afford to be courageous and politically principled. Even if being principled meant they would take a hit financially, it wasn't going to affect their principal, as Wasserman cleverly put it.

When Wasserman reached the 150th name, he called it quits. "You can be very cynical about them," he acknowledges, "and on alternate Wednesdays I am." However, he also feels gratitude toward people—both older and younger—whose money enabled left-wing institutions to survive. "Without Stanley Sheinbaum and Betty Warner's money, the ACLU wouldn't have a headquarters office in New York City and *Ramparts* wouldn't have survived as long as it did."[135] Another generous Hollywood donor was the producer Bert Schneider. In the fall of 1967, when Schneider visited antiwar activist Rennie

Davis of the National Mobilization to End the War in Vietnam, he asked what the group most needed. When Davis replied that the organization was deeply in the red and unable to pay its enormous telephone bills, Schneider reportedly wrote Davis a check on the spot for $170,000.[136] That's nearly 1.7 million in today's dollars.

These stories of financial generosity by rich left-of-center people are little known. Wasserman ventures that "the history of the moneyed left has never been truthfully told or written." It is, he claims, "the big taboo that dares not speak its name."[137] If this story has remained tabooed, under wraps all these decades later, it owes something to Wolfe's essay. Radical chic . . . few fessed up to belonging to *that* club.

In thinking about the relationship of the radical rich to the Panthers, it makes sense to pay attention to what Panther leader Elaine Brown wrote about the party's collaborators some 30 years ago. Brown resented Wolfe's depiction of them as insincere and ludicrous. She acknowledged that not everyone who gave money or attended a benefit did so because they were concerned about "the plight of poor and oppressed black people." However, she also pointed out that when it came to commitment, plenty of people fell short. Even within the ranks of the Panther party there were "ordinary black opportunists." Brown was less interested than rival Black Power activists in probing the intentions of those aiding the party. "None of that was the point. We were dying, and all of them, the strongest and the most frivolous, were helping us survive another day."[138]

Part Five chronicles the period after the publication of "Radical Chic" when the Panthers made an even firmer pivot away from armed struggle and began to focus much of their attention on survival programs—"survival pending revolution." Those programs cost money, and the Panthers gained some high-profile benefactors. While solidarity did not entirely disappear, it might make sense to characterize much of it as allyship. One key site in which solidarity or allyship played out, and sometimes quite vividly, was in America's courtrooms as the Panthers and their mostly white left-wing lawyers put prosecutors, Red Squad agents, and the whole apparatus of the state up against the proverbial wall.

PART FIVE

The Changing Fortunes of Cross-Racial Solidarity

Part Five: Introduction

As colleagues at *New York* magazine, Gloria Steinem and Tom Wolfe were friendly, even though she was a part of the Movement he mocked. Nevertheless, she saw up close how "Radical Chic" played out. "The power of ridicule," she later observed, "is quite profound."[1] Of course, the power of COINTELPRO, the Federal Bureau of Investigation (FBI)'s counterintelligence program, working in tandem with local Red Squads, was also profound. COINTELPRO amplified rivalries and ideological schisms to such an extent that the Black Panther Party became enveloped in a fog of debilitating paranoia. As the party's chief of staff, David Hilliard found himself face to face with the depressing reality that "the police dominate what we do, how we're seen." The terrible irony of this was not lost on him. "We wanted to create a party that would let us—and the black community—determine our own destinies," Hilliard wrote. "But now, because of the Party, the state—FBI, police, Red Squads—is deciding our fate."[2]

In the past, the coordinated efforts of law enforcement to neutralize the Panthers had encouraged the group to work in coalition with other radicals, and to even seek the support of left-leaning liberals. They sought allies, which led to cross-racial efforts at solidarity such as 1969's United Front Against Fascism. Until the late fall of 1970, the Panthers seemed likely to continue down this path, but within a year it became clear they were headed in a different direction.

As I demonstrate in Part Five, cross-racial solidarity did not entirely end, but it did develop differently. Often it came about spontaneously in courtrooms from San Jose, California, to New York City, where Black radicals, most of them Panthers, were on trial. In some of those courtrooms, everyday Americans, fulfilling their civic duty as jurors, turned the courtroom into

Image P5.1 Black Panther Chief of Staff David Hilliard speaking at the start of the Bobby Seale/Ericka Huggins trial in New Haven, Connecticut, May 1, 1970. Behind Hilliard, left to right: Tom Hayden, with his head down, longtime pacifist David Dellinger, Panther Elbert Howard in sunglasses, Lee Weiner and Rennie Davis, both bespectacled, and Abbie Hoffman.

Fred W. McDarrah, Getty Images

a site of solidarity as they thwarted the state's prosecutorial war against Black radicals. Theirs was not the "great refusal" that radicals had hoped for, but it signaled that the Movement could reach more middle-of-the-road Americans.

TWELVE

"Allies Everywhere"

The Panthers' Relations with Liberals and Radicals

Popular accounts of the Movement often treat it as a decade-bound phenomenon, but the era's engine of protest did not stall out at the dawn of the new decade. Instead, the Movement was growing and expanding its reach, but, it must be said (and this is an important caveat), without the benefit of robust, mass-based organizations. Left liberals played a role in the broadening of dissent.[1]

Certainly, Black left liberals continued to oppose the government's campaign against the Panthers. They did so in Detroit after a violent confrontation in fall 1970 between the police and local Panthers resulted in the murder of a police officer and the mass arrest of local Panthers on charges of conspiracy to murder. A coalition called the Michigan Committee Against Repression (MCAR) had formed earlier to protest the Detroit police department's relentless harassment of local Panthers for such activity as selling the party newspaper. MCAR, whose members included Congressman John Conyers, state representative (and future Detroit mayor) Coleman Young, local National Association for the Advancement of Colored People (NAACP) officials, and religious leaders, denounced the police department's attack on the Panthers as "part of a nation-wide government conspiracy that is mounting in fury against the Black Panther Party."[2]

One can find more mainstream liberal support for the Panthers, too. In late April 1970, Yale University president Kingman Brewster shocked many when he weighed in on the Panther case in New Haven. Brewster said he thought the Panthers were likely right: They could not get a fair trial in America, and he was "appalled and ashamed" that this should be so.[3] Later that same year, in November 1970, liberals and leftists came together to form the Committee for

Public Justice (CPJ) because they believed the country had entered a period of "political repression."[4] Lawyer and journalist Roger Wilkins was the group's chairman, and other familiar names were a part of the effort, including former Attorney General Ramsey Clark, Hannah Weinstein, writer Lillian Hellman, *New York Review of Books* editor Robert Silvers, the psychiatrist Robert Coles, and the Bernsteins.

One indicator of repression, in the CPJ's view, was the government's treatment of the Panthers. Clark publicly labeled as "absurd" Hoover's view of the Panthers as the most dangerous group in America.[5] Even several years later there were centrist liberals who blamed law enforcement for the violence between the Panthers and the police. When the commission investigating police–Panther violence, the one headed up by civil rights moderate Roy Wilkins and Ramsey Clark, issued its long-delayed 1973 report, *Search and Destroy*, it excoriated the government, particularly in relation to the Fred Hampton–Mark Clark murders in Chicago. Ramsey Clark put it this way: "In the raw, deliberate unnecessary use of violence, this stands alone. People are sleeping in the cold of night, and you come in with machine guns."[6]

Liberal support emerged in the South as well, as the historian Devin Fergus has demonstrated in his work on Black Power. Fergus focused on Winston-Salem, North Carolina, where local Panthers weathered all manner of police harassment, including the destruction by arson of their headquarters, the illegal seizure of their property, and arrest. The American Civil Liberties Union (ACLU) and its North Carolina chapter (NCCLU) proved crucial in helping the Panthers legally fight back against their treatment at the hands of law enforcement and the judicial system. Between 1969 and 1975, the NCCLU fought to protect the Panthers' constitutional rights. One went all the way to the Supreme Court, which, in March 1971, ruled in favor of the NCCLU. Oakland headquarters played a role in building support for the beleaguered Panthers of Winston-Salem. Following a January 1971 police raid, David Hilliard authorized Martin Kenner, who headed up the defense of the New York Panther 21, to build on the efforts of a committee of Panther moms to win the support of local church elders. From their successful campaign ("Support our children. Don't kill our children."), support from more Black and white liberals followed.[7] The Episcopal Church, on the recommendation of a local Episcopalian grant committee, gave $45,000 of funding to the Panthers' free ambulance service.[8]

However, complicating the Panthers' efforts to win the support of liberals was the steady stream of news stories about violence within the Black Panther Party. Details about the torture and murder of Alex Rackley coming out of the Panther trial in New Haven were especially troubling. If George Sams was such a violent and repellent person, as Panthers testified on the witness stand, why did the New Haven Panthers obey his order to murder Rackley?[9] Then there was the news in May 1970 about the arrests of 10 Panthers, including Don Cox, accused of murdering another suspected informer, this time in Baltimore.[10] Then in February 1971, the journalist Edward Jay Epstein (no relation to the aforementioned Epsteins), writing in *The New Yorker*, contested claims made by Panther lawyer Charles Garry that the police had killed 28 Panthers in the past year. Garry's allegation was widely covered, but so was Epstein's so-called correction in which he declared that only two deaths—those of Fred Hampton and Mark Clark—were directly attributable to the police. The others, Epstein argued, "start off as just ghetto incidents."[11]

A few left-liberal journalists continued to support the Panthers. Murray Kempton covered the Panther 21 trial in New York. "Murray Kempton was there every day in that courtroom," said Afeni Shakur. "God bless him." Kempton, who knew Don Cox from the defense committee benefits, provided him with bail money when Cox was charged with murder.[12] Donald Freed of Los Angeles wrote about the Bobby Seale–Ericka Huggins trial in New Haven. But more centrist liberals believed that the negative press signaled something was deeply wrong with the Panthers.

While liberals often were divided about the Panthers, leftists often behaved like the Panthers' cheering squad. It was an article of faith on the left that the Panthers were blameless in every one of their encounters with the police. One measure of contemporaneous left-wing support for the Panthers is the amount of newspaper coverage the alternative press devoted to Panther trials and the size and racial diversity of the crowds supporting incarcerated Panthers.

In early April 1970, the one-year anniversary of the arrests in the New York Panther 21 case, several thousand protestors, described by the *New York Times* as mostly white and young, marched and rallied "to put the pigs in the pokey and the Panthers on the street." A month later, on "May Day," May 1, 1970, as many as 15,000 people gathered on the New Haven Green to protest the prosecution of eight Panthers in the Rackley case and Nixon's expansion of the war. (Nixon and Agnew reportedly hoped for violent protests to break out at Yale, thereby deepening the silent majority's antagonism toward higher education.[13]) In courtrooms in New York and New Haven, the spectators included not just other Panthers, particularly relatives of the defendants, but also a larger number of young white supporters.

In the Bay Area, white radical enthusiasm for the Panthers, a homegrown phenomenon, was strong. On August 5, 1970, a sea of people—somewhere between 5,000 and 10,000—gathered at the Alameda County courthouse to greet Huey Newton upon his release on bail.[14] This was two months after Charles Garry won, on appeal, a reversal of Newton's conviction on the charge of manslaughter in the October 1967 death of Officer Frey. (The California Court of Appeals surprised many by ruling that the judge had failed to include in his instructions to jurors that if they accepted Newton's explanation that he had been unconscious when the police were shot, it constituted a complete defense.)[15] Newton would have to stand trial again, but he was free on bond.

Within a week of his release, Newton declared of the Panthers, "We have allies everywhere." It must have felt that way.[16] After all, much of his bond was reportedly provided by the white Episcopal bishop of New York, Paul Moore, who was a well-known liberal. Moreover, the people providing him a haven in his first three months of freedom were his lawyer Alex Hoffmann and Elsa Knight Thompson of the radical radio station KPFA, who lived together.[17]

One year later, in August 1971, the Panthers still had the support of many white radicals, as evidenced by the turnout to commemorate George Jackson. The incarcerated Panther had been gunned down, according to prison authorities, while trying to escape San Quentin.[18] Five thousand people attended his memorial. Many of the attendees were young people wearing "old shirts and Levi trousers," the downwardly mobile style now common among white radicals. When Jackson's body arrived, people "saluted him with clenched fists raised high."[19]

White radicals' support of the Black Panther Party remained robust through two key Panther-sponsored gatherings of the left in the fall of 1970. It was Eldridge Cleaver, still in exile in Algiers, who came up with the idea that the Panthers sponsor a Revolutionary People's Constitutional Convention (RPCC). Cleaver had long maintained that "neither white radicals nor black radicals are going to get very far by themselves, one without the other."[20] The plan was for a multiracial group of radical activists to meet Labor Day weekend in Philadelphia, where they would deliberate about how they might rewrite the country's constitution.

Image 12.1 Huey P. Newton, fist raised, addresses the Panthers' Revolutionary People's Constitutional Convention at Temple University in Philadelphia, September 5, 1970. Crowd estimates range between 6,000 and 15,000.
AP Photo

The Philadelphia convention, which drew somewhere between 6,000 and 15,000 people, 60–70 percent of whom were Black, was contentious.[21] Just before the convention, Huey Newton had declared his support for women's and gay liberation, but in the trenches Newton's words did not always carry much weight. In Philadelphia, white women's liberationists and Panthers were often at loggerheads.[22] Despite the tensions, participants hammered out the broad outlines of a constitution, which included community control of the police, courts, and schools.[23] However, the large number of white activists reportedly alienated some party members. The follow-up convention in Washington, DC, went forward but in a highly disorganized fashion, without even a proper convention site after Howard University pulled out of its agreement to host the event. This time, Black activists constituted only 30 percent of attendees.[24]

Image 12.2 Attendees of the Panthers' Revolutionary People's Constitutional Convention in Philadelphia respond to Newton's speech.
AP Photo

After the shambolic RPCC in Washington, DC, in late November 1970, some white radicals grumbled to each other about how little they mattered to the Panthers, little more than an afterthought. One white radical and Panther supporter, writing in the *Berkeley Barb*, agreed with that assessment. However, he blamed white activists who, back in 1967–68, when they first had contact with the Panthers, were too guilt-ridden to question the Panthers' subordination of them. "The Panthers could not respect the white movement when it failed to respect itself." Now it is time, he argued, for white radicals to absorb the Panthers' original message to them: "Go and organize your own community."[25]

The only problem with this analysis was that the Panthers had not usually leaned into the Student Nonviolent Coordinating Committee (SNCC)'s dictum to whites: "Organize your *own* community." Particularly from 1968 onward their message to white radicals was to support the Panthers, to serve as auxiliaries to the country's genuine revolutionaries. In March 1970, Hilliard told white college students in Connecticut that if they wanted to stop the state's prosecution of Bobby Seale in New Haven, they should follow the example of the Panthers by fighting back. "If you want to break windows, if you want to kill a pig, if you want to burn the courthouse, you would be moving against the symbols of oppression."[26]

This was precisely the direction that some white radicals already had taken and would continue to take. However, it was not the direction in which Newton wanted the Panthers to move. For the RPCC to foster the development of a multiracial left, something that for three years the Panthers had been attempting, albeit sometimes perfunctorily, Newton would have to be onboard. However, at this juncture Newton seemed more interested in delivering ponderous two-hour lectures about the ideas of Marx and Lenin. Newton's desire to get Panther members and college students up to speed about dialectical materialism was well-intentioned, but his talks were full of jargon, and he often came across as pretentious as he laid out his new and confusing theory of "intercommunalism." Audiences were left feeling perplexed and angry. Why are you lecturing us about these dead Marxist guys, audience members demanded, when you could be talking about what's happening right now? After witnessing one such long-winded performance, Stew Albert joked, "Right on, and on, and on."[27]

The more important reason the RPCC was going nowhere was that Newton wanted to marginalize its creator and instigator, Eldridge Cleaver. In Newton's view, Cleaver's militarism and his fixation on guerrilla warfare had taken the Panthers down the wrong road. What did Newton say to his friend David Hilliard shortly after being released from prison? "Everybody in the Party acts like Eldridge." Newton took steps to reorient the party away from Cleaver, but a lot of Panthers disagreed. Certainly, Cleaver, head of the party's international section in Algiers, was not giving up without a fight.[28]

COINTELPRO played a significant role in the bad blood between the two men, but so did strategic differences, particularly that Newton rejected as chimerical Cleaver's continued faith in armed struggle and that Cleaver derided as "revisionist" Newton's turn toward the pragmatic with the party's survival programs.²⁹ Mind you, Newton sometimes still sounded like his old self. In his August 1971 eulogy for slain writer and prisoner George Jackson, Newton declared that revolutionaries would "slit every throat that threatens our freedom."³⁰ However, Newton's rhetoric may have stemmed in large part from his fears about political rivals. Certainly, by spring 1971 the differences separating Newton and Cleaver hardened into a lethal conflict. There were two warring camps, with Newton's supporters often dubbed the West Coast faction and Cleaver's supporters the East Coast faction.

What happened was not just a war of words. People on both sides died. Consider Sam Napier, the Panther who ran the East Coast distribution of the Panther newspaper. Napier dedicated himself to getting out the paper; he was not involved in the military arm of the party. However, his centrality to the paper made him a target of Newton's enemies. On April 17, 1971, a group of pro-Cleaver Panthers, two of whom were among the Panther 21, broke into the Queens distribution center and set it on fire. But not before they found Napier, whom they tied to a bed, tortured, shot to death, and then burned. They also grabbed the two-year-old child whom Napier cared for and threw him out the door, leaving him with lasting injuries. Kenner called it "unspeakably brutal."³¹ Afeni Shakur agreed. When a friend of Shakur's expressed astonishment about Black people who became "pigs," Afeni did not miss a beat. "And what do you think of a brother who will go to another brother, and tie his hands and put plaster over his mouth and blindfold him and put three bullets in the back of his head?"³²

The same could have been asked about the shooting of the radical white lawyer Fay Stender, which was only very distantly related to the East-West conflict. Just as Beverly Axelrod played the key role in the editing and publication of her client/lover Eldridge Cleaver's *Soul on Ice*, so had Fay Stender played that role for George Jackson's *Soledad Brother*. Working with Garry, she played a critical role in the defense of Jackson, and before that, Newton. However, Stender fell out of favor with Jackson when she refused to facilitate his prison escape. Falling out with Jackson meant running afoul of the prison gang/political group he had formed, the Black Guerrilla Family (BGF). Eight long years after Jackson's death, a recently paroled BGF member broke into Stender's home and demanded she sign a statement admitting she had betrayed Jackson and the prison movement. Once she signed it, while declaring her innocence, the intruder shot her, leaving her paralyzed from the waist down. After testifying against her assailant, she flew to Tokyo, where she took her own life.³³

But that was 1980, and I have gotten ahead of my story. After his August 1970 release on bail, Newton pursued a two-pronged approach: a pragmatic aboveground strategy of Black community survival programs and a clandestine project to strengthen the party's militaristic arm. Newton continued to describe the Panthers as Marxist, but he departed from party orthodoxy when he extended an olive branch to Black churches and Black capitalists.[34] He also made a point of publicly disavowing the Panthers' relationship to the white left. In an April 1971 article, Newton criticized the Panthers' "hook-up with white radicals," which he blamed on Cleaver. It had alienated the Black community and left the Panthers in "a twilight zone." Moreover, Newton observed that because white leftists had little influence in their own communities, the Panthers were without "access to the white community."[35]

In 1973, Newton was more forthright, as he argued that white radicals' connections to the party had hurt them, too. Cleaver had "encouraged young whites to think of themselves as 'bad' Blacks, thus driving them even further from their own community," as they were "plunged deeper into their peculiar identity crisis." The result, Newton argued, was that the young Blacks and whites missed out on an opportunity "to express and make concrete their authentic underlying solidarity and love." He was not writing off such partnerships, but he wanted to rewrite their terms. True solidarity, he said, "still remains to be done."[36]

Where did this leave the white leftists who had imagined themselves an auxiliary to the Panther struggle? After all, although Newton had been moving toward survival programs since late 1968, Panthers, including those in powerful leadership positions, continued to demand that white radicals "pick up the gun." Some white radicals had obliged, or at least began taking target practice.[37] Roxanne Dunbar-Ortiz was part of a radical group in New Orleans and recalls that they were asked to "develop safe places that could be filled with guns for fugitive Panthers who never showed up."[38]

As for Weatherman, by late 1969, its members were underground and determined to "bring the war home." In March 1970, a Weatherman cadre set about making anti-personnel bombs similar to the ones America was dropping in Vietnam. They were filled with roofing nails to maximize maiming. The group's intended target was noncommissioned officers and their wives and dates at a dance at the Army base in Fort Dix, in New Jersey. Instead, one of the would-be bombers accidentally connected the wrong wire, setting off an explosion so massive it killed three Weathermen and leveled the Greenwich

Village townhouse where they were holed up.³⁹ Two months later, Weatherman announced a "Declaration of War" against "Amerika" to show that black revolutionaries would "never again . . . fight alone." As Weatherman Mark Rudd later pointed out, the group's communique was "suitably contradictory." They wanted to make common cause with the predominantly white counterculture—"freaks are revolutionaries, and revolutionaries are freaks," even though it seemed to contradict their conviction that whites were, across the board, racist.⁴⁰

Somehow, by the spring of 1970, Weatherman seemed to have moved several steps closer to where Abbie Hoffman had been some three years earlier during the Summer of Love, when he declared hippies his tribe, his community. In fact, Weatherman and Yippie grew closer in this period. But living as hippies and setting off the occasional bomb in support of Black revolutionaries or the North Vietnamese was not the difficult organizing work that Bayard Rustin had in mind when he first suggested whites undertake antiracist work in their own communities. Moreover, life underground consigned the members of the Weather Underground to living what Rudd called "shadowy, anonymous existences."⁴¹

Weatherman succeeded in doing more than just provoking the ire of the Nixon White House, the Federal Bureau of Investigation (FBI), and law enforcement more broadly. Recent scholarship shows that Weatherman's townhouse explosion, its promise of more violence, and its impermeability to surveillance and infiltration led the FBI to reframe clandestine left-wing guerrilla violence as "terrorism." This reframing enabled the FBI to reorder its domestic security operations and to develop different strategies and techniques, all in the name of national security.⁴²

Despite the extraordinary effort extended to put an end to Weatherman, they remained remarkably successful at eluding the authorities. That doesn't mean the group was politically successful. For the most part, the groups Weatherman hoped to incite to action—the "grease," the "freaks," maybe even Black people—were hostile or indifferent to them. Yet not all Americans were utterly obdurate. There were signs that consciousness was shifting among Vietnam veterans, and a group of people the hard left had disowned: students on college campuses.

Indeed, even if the "revolution" was a mirage, protest did not end with December 1969's disastrous concert at Altamont, or three months later with the townhouse explosion, or the National Guard's gunning down of students at Kent State in early May 1970—the events that histories typically invoke as the end of the era. Even after Kent State, college students were more united than ever in opposing the status quo. A Harris poll of college students in the summer of 1970 provided ample evidence of this attitudinal shift. According to the poll, 75 percent of college students said they agreed with the antiwar protests on campus and favored "basic changes in the system." A surprising 11 percent of students polled labeled themselves radical or far left.[43]

A year later when Nixon announced an incursion into Laos, antiwar activists took to the streets again, this time in Washington, DC. "If the government won't stop the war," they declared, "we'll stop the government." In early May 1971, tens of thousands of people came to Washington, DC, with the intention of nonviolently blocking key bridges and traffic circles, with vehicles, blockades, and their own bodies. Local law enforcement, supplemented by the National Guard, arrested 12,000 protestors, the largest number ever. Although they failed to shut down the government, they made themselves heard at the White House. CIA director Richard Helms later acknowledged that the protest put more pressure on the government to end the war. The release of the Pentagon Papers a few weeks after the May Day protests turned more mainstream Americans against the war in Vietnam, though their attitudes toward the antiwar movement remained negative.

Ironically, as the prospects for change brightened somewhat—whether in ending the government's war against the Vietnamese or the Panthers—the Movement, which might have taken advantage of these changing circumstances, was continuing to splinter. Its disarray nearly caused the shelving of 1971's May Day protest, which was the last big antiwar protest.[44]

There were some on the left, people such as Arthur Waskow of the Institute for Policy Studies, who tried to exert a moderating influence. In the wake of 1968's Democratic National Convention, Waskow counseled "guerrilla politics, not guerrilla war." In his view, the Movement needed to "invent a political course of action, not street tactics."[45] Even some activists to Waskow's left believed that the Movement needed to abandon its quixotic fantasies of revolution. Take the case of Bill Zimmerman, a dedicated radical whose activism stretched back to early-sixties Mississippi. He participated in 1971's May Day protest, and took up even riskier forms of activism, but as early as the fall of 1969, Zimmerman was brooding about the revolution that he and his friends

Image 12.3 Demonstrators, protesting the Vietnam War, gather in front of the Justice Department in Washington, DC, as part of the May Day Protest, May 4, 1971. AP Photo

were supposedly working toward. Of course, the right had been criticizing the left's lack of a plan since the dawn of the sixties. Radicals were accustomed to batting away such criticisms. But it increasingly seemed to Zimmerman that he and his comrades had little understanding of such essentials as a "practical strategy, an understanding of the balance of forces, the marshaling of resources, and workable tactics." Indeed, he had no "clear vision of a revolutionary future." His decision to embrace pragmatic politics was, he said, "simply a matter of weighing real political achievement against merely being politically correct."[46]

With Tom Hayden, Jane Fonda, and others, Zimmerman formed the Indochinese Peace Campaign (IPC), which played a role in key Congressional races in 1972. The IPC's immediate achievement was the passage in Congress of the War Powers Act on November 7, 1973. It became law after Congress overrode Nixon's veto. The act forced the president to provide official notice to Congress within 48 hours of the deployment of U.S. military forces abroad. If Congress failed to approve the deployment, our forces would have to be withdrawn within 60 days. The War Powers Act affected Nixon's ability to respond to what was a deteriorating military situation in South Vietnam. Later, it would limit the military actions Ronald Reagan could carry out in Central America, and it forced George H. W. Bush and George W. Bush to seek congressional approval before launching US invasions. "We had turned Congress into an antiwar battleground," Zimmerman wrote, "and had revealed the significant antiwar sentiment within it."[47]

Other left-wing young people pursued organizing that reached into white America, although not usually as emissaries of antiracism. They did so by working in the environmental, feminist, or lesbian and gay movements, or by becoming organizers in less easily managed unions or entirely new organizations such as 9to5, which organized women office workers.[48] One of the more promising efforts to organize white men in the latter half of the sixties had been the draft resistance movement. However, the Nixon administration's remaking of the Vietnam war from a ground war to an aerial war, and its launching of the draft lottery in late 1969, undercut that movement. In another promising innovation, some young white radicals established GI coffeehouses to foster antiwar activism on and around military bases.

By 1972, cross-racial collaborations between the Panthers and the white left were largely a thing of the past. It is true that the United Front to Combat Fascism and the RPCC had not nourished a durable multiracial left. Certainly, the Panthers' focus on survival programs, which prioritized Black self-sufficiency, offered no obvious or meaningful role for self-declared white revolutionaries. But even had Newton and the Panthers wanted to work with white leftist groups, to which groups would the Panthers have turned? The left was too riven, and for that matter so were the Panthers.

One measure of the Movement's crack-up is what happened in December 1971 when the manslaughter charges against Huey P. Newton were dismissed. Just 16 months earlier Newton was mobbed when he walked out of the Alameda County courthouse. This time, there were no crowds to greet the man who had inspired cries of "Free Huey!" One reason activists greeted his freedom indifferently was that the FBI made sure that news of Newton's lifestyle, particularly his $650 a month penthouse apartment, was widely circulated. Within the party there was considerable grousing. One of the New York Panthers, Cetewayo, accused Newton and Hilliard of "squandering money while most party members are starving to death." The *New York Times* quoted someone familiar with the Panthers who echoed that charge. "His cadre doesn't even have clothes, and [Newton's] in a penthouse." Once again, a plush penthouse proved an effective attack line against the Panthers.[49]

Since his release on bail in August 1970, Newton had been charting the party's course, and he was determined to make it into a "stronghold" in the city of its birth. In 1971, the party closed ranks and closed chapters across the country. It made Oakland its base, its stronghold, as it focused on developing programs to facilitate the new party mandate of "survival pending revolution."[50] Martin Kenner believes that these programs represented "Huey's most brilliant insight." Kenner claims that Newton understood, and well before other left leaders, that the United States was "headed toward a counter revolution," one that set the stage for the income inequality and the stagnation of wages that came to prevail.[51] By 1972, Newton, who had long sworn off electoral politics, made another turn, as he pushed the Panthers into local Democratic Party politics, with Seale and Elaine Brown running for mayor and a seat on the Oakland City Council respectively. "We have to start talking about how to win, not how to get killed," was how Brown put it to a pro-Panther audience at Merritt College.[52] The Panthers' embrace of electoral politics was not unique to them. Some white left-wingers such as Tom Hayden tried their hand at electoral politics, too.

In this period, cross-racial partnerships faded as the Movement, admittedly never a cohesive whole, further unraveled. Yet even after the Panther leadership in Oakland largely abandoned the solidarity politics that had animated the RPCC in the summer of 1970, cross-racial solidarity persisted in two connected areas where it had first emerged in 1967: the financial and the legal.

Stronghold and Its White Supporters

Not much has been written about Panther finances, largely because most scholars have been absorbed in chronicling the party's ideological twists and turns or, especially in the post-1970 period, in documenting the criminality of some of its leaders. Panther finances are an important part of the story, though. In the early 1970s, the Panthers had what seemed like "incredible amounts of money," to the Berkeley radical Anne Weills.[53] Their money aroused the interest of both the FBI and Panthers in other cities struggling to keep their chapters afloat. Of course, keeping the party going, particularly its survival programs, required money. Providing legal defense for even some incarcerated Panthers was even costlier and made more so when defendants jumped bail. Still, the presence of money and the rumors of its misuse, which were amplified by the FBI, had an undeniably corrosive effect on the party.

Writing about the Panthers and money necessarily involves writing about the people who funded them, an overwhelmingly white and privileged group that most scholars have steered clear of. However, the Panthers' success in fundraising bears further examination, especially because it stands in such contrast to SNCC's fundraising woes. Even though SNCC kept its distance from actual violence, in contrast to the Panthers, it faced more formidable obstacles when it came to fundraising. Perhaps it was a matter of timing, that SNCC's disavowal of interracialism felt extreme in 1966, and within a few years was normalized. While it is true that the controversy surrounding Felicia Bernstein's benefit made the Panthers persona non grata among many Manhattan left liberals, the same was not true on the West Coast. The charge of radical chic had virtually no impact in Hollywood.[54] Nor did all the troubling news stories about the Panthers make any real dent in their support there.

Donations by wealthy Hollywood supporters proved crucial in sustaining the Panthers. No one's support was more important than that of Bert Schneider, the glamorous, risk-taking Hollywood producer. Schneider was highly successful, and the scion of a powerful Hollywood insider, but that did not stop him from routinely giving the middle finger to the Hollywood establishment. The filmmaker Henry Jaglom believed that "having a father who ran Columbia Pictures gave Bert great security and an even greater desire to rebel." With his friend Bob Rafelson, Schneider developed and produced the hit TV series *The Monkees*, which gave American audiences their own not exactly homegrown version of the Beatles, but something rather akin to the Fab Four's *A Hard Day's Night* hit movie. It debuted in 1966 and kept Schneider flush for years. He made a bigger splash as the executive producer of 1969's *Easy Rider*, the first truly "sixties" youth movie. *Easy Rider* cost nothing to make and it made millions. Schneider was a central figure in the "New Hollywood," which took a sledgehammer to the old studio system and revolutionized the industry. No more would directors toil to please an imperious studio head. The New Hollywood empowered directors, who began to see themselves as auteurs. No one took greater pleasure in this revolution than Schneider.[55]

Schneider's string of hits made him rich. Despite his reputation as a hedonist, he was not a frivolous man. Yes, he apparently was "an extreme pothead and cokehead," as Martin Kenner puts it, but he was also well-read and

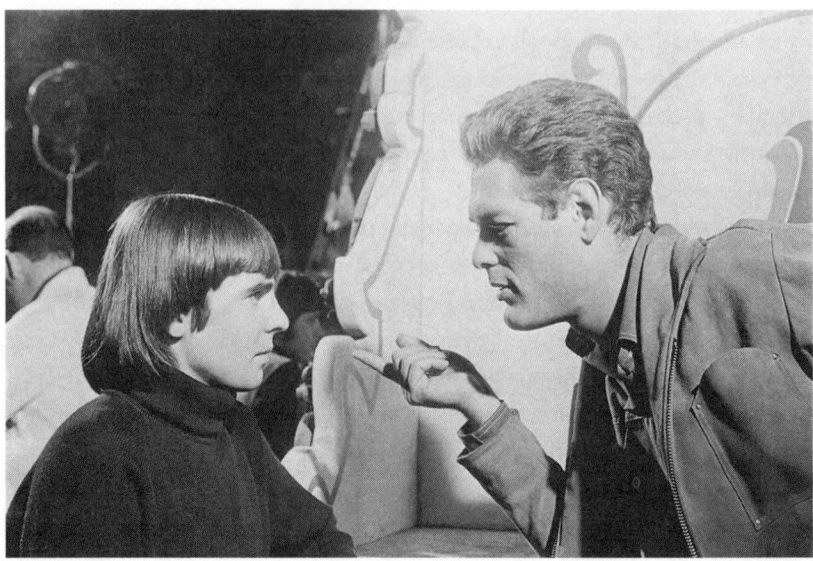

Image 12.4 Hollywood producer Bert Schneider with the British singer Davy Jones of the Monkees, December 19, 1966. Schneider became a key benefactor of the Black Panther Party.
Cyril Maitland/Express/Hulton Archive/Getty Images

intelligent.⁵⁶ Most likely because of his experience as a producer, he was an able problem-solver. The combination of his money, intelligence, chutzpah, and problem-solving capabilities must have made him irresistible to two high-profile rebels in need of assistance: Abbie Hoffman and Huey Newton. Both men became central people in Schneider's life. Before Schneider met Newton, he had already been linked to Elaine Brown, who was the Panthers' liaison to Hollywood liberals. She judged him "a unique 'white boy'" because he had none of the "annoyingly patronizing attitude of ingratiation" that so many white liberals had. Perhaps Newton appreciated Schneider's naturalness, too.⁵⁷ As for Schneider, once he met Newton, whom he regarded as the smartest man he had ever met, he became committed to the Panther leader. The two men saw something in each other . . . perhaps their shared love of rebellion, cocaine, and heterosexual adventuring. Although it is hard to imagine that Schneider's wealth was not a complicating feature of their friendship, Kenner emphasizes that they were "really like brothers."⁵⁸

Schneider introduced the Panthers to sympathetic Hollywood stars. He also became their biggest donor. He picked up much of the tab for the Panthers' programs and helped the much-honored Oakland Community Learning Center, which brought the Panthers good press. He also helped to cover Newton's rent and his legal expenses, which were substantial and remained ongoing. Journalist Kate Coleman estimated that Schneider spent millions on Newton and the Panthers. Newton gave Schneider a gold Panther ring, and he took to calling him an honorary Panther. According to some people, Schneider spoke as if he were a party member, a view likely not shared by actual members. Still, Schneider went to the mat repeatedly for Newton. In 1974, when the Panther was charged with murder, Schneider led the effort to help him avert prosecution by spiriting him out of the country to Cuba. In 1977, when Newton returned to the United States, Schneider paid for his legal defense.

Schneider remained an antiwar stalwart, too, producing the 1974 Oscar-winning antiwar documentary *Hearts and Minds*. Its filmmaker was Peter Davis, the son of writers Tess Slesinger and Frank Davis. During his acceptance speech at the Academy Awards, Schneider angered establishment Hollywood by reading a telegram from the head of the North Vietnamese delegation at the Paris peace talks, thanking America's antiwar movement. Over time, as Hollywood became obsessed with blockbuster movies, Schneider lost interest in making films. Later in the decade, Bob Rafelson says Schneider "shifted more of his energy into political activism," though it is not clear whether that involved more than what he had been doing in supporting Newton and Hoffman.[59]

One difficulty in researching Schneider is that he took a hyperlitigious stance toward the press. To maximize his chances of winning libel suits, he deliberately left as small a footprint in the press as possible, which meant rejecting virtually all interview requests. Still, stories of his bankrolling of the Panthers and others circulated. The left-wing film historian Peter Biskind maintains that Schneider, in contrast to "many Hollywood radicals in those days, acted on his convictions at great personal risk to himself, and was prepared to pay the price."[60] Biskind's point is a crucial one. However, over time it seems that Newton, rather than the party, became the primary beneficiary of Schneider's largesse.[61]

Martin Kenner was not a benefactor, but he was a Panther ally whose knowledge of finances helped to keep the party afloat. Kenner was especially close to David Hilliard, who said Kenner was "as valuable a confidant and advisor to the Party as Stanley Levison was to Martin Luther King's SCLC."[62] Kenner's role as the head of the defense committee for the Panther 21 put him in the position of handling money for the Panthers. His financial know-how, his honesty, and his willingness to "subordinate" himself to the political leadership of the Oakland Panthers led them to entrust him with managing their money. This would have been in fall 1970, while Kenner was still with the Panther 21 defense committee. The reason that money management was an issue at all was that the Panthers were "besieged with offers for books and movies," according to Kenner. Newton believed the Panthers should form a corporation called Stronghold to take advantage of the media's interest in them. The lawyer Alex Hoffmann was also there at Stronghold's creation and claims its primary attraction was as an offshore corporation that would be free of taxes, and through which money from North Korea and other countries could be funneled.[63]

Kenner was the one who facilitated the formation of the new Panther corporation. He put Newton and Hilliard in contact with David Lubell, an older white left-wing member of the National Lawyers Guild, who was an entertainment lawyer, someone who likely knew Hannah Weinstein. With his assistance, they drew up the papers for Stronghold Productions. Lubell served as Stronghold's president, but it was Kenner, as its executive vice president, who handled the corporation's day-to-day management. Kenner negotiated lucrative book deals for Panther leaders, and the advances publishers offered helped to fund the purchase of buildings where the Panthers operated health clinics and schools.

Stronghold assumed control of the party's assets, and the receipt of all income, whether it was through campus lectures, book deals, television appearances, records, or films. Party members writing books or recording music were given a contract that assigned rights and royalties to Stronghold. *The Black Panther* newspaper, which started publishing weekly in April 1967, had been the Party's most lucrative source of revenue. That revenue would now flow into the coffers of Stronghold. As the president of Stronghold, Lubell exploited the Party's cultural assets. He copyrighted as Stronghold's own the artwork of Emory Douglas and charged for any reprinting of the Ten-Point Party Program. Most of Stronghold's money was plowed into acquiring property or to pay existing mortgages. Assisting the party in that effort was the Panthers' longtime real estate agent Arlene Slaughter and her son Mickey Phillips. In its first year, Stronghold generated more than $200,000 from its newspaper, book contracts, and lecture fees. It turned a net profit of $94,000 in its first year.[64]

Kenner spent a lot of time hanging out with Hilliard, Newton, and other Panthers. Besides also helping to set up defense committees in various cities for incarcerated Panthers, he accompanied the French writer and Panther supporter Jean Genet when he toured the country in 1970 in support of the Panthers. Kenner had contacts in academia, and it became his job to introduce Newton to intellectuals such as Franz Schurmann, the sociologist who wrote sympathetically about China. It was Kenner who set up the 1971 trip that Newton and a delegation of Panthers took to China, where they met with Premier Zhou Enlai.[65] Kenner finally quit working for the Panthers in 1972, primarily because he had not become a Movement activist to end up a businessman, even one working for the Panthers. Accelerating his exit were Newton's emotional volatility and his conviction that the Panthers should emulate the mafia, albeit below the radar. Newton was apparently inspired by Mario Puzo's bestselling 1969 novel, *The Godfather*, which Kenner had recommended to him.[66]

Kenner and Schneider were not the only white allies who could be said to have collaborated closely with the Panthers in this period, but there were not many others. Robert Scheer continued to work together with Eldridge Cleaver, but this was, by necessity, mostly at a distance since Cleaver resided in Algiers. Moreover, the nature of white radicals' connection, which was with the Oakland leadership rather than the rank and file, illustrates how much the Panthers' practice of cross-racial partnerships had contracted since the high tide of the summer of 1970.

Forging Cross-Racial Solidarity in the Courtroom: Free Huey!

Nevertheless, there were still white Movement people supporting the Panthers in the early 1970s. Many of them did so as members of defense committees active in some of the places where Panthers were on trial. Their work, whether in the Free Huey! campaign, the New York Panther 21 case, or the New Haven trial of Bobby Seale and Ericka Huggins, was consequential.

Gerald Lefcourt of the Panther 21 defense team credits their defense committee in New York with mobilizing critical support among white activists. Lefcourt remembers there being "signs on almost every street corner that read 'Free the Panther 21.'"[67] When the process of questioning prospective jurors (known as voir dire) began on September 8, 1970, the courtroom and hallways were packed with supporters. Outdoors there were demonstrations.[68]

In Lefcourt's view, the committee's success in generating publicity and support for the defendants, who numbered only 12 by the start of the trial, ended up "making incredible inroads" on behalf of the defendants.[69] For one, the protests meant that the press showed up in the courtroom. And not just the alternative press, but the *New York Times*, too. Although the judge in the Panther 21 trial was openly hostile to the defendants and their lawyers, he understood, perhaps especially in the wake of Garry's successful appeal of the verdict in Newton's case in Oakland, that any misstep on his part would lead to an appeal.

The press coverage may have had a moderating effect on the judge in the New Haven case against Panthers Bobby Seale and Ericka Huggins, too. Certainly, Seale's lawyer, Charles Garry, was almost always in the news, and not just for his courtroom theatrics. "Judicial System Geared to Power, Can't Get a Fair Trial, Garry Says" was a fairly typical headline in New Haven.[70] As for the case in San Jose, California, involving Angela Davis, the former Panther and current Communist Party (CP) member, one of the key people on her team, Doris Bin Walker, thought the support generated by the defense committee had a "profound" effect on how the trial unfolded. It prevented the prosecution from engaging in the "more overt and objectionable and most prejudicial manifestations of racism and chauvinism."[71]

Many came to these defense committees with some understanding of the workings of racism in America. But for most white Americans, "the news of an indictment [against a Panther] read like news of a conviction," as the journalist Gilbert Moore put it.[72] The task in all the Panther trials was to help the jurors grasp something of the contours and impact of racism in America. Many of the people who served on these juries came to their service with a good deal of trust in the fairness of law enforcement and the judicial system. What they witnessed in these courtrooms, including the behavior of the prosecuting attorneys and often the judges, rattled their trust that the system really was fair. It changed them.

Jurors' growing willingness to question the state's assertions of guilt reflect the success of defense teams in flipping the script on the prosecution. Prosecuting attorneys imagined they were prosecuting the Panthers, but at a certain point in these trials they realized that the defense was putting on trial the very methods and assumptions that undergirded the prosecutors' cases. What started out as trials about the criminal actions of the Panthers became trials about the government's persecution of the Panthers. Indeed, one important site of cross-racial solidarity in this period of 1970–72 is in the courtrooms of these political trials where jurors came to question the prosecution's presumption of Panther culpability.

The first real sign that Panther trials might not unfold as the government expected, that indictment was *not* tantamount to conviction, occurred on September 1968, when the Alameda County Assistant District Attorney failed to secure a first-degree murder conviction against Newton. At a news conference immediately following the verdict, the lead defense lawyer, Charles Garry, told the assembled reporters that he was "keenly and absolutely disappointed" with the manslaughter conviction. But after the press conference ended, Garry walked over to a sympathetic Black journalist, nudged him in the ribs, and whispered, "We got 'em. We got 'em." It was not an acquittal, but Newton had been saved from the electric chair that many assumed was his fate.

How did Garry and his legal team of Fay Stender and Alex Hoffmann upend the government's plans? Their first step was to use the media to challenge the government's depiction of Newton as a killer. They organized press conferences in which Newton explained why and how the Panthers came to be. They had sympathetic journalists interview Newton, who invariably came across as composed, intelligent, and likable. There were all those enormous "Free Huey!" rallies, too. All of it made for what Garry called "tremendous public relations." Kathleen Cleaver, who helped with the media makeover of Newton, said its point was to make it "politically very, very difficult for Huey Newton to get the death penalty."[73]

Then there were the pretrial motions in which Garry came out punching. The indictment against his client emerged from a grand jury system that he argued was unconstitutional and racist since Blacks were rarely chosen to serve on grand juries. He was relentless about the unfairness of the jury pool, which was drawn from voter registration lists in which Blacks were disproportionately underrepresented. To obtain a jury panel that came even a bit closer to being a jury of Newton's peers, Garry made the unusual move of staging an exceedingly long voir dire process in which he eliminated jurors with openly racist attitudes. The voir dire lasted two weeks, during which lawyers from both sides questioned nearly 160 prospective jurors. Prosecuting attorney Lowell Jensen used 15 preemptive challenges, and Garry used all 20 of his as he tried to eliminate the most worrying racists.

With nine whites, one African American, one Cuban-born American, and one Japanese American, the panel fell far short of what the defense team would have wanted. Bob Blauner, the Berkeley sociologist who appeared as an expert witness, was scathing about the voir dire. Even with Newton's defense team doing its best, the process demonstrated that "total ignorance and indifference to racial matters" proved no bar to serving on the jury.[74] Still, Garry achieved some racial diversity and a surprising degree of gender diversity, with seven female jurors. "Before then," observes the Bay Area lawyer Lise Pearlman, "trial lawyers took the first twelve men who didn't have two heads." Women jurors were a rarity until 1968.[75]

The aim of Newton's attorneys was not just to eliminate racists from the jury; it was to sensitize jurors to their own perhaps unrecognized racism.[76] Both the voir dire process and the trial itself featured expert witnesses giving disquisitions about racism, Black Power, and the meaning of certain expressions or jargon (e.g., "taking care of business") in Black communities. When Newton took the stand, Garry questioned him in a way that enabled him to respond with lengthy, thoughtful answers. It was as if Newton was conducting a seminar about racism, Black history, and the Black Panther Party.

Garry's explicitly political approach in the trial marked a departure from the civil liberties defense typically used by most left-wing National Lawyers Guild attorneys. Explaining his methods to the National Lawyers Guild a year later, Garry stressed the importance of projecting "certain images and issues into the courtroom. Ghettoes are Colonies of the U.S., Huey can't get a fair trial." Garry was also determined to "present Huey as I saw him ... selfless and beautiful."[77]

Garry's efforts to make jurors admirers of Newton persuaded few, most of whom reportedly felt Newton was guilty of *something*. Had it not been for the shrewdness of David. B. Harper, whom the jurors elected their foreman, they would have allowed their gut feelings to prevail. The sole Black juror, Harper, a top officer at the Bank of America in San Francisco, commanded their respect. After being chosen foreman, he readily assumed a position of authority. During their deliberations, he stood at the blackboard in front of the other jurors as if he was teaching a "class."[78] When the jury sat down to deliberate, they were eager to learn what Harper thought about Newton and the Panthers, and the ubiquity of racism in America. Harper "charmed" his fellow jurors and to such an extent that the journalist Gilbert Moore said that he "*hustled* them into the proper administration of justice," so that they would not just rely on their gut feelings. Throughout, he kept his preference for acquittal to himself. When he realized a bloc of jurors could not be talked out of a murder conviction, he was able to pivot and achieve consensus on the lesser charge of manslaughter.[79]

It is impossible to know whether Harper's effectiveness stemmed in part from the way in which Garry foregrounded Black Americans in the courtroom, including the defendant Huey P. Newton. But the Black witnesses called by the defense had an impact on some of the jurors. Speaking of J. Herman Blake, the Black sociologist who explained the meaning of such "ghetto" expressions as "taking care of business," one juror said, "I liked that black professor." Blake told her "a lot about the ghetto and what it's like." She admitted to being "surprised" by him because "with that beard and all over his face, he looked like a bum."[80] That's how the trial worked on these jurors, provoking them to rethink seemingly commonsensical assumptions.

Charles Garry had many opportunities to use these methods in other political trials. In 1969, he turned the courtroom into an antiwar teach-in when defending the Oakland Seven, who were charged with conspiracy for their activism during the fall 1967 Stop the Draft Week. Jurors who had been pro-war emerged from the trial either opposing it or viewing it skeptically. They acquitted all seven defendants.[81] Then, in New Haven, Connecticut, where Panthers Bobby Seale and Ericka Huggins were on trial for kidnapping and murder, Garry, who was defending Seale, and Catherine Roraback, who was defending Huggins, insisted the jury panel include Blacks. After a 17-week voir dire, the longest ever in the state's history, in which 1,034 potential jurors were questioned, the lawyers managed to seat five Blacks on the jury panel.[82] As for Newton, after two mistrials, in which Garry defended Newton, the District Attorney unhappily dropped all charges against him in December 1971. The District Attorney saw no point in another trial when the outcome was likely another deadlocked jury.

Other left-wing lawyers took note of what Garry's legal team was accomplishing. Left-leaning and liberal defense attorneys began incorporating methods they used to challenge the systemic racism embedded in the jury selection process. The National Lawyers Guild published a handbook based on the case, "Minimizing Racism in Jury Trials." They, too, began to use the courtroom to raise the consciousness of the jurors, the judges, the journalists, and everyone else.

The Trials of the Panther 21 and Bobby Seale/Ericka Huggins

However, it was not in Alameda County, California, or in New Haven, Connecticut, that juries first thwarted the government's prosecution by returning acquittals. Those first shocking acquittals of Black Panthers happened in New York City in the spring of 1971. In many ways, the defense team followed the playbook that Garry and his team had written.

Readers will recall that the Panther 21 were charged with conspiracy to commit a battery of crimes: killing policemen, blowing up two police stations, tracks of the New Haven branch of the Penn Central Railroad, several subway stations, a Queens Board of Education office, the Bronx Botanical Garden, and five Midtown department stores that ranged from the down-market Korvette's to the high-end Abercrombie & Fitch. The arrests were carried out on April 2, 1969, and dominated the headlines in the city's papers. Each defendant was slapped with $100,000 bail, and despite many efforts by the defense team to lower their bail, judges refused to budge.[83] By the time the trial began, the number of Panthers in the courtroom was 12. Two of those charged could not be found, and others were in jail elsewhere on other charges or had been severed from the case because they were too sick or too young.[84]

Some of the Panthers' lawyers were inexperienced, which exasperated both the prosecutor, the Assistant District Attorney Joseph A. Phillips and Judge John M. Murtagh. However, the conditions of the trial would have left any defense attorney feeling handicapped. Because the government's case was built on the testimony of six undercover agents, the Panthers' lawyers had no idea what the evidence against their clients was until the first day of the trial. That's when they learned of the central role played by undercover agents. Moreover, the decision of the corrections department to keep defendants in separate facilities made coordinating their defense impossible. The authorities did not alter their position until about a month from the start of the pretrial hearing, leaving the lawyers to at first stumble in the courtroom as they struggled to put names to the faces of their clients. Complicating matters further for the defense was that two defendants—Afeni Shakur (Alice Williams) and Cetawayo (Michael Tabor)—chose to defend themselves.

Voir dire began September 8, 1970, and lasted a full five weeks. About half of the 215 people questioned were immediately dismissed because they already had formed views about the case, or they could not serve for the expected three months. Judge Murtagh admonished the defense for conducting such an abnormally long voir dire, but he permitted it.[85]

In the end, the panel of 12 jurors consisted of six white men, four Black men, one Black woman, and one Puerto Rican man.[86] Lefcourt thought the jurors were a "real mix," although it's worth noting that half of them were well educated. Still, most of them were faithful readers of the city's most conservative newspaper, the *New York Daily News*. Edward Kennebeck, a white book editor who leaned liberal, found this worrying.[87] He was also concerned about their foreman, Ingram Fox, a Black man born in Guyana. A musician and composer, Fox came off "like a pillar of West Indian rectitude," as one journalist put it.[88] He could be stern, and he was known to reprimand other jurors for minor infractions.

Even though the jury panel was decidedly more racially and ethnically diverse than the panel in the first Newton trial, none of its members seemed predisposed to side with the defendants at the start of the trial on October 19, 1970. The Assistant District Attorney Phillips seemed completely confident that they would accept the state's case against the Panthers. Moreover, with six agents ready to testify about the Panther plot to blow up New York, Phillips had amassed an armload of evidence. Then there were the Panthers themselves, who broke all the rules of courtroom decorum. They were not going to play nice the way that Huey Newton had in Oakland. By the time they entered the courtroom for pretrial motions in February 1970, they had been in jail since April 2, 1969, nearly a year. Their appeals for lower bail, decent prison conditions, and access to their lawyers had been denied. Convinced they were being railroaded and that they would be convicted, they decided—and apparently individually—to resist. To juror Stephen Chaberski, a white graduate student in political science, it seemed as if the Panthers arrived in court determined that they would not "cooperate in their own destruction."[89]

Their behavior was so rowdy, their talk so profane that Judge Murtagh, who had been the presiding judge in the trial and conviction of the edgy comic Lenny Bruce, took extreme action.[90] Not even a month into the pretrial hearing, he called a recess, which lasted until April 7. When they returned, they were quieter. But when jury selection began in September, the defendants had a lot more to complain about, including the fact that their legal team could not afford the daily transcripts of the trial, and that the judge had limited the first five rows of the courtroom to members of the press. He put them off limits to the defendants' families and their supporters. Lefcourt remembers that there was a "near riot" over this. "The rebellion in the courtroom was front page news almost daily." If you were the prosecuting attorney, you likely figured that the Panthers' behavior was so appalling that they would have alienated the jurors.[91]

So how did these jurors get turned around? How did they come to sympathize with these unabashedly militant Panthers? For one, Assistant District Attorney Phillips's decision to try it as a political case ended up playing into the hands of the defense. Take Phillips's decision at the trial's outset to have the jurors view *The Battle of Algiers*, a documentary-like film about the Algerian anticolonial struggle for independence against France. Because an undercover agent reported that the Panthers planned to copy the tactics used by the film's rebels, Phillips argued that the film was relevant, that it had bearing on the defendants' intent. The prosecutor took for granted that the jurors would identify with the victims of terrorists so fanatical that they would "blow up little children." For that reason, the defense team also worried that the film might influence the jurors to support conviction.[92]

However, the film landed differently than either side imagined, though it is not too hard to imagine why. *Battle* was widely understood to favor the insurgent Arabs of the National Liberation Front. The filmmaker Gillo Pontecorvo had said of his film that he had wanted to show the "unstoppable process of liberation, not only in Algeria, but throughout the entire world."[93] Although the film showed rebels carrying out brutal bombings in which ordinary people were killed, the French came off far worse. "I'm sure the film did more to help me see things from the defense point of view than the DA suspected," wrote juror Edwin Kennebeck. He was not alone.[94]

The prosecutor's decision to politicize the trial should have made him sensitive to the politics of the courtroom, but it did not. As the journalist Murray Kempton observed, Phillips made plain his contempt for the defendants, speaking condescendingly of their "uneducated minds."[95] Indeed, critical to the jurors' growing sympathies for the defendants were the power dynamics in the courtroom, including the District Attorney's cozy relationship to Judge Murtagh. The defendants suspected the two men were meeting secretly, and a lawyer in the District Attorney's office later confirmed that Murtagh and Phillips frequently conferred. If Phillips wanted to highlight politics, he would have been smart to suggest to the judge with whom he was conferring that he at least try to appear evenhanded. Instead, the judge's bias against the defendants and their lawyers was unmistakable. Lefcourt and his colleagues on the defense team could not get a break as Murtagh overruled them time and again. As the juror Chaberski saw it, the judge, who should have been "a referee," was instead behaving like "a combatant." In the end, Murtagh's unabashed prejudice, his willingness to be the "prosecutor's ally," made him "an inviting target" for the defense. If your argument hinged on the pervasiveness of racism in America, as much of the defense's argument did, you had all the proof you needed every day that court was in session.[96]

One telling moment, at the very end of December, reveals how jurors were absorbing this. That day, the prosecuting attorney Phillips questioned one of his expert witnesses about how much damage a hypothetical blast from a Panther bomb would cause. The defense objected time and again but were consistently overruled. After the judge called for a brief recess, the jury left the courtroom and gathered in their designated room. The jurors were meant to never discuss the case among themselves, but this day a Black juror, Ben Giles, a retired longshoreman, was beside himself with anger. "He's bulldozing them," he said of the judge. He was so furious he wanted to quit. It was one of the very few times that the jurors spoke about the trial as they tried to calm him. As Giles fumed about the trial, several jurors persuaded him to continue serving. Later that evening, Kennebeck wrote in his diary, "Giles, who seemed conservative, has exploded. Has Giles been radicalized?" Giles was not the only frustrated juror. Another Black juror, postal worker James Gary, later said that "some of the jurors were so angry about the Judge's bias they wanted to come out of the jury box and say, 'you're biased . . . this is it—we're gonna acquit.'"[97]

Another reason the jurors grew skeptical of the state's case was that so much of it relied upon the testimony of police agents. The prosecution tried its best to use their testimony to "weave a tapestry of insinuations into a solid piece of conspiracy," but fell short.[98] Take the case of Gene Roberts, a longtime member of the Bureau of Special Services (BOSS), the undercover branch of the New York Police Department. (He had been working for BOSS while serving as Malcolm X's bodyguard at the time of his murder in 1965.) Roberts began confidently, describing the nighttime "recons" he and the Panthers made of downtown department stores. But as the defense team grilled him, these reconnaissance missions turned out to have been curiously haphazard, even laughable affairs. How much time had the Panthers spent checking out the department stores? Two hours. Nor had they produced any drawings of Alexander's or Bloomingdales or provided any reports to the larger group about their findings. Asked what day the group planned to bomb the stores, Roberts admitted they had not settled on a date for the bombing, nor had they decided which stores were meant to be the "jackpot."[99] If the Panthers were going to deliver a day of carnage to New York, it was not anytime soon.

What Roberts and the other five informants did witness (and report on) was what the defendant Dhoruba bin Wahad called a lot of "shucking and jiving," that is, loose talk, often driven by weed and alcohol.[100] During his cross-examination, agent Ralph White admitted that when the Panthers talked about offing the pigs or blowing up this or that building, he never knew whether they were serious or if it was just a matter of "rhetoric."[101] And during his cross-examination, Roberts acknowledged that not one of the Panthers had ever told him to blow up anything. In fact, Roberts was the only "Panther" to acquire aerosol cans for bomb-making. This is consistent with the profile of an infiltrator, invariably the hothead eager to up the ante by acquiring weapons and calling for violence. Captured on his own tiny microphone, Roberts came off "eager and jivey . . . and with a hip drawl"—nothing like the sober agent on the stand.

Yes, there was incriminating evidence against the Panthers, but it was not iron tight, and it never matched the grandiosity of the Panthers' alleged plot. It is true that one of the defendants had written a manual, "Urban Guerilla Warfare," which the police found in several Panther residences.[102] Yet that was not in and of itself proof of guilt. There was also that botched sniper attack on the police and bombings of police stations and the board of education building back in January 1969 when Kuwasi Balagoon (Donald Weems) and Sekou Odinga (Nathaniel Burns) fled the scene of a shooting, leaving Joan Bird hovering in the car to be arrested. Even the journalist Murray Kempton, whose sympathies were with the defendants, acknowledged, "Something *had* happened on the night of January 17."[103] But much of the case against the Panthers focused on their Easter attack on the city. Phillips had emphasized that the police had found pipe bombs that suggested an imminent attack. In truth, all they had found were capped iron pipes, a milk carton half-full of gunpowder, and a few empty aerosol cans. As juror Chaberski notes, "these were the only 'bombs' ever discovered." While the police seized some firearms, they hardly constituted a cache, and they could be justified as needed for self-defense.[104]

Lefcourt's explanation of how the mind of an infiltrator works seems to have made sense to these jurors. His mind is "unreliable because it has a purpose," the lawyer explained. "It needs subversion like a private detective needs an adulteress or adulterer. . . . It extracts sinister language and excludes the good or the explanation for the acts." Moreover, the "infiltrator, the agent, is the heart of the police state," which Lefcourt and the other lawyers believed America was becoming.¹⁰⁵ It was a threat to all Americans.

As the defense team intensely cross-examined three of these infiltrators, it became clear that the agents themselves were central actors in this much hyped Easter Plot. After all, two of the agents had been with the Panthers pretty much since the Panthers' first Brooklyn chapter formed in June 1968. "I told the jury that maybe the police started the party," Lefcourt later recalled. The heart of the case against the Panthers was a conspiracy to destroy key parts of the power structure in the city. But the jurors came to agree with the defendants and their lawyers that the real conspiracy was the government's framing of the Panthers.¹⁰⁶

The racist dynamics of the courtroom, the flimsiness of the evidence, the ease with which the defense team took apart the testimony of the undercover agents meant that members of the jury came to believe that the defendants really were being railroaded. There was another feature of the courtroom that may have enabled the jurors to share the Panthers' view of the state's case, and that was the Panthers' lawyers, many of whom shared their clients' view of the system. Lefcourt stood out for the way he modeled cross-racial solidarity for others in that courtroom. The 27-year-old, white lawyer Gerry Lefcourt recalled feeling "as much a Panther as any one of them in my heart. I felt so emotionally involved." For all the defense lawyers in the Panther 21 case, the trial became a crucible. Pretrial proceedings began in early February 1970, just weeks after the Bernstein benefit, and lasted four months. Then the trial dragged on for nine long months. "What people thought would be two months," Lefcourt remembers, "became a whole life." There was very little down time. Often when the lawyers were not in court they would be speaking at fundraisers and rallies. "It was all consuming," he remembers, "as it became our work life, our social life, play life, our political life."¹⁰⁷

And, of course, the defendants had something to do with the way in which jurors began to see things their way. At least those who stuck around for the entirety of the trial. It did not help their cause when two Panthers out on bail, Cetewayo and Dhoruba bin Wahad, disappeared in early February 1971. But even when the Panther defendants were angry, indignant, and defiant, they were also smart and funny. When Assistant District Attorney Phillips showed *The Battle of Algiers*, some of the defendants complained that they had paid $100,000 for seats that didn't give them a view of the screen, whereupon their chairs were rearranged.¹⁰⁸

No single defendant did more to counter the prosecution's portrait of the Panthers as violent terrorists than Afeni Shakur. From the beginning, people were taken with the striking-looking Shakur, who was unusually self-possessed. The writer Honor Moore, who, with other women's liberation activists, helped provide the bail for Joan Bird, observed that Afeni Shakur was "a natural star, intellectually sophisticated, articulate, charismatic—and pregnant." She rebutted the prosecution's claim that they intended to bomb department stores. The people crowding into many of these stores before a holiday were poor people, she argued, the very people the Panthers had sworn to protect.[109] She could be quietly devastating in cross-examining the undercover agents on the stand. Her grilling of police agent Ralph White (or Yedwah, as he was known to the Panthers) had what Kempton called a "fierce, calm concentration on necessity." She forced him to admit he had never seen her commit an act of violence but *had* witnessed her working to lift up and organize the community.[110]

By the trial's end, Shakur had not lost her toughness, but she was also "very pregnant, very weary."[111] Kempton thought he discerned a shift in her demeanor, which he attributed to her imminent motherhood. Her closing remarks revealed, he thought, that she had become "vulnerable, softened, pleading," albeit "with anger and dignity to be sure."[112] More than anything, she was eloquent, though her voice was trembling, either from emotion or from a bad cough. She walked over to the jurors and spoke directly to them. She was personal, eschewing the political rhetoric she might have used. "I don't know what I'm supposed to say," she began. "But I do know that none of these charges has been proven, and I'm not talking about proven beyond a reasonable doubt." Calling attention to the weakness of the state's case, she asked why she and her fellow defendants had been stuck in "this nightmare" for two years. Please end it, she implored them. "Please don't forget what you heard and saw in this courtroom. Don't forget any of it," she urged them. "Let history record you as a jury that would not kneel to the outrageous bidding of the state." Making herself more vulnerable, she said, "Show us that we were not wrong in assuming that you would judge us fairly. And remember that that's all we're asking of you."

The People of New York Against Lumumba Abdul Shakur et al. was the longest and most expensive trial in the history of New York State. Yet 20 minutes into their deliberation, a consensus developed among the jurors that "there just wasn't any case—the evidence wasn't there." Jurors who had worried that others might vote to convict were shocked to discover that there was broad

Image 12.5 Panther 21 defendant Dhoruba bin Wahad (Richard Moore); his wife, Iris Moore; and his co-defendant Afeni Shakur, leaving the Criminal Courts Building in Manhattan for lunch April 9, 1970. Walking a few steps behind them is the journalist Murray Kempton, who covered the trial.
Leonard Detrick/NY Daily News Archive via Getty Images

agreement on acquittal. To be clear, several jurors believed the Panthers might have been guilty of many of the charges, but they were just as sure that the government failed to prove their guilt.[113] They were skeptical of the prosecution's heavy reliance on undercover agents whose testimony was not corroborated by even one disinterested witness.[114]

One curious and relevant wrinkle involved Judge Murtagh's directions to the jurors just prior to their deliberations. Murtagh whittled down the charges to 12, dropping all the gun charges, which were the case's rock-solid charges. Had these charges been included, the verdict likely would have been different. The defense thought Murtagh did this to eliminate the possibility of "compromise points" that would permit the jurors to find the defendants guilty of something, but not the heavy charges. Without those compromise points, the jury would have to find the defendants guilty on the heavy charges or acquit, an outcome that Murtagh likely never anticipated.[115] But even Ingram Fox, the Black foreman whom the defense lawyers worried might be "too establishment" and whom one reporter called an "Uncle Tom," was for acquittal. "It's collusion by police," he said. Fox noted that the judge had likened a conspiracy to a play in which everyone plays a role. "Well, we have seen the play," Fox said, "but the police wrote the prologue."[116] And all along the "infiltrators were aiding and abetting."[117]

The jurors briefly disagreed about what to do about Cetewayo and Dhoruba bin Wahad, who had jumped bail three months earlier. However, once that was resolved, "no one could find anyone else to argue with and no one was willing to take the District Attorney's side." The consensus was that it made little sense to prolong their discussion. Because "the mountain had labored mightily and brought forth a mouse, it was not worth the effort of dissecting the mouse." The book editor Fred Hills believed there was another reason to end their deliberations. "Think of the drama of the statement we'd be making by returning in two hours with verdicts on everyone." They came close. Deliberations started at 1:35 p.m., and by 4:00 p.m. they had finished voting on all the charges.[118]

When the jurors returned to the courtroom, they were surprised to see "wall to wall a sea of blue," to prevent a riot from breaking out when the verdict was read. The defense lawyers, depressed and drunk from the jug of martinis they had downed at lunch, were surprised by the demeanor of the jury. Had the juror Fred Hills, the other white book editor, "flashed a triumphant smile" or was it the alcohol? When the clerk of the court asked if the members of the jury had reached a verdict, their foreman said, "Yes." The way that Fox uttered the word "Yes" sent journalist Murray Kempton on a reverie. He wondered "what fugitive echo of Joe Turner singing it's your dollar now but it's gonna be mine some sweet day had entered with so many other intricacies into the orchestration of this single syllable." After Fox uttered "Not guilty" 12 times for Lumumba Shakur, Afeni Shakur and Joan Bird "shrieked and sobbed." As Lumumba Shakur comforted his wife, his face was set in disbelief. An outright acquittal?[119]

By this time, "the lawyers were staring at the jurors and beginning to smile." In total, Fox said the words "Not guilty" 156 times, each time in a slightly different register. After he finished, there were "cries of happiness throughout the room."[120] One reporter noted that "male Panthers don't cry in public, but their Jewish lawyers went to pieces." Some of the jury members were also crying.[121] Prosecutor Phillips "turned ash-white," and Judge Murtagh was "stone-faced." As the jurors filed out of the courtroom to people shouting, "Power to the people!" and "Power to the jury!" a policeman "shot a fat wad of spit towards their feet." As they walked past the defendants, and filed out of the courtroom, juror Kennebeck raised his fist. A "tornado of joy" followed them into the jury room.[122]

When the jurors reached the first-floor lobby, the scene was absolutely "chaotic." Then, the defendants and their lawyers appeared, and "frenzied handshaking and shouting" lasted almost an hour.[123] The journalist who had covered the trial for Liberation News Service (LNS) wrote that "months of agonizing, depressing, frustrating trial magically became instant joy." Panther supporters thanked and hugged the jurors. "It was pandemonium," recalled Lefcourt. "Pandemonium not only in the courtroom, but in the courthouse and in the streets. People in Harlem went into the streets."[124]

In the immediate aftermath of the trial, the LNS reporter observed that the "indictment had read the People of New York against Lumumba Abdul Shakur, et al. But it was the people who freed the New York Panther 21. And the people grouped and clung together long after the verdict was in, the most fantastic community of joy between defendants, their lawyers, family, friends, and their jury perhaps this country has ever witnessed." Lefcourt agreed and later called the jury's verdict "the most stunning, most incredible, rejection of the government." He emphasized how much the jurors were a part of them. "They weren't like acquitting jurors, who said, 'Well, they didn't really prove it.' They were just thrilled to be there, to be a part of this rejection."[125]

The jurors *were* thrilled. Later that evening they reconvened for a party at the Law Commune. The lawyers' office was reportedly not where Judge Murtagh expected the jurors would be celebrating the trial's end. He had planned for the 12 jurors and 64 guards to eat dinner together at Doyle's Corner Pub. Instead, the jurors were at the funky Law Commune at 640 Broadway, "swigging the Asti Spumante from the bottle" and enveloped in what one juror described as "'a warm goo of hugs and tears." Everyone there treated this distinctly non-countercultural group of jurors as though each one was a "conquering hero." As the first juror walked into the Law Commune, people cheered loudly. Alternate juror, Joe Rainato, a white mechanical engineer, said it was the happiest day of his life. Another alternate juror, Claudette Sullivan, a Black woman who worked as a finance officer, said that even at her own wedding she had not felt like she did in this moment.[126] Lumumba Shakur told one juror that the verdict "restored my faith in humanity." Afeni Shakur later explained, "You can translate that as 'whites.'"[127]

Over the next year, the group held two more reunions. There was some socializing among jurors and those defendants who were not in jail on other charges. Take Ingram Fox, who invited some of the Panther defendants to his house to listen to his music. Before the trial, he would never have allowed a Black Panther in his home. A couple of the jurors became more politically active as a result of the trial. For a while, Kennebeck and Rainato "dragged each other to every radical demonstration." But even many of those jurors who weren't at every demo were changed by the trial. In some cases, so were their close friends and family members. If they accompanied one of the jurors to one of the parties, they saw the Panthers up close. Sometimes they were given a big bear hug by Joan Bird or they spoke to Afeni Shakur and bounced her baby, then named Parrish but soon to be Tupac, on their laps.[128]

Ironically, one person who did not attend the celebration was the white radical in charge of the Panther 21 defense committee, Martin Kenner. He had been working to raise money for the Panther 21 and their lawyers since fall 1969, but when asked if he had attended the postacquittal party, he says, "That is such a crazy question." Kenner deliberately avoided the party because he had run afoul of some of the New York Panthers. They hated him first and foremost because he had sent some of the money the committee had raised to Oakland, which needed it for the defense of other Panthers. Kenner's willingness to siphon off money the New York Panthers thought was meant solely for their defense infuriated the 21 and their lawyers. Moreover, by spring 1971 Kenner and the Panther 21 were on opposite sides of the Newton-Cleaver split. Kenner had to have been glad about their acquittal, but he was afraid that some of the Panthers might come after him.[129] It had not been even a month since Sam Napier had been murdered.

As for the mainstream press, the jubilation at the Law Commune party did not extend to it. The day after the verdict, the editorial Board of the *New York Daily News* weighed in. "We are profoundly bored with the beefs and bawls of some of the acquitted."[130] Two days later, the editorial board of the *New York Times* claimed to be reassured, "at a time when the government so often confuses invective with insurrection," that the jury in the trial "insisted on evidence of wrong-doing rather than wrongthinking." However, the board also said the verdict "exposes as a fraud the Panthers' noisy and noisome oratory about the 'fascist' nature of justice in America."¹³¹ Some radicals forcefully rejected the idea that the acquittal exonerated the American justice system. "The system did not come through," argued stalwart left-wing lawyer William Kunstler. "What came through was the jury. This was not a victory for the system, that was a defeat. The sewer was open for one brief moment and the odor was smelled by everyone."¹³²

The odor from that Manhattan courtroom may have reached jurors in other cases involving Panthers. Juror Steven Chaberski, who wrote a dissertation about strategies in political trials, claimed that the Panther 21 trial and subsequent political trials marked the first time in U.S. history that juries began to set radicals free. It happened in many such trials, including the New Haven trial against Bobby Seale and Ericka Huggins, which was happening the same time as that of the Panther 21. Lefcourt claimed that the day after the Panther 21 acquittal, Garry told him he saw a change in the jury. "You could see the difference in the jury's eyes. They were thinking, 'Maybe the government could be wrong.'"¹³³ Of course, in the New Haven case, some Panthers had admitted to murdering another member they believed was an agent. The police even possessed a voluntary recording that the Panthers made of their torture of the suspected agent, Alex Rackley, and Huggins was captured saying things that were hard to explain away.

During their deliberations, the New Haven jurors moved quickly on Bobby Seale's case. Within two hours, they had agreed to vote not guilty. The prosecutor had not come close to making the case against him. Huggins's case was trickier, and when one white female juror pressed for a guilty verdict and met hard resistance, she withdrew her vote for Seale's acquittal. In another contrast to the jury in Manhattan, the New Haven jury included two women who came to the case as pro-Panther supporters. Still, eight other jurors wanted to find her not guilty. After five days of rancorous discussion, the jury foreman reported to the judge that they were hopelessly deadlocked and unable to move past their current divided vote of 10 for acquittal and 2 for conviction.¹³⁴

On May 25, the judge in the trial shocked the courtroom by dismissing the charges against both defendants. Judge Mulvey was a conservative man and had been eager to prove Yale's president Kingman Brewster wrong. In his court, the Panthers would get a fair trial. He explained his decision to dismiss by citing his nearly two years of experience with the case. He then said something entirely unexpected. "I have observed a rather remarkable change in the attitude of these defendants during the time they have been before me, and I don't think it is feigned." It was his gut feeling, and Mulvey led with it. Then he explained the pragmatic difficulties of continuing the case. The state could retry Seale and Huggins, but with the array of jurors for that year nearly exhausted, the chance that a jury could be constituted was "practically nil." He also noted that with the "massive publicity" the trial had received it would be impossible to select an unbiased jury. He also acknowledged, almost in passing, that the state had failed to convince the jury of the defendants' guilt.[135]

The Seale-Huggins trial had been the most expensive and the longest in the history of Connecticut. It was an extraordinary move, in which Judge Mulvey was, effectively, confirming the accusation that Yale's president had leveled at the country. The white left-wing writer Donald Freed wrote a book about the trial which he witnessed. Freed thought that during the past two years, "Mulvey had begun to get to know different black people." He thought the voir dire strategy enabled Mulvey to see that almost all the prospective jurors "had been blinded as he once, perhaps, was."[136]

The defense team's strategy also worked on some of those jurors, too. Two months after the trial had ended, the Black Panther Party invited all the jury members to come to Oakland. Eight jurors accepted the Panthers' invitation, which included picking up their travel and hotel costs. The white state police sergeant who accompanied Seale on the 100-mile round trip to the courthouse in New Haven was also invited and joined the jurors.[137] In talking over with the Panthers what had happened in their deliberations, a juror revealed that one of the women jurors whom Seale suspected of being racist, supported his acquittal. "He's not guilty," she insisted, pounding her hand against the table.[138]

The Trial of Angela Davis

Throughout 1971 and 1972, the government suffered defeat after defeat as juries acquitted Black Panthers, or deadlocked on the verdict, or found them guilty of lesser charges. In New Haven, the judge called it quits. Often, as in the case of the Harlem 5, which was decided the same day as the bigger Panther 21 case, jurors rejected conspiracy charges. In Detroit, the jury rejected the government's case against the 12 Panthers accused of murdering a Black policeman

Image 12.6 Ericka Huggins, free from jail for the first time in two years, joins her lawyer Catherine Roraback in a smile, May 25, 1971. The judge in the trial dismissed charges of murder and kidnapping against Huggins and Bobby Seale.
Dave Pickoff/AP Photo

during the October 1970 confrontation about selling the Panther newspaper. The jury consisted of 10 Blacks and two whites.[139]

One of the government's biggest defeats came with the acquittal of the Black scholar and CP member Angela Davis on June 4, 1972. Of all the many defense committees formed to aid indicted sixties radicals, none was as successful as the CP-organized committee that supported Davis. It is telling that in a period dominated by young New Left activists, the last political trial to mobilize thousands was one in which that relic of the Old Left, the CP, made itself relevant. Of course, it was the CP's defense committee strategy that had guided those earlier Panther cases. But the CP was not running their defense committees. With little competition from New Left groups, the Free Angela! defense committee made the CP seem suddenly alive as the committee oriented itself to the political sensibility of the New Left.[140]

All the campaigns to free various Panthers involved Blacks and whites working together to varying degrees, whether as lawyers, donors, or defense committee volunteers. However, the Free Angela campaign, which built on the

CP's decades of experience in mounting robust defenses in political trials, featured an even greater degree of collaboration across the color line. The CP had long understood defense committees as vehicles of movement building that often involved multiracial partnerships. So it is not surprising that the National United Committee to Free Angela Davis (NUCFAD) represented something of a throwback in terms of its racial politics. Certainly, strong currents of Black Power ran through the leadership of NUCFAD, which was drawn from the Che-Lumumba Club. Yet Davis's legal team, its support staff, and its volunteers worked together in an interracial collaboration more typical of the early sixties than the early 1970s.

It was Angela Davis's membership in the CP that first landed her in the headlines. In September 1969, UCLA fired the doctoral candidate in philosophy from her position as a lecturer, claiming her membership in the party disqualified her as a teacher there. The next time she was in the news, in August 1970, it was for making the FBI's Ten Most Wanted List. The 26-year-old graduate student found herself hunted by the FBI because she had become involved in a defense committee for the trio of Black Panther inmates known as the Soledad Brothers who stood accused of murdering a prison guard. By this point, Soledad Brother George Jackson, the founder of the Panthers' San Quentin chapter, was already famous as the author of a recently published collection of letters. *Soledad Brother* made him famous, just as *Soul on Ice* made a celebrity of Eldridge Cleaver. Fay Stender, the radical white lawyer who had worked with Garry on Newton's case, formed the Soledad Brothers Defense Committee (SBDC). It included white and Black radical activists, and inmates' relatives, including George Jackson's younger brother, Jonathan. When Angela Davis joined the SBDC, she soon became friendly with Jonathan, who acted as her bodyguard.

However, Jonathan Jackson wanted to be more than a mere bodyguard. Convinced his older brother would be convicted, he devised a scheme to free the Soledad Brothers. In August 1970, the armed 17-year-old entered a Marin County courtroom, and with three Black radical inmates assisting him, took five white hostages, including the District Attorney and the Superior Court Judge. It was a deadly gambit that left Jackson, two inmates, and the judge dead. The District Attorney and another inmate were badly wounded. (One year later, George Jackson, in an apparent effort to escape San Quentin that left three white guards and two white prisoners dead, was himself gunned down in the prison yard by a tower guard.) Within a week of Jonathan's Jackson's failed mission, the state accused Angela Davis of having supplied the guns that Jackson used in the shoot-out. The FBI announced a nationwide hunt for Davis that ended two months later in New York.

A grand jury indicted Davis on counts of aggravated kidnapping, first-degree murder, and conspiracy. It was a capital offense, and her guilt was widely assumed. Two days after her capture, President Nixon, at his signing of the Organized Crime Control Act of 1970, congratulated FBI director Hoover for capturing the "dangerous terrorist Angela Davis." One day later, an editorial in the *New York Times* called it a tragedy that Davis, "who could have made a significant contribution to the nation's normal political debate and its needed processes of peaceful change became so alienated that she finally went over to revolutionary words and perhaps even worse." A racial divide quickly opened as prominent Black politicians, pundits and entertainers argued the charges were trumped up.[141]

Although most white politicians and the mainstream press treated Davis as guilty as charged, the prosecutor in the case, Albert Harris, had a problem on his hands. His case against her, resting largely on circumstantial evidence, was wobbly. Yes, she had purchased the guns and registered them in her name—the same guns that Jonathan Jackson used in the Marin shoot-out. But she bought the guns and ammunition for the Che-Lumumba Club to use for target practice, not to arm Jonathan Jackson.[142] Davis reportedly began carrying a gun after a member of the Los Angeles chapter of the Panthers threatened her at gunpoint.[143]

Davis and her comrades in the Che-Lumumba Club determined early on that her case could not be won solely by "legal maneuvering." It was going to require a campaign of "massive pressure, exerted by millions of Americans on state and local authorities" to counter the state's megaphone. At first, the CP resisted getting involved with Davis's case, despite the party's decades of experience in mounting defense campaigns. It determined it would support Davis but condemn Jonathan Jackson's "adventurism," a move that infuriated Davis.[144] Eventually, the CP did come around, perhaps because of Davis's substantial support within Black communities. Within nine months of her arrest, there were 60 fully operational local committees of NUCFAD that focused most of their energy on publicity, fundraising, and event planning. Fundraisers were especially important, given that the cost of her large legal team could run as high as $1 million.[145] To create what Hannah Weinstein had done in the past—a countervailing force—seven full-time national staff members were drawing salaries of $75 a week.

The campaign to free Angela recruited support from civil rights activists at home, including Coretta Scott King and Ralph Abernathy of the Southern Christian Leadership Conference. Writing about his time on a picket line in Portland, Oregon, shouting, "Free Angela! Free all political prisoners!" former New Left activist Maurice Isserman attributed the support Davis received both to the "efficiency" of local CP organizers, and to Davis herself. It was "her ability to combine the image of street-tough activist with serious intellectual credentials: Brandeis, Marcuse, the Sorbonne, the University of Frankfurt" that made her attractive to New Leftists like him.[146]

Arguably, where the CP truly excelled was in the astonishingly broad global support it garnered for Davis. Communists provided the foundation of those Free Angela committees that emerged almost everywhere, from France and India to Chile and South Africa and beyond. Boosting support were CP-sponsored trips abroad by NUCFAD members who were close to Davis. Protests included those staged by 2,500 Ceylonese women at the American embassy and a march by 700 Australian women in Sydney. Support in Communist Cuba, East Germany, and the Soviet Union was very robust.[147] Worth mentioning as well were the letters of support penned by leading European intellectuals and artists such as Michel Foucault, Günter Grass, Pablo Picasso, and Davis's mentor Herbert Marcuse, and songs of support recorded by the Rolling Stones ("Sweet Black Angel") and John Lennon and Yoko Ono ("Angela").

It doubtless helped the defense that there was such a resounding groundswell of support for Davis. It may have played a role in the judge's decision, finally, to grant her bail request. That decision mattered because it allowed jurors to observe Davis, not as a shackled prisoner, but as a free woman, wearing her own clothes, talking casually to her lawyers and supporters, and when permitted, addressing the court.

When Davis was finally freed on $102,500 bail, just days before her trial began in late February 1972, the crucial benefactor was not someone easily ridiculed as a radical chic supporter. Rodger McAfee was a 33-year-old white dairy farmer in the San Joaquin Valley who handed over the deed to the 405 acres of rich farmland he owned to the chairman of the CP in Northern California. McAfee had lived in the area since he was eight, but he was not your typical resident. Raised by left-wing schoolteachers, McAfee started to travel

Image 12.7 The German American philosopher and social critic Herbert Marcuse, with whom Angela Davis had studied, addresses the Angela Davis Solidarity Congress on Frankfurt's Opernplatz, June 3, 1972.
DB/picture-alliance/dpa/AP Photo

widely by the time he was 15. He read Marx, and he eventually began calling himself a communist. He met Davis at a 1970 antiwar rally and was impressed by her style and ideas as well as her personality. He told the *New York Times* that having a role in Davis's release from jail was "the thrill of a lifetime." However, within days, racist death threats against McAfee and his family forced them to leave the area. Three weeks later, it was reported that he had suffered such steep financial losses he was forced to sell his herd of cows.[148]

Financial support was crucial to getting bail, and the voir dire, as Garry had proven, was critical to ensuring a fair trial. Davis's defense team had tried but failed to get the trial moved to San Francisco. They did succeed in getting it moved from Marin County to the more diverse San Jose. One of Davis's lawyers told a reporter that the presence of Black jurors was why recent Panther trials had resulted in acquittals. They were determined to get Black people on the jury panel, but that was not to be. After only nine days of jury selection in which only 41 prospective jurors were questioned, the defense team surprised some by deciding to accept the jury. Angela Davis rose from her seat and declared that the defense was ready to move forward and begin the

Image 12.8 Farmer Rodger McAfee of Fresno, California, put up 405 acres of farmland to assure Angela Davis's release on $102,500 bail the week before. He brought his family to meet Davis outside the Santa Clarita courthouse on March 3, 1972.
Robert W. Klein/AP Photo

trial. She acknowledged that this was not a jury of her peers. The panel consisted of 11 whites (eight of them women) and one Mexican American man, though most newspapers called the jury "all-white." Despite the jury's racial composition, Davis said she and her lawyers had confidence in the fairness of the jurors chosen.

Perhaps one reason that Davis and her team trusted this jury panel was the way that its members reacted when the sole prospective Black juror was challenged by the prosecuting attorney, Harris. Both sides imagined that Janie L. Hemphill might be the juror to dig in her heels and vote against conviction. Harris questioned Hemphill at length because of a saloon she and her husband operated. He revealed that the state had refused to renew the financially troubled business's license after the authorities determined the couple permitted gambling on its premises. Hemphill explained that this was true, but that she and her husband had already decided to give up the bar. In an obvious effort to get her dismissed, Harris kept pushing her to admit that she was biased against the state of California.

The interaction between Hemphill and Harris grew tense as the prosecutor continued badgering her. Looking straight at Harris (and apparently straight through him), Hemphill reiterated that she would be a fair juror. "For so many years," she said, "I have had to blot out so many things . . . I could blot this part out." Her rejoinder, which likely left people thinking that racism constituted a large part of what she had been blotting out, silenced the courtroom, even Harris.[149]

In the view of defense lawyer Doris Bin Walker, Harris hurt his cause with his "humiliating" interrogation. It was not just that it had upset Hemphill, it was also that "the rest of the prospective jurors in the box were becoming emotionally and psychologically involved." Walker called it "one of the most moving experiences [she had] had in a courtroom." The prosecutor's behavior dramatized the pervasiveness of white racism for the prospective jurors in a way that was helpful to the defense. If the white jurors did not understand how profoundly racism shaped life before Hemphill's questioning, they likely did now. When the prosecutor later exercised a peremptory challenge, the defense quickly responded. They thought they had won the battle to keep Hemphill on the jury, but Harris eventually managed to have her removed from the panel.[150]

Yet even without Janie Hemphill, the jury in Angela Davis's case seems to have favored the defense. One reason they may have been favorably inclined was the role played by some members of the NUCFAD. Early on, Davis's defense team, particularly longtime communist Doris Bin Walker put the defense committee to work, performing granular research on the jury pool to aid with the voir dire. Members went to communities where prospective jurors lived to get a sense of their racial and economic make-up. Sometimes they were able to speak to people who knew something about the people the lawyers would be questioning. Getting into the investigative trenches paid off, and this is likely another reason that Davis and her team stopped the process after only nine days.[151]

By the time Harris finally settled on Davis's motive, the jury had already heard two months of testimony. Harris argued that Davis was so in love with George Jackson that she plotted with Jonathan Jackson to free the Soledad Brothers. The judge allowed the prosecutor to introduce as evidence newly discovered love letters that Davis had written to Jackson. The defense team countered Harris's theory of the case by refusing to treat the letters as humiliating and incriminating. Here's an opportunity, they told the jurors, for you to identify with Davis's love of Jackson, just "as they would seek to identify with any other human experience." Davis's lawyers were confident that the jurors would vote for acquittal. Their hopes were perhaps boosted by the recent verdict in the trial of the two remaining Soledad Brothers. An all-white jury in San Francisco had voted for acquittal.

The trial of Angela Davis, which lasted from late February until early June, was one of the longest, costliest, and most controversial trials in the history of the state. Obviously, the jury's verdict was much anticipated. When the jury broke off its deliberations because it had reached an impasse, court watchers thought it might be deadlocked. In fact, in the three votes that were taken, the votes were lopsidedly in favor of acquittal. Only once, and briefly at that, did a juror vote guilty.[152] In deciding to acquit Davis, the jurors deliberated a full 13 hours over the course of three days. Throughout, the process was amicable. "There was no table-pounding or anything like that," according to one jury member. The lone person of color on the jury later said that as a Mexican American man he had been moved by the closing comments of Davis's lawyer, who had lingered on America's centuries-long persecution of Black people.

When the jury returned to the courtroom and the clerk read the verdict of not guilty three times, the courtroom erupted with screaming and crying. Angela Davis, who had shown virtually no emotion during the trial, was sobbing, her body shaking. By the time Judge Arnason threatened to clear the courtroom because of the noise, even the jurors had tears in their eyes. After the court was adjourned, Davis went into the press room for a news conference, where she hugged each member of the jury.

Outside the courtroom, the jury's not-guilty verdict registered immediately. At San Francisco's Candlestick Park, the announcer interrupted the baseball game to announce the verdict. The crowd reacted as if the Giants had "scored the winning run." In Watts, where Democratic candidate George McGovern was campaigning, news of Davis's acquittal circulated. Soon, the crowd was chanting "Power of the people set Angela free!"[153]

The June 4 evening of Davis's acquittal brought . . . a party. Present at the private affair were Davis, her family and friends, the defense team, and nine of the jurors and their spouses, who wanted to meet Davis. They celebrated her

Image 12.9 Angela Davis and juror Stephanie Ryon hug after the jury acquitted her of all charges, June 4, 1972.
AP Photo

victory with champagne. "This is the happiest day of my life," Davis said. What had happened that day in court was "a people's victory," she declared.[154]

In speaking about the trial, Davis insisted that despite its outcome, it had not been fair. "A fair trial," she declared, "would have been no trial at all." Davis had a point, of course. Moreover, she likely wanted to challenge all the politicians and pundits who claimed that her acquittal (and the acquittals of so many other Black radicals) vindicated the essential fairness of the American legal system. Yet her proclamation, which was widely quoted, breezed right past the enormity of this extraordinary verdict. Why not admit that the outcome of her trial (and those of so many others) showed that American society *had* changed. "A Communist and a Black militant *could* get a fair trial in 1972," her comrade Dorothy Healey later wrote of Davis's trial. It represented a genuine shift from what would have happened just a few short years earlier.[155]

Admittedly, these verdicts were not the revolution that SNCC and the Black Panther Party sought. Moreover, there is no denying that these prosecutions and lengthy trials hobbled radicals, particularly the Black Panther Party. They were meant to do precisely that. The Special Agent in charge of the New

Haven case boasted that the combined actions taken by the FBI's New Haven office and the New Haven police department had succeeded in disrupting the Panther leadership.[156] A lawyer involved in prosecuting the Panther 21 case later admitted that the state's case against the Panthers was "flimsy." However, he justified it on the grounds that the Panthers were pushing the police to see what they could get away with. "If we hadn't acted to prosecute, and *tied them up in a trial*, they would have continued to go further and further" [emphasis added].[157] The trials were debilitating. Yet what happened in that San Jose courtroom and in the other courtrooms where jury members thwarted the government would not have happened without the Movement. It was astonishing.

At the time of Angela Davis's arrest in fall 1970, James Baldwin wrote her an open letter. Writing of the widely circulated picture of Davis in handcuffs, Baldwin excoriated white Americans for failing to "spontaneously rise up and strike off the manacles."[158] As Davis's friend and CP comrade Bettina Aptheker subsequently pointed out, Americans, with help from millions globally, did eventually free Angela Davis.[159] These were everyday Americans, and they were crucial to securing Davis's freedom, just as the jurors, lawyers, and supporters involved in similar cases had been in Oakland, New Haven, and New York City.

Conclusion

After her victory, Angela Davis went on the road to raise the more than $200,000 needed to pay her legal expenses. Over three weeks, she appeared at four rallies. Her final stop at New York City's Madison Square Garden drew 15,000 people who listened to her as she spoke from within a four-sided shield of bulletproof glass. "We have come together," Davis said, "blacks and Puerto Ricans and white people and Asians and women and men and students and workers and entertainers and professionals—we have come to tell [the rulers] that this victory that we are celebrating, a victory that we ourselves brought into being, is just a bare small taste of what they can expect from us from now on."[1] Davis vowed to continue the struggle with the formation of a new organization focused on prisoners' rights.[2]

Even after the signing of the Paris Peace Accords in January 1973, officially ending America's war in Vietnam, signs of the sixties were still in evidence. However, movements don't last forever, and neither the Communist Party (CP) nor the CP-aligned group she was forming was going to extend the longevity of this one. Not even Angela Davis could overcome the party's reputation as a sclerotic has-been organization. By this juncture only the most deluded—the Weather Underground, the Black Liberation Army, and the Black-led, white-majority Symbionese Liberation Army—believed revolution was still around the corner. Many decades later, Angela Davis said that she was glad the sixties revolution had not come to pass "because there would still be male supremacy. . . . There would be all these things that we had not yet come to consciousness about."[3] Certainly, public awareness about the prejudice and systemic discrimination facing LGBTQ people, which was part of what Davis had in mind, was minimal in the sixties.

Yet, at the time, few Movement veterans, even those suffering burnout, welcomed the return to civilian life. Indeed, the dawning realization that the system was resilient, much more so than the Movement fighting it, left many activists feeling disoriented, even crushed. They had believed they could remold America and now as the "surge of that promise" receded, they were "left with the ebb."[4] Roxanne Dunbar-Ortiz, who had been active in women's liberation and the larger Movement, recalled "all of us having to adjust to a different life."[5]

Take the example of Jerry Rubin. In no time, Rubin went from being at the Movement's epicenter to living in a high-rise apartment in New York City struggling to make a living by talking and writing about his former life as a sixties activist. Trying to figure out his next joyless career move, he wondered if it made sense to pursue a career as a sex therapist. "If we knew in 1963 where we would be in 1973," he admitted, "we would have all considered suicide." Rubin went on to do a brief stint on Wall Street, which was ironic and/or sad, given the Yippies' anticapitalist zap of Wall Street in 1967. At some point, he began hawking Wow, a nutritional drink for which he assembled a sales force that included his former Chicago 8 codefendant, Bobby Seale.[6]

Seale remained politically active longer than Rubin. As the Panther's candidate in 1973's mayor's race in Oakland, he outperformed expectations, coming in second in a nine-person race. Not long after, having come up against Huey Newton's complicated scorecard, he exited the Panthers. As for Newton, life remained a struggle marked by substance abuse and episodes of violence, though he did earn his PhD in UC–Santa Cruz's History of Consciousness Department in 1980.[7] Don Cox believed "the actual Huey could not survive the Huey we created." Martin Kenner probably would not disagree, but for him the larger problem was that Newton, whom he knew well, was "a rebel, not a revolutionary." By the time Kenner ended his relationship with the Panthers in 1972, it was clear to him that Newton wanted to be done with the party. Two years after the party officially ended, Newton said of his critics that he was not going to be "enslaved" by people's expectations of him. "I never contracted to do that in the first place."[8]

One way for Black activists to take a break from the Movement or to put themselves in a more global struggle or perhaps to make their way "home" was to move to Africa. Bob Moses was already living in Canada to avoid being drafted when he moved to Tanzania in 1969. He spent seven years there, mostly working as a math teacher. He and his wife, another Student Nonviolent Coordinating Committee (SNCC) staffer, started a family abroad, before returning to the States after Jimmy Carter's pardoning of draft resisters. Moses's colleague Stokely Carmichael also relocated to Africa. He settled in Conakry, Guinea, in 1968 with his wife, the popular South African singer

Miriam Makeba. Precipitated in part by the Federal Bureau of Investigation campaign against Carmichael and Makeba, the move felt like "home to Africa." Carmichael organized the All-African People's Revolutionary Party, which he took in a Marxist direction, a surprising turn after his blanket rejection of all things left-wing.[9]

Several Panthers made their way to Africa, too, among them, Michael Tabor (Cetewayo) of the Panther 21, Don Cox, and Eldridge Cleaver. Cleaver headed up the Panthers' International Section in Algiers for several years. His unseriousness became clear to Algerian officials almost immediately. One observed that his apartment was "full of hi-fi equipment [and] his mind full of wild slogans." He was stunned to discover that America's "black revolutionaries were so corrupted by Yankee individualism and bourgeois materialism."[10] After failing to win over the governments of Cuba, Algeria, North Vietnam, and North Korea, Cleaver, fed up with communism, moved to France with Kathleen and the children. In 1975, they returned to America, where Cleaver spent his first nine months in prison on 1968's attempted murder charge. His commitment to reaching across the racial divide remained intact, but much else about his thinking shifted as he started cozying up to the religious right, whose support proved crucial. "I have had to get me some brand new friends," he wrote a friend in Paris. "All of the bastards who called themselves Black Panthers, Communists, etc., have tried to crucify me with lies."[11] Eventually, through a plea bargain deal, Cleaver was spared further prison time, but he remained estranged from the Movement.[12]

Cleaver's turn to conservatism was not typical of sixties radicals, few of whom became apostates in the way that many thirties leftists had. However, one ex-radical who made a hard-right turn, and not, it appears, opportunistically, was David Horowitz, Robert Scheer's former colleague at *Ramparts*. Horowitz was raising funds for the Panthers' Oakland Community School when the scales fell from his eyes in 1974, a while after they had fallen for some other Panther allies. It began when a white leftist bookkeeper whom the Panthers had hired on Horowitz's recommendation went missing the same day that she told a party leader about the illegal activity she had discovered. More than a month later, her body, badly beaten and decomposed, was found in the San Francisco Bay.[13] Horowitz maintained that his disillusionment with the Panthers and his anger at Bay Area white leftists who preferred not knowing too much about the group they once valorized were crucial to his switching sides.[14]

Much more typical were the many activists who pulled away from the Movement, but not to repudiate the larger project of social justice. Many were still engaged in that project, often locally, and in a more pragmatic, hands-on way. Charles Sherrod founded a Black-owned cooperative farm called New Communities in what had become his bailiwick, Southwest Georgia. Casey Hayden helped to form a commune in Vermont with some of her former SNCC colleagues. She continued to move around—physically and spiritually—becoming a student of Tibetan Buddhism and yoga, and a pioneer of the home-birth movement. Maria Varela moved to northern New Mexico, where she became a part of the Land Grant movement and organized a successful health clinic. Dottie Zellner became a licensed practical nurse and organized a union in the New Orleans Home for Incurables. Muriel Tillinghast was a pioneer in fighting for better institutional responses to domestic violence.

Others moved into electoral politics and government service, including Tom Hayden, who served in the California legislature, and Julian Bond, whose election the Supreme Court validated, allowing him to serve in the Georgia House of Representatives. Additionally, John Lewis and Panther Bobby Rush won seats in the U.S. House of Representatives, and Marion Barry was elected mayor of Washington, DC. Former SNCC staffers Lawrence Guyot, who earned his law degree in 1971, and Ivanhoe Donaldson advised Barry. Mary King worked in the federal government, including with the Peace Corps and Vista. Ericka Huggins was the director of the Panthers' Oakland Community School. In 1976, she became the first woman and the first Black person appointed to the Alameda County Board of Education. In 1970, Robert Scheer ran in California for U.S. Senate as the nominee of the Peace and Freedom Party. His brief and unsuccessful return to electoral politics happened after David Horowitz fired him from *Ramparts*, Scheer says, for being insufficiently radical.[15] He remained a radical presence within the world of mainstream journalism.

Many Movement veterans, including quite a few who had earlier foresworn universities for "the people," would work inside them. Some, including Joyce Ladner and Todd Gitlin, became well-known scholars. Another academic, SNCC alumnus Michael Thelwell, wrote the best-selling novel, *The Harder They Come*, which was then made into a highly regarded 1973 movie of the same name. A cult classic, the movie played a role in introducing reggae to Americans.

Many more Movement veterans earned credentials that enabled them to teach in universities, while doing other kinds of work, often activism. James Forman entered a PhD program after spearheading the 1969 campaign for reparations to African Americans. After earning his doctorate, he taught classes at American University in Washington, DC, but he remained an organizer. Shortly after the musician Bernice Johnson Reagon founded the a cappella group Sweet Honey and the Rock in 1973, she completed her doctorate in U.S. history at Howard University. She was appointed a cultural historian at the Smithsonian Institution, where SNCC alumnus Worth Long was also working. Bob Zellner earned his PhD in history at Tulane University and taught college classes about the freedom movement. Martin Kenner remained involved in the world of investment, but he also completed a doctorate in economic history from Columbia University.

For Angela Davis and Bob Moses, it was a matter of resuming their academic studies. After returning to Harvard and earning his PhD, Moses launched a project to teach algebra to Black schoolchildren, whom he believed needed proficiency in algebra if they were to succeed in math, technology, and science. Other movement veterans, including Mendy Samstein and Dave Dennis, worked with Moses. Angela Davis resumed college teaching after her trial ended, but a tenured position initially eluded her. In time, and with her well-respected writings, she achieved both academic celebrity and security. She remained a leader in the CP until the unraveling of the Soviet Union, when she finally left the party.

Many of the people featured in these pages continued working as full-time activists. Betita Martínez was involved in several left-wing groups in the Bay Area and in 1982 ran for California governor on the Peace and Freedom ticket. Courtland Cox was committed to building alliances across the Black Diaspora and helped to organize the Sixth Pan African Congress in Tanzania in 1974. Marshall Ganz worked for years with the United Farm Workers in California. Mike Miller became staff director on a Kansas City project in a Black neighborhood for organizer Saul Alinsky's Industrial Areas Foundation. He then founded the ORGANIZE Training Center in the Bay Area. Anne Weills became a union organizer before going to law school and becoming a civil rights lawyer and working on prisoners' rights.

Just this partial discussion of what activists did after the Movement's fade-out suggests the seriousness of their resolve. It also suggests that in the seventies working across difference diminished somewhat as women, racial and ethnic minorities, and sexual minorities struggled to create a common consciousness, a sense of "we-ness."[16] One effort that went against this current involved two people familiar with working across difference—Angela Davis and former SNCC staffer Bernice Johnson Reagon. What motivated them was Joanne (Joan) Little, a 21-year-old Black woman who in 1974 was charged with murdering her jailer in a North Carolina prison. Little insisted that the guard was sexually assaulting her, and that she killed only in self-defense. For many feminists, Little's situation consolidated their growing consciousness about how deeply sexual violence shaped women's lives. A range of feminists from radical women's liberationists to NOW activists, Black and white women, and even Black Power leaders Amiri Baraka and Maulana Karenga joined the Free Joanne Little Movement. Little was acquitted in 1975.[17]

Four years later, in 1979, another predominantly female multiracial group formed in Boston after the murders of 13 women, 12 of them Black. White women positioned themselves as allies in this coalition, which included Mel King, a Black Boston state legislator. Barbara Smith of the feminist Combahee River Collective called the Coalition for Women's Safety "unprecedented in Boston's political history." It became the basis for the Rainbow Coalition that powered progressive Mel King's 1983 run for mayor, in which he received a startling 20 percent of the vote.[18]

In 1983, Mel King was not the only Black person running for office with a Rainbow Coalition propelling him.[19] Readers will remember that the original Rainbow Coalition stretched back to 1969, when Fred Hampton and Bobby Lee of the Illinois Black Panther Party chapter brought together people who seemed like nothing so much as natural antagonists: the Black Panthers, the Puerto Rican Young Lords, and the Confederate-flag-waving Appalachian whites of the Young Patriots. Although that first Rainbow Coalition ended in 1971, it was revived by the Black politician Harold Washington more than a decade later. Washington was a career politician who had been shaped years earlier by his visit to the bullet-ridden apartment where Fred Hampton and Mark Clark met their death at the hands of the Chicago police.

That experience stuck with Washington, and soon he was working with some of the very people involved in Hampton's multiracial project. In 1983, when he ran for mayor, Washington spoke of building a Rainbow Coalition to pursue "racial justice and equality for working people and the poor." José "Cha Cha" Jiménez of the Young Lords and Bobby Rush of the Panthers, who had been a part of the original coalition, worked as community organizers for his campaign. For the former Panther Bobby Lee, Washington's victory vindicated their multiracial strategy. Chicagoan Jesse Jackson tried to expand that same coalition in his 1984 and 1988 presidential runs, even going so far as to trademark the term "Rainbow Coalition." In the Democratic primary, Jackson succeeded in earning over three million votes, a figure he nearly doubled four years later when he ran again.

Twenty years after Jackson's last run, in his 2008 presidential campaign, Barack Obama went all the way to the White House by harnessing the Rainbow Coalition. He won it with the help of Mayor Washington's one-time campaign advisor, David Axelrod. Yet Obama's Rainbow Coalition was far from what Fred Hampton had imagined: a coalition that would bring on the revolution. The anticapitalist radicalism of the original Rainbow was long gone.[20]

*****

Advocates of solidarity often quote Toni Morrison's wonderfully quotable line, "The function of freedom is to free someone else." But how does one go about freeing someone else without also reifying existing power relations? How does one avoid the snare of paternalism? One way that SNCC staffers tried in 1964 was to counsel summer volunteers to take part in the Mississippi Project not to help Black Mississippians, but to help themselves. To achieve legitimacy, volunteers, most of whom were white and relatively privileged, would have to turn themselves into critics and adversaries of the "system." They had to find their own stake in the fight to change America.

As readers know, in certain respects this strategy worked, but it also came up against all kinds of obstacles, external and internal. Yet, the process of creating stakeholders did begin a process, accelerated by Black Power, that changed the country as veterans of the struggle began to identify multiple kinds of inequity and unfairness. Encouraging people to organize around their own oppression was a brilliant move, but not a magic bullet. Identity-based organizations have limitations, beginning with the difficulties involved in ensuring that they can also come together in a larger movement. And then there's the irony that identity-based groups, meant to build group cohesion, are often riven by conflict, as with the battles between the Panthers and their rivals over the meaning of nationalism. In any case, by 1968, much of the New Left had given up on the radical potential of their largely white, middle-class constituency. Instead, many New Leftists opted to become again an adjunct to someone else's struggle, in this case, that of the Panthers. In becoming an essential, if largely adjacent part of the party, the New Left succeeded in extinguishing much of its own creativity.

Illustrating the difficulty of cross-racial solidarity in the sixties are the Movement postmortems of Huey Newton and Jerry Rubin. In 1984, Huey Newton spoke about the Black Panther Party as he never had before. By this point the party had been dead for two years and Newton seemed wistful and aggrieved. "The Panthers," he explained, "only existed in the context of a movement of Progressive whites."[21] Once the white Movement slipped away, he said, it was only a matter of time before the Panthers did as well. Recall that it was the Black freedom movement, more than a decade earlier, that had animated left-wing college students. Newton's admission of how much the white Movement had mattered to the Panthers is startling, given the Panthers' long-standing cageyness about it. But Newton's larger point was that white radicals had been the first to abandon the struggle, and worse, they had then criticized the Panthers, and at a time when the party was just barely holding on.

Jerry Rubin had been a part of that movement of progressive whites and knew its importance to the Panthers. As law enforcement waged its campaign against the Panthers, the Yippie leader had called on white radicals to put themselves at risk to the same degree that Black radicals were, even if it meant risking death.[22] Yet in an unpublished 1973 interview, Rubin, sounding petulant and aggrieved, revealed his ambivalence about the power dynamics between white and Black radicals, particularly the Panthers. He emphasized the authority and the power—"smoking-gun power"—that Black activists possessed in the sixties. Rubin understood why this was so, but he resented how Black power had delegitimated white radicals whose participation was limited to "supporting roles" only.[23]

Huey Newton and Jerry Rubin understood the benefits of interdependence, but they resented what followed from it. For the Panthers, being dependent upon the money and resources of whites, as their enemies alleged, was as uncomfortable as it was necessary. For white radicals, though they basked in the glow of the Panthers' approval, when it came their way, they bristled at the Panthers' insistence on their deference. For people on both sides, interdependence was often productive, but it rankled. Rubin ended up feeling that the relationship between Blacks and whites was "the whole story of the Sixties."[24]

The collaborations and alliances between Black and white activists, while not the whole story of the sixties, was a crucial piece of it. If "black and white together" was SNCC's radical underpinning—central to the project of overcoming racism—within a few short years, it became instead its albatross, what needed to be overcome. The Panthers developed a different and more flexible approach to working with whites, but the stigma attached to Black-and-white-together proved hard to shake. And, as the reflections of Newton and Rubin suggest, cross-racial collaborations sometimes brought to the surface feelings so uncomfortable that participants likely would have preferred retreating to their own comfort zones.

Roxanne Dunbar-Ortiz, a white working-class feminist and socialist, has written incisively about solidarity. Reminiscing about her long history as an activist, she recalled the time in December 1968 when her efforts to spread the word about women's liberation had taken her to Smith College, where she met with a group of undergraduates. Sitting in an elegant residence hall with young women whom the 30-year-old Dunbar characterized as "daughters of the ruling class," it struck her that the feminist mantra of sisterhood had distinct limitations. The next day she found herself in much more congenial circumstances: a rowdy protest sponsored by the National Welfare Rights Organization in Cambridge, Massachusetts. Three hundred women—one-third of them Black and Puerto Rican, the rest of them white—were just outside the Sears store, where they were demanding supplemental funds from the welfare department for winter clothing for their children.

Dunbar-Ortiz wasn't sure why they were protesting at Sears until someone yelled, "Let's go." Suddenly, the protestors rushed into the store and headed for the children's department. As they grabbed coats, boots, and anything to keep their kids warm, they yelled at stunned saleswomen, "Charge it to welfare!" Dunbar-Ortiz recalled watching in amazement. In her bones she felt at home with these women, whereas she felt like an outsider with the Smith students. But she also realized that strategy mattered. "The trick would be to organize the privileged women to join the poor, otherwise the poor would be once again abandoned."[25]

That had indeed been the trick in Mississippi, and it was to remain the key moving forward.

Afterword

I opened this book with a discussion of how the far right usefully invoked Tom Wolfe's 1970 essay in its battle against "wokeness." Wolfe's long-simmering disdain for the country's liberal elites aligned with that of Richard Nixon, whose campaign operatives used the charge of radical chic against his liberal opponent George McGovern in 1972. Although Wolfe's ridicule may have laid the foundation for today's assaults on left-of-center America, what we are currently witnessing has morphed into something else. The right now routinely denounces "liberal elites" and/or "radical left lunatics," going so far sometimes as to describe them as "vermin," just as Hitler and Mussolini once did. As scholars have shown, attacking liberal elites and the institutions with which they are identified—universities, libraries, museums, the fourth estate, the legal profession, and the culture industry—is part of the authoritarian playbook. Such attacks also divert attention from what is happening under our noses: the power being wielded by America's right-leaning oligarchs, by any measure the real elite.

Then there is the right's return to attacking the left as anti-Semitic. This, too, harks back to 1970, when the Federal Bureau of Investigation (FBI) reportedly coordinated with the Jewish Defense League to attack the Bernsteins. Ten years after the Panther benefit, when Bernstein finally got hold of the relevant FBI files, it was clear to him that the FBI had "conspired to foment hatred and violent dissension among blacks, among Jews and between blacks and Jews."[1] This is not to say that anti-Semitism was (or is) entirely a cooked-up charge. Rather, it is to say that the charge of anti-Semitism was used opportunistically to discredit left liberals and drive a further wedge between Black radicals and the Jewish progressives who supported them, and at a moment when those bonds were already fraying. Today, the right is using the accusation of anti-Semitism, now so expansively defined as to include even mild criticism of Israel, as a pretext to take a sledgehammer to the country's elite universities. Not incidentally, the right's reframing of anti-Semitism has also undermined efforts to fight Islamophobia.

With America so clearly in the hard right's crosshairs, it may be time for people to pay heed to what Bernice Johnson Reagon said about working across difference over 40 years ago. "You don't go into coalition because you just *like* it," Reagon said. You do it "because that's the only way you can figure you can stay alive."[2]

Los Angeles
April 2025

Acknowledgments

I am no stranger to writing about easily maligned or misunderstood subjects: disco, the hippie counterculture, women's liberation. I am also accustomed to going against the tide. In writing about the partnerships forged decades ago by Blacks and whites in the freedom movement, I knew I was going against the historiographical current. And I soon discovered that I would also be pushing back against a widely shared cultural skepticism about the usefulness, even desirability of working across difference.

One reason I decided to take on this project was my students' cynicism about allyship, particularly when it involves privileged people's participation in and support for the struggles of those with less power. Honestly, my initial motivation in writing this book was not much more complicated than this: "Look, people united across difference in the sixties; they can do it again!" I still believe that in America no one group can successfully go it alone in making change. However, as I worked on *Black Power, White Heat*, I developed a deeper understanding about how and why these partnerships mattered, even when they fell apart. I came to see that there was a story here, a story that goes some way toward explaining the sixties. A lot of people helped in getting me to this place, and it is to them that I now turn.

Many thanks go to these colleagues and friends who read various iterations of my book proposal: Elinor Accampo, Julia Brown Bernstein, Wini Breines, Howard Brick, Ellen DuBois, Kate Flint, Daniel Geary, Susan Johnson, Jane Kamensky, Seth Koven, Mike Messner, Paula Rabinowitz, Steve Ross, Vivian Rothstein, Connie Samaras, Beryl Satter, and Alice Wexler. Although they appreciated what I was attempting, some of them disagreed with at least parts of my argument. Their support and their criticism proved invaluable. I also am indebted to Domna Stanton, who had been a guest at Felicia Bernstein's 1970 benefit for the Black Panthers. Her comments on Part Four of this book were exceedingly helpful.

Over the years, I spoke with a variety of scholars and friends about this project, including Anthony Chase, Martha Jane Echols, Phil Ethington, Adam Goodman, Sofia Gruskin, Pierrette Hondagneu-Sotelo, Scott Johnson, Lon Kurashige, Maria Lepowsky, Beth Meyerowitz, Allison Miller, Nathan Perl-Rosenthal, Nayan Shah, Marla Stone, Joan Flores Villalobos, Devra Weber, and Patricia Yeghessian. I also interviewed three historians whose work on the freedom struggle helped to shape my own thinking about it. My interviews with Clayborne Carson, Wesley Hogan, and Donna Murch usefully clarified some pieces of the story I tell here.

Although this book does not rely heavily on interviews, I owe a lot to all 33 people who agreed to talk with me. They were unfailingly thoughtful and self-reflective. Even the person who said, teasingly, "Oh, you're writing about do-gooders," made me think about what it was I thought I was doing. As it happened, I conducted only one interview before the pandemic hit. By the time I was ready to resume interviewing people, in the summer of 2020, we were deep into the pandemic. I pivoted to Zoom or the telephone, and stayed there, even after the pandemic receded. One exception was Gay Falk, who met me at an Echo Park café to talk about her friend Beverly Axelrod. Gay also generously shared with me some of Axelrod's papers. In one case, I conducted the interview entirely by email. Not everyone I interviewed is quoted in the text or even in a footnote. Yet every single interview enhanced my understanding of solidarity in the sixties. Unsurprisingly, some of the people I most wanted to interview had passed, in one case just days before I intended to make contact. Predictably, several interview requests went unanswered. In those cases, I tried to compensate as best I could with the memoirs, oral histories, and autobiographies I could locate.

I also want to thank those who took part in the October 2023 conference, "Insurgents and Intellectuals: Thought and Practice on the Left in U.S. History," in honor of Howard Brick. It was exciting to present a piece of this book and to be in dialogue with such a thoughtful group of scholars. I also presented a much more schematic version of this project at USC's Society of Fellows. As for USC, in many ways it has been a remarkable community in which to work. I want to express my deep gratitude to Barbra Streisand for her commitment to progressive causes, and for funding USC's Barbra Streisand Chair of Contemporary Gender Studies, which I hold. Thanks also to Humanities' vice-deans Rebecca Lemon and Sherry Velasco and the Chair of the Gender and Sexuality Department, Karen Tongson, who provided timely assistance in helping me to bring this project to completion. I also want to give a shout-out to the History Department's office manager. Lori Rogers is efficient, thoughtful, and kind. She also has a great sense of humor, particularly about our football team.

When I was just starting to do the research for this book, I was represented by Geri Thoma of Writers House. Geri became my agent back in the mid-1990s, when I was working on my biography of Janis Joplin. Early on, she offered encouragement and useful feedback, but she retired before I had made much headway. Retiring was doubtless good for her, but I imagine I am not the only historian and former client who misses Geri's commitment to histories that are at once serious and readable. I worked briefly with one of her colleagues at Writers House before arriving at an amicable parting.

As I negotiated the book world agent-less, I benefited from enormously helpful discussions with Brandon Proia at Basic Books. Brandon offered me crucial advice on my proposal, and his enthusiasm gave me a much-needed lift. However, I began to think that this book needed to find a home with a university press. My colleague Steve Ross recommended David McBride at Oxford University Press. As it happened, I knew Dave slightly from when he was a graduate student at UCLA in the mid-1990s when he had been a teaching assistant in my twentieth-century U.S. history survey class. He immediately understood my book and expertly shepherded it through the acquisitions process. We have had some terrific conversations, but he left OUP for Princeton University Press just before I submitted my manuscript. Thankfully, my new editor, Angela Chnapko, also "gets" this book and is an extremely talented editor. Sarah Ebel, the project editor with whom I worked on the book's production, was unfailingly efficient, helpful, and calm.

Speaking of the acquisitions process, I want to give a shout-out to the anonymous readers of my book proposal. All three readers gave it a careful and thoughtful reading and made very useful suggestions. I was also very lucky in that one of them signaled to Dave his willingness to be in conversation with me. Devin Fergus, the author of an important book about liberalism and Black Power, was exceptionally clear-eyed about my project in our conversation.

Archivists and librarians at the Brooke Russell Astor Reading Room for Rare Books and Manuscripts at the New York Public Library, Special Collections at the University of Michigan, the University of Iowa, and the University of Delaware provided essential help and know-how. I also used many digital collections, none more useful than that of the State Historical Society of Wisconsin, which has a searchable digital collection related to 1964's Freedom

Summer, SNCC, and much more. I was on their site day after day. I had hoped that several Freedom of Information Act requests I made in 2022 might turn up some interesting findings, but those requests remain outstanding, and likely will remain so. Thanks to Simon Judkins for his assistance in navigating it all.

By a very long ways, my biggest and most heartfelt thanks is to the cultural historian Kate Flint. There had to be moments during the past six years when she questioned the wisdom of marrying me. How many times did I ask Kate to read a part—usually a very long part—of this book? Too many . . . and then the whole frigging book. Kate made time, despite writing her own book and having a demanding schedule that involves teaching and unending administrative work. Her generosity did not stop there. Who else would have given me as a birthday present a copy of Leigh Claire La Berge's *Marx for Cats: A Radical Bestiary*? Who but Kate would have had the good sense to do a search of Project 2025 to see if it includes a mention of radical chic? Who else would remind me to acknowledge not only our cats Moth and Gramsci . . . but also our beloved but now-deceased LucyFur? I am very lucky to have Kate's love, and to experience her great generosity of spirit each and every day.

Notes

Links to the Wisconsin Historical Society, whose digitally available SNCC collections I have consulted, may not work by the time of this book's publication, as the WHS is transitioning to a new platform. However, endnotes should contain sufficient information to permit future researchers to locate the material cited. Abbreviations used in the Notes can be found on pp. xiii–xiv.

INTRODUCTION

1. Larry Buchanan, Quoctrung Bui, and Jugal K. Patel, "Black Lives Matter May Be the Largest Movement in U.S. History," *NYT*, July 3, 2020.
2. Keeanga-Yamahtta Taylor, "How Do We Change America?" *The New Yorker*, June 8, 2020.
3. Martin Luther King often invoked the words of the nineteenth-century abolitionist Theodore Parker, who coined this by-now familiar expression. Thomas J. Sugrue, "2020 Is Not 1968," *National Geographic*, June 11, 2020. Accessed June 15, 2022: https://www.nationalgeographic.com/history/article/2020-not-1968
4. Nikole Hannah-Jones, Caitlin Roper, Ilena Silverman, and Jake Silverstein, eds., *The 1619 Project* (One World, 2021), 455. In retrospect, people may have taken to the streets, not despite the pandemic, but because of it. Certainly, many people were starved for contact and a feeling of community.
5. McAdam quoted in Buchanan et al., "Black Lives Matter"; Amy Harmon and Sabina Tavernise, "One Big Difference About George Floyd Protests: Many White Faces," *NYT*, June 17, 2020.
6. There is no one agreed-upon definition of "woke." Here I use the term to denote an acknowledgment of systemic racism and the role it has played in American history.
7. My account relies on the following articles: Nicholas Kulish, "After Raising $90 Million in 2020, Black Lives Matter Has $42 Million in Assets," *NYT*, May 17, 2022; Jelani Cobb, "The Matter of Black Lives," *The New Yorker*, March 6, 2016; Alex Thompson, "White America Is Reckoning with Racism," *Politico*, June 9, 2020, https://www.politico.com/news/2020/06/09/white-voters-2020-biden-304804; Matthew Yglesias, "The Great Awokening," *Vox*, April 1, 2019, about white liberals' growing awareness about racism, https://www.vox.com/2019/3/22/18259865/great-awokening-white-liberals-race-polling-trump-2020; "Holding Corporations Accountable to Their Black Lives Matter Pledges," *Green America*, undated, https://greenamerica.org/show-ga-blog?nid=18648
8. Biden also acknowledged that 1994's crime bill, which he sponsored, in many ways failed. He blamed its failure on what happened locally, that is how the *states* behaved after its passage. See Lauren Gambino, "Things Have Changed," *Guardian*, October 17, 2020. The 1994 crime bill has been attacked for exacerbating racist policing and causing mass incarceration. One such example is Taylor's "How Do We Change America?" As others have pointed out, however, the bill was supported by Black communities and the Congressional Black Caucus. For a rich historical study, see James Forman Jr., *Locking Up Our Own: Crime and Punishment in Black*

America (Farrar, Straus and Giroux, 2017). For a useful journalistic summary, see Rashawn Ray and William A. Galston, "Did the 1994 Crime Bill Cause Mass Incarceration?" Brookings, August 28, 2020, https://www.brookings.edu/articles/did-the-1994-crime-bill-cause-mass-incarceration/

9. Mie Inouye, "Solidarity Now," *Boston Review*, September 19, 2023. She writes of the post-2020 pessimism about cross-racial solidarity. As for BLM's decline, it had multiple sources, but surely one was the group's well-publicized financial missteps. They may have resulted primarily from poor management and understaffing, but the optics were bad and the fallout damaging. Kulish, "After Raising $90 Million in 2020."

10. For a brilliant dissection of allyship that examines its shortcomings, both for allies and the activists they support, see Robin Givhan, "The Black Lives Matter Movement Hits a Different Kind of Wall," *Washington Post*, August 6, 2020. "There are so many ground rules for allyship," wrote Givhan, "that the list reads like a series of impossible tasks."

11. See Hajar Yazdiha, *The Struggle for the People's King: How Politics Transforms the Memory of the Civil Rights Movement* (Princeton University Press, 2024); Jeanne Theoharis, *A More Beautiful and Terrible History: The Uses and Misuses of Civil Rights History* (Beacon Press, 2018).

12. Jelani Cobb, "The Matter of Black Lives," *The New Yorker*, March 6, 2016. It was the rapper Tef Poe, whose 2014 track "War Cry" boasted the refrain, "This ain't your daddy's civil rights movement, nah / This ain't your mama's civil rights movement, nah." Lanre Bakare, "St Louis Rapper Turned Activist," *Guardian*, November 12, 2014. It then mutated into "not your grandfather's civil rights movement." For the track, accessed January 27, 2025: https://soundcloud.com/tef-poe/war-cry-produced-by-dj-smitty-jay-nixon-diss-record? utm_source=www.theguardian.com&utm_campaign=wtshare&utm_medium=widget&utm_content=https%253A%252F%252Fsoundcloud.com%252Ftef-poe%252Fwar-cry-produced-by-dj-smitty-jay-nixon-diss-record

13. Tom Cotton, "Send In the Troops," *NYT*, June 3, 2020.

14. The pdf of the Heritage Foundation's Project 2025 can be found on the foundation's website: chrome-extension://efaidnbmnnnibpcajpcglclefindmkaj/https://static.project2025.org/2025_MandateForLeadership_FOREWORD.pdf. A sampling of conservative critics who treat wokeness as radical chic redux: Lorrie Goldstein, "Why Black Lives Matter, Matters," *Toronto Sun*, July 9, 2016; John Loftus, "'Radical Chic' Turns 50," *National Review*, June 9, 2020; James Pinkerton, "'Radical Chic': Still Cringey After All These Years," *The American Conservative*, June 10, 2020; Leo Morris, "From Radical Chic to 'Woke' All of a Sudden," *Monticello Herald Journal*, June 17, 2020; "The Classicist: Radical Chic and Its Terrified Enablers," Interview with Victor Davis Hanson, Hoover Institution webpage, July 10, 2020.

15. It is fair to say that politics practiced in the name of woke could give pause. Examples of leftists and moderates who have criticized liberal elites and/or wokeness, often with real insight, include Susan Neiman, *Left Is Not Woke* (Polity, 2023); Frederik DeBoer, *How Elites Ate the Social Justice Movement* (Simon & Schuster, 2024); Olúfémi O. Táíwò, *Elite Capture* (Haymarket, 2022); Musa al-Gharbi, *We Have Never Been Woke*

16. (Princeton University Press, 2023); Michelle Goldberg, "The Awful Advent of Reactionary Chic," *NYT*, April 25, 2022; David Brooks, "This Is How Wokeness Ends," *NYT*, May 13, 2021.
16. Historians debate whether it is best to treat the struggle for civil rights and the pursuit of Black Power as two distinct movements or as one movement. I write of them as one movement, while paying attention to the important differences between the two.
17. Not everyone will agree with my decision to include people who might be considered patrons. The historian Eduardo Galeano believes the power dynamics underlying solidarity and charity are fundamentally and irreconcilably different. "Unlike solidarity, which is horizontal and takes place between equals, charity is top-down, humiliating those who receive it and never challenging the implicit power relations." However, solidarity often happens between people who are not equals. Moreover, when it comes to "charity," the sixties donors in my study did not regard their support as charity. The lines between solidarity, allyship, and patronage are murkier than one might think. Galleano quoted in Paul Haacke, *The Vertical Imagination and the Crisis of Transatlantic Modernism* (Oxford University Press, 2021), 310.
18. Corey Richardson used the term "awkward ally" to defend Joe Biden. "Black folks who have been black for long enough can identify the difference between an awkward ally and a virulent racist. We good." Richardson quoted in Gregg Hurwitz, "Is the Spell of Political Correctness Breaking," https://www.thebulwark.com/p/is-the-spell-of-political-correctness-breaking. As for the use of the term "comrade," Bill Ayers, a leader of the white militant group Weatherman, said that he and other Weathermen saw themselves as the Black Panthers' "comrades," not allies. "Mother Country Radicals," on "Democracy Now!" August 1, 2022.
19. Charles M. Payne, *I've Got the Light of Freedom: The Organizing Tradition and the Mississippi Freedom Struggle* (University of California Press, 1995), 88, 177.
20. Robin Kelley, Society for Cultural Anthropology, July 8, 2019, accessed October 29, 2024: https://culanth.org/fieldsights/recording-culture-at-large-2018-with-robin-kelley
21. Inouye, "Solidarity Now." See also Michael Rothberg, *The Implicated Subject: Beyond Victims and Perpetrators* (Stanford University Press, 2019).
22. I capitalize "Movement" when writing about the larger Movement that included the intersecting left-wing causes of the day. Otherwise, I use "movement," as in the Black freedom movement, in lowercase.
23. Clayborne Carson, *In Struggle: SNCC and the Black Awakening of the 1960s* (Harvard University Press, 1981), 98.
24. For an exemplary critique of the collective fables that constitute this version of civil rights history, and a counterhistory, see Theoharis, *A More Beautiful and Terrible History*.
25. Several books have since revealed the extent of racism in the North, including Thomas Sugrue's *Origins of the Urban Crisis: Race and Inequality in Postwar Detroit* (Princeton University Press, 1996).
26. Over the years, Bond gave slightly different versions of this. For another, see Wesley Hogan, "Freedom Now! SNCC Galvanizes the New Left," in *Rebellion in Black and White: Southern Student Activism in the 1960s*, ed. Robert Cohen and David J. Snyder (The Johns Hopkins University Press, 2013), 48.

27. Taylor Branch, author of the riveting trilogy *America in the King Years*, likened Black Power to an "extravagant death rattle" in its final volume, *At Canaan's Edge*, 494. Todd Gitlin, *The Sixties: Years of Hope, Days of Rage* (Bantam Books, 1987); Tom Hayden, *Reunion: A Memoir* (Random House, 1988), 308–9, 419. Maurice Isserman takes issue with the Good Sixties/Bad Sixties dichotomy, but he considers the influence of the Panthers on the African American left an "unmitigated disaster." See Isserman, "Where Have All the Convict Heroes Gone, Long Time Passing?" *Radical History Review* 64 (1996): 115. For two critiques of the "declension narratives" that characterize many accounts of the sixties, see Wini Breines, "Whose New Left?" *Journal of American History* 75 (Sept. 1988), 528–45, and Alice Echols, "'We Gotta Get Outta of This Place': Notes Towards a Remapping of the Sixties," in Echols, *Shaky Ground: The Sixties and Its Aftershocks* (Columbia University Press, 2002).
28. Peniel E. Joseph, *Waiting 'til the Midnight Hour: A Narrative History of Black Power in America* (Henry Holt, 2006); Komozi Woodard, *A Nation with a Nation: Amiri Baraka (LeRoi Jones) and Black Power Politics* (University of North Carolina Press, 1999); Jeffrey O. G. Ogbar, *Black Power: Radical Politics and African American Identity* (Johns Hopkins University Press, 2004); Tyson, *Radio Free Dixie;* Matthew J. Countryman, *Up South: Civil Rights and Black Power in Philadelphia* (University of Pennsylvania Press, 2005); Donna Jean Murch, *Living for the City: Migration, Education, and the Rise of the Black Panther Party in Oakland, California* (University of North Carolina Press, 2010); Joshua Bloom and Waldo Martin, *Black Against Empire: The History and Politics of the Black Panther Party* (University of California Press, 2013); Hasan Kwame Jeffries, *Bloody Lowndes: Civil Rights and Black Power in Alabama's Black Belt* (New York University Press, 2009); Dan Berger, *Stayed on Freedom: The Long History of Black Power Through One Family's Journey* (Basic Books, 2023); Charles M. Payne, *I've Got the Light of Freedom: The Organizing Tradition and the Mississippi Freedom Struggle* (University of California Press, 2007); Wesley Hogan, *Many Minds, One Heart: SNCC's Dream for a New America* (University of North Carolina Press, 2007). A crucial text that bridges these two historiographical moments is Carson, *In Struggle*.
29. For a newer work that challenges head-on earlier narratives that positioned Black Power as "the evil twin" that doomed the movement, see Shirlette J. Kinchen, *Black Power in the Bluff City: African–American Youth and Student Activism in Memphis, 1965–1975* (University of Tennessee Press, 2016).
30. It is, however, worth noting that staffers sang this song with hard-hitting improvised lyrics. Staughton Lynd, *Living Inside Our Hope: A Steadfast Radical's Thoughts on Rebuilding the Movement* (Cornell University Press, 1997), 32. For an incisive piece about how "Kumbaya" has been unfairly depicted as a cuddly, feel-good song, see Samuel G. Freedman, "A Long Road from 'Come by Here' to 'Kumbaya,'" *NYT*, November 30, 2010.
31. See Carson, *In Struggle*, 96–110.
32. The book that helped to establish this view of the Panthers is the Black journalist Hugh Pearson's *The Shadow of the Panther: Huey Newton and the Price of Black Power in America* (Da Capo Press, 1994). Almost everything that's been written in the wake

of Pearson's book pushes back hard against it. But, as David Garrow has noted, scholars' negative treatment of Pearson's book is curious, given that much of his account is corroborated by the memoirs and autobiographies of former Panthers. Still, Pearson's journalistic odyssey, from admirer to critic, becomes too much the story here. The reader is meant to share Pearson's disillusionment with his one-time heroes as he details one terrible story of abuse and exploitation after another, and what was admirable about the Panthers is lost. Roz Payne challenges the view of the Panthers as "gun-toting thugs" in her article, "WACing Off: Gossip, Sex, Race, and Politics in the World of FBI Special Case Against William A. Cohendet," in *In Search of the Black Panther Party*, ed. Jama Lazerow and Yohuru Williams (Duke University Press, 2006), 175.

33. Murch, *Living for the City*; Bloom and Martin, *Black Against Empire*; Jakobi Williams, *From the Bullet to the Ballot: The Illinois Chapter of the Black Panther Party and Racial Coalition Politics in Chicago* (University of North Carolina Press, 2013); Jane Rhodes, *Framing the Panthers* (The New Press, 2007); Woodard, *Nation Within a Nation*; David Hilliard and Lewis Cole, *This Side of Glory: The Autobiography of David Hilliard and the Story of the Black Panther Party* (Little, Brown and Company, 1993); Judy Tzu-Chun Wu, *Radicals on the Road* (Cornell University Press, 2013).

34. Peniel E. Joseph, "Black Power Studies I," *Black Scholar* 31 (Fall–Winter 2001): 1–26.

35. As Brenda Gayle Plummer incisively observes, scholars of Black Power sometimes have treated the early civil rights movement as insufficiently revolutionary, "not 'black' enough, and tainted by liberalism's universalist assumptions, in order that Black Power militancy might not only shine in contrast, but also take on legibility based on what it is perceived *not* to be." See Plummer, *In Search of Power: African Americans in the Era of Decolonization, 1956–1974* (Cambridge University Press, 2012), 15–16. Two recent efforts that acknowledge the complex relationship between Dr. King and more militant activists are Jeanne Theoharis, *King of the North: Martin Luther King's Life of Struggle Outside the South* (New Press, 2025), and Peniel E. Joseph, *The Sword and the Shield: The Revolutionary Lives of Malcolm X and Martin Luther King Jr.* (Basic Books, 2020).

36. Exceptions include Hogan, *Many Minds*; Payne, *I've Got the Light of Freedom*; Simon Hall, *Peace and Freedom: The Civil Rights and Antiwar Movements in the 1960s* (University of Pennsylvania Press, 2005); David Barber, *A Hard Rain Fell: SDS and Why It Failed* (University Press of Mississippi, 2008). In *Black Against Empire*, Bloom and Martin very usefully document the Panthers' "allies," but they don't probe what they meant for the Panthers. The autobiography that consistently draws attention to the party's collaborators is Hilliard and Cole, *This Side of Glory*.

37. Ernst Borinski is largely unknown. Lawrence Guyot of SNCC cited his influence in Cheryl Lynne Greenberg, ed., *A Circle of Trust: Remembering SNCC* (Rutgers University Press, 1998), 66, 9.

38. Stokely Carmichael, with Ekwueme Michael Thelwell, *Ready for Revolution: The Life and Struggles of Stokely Carmichael (Kwame Ture)* (Scribner, 2003), 426. SNCC workers' memories about the number and make of these cars differ. SNCC obtained a lower insurance rate by naming their cars a fleet. SNCC called it the Sojourner Motor Fleet, after Sojourner Truth. See "Sojourner Motor Fleet," SNCC Digital: https://snccdigital.org/inside-sncc/sncc-national-office/sojourner-motor-fleet/

39. Journalists who recently have written critically about Wolfe's journalism include Osita Nwanevu, "The Electric Kool-Aid Conservative," *The New Republic*, January 5, 2024; Benjamin Ivry, "That Time Tom Wolfe Lampooned Leonard Bernstein and 'Radical Chic,'" *The Forward: News That Matters to American Jews*, May 16, 2018.
40. One astute effort to analyze "Radical Chic" is Michael Staub's "Black Panthers, New Journalism, and the Rewriting of the Sixties," *Representations* 57 (Winter 1997), 52–72.
41. However, someone who did not appreciate Ochs's song was the left-wing muckraker I. F. Stone. For someone whose politics were more Old than New Left, Stone was unusually supportive of radicalism, including Black Power and the militant New Left. Yet he objected to Ochs's song. Doug Rossinow, *Visions of Progress: The Left-Liberal Tradition in America* (University of Pennsylvania Press, 2008), 246–47.
42. Today, many twentieth-century U.S. historians reject the familiar story of the sixties as a time of political polarization. Instead, they argue for the essential congruence between liberals and conservatives. This historiographical shift, dubbed by one historian "neo-consensus history," follows in part from the growing attention paid to mass incarceration and neoliberalism, developments in which liberals certainly played a role. See Bruce Schulman, "Post-1968 US History: Neo-Consensus History for the Age of Polarization," *Reviews in American History* 47, no. 3 (Sept. 2019): 479–99. For a critique of "neo-consensus history," see Ariane Leendertz, "A View from Abroad: Post-1968 U.S. History, the End of the New Deal Order, and Neoliberalism," *Reviews in American History* 49, no. 4 (Dec. 2021): 633–48. For their nuanced treatment of post-1970 liberalism, see Nelson Lichtenstein and Judith Stein, *A Fabulous Failure: The Clinton Presidency and the Transformation of American Capitalism* (Princeton University Press, 2023).
43. This is the characterization advanced by Richard Flacks and Nelson Lichtenstein in their Introduction to their co-edited volume, *The Port Huron Statement* (University of Pennsylvania Press, 2015), 2. In that same volume, see, Daniel Geary, "The New Left and Liberalism Reconsidered: The Committee of Correspondence and the Port Huron Statement," 85–106.
44. For liberals' reaction to the Kerner Commission's Report, see David C. Carter, *The Music Has Gone Out of the Movement* (University of North Carolina Press), 226. For Humphrey's tough-on-crime stance, see Steve Gillon, *Separate and Unequal: The Kerner Commission and the Unraveling of American Liberalism* (Basic Books, 2018), 294–95. An article detailing FBI director J. Edgar Hoover's campaign against the party is John Kifner's, "F.B.I. Sought Doom of Panther Party," *NYT*, May 9, 1976. For antiwar liberals finally coming together with radicals for the October and November 1969 Moratoriums, see David Greenberg, *Nixon's Shadow: The History of an Image* (Norton, 2003), 88.
45. Rothberg, *The Implicated Subject*.
46. Julius Lester, *All Is Well* (William Morrow & Co., 1976), 80.
47. Elaine Mokhtefi, *Algiers, Third World Capital* (Verso Press, 2018), 166–67, and "Diary: Panthers in Algiers," *London Review of Books* 39, no. 11 (June 1, 2017), accessed August 4, 2025: https://www.lrb.co.uk/the-paper/v39/n11/elaine-mokhtefi/diary
48. Originally, the group was called the Progressive Labor Movement, and then took the name, the Progressive Labor Party. It was widely known as PL. The meltdown

at SDS's final national conference, in Chicago, is amply covered in many sixties histories, including Gitlin's *The Sixties* and Mark Rudd's *Underground: My Life with SDS and the Weathermen* (Harper-Collins, 2009). Gitlin provides a good introduction to the sectarian left in his book; *The Sixties*, 179–83. For an account that appeared in the local underground paper, *The Washington Free Press*, see "Kommie Kapers," July 1–15, 1969, https://washingtonspark.files.wordpress.com/2020/05/1969-07-01-wfp-vol-3-no-6.pdf

49. Bryan Burrough, *Days of Rage* (Penguin, 2015), 74.
50. I am almost certain this was Bill Ayers. For more on the relationship between Weatherman and the Black Panther Party, see Hilliard and Cole, *This Side of Glory*; Rudd, *Underground*; Williams, *From the Bullet to the Ballot*; David Barber, "Leading the Vanguard," in *In Search of the Black Panther Party*, ed. Jama Lazerow and Yohuru Williams (Duke University Press, 2006).
51. https://www.washingtonpost.com/archive/local/2005/08/28/you-better-sit-down-the-big-chairs-gone/f08bd4df-14a7-48bd-87a8-290a94b85d26/
52. Terry Becker, "Bridging the Gap: SDS," *Quicksilver Times* 1, no. 1 (June 16, 1969), 5, https://washingtonspark.files.wordpress.com/2020/04/1969-06-16-quicksilver-vol.-1-no-1.pdf
53. I have come to appreciate PL's long-game approach to organizing, but its dogmatism was off-putting, and its faith that the white working class could be easily radicalized in 1969 was misplaced. As Robert F. Williams, the original advocate of Black self-defense, said in 1969 of the Panthers' imagined alliance with the white working class, "I don't know what white proletariat they have found to unite with." See Timothy Tyson, "Robert F. Williams, 'Black Power,' and the Roots of the African American Freedom Struggle," *Journal of American History* 85, no. 2 (Sept. 1998): 567n61.
54. For Susan Brownmiller's account, see Brownmiller, *In Our Time: A Memoir of Revolution* (Dial Press, 1999), 252. Amiri Baraka characterized Cleaver as a trickster, though not in relation to this incident. It is worth noting that Cleaver was, by this juncture, turning to the right. Nevertheless, it's hard to see what political advantage would have accrued to Cleaver by warning Brownmiller that she needed to attend to, rather than alienate, a crucial constituency. Baraka is quoted in Ishmael Reed's new introduction to the 1999 edition of Eldridge Cleaver, *Soul on Ice*, 16th ed. (Delta, 1999), 5–6.
55. The date of their appearance on *The Phil Donahue Show* was October 5, 1976, less than two months after he had been released from prison on parole. Cleaver's turn to the religious right deepened in the months ahead. Justin Gifford, *Revolution or Death: The Life of Eldridge Cleaver* (Lawrence Hill Books, 2020), 250.
56. By now, the ranks of voters drawn to the Republican Party include significant numbers of non-white voters. See Daniel Martinez HoSang, "Inside the Rise of the Multiracial Right," *NYT,* July 24, 2025.
57. Karen E. Fields and Barbara J. Fields, *Racecraft: The Soul of Inequality in American Life* (Verso, 2012), 63.

PART ONE

1. When Jackson, Mississippi's Chamber of Commerce signaled its willingness to abide by the accommodations section of 1964's civil rights law and when white housewives

opposed the formation of state-funded private segregated schools, which would damage public schools, one Jackson lawyer noted, "some crack has been made in that wall of Never." Calvin Trillin, "The Struggle for Civil Rights in Mississippi," *The New Yorker*, August 21, 1964.

2. Jacqueline Dowd Hall, "The Long Civil Rights Movement and the Political Uses of the Past," *Journal of American History* 91, no. 4 (March 2005): 1233–63. Hall's influential article reperiodized the Black freedom movement, whose beginnings many historians had traced to the mid-1950s. Hall contended that the civil rights movement has a longer, and a more radical, trajectory whose politics she calls "civil rights unionism." The Communist Party played a prominent role in this political formation. Hall's article has come in for criticism for its lionizing of mostly communist left-wing activists of the 1930s and '40s, and for its somewhat dismissive treatment of the movement in its classic "civil rights" phase. For example, Eric Arnesen questions whether "the existence of individual activists or even a small and often stigmatized left-wing organization allow us to talk about a movement or suggest an ongoing, relentless struggle?" Arnesen also argues that communists' interest in promoting civil rights was primarily about defeating capitalism; it wasn't always rooted in a deep commitment to racial equality. See Eric Arnesen, "Reconsidering the 'Long Civil Rights Movement,'" *Historically Speaking*, April 2009, 32. Other skeptical accounts of the Communist Party's relationship to civil rights, which stress its opportunism, include Sundiata Kieta Cha-Jua and Clarence Lang, "The 'Long Movement' as Vampire: Temporal and Spatial Fallacies in Recent Black Freedom Studies," *Journal of African-American History* 92, no. 2 (Spring 2007): 265–88; Steve Lawson, "Long Origins of the Short Civil Rights Movement," in *Freedom Rights: New Perspectives on the Civil Rights Movement*, ed. Danielle L. McGuire and John Dittmer (University of Kentucky Press, 2011); see also Peniel E. Joseph, *Waiting for Midnight: A Narrative History of Black Power in America* (Henry Holt, 2006), 3–7. John Dittmer has argued, also influentially, for the years surrounding World War II as the starting point of the movement. Dittmer, *Local People: The Struggle for Civil Rights in Mississippi* (University of Illinois Press, 1994).

3. Glenda Elizabeth Gilmore, *Defying Dixie: The Radical Roots of the Civil Rights Movement* (Norton, 2009), 384–93. Gilmore emphasized the role played by Howard Law School student and activist Pauli Murray, whose intersectional analysis of racism and sexism would prove so influential.

4. These are the words of white New Leftist Tom Hayden after a visit to McComb, Mississippi. See Tom Hayden's January 1962 pamphlet, "Revolution in Mississippi," 21, accessed November 4, 2023: chrome-extension://efaidnbmnnnibpcajpcglclefindmkaj/https://www.crmvet.org/info/62_hayden_mccomb.pdf. Parts of it are included in Tom Hayden, "SNCC in Action," in *Writings for a Democratic Society: The Tom Hayden Reader* (City Lights Books, 2008), 34.

5. Greenberg, *Circle of Trust*, 23.

6. Take the influential exhortation that activists put their bodies on the line. It was Mario Savio, a leader of UC–Berkeley's Free Speech Movement, who uttered those words, but they grew out of his life-changing experience months earlier at a SNCC project in Mississippi. For a discussion of living in the solution or personal politics, see Wesley

C. Hogan, *Many Minds, One Heart: SNCC's Dream for a New America* (University of North Carolina Press, 2007), 23.
7. Mary King, *Freedom Song: A Personal Story of the 1960s Civil Rights Movement* (William Morrow, 1987), 275.
8. Laura Visser-Maessen, *Robert Parris Moses: A Life in Civil Rights and Leadership at the Grassroots* (University of North Carolina Press, 2016), 72; Taylor Branch, *Parting the Waters: America in the King Years, 1954–63* (Simon & Schuster, 1988), 500.
9. King, *Freedom Song*, 405.
10. Carmichael, *Ready for Revolution*, 309.
11. For Zellner, see Hogan, *Many Minds*, 63. See also Bernice Johnson Reagon, "Coalition Politics: Turning the Century," in *Home Girls: A Black Feminist Anthology*, ed. Barbara Smith (Rutgers University Press, 1983), 363.

CHAPTER ONE

1. SNCC workers were frequently called "shock troops." On at least on one occasion, Martin Luther King Jr. called them the "storm troopers" of the movement, whose full-bore activism was not constrained by adult responsibilities. See Hogan, *Many Minds*, 8. At the February 7, 2005, memorial service for James Forman, Annie Pearl Avery of SNCC spoke of how the organization did crucial work in confronting terror. SNCC, she said, "softened up places" to the point where "you could walk the streets at least, without getting arrested." Accessed on C-SPAN, November 5, 2024: https://www.c-span.org/video/?185459-1/memorial-service-james-forman
2. See https://snccdigital.org/events/freedom-rides/
3. Moses quoted in Visser-Maessen, *Robert Parris Moses*, 67.
4. Julian Bond said that in going into the Deep South, SNCC was "daring to take the message of freedom" into regions where "the bigger civil rights organizations feared to tread." Julian Bond, "The Movement We Helped to Make," in *Long Time Gone: Sixties America Then and Now*, ed. Alexander Bloom (Oxford University Press, 2001), 16.
5. Thurgood Marshall and other civil rights lawyers were initially confused by the Court's language. When they consulted a dictionary, they learned that, as they had suspected, "all deliberate speed" actually meant slow. See Charles J. Ogletree, "All Deliberate Speed," The Center for American Progress, April 12, 2004, https://www.americanprogress.org/article/all-deliberate-speed/. Also see Julian Bond, "What We Did," adapted from a 2000 talk that Bond delivered at Harvard's W. E. B. Du Bois Institute for Afro-American Studies. https://static1.squarespace.com/static/5b390ebb7e3c3a94b302e525/t/5c129d1621c67c252de89e54/1544723735121/Julian+Bond-What+We+Did.pdf
6. King, *Freedom Song*, 35. King claims this was the number that James Forman cited when she joined the organization. However, Clayborne Carson put the number at 20 in April 1962. See Carson, *In Struggle*, 67.
7. Hogan, *Many Minds*, 114.
8. Julian Bond, "SNCC: What We Did," *Monthly Review*, October 2000, https://monthlyreview.org/2000/10/01/sncc-what-we-did/

9. Moses had been in Mississippi briefly in 1960. When he returned a year later, he was working for SCLC, but he had his eye on joining SNCC. When he requested official status as a voluntary field secretary for SNCC, it initially provoked some debate in SNCC because he was already working for SCLC. Minutes from SNCC Meeting; July 16, 1961, SAVF-SNCC, Mss. 577, Box 47, Folder 2, Wisconsin Historical Society (WHS). According to Tim Jenkins, Moses had checks from both CORE and SCLC, which wanted him to work for them. See Howard Zinn Interview Transcripts, 1963–65; Interview with Tim Jenkins, Mss. 588, Box 3, Folder 10.
10. Visser-Maessen, *Robert Parris Moses*, 122.
11. Interview with Charles Sherrod, June 23–24, 1997, Veterans of Hope Project, Emory University, accessed July 2025: https://aviary.libraries.emory.edu/collections/1344/collection_resources/44039/file/149358
12. Hogan, *Many Minds*, 3.
13. Bernice Reagon, "The Borning Struggle: The Civil Rights Movement," in *They Should Have Served That Cup of Coffee: 7 Radicals Remember the 60s*, ed. Dick Cluster (South End Press, 1979), 23.
14. Carson, *In Struggle*, 78.
15. Bob Moses describes this method in detail in relation to McComb, Mississippi, where he and Amzie Moore had been invited by local NAACP leader C. C. Bryant to take preliminary steps for launching a voter registration drive. For the first two weeks, Moses spoke to business leaders, ministers, and other local people to see if they would be willing to support 10 students to lead this drive. They agreed, and the drive began August 1, 1961, and lasted through December. Robert Moses Account of Voter Registration Drive in Mississippi in 1961, February 1963, Carl and Anne Braden Papers, 1926–2006; Archives Sound Holdings, Audio 443A/18–19, WHS, https://content.wisconsinhistory.org/digital/collection/p15932coll2/id/55798/rec/3. John Dittmer quoted in Visser-Maessen, *Robert Parris Moses*, 66. About Albany, see Sherrod Interview, June 23–24, 1997, Emory University, accessed November 5, 2024: https://aviary.libraries.emory.edu/collections/1344/collection_resources/44039/file/117251
16. Here, my understanding of SNCC's organizing style is enhanced by email discussions with Mike Miller, a SNCC veteran and a longtime organizer who worked with Saul Alinsky. Email correspondence with author, June 13, 2021.
17. Courtney Pace, *Freedom Faith: The Womanist Vision of Prathia Hall* (University of Georgia Press, 2019); author's interview with Mike Miller, July 2, 2021. As Wesley Hogan and Clayborne Carson note, the distinctiveness of SNCC's style owed a lot to Ella Baker.
18. The organizer, Charles McLaurin, is quoted in Hogan, *Many Minds*, 60.
19. Charles Sherrod, Interview, June 23–24, 1997, Emory University, https://aviary.libraries.emory.edu/collections/1344/collection_resources/44039/file/117251
20. See Carson, *In Struggle*, 75–77.
21. Anne Braden, quoted in Hogan, *Many Minds*, 72.
22. Jean Smith, "The Borning Struggle," in Cluster, *They Should Have*, 31.
23. This is Casey Hayden's description in her article "Fields of Blue," in *Deep in Our Hearts: Nine White Women in the Freedom Movement*, ed. Joan C. Browning et al. (University of Georgia Press, 2000), 347.

24. Casey Hayden, Interview, "Eyes on the Prize," May 15, 1986, Blackside, Inc., accessed November 6, 2024, through American Archive of Public Broadcasting: https://americanarchive.org/catalog/cpb-aacip_151-kd1qf8kc1r
25. Pete Daniel, Interview with Jane Stembridge, December 5, 1996, Southern Oral History Program, https://dc.lib.unc.edu/cdm/compoundobject/collection/sohp/id/6910/rec/5
26. Bob Zellner, *The Wrong Side of Murder Creek: A White Southerner in the Black Freedom Movement* (NewSouth Books, 2008), 154.
27. King, *Freedom Song*, 144.
28. Francesca Polletta, *Inventing the Ties That Bind: Imagined Relationships in Moral and Political Life* (University of Chicago Press, 2020), 50; Zellner, *Wrong Side*, 154–55.
29. Lawson quoted in Barbara Ransby, *Ella Baker and the Black Freedom Movement: A Radical Democratic Vision* (Chapel Hill: University of North Carolina Press, 2003), 263.
30. Lawson could be fearless, reprimanding the NAACP for focusing on fundraising and the courts instead of civil disobedience and direct action, when it should be "developing our greatest resource, a people . . . who can act in a disciplined manner to implement the [country's] constitution." Lawson quoted in Carson, *In Struggle*, 23.
31. Hogan, *Many Minds*, 249.
32. Those SNCC people whose fathers were ministers or preachers include Prathia Hall, Charles Cobb, Bernice Johnson Reagon, Jane Stembridge, Bob Zellner, Charles Jones, and Sam Shirah.
33. Peggy Trotter Dammond Preacely, "It Was Simply in My Blood," in *Hands on the Freedom Plow*, ed. Faith S. Holsaert et al. (University of Illinois Press, 2012), 169, hereafter cited as *Hands*; Joann Christian Mantis, "We Turned This Upside-Down Country Right Side Up," in *Hands*, 130.
34. Prathia Hall, "Freedom-Faith," in *Hands*, 178.
35. Hogan, *Many Minds*, 87.
36. Payne, *I've Got the Light of Freedom*, 260.
37. According to one obituary, Anne Braden declined publicly to confirm or deny her or her husband Carl's membership in the Communist Party. See Margalit Fox, "Anne Braden, 81, Activist in Civil Rights and Other Causes, Dies," *NYT*, March 17, 2006. Civil rights activists' fears about the Bradens' possible communism lingered. Anne Braden's letter to Ed Hamlett, whose involvement with the proposed White Folks' Project that the Bradens' group, SCEF, planned to subsidize, references Hamlett's concerns that SCEF might be a communist group. She assured him that neither she, her husband, nor SCEF was communist and explained they had been red-baited. See Anne Braden, Letter to Ed Hamlett, May 19, 1963, The Ed Hamlett Collection, the University of Southern Mississippi, accessed November 15, 2023: https://usm.access.preservica.com/uncategorized/IO_d256f06b-7d37-49e9-a23a-b647022921bb/
38. Ransby, *Ella Baker*, 74.
39. SNCC owed its very existence to Baker, who opposed the efforts of King's SCLC to annex the nascent group of sit-in students as its youth wing. For her influence on SNCC people's understanding of themselves as full-time freedom fighters, see Carmichael, *Ready*, 298.
40. Ransby, *Ella Baker*, 188.

41. Hayden, "Fields of Blue," 345.
42. Payne, *I've Got the Light*, 88, 177.
43. See Carson, *In Struggle*, 25–26. Baker quoted in Howard Zinn, *SNCC: The New Abolitionists* (Beacon Press, 1964), 106.
44. Baker quoted in Davis W. Houck and David E. Dixon, eds., *Women and the Civil Rights Movement, 1954–1965* (University Press of Mississippi, 2009), 249; McDew quoted in Joanne Grant, A "Peek Around the Mountain," in *Hands*, 309.
45. Carmichael, *Ready*, 95.
46. About the marginalizing role played by Rustin's homosexuality, see John D'Emilio's *Lost Prophet: The Life and Times of Bayard Rustin* (University of Chicago Press, 2003); Ella Baker saw it this way as well. See Ransby, *Ella Baker*, 163.
47. Aldon Morris, *Origins of the Civil Rights Movement* (Free Press, 1984), 83. In interviews with Aldon Morris, Ella Baker and Stanley Levison gave slightly different versions of this story, but all three stress the centrality of those three New Yorkers. See also D'Emilio biography of Bayard Rustin. Baker also suggested this as well. See Ransby, *Ella Baker*, 163.
48. Gerald Horne and Mary E. Young, *W. E. B. Du Bois: An Encyclopedia* (Greenwood Press, 2001), 10.
49. This quotation is drawn from Eric J. Sundquist's provocative book, *Strangers in the Land: Blacks, Jews, Post-Holocaust America* (Harvard University Press, 2005), 30.
50. Jonathan Kaufman, *Broken Alliance: The Turbulent Times Between Blacks and Jews in America* (Scribner, 1988), 67.
51. Joyce Ladner says that within SNCC these men were known as the "Howard University Crew." See Greenberg, *Circle of Trust*, 139. Another Rustin protégé was Tom Kahn, who was white and Jewish and played a role in writing the famously militant speech that John Lewis was prevented from delivering at 1963's March on Washington. Lewis gave a milder speech lest SNCC further antagonize the Kennedy administration. See Dennis C. Dickerson, *Militant Mediator: Whitney M. Young, Jr.* (The University of Kentucky Press, 1998), 168. Rachelle Horowitz, who worked with Kahn and Rustin, remembers Rustin being "very popular with the SNCC kids." Michael G. Long, ed., *I Must Resist: Bayard Rustin's Life in Letters* (City Lights Press, 2012), 259–60.
52. Jonathan Kaufman, *Broken Alliance: The Turbulent Times Between Blacks and Jews in America* (Scribner, 1988), 67.
53. I say "white Jewish members" because Charles McDew converted to Judaism.
54. See Clayborne Carson, "Blacks and Jews in the Civil Rights Movement," in *Bridges and Boundaries: African Americans and American Jews* (George Braziller, Inc. and The Jewish Museum, 1992), 37.
55. See Carson, *In Struggle*, 107. NLG lawyer Victor Rabinowitz forged the connection with SNCC, where his daughter briefly worked and his son volunteered. Joni Rabinowitz was a field staffer for six months in spring and summer of 1963 in Albany, Georgia; her brother was a Freedom School teacher the following year.
56. Carson, "Blacks and Jews," 37. Elizabeth Betita Sutherland Martínez headed up SNCC's New York office and focused her fundraising efforts on the city's left-liberal Jews. Contributions to the New York office far outpaced those made to other offices

57. Tyson, "Robert F. Williams," 562. Carmichael includes a wonderful discussion of nonviolent direct action in *Ready*, 166.
58. Howard Zinn notes of November 1963 meeting about whites in the movement, Howard Zinn Papers at Wisconsin Historical Society (HZP/WHS), 1956–94; Mss 588, Box 2, Folder 10, WHS, https://content.wisconsinhistory.org/digital/collection/p15932coll2/id/26925/rec/1
59. Carson, *In Struggle*, 100.
60. Martha Prescod Norman Noonan, "The Constant Struggle," in *Hands*, 500. Others, such as Betty Garman, make this point, too. Interview, Julian Bond Oral History Project.
61. Carson, *In Struggle*, 52.
62. Carmichael, *Ready*, 306–9.
63. Schwerner confided to his Black friend and CORE comrade, David Dennis, that he wanted to be Black and thought of himself as Black. David J. Dennis Jr. and David J. Dennis Sr., *The Movement Made Us: A Father, a Son and the Legacy of a Freedom Ride* (Harper Collins, 2022), 202, Kindle edition.
64. Casey Hayden, "Returning to Ann Arbor," in *A New Insurgency: The Port Huron Statement*, ed. Howard Brick and Gregory Parker (Maize Books, University of Michigan, 2015), 76.
65. Pete Daniels, Interview with Jane Stembridge, September 17, 1997, the Southern Oral History Program at UNC. https://dc.lib.unc.edu/cdm/compoundobject/collection/sohp/id/6883/rec/4
66. Interview with Timothy Jenkins, HZP/WHS, 1956–94, Zinn Interviews, 1963–65, MSS. 588, Box 3, Folder 10.
67. In his short story, "The Organizer," Michael Thelwell wrote about Truman, whom he modeled on Forman. See Sharon Monteith, *SNCC's Stories at the Barricades: The African American Freedom Movement in the Civil Rights South* (University of Georgia Press, 2020), 143.
68. A financial audit of SNCC, performed in the spring of 1964, detailed the group's sources of income. See audit at the Civil Rights Movement Archive: chrome-extension://efaidnbmnnnibpcajpcglclefindmkaj/https://www.crmvet.org/docs/63_sncc_financial_audit.pdf. The accountant's description of SNCC's sources of income is borne out by a set of SNCC's meeting notes. See Report from the SNCC Meeting, April 23, 1961, SAVF/SNCC, Box 47, WHS. Donations included $10 from the theologian James A. Dombrowski, who was a founder of the Highlander School and the executive secretary of SCEF; amounts from Episcopalian, Methodist, and Presbyterian parishes, and rabbis and ministers such as Rev. W. H. Moore; NSA: $40; four donations of $1,000 from SCLS; $200 from the National Council of Churches; very small amounts from activists such as Julian Bond, Vivian Franklin, Casey Hayden, future Bay Area journalist Kate Coleman of SLATE in Berkeley, and Tom Kahn of Howard University. Accessed October 10, 2023: https://content.wisconsinhistory.org/digital/collection/p15932coll2/id/64494/rec/26
69. Hogan, *Many Minds*, 98–99.
70. Greenberg, *Circle of Trust*, 132–33.

71. Hayden, Interview, "Eyes on the Prize"; Constance Curry, "Wild Geese to the Past," in Browning et al., *Deep in Our Hearts*; Hayden, "Fields of Blue."
72. Hayden, "In the Attics of My Mind," in *Hands*, 387.
73. Most people did not have the stomach to risk arrest unless they were assured of being bailed out quickly. Carson, *In Struggle*, 28–32.
74. Julian Bond Oral History Project: Betty Garman Robinson.
75. Long-distance calls were expensive, and many of the rural communities in the South where SNCC was operating did not yet have direct-dial long-distance service, which meant using a local operator who was white because the phone company did not hire Blacks for those jobs. SNCC paid for a WATS line because safe, reliable long-distance service was essential to the safety of SNCC workers. See this link: https://www.crmvet.org/disc/jews.htm
76. Julian Bond Oral History Project: Betty Garman Robinson, https://www.julianbondoralhistoryproject.org/betty-robinson
77. Julian Bond Oral History Project: Betty Garman Robinson.
78. Dittmer, *Local People*, 145.
79. Hogan, *Many Minds*, 115.
80. See Judy Richardson, "In Memoriam: Jack Minnis," https://sncclegacyproject.org/in-memoriam-jack-minnis//
81. For remembrances, see https://www.crmvet.org/mem/minnis.htm. Greenberg, *Circle of Trust*, 108. Mary King says that Minnis "singlehandedly popularized" the term "power structure," but that it was the political scientist Floyd Hunter who originally conceptualized it. King, *Freedom Song*, 490.
82. Dorothy M. Zellner, "My Real Vocation," in *Hands*, 315.
83. Tillinghast quoted in Belinda Robnett, *How Long, How Long? African-American Women in the Struggle for Civil Rights* (Oxford University Press, 1997), 127.
84. Trillin, "The Struggle for Civil Rights in Mississippi," *New Yorker*, August 21, 1964.
85. Payne, *I've Got the Light*, 355.
86. Hayden, "Attics," in *Hands*, 387.
87. Cathy Cade, "Caught," in *Hands*, 207.
88. Ed Hamlett, "SNCC's Relationship to White-Dominated Organizations," undated, Mary King Papers, SNCC Position Papers and Reports (1962–99). M82-445, Box 1, Folder 19, WHS. See also Carson, *In Struggle*, 52.
89. Zellner, *Wrong Side*, 159; Hogan, *Many Minds*, 62–63.
90. Hayden, Interview, "Eyes on the Prize."
91. In Mississippi and in Alabama, one did not simply register to vote; one applied to register. Applying involved filling out a form with questions. In Alabama, applicants answered 21 written questions, which was followed by an oral questioning. See Howard Zinn, *SNCC: The New Abolitionists* (Beacon Press, 1965), 153.
92. Hogan, *Many Minds*, 155.
93. Taylor Branch, *Pillar of Fire: America in the King Years, 1963–65* (Simon & Schuster, 1998), 51.
94. Carson, *In Struggle*, 114.
95. Kennedy did push for important changes in the powerful House Rules Committee, whose conservatives blocked legislation coming to the floor. Those 1961 changes enabled passage of civil rights bills and Johnson's Great Society legislation in the years to come. Richard Reeves, "How Kennedy Won the House and Lost the South," *NYT*, March 9, 2009.

96. See the SNCC Digital Gateway on Herbert Lee's murder: https://snccdigital.org/events/herbert-lee-murdered/
97. Doug McAdam, *Freedom Summer* (Oxford University Press, 1988), 27.
98. Visser-Maessen, *Robert Parris Moses*, 184.
99. Hayden, Interview, "Eyes on the Prize."

CHAPTER TWO

1. SNCC people were cynical about the march, whose organizers censored the speech delivered by their chairman, John Lewis. Nonetheless, some activists came to think it marked a turning point in the movement for equal rights. For SNCC's lack of enthusiasm, see Danny Lyon, *Memories of the Southern Civil Rights Movement* (University of North Carolina Press, 1992), 84. A few years later, Mendy Samstein of SNCC called it a "turning point," in Part III of his interview with Anne Romaine. Anne Romaine Papers, SC 1069, Folder 1, WHS.
2. Lawrence Guyot quoted in Greenberg, *Circle of Trust*, 66.
3. Mary King called it a "shell." See King, *Freedom Song*, 401; Sally Belfrage called it a "spine." See Sally Belfrage, *Freedom Summer* (Viking Press, 1965), 4.
4. Holt notes that SNCC provided the personnel in four of the five Congressional districts, "95% of the staff in state headquarters in Jackson, and 90 to 95% of the money operating the civil rights program and facilities throughout the state." Len Holt, *The Summer That Wouldn't End* (William Morrow, 1965), 33.
5. Hogan, *Many Minds*, 60; Payne, *I've Got the Light*, 105–6.
6. James Farmer, *Lay Bare the Heart: An Autobiography of the Civil Rights Movement* (Texas Christian University Press, 1998), 219.
7. See Carson, *In Struggle*, 39–40.
8. Payne, *I've Got the Light*, 108–10. Payne notes that the memories of some administration officials are at odds with those of the activists. While activists believed that the administration had their backs, the officials remember stressing the limitations of the support they could provide.
9. Carson, *In Struggle*, 40. Belafonte quoted in John Leland, "Harry Belafonte Knows a Thing or Two About New York," *NYT*, February 3, 2017.
10. See Payne, *I've Got the Light*, 110–11.
11. M. J. O'Brien, *We Shall Not Be Moved: The Jackson Woolworth Sit-In and the Movement It Inspired* (University of Mississippi Press, 2013), 24–25.
12. Lawrence Guyot of SNCC cited his influence in Greenberg, *Circle of Trust*, 9, 66.
13. See Howard Zinn's Interview with Tim Jenkins: HZP/WHS: https://content.wisconsinhistory.org/digital/collection/p15932coll2/id/11925
14. Hogan, *Many Minds*, 144.
15. Walter White of the NAACP had made this discovery after World War II when he got journalist Jimmy Sheean to cover the trial of several Black World War II veterans in Columbia, Tennessee. "For Walter White, the verdict was proof that publicity, providing the glare was sufficiently harsh, could have a chastening effect in even the most obdurate bastions of white supremacy." Deborah Cohen, *Last Call at the Hotel Imperial: The Reporters Who Took on a World at War* (Random House, 2023), 373–74.

16. Lowenstein first encountered people engaging in something like a protest vote when traveling in South Africa. For more on Lowenstein, including that description, see Branch, *Pillar of Fire*, 274, 118–23.
17. Lowenstein's bouts of intense activism were often followed by sudden disappearances, a pattern that would come to strike many in SNCC as peculiar, possibly even sinister.
18. In the end, somewhere between 70 and 100 students came to Mississippi. For more about the discussion and about the numbers of students involved, see Dittmer, *Local People*, 203. Another way that Lowenstein alienated SNCC staffers was by trying to take control of the Summer Project. See Dittmer, *Local People*, 232–34.
19. In fact, four SNCC people—Tim Jenkins, Casey Hayden, Jim Monsonis, and Bob Zellner—were also members of SDS. See Carson, *In Struggle*, 53–54.
20. See Gitlin, *The Sixties*, 147, 165; James Miller, *Democracy Is in the Streets: From Port Huron to the Seige of Chicago* (Harvard University Press, 1987), 187; and Hogan, *Many Minds*, 133–34, 340n12.
21. This enthusiasm for action is perhaps not too surprising, given that at this juncture some of its most influential members included graduate students for whom the university had come to "feel like a cage," as Todd Gitlin put it. See Hogan, *Many Minds*, 132; Richard Rothstein, "A Short History of ERAP," *SDS Bulletin* 4, no. 2, February–March 1965. https://oac.cdlib.org/view?docId=kt4k4003k7&brand=oac4
22. Bob Moses, Interview with Anne Romaine, part III, Anne Romaine Papers, SC 1069, Folder 1, WHS.
23. Mike Miller quoted in Mississippi Freedom Vote, SNCC Digital: https://snccdigital.org/events/mississippi-freedom-vote/
24. For a more cautionary take on the Freedom Vote Campaign, see Dittmer, *Local People*, 205–6.
25. Ivanhoe Donaldson quoted in Dittmer, *Local People*, 205.
26. See Hogan, *Many Minds*, 147. Carson, *In Struggle*, 97–98.
27. McAdam, *Freedom Summer*, 37.
28. Dittmer, *Local People*, 206.
29. Howell Raines, *My Soul Is Rested: The Story of the Civil Rights Movement in the Deep South* (Penguin, 1983), 287.
30. Dittmer, *Local People*, 206.
31. HZP/WHS, 1956–94; Mss 588, Box 2, Folder 10, "Whites in the Movement," 1963, https://content.wisconsinhistory.org/digital/collection/p15932coll2/id/26907/rec/1; Hogan, *Many Minds*, 149.
32. Guyot quoted in McAdam, *Freedom Summer*, 40.
33. Carson, *In Struggle*, 108.
34. Robert P. Moses and Charles E. Cobb, Jr., *Radical Equations: Civil Rights from Mississippi to the Algebra Project* (Beacon Press, 2001), 74–75.
35. Moses and Cobb, *Radical Equations*, 76. See James Forman's recollection about the decision to move forward with the project, despite the opposition of the Mississippi staff in Greenberg, *Circle of Trust*, 78–80.
36. Carson, *In Struggle*, 112.
37. Carson, *In Struggle*, 98.
38. The label of Northerner was attached to all white volunteers even if they were—and many were—from the West. See Maria Gitlin, *This Bright Light of Ours: Stories from the 1965 Voting Rights Fight* (University of Alabama Press, 2014), 37.

39. Holt, *The Summer*, 44.
40. Hogan, *Many Minds*, 155.
41. Emilye Crosby, "'I Just Had a Fire': An Interview with Dorie Ladner," *Southern Quarterly* 52, no. 1 (Fall 2014): 102.
42. Hogan, *Many Minds*, 202; Carson, *In Struggle*, 100.
43. Wesley Hogan notes that even before the Freedom Vote, people in SNCC's national headquarters in Atlanta tended to be more open to using whites in the field than were many of the Black staffers in the field. See Hogan, *Many Minds*, 271n22. Staff numbers vary. Charles Payne says that in late 1963 SNCC had 150 full-time staffers. By the summer of 1965, there were more than 200 staff and 250 volunteers (p. 368). However, the accountant, who provided SNCC with an audit, said that the group listed 175 employees on its W2 form to the Internal Revenue Service in 1963. See SNCC Financial Audit: chrome-extension://efaidnbmnnnibpcajpcglclefindmkaj/https://www.crmvet.org/docs/63_sncc_financial_audit.pdf. According to the SNCC Executive Committee Meeting Minutes, by September 1964 SNCC had 144 staff members overall. chrome-extension://efaidnbmnnnibpcajpcglclefindmkaj/https://www.crmvet.org/docs/640905_sncc_projects.pdf
44. Dittmer, *Local People*, 209.
45. Sherrod would eventually decide to "use the system," that is, local Blacks' deference to whites to get them involved. See David P. Cline, *From Reconciliation to Revolution: The Student Interracial Ministry, Liberal Christianity, and the Civil Rights Movement* (University of North Carolina Press, 2016), 105.
46. "Transcript Black Nationalism," SAVF-SNCC, MSS577, Box 47, F 12, WHS, 9, https://content.wisconsinhistory.org/digital/collection/p15932coll2/id/66642
47. All the quotations in this discussion, unless otherwise noted, are drawn from Howard Zinn's meeting notes—all 46 pages. Whites' roles are defined on page 19. Moses's failed efforts to find Black locals to work in Jackson are on page 4. Moses's criticism of those calling for restrictions on what whites could do is on page 21; Dona Richards's dictum regarding whites is on page 25. See "Whites in the Movement, 1963," HZP/WHS, 1956–94; Mss 588, Box 2, Folder 10, WHS, https://content.wisconsinhistory.org/digital/collection/p15932coll2/id/26907/rec/1
48. Long-distance calls were expensive, and many of the rural communities in the South where SNCC was operating did not yet have direct-dial long-distance service, which meant using a local operator who was white because the phone company did not hire Blacks for those jobs. SNCC paid for a WATS line because safe, reliable long-distance service was essential to the safety of SNCC workers. Even so, SNCC people understood the line was tapped. See this link: https://www.crmvet.org/disc/jews.htm
49. It was the view of one staffer—quite possibly Joan Browning—that some Black staffers were opposed to working with white staffers. Zinn interview notes, 21.
50. Mike Miller, The Stansbury Forum, "Bob Moses, 1935–2021," July 28, 2021. https://stansburyforum.com/2021/07/28/bob-moses-1935-2021
51. Moses quoted in Visser-Maessen, *Robert Parris Moses*, 199.
52. SNCC's Mississippi staff did not support the Project, but James Forman maintains that SNCC's Executive Committee did support it. See Greenberg, *Circle of Trust*, 78. For COFO, see Council of Federated Organizations, Minutes on Staff Meeting, January 18, 1964. https://content.wisconsinhistory.org/digital/collection/p15932coll2/id/29501

53. Maria Varela, "Time to Get Ready," in *Hands*, 560.
54. "Working Notes on SNCC Executive Committee . . . ," Mary King Papers, 1962–1999; SNCC Position Papers, Waveland, Mississippi, meeting, Accessions, M82-445, Box 1, Folder 18, WHS. The writer here is clearly Bob Moses.
55. Hogan, *Many Minds*, 153–54; SNCC Digital: https://snccdigital.org/events/sncc-debates-freedom-summer/
56. Carson, *In Struggle*, 99.
57. Greenberg, *Circle of Trust*, 79.
58. Sally Belfrage, Miscellaneous COFO and SNCC Papers, 1963–4, WHS, Micro 599, Reel 1, Segment 6, Dona Richards, "Memorandum to Mississippi Field Staff Regarding Tougaloo Work-Study Project," August 1963. More scholarship money was soon available for SNCC staff through other foundations. See "Do You Want a Scholarship," in Stuart Ewen Papers, 1961–65; SNCC Proposals for the Waveland Retreat, WHS, MSS 531, Box 1, Folder 4.
59. The following year SNCC had plans to expand it. See "Memo: Tougaloo Work-Study Project," CORE Educational Programs (CORE, COFO)—Correspondence and Memoranda, Mississippi 4th Congressional District Records, 1961–66, WHS, Micro 793, Reel 2, Segment 21. It was sufficiently successful that it received funding for 42 students to take part in the 1964–65 academic year. For a more detailed follow-up presented at the Waveland Conference, see "Education Committee, SNCC: Work-Study Program," Stuart Ewen Papers, 1961–65; SNCC Proposals for the Waveland Retreat, WHS, MSS 531, Box 1, Folder 4, https://content.wisconsinhistory.org/digital/collection/p15932coll2/id/19615/rec/157
60. McAdam, *Freedom Summer*, 42; Greenberg, *Circle of Trust*, 79.
61. Sellers claims that there were about 135 Black volunteers and that most of them, "feeling outnumbered and misunderstood," withdrew. Cleveland Sellers, *The River of No Return: The Autobiography of a Black Militant and the Life and Death of SNCC* (University of Mississippi Press, 1990), 82. Carmichael mentions family resistance, too, in *Ready*, 358; Carson tells a somewhat different story of Blacks' alienation. *In Struggle*, 112.
62. McAdam, *Freedom Summer*, 40.
63. McAdam, *Freedom Summer*, 40. For further evidence, see Dottie Zellner's letter to Jim Forman, March 1964 "letters concerning SNCC fund-raising," in HZP/WHS, 1956–64; Zinn-SNCC Paper, administration, 1963–65, Mss 588, Box 2, Folder 11.
64. In SNCC Executive Committee minutes, Mendy Samstein says that most of the students were bringing $150 with them. Minutes, May 10, 1964, p. 4. chrome-extension://efaidnbmnnnibpcajpcglclefindmkaj/https://www.crmvet.org/docs/640410_sncc_excom_min.pdf. See the memo on the SNCC Summer Project: https://content.wisconsinhistory.org/digital/collection/p15932coll2/id/66317/rec/23. However, Len Holt asserts that volunteers had to have a source of getting a $500 bond when arrested, pay for transportation to Oxford, Ohio, and to Mississippi, pay for living and eating expenses in Mississippi, and take care of any medical or hospitalization bills they incurred during the summer. They were also on the hook for the cost of getting back home at summer's end. See Holt, *The Summer*, 46. Given this, it's perhaps not surprising that in a fall 1964 memo on subsistence for volunteers, Barbara Jones notes that many volunteers have no money and are borrowing from SNCC staff whose weekly stipend comes to only $9.64 after taxes.

chrome-extension://efaidnbmnnnibpcajpcglclefindmkaj/https://www.crmvet.org/docs/640900_sncc_subsistence.pdf
65. Interview with Bob Moses, Julian Bond Oral History Project, November 18, 2018.
66. In 1962–63, SNCC received less than $24,000 of the more than $500,000 that the Voter Education Project (VEP) dispersed. This seems odd, given that of all the organizations involved, SNCC had the largest staff of full-time voter registration workers. VEP's funds came from contributions from the Taconic Foundation, Field Foundation, Stern Family Fund, and other liberal foundations. See Carson, *In Struggle*, 70. Carson attributes VEP's underfunding of SNCC to the fact that it focused its efforts on the most difficult regions, where the payoff, in terms of voters registered, was negligible. Indeed, right on the heels of the Freedom Ballot initiative in November 1963, VEP's head, Wiley Branton, informed Bob Moses and Aaron Henry that VEP would no longer fund its efforts in Mississippi. John Dittmer's research suggests the possibility that COFO ran afoul of the VEP by not following its stricture forbidding "partisan political activity." In their accounts, it is worth noting that Dittmer writes of COFO, which was indeed SNCC-dominated, and Carson writes of SNCC. See Dittmer, *Local People*, 212.
67. It is ironic that Forman was the one who advanced SNCC's fundraising, targeting white left liberals, when he earlier criticized King for wanting to "protect his 'fundraising base'" among the white people who read the *New York Times*. See Branch, *Parting the Waters*, 614.
68. Holt, *The Summer*, 156.
69. Ruth Howard Chambers, Interview by Gretchen Howard, November 15, 1994, the Civil Rights Movement Archive, accessed November 3, 2024: chrome-extension://efaidnbmnnnibpcajpcglclefindmkaj/https://www.crmvet.org/nars/9410_howard.pdf
70. Moses quoted in Holt, *The Summer*, 36.
71. Zellner, "My Real Vocation," in *Hands*, 321–22.
72. Dittmer, *Local People*, 232.
73. Hogan, *Many Minds*, 160.
74. Givhan, "The Black Lives Matter Movement Hits a Different Kind of Wall."
75. Harding quoted in Belfrage, *Freedom Summer*, 7; Moses quoted in Carol V. R. George, *One Mississippi, Two Mississippi: Methodists, Murder and the Struggle for Racial Justice in Neshoba County* (Oxford University Press, 2015), 130.
76. LeRoi Jones, "Tokenism: 300 Years for Five Cents," in Jones, *Home: Social Essays* (William Morrow, 1965), 72.
77. Interview with Betty Garman, Julian Bond Oral History Project.
78. Mike Miller, Interview with author by email, June 13, 2021.
79. McAdam, *Freedom Summer*, 103.
80. David Harris, *Dreams Die Hard* (St. Martin's Press, 1982), 14.
81. Sweeney quoted in Branch, *Pillar of Fire*, 156.
82. McAdam, *Freedom Summer*, 29.
83. Doug McAdam, the leading historian of Freedom Summer, notes that it is impossible to pin down precisely the percentage of volunteers who were Jewish. The main reason for this is that the application did not require volunteers to identify their religious background or orientation. The application did ask applicants to list organizations,

both on and off campus, to which they belonged, and these might include a church, synagogue, or campus religious organization. He notes that "a fair number of applicants mentioned religious values or background." Although many Christian students listed church membership or involvement in campus Christian groups, the number of applicants who cited membership in synagogues or the influence of Judaism was very small. This is likely because they were not observant Jews. However, even in his own random sample of volunteers with whom he conducted intensive interviews, only about 7 of 40 identified as Jewish. Moreover, McAdam notes that the bulk of volunteers were students at Harvard, Yale, Princeton, and Stanford, all of which had small numbers of Jewish students. I have delved into this in such detail because it has become common for people writing about Freedom Summer to assert that nearly two-thirds of the volunteers were Jewish. This seems very unlikely. McAdam thinks the number is likely closer to 20–30 percent. Author's email exchange with Douglas McAdam, June 26, 2023. How the idea took hold that the number was far higher is not entirely clear. However, the journalist Jonathan Kaufman ventured that "well over half of the white students heading South that summer were Jewish." See Kaufman, *Broken Alliance*, 19. Kaufman cites as his source Murray Friedman, "Jews, Blacks and the Civil Rights Revolution," *New Perspectives* (U.S. Commission on Civil Rights, Fall 1985), 285. Others who cite large numbers are Edward S. Shapiro, *A Time for Healing: American Jews Since World War II* (Johns Hopkins University Press, 1995), 223; Matthew Frye Jacobson, *Roots, Too: White Ethnic Revival in Post–Civil Rights America* (Harvard University Press, 2006), 216; Melanie Kaye/Kantrowitz, *The Colors of Jews: Racial Politics and Radical Diaspora* (Indiana University Press, 2007), 57.

84. Even Stokely Carmichael spoke of the parallels in Black and Jewish experiences, and as late as 1966. Carson, "Blacks and Jews," *Bridges*, 40.

85. For a discussion of relations between Blacks and Jews, see Michael E. Staub, *Torn at the Roots: The Crisis of Jewish Liberalism in Postwar America* (Columbia University Press, 2002), 22–43. He points out that the Nazi analogy, by virtue of its association with the American Communist Party, fell out of favor during McCarthyism. It would be revived after the worst of McCarthyism ended.

86. Prinz was himself a victim of German fascism. He had been a rabbi in the Berlin Jewish community from 1925 to 1937, when he was expelled by the Gestapo. See Staub, *Torn at the Roots*, 46.

87. SNCC Digital, chrome-extension://efaidnbmnnnibpcajpcglclefindmkaj/https://snccdigital.org/wp-content/uploads/2017/12/SWGA_Transcript02.pdf

88. Howard Zinn writes of Samstein that the leftist philosopher Herbert Marcuse was "his God." See Robert Cohen, *Howard Zinn's Southern Diary* (University of Georgia Press, 2018), 133.

89. The Nazi Germany–Mississippi analogy was a part of the Freedom Schools' curriculum. See Holt, *The Summer*, 113.

90. Hayden quoted in Hogan, *Many Minds*, 351n20.

91. David Dennis was friends with Chaney and Schwerner. He says that although the nickname originated with the Klan, Black people took to calling Schwerner "Goatee," too. See David J. Dennis Jr. in collaboration with David Dennis Sr., *The Movement Made Us: A Father, A Son, and the Legacy of a Freedom Ride* (Harper Collins, 2022), Kindle edition, 197.

92. Branch, *Pillar of Fire*, 430–34.
93. King, *Freedom Song*, 398.
94. On LBJ's decision to have a surrogate call James Chaney's family, see King, *Freedom Song*, 388. For Lewis's reaction, see Carson, *In Struggle*, 115. White SNCC staffer Jane Stembridge says that in her experience most white workers received preferential treatment from the authorities, even in jail. Southern Oral History Program, Interview with Jane Stembridge, September 17, 1997, by Pete Daniel, 11. https://dc.lib.unc.edu/cdm/ref/collection/sohp/id/6883
95. Carmichael, *Ready*, 368.
96. This is the judgment of the Black protagonist in Lore Segal's novel, *Her First American: A Novel*, 20th ed. (The New Press, 2004), 15.
97. According to the lawyer, Len Holt, the workshops were staggered with roughly 250 students at each one-week session. Holt, *The Summer*, 48.
98. Holt, *The Summer*, 49.
99. McAdam, *Freedom Summer*, 88; Hogan, *Many Minds*, 173.
100. For the willingness of local Blacks to open themselves to retaliation, see Anne Romaine Interview with Mendy Samstein, Part II, February 1967, Anne Romaine Papers, SC 1069, Folder 1, WHS. https://content.wisconsinhistory.org/digital/collection/p15932coll2/id/13855.For more on the response of white Mississippians to the volunteers, see Trillin, "The Struggle for Civil Rights in Mississippi," *New Yorker*, August 21, 1964.
101. Visser-Maessen, *Robert Parris Moses*, 217.
102. McAdam, *Freedom Summer*, 89.
103. In some communities, church women provided home-cooked meals every day to schoolteachers working in the Freedom Schools. Sometimes as volunteers walked down dusty roads, children cheered them on. See McAdam, *Freedom Summer*, 89–92.
104. Sally Belfrage, *Freedom Summer* (Viking Press, 1965), 81. Belfrage believed that the SNCC veterans were invested in developing their own Black identity and didn't want to "bend" to the volunteers. Perhaps, but they also had no need for friends. Others have written about these tensions, which were obvious during the training sessions in Ohio. Holt acknowledges, but downplays racial tensions in *The Summer*, 49–50; Carson, *In Struggle*, 112–13.
105. Sellers, *The River*, 54.
106. Hogan, *Many Minds*, 218.
107. As already noted, accounts of SNCC's staff numbers vary. As for the 1,000 volunteers who came to the state, they were spread out over five Congressional districts, only four of which SNCC controlled. The fifth was operated by CORE. Doug McAdam points out that it is not the case that all 1,000 volunteers arrived early on and stayed. The first wave consisted of about 550 volunteers, who were joined by an estimated 400–450 volunteers who kept arriving, and well into August. He believes that there were never more than about 600 volunteers in the state at any one time. See McAdam, *Freedom Summer*, 77.
108. King, *Freedom Summer*, 369; Hayden, "Fields of Blue," 358.
109. Sellers, *The River*, 82–83.
110. Visser-Maessen, *Robert Parris Moses*, 276–77.
111. McAdam, *Freedom Summer*, 142–43.

112. Lynd quoted in Jon N. Hale, *The Freedom Schools: Student Activists in the Mississippi Civil Rights Movement* (Columbia University Press, 2014), 78.
113. McAdam, *Freedom Summer*, 110; Carmichael, *Ready*, 388.
114. McAdam, *Freedom Summer*, 79.
115. Muriel Tillinghast, "Depending on Ourselves," in *Hands*, 251–53.
116. Many people were involved in the planning of the curriculum and would include Cobb, Bob Moses, Dona Richards, Staughton Lynd, Casey Hayden, Mendy Samstein, Lois Chaffee, Noel Day, Jane Stembridge, and Jack Minnis. See Liz Fusco, "Freedom Schools in Mississippi, 1964," in Holt, *The Summer That Wouldn't End*, 332. Fusco was coordinator of the COFO Freedom School Project. See King, *Freedom Song*, 368, and Staughton Lynd, "The Freedom Schools, An Informal History," in *Against the Current*, February 2004: https://againstthecurrent.org/atc108/p477/
117. The coinage was that of Dr. Carter G. Woodson. See his 1933 book, *The Mis-Education of the Negro* (12th Media Services, 1999).
118. These figures are drawn from Carson, *In Struggle*, 119; Holt, *The Summer*, 318; and McAdam, *Freedom Summer*, 84.
119. McAdam, *Freedom Summer*, 83–85.
120. Carmichael, *Ready*, 389.
121. Chude Pamela Parker Allen, quoted in McAdam, *Freedom Summer*, 86. See Mendy Samstein's memo on the schools in Holt, *The Summer*, 325–26.
122. Carmichael, *Ready*, 387.
123. See Fusco, "Freedom Schools," in Holt, *The Summer*, 331–35.
124. Holt, *The Summer*, 333.
125. "Interviews with Amiri Baraka, Askia Touré, and Sonia Sanchez," in Joyce A. Joyce, *Black Studies as Human Studies* (State University of New York Press, 2004), 144. The speaker making this claim is Askia Touré, who went by the name of Roland Snellings and was a part of the militant group RAM, which infiltrated SNCC. He also claims that Black field staff resented white administrative staff for keeping the cushy jobs for themselves and pushing Black staff to take on dangerous work.
126. Dittmer usefully summarizes this activity in *Local People*, 264.
127. Lynd, "The Freedom Schools."
128. Staughton Lynd, *From There to Here* (PM Press, 2010), 82 of Kindle.
129. This is rarely mentioned by historians, but activists sometimes mention it in their memoirs. King makes this argument in *Freedom Summer*, 408, and so does Harris in *Dreams Die Hard*, 67.
130. King, *Freedom Song*, 352–58; Greenberg, *A Circle*, 67–68.
131. Ex-communists rather than current members of the CPUSA were the ones who contributed most to the upsurge of protest in the sixties. See Maurice Isserman, *Reds: The Tragedy of American Communism* (Basic Books, 2024), 140–41; Gilmore, *Defying Dixie*, 400–444.
132. Carson, *In Struggle*, 136–37.
133. Zellner quoted in Robnett, *How Long*, 131; Carmichael, *Ready*, 427.
134. Tom Wolfe, *Radical Chic and Mau-Mauing the Flak Catchers*, 2nd ed. (Bantam Books, 1971).
135. Doug McAdam reprinted the list as Appendix D in *Freedom Summer*, 257–82.
136. Hogan, *Many Minds*, 166.
137. McAdam, *Freedom Summer*, 101.

138. Taylor Branch suggests that by the spring of 1963, SNCC people had been "tiptoeing around the gaping cultural and racial differences between them." Branch, *Parting the Waters*, 734. Intraracial differences were evident. Barry quoted in David Halberstam, *The Children* (Open Road Media, 2012), 808, online e-book. He claimed he noticed this as early as 1961, when more Northern Blacks came South. Gwen Patton, who singled out Stokely Carmichael as particularly patronizing, is quoted in her interview with Joseph Monier, Library of Congress, June 1, 2011. https://www.loc.gov/item/2015669119/
139. James Forman, *The Making of Black Revolutionaries* (University of Washington Press, 1972), 366. Bob Moses also notes that in discussions about the Summer Project, the staff's objections to "outsiders" extended to Black outsiders. *Radical Equations*, 79.
140. Carmichael, *Ready*, 357.
141. See Payne, *I've Got the Light*, 387.
142. Martha Prescod Norman Noonan, "Captured by the Movement," in *Hands on the Freedom Plow*, 501.
143. I discuss this at greater length later in this chapter. One of the first stirrings of Black feminism emerged in a group, Third World Women's Alliance, that grew out of an earlier group in SNCC. Black Power was empowering to Black women, but its reliance on conventional gender norms also made it constraining, as Frances Beal, a member of that group, argued in 1969. See Beal, "Double Jeopardy: To Be Black and Female," reprinted in Judith Clavir Albert and Stewart Edward Albert, eds., *The Sixties Papers: Documents of a Rebellious Decade* (Praeger, 1984), 500–508.
144. Hogan, *Many Minds*, 151. "Some Aspects of Black-White Problems as Seen by Field Staff," Sally Belfrage Papers, 1962–66, Historical Library Microforms Room, Micro 599, reel 1, segment 6, WHS. https://content.wisconsinhistory.org/digital/collection/p15932coll2/id/37678/
145. Phyllis Cunningham, "Hattiesburg," First District Report, Samuel Walker Papers, SNCC and COFO Papers, 1964–66, MSS 655, Box 1, Folder 6, WHS.
146. Wynn quoted in Robnett, *How Long*, 126.
147. Francesca Polletta, *Freedom Is an Endless Meeting: Democracy in American Social Movements* (University of Chicago Press, 2012), 105.
148. CORE—Staff Meetings (Canton and Meridian, CORE and COFO), Micro 793, Reel 4, Segment 90, SHSW. https://content.wisconsinhistory.org/digital/collection/p15932coll2/id/43792/rec/1
149. McAdam, *Freedom Summer*, 104.
150. Hogan, *Many Minds*, 171.
151. As previously mentioned, Mickey Schwerner reportedly came to see himself as Black. Many white radicals said they were ashamed of being white and even wished they could be Black. In an April 2007 discussion between three white women, all of them on an exchange program at Spelman College at various points between 1962 and 1964, the topic of not wanting to be white came up. Two of the three women—Cathy Cade and Karen Haberman Trusty—admit to that feeling. Cade said that within a few years "you really weren't allowed to say, 'I don't want to be white'—it was politically incorrect—but that's exactly how I felt." Chude Pam Parker Allen says she didn't feel that way, but she nonetheless felt ashamed of being white. "How could you not feel ashamed," Allen asked, "when white people were doing these horrendous things?" See https://www.crmvet.org/disc/spelman.htm

152. Hogan, *Many Minds*, 153.
153. King, *Freedom Song*, 498. She says this was especially true after 1964, however.
154. "Interviews with Amiri Baraka, Askia Touré, and Sonia Sanchez," in Joyce, *Black Studies*, 144.
155. John Lewis with Michael D'Orso, *Walking with the Wind: A Memoir of the Movement* (Simon and Schuster, 2015), 272.
156. Bill Hansen and Ruth Buffington; Alice Walker and Melvyn Leventhal.
157. His research into the Summer Project led sociologist Doug McAdam to conclude that there was a lot of sex during the summer. See McAdam, *Freedom Summer*, 93–96, 143–45; Staughton Lynd, who directed the Freedom Schools, remembers a lot of sex between Black male staffers of SNCC and CORE and white female volunteers. This happened despite "constant public pronouncements that it should not happen." See Lynd, *Living Inside Our Hope*, 3.
158. Harris, *Dreams Die Hard*, 67; McAdam, *Freedom Summer*, 106.
159. Chana Kai Lee, *For Freedom's Sake: The Life of Fannie Lou Hamer* (University of Illinois Press, 1999), 76.
160. Some white women report that they made a point of sidestepping romantic and sexual entanglements and practiced a form of "self-imposed celibacy." See Mary A. Rothschild, "White Women Volunteers in the Freedom Summers: Their Life and Work in a Movement for Social Change," *Feminist Studies* 5, no. 3 (Fall 1977): 485.
161. Robnett, *How Long*, 131, 138.
162. Bob Moses said Mississippi was the "middle of the iceberg." See Moses and Cobb, *Radical Equations*, 23.

CHAPTER THREE

1. Todd Gitlin says that Atlantic City became "synonymous with liberal betrayal." Gitlin, *The Sixties*, 161.
2. Here I am influenced by John D'Emilio's' treatment of the Convention in *Lost Prophet*, 389–92.
3. Carmichael, *Ready*, 400. In his memoir, Tom Hayden, husband of Casey and SDS leader, claimed that he had suggested to Bob Moses that SNCC organize a challenge to the seating of the racist Mississippi Democratic Party at the upcoming party convention. Hayden, *Reunion: A Memoir* (Random House, 1988), 116.
4. Holt, *The Summer*, 158.
5. Holt, *The Summer*, 154. See also Anne Romaine's Interview with Mendy Samstein, SHSW, https://content.wisconsinhistory.org/digital/collection/p15932coll2/id/13870
6. Doug McAdam and Karina Kloos, *Deeply Divided: Racial Politics and Social Movements in Post-War America* (Oxford University Press, 2014), 99 and 75.
7. McAdam and Kloos, *Deeply Divided*, 79.
8. See Steven F. Lawson, *Black Ballots: Voting Rights in the South, 1944–1969* (Columbia University Press, 1976); McAdam and Kloos, *Deeply Divided*, 80–81. Timothy Shenk called the coalition a "brittle colossus" in his book, *Realigners: Partisan Hacks, Political Visionaries, and the Struggle to Rule American Democracy* (Farrar, Straus and Giroux, 2022), 1900 on Kindle.
9. See Rossinow, *Visions of Progress*, 122–24, 209–17.

10. McAdam and Kloos also argue that the Mississippi Summer Project was LBJ's "worst nightmare" in that it was a highly public civil rights campaign right before the election, completely out of line with the president's call for a "cooling-off period." *Deeply Divided*, 89.
11. Len Holt relates that at a meeting in Jackson, Mississippi, with King, James Farmer of CORE, Ella Baker, James Forman, and Bob Moses of SNCC, Rustin seemed to turn on a dime regarding the advisability of the challenge. Holt traced Rustin's equivocation to a phone call he had with a friend in Detroit. One imagines that Holt is suggesting that Rustin was corralled by a labor leader, who talked him out of his support for the challenge. However, Rustin's communication with King suggests that he was bothered by the cynicism of SNCC staffers about the Democratic Party, which they believed would sell the MFDP out. See D'Emilio, *Lost Prophet*, 387.
12. Sellers quoted in Gitlin, *The Sixties*, 152.
13. Staughton Lynd and Alice Lynd, *Stepping Stones: Memoir of a Life Together* (Rowman & Littlefield, 2009), 74.
14. D'Emilio, *Lost Prophet*, 387.
15. Holt, *The Summer*, 164.
16. D'Emilio, *Lost Prophet*, 386–87.
17. Casey Hayden quoted in Tom Hayden, *Reunion*, 118. Ella Baker, who had coordinated the campaign for the MFDP in Washington, DC, seems to have doubted the delegation would be seated. See Ella Baker, interviewed by Anne Romaine, February 1967, Anne Romaine Papers, SC 1069, Folder 1, WHS.
18. Lynd and Lynd, *Stepping Stones*, 73–74. The dissenters spoke at a June 9–11, 1964, meeting.
19. They even brought with them the burned-out remnant of the blue Ford Fairlane station wagon in which Chaney Goodman and Schwerner had been traveling. They made sure that the car, which had been purchased with money raised at a benefit held by the playwright Lorraine Hansberry, was visible for all to see on the boardwalk. See Joan Steinau Lester, *Loving Before Loving: A Marriage in Black and White* (University of Wisconsin Press, 2021), 79.
20. Belfrage, *Freedom Summer*, 241.
21. This is Taylor Branch's characterization in *Pillar of Fire*, 473.
22. Beverly Gage, *G-Man: J. Edgar Hoover and the Making of the American Century* (Viking, 2022), 598–99; McAdam and Kloos, *Deeply Divided*, 93.
23. Forman, *The Making*, 392.
24. SNCC withdrew a speaking invitation to Rustin in 1960. Carson, *In Struggle*, 29.
25. Carmichael, *Ready*, 402.
26. Branch, *Pillar of Fire*, 468.
27. John Dittmer emphasizes that the MFDP would have voted the same way even had its members been permitted to choose the two delegates. It was the two seats that doomed its approval. Dittmer, *Local People*, 298.
28. Branch, *Pillar of Fire*, 473.
29. Branch, *Pillar of Fire*, 471.
30. Nelson Lichtenstein, "Labor, Liberalism, and the Democratic Party," in *Making Sense of American Liberalism*, ed. Jonathan Bell and Timothy Stanley (University of Illinois Press, 2012), 232–33. It was the British historian D. W. Brogan, who argued, in 1957, that "the American liberal today is confronted first of all by the memory of something

that did not happen." He meant the social democracy akin to what was developing in Western European countries. On liberals' wariness about SNCC's policy of "free association," see Carson, *In Struggle*, 105–107.
31. Branch, *Pillar of Fire*, 404.
32. Branch, *Pillar of Fire*, 405.
33. McAdam and Kloos, *Deeply Divided*, 105; Nelson Lichtenstein, *Walter Reuther: The Most Dangerous Man in Detroit* (University of Illinois Press, 1997), 393.
34. Branch, *Pillar of Fire*, 340.
35. Lichtenstein, *Walter Reuther*, 393.
36. D'Emilio, *Lost Prophet*, 401. Rustin's critics believe his turn was not entirely a matter of political principle. Movement activist William Strickland said Rustin's sexual orientation made him vulnerable, and he suggests that he was "kept" by the labor movement, specifically the ILGWU. William Strickland Oral History with Robert S. Cox and Jeremy Smith, March 25, 2015, Amherst Sesquicentennial Oral History Collection, University of Massachusetts. However, Edwin King of the MFDP believes that Rustin was indeed motivated by fears of a white backlash. He also claims that Rustin saw LBJ as the "peace candidate." Ed King interviewed by Anne and Howard Romaine, 1966, Anne Romaine Papers, WHS.
37. Rustin quoted in D'Emilio, *Lost Prophet*, 392.
38. D'Emilio, *Lost Prophet*, 390.
39. D. D. Guttenplan, *American Radical: The Life and Times of I.F. Stone* (Farrar, Straus and Giroux, 2009), 316, 324, 382–85.
40. Arthur Waskow letter to Bob Moses, September 9, 1964, Arthur Ocean Waskow Papers, 1943–77, MSS Box 5, Box 10, Folder 30, WHS. https://content.wisconsinhistory.org/digital/collection/p15932coll2/id/29596/rec/5
41. Dorothy Healey and Maurice Isserman, *Dorothy Healey Remembers: A Life in the American Communist Party* (Oxford University Press, 1990), 203.
42. See Doug Rossinow's clarifying discussion in *Visions of Progress: The Left-Liberal Tradition in America* (University of Pennsylvania Press, 2008), 246–47. Scheer quoted in Peter Richardson, *A Bomb in Every Issue* (The New Press, 2009), 66. At the time, that is, in March 1965, Virginia Durr complained to her friend Jessica Mitford, whose daughter Dinky Romilly was in SNCC, that the politics of the SNCC kids seemed "pretty vague." Worse still, "they don't seem to make any effort to win people over, and in fact seem to delight in offending their most deeply felt standards." Sullivan, *Freedom Writer*, 323.
43. James F. Findlay, *Church People in the Struggle: The National Council of Churches and the Black Freedom Movement, 1950–1970* (Oxford University Press, 1993), 115.
44. Charles Sherrod, SNCC Proposals for the Waveland Retreat, Stuart Ewen Papers, Freedom Summer Digital Collection, University of Wisconsin. Theresa de Pozzo wrote of the skirmishes of whites and Blacks that happened near the SNCC Atlanta office. Hogan, *Many Minds*, 338n2. https://content.wisconsinhistory.org/digital/collection/p15932coll2/id/19606/rec/7
45. Betty Garman of SNCC notes that agents were more likely to investigate a situation, but rarely did their investigations result in arrests being made. Letter to All Friends of SNCC, Fall 1964: chrome-extension://efaidnbmnnnibpcajpcglclefindmkaj/https://www.crmvet.org/docs/640900_sncc_mccomb_memo.pdf
46. Harris, *Dreams Die Hard*, 79–80.

47. Samstein quoted in Visser-Maessen, *Robert Parris Moses*, 262.
48. Constance Curry, "'Silver Rights': One Family's Struggle for Justice in America," *The Virginia Quarterly Review* 68, no. 1 (1992): 31. See also King, *Freedom Song*, 422.
49. I go on to discuss the victories, but one case in point: The Marshall Field Foundation continued supporting the Quaker-led FAF in Mississippi. For a clarifying discussion of the divisions within the Johnson administration on civil rights, see David C. Carter, *The Music Has Gone Out of the Movement* (University of North Carolina Press, 2009), 243.
50. Robert Coles served as staff psychologist for the Summer Project and found that SNCC veterans were often experiencing "exhaustion, weariness, despair, frustration and rage." Quoted in McAdam, *Freedom Summer*, 33.
51. Carmichael, *Ready*, 415.
52. Hayden, "Fields of Blue," 360.
53. Forman and Moses believed the timing of the trip destabilized SNCC. See Visser-Maessen, *Robert Parris Moses*, 265n31.
54. Carmichael, *Ready*, 426.
55. For the Sojourner fleet, and that "hot minute," see Carmichael, *Ready*, 426; Hogan, *Many Minds*, 366n13. The building was a church in Atlanta that SNCC would have to begin making payments on in February 1965. "The Building," Stuart Ewen Papers, 1961–65; SNCC Proposals for the Waveland Retreat, WHS, MSS 531, Box 1, Folder 4. https://content.wisconsinhistory.org/digital/collection/p15932coll2/id/19534/rec/157
56. According to the September 4, 1964, Executive Committee meeting minutes, it cost SNCC $1,000 for each person who traveled. Moses and Richards may have paid their own way. See chrome extension: chrome-extension://efaidnbmnnnibpcajpcglclefindmkaj/https://www.crmvet.org/docs/640904_sncc_excom.pdf
57. Gas cost 30 cents a gallon for what was likely a 20-gallon gas tank. Cleveland Sellers, Holly Springs Project, undated but post-Waveland, November 1964, Samuel Walker Papers, SNCC and COFO Papers, 1964–66, MSS 655, Box 1, Folder 6, WHS. https://content.wisconsinhistory.org/digital/collection/p15932coll2/id/12228/rec/2
58. Historians usually write about the salaries that SNCC workers earned, but Mary King says they were subsistence stipends. King, *Freedom Song*, 405.
59. These numbers vary from source to source. See Hogan, *Many Minds*, 202; Greenberg, *Circle of Trust*, 5.
60. What is clear is that one reason that SNCC's payroll costs ballooned was the decision to pay Mississippi staff $20 a week, to match what staffers in other states were earning. Although $10 had seemed sufficient when they were living with locals, it was no longer adequate when they began to move around. See Forman, memo on SNCC finances, December 1964, post-Waveland: chrome-extension://efaidnbmnnnibpcajpcglclefindmkaj/https://www.crmvet.org/docs/6412_sncc_finances.pdf
    The story of the volunteers is confusing because accounts so vary. Betty Garman, Northern Coordinator, sent a memo about recruiting new volunteers to the Project's Parents' Committees. In it, she explained that 200 volunteers have elected to stay on for six months or more. However, they were still looking to recruit more volunteers because the Summer Project would be continuing

throughout the year. She doesn't mention if the 200 will be put on payroll or not. See chrome-extension://efaidnbmnnnibpcajpcglclefindmkaj/https://www.crmvet.org/docs/640820_sncc_ms_recruit.pdf

In his August or September memo to Project directors, Courtland Cox writes of the "knotty problem" of how many volunteers should be put on staff and the appropriate criteria for their selection. chrome-extension://efaidnbmnnnibpcajpcglclefindmkaj/https://www.crmvet.org/docs/640000_sncc_cox_staff.pdf

At the September 5, 1964 meeting, Cox says that 200 want to stay on and 109 volunteers need subsistence: chrome-extension://efaidnbmnnnibpcajpcglclefindmkaj/https://www.crmvet.org/docs/640905_sncc_projects.pdf

James Forman claimed that a vote had been taken at an October staff meeting to add 85 volunteers to the staff. Forman, *The Making*, 420. However, according to Wesley Hogan, it's not clear that such a vote was ever taken. Some say that they received a memo at the summer's end announcing the volunteers who had chosen to stay in Mississippi. See Hogan, *Many Minds*, 370n39. Taylor Branch claims that more than 100 summer volunteers wanted to stay on. See also SNCC's Digital Gateway: "Fundraising and the New York Office," https://snccdigital.org/inside-sncc/sncc-national-office/fundraising-new-york-office/

61. Forman, *The Making*, 420. Lewis, *Walking*, 304; Hogan, *Many Minds*, 375n6; Judy Richardson, "My Enduring 'Circle of Trust,'" in *Hands*, 363; Mary King covers the period 1964–65 in *Freedom Song*, 518–20.
62. By contrast, Mary King says that in 1963 SNCC's yearly budget was $250,000, with almost all of it coming from donations from individuals, churches, and private organizations. King, *Freedom Song*, 163.
63. Jack Newfield, "The Liberals' Big Stick," *Cavalier*, June 1965.
64. Sellers, *The River*, 111. White volunteer David Harris put it this way: "The change that [the Movement] wanted, once minimal, now seemed deep and massive." Harris, *Dreams Die Hard*, 92.
65. Harris, *Dreams Die Hard*, 88. There is disagreement about what this phrase actually meant. When used by Sweeney, it was an indictment of electoral politics. However, Moses said something similar, but he used the phrase to describe SNCC, where consensus making had given way to top-down centralized leadership. See Visser-Maessen, *Robert Parris Moses*, 278.
66. Political Programs Workshop, Stuart Ewen Papers, 1961–65; SNCC Proposals for the Waveland Retreat, WHS, MSS 531, Box 1, Folder 4.
67. Zinn, *SNCC: The New Abolitionists*, 139.
68. Bob Moses used those words to describe the poor. Moses quoted in Visser-Maessen, *Robert Parris Moses*, 215.
69. Staughton Lynd usually agreed with Bob Moses, but he said that "if voting is a snare and a delusion, what is not?" Lynd, "The New Radicals and 'Participatory Democracy,'" appeared in *Dissent*, Summer 1965, and was reprinted in Teodori Massimo, ed., *The New Left: A Documentary History* (Bobbs Merrill, 1969), 229.
70. For the Cobb reference, see Lynd and Lynd, *Stepping Stones*, 74.
71. For the growing divide between SNCC and the MFDP, see Dittmer, *Local People*, 421; Payne, *I've Got the Light*, 323; Carson, *In Struggle*, 149–50. Dittmer argues that

as the movement went mainstream, it attracted the middle-class people who he claims had chosen to sit out those punishing early years of protest. *Local People* is an award-winning book, and deservedly so. However, as Alan Draper argues, Dittmer overstates the political reticence of middle-class Blacks through a sleight of hand in which his middle class consists of ministers and teachers, but not businessmen, many of whom, as his own account indicates, played an active role in the movement. Draper points out as well that Dittmer associates the middle class with a more moderate or even conservative political orientation and the more disenfranchised citizenry with a more radical political orientation. This is not how it always played out, however. See Alan Draper's incisive review of John Dittmer's *Local People*, in *The Journal of Negro History* 83, no. 3 (Summer 1998): 205.

72. Ed Brown of SNCC, quoted in Visser-Maessen, *Robert Parris Moses*, 255.
73. Barbara Schwartzbaum in a November 1964 memo, quoted in Francesca Polletta, *It Was Like a Fever: Storytelling in Protest and Politics* (University of Chicago Press, 2006), 66.
74. See Charles Payne's incisive discussion in *I've Got the Light*, 359.
75. My discussion here of organizers and the people they were organizing inventing each other is indebted to Polletta, *Inventing the Ties*, 43–44.
76. Polletta, *Inventing the Ties*, 44.
77. Gitlin, *The Sixties*, 161–62.
78. About Rustin's influence, see John D'Emilio's *Lost Prophet*, 276–77; William Strickland Oral History with Robert S. Cox and Jeremy Smith, March 25, 2015, Amherst Sesquicentennial Oral History Collection, University of Massachusetts. For Rustin's feelings about Carmichael, *I Must Resist: Bayard Rustin's Life in Letters*, ed. Michael G. Long (City Lights Press, 2012), 323.
79. Michael G. Long, ed., *I Must Resist: Bayard Rustin's Life in Letters* (City Lights Books, 2012), xxii
80. For a sobering account of Southern unionized workers' opposition to the movement, see Alan Draper, *Conflict of Interests: Organized Labor and the Civil Rights Movement in the South* (Cornell University Press, 1994).
81. Take Macomb County, Michigan, a white working-class enclave north of Detroit. It had been reliably Democratic for decades, but school busing and the prospect of integrated neighborhoods turned it red in 1972's presidential race. See Lichtenstein, *Walter Reuther*, 443.
82. Long, *I Must Resist*, 323.
83. Victoria Gray Adams, "They Didn't Know the Power of Women," in *Hands*, 238.
84. Carmichael, *Ready*, 423–24; McAdam, *Freedom Summer*, 81; Victoria Gray Adams, "They Didn't Know the Power of Women," in *Hands*, 236; Julian Zelizer, *The Fierce Urgency of Now: Lyndon Johnson, Congress, and the Battle for the Great Society* (Penguin, 2015), 220.
85. Lewis, *Walking*, 282.
86. Hogan, *Many Minds*, 363.
87. Forman quoted in Greenberg, *Circle of Trust*, 79.
88. Bob Moses quoted Payne, *I've Got the Light*, 333.
89. Emmie Schrader Adams, "An Interracial Alliance of the Poor: An Elusive Populist Fantasy?" in *Hands*, 424-5.
90. Lane quoted in Visser-Maessen, *Robert Parris Moses*, 216.

91. Ruth Howard Chambers emphasized that the issue "crossed color lines." Interview by Gretchen Howard, November 15, 1994: chrome-extension://efaidnbmnnnibpcajpcglclefindmkaj/https://www.crmvet.org/nars/9410_howard.pdf
92. Payne, *I've Got the Light*, 328–29.
93. Elaine DeLott Baker, "They Sent Us This White Girl," in *Deep in Our Hearts*, 273. Other volunteers became involved in such efforts, too. For example, in the fall of 1965, Barbara Brandt also got involved in the Agricultural Stabilization and Conservation Service project, which helped Black farmers and sharecroppers participate in local elections for the county committees in which cotton allotments were determined. "We Weren't the Bad Guys," in *Hands*, 434–35.
94. Patricia Sullivan, *Freedom Writer: Virginia Foster Durr, Letters from the Civil Rights Years* (Routledge, 2003), 383.
95. Moses quoted in Visser-Maessen, *Robert Parris Moses*, 255. The proposal was voted down at the fall 1964 Waveland retreat.
96. For the putdown of nursery schools, see Barbara Schwartzbaum, MFDP Lauderdale County, Hattiesburg Report, Micro Film 55, Reel 2, Segment 50. Samuel Walker Papers, SNCC and COFO Papers, 1964–66, MSS 655, Box 1, Folder 6, WHS. One worker, probably a volunteer who had stayed on, wrote in late November 1964 that he and many others failed to see the relationship between community centers and sewing classes, on the one hand, and political and economic freedom, on the other. See CORE, Micro 793, Reel 2, Segment 19, WHS. For the view that government programs were a "sham," see Jesse Morris, Federal Programs, in Samuel Walker Papers, SNCC and COFO Papers, 1964–66, MSS 655, Box 1, Folder 6, WHS. See also Carter, *The Music Has Gone Out of the Movement*, 38-39; Lynd, *From There to Here*, 82 of Kindle; Payne, *I've Got the Light*, 342-62.
97. For Allen's remarks, see "Exchange with Three White Women at Spelman, 1962–64, a Discussion," April 2007: https://www.crmvet.org/disc/spelman.htm
98. Carmichael, *Ready*, 416.
99. Mike Miller, "Bob Moses, 1935–2021," July 28, 2021, The Stansbury Forum, https://stansburyforum.com/2021/07/28/bob-moses-1935-2021
100. Carson, *In Struggle*, 187; Maria Gitin, *This Bright Light of Ours: Stories from the Voting Rights Fight* (University of Alabama Press, 2014) is about SCLC's Summer Community Organization and Political Education (SCOPE) project.

CHAPTER FOUR

1. The Atlanta office staff met several times in September and October to energize the group. When the meetings ended with the staff at an impasse, it was decided that SNCC would convene in Waveland, Mississippi, that November to hash out their differences and a chart a way forward. See Hogan, *Many Minds*, 197–98.
2. Richardson, "My Enduring 'Circle of Trust,'" in *Hands*, 363.
3. Hayden, "Fields of Blue," in *Deep in Our Hearts*, 360. There is considerable confusion about how those volunteers, some of whom were Black, came to stay. According to Visser-Maessen, at a mid-August conference at Tougaloo College that Moses organized, people agreed that volunteers could stay on as a "SNCC-supervised, but Northern-financed freedom force." See Visser-Maessen, *Robert Parris Moses*, 257. Some people say that a vote was taken at the October 1964 staff meeting. However,

Wesley Hogan finds no mention in the notes of a vote at that meeting. See Hogan, *Many Minds*, 370n39. Forman claims the vote was taken at Waveland that November. See Forman, *The Making of Black Revolutionaries*, 465–72.
4. Hayden, "Fields of Blue," in *Deep in Our Hearts*, 360.
5. "Working Notes on SNCC Executive Committee . . .," Mary King Papers, 1962–1999; SNCC Position Papers, Waveland, Mississippi, meeting, Accessions, M82-445, Box 1, Folder 18, WHS. The writer here is clearly Bob Moses. Visser-Maessen says, "Do we build a SNCC machine?"; Moses at February 1965 meeting, p. 274.
6. [Bob Moses], "Working Notes on SNCC Executive committee and Membership," SNCC Position Papers, Waveland Mississipp, meeting, November 1964, M82-445, Box 1, Folder 18, Mary King Papers, 1962–99, 1. https://content.wisconsinhistory.org/digital/collection/p15932coll2/id/24553/rec/1
7. "SNCC: Southern Campus Travel," Stuart Ewen Papers, 1961–65; SNCC Proposals for the Waveland Retreat, WHS, MSS 531, Box 1, Folder 4, https://content.wisconsinhistory.org/digital/collection/p15932coll2/id/19548/rec/157. See also Carson, *In Struggle*, 141, and Visser-Maessen, who explains Moses was riffing on the work of philosopher Otto Neurath. Visser-Maessen, *Robert Parris Moses*, 270.
8. See the remarks of Moses and Zinn at a 1986 conference: https://www.howardzinn.org/collection/bob-moses-howard-zinn-mlk-legacy-forum/
9. Forman's speech is available in PDF form on the civil rights movement archive. It is also quoted in Visser-Maessen, *Robert Parris Moses*, 271, and in Hogan, *Many Minds*, 273–76. Sellers gives it a different meaning, and offers a somewhat different account in his memoir, *The River*, 115.
10. Sellers, *The River*, 133.
11. According to Moses, all papers were meant to be anonymous. https://www.howardzinn.org/collection/bob-moses-howard-zinn-mlk-legacy-forum/
12. [Michael Thelwell], "Mississippi's Metaphysical Mystics: A Sect Wrapped Up in a Clique Within a Cult (a Thumbnail Sketch of the New Revolutionary Vanguard)," in Mary King Papers, 1962–99; M82-445, Box 1, Folder 19, WHS, https://content.wisconsinhistory.org/digital/collection/p15932coll2/id/24624/rec/1
13. Constance Curry knew Moses very well and observed that he "used to get hurt anytime anybody would look mean at him." See Visser-Maessen, *Robert Parris Moses*, 262.
14. Visser-Maessen, *Robert Parris Moses*, 272.
15. Sellers, *The River*, 132.
16. Hogan makes a point, correctly, of emphasizing just how offbase the class analysis was. See also Polletta, *Fever*, 68–71. Ruth Howard Chambers emphasized that the issue "crossed color lines." Interview by Gretchen Howard, November 15, 1994: chrome-extension://efaidnbmnnnibpcajpcglclefindmkaj/https://www.crmvet.org/nars/9410_howard.pdf
17. "SNCC in the North," Mary E. King Papers: SNCC Position Papers, Waveland, Mississippi, meeting, Accessions, M82-445, Box 1, Folder 18, accessed November 6, 2023: https://content.wisconsinhistory.org/digital/collection/p15932coll2/id/24576
18. March 1964 letters concerning SNCC fundraising, in HZP/WHS, 1956–64; Zinn-SNCC Paper, administration, 1963–65, Mss 588, Box 2, Folder 11.

19. Betty Garman, "A Note to SNCC Staff." This note was filed, incorrectly, it seems, under "The Building," Stuart Ewen Papers, 1961–65; SNCC Proposals for the Waveland Retreat, WHS, MSS 531, Box 1, Folder 4, https://content.wisconsinhistory.org/digital/collection/p15932coll2/id/19534/rec/157
20. Known as Elizabeth Sutherland until the late sixties, she decided to begin using her father's surname, Martínez, and the nickname "Betita." Tony Platt, "The Heart Just Insists: In the Struggle with Elizabeth 'Betita' Sutherland Martínez," *Social Justice* 39, no. 2–3 (2012): 26–60.
21. Forman's Undated 1964 Paper on the Salary Structure of SNCC: chrome-extension://efaidnbmnnnibpcajpcglclefindmkaj/https://www.crmvet.org/docs/640000_sncc_salarystructure.pdf
22. "Fairy Tale," Stuart Ewen Papers, 1961–65; SNCC Proposals for the Waveland Retreat, WHS, MSS 531, Box 1, Folder 4. This was hardly an isolated example. See Barbara Schwartzbaum letter, Samuel Walker Papers, SNCC and COFO Papers, 1964–66, MSS 655, Box 1, Folder 6, WHS.
23. King, *Freedom Song*, 451–52. Casey Hayden agrees with King. However, Eleanor Holmes Norton later said, "Yeah, my ass he was joking. People don't joke about things they don't believe." Norton quoted in Joan Steinau Lester, *Loving Before Loving*, 126. See also Sara Evans, *Personal Politics: The Roots of Women's Liberation in the Civil Rights Movement and the New Left* (Vintage Books, 1979). For an indispensable treatment of the gender relations in SNCC, see Wini Breines, *The Trouble Between Us: An Uneasy History of White and Black Women in the Feminist Movement* (Oxford University Press, 2006).
24. Adams quoted in Breines, *The Trouble*, 208n37. Adams discusses this in her essay, "Fighting Another Day," in *Hands*, 426. Casey Hayden admitted that his comment made him sound like a sexist, but she insists, "he was quite the opposite." Hayden, "Fields of Blue," 366.
25. Sherrod, Memo from Charles Sherrod, Waveland, Mississippi, meeting, Mary King Papers, 1962–99; M82-445, Box 1, Folder 18, WHS.
26. Elizabeth "Betita" Sutherland Martínez, "Neither Black or White," in *Hands*, 535. The historian Charles Payne has argued that SNCC's floundering also owed something to its success. See Payne, *I've Got the Light*, 362. See also Harris, *Dreams Die Hard*, 92.
27. As Clayborne Carson points out, SNCC people had long spoken of revolution, but they had not meant overthrowing the government. See Carson, *In Struggle*, 51.
28. Moses quoted in Jack Newfield, "The Liberals' Big Stick: Ready for Snick?" *Cavalier*, June 1965, 34.
29. One idea that was seriously explored by Jean Smith, Frank Smith, and others was building a brick factory that would employ sharecroppers displaced by the ongoing mechanization of agriculture. See Jean Smith, "How to Help the Ones at the Bottom," in *Takin' It to the Streets: A Sixties Reader*, ed. Alexander Bloom and Wini Breines (Oxford University Press, 2015), 81. Lucille Montgomery, the Illinois-based white philanthropist, helped to fund the initial explorations. Tribbett and Brick Factory, Lucille Montgomery Papers, 1963–67, Micro 44, Reel 2, Segment 25, WHS: https://content.wisconsinhistory.org/digital/collection/p15932coll2/id/34315/
30. Memo from Charles Sherrod, Waveland meeting, Mary King Papers, 1962–99; M82-445, Box 1, Folder 18, WHS.

31. Hayden, "Fields of Blue," 365.
32. Emmie Schrader Adams, "From Africa to Mississippi," in Browning et al., *Deep in Our Hearts*, 325–26.
33. Reagon, "The Borning Struggle," in *They Should Have*, 23.
34. Samstein quoted in Visser-Maessen, *Robert Parris Moses*, 276.
35. King, *Freedom Song*, 439.
36. Moses quoted in Visser-Maessen, *Robert Parris Moses*, 257.
37. Carson, *In Struggle*, 144. COFO's state headquarters in Jackson was one especially bad example, in which race riots and thievery had become expectable. See Dittmer, *Local People*, 330.
38. Lewis quoted in Carson, *In Struggle*, 101. In his February 1, 1964, speech at the 26th Anniversary Meeting of the staff of the *People's World*, Mike Miller noted that on his recent visit to the Bay Area, John Lewis expressed his commitment to the Black revolutions of Africa. Accessed November 5, 2024: https://www.crmvet.org/info/6402mike.htm. See also Howard Brick and Christopher Phelps, *Radicals in America: The US Left Since the Second World War* (Cambridge University Press, 2015), 110.
39. As Komozi Woodard helpfully points out, nationalism is a heterogeneous ideological formation. Not all nationalists advocated land-based solutions, looked to the countries of Africa for spiritual and cultural guidance, eschewed alliances with non-Blacks, were suspicious of the left, and supported armed self-defense. However, some did favor the whole ensemble, and many embraced some combination of those features. Woodard defines Black nationalism as "an ideological movement for the attainment and maintenance of autonomy and individuality for a social group, some of whose members conceive it to constitute an actual or potential nation." See Woodard, *Nation Within a Nation*, 9.
40. Loren Miller quoted in Amina Hassan, *Loren Miller: Civil Rights Attorney and Journalist* (University of Oklahoma Press, 2015), 196.
41. Many scholars have noted this. Tom Adam Davies contends that Black Power was an "ambiguous concept." See Davies, *Mainstreaming Black Power* (University of California Press, 2017), 218; Devin Fergus showed that it was in practice, too. See Fergus, *Liberalism, Black Power, and the Making of American Politics, 1965–1980* (University of Georgia Press, 2009).
42. Author's interview with Wesley Hogan, May 23, 2021.
43. Hogan, *Many Minds*, 284.
44. Oakland activist Donald Warden, whom I discuss in Part Three claims he advised Brown to "talk to the race," and in contrast to Dr. King, to "assume no white people exist." I discuss this in Alice Echols, "The Land of Somewhere Else: Reconfiguring James Brown in Seventies Disco," *Criticism* 50, no. 1 (January 1, 2008), 26.
45. Horne quoted in Matthew Frye Jacobson, *Dancing Down the Barricades: Sammy Davis Jr. and the Long Civil Rights Era* (University of California Press, 2023), 211.
46. According to Carson, the proposal was floated by Mississippi field secretary Jesse Morris. See Carson, *In Struggle*, 151. Visser-Maessen and Forman claim that Moses reintroduced the motion. See Visser-Maessen, *Robert Parris Moses*, 255, and Forman, *The Making of Black Revolutionaries*, 438.
47. See Tyson, "Robert F. Williams."
48. In *Ready for Revolution*, Stokely Carmichael emphasizes that SNCC's thinking about Black Power evolved from staffers' experiences in Southern Black communities.

49. Ransby, *Ella Baker*, 257. See also Joyce Ladner's observation in Cynthia Griggs Fleming, *Soon We Will Not Cry* (Rowman & Littlefield, 1998), 112.
50. A fellow activist, quoted in Charles Cobb, *This Nonviolent Stuff'll Get You Killed: How Guns Made the Civil Rights Movement Possible* (Basic Books, 2014), 7.
51. Tyson, "Robert F. Williams," 562.
52. Marlene Nadle, "Malcolm X: The Complexity of a Man in the Jungle," *Village Voice*, February 25, 1965. "We nationalists used to think we were militant. We were just dogmatic. It didn't bring us anything." Accessed April 10, 2025: https://www.villagevoice.com/malcolm-x-the-complexity-of-a-man-in-the-jungle/
53. Carmichael, *Ready*, 427. Carson, *In Struggle*, 135–36.
54. Clayborne Carson, "Two Cheers for Brown," *Journal of American History* 91, no. 1 (June 2004), 26-31. Carson offers a sobering account of the *Brown* decision, one that argues that it unleashed a backlash that intensified racism, and that its failure to deliver led to resentment and anger among many Black Americans, which made Black Power even more appealing.
55. Clayborne Carson, "A Scholar in Struggle," *Souls* 4, no. 2 (2002): 29.
56. Bruce Hartford, *Troublemaker: Memories of the Freedom Movement* (Westwind Writers, 2019), 67.
57. "Salary Structure of SNCC," Stuart Ewen Papers, 1961–65; SNCC Proposals for the Waveland Retreat, WHS, MSS 531, Box 1, Folder 4.
58. Forman, *The Making of Black Revolutionaries*, 445.
59. Sellers, *The River of No Return*, 142; Sellers quoted in Jeffries, *Bloody Lownde*, 180.
60. King, *Freedom Song*, 490.
61. Stories certainly differ, but I have leaned heavily on two accounts: Dottie Zellner's story and Ruth Howard Chambers's oral history, conducted by Gretchen Howard, November 15, 1994, 13, 14. In this interview, immediately after identifying Jim Forman as the original Black Panther, Ruth Howard shows her original sketch of the black panther for the LFCO. Jim and the black panther in her drawing are linked in this interview, but it is not clear whether she means that Forman was the model of the panther in her drawing. Her panther had a very humanlike face, so this is plausible. chrome-extension://efaidnbmnnnibpcajpcglclefindmkaj/https://www.crmvet.org/nars/9410_howard.pdf
62. Jeffries, *Bloody Lowndes*, 79.
63. Jeffries, *Bloody Lowndes*, 147–48; Carmichael, *Ready*, 462.
64. Zellner, "My Real Vocation," in *Hands*, 324; Zellner, *Wrong Side*, 286; Hasan Kwame Jeffries, *Bloody Lowndes*, 152. Benjamin Hedin, "From Selma to Black Power," *Atlantic*, March 6, 2015.
65. Stokely Carmichael and Charles Hamilton, *Black Power: The Politics of Liberation in America* (Vintage, 1967), 44.
66. Polletta, *Fever*, 71.
67. Zellner, *Wrong Side*, 286.
68. "Black Nationalism," undated and anonymous, SAVF, SNCC vertical file, circa 1930–2002, MSS 577, Box 47, Folder 12, WHS, https://content.wisconsinhistory.org/digital/collection/p15932coll2/id/66644
69. Martínez quoted in Tony Platt, "Legendary Chicana Organizer Betita Martínez Wrote a Perfect Parody for the Trump Era," *Nation*, September 11, 2017.

70. D. Gorton quoted in the comments section of an article featuring him and his photographic work documenting white Southerners, in James Estrin, "Photographing the White South in the Turbulence of the 1960s," *NYT*, September 13, 2018.
71. The Black novelist and editor Toni Morrison grappled with this in the mid-seventies. What if you liked watching the *Amos 'n' Andy Show* or reading *Little Black Sambo*, she asked? Was this proof that "many dark valleys of unraised consciousness dotted [her] perceptions," as Black Power suggested? She didn't think so. The people who were dupes were the purveyors of this new Black consciousness who "were rejecting parts of their culture" and depriving themselves of the "the old verities that made being black and alive in this country the most dynamite existence imaginable." See Morrison, "Recovering Black History," *NYT Magazine*, August 11, 1974, 220.
72. Carson, *In Struggle*, 238.
73. Lester, *Loving Before Loving*, 106.
74. Payne, *I've Got the Light*, 388.
75. Mike Miller discusses Lewis's view in his 1964 speech. chrome-extension://efaidnbmnnnibpcajpcglclefindmkaj/https://www.crmvet.org/docs/6402_sncc_mikemiller.pdf
76. Lewis, *Walking*, 306–7. Likewise, Julius Lester believed that it was indeed the Northerners who were most likely to be stridently militant. He came to consider "their rage at whites, misdirected self-hatred." Lester, *All Is Well*, 130.
77. At Waveland, Silas Norman Jr. did not endorse separatism, but he did contend that some geographic areas required separate organizing. Norman, "What Is the Importance of Racial Considerations Among the Staff?" Stuart Ewen Papers, 1961–65; SNCC Proposals for the Waveland Retreat, WHS, MSS 531, Box 1, Folder 4.
78. Rustin's 1963 speech was covered in a SNCC publication. See "Whites Stay North," *The Student Voice* 4, no. 7, December 9, 1963. Rustin discouraged whites from going South and donning overalls. Whites, he said, needed to work with unemployed whites in depressed areas of Kentucky, West Virginia, and the North. "When the day comes that the white unemployed adopt the spirit and tactics of the civil rights movement, we are on our way to a revolution in this country." Simon Hall quotes from this same speech, but he characterizes it as Black nationalist. See Hall, *Peace and Freedom: The Civil Rights and Antiwar Movements in the 1960s* (University of Pennsylvania Press, 2005), 58.
79. For White Folks Project, see David Cline, *From Reconciliation to Revolution: The Student Interracial Ministry, Liberal Christianity, and the Civil Rights Movement* (UNC Press, 2016); Lewis, *Walking*, 250. "Can Freedom Get to Poor White Folks," in *Bay Area Friends of SNCC*, November 1964. One staff member quoted for the piece said that those who believed in an "interracial movement of the poor" needed to come to Mississippi. However, he acknowledged that it was a "near impossible task" building such a movement. For the Southern Students Organizing Committee, see this link: https://www.crmvet.org/docs/64_ssoc_about.pdf
80. Carson, *In Struggle*, 203.
81. Lyon, *Memories*, 175.
82. Carmichael, *Ready*, 52.
83. Carmichael was quoted in the *NYT*, May 28, 1966. See Joseph, *Waiting 'til the Midnight Hour*, 131.

84. Here, Carmichael was referencing a popular Pepsi Cola commercial and asked white activists if they couldn't "stop trying to be a [member of the] Pepsi generation who comes alive in the black community?" Carmichael, *Stokely Speaks: From Black Power to Pan-Africanism* (Lawrence Hill, 2007), 51.
85. Carmichael, *Stokely Speaks*, 27.
86. Julius Lester, *Look Out, Whitey! Black Power's Gon' Get Your Momma!* (Grove Press, 1968), 103.
87. James Garrett, "From the Streets of LA," Civil Rights Movement Veterans, September 30, 2018, https://www.crmvet.org/nars/1809jimy.htm
88. Tom Hayden, on one visit to a SNCC retreat in Mississippi, witnessed Black staffers "withdrawing from whites, who were reacting with painful defensiveness." Hayden, *Reunion*, 129.
89. Zellner, *Wrong Side*, 296. Mary King observed there was no potential for insurgency in white communities. King, *Freedom Song*, 499. White activist Bruce Hartford, who came South to work with SCLC, discovered that antiracist organizing with Southern whites was "at best ineffective and at worst impossible." Hartford, *Troublemaker*, 252.
90. Carson, *In Struggle*, 118; Cline, *From Reconciliation to Revolution*, 118.
91. Emmie Schrader Adams, "An Interracial Alliance of the Poor: An Elusive Populist Fantasy?" in *Hands*, 422.
92. HZP/WHS, 1956–94; Mss 588, Box 2, Folder 10, "Whites in the Movement," 1963, WHS.
93. Wesley Hogan makes this argument in *Many Minds*, 158.
94. Theresa Del Pozzo, "The Feel of a Blue Note," in Browning et al., *Deep in Our Hearts*, 184.
95. Block quoted in Gitlin, *This Bright Light of Ours*, 182.
96. Carson, *In Struggle*, 217.
97. Lewis, *Walking*, 382–83; Sellers, *The River*, 157; Martínez quoted in Platt, "The Heart Just Insists"; Adams, "An Interracial Alliance," in *Hands*, 424.
98. Carson, *In Struggle*, 189–95; Carmichael, *Ready*, 565–71; Stanford later said that he envisioned RAM as a "third force" operating between SNCC and the Nation of Islam. Manning Marable, *Malcolm X: A Life of Reinvention* (Penguin, 2011), 353.
99. Carmichael did not mention in his memoir that RAM's leader, Max Stanford, was a close friend in this period.
100. In his essay about RAM, Ahmad says the group formed secret political cells that were meant to be "the support apparatus for field organizers who were openly trying to transform the Civil Rights Movement into a revolutionary Black nationalist movement." Akbar Muhammad Ahmad, "The Revolutionary Action Movement," in Judson L. Jeffries, *The Black Power Movement: In the Belly of the Beast* (University of Illinois Press, 2006), 267. Guyot and Peacock quoted in Discussion Notes, June 10, 1964, Minutes of Meetings, Mary King Papers, 1962–99; M82-445, Box 3, Folder 2, WHS. https://content.wisconsinhistory.org/digital/collection/p15932coll2/id/25825/rec/7
101. Carson, *In Struggle*, 189–201, 261; Thelwell's account appears in one of the many extended sidebars in Carmichael's *Ready for Revolution*, 569. White SNCC staffer Bill Hansen maintains "there is no question in my mind—virtually all SNCC veterans agree with me here—that we were infiltrated." He attributes SNCC's decline to

a "loony ultra-nationalist fringe" whom he suspects were connected to COINTELPRO, the FBI's secret program. Hansen is quoted in Brent Riffel's article "In the Storm," in *Arsnick: The Student Nonviolent Coordinating Committee in Arkansas*, ed. Jennifer Jensen Wallach and John A. Kirk (University of Arkansas Press, 2011), 33. Mary King believes agents provocateurs helped to bring SNCC down. See King, *Freedom Song*, 526–29; Emmie Schrader Adams suspects they were. See Adams, "Interracial Alliance of the Poor," in *Hands*, 425. In another piece, she reports that the white Citizens' Council archives show that by April 1964 the group had at least one agent working inside COFO in Jackson, Mississippi. Adams, "From Africa to Mississippi," in Browning et al., *Deep in Our Hearts*, 316. Sellers and Thewell seem to have their suspicions, but they never go so far as to suggest that anyone in RAM was knowingly doing the bidding of the FBI. Bob Zellner believes that the FBI's COINTELPRO operation was targeting SNCC, with agents who "seemed to encourage divisiveness and confrontation on the black/white and other issues." However, even if the FBI was involved, as he believes it was, he thinks that it probably only succeeded in "nudging SNCC to go ahead and do what it was already inclined to do." See Zellner, *Wrong Side*, 283–94.

102. Mark Whitaker, *Saying It Loud: 1966—The Year Black Power Challenged the Civil Rights Movement* (Simon & Schuster, 2023), 184–85. Whitaker notes a curious detail about the position paper, that is, the appearance on its title page of the seal of the USNSA, as the organization responsible for its reprinting. The USNSA, which was more commonly known as the National Student Association, was secretly underwritten by the Central Intelligence Agency (CIA). Very secretly, for even as high-ranking an official as Vice-President Hubert Humphrey had not known of the CIA's involvement in it until *Ramparts* magazine published an exposé less than a year later. The copy to which Whitaker refers is not identified as a position paper of SNCC, but of the SNCC Vine City Project, which was the Atlanta Project. Whether this was what was leaked to the *Times* is not clear. The document can be found online through the Freedom Archives.

103. Some, such as Lucille Montgomery, continued to give. Thelwell quoted in Carmichael, *Ready*, 567–68. The piece remains erroneously identified in one popular sixties anthology. See SNCC, "The Basis of Black Power," in Bloom and Breines, *Takin' It*, 131.

104. Carson, "Blacks and Jews," 42.

105. Payne, *I've Got the Light*, 372.

106. Richardson, "My Enduring 'Circle of Trust,'" in *Hands*, 365.

107. These are the adjectives that Michael Thelwell says that participants used to describe the meeting. Carmichael, *Ready*, 570.

108. Carson, *In Struggle*, 240.

109. Ethel Minor, a Black staffer recalled feeling guilty afterward because Bob Zellner "had been on the front lines long before I came into the organization. No one wanted to look at Bob afterwards." Minor quoted in Carson, *In Struggle*, 241.

110. Julius Lester, *All Is Well*, 135–36. A few months later, when SNCC refused to give the Zellners voting rights as SNCC members, as they worked to organize whites in an already funded project in New Orleans, Payne writes that the SNCC leadership rejected it, but uneasily. "They were doing something that just did not sit right in the gut." Payne, in *I've Got the Light*, 384.

111. Carmichael, *Ready*, 564–71.
112. Charles Payne stresses this, too, in *I've Got the Light*, 384–85.
113. Lyon, *Memories*, 175.
114. Hall's remark part of a transcript of SNCC Central Committee meeting of May 1967, in Lyons, *Memories*, 181.
115. Carson, *In Struggle*, 199.
116. Thelwell, quoted in Greenberg, *Circle of Trust*, 153.
117. Thelwell, quoted in Carmichael, *Ready*, 570.
118. On this matter, Stokely Carmichael's memoir, which includes recollections of some of his comrades, *Ready for Revolution,* is suggestive. Carmichael is critical of the separatists from RAM, but far more critical is Michael Thelwell, who insinuates that something was deeply amiss with the RAM infiltrators. Perhaps Carmichael's friendship with RAM leader Max Stanford, who was a follower of Malcom X, explains his relatively constrained response. See Carmichael, *Ready*, 566–71, and Hogan, *Many Minds*, 157.
119. Carson notes this, arguing that in an ironic turn, "the bonds that held the staff together loosened while SNCC became more racially homogeneous." *In Struggle*, 237.
120. See Payne, *I've Got the Light*, 385–87.
121. Cline, *From Reconciliation to Revolution*, 91.
122. Sherrod, quoted on SNCC Digital page: https://snccdigital.org/people/charles-sherrod/
123. Platt, "The Heart," 34.
124. Lewis, *Walking*, 385.
125. King, *Freedom Summer*, 503; Visser-Maessen, *Robert Parris Moses*, 289.
126. He suspected that his antiwar activism led the FBI to apply pressure on his New York City draft board. Visser-Maessen, *Robert Parris Moses*, 292.
127. Payne, *I've Got the Light*, 373.
128. Guyot quoted in Dittmer, *Local People*, 411.
129. Cruse quoted in Carson, *In Struggle*, 227–28; Cornel West, "The Paradox of the Afro-American Rebellion," in *The 60s Without Apology*, ed. Sonya Sayres, Anders Stephanson, Stanley Aronowitz, and Fredric Jameson (University of Minnesota Press, 1984), 52.
130. Black Nationalism, unnamed author, undated, WHS, 11 SAVF- SNCC, circa 1930–2002, Archives Main Stacks, Mss 577, Box 47, Folder 12. The author signals that "black power" is already in the air, so it is probably post March 1966. https://content.wisconsinhistory.org/digital/collection/p15932coll2/id/66644
131. Carmichael quote, see Carson, *In Struggle*, 229. For Ruby Doris Smith Robinson's lambasting Carmichael in that October 21, 1966, internal memo, see chrome-extension://efaidnbmnnnibpcajpcglclefindmkaj/https://www.crmvet.org/docs/661021_sncc_org-rpt.pdf
132. Stokely Carmichael, "You Better Come on Home," *The Movement* 3, no. 6 (June 1967): 4. As Carson notes, SNCC's public pronouncements of Black Power tended to be ambiguous, but he notes that in 1966 Carmichael spoke in ways that suggested "vague implications of future racial retribution." Carson, *In Struggle*, 219–21.
133. "From the Streets of L.A. . . . Interview with James Garrett," conducted at UC Berkeley September 30, 2018, and accessed on May 31, 2020: https://www.crmvet.org/nars/1809jimy.htm

134. The decision of some SNCC leaders to oppose the war as individuals was already affecting the group's fundraising. In an October 1965 letter, Pamela (Chude) Parker Allen noted that SNCC's stance on the war had caused a dropoff in contributions. Letter from Chude Pamela Parker Allen to Gloria Xifaras Clark, October 21, 1965, Gloria Xifaras Clark Papers, Robert S. Cox Special Collections, University of Massachusetts, Amherst Library, https://credo.library.umass.edu/view/full/mums865-b002-f039-i001
135. Carson, *In Struggle*, 187–90.
136. Carson, "Blacks and Jews," 44. In her interview with Carson, SNCC staffer Ethel Minor claimed that on one occasion Stokely Carmichael and H. Rap Brown drove through a Black neighborhood, shouting, "Guns for Arabs, sneakers for Jews." Carson, *In Struggle*, 340n10.
137. Forman, *The Making of Black Revolutionaries*, 498–503.
138. The speaker is Cleveland Sellers, quoted in Carson, *In Struggle*, 268. Carson points out that in the aftermath of Freedom Summer, the money from labor unions, churches, and foundations, which had made the Summer Project possible, ended. SNCC was forced to rely on personal donations. Carson, *In Struggle*, 173. On the plunge in donations, Betita Martínez in SNCC's New York City office, which focused on fundraising, reported that her office received $12,360 from direct mailings in 1965, but only $632 in 1966 after SNCC publicly promoted Black Power. She laid this out in her "Desperation Memorandum." See Hogan, *Many Minds*, 221, 375n6.
139. Interview with Bob Moses, Julian Bond Oral History Project, accessed April 3, 2025: https://www.youtube.com/watch?v=47_A1U4vbFk
140. Greenberg, *Circle of Trust*, 153.
141. Carson, *In Struggle*, 262–63; Cleveland Sellers emphasized how law enforcement prosecuted him again and again, effectively neutralizing him as a leader. See Greenberg, *Circle of Trust*, 158.
142. The evidence suggests that this began to happen before the end of 1964. Hogan says that throughout 1965, the virtual absence of funds forced people to ditch local projects throughout the South. See Hogan, *Many Minds*, 213. John Lewis notes that donations to SNCC "drastically decreased after its turn to Black Power, leaving the organization barely able to function." See Lewis, *Walking*, 277.
143. After another electoral defeat in 1968, and with SNCC activists gone from the county, the LFCO decided to abandon its emblem. See Jeffries, *Bloody Lowndes*, 212. Jeffries explains this as the result of SNCC's philosophical commitment to organizing a community, helping to develop leadership, and leaving. SNCC people said, "They worked themselves out of a job." Jeffries does cite other reasons, including SNCC's commitment to expanding its third-party-organizing initiative beyond Lowndes County.
144. Hogan, *Many Minds*, 25n17.
145. Carson, "A Scholar in Struggle," *Souls* 4, no. 2 (2002): 32.
146. Faith Holsaert Papers, 1950–2011, Duke University, Southwest Georgia Voter Registration Project, Correspondence, Friends, "Letter from Wendy," December 8, 1964. This letter is signed by two people. The archive's staff have listed its author as "Wendy." However, the letter might be from Mendy Samstein and Dennis Sweeney. Dennis is the second signatory, and the two men were friends. https://archives.lib.duke.edu/catalog/holsaertfaith_aspace_ref438_wx8

In meeting notes from early May 1965 in Waveland, Jim Forman asks Cordell Reagon, who headed up the SW Georgia Project, if he wants to attend "Synanon House (for junkies) for a couple of months, and come back and get the same thing going here." This suggests that hard drugs were impacting these communities. Minutes of Meetings, Mary King Papers, 1962–99; M82-445, Box 3, Folder 2, p. 3, https://content.wisconsinhistory.org/digital/collection/p15932coll2/id/25933/rec/9

147. Visser-Maessen, *Robert Parris Moses*, 264.
148. Ruth Howard Chambers, Interview by Gretchen Howard, November 15, 1994: 41.
149. See the comments of Mendy Samstein and Casey Hayden in Greenberg, *Circle of Trust*, 82, 86.
150. Darlene Clark Hine and Kathleen Thompson, *A Shining Thread of Hope: The History of Black Women in America* (Crown, 2009), 283. Joan Steinau Lester references this in her biography, *Eleanor Holmes Norton: Fire in My Soul* (Atria, 2003), 126. Still, it is important to note that the MFDP remained marginalized within the Democratic Party, which allotted it only one-quarter of the seats at its 1968 convention. See Mike Miller's "From Protest to Power": https://www.crmvet.org/comm/miller19.htm

PART TWO

1. Hayden, "Fields of Blue," 341. Hayden quoted in Hogan, *Many Minds*, 377. Black staffer and friend Ivanhoe Donaldson later told her, "Casey, when we said whites should work with whites, we didn't mean you," which was rather bittersweet all those years later. Hayden, "In the Attics of My Mind," in *Hands*, 383. Donaldson seems to have said pretty much the same thing to Mary King. See King, *Freedom Song*, 530.
2. Zellner, "My Real Vocation," in *Hands*, 325. As for Mary King, she felt "lost to myself" for three years. See King, *Freedom Song*, 496. King's pain was amplified by her marriage to another white ex-SNCC activist Dennis Sweeney. Sweeney began to come apart during their marriage, and they soon divorced. King regained her bearings, but Sweeney grew more psychologically unhinged. In 1980, he killed Allard Lowenstein, the man who had recruited him to the Freedom Vote campaign. Sweeney had been Lowenstein's one-time protégé, and he came to feel, as did many in SNCC, that Lowenstein was the embodiment of all that they hated about liberals. See Harris, *Dreams Die Hard*, which focuses on his relationship to Sweeney and Lowenstein. At the 1989 Freedom Summer reunion, Bob Moses later spoke tenderly of Sweeney as "someone whom the Movement had failed." Visser-Maessen, *Robert Parris Moses*, 262.
3. Miller made these remarks following 2014's Freedom Summer Reunion. Mike Miller, "The Mississippi Summer Project 50th Anniversary Reunion: Notes of a Veteran," originally published in *Counter Punch*, July 11–13, 2014, https://www.crmvet.org/comm/miller14.htm
4. King, *Freedom Song*, 530; Zellner, "My Real Vocation," in *Hands*, 325; Payne, *I've Got the Light*, 384.
5. In Chicago, the ERAP project went by the name Jobs or Income Now or JOIN. Casey Hayden notes in a 2010 autobiographical essay that SNCC's underwriting of her work was "a generous move toward interracial class solidarity that has not been recognized." See Hayden, "In the Attics of My Mind," in *Hands*, 384.

6. The person who critiqued altruism, especially "pure altruism," was a white SNCC staffer, writing about the effects of Black nationalism on white activists. He argued, "while altruism may be possible, *pure* altruism without reference to the needs of the self is hypocritical and transparently self-deceptive." "Black Nationalism," undated and anonymous, SAVF, SNCC vertical file, circa 1930–2002, MSS 577, Box 47, Folder 12, WHS.

CHAPTER FIVE

1. Norman Mailer, *The Armies of the Night: History as a Novel, The Novel as History* in *Norman Mailer, Four Books of the 1960s*, ed. J. Michael Lennon (Library of America, 2018), 450.
2. Mills's opposition to the Old Left's kneejerk positioning of the working class as *the* agent of radical change—what he called the "labor metaphysic"—helped to lay the foundation for the New Left's relative openness to other actors. So did liberal social democrats, whose understanding of postindustrial development suggested that the university could be a site of change, and that students and intellectuals could be "independent catalysts" of change. Mills's "'labor metaphysic,'" recalled Richard Flacks, "that phrase, was constantly reverberating for us. We didn't want to be guilty of it. And we weren't." Flacks quoted in Miller, *Democracy*, 177. Another key early sixties activist who was never seduced by the certitudes of Marxism was Mario Savio. Savio was not an SDS'er, but like many of them, he did not believe that America's problems were reducible to capitalism. See Robert Cohen, *Freedom's Orator* (Oxford University Press, 2009), 371.
3. SDS'ers were also influenced by liberals in the anti-nuclear campaign and in the labor movement, particularly the United Automobile Workers. See Nelson Lichtenstein, "A Moment of Covergence," in *The Port Huron Statement*, 95–124; Daniel Geary, "The New Left and Liberalism Reconsidered: The Committee of Correspondence and the Port Huron Statement," in *The Port Huron Statement*, 83–94.
4. The *Port Huron Statement*, reprinted in Bloom and Breines, *Takin' It*, 70.
5. Twenty years later, Savio admitted, "I wanted to be like Bob Moses. I wanted to *be* Bob Moses if I could do it." Savio quoted in Cohen, *Freedom's Orator*, 52. Underscoring Moses's influence on Savio and FSM is FSM's adoption of the same organizational structure—nonhierarchical and highly democratic—that Moses favored. See Doug Rossinow, "Mario Savio and the Politics of Authenticity," in *The Free Speech Movement: Reflections on Berkeley in the 1960s*, ed. Robert Cohen and Reginald E. Zelnick (University of California Press, 2002), 541.
6. Howard Brick and Christopher Phelps, *Radicals in America: The US Left Since the Second World War* (Cambridge University Press, 2015), 114.
7. According to Mike Miller, the former SNCC field secretary, who now directed the local FOS chapter, students were "really upset about that." Martin Meeker Interview with Miller, UC Berkeley Oral History Center, 49: https://digicoll.lib.berkeley.edu/record/219284?ln=en&v=pdf. Miller also notes that over 100 UCB students took part in the Mississippi Summer Project. Author's interview with Miller, July 9, 2021.
8. Savio credited the FSM with his overcoming his stutter. Cohen, *Freedom's Orator*, 7.
9. Likening Cal to a knowledge factory, its students treated like IBM cards, was common. Citing the work of Paul Goodman, Savio told a reporter from *Life* magazine, who was writing a feature about him, that students were an "exploited class," subjected to "all

the techniques of the factory methods." See Robert Cohen, "This Was Their Fight and They Had to Fight It: The FSM's Nonradical Rank and File," in *The Free Speech Movement: Reflections on Berkeley in the 1960s*, ed. Robert Cohen and Reginald E. Zelnick (University of California Press, 2002), 240.

10. Savio, "An End to History," in Hal Draper, *Berkeley: The New Student Revolt* (Grove Press, 1965), 179.
11. Mario Savio, "Introduction," in Draper, *Berkeley*, 7.
12. Savio, "Introduction," 6. Before long, white student radicals were declaring that the "campus was another ghetto." The phrase is Doug Rossinow's in his article, Doug Rossinow, "Mario Savio and the Politics of Authenticity," in *The Free Speech Movement*, 541.
13. Visser-Maessen, *Robert Parris Moses*, 286.
14. Flacks recalled Hayden posing the question in this way, but Hayden might have said a Frankenstein's monster, the proper expression. Flacks quoted in Miller, *Democracy*, 195.
15. Miller, *Democracy*, 196.
16. Gitlin, *The Sixties*, 165. In the Newark ERAP, Hayden tried to organize the project's Black constituency around being "poor and powerless, rather than being black." Hayden, quoted in Jennifer Frost, *An Interracial Movement of the Poor: Community Organizing and the New Left in the 1960s* (New York University, 2001), 115. Paul Potter claims that there was in ERAP an "implicit" critique of SNCC for "organizing around the divisive issue of race" in "An Interracial Movement of the Poor?," the influential paper coauthored by Tom Hayden and Carl Wittman. See Potter, *A Name for Ourselves* (Little, Brown & Company, 1971), 143.
17. Alyosha Goldstein, *Poverty in Common: The Politics of Community Action During the American Century* (Duke University Press, 2012), 165.
18. Hayden, quoted in Frost, *An Interracial Movement*, 115. Perhaps this is what also motivated Carl Wittman, Hayden's coauthor on "An Interracial Movement of the Poor?" Wittman argued in an April 1964 SDS pamphlet that "the problems of the American Negro are not essentially racial, but are problems of poverty focused on a racial minority." It's one of many examples of the arrogance of Northern white students. Perhaps Wittman took this position because he was a red-diaper baby who, like his communist parents, generally believed class trumped race. Whatever the case, pronouncements of this sort by white radicals understandably annoyed Black activists.
19. Potter, *Name*, 147, 152.
20. Gitlin quoted in Goldstein, *Poverty*, 164.
21. Here, I depart from the view of James Miller, who argued that it was SNCC following SDS in this period. See Miller, *Democracy Is in the Streets* (Simon and Schuster, 1987), 212–13.
22. Frost, *Interracial Movement*, 149–50; Potter, *Name*, 149. The phrase that was often used to describe ERAP organizers was "catalyst." See Staughton Lynd, "The New Radicals and 'Participatory Democracy,'" which appeared in *Dissent*, Summer 1965. It was reprinted in Massimo, *The New Left*.
23. Frost, *Interracial Movement*, 174.
24. Potter, *Name*, 149.
25. Peter Countryman, "Race and the Movement," *ERAP Newsletter*, August 21, 1965. The concern about manipulation troubled some SNCC staffers, too.

26. Gitlin, *The Sixties*, 165–67.
27. See Miller, *Democracy*, 200,
28. Frost, *Interracial Movement*, 157–58; Potter, *Name*, 139.
29. The number of projects, see Frost, *Interracial Movement*, 1. On "feeling real, see Tom Hayden, "The Politics of the Movement," originally published in *Dissent*, January/February 1966, and reprinted in Massimo, *The New Left*, 207. On his hopes for ERAP, Hayden, quoted in Frost, *Interracial Movement*, 158. Potter, *Name*, 138.
30. On expectations, see Frost, *An Interracial*, 2; on being worn down, Frost, *Interracial Movement*, 148.
31. Potter, *Name*, 145.
32. Frost, *Interracial Movement*, 114.
33. The speaker is Vivian Rothstein. See Frost, *Interracial Movement*, 175, 154–55, 150.
34. Potter, *Name*, 148.
35. Frost, *Interracial Movement*, 148–50. Miller, *Democracy*, 212.
36. Hayden, quoted in Frost, *Interracial Movement*, 150.
37. Eric Mann, quoted in Frost, *Interracial Movement*, 161.
38. On the Du Bois Clubs, see Maurice Isserman, *Reds: The Tragedy of American Communism* (Basic Books, 2024), 282. For PL, see Miller, *Democracy*, 284–85; Gitlin, *The Sixties*, 180. Anne Weills was a member and says they were a vehicle to recruit people into the Communist Party. Jean Stein's Interview with Anne Weills, JSP/NYPL, Box 161, F4.
39. Potter, *Name*, 66.
40. Gregory Calvert, "In White America: Radical Consciousness and Social Change," originally delivered in February 1967, published in the *National Guardian*, March 25, 1967, and reprinted in Massimo, *The New Left*, 414.
41. Greg Calvert, "Shake the Empire," *The Movement*, December 1967, 6.
42. Calvert, "In White America," 413.
43. Calvert, "Shake the Empire," 6.
44. Someone who tried to figure out what a liberated identity might look like for white middle-class radicals was Paul Potter. He contended they needed to undo their socialization as middle-class Americans, but not with the aim of making themselves over as working class. Potter, *Name*, 100–128.
45. Julius Lester, *Look Out, Whitey*, 139. The footnotes suggest that Lester likely wrote this before 1968.
46. Antiwar sentiment had been bubbling up in both SNCC and SDS since August 1964, in the wake of Congress's Gulf of Tonkin resolution, which effectively gave Johnson a blank check to wage war in Vietnam. When it came to draft resistance, the May 2 Movement, a PL-derived groupuscule, was the first group to circulate a "We Won't Go" petition in fall 1964. However, by late 1964, some people in SNCC and SDS were in favor of opposing the war and the draft. The MFDP, in its July 1965 newsletter, called on Mississippi Blacks to not fight in Vietnam. Muhammad Ali refused to be drafted in 1966 on religious grounds, though he opposed it politically, too. In July 1966, Carmichael and SDS president Carl Oglesby cosigned a statement to the House Committee on the Armed Services criticizing the draft. It was Carmichael who approached Oglesby to cosign. See Carson, *In Struggle*, 183–85; Gitlin, *The Sixties*, 179–83; Lyon, *Memories*, 177; Bloom and Martin, *Black Against Empire*, 128–29.

47. Michael Foley, *Confronting the War Machine: Draft Resistance During the Vietnam War* (University of North Carolina Press, 2003), 39.
48. Stokely Carmichael, speech at Berkeley, https://americanradioworks.publicradio.org/features/blackspeech/scarmichael.html
49. On Carmichael, see his fall 1965 Berkeley speech. He took this position from the summer of 1965 through 1966, and perhaps longer. H. Rap Brown's appreciation of his white comrades was short-lived. Brown is quoted here in Hall, *Peace and Freedom*, 126.
50. It was held on the 20-year anniversary of the bombing of Hiroshima and Nagasaki. The protestors presented the U.S. government with a Declaration of Conscience, condemning U.S. foreign policy. See Vanessa Cook, *Spiritual Socialists: Religion and the American Left* (University of Pennsylvania, 2019), 189.
51. Visser-Maessen, *Robert Parris Moses*, 290. For the Executive Committee decision, see Greenberg, *Circle of Trust*, 80. Moses's explanation stands as a rare acknowledgment of his influence among other Movement people.
52. Bob Moses and Dona Richards were two of the five people who attended the wedding of Sweeney and King in late 1964.
53. They were not the first white activists to push for draft resistance. The May 2 Movement, a PL spin-off, circulated a "We Won't Go" petition in the fall of 1964. Not wanting to be outflanked, SDS, in late 1964, made plans for what turned out to be the largest antiwar march yet, April 1965's march in Washington, DC. See Gitlin, *The Sixties*, 179–83. But neither SDS nor M2M was suggesting draft resistance as a way in which white radicals could satisfy the demands of Black Power advocates that they organize white people.
54. Bruce Dancis, *Resister: A Story of Protest and Prison During the Vietnam War* (Cornell University Press, 2014), 66.
55. Foley, *Confronting*, 79.
56. Staughton Lynd, "The Movement: A New Beginning," *Liberation* 14, no. 2 (May 1969): 14.
57. This quote is not attributed to anyone. The article was collectively written by people associated with the periodical *The Movement*, where it appeared in its November 1967 issue. "The Movement: We've Got to Reach Our Own People," reprinted in Massimo, *The New Left*, 306.
58. Harris, *Dreams Die Hard*, 204. The draft resistance movement contained different approaches: those who, like David Harris, believed in resistance as moral witness and those who criticized it as middle-class and self-indulgent when the task should be trying to reach the working-class whites who had no 2-S exemption.
59. Indeed, Greg Calvert in his February 1967 speech spoke approvingly and at some length about new working-class theory.
60. Gareth Stedman Jones, "The Meaning of the Student Revolt," in *Student Power*, ed. Alexander Cockburn and Robin Blackburn (Penguin Books, 1969), 32.
61. One of its authors was David Gilbert, who later joined Weatherman. See David Gilbert, *Love and Struggle* (PM Press, 2012), 70–75.
62. Jonah Raskin, *For the Hell of It: The Life and Times of Abbie Hoffman* (University of California Press, 1996), 97.
63. Hoffman antagonized people in SNCC by writing about Blacks' hostility toward their white coworkers. In late 1966, he submitted two articles to the *Village Voice*, which

published both. He blasted SNCC's treatment of whites and controversially claimed that Black men in SNCC took sexual advantage of white female staffers. In a follow-up piece, he voiced his fears about dying "at the hands of one of my black brothers." Hoffman's decision to air his grievances about SNCC, something other whites in SNCC did not do, ended his relationship with his friend, Mendy Samstein. See Raskin, *For the Hell*, 75–79.
64. Hoffman quoted in Raskin, *For the Hell*, 99 and 109.
65. Frost, *Interracial Movement*, 153–54.
66. Tepperman quoted in Frost, *Interracial Movement*, 163.
67. Mimi Feingold, quoted in Evans, *Personal Politics*, 182.
68. To be clear, Staughton Lynd was not criticizing the machismo of draft resistance. See Lynd, "The Movement," 14.
69. For more on the influence of this concept, see Evans, *Personal Politics*; Alice Echols, *Daring to Be Bad: Radical Feminism in America, 1967–75*, 2nd ed. (University of Minnesota Press, 2019).
70. Gloria Steinem, "After Black Power, Women's Liberation," *New York Magazine*, April 4, 1969, https://nymag.com/news/politics/46802/
71. Bob Gottlieb and Marge Piercy, "Movement for a Democratic Society, Beginning to Begin to Begin," *Radicals in the Professions Newsletter*, March 1968, reprinted in Massimo, *The New Left*, 409.
72. Gitlin, *The Sixties*, 168.
73. Foley, *Confronting*, 337.
74. Gitlin, *The Sixties*, 379.
75. Foley, *Confronting*, 141.
76. *New York Times* reporter James Reston reported this in the *Times*. See Foley, *Confronting*, 90.
77. Foley, *Confronting*, 338.
78. Greg Calvert, "In White America: Radical Consciousness and Social Change," in *Takin' It to the Streets*, 113.
79. Heterosexuals who cohabitated in this period still encountered discrimination. See Elizabeth H. Pleck, *Not Just Roommates: Cohabitation After the Sexual Revolution* (University of Chicago Press, 2012).
80. C. Wright Mills, "Letter to the New Left," reprinted in *Takin' It to the Streets*, 74.
81. Raskin, *For the Hell*, 128.
82. Judy Gumbo, *Yippie Girl* (Three Rooms Press, 2022), 53.
83. Frost, *Interracial Movement*, 150. Hayden, "Fields of Blue," 371. Hayden reworked the Waveland paper during the summer of 1965, when she was part of the Chicago ERAP project, called JOIN. Hayden's comments appeared in this preface to "Sex and Class," accessed April 4, 2026: https://documents.alexanderstreet.com/d/1006932381
84. Breines, *The Trouble Between Us*, 31.
85. Andrew Kopkind, "The New Left: Chicago and After," *The New York Review of Books*, September 1967.
86. Arthur Waskow, *Running Riot* (Herder & Herder, 1970), 99.
87. Clay Carson, "New Politics, Black Power," *New West Magazine* 2 (Spring 1967).

88. Carl Davidson of SDS put forward this analysis. Carl Davidson, the *Guardian*, March 23, 1968.
89. Earl Caldwell, "2 Negro Militants See Serious Split," *NYT*, October 2, 1967, 41. Others also alleged that police or FBI agents, posing as hardcore nationalists, caused the fireworks at the NCNP. However, the Black caucus was apparently fully supportive of a nationalist agenda. Other accounts that emphasize agents include Nancy Zaroulis and Gerald Sullivan, *Who Spoke Up: American Protest Against the War in Vietnam, 1963–1975* (Doubleday, 1984), 129; Gitlin, *The Sixties*, 245; Healey and Isserman, *Dorothy Healey*, 206; Hall, *Peace and Freedom*, 68.
90. Roy Innis quoted in Robert Weisbrot, *Freedom Bound: A History of America's Civil Rights Movement* (Norton, 1990), 256. In 2005, Innis supported the conservative Samuel A. Alito Jr., who had been nominated to the Supreme Court by George W. Bush. Robert D. McFadden, "Roy Innis, Black Activist with a Right-Wing Bent, Dies at 82," *NYT*, January 10, 2017.
91. Hall, *Peace and Freedom*, 119.
92. Arthur Waskow quoted in Hall, *Peace and Freedom*, 116.
93. Waskow, *Running Riot*, 99.
94. See Zaroulis and Sullivan, *Who Spoke Up*, 128.
95. Quoted in Simon Hall, "On the Tail of the Panther: Black Power and the 1967 Convention of the National Conference for New Politics," *Journal of American Studies* 37, no. 1 (2003): 75n80.
96. Berman, writing in 1971, is quoted in Michael Kazin, *American Dreamers: How the Left Changed a Nation* (Knopf, 2011), 215.
97. Martin Kenner, Interview with Lewis Cole, n.d., Columbia University Black Panther Project.
98. John Veneziale, "Students," *New Left Notes*, 2, no. 33 (September 25, 1967): 8.
99. Carl Oglesby, "Notes on a Decade Ready for the Dustbin," *Liberation* 4, nos. 5 & 6 (August/September 1969): 17.

PART THREE

1. Reginald Major, "Stealth History," *The Black Scholar* 24, no. 4 (Fall 1994): 40. Major was a journalist with an intimate knowledge of the Panthers. Sol Stern, "The Call of the Black Panthers," *NYT Magazine*, August 6, 1967; Bloom and Martin, *Black Against Empire*, 58.
2. "Armed Negroes Protest Gun Bill," *NYT*, May 3, 1967, 23.
3. Bloom and Martin, *Black Against Empire*, 61.
4. Stern, "The Call," 68.
5. David Talbot and Margaret Talbot, *By the Light of Burning Dreams: The Triumphs and Tragedies of the Second American Revolution* (HarperCollins, 2021), 80.
6. Bobby Seale's recollection appears in the documentary *Berkeley in the Sixties*. For footage of the demonstration, see the Center for Sacramento History's webpage: https://www.youtube.com/watch?v=6woXE-RPY7A
7. Here I am paraphrasing Jane Rhodes in her astute book *Framing the Panthers* (The New Press, 2007), 74.
8. Bobby Seale provides a full account in *Seize the Time* (Random House, 1970), 160–72.

9. Rhodes, *Framing*, 131. One exception was an early piece written by the *Ramparts* writer Sol Stern for the *New York Times Magazine*. Stern emphasized that the Panthers "were conscious of the dangers of simple-minded anti-white hostility." Stern, "The Call of the Black Panthers," 68.
10. See the Center for Sacramento History: https://www.youtube.com/watch?v=6woXE-RPY7A
11. Peniel E. Joseph attributes the bad blood between the Panthers and their nationalist rivals to the Panthers' faith in white radicals and Marxism, a belief "shared by no other major Black Power organizations." Joseph, *Waiting for Midnight*, 219.
12. There is another problem: the difficulty of determining authorship. How many of the books allegedly written by the Panthers really were written by them? There is no doubt that Eldridge Cleaver was a writer, but the same cannot be said about Bobby Seale or Huey Newton. The books that bear Newton's name were likely written instead by the scholar and Panther ally J. Herman Blake. "He wasn't a writer," said Blake of Newton. "I was the writer." Similarly, Bobby Seale's 1970 memoir, *Seize the Time*, was written by the white left-wing journalist Art Goldberg. Blake worked from taped interviews he conducted with Newton, whereas Goldberg appears to have worked from written notes of his conversations with Seale. Many of these interviews and conversations occurred when Seale and Newton were incarcerated. One cannot be certain about the reliability of these texts because we don't know just how involved Seale and Newton were in reading and correcting drafts of the final manuscripts. The historian David Garrow has noted the significance of Blake's contribution to work that carries the name of Huey P. Newton. David J. Garrow, "Picking Up the Books: The New Historiography of the Black Panther Party," *Reviews in American History* 35 (2007): 668n29. See also documentarian Roz Payne's article, "WACing Off: Gossip, Sex, Race, and Politics in the World of the FBI Special Case Agent William A. Cohendet," in *In Search of the Black Panther Party: In Search of a Revolutionary Movement*, ed. Jama Lazerow and Yohuru Williams (Duke University Press, 2006), 180n22. Payne says that she reached out to Blake, who responded by email to say that he wrote Newton's autobiography *Revolutionary Suicide*, most of the articles in Newton's collection *To Die for the People*, and many of the articles under Newton's byline in the *Black Panther* newspaper. Blake says that initially he intended to write Newton's biography. However, when Newton's conviction for police officer John Frey's death was overturned in the summer of 1970, it was decided that the book should be an autobiography, with the hope that it would become a bestseller like *The Autobiography of Malcolm X*, which it didn't. He had many conversations with Newton in prison, which Blake taped, and which were subsequently transcribed by Blake's students. However, Blake says here that he wrote every line of the book, not Newton. For Blake's version, see https://www.thehistorymakers.org/biography/j-herman-blake-41

According to the sociologist Andrew Fearnley, who has written the fullest treatment of this, the publisher's records show that in June 1970 Blake and Newton signed a contract agreeing to coauthor *Revolutionary Suicide* and to split the advance. Five months later, the newly formed Panther corporation, Stronghold Consolidated, inherited the deal. Once the book appeared in print, Blake charged that Stronghold had not honored its agreement. As a result, he said he had been forced to "beg . . . for what I should be able to expect with dignity." Under oath during the lawsuit, he insisted he was the book's principal author, the one who had produced rough drafts and the original manuscript to the publisher. Stronghold countered that the manuscript was so inadequate that the writer Donald Freed and Huey's brother, Melvin Newton, had to undertake more writing and editing of the taped interviews. Records indicate the involvement of still others, including Panther financier Martin Kenner. Had the court interviewed the book's editor, the evidence would have corroborated Newton's noninvolvement as a writer. Fearnley's own judgment is that "the only one never mentioned as having written any part of the work was Newton." Indeed, in June 1976, Stronghold was ordered to pay Blake $8,250, though by that point the corporation was reportedly "defunct with no assets." For his fascinating discussion of this episode and much more, see Andrew M. Fearnley, "The Black Panther Party's Publishing Strategies and the Financial Underpinnings of Activism, 1968–1975," *Historical Journal* 62, no. 1 (2019): 214–15.

13. Scholars have relied on government records, mainstream and alternative newspaper accounts, the Panthers' own weekly newspaper, and oral histories and autobiographies. For one very focused history that is nevertheless groundbreaking, see Murch, *Living for the City*. The most comprehensive history is Bloom and Martin, *Black Against Empire*. Although outsider accounts of the Panthers, whether FBI reports or articles in the mainstream press, are often full of distortions, insider accounts have drawbacks, too. As for the party's newspaper, the *Black Panther*, it usefully documents the party's tactical lurches—from armed self-defense in 1966 to revolutionary insurrection to "survival programs," to its final pivot, electoral politics in 1972—and its changing cast of preferred revolutionary icons. But the paper was a propaganda sheet committed to putting forward what its leaders considered the party's best face.

14. Allen quoted in Garrow, "Picking Up the Books," 658. Panther memoirs have been more forthright about this duality than most histories of the Panthers. See Hilliard and Cole, *This Side of Glory*; Don Cox, *Just Another N****r: My Life in the Black Panther Party* (Heyday, 2019); Elaine Brown, *A Taste of Power: A Black Women's Story* (Pantheon, 1992); Aaron Dixon, *My People Are Rising* (Haymarket, 2012); Curtis J. Austin, *Up Against the Wall: Violence in the Making and Unmaking of the Black Panther Party* (University of Arkansas Press, 2006); Flores A. Forbes, *Will You Die with Me? My Life and the Black Panther Party* (Atria, 2006).

15. James Baldwin, "No Name in the Street," in James Baldwin, *The Price of the Ticket* (St. Martin's Press, 1985), 546.

16. Angela Davis, "The Making of a Revolutionary," *Women's Review of Books* 10, no. 9 (June 1993), 3. Davis writes that she came to understand that some of the "danger and chaos" enveloping the group stemmed "from the very core of the Black Panther Party." This is Davis's review of Elaine Brown's 1993 memoir, *A Taste of Power*.

17. Carson makes this judgment in Stanley Nelson's documentary *Black Panther: The Vanguard of the Revolution*. Murray Kempton's observation appears in his blurb of David Hilliard's *This Side of Glory*.

CHAPTER SIX

1. Tyson, *Radio Free Dixie*, 289.
2. Stern, "The Call of the Black Panthers," 67.
3. Amari Baraka, *The Autobiography of Leroi Jones/Amiri Baraka* (Freundlich Books, 1984). Karenga told Baraka that it did not mean United Slaves; it meant "US" as

opposed to "THEM," 252. Scot Brown, "A Conversation with Amiri Baraka: Politics, Class Struggle and Black Culture, January 5, 1996—A Retro-Engagement," *Langston Hughes Review* 25, no. 2, 38; Murch, *Living for the City*, 82.
4. Some say that SSAC was a front group for the local chapter of RAM. Bloom and Martin, *Black Against Empire*, 31.
5. Donna Murch, "When the Panther Travels: Race and the Southern Diaspora in the History of the BPP, 1964-1972," in *Black Power Beyond Borders: The Global Dimensions of Black Power*, ed. Nico Slate (Palgrave Macmillan, 2012), 69; Bloom and Martin, *Black Against Empire*, 32, 70.
6. Huey P. Newton, "Intercommunalism: February 1971," in *The Huey P. Newton Reader*, ed. David Hilliard and Donald Weise (Seven Stories, 2002), 184.
7. Victoria J. Gallagher, "Black Power in Berkeley: Postmodern Constructions in the Rhetoric of Stokely Carmichael," *Quarterly Journal of Speech* 87, no. 2 (May 2001): 144–45.
8. Lawrence E. Davies, "Carmichael Asks Draft's Defiance," *NYT*, October 30, 1966. 62. The speaker here seems to be Carmichael, but, as written, it is ambiguous.
9. See the Voices of Democracy link: https://voicesofdemocracy.umd.edu/carmichael-black-power-speech-text/. Bloom and Martin, *Black Against Empire*, 40–44.
10. See Murch, "When the Panther," 63.
11. Carmichael, *Ready*, 664, 475.
12. David Hilliard says Newton read in the newspapers about the formation of the Community Alert Patrol (CAP) in Watts. See David Hilliard, *Huey: Spirit of the Panther* (Thunder's Mouth Press, 2006), 39–40.
13. Carmichael, *Ready*, 476.
14. In 2012, a well-regarded journalist revealed that Aoki had been an FBI informant. Seth Rosenfeld, *Subversives: The FBI's War on Student Radicals, and Reagan's Rise to Power* (Farrar, Straus and Giroux, 2012), 418–24. Richard Aoki's FBI file: https://vault.fbi.gov/richard-m.-aoki/Richard%20Matsui%20Aoki%20Part%2016%20of%2016/view
15. Seale, *Seize*, 79–80.
16. Seale, interviewed in the documentary, *Berkeley in the Sixties*; Seale, *Seize*, 79–85.
17. Seale, *Seize*, 183.
18. Huey P. Newton, *Revolutionary Suicide* (Penguin Classics Edition, 2009, original publication 1973), 59–62. Andrew Lester, "'This Was My Utopia': Sexual Experimentation and Masculinity in the 1960s Bay Area Left," *Journal of the History of Sexuality* 29, no. 3 (Sept. 2020): 366–68.
19. Author's Interview with Steve Wasserman, August 21, 2020.
20. Robert O. Self, *American Babylon: Race and the Struggle for Postwar Oakland* (Princeton University Press, 2003), 4.
21. Gerald Horne says that Goodlett was close to William Patterson, the most powerful African American in the Communist Party, and had extensive ties to people in the CPUSA. Gerald Horne, *Black Revolutionary: William Patterson and the Globalization of the African American Freedom Struggle* (University of Illinois Press, 2013), 198–99.
22. The CRC represented the Communist Party's merger in 1946 of two organizations, the National Negro Congress and the International Labor Defense (ILD), which decades earlier had played a critical role in the defense of the "Scottsboro Boys" case

in Alabama in the early 1930s. For more on the ILD, see Rebecca N. Hill's useful book, *Men, Mobs, and Law: Anti-Lynching and Labor Defense in U.S. Radical History* (Duke University Press, 2008), 248.
23. Horne, *Black Revolutionary*, 339.
24. Interview with Treuhaft: https://oac.cdlib.org/view?docId=kt4xonbobf;NAAN=13030&doc.view=frames&chunk.id=d0e1426&toc.id=d0e252&brand=calisphere
25. Anthony Ashbolt, *A Cultural History of the Radical Sixties in San Francisco* (Routledge, 2016), 53. Some say that there was a lot of overlap in membership between the Communist Party and the Du Bois Clubs. Left-liberal journalist Jack Newfield maintained that although the Du Bois Clubs would deny it, they were the youth wing of the Communist Party. Their leadership was dominated by kids of Communist Party members. Jack Newfield, *A Prophetic Minority* (Signet, 1967), 124. Howard Brick and Christopher Phelps echo Newfield in *Radicals in America: The US Left Since the Second World War* (Cambridge University Press, 2015), 107. By contrast, O'Shaughnessy's Online argues that the Du Bois Clubs were not a Communist Party front. https://beyondthc.com/remembering-kayo-1/
26. Seale, documentary film, *Berkeley in the Sixties*.
27. The actual membership numbers are a matter of dispute. Huey Newton claimed that after the Sacramento action, the Panthers' phone rang off the hook as they heard from people across the country eager to set up Panther chapters. Newton, quoted in Hilliard, *Huey*, 74. Bobby Seale claimed the Panthers numbered about 75. However, the historian David Garrow usefully notes that David Hilliard put the figure at 12 and Don Cox at between 5 and 10. See Garrow, "Picking Up," 652.
28. Lewis Cole, Interview with Alex Hoffmann, Columbia University Black Panther Project (CUBPP), 6.
29. Melanie Kask, "Soul Mates: The Prison Letters of Eldridge Cleaver and Beverly Axelrod," PhD diss. (University of California, Berkeley, 1971), 195.
30. Cleaver had taken classes in San Quentin as part of a short-lived experimental program with Chris Lovdjieff, a teacher who exposed his pupils to literature, world history, philosophy, economics, and comparative religion. Cleaver wrote an article about him for *Esquire*. Kathleen Rout, *Eldridge Cleaver* (Twayne Publishers, 1991), 81.
31. For the back story of their relationship, see Kask, "Soul Mates," 3–4.
32. Lise Pearlman, *Call Me Phaedra: The Life and Times of Movement Lawyer Fay Stender* (Regent, 2018), 113.
33. Nancy Zaroulis and Gerald Sullivan, *Who Spoke Up? American Protest Against the War in Vietnam, 1963–1975* (Doubleday, 1984), 51.
34. As evidence of Axelrod's having a foot in both the Old and New Left, when she served as Jerry Rubin's attorney in his August 1966 appearance in Washington, DC, before the House Committee on Un-American Activities, she stayed with the longtime left-wing peace activist and DC resident, Donna Allen.
35. Elizabeth Martínez, "*Social Justice* Salutes Beverly Axelrod," *Social Justice* 29, no. 1–2 (2002): 186.
36. https://www.sfchronicle.com/bayarea/article/Beverly-Axelrod-attorney-to-Black-Panthers-2805883.php

37. The memories of her friend Patrick and of Frank Browning are in Beverly Axelrod File, Box 6, Stew Albert and Judy Gumbo Albert Papers, Labadie Collection, University of Michigan, hereafter SAJGAP-UMSCRC.
38. In 1954, when Axelrod moved to San Francisco, Garry was himself head of the city's chapter of the National Lawyers Guild. Kask, "Soul Mates," 27.
39. Author's Interview with Anne Weills.
40. Kask, "Soul Mates," 56.
41. Cleaver himself would write about the Twist, calling it "a guided missile launched from the ghetto into the heart of suburbia." Cleaver, *Soul on Ice* (Delta Books, 1968), 191–204.
42. Kask, "Soul Mates," 29.
43. Kask, "Soul Mates," 155.
44. Kask, "Soul Mates," 1401–404.
45. Cleaver, *Soul on Ice*, 21.
46. Kask, "Soul Mates," 79n74.
47. Axelrod wrote Cleaver about sharing their story with the lawyer, Fay Stender. Kask, "Soul Mates," 1812.
48. Kask, "Soul Mates," 66.
49. Alex Hoffmann, quoted in Hilliard, *This Side*, 144.
50. Jasmine Guy, *Afeni Shakur: Evolution of a Revolutionary* (Atria Books, 2004), 143.
51. Kask, Soul Mates," xix.
52. Kask, Soul Mates," 35.
53. Lewis Cole Interview with Dan Siegel, Columbia University Black Panther Project, 2–3.
54. Bill Bradley (now Dr. Oba T'Shaka) was the head of SF CORE.
55. Letters from Laverne Williams, BAP-DU, Box 1.B, Box 2, F 25; Kask, "Soul Mates," 961.
56. Kask, Soul Mates, 116.
57. Kask, "Soul Mates," 393.
58. Journalist Don Schanche spent time with Cleaver, and is quoted in Rout, *Eldridge Cleaver*, 81.
59. Kask, "Soul Mates," 974.
60. Hilliard, *Huey*, 109.
61. Hilliard, *Huey*, 112.
62. Rout, *Eldridge Cleaver*, 133.
63. Eldridge Cleaver, Introduction to Jerry Rubin, *Do It!* (Simon and Schuster, 1970), 10–11; Stew Albert, "White Radicals, Black Panthers, and a Sense of Fulfillment," in *Liberation, Imagination, and the Black Panther Party*, ed. Kathleen Cleaver and George Katsiaficas (Routledge, 2001), 189; Rout, *Eldridge Cleaver*, 23.
64. Newton had been incarcerated with FSM protestors, too, but it was Cleaver who brokered the partnership.
65. Cleaver, "Introduction to Rubin," in *Do It*, 10–11; Kask, "Soul Mates."
66. Albert, "White Radicals," 188.
67. Amiri Baraka claims that he, Ed Bullins, and Marvin X had been operating out of the Black House in San Francisco. When Baraka was out of town, Eldridge Cleaver came on the scene and forced out Bullins and Marvin X. See Brown, "A Conversation with Amiri Baraka."

68. Hilliard, *Huey*, 114; Rout, *Eldridge*, 44.
69. Newton, *Revolutionary Suicide*, 194.
70. Hilliard, *This Side*, 438.
71. Jo-Ann Morgan, *The Black Arts Movement and the Black Panther Party in American Visual Culture* (Taylor & Francis, 2018), 80.
72. Kask, "Soul Mates," 119; Seale, *Seize*, 182; Morgan, *Black Arts*.
73. While Cleaver was in prison, Axelrod's life contracted and his began to expand as word of his talent spread. They fought, and at least one friend says that he beat her, which was not, it seems, uncharacteristic of Cleaver.
74. Beverly Axelrod, Interview with Roz Payne, "Movement Lawyers Tell Their Stories About BPP Legal Cases." https://video-alexanderstreet-com.libproxy1.usc.edu/watch/movement-lawyers?utm_campaign=Video&utm_medium=MARC&utm_source=aspresolver
75. Baraka says that "the sisters" at the Black House were very critical of Cleaver for still "tipping around seeing his lawyer and old love, Beverly Axelrod." Baraka, *The Autobiography*, 251.
76. Baraka, *The Autobiography*, 251.
77. Hilton Als, "Amiri Baraka's First Family," *The New Yorker*, January 11, 2014.
78. Hoffmann quoted in Kask, "Soul Mates," xx.
79. Newton, *Revolutionary Suicide*, 194–95.
80. Cleaver's ambivalence about his relationship to Axelrod grew untenable. But even as his relationship with Neal deepened, Cleaver insisted in a letter to Axelrod that he loved her and believed she belonged to him and that they were "as one." Eldridge Cleaver Letter to Beverly Axelrod, November 6, 1967, Box 12, F 12, Beverly Axelrod Papers, University of Delaware (BAP-UD).
81. Letters from Laverne Williams, BAP-UD, C., Box 7, F 18–19; Hilliard, *This Side*, 146. The letter was sent by Newton, then incarcerated in Oakland, to Williams on December 7, 1967.
82. Author Interview with Melanie Kask, April 16, 2021.
83. Cox, *Just Another*, 55. Cox says that the Panthers abandoned the scheme after Eldridge Cleaver's violent ambush of the police in the wake of Martin Luther King's murder in April 1968. However, Axelrod was already living in New Mexico by that point.
84. William E. Berry, "Ex-Black Panther Leader Eldridge Cleaver," *Jet*, October 18, 1973.
85. Martínez, "*Social Justice* Salutes Beverly Axelrod," 186.
86. Cecil Brown, "Afterword: Eldridge Cleaver, My Running Buddy," in Eldridge Cleaver, *Target Zero: A Life in Writing* (St. Martin's Press, 2015), 321–22.
87. Murch, *Living for the City*, 84; Author's Interview with Kask.
88. Judy Gumbo, *Yippie Girl* (Three Room Press, 2022), 322. Author's Interview with Kate Coleman, August 9, 2020.

CHAPTER SEVEN

1. Patterson claims that the idea for the "Free Huey!" campaign originated with him. Panther leader Dave Hilliard backs up Patterson's account. He says Patterson even tried to talk Huey Newton's mother into going on a Communist Party–sponsored world tour to talk about her son's case. Mamie Till-Mobley gave talks around the country to shine a light on the horrors of her son Emmett's death in 1955. It is true that Patterson was an old hand at organizing defense committees of this kind. His biographer Gerald

Horne believes that he did play an outsized role in the Free Huey! campaign. However, the evidence cited by Horne is mostly from 1969, which is after the Free Huey! campaign was launched in the fall of 1967. See Hilliard and Cole, *This Side*, 144–45, and Horne, *Black Revolutionary*, 195–97.
2. On Garry and his relationship to the Panthers, see Katherine Bishop, "Charles R. Garry, 82, a Lawyer Known for Radical Clients in 60's," *NYT*, August 18, 1991; Hilliard, *Huey*, 91, 185–86; Newton, *Revolutionary Suicide*, 194–95; Roz Payne Interview with Beverly Axelrod: Movement Lawyers Tell Their Stories About BPP Legal Cases: https://video-alexanderstreet-com.libproxy1.usc.edu/watch/movement-lawyers?utm_campaign=Video&utm_medium=MARC&utm_source=aspresolver
3. Stew Albert said he was an ex-communist. Albert, "White Radicals," 189; Luca Falciola, *Up Against the Law: Radical Lawyers and Social Movements, 1960s–1970s* (University of North Carolina Press, 2022), 273–74.
4. Hill, *Men, Mobs, and Law*, 248.
5. Hilliard says that it was Cleaver who pushed for the party to hire Garry. Hilliard, *This Side*, 144.
6. Joel Wilson alleges that Axelrod was a communist, but there's no evidence she was, beyond the FBI's belief she was. Wilson, "Invisible Cages: Racialized Politics and the Alliance Between the Panthers and the Peace and Freedom Party," in *In Search of the Black Panther Party*, ed. Jama Lazerow and Yohuru Williams (Duke University Press, 2006), 217n17.
7. Healey and Isserman, *Dorothy Healey*, 212.
8. Hilliard, *This Side*, 127; [Eldridge Cleaver], Editorial: "White 'Mother Country' Radicals," *Black Panther*, July 20, 1967, 1.
9. Hilliard, *This Side*, 144–45.
10. Bloom and Martin, *Black Against Empire*, 109.
11. Wilson, "Invisible Cages," 194.
12. FBI memo, CounterIntelligence Program, October 14, 1968, in Box 12, FBI—Huey P. Newton folder, SAJGAP-UMSCRC.
13. Eldridge Cleaver, "*Playboy* Interview," in *Eldridge Cleaver, Post-Prison Writings and Speeches*, ed. Robert Scheer (Ramparts, 1969), 198.
14. Charles E. Jones and Judson L. Jeffries, "'Don't Believe the Hype': Debunking the Panther Mythology," in *The Black Panther Party Reconsidered*, ed. Charles E. Jones (Black Classic Press, 1998), 39.
15. Hilliard, *This Side*, 141.
16. Huggins quoted in Murch, "When the Panther Travels," 59. See also Eldridge Cleaver's October 1968 "The Stanford Speech," in *Eldridge Cleaver, Post-Prison*, 143–44.
17. Ramparts writer Gene Marine quoted in Wilson, "Invisible Cages," 204.
18. Cleaver quoted in Gilbert Moore, *A Special Rage* (Harper & Row, 1971), 73.
19. Hilliard, *This Side*, 147.
20. This is also the view advanced in Bloom and Martin, *Black Against Empire*, 109.
21. Robyn C. Spencer, *The Revolution Has Come: Black Power, Gender, and the Black Panther Party in Oakland* (Duke University Press, 2016), 80.
22. Falciola, *Up Against the Law*, 93.

23. Andrew Fearnley, "The Black Panther Party's Publishing Strategies and the Financial Underpinnings of Activism, 1968–1975," *Historical Journal* 62, no. 1 (2019): 200.
24. Bloom and Martin, *Black Against Empire*, 2.
25. Seale, *Seize*, 213–14.
26. Payne, *I've Got the Light*, 380. Cleveland Sellers claims that by February 1968 SNCC was "virtually defunct." Sellers, *The River*, 247.
27. Payne, *I've Got the* Light, 111–12.
28. Hall, *Peace and Freedom*, 126.
29. Forman, *Black Revolutionaries*, 528.
30. Carmichael quoted in Hall, *Peace and Freedom*, 144.
31. Robert Williams quoted in Hall, *Peace and Freedom*, 190n11.
32. Carmichael, *Ready*, 660. Cleveland Sellers claims that James Forman wanted to take over the Panthers. See Sellers, *The River*, 247.
33. Carmichael, *Ready*, 660.
34. Sellers, *The River*, 247.
35. Newton, *Revolutionary Suicide*, 162.
36. Carmichael, *Ready*, 670.
37. Carmichael, *Ready*, 662; Healey and Isserman, *Dorothy Healey*, 211.
38. Forman, *The Making*, 534. See Rhodes, *Framing*, 83; Kask, "Soul Mates," viii.
39. Brown quoted in Bloom and Martin, *Black Against Empire*, 112; Rickey Vincent and Boots Riley, *Party Music: The Inside Story of the Black Panthers' Band* (Lawrence Hill Books, 2013), 234.
40. Brown, "A Conversation with Amiri Baraka," 179–95.
41. Cleaver on SNCC people being Black hippies, *Ramparts* 6, no. 7 (Dec. 14–28, 1968): 44.
42. Bloom and Martin, *Black Against Empire*, 123. The *NYT* claimed that the Panthers forced Forman into a game of Russian roulette, with a gun he believed was loaded. Forman denied that story, calling it a "vicious lie," but he admitted that the Panthers had threatened him. Forman, *The Making*, 522.
43. Carmichael, *Ready*, 671, 664–72.
44. "B.P.P. and P.F.P.," Editorial, *Black Panther*, March 16, 1968.
45. "Huey Talks to *The Movement*," August 1968. Newton said that the Panthers have "NEVER been controlled by white people." Hilliard, *This Side*, 168–70.
46. Forman, *The Making*, 459.
47. Wilson, "Invisible Cages," 204.
48. Ernie Mkalimoto, "Revolutionary Black Culture: The Cultural Arm of Revolutionary Nationalism," *Negro Digest* 19, no. 2 (Dec. 1969): 16.
49. Anthony was also an informant. https://www.aaihs.org/earl-anthony-and-the-black-panther-party/
50. Joseph, *Waiting 'til the Midnight Hour*, 219.
51. For the FBI involvement, see the October 10, 1968, memo from the Los Angeles Bureau to Hoover regarding the bureau's plan to intensify the tensions. FBI memo, CounterIntelligence Program, in Box 12, Huey P. Newton folder, Stew Albert and Judy Gumbo Albert Papers, University of Michigan Special Collections Research Center, hereafter SAJGAP-UMSCRC.
52. Amiri Baraka was with Karenga the night of the shoot-out. His account of Karenga's nearly hysterical reaction to the phone call alerting him to the shoot-out suggests that

US had not planned the deadly attack. Woodard, *Nation Within a Nation*, 119–20; Scot Brown, *Fighting for US* (NYU Press, 2003), 98–99.
53. Newton, *Revolutionary*, 183.
54. Joy Ann Williamson, "Community Control with a Black Nationalist Twist," *Counterpoints* 237 (2005): 150.
55. See Donna Murch on the Panthers: https://isreview.org/issue/100/roots-black-panther-party
56. Spencer, *The Revolution*, 82–83.
57. "Editorial: BPP and PFP," *Black Panther*, March 16, 1968, 3.
58. James T. Campbell, "The Panthers and Local History," in *In Search of the Black Panther Party*, ed. Jama Lazerow and Yohuru Williams (Duke University Press, 2006), 99; Cox, *Just Another*, 73.
59. Kathleen Cleaver quoted in Murch, *Living for the City*, 235.
60. Cox, *Just Another*, 107; Murch, *Living for the City*, 186.
61. Hilliard, *This Side*, 168.
62. Hilliard, *This Side*, 168.
63. T. J. English, *The Savage City* (William Morrow, 2011), 290–91.
64. Seale, *Seize*, 256.
65. "B.P.P. and P.F.P.," Editorial, *Black Panther*, March 16, 1968.
66. Hilliard recalls seeing Carmichael on TV, waving a .22 and advocating retribution. Hilliard, *This Side*, 183. Tom Hayden says that he heard this from friends. See Hayden, *Reunion*, 269.
67. Cole Interview with Siegel, CUBPP, 30–34.
68. Murray Kempton, *The Briar Patch: The People of the State of New York v. Lumumba Shakur et al.* (Delta, 1973), 75; English, *The Savage City*, 266–69.
69. Justin Gifford, *Revolution*, 172. For a wonderful reminiscence, see Bud Johns, "My Tenants, the Black Panthers," *The New Fillmore*, December 1, 2009, accessed April 5, 2025: https://newfillmore.com/2009/12/01/my-tenants-the-black-panthers/
70. Hilliard, *This Side*, 289.
71. Healey and Isserman, *Dorothy Healey*, 211.
72. Interview with Elsa Knight Thompson, Oral History of the Black Panther Party, BAP-UD, Box 1.B, Box 2, F 25, 12. Thompson and Hoffmann were very close, and both were friends of Beverly Axelrod.
73. Fearnley, "The Black Panther Party's Publishing Strategies," 209.
74. Morrison quoted in Joy James, "The Other Toni Morrison," *Boston Review*, August 7, 2019. The interview was with Hilton Als.
75. Curt Schleier, "How It Was Done," *NYT*, July 12, 1970, 197.
76. Hoffmann quoted in Hilliard, *This Side*, 146.
77. Pearlman, *Call Me*, 144.
78. Spencer, *The Revolution*, 82.
79. One noteworthy exception is Fearnley, "The Black Panther Party's Publishing Strategies."
80. Jane Rhodes, relying on a government investigation of the Black Panther newspaper, says that by 1970 circulation of the paper reached 140,000 copies, providing a monthly revenue of $40,000. Fully one-third of all papers were sold in the Bay Area, and the rest shipped to cities across America, with a small number shipped abroad. Rhodes, *Framing*, 105, 296. According to Congressional investigators, in 1969 alone, the Panthers

made 189 appearances on high-school or college campuses and charged speaking fees that went as high as $1,900. Both the number of talks and the fees seem very high for 1969. See "Gun-Barrel Politics: The Black Panther Party, 1966–71," U.S. House of Representatives, 1971, 85.
81. The Episcopalian ministers stipulated that their money not go to the purchase of guns, although it's not clear that requests of that sort were honored. Fearnley, "The Black Panther Party's Publishing Strategies," 200.
82. Author's Interview with Wasserman.
83. Bloom and Martin, *Black Against Empire*, 211.
84. Fearnley, "The Black Panther Party's Publishing Strategies," 207.
85. Hilliard, *This Side*, 197; Michael Levenson, "FBI Monitored Aretha," *NYT*, October 12, 2022.
86. It was the funeral for Bobby Hutton. Stefan Kanfer, *Somebody: The Reckless Life and Remarkable Career of Marlon Brando* (Vintage, 2008), 229. Author's Interview with Wasserman.
87. Hilliard, *This Side*, 259.

CHAPTER EIGHT

1. Healey and Isserman, *Dorothy Healey*, 204.
2. Huey Newton, "The Correct Handling of a Revolution," *The Black Panther* 1, no. 5 (July 20, 1967): 5.
3. Huey P. Newton, *Revolutionary*, 354–55; Hilliard, *Huey*, 126–27.
4. Hilliard, *This Side*, 175–76.
5. Karen Grigsby Bates, "Bobby Hutton: The Killing That Catapulted the Black Panthers to Fame," NPR, April 6, 2018, https://www.npr.org/2018/04/06/600055767/bobby-hutton-the-killing-that-catapulted-the-black-panthers-to-fame
6. Hilliard, *This Side*, 183; Kate Coleman, "Souled Out," *New West* Magazine, May 19, 1980.
7. Had Hutton listened to Cleaver and not been too embarrassed to shed all his clothes, the police likely would not have killed him. Bates, "Bobby Hutton."
8. Hilliard, *This Side*, 328.
9. This is Alex Hoffmann's memory. See Hilliard, *This Side*, 194.
10. Cleaver made that statement in an interview with a producer for PBS's *Frontline*. See David and Margaret Talbot, *By the Light of Burning Dreams* (Harper Collins, 2019), 89. And Gifford, *Revolution or Death*, 160–61.
11. Dixon, *My People*, 123. Brown, *A Taste of Power*, 151–52. "Fired on Police," *Madera Tribune*, August 6, 1968. https://cdnc.ucr.edu/?a=d&d=MT19680806.2.3&e=------en--20--1-txt-txIN———1
12. Dixon, *My People*, 126–28.
13. Bay Area TV Archive at San Francisco State University, accessed April 6, 2025: https://batv.quartexcollections.com/Documents/Detail/opd-officers-attack-black-panther-headquarters/155
14. Gifford, *Revolution or Death*, 168.
15. David Farber, *Chicago '68* (University of Chicago Press, 1988), 190.
16. The Yippies were a part of the coalition staging the Chicago demonstrations, and Seale reportedly agreed to address the rally after Cleaver, who was still close to Yippie leaders Jerry Rubin and Stew Albert, urged him to do so. Cleaver argued that the Panthers

should judge these young white rebels generously. Their cultural rebelliousness might mature into genuine revolutionary politics. Cleaver spoke of "disenchanted alienated white youth, the hippies, the yippies . . . as our allies." See Cleaver's statement in the Yippie Panther Pact issue of the *Berkeley Barb*, October 4–20, 1968.
17. Hilliard, *This Side*, 264–65. Hilliard served time for his role in the Panthers' April 1968 ambush of the Oakland police, but a federal judge dismissed the indictment against Hilliard for threatening the life of President Nixon. See Earl Caldwell's account of the alleged death threat saga in "Panther Is Released Because of Wiretap, *NYT*, May 5, 1971, https://www.nytimes.com/1971/05/05/archives/panther-is-released-because-of-wiretap-panther-released-because-of.html
18. Hoffmann quoted in Hilliard, *This Side*, 179; Hilliard, *Huey*, 166.
19. See Gumbo, *Yippie Girl*, 116–21. Also useful is the remembrance of the Cleavers by the man who was briefly their landlord when they lived at 2777 Pine Street. Jones, "My Tenants, The Black Panthers."
20. Gifford, *Revolution or Death*, 172–73.
21. Brown, *A Taste of Power*, 216–25; Hilliard, *This Side*, 158.
22. Hilliard, *This Side*, 158.
23. Hilliard, *This Side*, 182. Phyllis Willner offers a corroborating story. She remembers the Panthers coming to the Diggers' Free Store because the Panthers were interested in doing something similar and in offering free food. The Panthers were not interested in maintaining a steady relationship with the Diggers. However, when Emmett Grogan died in 1978, Huey Newton came to the party to celebrate his life. Jay Babcock, "For the Duration of Our Parallel Flow: An Epic Interview with Phyllis Willner," Diggers Docs, accessed July 6, 2024: https://diggersdocs.org/. According to Aaron Dixon, the idea for the Breakfast for School Children Program was first advanced by Oakland member Glen Stafford. Dixon notes that some Panthers doubted that this was a revolutionary program. See Dixon, *My People Are Rising*, 167.
24. The September 7, 1968, edition of *The Black Panther* includes an announcement from Cleaver and Newton about breakfast for Black children being served at three locations in North and West Oakland, 7. Murch notes that there is a discrepancy in the timing and the location of the first Breakfast for School Children Program. She puts the date in October or November 1968. See Murch, *Living for the City*, 264n2.
25. Bloom and Martin, *Black Against Empire*, 13.
26. Panther artist Emory Douglas, the party's Minister of Culture, captured this shift in his depiction of a "survival nurse" in the March 21, 1970, issue of the party newspaper. Spencer, *The Revolution*, 117.
27. "The Panther and the Law," *Newsweek* 75, no. 8 (Feb. 23, 1970).
28. Eldridge Cleaver made this claim about Newton's prediction in his introduction to Rubin's *Do It*, 8.
29. Alex Hoffmann remembers this detail in Hilliard, *This Side*, 261. Hoffmann, who often visited Newton in prison, had been a member of the CP front group, the Labor Youth League (LYL), which was responsive to the critique of Stalinism. Hoffmann never joined the CP. He likely was the person who gave Newton the biography. Cole Interview of Alex Hoffmann, CUBPP. When he was in the Bay Area, Cleaver reportedly hung a poster of Stalin in his office and home. Cleaver remained involved in editing the party's newspaper even after he had left the United States. See Kathleen Rout, *Eldridge Cleaver* (Boston: Twayne Publishers, 1991), 123.

30. Cox, *Just Another*, 126.
31. Kathleen Cleaver quoted in Stanley Nelson's documentary, *Black Panther: The Vanguard of the Revolution*.
32. Bloom and Martin, *Black Against Empire*, 184–87; Edward P. Morgan, "Media Culture and the Public Memory of the Black Panther Party," in *In Search of the Black Panther Party*, ed. Jama Lazerow and Yohuru Williams (Duke University Press, 2006), 335.
33. Paul Bass and Douglas W. Rae, *Murder in the Model City: The Black Panthers, Yale, and the Redemption of a Killer* (Basic Books, 2006), 102–4; "Hoover Calls Panthers Top Threat to Security," *Washington Post*, July 16, 1969.
34. These figures were the FBI's own. Paul Alkebulan, *Survival Pending Revolution: The History of the Black Panther Party* (University of Alabama Press, 2007), 49.
35. FBI memo, CounterIntelligence Program, October 14, 1968, in Box 12, FBI—Huey P. Newton folder, SAJGAP-UMSCRC; Bass and Rae, *Murder*, 114–15.
36. Dixon, *My People*, 243.
37. Lewis Cole Interview with Martin Kenner, CUBPP, 67.
38. Cox, *Just Another*, 88–92; Carmichael, *Ready*, 670.
39. Forbes, *Will You*, 2.
40. Peniel E. Joseph described it as Janus-faced as well. See Peniel E. Joseph, "The Black Power Movement, Democracy, and America in the King Years," *American Historical Review* 114, no. 4, October 2009. For the party's growth, see Bloom and Martin, *Black Against Empire*, 2.
41. Robert E. Lee (Bob Lee), quoted in Jeb Aram Middlebrook, "Organizing a Rainbow Coalition of Revolutionary Solidarity," *Journal of African American Studies* 23 (2019): 427.
42. Hilliard, *This Side*, 258–59.
43. Nixon's domestic policy chief, John Ehrlichman, later admitted that the Nixon campaign and White House believed it "had two enemies: the antiwar left and black people." Ehrlichman also claimed that because the administration knew it could not outlaw protests, it "staged a War on Drugs" to disrupt the Movement. Ehrlichman quoted in Steve Gillon, *Separate and Unequal: The Kerner Commission and the Unraveling of American Liberalism* (Basic Books, 2018), 296. In a December 17, 1968, editorial, the *New York Times* questioned Nixon's decision to retain Hoover. "Only a few weeks ago he declared that 'justice is incidental to law and order,'" which the *Times* noted was a strange comment from the head of an agency which at least theoretically comes under the Department of Justice."
44. David Burnham, "Panthers to Seek Voice over Police," *NYT*, September 11, 1968.
45. Burnham, "Panthers to Seek Voice."
46. Catherine Breslin, "One Year Later: The Radicalization of the Panther 13 Jury," *New York Magazine*, May 29, 1972, 59.
47. Stephen George Chaberski, "The Strategy of Defense in a Political Trial: The Trial of the 'Panther 21,'" PhD diss. (Columbia University, 1975), 23.
48. Chaberski, "The Strategy," 30–31.
49. Earl Caldwell, "Panther Is Given 15-Year Sentence," *NYT*, October 30, 1969, 39.
50. For a solid account of Hampton's murder and the effort to seek justice, see the book by lawyer Jeffrey Haas, *The Assassination of Fred Hampton* (Chicago Review Press, 2019).

51. Matthew Fleischer, "Opinion: Fifty Years Ago, LAPD Raided the Black Panthers," *LAT*, December 8, 2019.
52. Cleaver, quoted in the documentary *The Black Panthers: Vanguard of the Revolution* (Stanley Nelson, 2015).
53. Bass and Rae, *Murder*, 102–4.
54. Yohuru Williams, "No Haven: From Civil Rights to Black Power in New Haven, Connecticut," *The Black Scholar* 31, no. 3–4 (2001): 61.
55. Frances Carter quoted in Williams, "No Haven"; Bass and Rae, *Murder*, 102–5.
56. Jessica Seigel, "New Haven," *Liberation News Service*, April 24, 1971, 1. Gail Sheehy, "The Consequences of Panthermania," *New York*, November 23, 1970, 62.
57. Carmichael argued that the actions of white radicals were leading the country into fascism. James M. Fallows, "Carmichael Attacks White Radicals for Causing Repression of Blacks," *Harvard Crimson*, April 23, 1970. About Sams, Carmichael said that he had learned in May 1969 that he was an agent but had been unable to inform the Panthers because he was living in Africa. Some accounts suggest that Sams may have been an agent, but Bass and Rae, authors of *Murder in the Model City*, insist there is no corroborating evidence. Joseph Lelyveld, "Former Panther Tells of Dispute," *NYT*, August 8, 1970; Joseph Lelyveld, "Prosecution Rests in Panther Trial in New Haven," *NYT*, August 12, 1970; Garrett Epps, "The Trial of Bobby Seale," *Harvard Crimson*, April 28, 1970.
58. See Morgan, "Media Culture."
59. "Times Reporter Gets a Subpoena," *NYT*, February 3, 1970.
60. Richard Prince, *Journal-isms*, October 21, 2023, https://www.journal-isms.com/feds-targeted-black-reporter-author-says/
61. J. Anthony Lucas, "Seale Found in Contempt," *NYT*, November 6, 1969. It was one of many first-page, above-the-fold stories that the *Times* ran on the Panthers.
62. Hilliard, *This Side*, 181; Gumbo, *Yippie Girl*, 117–18.
63. Email correspondence with Martin Kenner, February 16, 2022. Kenner recalls having dinner with Hoffman at Max's Kansas City in New York when he turned over the entire advance for *Revolution for the Hell of It*. Hoffman did not come from money, nor did he have much money; Edith Evans Asbury, "Panther Counsel Pressed by Judge," *NYT*, March 25, 1970.
64. Gumbo, *Yippie Girl*, 116.
65. Committee on Internal Security, House of Representatives, Black Panther Party, Part 1, Testimony of Richard A. Shaw, March 1970, 4737–38, https://books.google.com/books?id=193zTOIPNwMC&newbks=1&newbks_redir=0&printsec=frontcover&source=gbs_ge_summary_r&cad=0#v=onepage&q&f=false
66. See the March 1970 Hearings on the Black Panther Party before the Committee on Internal Security, House of Representatives, 4737–38, https://www.google.com/books/edition/Black_Panther_Party_Hearings_Before/193zTOIPNwMC?hl=en&gbpv=1&dq=panther+mark+comfort+CPUSA&pg=RA4-PA4737&printsec=frontcover
67. Healey and Isserman, *Dorothy Healey*, 212. In an article in *Public Affairs*, William Patterson argued that the Panthers were beginning to see the error of the Maoist "go-it-alone" approach to change, that they needed to achieve working-class unity across the color line. His article is quoted in the California State Legislature, "Un-American Activities in California," *Journal of the Senate*, 1970.

68. Joan Didion, *The White Album* (Pocket Books, 1979), 31. Garry quotation drawn from the actual interview: https://americanarchive.org/catalog/cpb-aacip_28-b853f4m063
69. Carmichael, *Ready*, 662.
70. Patterson quoted in Horne, *Black Revolutionary*, 198; Cleaver quoted in Dixon, *My People*, 140.
71. Kask, "Soul Mates," 1228; Cleaver quoted in Gifford, *Revolution or Death*, 130. This quote is from the paper "The New National Black Leadership," n.d., in Kathleen Cleaver's archive.
72. Art Goldberg, who had been an editor at *Ramparts* magazine, wrote the book based on barely edited transcribed conversations with Seale. See Fearnley, "The Black Panther Party's Publishing Strategies," 211.
73. The *Black Panther*, June 7, 1969.
74. His stance may not have reflected the influence of the CP. Newton could have come to this position after reading the left-wing literature on imperialism. See Huey P. Newton, "On the Peace Movement: August 15, 1969," in *The Huey P. Newton Reader*, ed. David Hilliard and Donald Weise (New York: Seven Stories, 2002), 152.
75. Bob Avakian, *From Ike to Mao and Beyond: My Journey from Mainstream America to Revolutionary Communist: A Memoir* (Insight Press, 2005), 213–14; Dorothy Healey attested to the CP's involvement in Healey and Isserman, *Dorothy Healey*, 208.
76. Bloom and Martin, *Black Against Empire*, 300.
77. Earl Anthony, "3000 Radicals, Mostly Whites, Open Panther-Led Unity Parley," *NYT*, July 10, 1969.
78. Advertisements for showings of the movie *Z* in Los Angeles at UCLA and the Europa at Beverly and La Brea appeared in *The Black Panther*, June 7, 1969.
79. Horne, *Black Revolutionary*, 194–95.
80. For his fascinating discussion of Patterson's relationship to the Panthers, see Horne, *Black Revolutionary*, 198–203. On this trip to Oakland, Patterson met other long-time Bay Area CP leaders, including Harry Bridges, who shared with him their deep skepticism about the Panthers.
81. Horne, *Black Revolutionary*, 194–98. The FBI was also concerned about any partnerships between the Panthers and the New Left. See Hoover's June 23, 1969, memo to the San Diego bureau about the forthcoming UFAF conference, Box 12, FBI folder, SAJGAP-UMSCRC.
82. Rudd, *Underground*, 148, 192.
83. Lewis Cole Interview with Martin Kenner, CUBBP.
84. Wilkerson quoted in Burrough, *Days of Rage*, 68.
85. Author's email exchange with Mark Rudd, April 6, 2022.
86. "Panthers Sound Off," *The National Guardian*, June 1968.
87. Rout, *Eldridge*, 73.
88. Ayers said this in an interview with Amy Goodman, on the occasion of his son's podcast, "Mother Country Radicals," August 1, 2022.
89. Jane Alpert, *Growing Up Underground* (William Morrow & Company, 1981), 199.
90. David Barber, "Leading the Vanguard," in *In Search of the Black Panther Party*, ed. Jama Lazerow and Yohuru Williams (Duke University Press, 2006), 234–38.
91. "UFAF Conference," *Old Mole*, August 1969, reprinted in *The U.S. Antifascism Reader*, ed. Bill V. Mullen and Christopher Vials (Verso, 2020), 274–76.

92. Harold Jacobs, ed., *Weatherman* (Ramparts, 1971), 143. Rudd, *Underground*, 192.
93. Bill Ayers quoted in Jeremy Peter Varon, *The Weather Underground, The Red Army Faction, and Revolutionary Violence in the Sixties and Seventies* (University of California Press, 2004), 155.
94. Hampton quoted, by way of Tappis, in Hilliard, *This Side*, 258.
95. Burrough, *Days of Rage*, 73. For another account, see Jonathan Lerner, *Swords in the Hands of Children* (OR Books, 2017), 98–124.
96. Arthur Eckstein, *Bad Moon: How the Weather Underground Beat the FBI and Lost the Revolution* (Yale University Press, 2016), 71–72.
97. Eckstein, *Bad Moon*, 68–71.
98. Eckstein, *Bad Moon*, 66–69.
99. Hampton quoted in David Barber, "Leading the Vanguard," 239.
100. Eckstein, *Bad Moon*, 73.
101. Hilliard claims the police invaded the Black community and killed two kids. Hilliard, *This Side*, 258.
102. Eldridge Cleaver, "Cleaver on Weathermen," *The Berkeley Tribe*, 7–13, 1969, 22.
103. Barber, "Leading the Vanguard," 240.
104. Eckstein, *Bad Moon*, 31–32.
105. Eckstein, *Bad Moon*, 37.
106. Kopkind quoted in Eckstein, *Bad Moon*, 39; 37–40. A full 10 months later, Bernardine Dohrn revealed that a Weatherman cell was responsible for the bombing of Judge Murtagh's home.
107. Barber, "Leading the Vanguard," 243.
108. Eckstein, *Bad Moon*, 40.
109. Barber, "Leading the Vanguard," 214.
110. Brown recalls him saying, "Weatherman and all that, and these motherfuckers." Cleaver quoted in Brown, *A Taste of Power*, 223. Cleaver told Elaine Brown this in the summer of 1970, when she was part of a delegation of journalists, including Robert Scheer, in Moscow, on their way to North Korea.
111. One piece of evidence pointing to frayed relations between the Black Panther Party and the CP was Huey Newton's November 9, 1970, letter to Angela Davis, who was then in prison. Davis was briefly a member of both the CP and the Los Angeles Panthers but chose to commit herself exclusively to the CP. Newton assured Davis that even though she was a CP member, that the Panthers would work with the CP to free her. However, he said the Panthers would be doing so despite the "ideological contradictions" between the two organizations. See Huey Newton's FBI file: chrome-extension://efaidnbmnnnibpcajpcglclefindmkaj/https://blackfreedom.proquest.com/wp-content/uploads/2020/09/blackpanther6.pdf
Another piece of evidence is that the CP seems to have not participated in the Panther-organized second Revolutionary People's Constitutional Conference in late November 1970. The CP had been centrally involved in the earlier UFAF conference a year earlier. According to Gerald Horne, the two organizations definitively fell out sometime in 1972–73. In 1972, Newton denounced William Patterson, and the latter attacked as "counterrevolutionary" both Newton's idea of "revolutionary suicide" and Seale's embrace of the Democratic Party. See Horne, *Black Revolutionary*, 203.
112. Author's email exchange with Mark Rudd, April 6, 2022.

PART FOUR

1. Earl Caldwell, "Declining Black Panthers Gather New Support from Repeated Clashes with the Police," *NYT*, December 14, 1969.
2. *Washington Post* reporter Karl Meyer was not a Panther supporter, but he opposed the lack of justice accorded the group. He made this observation in a story Meyer's *Post* editors chose not to run as written. Meyer attached the original article to his January 26, 1970, letter to Felicia Bernstein. See "Materials Related to the Black Panther Fundraiser," 1970, Leonard Bernstein Collection, LOC. https://www.loc.gov/item/2023778824/
3. David Shaw, "Who Are They? What Do They Want?" *Los Angeles Times*, June 15, 1969.
4. The *Wall Street Journal* article appeared above the fold on page 1, January 6, 1970. It was quoted in *Newsday* editorial, "'Out to Get the Panthers,'" January 19, 1970, Box 96 F 1 (1970), TWP/NYPL.
5. Originally, the group was formed by Wilkins and ex–Supreme Court Justice Abe Goldberg, who was replaced by Ramsey Clark. The report, which was delayed for months, excoriated the government. See Thomas A. Johnson, "Report Assails Inquiry on Slaying of Black Panthers," *NYT*, March 17, 1972; "The Panther and the Law," *Newsweek* 75, no. 8 (Feb. 23, 1970); Seth S. King, "Lawyer to Head Panther Inquest," *NYT*, January 1, 1970.
6. In the Bay Area, people holding benefits were more likely to be solidly left-wing. They would include the white Berkeley activist couple Robert Scheer and Anne Weills; Weills recalls that she and her white comrades had "very intimate relationships and alliances with the Panthers." Author's Interview with Weills, November 4, 2021. The Bay Area Movement couple Fay and Marvin Stender, both lawyers, held benefits for SNCC and the Panthers. See Pearlman, *Call Me Phaedra*, 374.
7. Christopher Bonanos, "The Making of Tom Wolfe's 'Radical Chic,'" *Vulture*, May 18, 2018, accessed December 7, 2024: https://www.vulture.com/2018/05/tom-wolfe-radical
8. Joseph Epstein, "The Party's Over," *Commentary* 51, no. 3, March 1, 1971.

CHAPTER NINE

1. Epstein, "'The Party's Over'; Tom Wolfe, 'A City Built of Clay,'" *New York*, July 6, 2008.
2. Christine Stansell, *American Moderns: Bohemian New York and the Creation of a New Century* (Metropolitan Books, 2000), 1, 121. It is worth noting that the involvement of entertainers in charitable work stretches back at least as far as late nineteenth century England. In London's stage culture, women, particularly actresses, made charitable work public facing with the introduction of the fund-raiser. See Catherine Hindson, *London's West End Actresses and the Origins of Celebrity Charity, 1880–1920* (University of Iowa Press, 2016).
3. Stuart Hall coined the phrase "prestige from below" that defined this process. Hall quoted by George Lipsitz, *Time Passages: Collective Memory and American Popular Culture* (University of Minnesota Press, 1990), 283.
4. Stansell, *American Moderns*, 109, 103, 106.
5. Stansell, *American Moderns*, 103–10, 144.

6. Stansell, *American Moderns*, 183, 10.
7. Ellen Carol DuBois, *Suffrage: Women's Long Battle for the Vote* (Simon & Schuster, 2020), 162.
8. Stansell, *American Moderns*, 141, 182.
9. Stansell, *American Moderns*, 313.
10. Tess Slesinger, *The Unpossessed: A Novel of the Thirties* (New York Review of Books Classics, 2002), 213, 219.
11. For a brilliant reflection on Slesinger's work, see Paula Rabinowitz's afterword, "She Had Done It as a Girl," in Tess Slesinger, *Time: The Present—Selected Stories* (Boiler House Press, 2022). Murray Kempton wrote about *The Unpossessed* in his 1955 book, *Part of Our Time: Some Ruins and Monuments of the Thirties* (NYRB, 1998), 121–23.
12. Rebecca Prime, *Hollywood Exiles in Europe* (Rutgers University Press, 2014), 49.
13. Wolfe interviewed MacLeish in June 1955. A transcript of his interview is in Box 75, F 1, TWP/NYPL.
14. For the Sleepy Lagoon defense committee, see Ralph Armbruster-Sandoval, "The Life of the Party: Alice McGrath, Multiracial Coalitions, and the Struggle for Social Justice," *Aztlan: A Journal of Chicano Studies* 36, no. 1 (Spring 2011): 69–98.
15. Armbruster-Sandoval, "The Life of the Party," 72.
16. The GOP often attacked the New Deal for "soaking the poor" through taxation. See, for example, a fall 1936 speech by the Republican vice-presidential nominee that was covered in the *Colorado Springs Gazette*, Oct. 1, 1936.
17. Michael Staub argued that the NAACP's effort to taint Robeson in some respects prefigured the attack on Leonard Bernstein as radical chic. Just as Robeson was attacked as insufficiently Black, so was Leonard Bernstein criticized for being insufficiently Jewish. See Michael E. Staub, *Torn at the Roots: The Crisis of Jewish Liberalism in Postwar America* (Columbia University Press, 2002), 27.
18. I. F. Stone quoted in Sally Belfrage, *Un-American Activities: A Memoir of the Fifties* (HarperCollins, 1994), 131. For the polling, see Belfrage, *Un-American Activities*, 176.
19. Kaufman, *Broken Alliance*, 110.
20. Truman quoted in Stephen J. Whitfield, *The Culture of the Cold War* (Johns Hopkins University Press, 1991), 124.
21. In 1963, Baez took Dylan to the homes of activists Bernard Brighton and Corliss Lamont for fundraising events to benefit the ECLC; another time they visited Clark Foreman at his "grand apartment on Riverside Drive and talked politics all night." David Hajdu, *Positively 4th Street: The Lives and Times of Joan Baez, Bob Dylan, Mimi Baez Fariña, and Richard Fariña* (Farrar, Straus and Giroux, 2001), 168.
22. Elissa Harbert, "1600 Pennsylvania Avenue," in *Leonard Bernstein and Washington, D.C.*, ed. Daniel Abraham et al. (Boydell & Brewer, 2020), 197.
23. Norman Mailer wrote witheringly about "the liberal party." Mailer, *The Armies of the Night*, 375–78.
24. Robert McG. Thomas Jr., "Two Different Parties Were 'The' Place to Be," *NYT*, April 19, 1969.
25. Steinem said that she warned him that some reporters might attack the benefit as a "radical chic" event. She said he was happy to be accused of being chic because the money could do so much for striking farmworkers. Author Interview of Gloria Steinem, July 30, 2020.

26. William F. Buckley Jr., "Don't Go Near the Grapes, Ethel," *Boston Globe*, July 1, 1969, 13.
27. Her colleague David Schneiderman is quoted in Liz Smith, Foreword, Marilyn S. Greenwald, *A Woman of the Times: Journalism, Feminism, and the Career of Charlotte Curtis* (Ohio University Press, 1999), xi.
28. Charlotte Curtis, "Southampton Meets 'La Causa,'" *NYT*, June 30, 1969. Curtis reported that one farmworker said of the appetizers on silver trays being offered guests by uniformed waitresses, "I didn't know if I was allowed to pick up anything or not." However, the farmworker in question was the wife of a high-ranking union official who apparently was joking. See Sydney Ladensohn Stern, *Gloria Steinem: Her Passions, Politics, and Mystique* (Open Road Media, 2023), 170.
29. Steve Fraser, *The Limousine Liberal* (Basic Books, 2016), 21. For an incisive discussion of how white working-class views of liberal politicians shifted, see Robert O. Self, *All in the Family: The Realignment of American Democracy Since the 1960s* (Hill & Wang, 2012), 8–11. Liberals whom the white working class had once believed provided a much-needed financial safety net, were now maligned for making their lives harder, economically and morally, as liberals pushed for racial, gender, and sexual equality.
30. Fraser, *Limousine Liberal*, 17.
31. Author interview of Steinem. One of Steinem's colleagues at *New York* was Pete Hamill, who wrote the much-cited article, "The Revolt of the White Lower Middle Class," *New York*, April 14, 1969.
32. Seymour Krim, "Norman Mailer, Get Out of My Head!" in Seymour Krim, *Missing a Beat: The Rants and Regrets of Seymour Krim* (University of Syracuse Press, 2010), 154.
33. Vivian Gornick, *The Situation and the Story* (Farrar, Straus and Giroux, 2001), 52.
34. Dan Wakefield, *New York in the 50s* (Houghton Mifflin, 1992), 132–33. Wakefield offers a respectful and empathic portrait of Krim. See 132–36, 325, 340–41.
35. Krim quoted in Mark Cohen, "Editor's Introduction," in *Missing a Beat*, xviii.
36. See Krim's "Black English" and "Ask for a White Cadillac" in his *Missing a Beat*. Baldwin defended Krim against his attackers. He claimed he was alone among writers of his generation in being neither "romantic or defensive" about Black people. But if some white writers' idealizing of Black Americans was problematic so was Krim's tendency to pathologize marginalized Black people and their culture. See Cohen, "Editor's Introduction, in Krim, *Missing a Beat*, xxvii.
37. Krim was active in the Peace and Freedom Party in 1968. See Krim, "Black English, or the Motherfucker Culture" in Krim, *Missing a Beat*, 121.
38. "Seymour Krim, "Who's Afraid of the New Yorker Now?" in Krim, *Shake It for The World, Smartass* (Delta, 1970), 171.
39. When Baldwin's "Letter" appeared in book-form it appeared as "Down at the Cross: Letter from a Region in My Mind" in *The Fire Next Time* (The Dial Press, 1963).
40. Krim, "Who's Afraid," 174.
41. Krim, "Who's Afraid," 180.
42. Krim, "Who's Afraid," 185–86.
43. Lynn Nesbit, Letter, Seymour Krim Papers–University of Iowa (hereafter SKP-UI), Box 1, F4. Nesbit represented Tom Wolfe for his long career.

44. In 1969, a year before the publication of "Radical Chic," Krim said that Wolfe was one of the writers whose work he promoted, though he did not need it by then. See Krim, "Norman Mailer," in Krim, *Missing a Beat*, 154.
45. Evidence that people on the left were critiquing the way in which radicalism was becoming "chic" includes Irving Howe's reply to fellow leftist Philip Rahv in which he wrote, "Radicalism is becoming chic in the intellectual world." See Irving Howe, "An Exchange on the Left," *NYRB*, November 23, 1967. Another example is a taped interview with Gloria Steinem, said to be from 1967, in which she criticizes the way that opposing the Vietnam War was becoming chic among intellectuals. Accessed August 2, 2025: https://www.youtube.com/watch?v=ZCi7fdHZ41U
46. Krim's phrase was also used in the spring of 1970 by the left-wing journalist Sidney Bernard about a "radical chic" party held by the *Village Voice* writer Dodson Rader. Bernard said it was a "Mayday extravaganza that *had* to be the New Left's answer to Truman Capote's at the Plaza a few years back.'" Bernard quoted in Kevin T. McEneaney, *Tom Wolfe's America: Heroes, Pranksters, and Fools* (Praeger, 2009), 62.
47. Krim, "Who's Afraid," 186.
48. Ishmael Reed, "Eldridge Cleaver—Writer," in *The Portable Sixties Reader*, ed. Ann Charters (Penguin, 2003), 475. Krim directed his anger toward the magazine, not Baldwin. However, Black writers may have criticized Baldwin's decision to publish in *The New Yorker*. Amiri Baraka (then LeRoi Jones) attacked James Baldwin for being the darling of white liberals in his cruel essay, "Brief Reflections on Two Hot Shots," *Kulchur* 3 (Winter 1963), reprinted in Amiri Baraka, *Home: Social Essays* (William Morrow, 1966). See Zadie Smith on Baraka and the writer Darryl Pinckney's reaction to Baraka's attempted takedown of Baldwin in her foreword, "Thus Far on the Way," in Darryl Pinckney, *Busted in New York and Other Essays* (Farrar, Straus and Giroux, 2019), xviii.
49. Irving Howe, "An Exchange on the Left," *The New York Review of Books*, November 23, 1967.
50. Kazin is quoted in Isaac Chotiner, "Can the Democratic Party Define Itself?" *The New Yorker*, April 19, 2022. For the Democratic Party's platform, see https://www.presidency.ucsb.edu/documents/1968-democratic-party-platform
51. Merle Miller may have been the first person to reveal that Wolfe had not actually coined the term. See Miller, "Why Norman and Jason Aren't Talking," *NYT Magazine*, March 26, 1972. Then, in a June 21, 1987, letter to the *NYT* Book Review, Pamela Walker corrected the reviewer of a recent Bernstein biography who had wrongly attributed the term to Wolfe. For Wolfe's claim, see his letter to the editor of the *NYT Magazine*, March 31, 1972. Box 12, F4, TWP/NYPL. In a *Rolling Stone* interview, Wolfe had this to say: "it took me an awful long time to work out the concept [of radical chic.] I had the phrase in my mind already, radical chic, 'cause I knew that by then there was a fashionable quality to certain radical causes." Chet Flippo, "Tom Wolfe: the *Rolling Stone* Interview," August 21, 1980, reprinted in Dorothy M. Scura, *Conversations with Tom Wolfe* (University Press of Mississippi, 1990), 136. Over the years, the two men exchanged the occasional letter or postcard, but in their archived correspondence, there is no record of Krim objecting to Wolfe's having lied about coining the term.
52. Patricia Sullivan, *Freedom Writer: Virginia Foster Durr, Letters from the Civil Rights Years* (Routledge, 2003), 334.

53. Author's Interview with Robert Scheer, July 30, 2020.
54. For *On the Town*, see Carol J. Oja, *Bernstein Meets Broadway: Collaborative Art in a Time of War* (Oxford University Press, 2014), 180; Barry Seldes, *Leonard Bernstein: The Political Life of an American Musician* (University of California Press, 2009), 43.
55. Seldes, *Leonard Bernstein*, 45.
56. Seldes, *Leonard Bernstein*, 57.
57. Robbins's cooperation with HUAC cost him friends. Zero Mostel, whose name Robbins had named at the HUAC hearing, worked with Robbins, but disdained him. He would not speak to him outside of rehearsals. Author's Interview with Domna Stanton, whose husband was among Mostel's good friends.
58. Sidney Lumet quoted in Jay Rothermel, "Politics & Sidney Lumet," in the blog, Marxist Update, April 16, 2011, http://marxistupdate.blogspot.com/2011/04/politics-sidney-lumet.html
59. The McCarran Act required that organizations that the U.S. government deemed communist register with the government and submit information about their organizations' members, activities, and finances.
60. For Bernstein's blacklisting, see Seldes, *Leonard Bernstein*, 44–86.
61. Nigel Simeone, *The Leonard Bernstein Letters* (Yale University Press, 2014), 310. For his letter, see https://vault.fbi.gov/leonard-bernstein/leonard-bernstein-part-02-of-04/view from 102 to end.
62. Seldes, *Leonard Bernstein*, 70–71.
63. Seldes, *Leonard Bernstein*, 77–79.
64. Seldes, *Leonard Bernstein*, 52–79.
65. Homer Bigart, "McCarthy Talks at Garden; Urges a Vietnam Coalition," *NYT*, Friday August 16, 1968.
66. Seldes, *Leonard Bernstein*, 114.
67. Hoover quoted in "Black Panther Threat to U.S. Security," *Desert Sun*, v. 42 #296, July 16, 1969. Hoover's view was widely covered in the press.
68. Hill, *Men, Mobs, and Law*, 288.
69. Author's Interview with Robert Scheer, July 30, 2020.
70. Morris Kaplan, "Bomb Plot Is Laid to 21 Panthers," *NYT*, April 3, 1969, 1.
71. Kempton, *The Briar Patch*, 33.
72. Interview of John Seale by Lewis Cole, CUBPP, 128.
73. Jasmine Guy, *Afeni Shakur: Evolution of a Revolutionary* (Atria Books, 2004), 79.
74. Mark Rudd, email to author, April 6, 2022. For Rudd's description of the crowd rampaging, see Rudd, *Underground*, 133–34. Jane Alpert wrote about attending a demo for the Panther 21 in December 1969 and seeing Mark Rudd there. Alpert, *Growing Up Underground*, 240.
75. Kempton, *The Briar Patch*, 38–39.
76. The *Washington Post* reporter Karl Meyer laid out the troubling details of the state's treatment of the defendants. See Meyer letter to Bernsteins, Material Related to the Black Panther Fundraiser, LOC. See also Kempton, *The Briar Patch*.
77. Interview with Gerald Lefcourt, Roz Payne Movement Lawyers. Link accessed May 6, 2021, no longer available. Jan Hoffman, "Public Lives: A Witness to the Revolution Recalls Abbie," *NYT*, August 24, 2000.
78. Interview of Martin Kenner by Lewis Cole, CUBPP, 50.

79. Interview of Kenner, CUBPP, 13; author's Interview with Martin Kenner, November 30, 2020.
80. Interview of Kenner, CUBPP, 47–49.
81. The following account of Hannah Weinstein draws heavily from Julia Bricklin, *Red Sapphire: The Woman Who Beat the Blacklist* (Rowman & Littlefield, 2023).
82. For *Mademoiselle*'s description, see Bricklin, *Red Sapphire*, 33. Ring Lardner's speech at the memorial for Hannah Weinstein, quoted in Bricklin, *Red Sapphire*, 3.
83. John J. Abt with Michael Myerson, *Advocate and Activist: Memoirs of an American Communist Lawyer* (University of Illinois Press, 1993), 141.
84. One such response was William Barrett's "On the Horizon: Culture Conference at the Waldorf," *Commentary*, May 1949.
85. Richard Polenberg, *In the Matter of J. Robert Oppenheimer: The Security Clearance Hearing* (Cornell University Press, 2002), 24. For the exchange between Robert Oppenheimer and Hannah Dorner, see United States Atomic Energy Commission, vol. 3, In the Matter of Robert Oppenheimer, April 14, 1954, 342–50, accessed December 19, 2024: chrome-extension://efaidnbmnnnibpcajpcglclefindmkaj/https://upload.wikimedia.org/wikipedia/commons/5/5b/J._Robert_Oppenheimer_Personnel_Hearings_Transcripts%2C_vol._III.pdf
86. Heiko Feldner et al., eds., *The Lost Decade? The 1950s in European History, Politics, Society and Culture* (Cambridge Scholars Publishing, 2011), 233.
87. Weinstein's name did not appear in the credits of Robin Hood, at least not at first. Sid Cole, the associate producer at Ealing Studios, suggested that Weinstein's proposed series be about Robin Hood. "The great thing about Robin Hood is that it enables you to identify with outlaws." Cole had no idea how ideally that resonated with the writers Ring Lardner Jr. and Ian McLellan Hunter and with Howard Koch revising scripts in London. Prime, *Hollywood Exiles in Europe*, 5. On Robin Hood's possible influence on young Americans, see Lardner, *I'd Hate Myself in the Morning* (Prospecta Press, 2017), 134.
88. Interview of Kenner, CUBPP, 53.
89. Author's Interview of Kenner.
90. John Anderson, "Walter Bernstein, Celebrated Screenwriter, Is Dead at 101," *NYT*, January 23, 2021.
91. Wolfe's researcher asks this question in a note to him. Box 96, F 1, TWP/NYPL.
92. Interview of Kenner, CUBPP, 54. Author's Interview with Lisa Weinstein, December 2, 2020, about her family's friendship with the Bernsteins.
93. Marin Alsop, "Bernstein the Inspiration," *The Guardian*, July 12, 2018; Author's Interview with Domna Stanton, September 13, 2019.
94. Roger Wilkins, *A Man's Life: An Autobiography* (Simon & Schuster, 1982), 269.
95. Interview of Kenner, CUBPP. Wolfe thought the planners wanted to attract Bigart. See Elon Green, "Annotation Tuesday! Tom Wolfe and Radical Chic," May 13, 2014, https://niemanstoryboard.org/stories/annotation-tuesday-tom-wolfe-and-radical-chic/
96. Patrick J. Buchanan, *Nixon's White House Wars: The Battles That Made and Broke a President and Divided America Forever* (Crown, 2017), 326.
97. Kenner Interview, CUBPP, 62. Author's Interview with Kenner, September 23, 2020.

98. Jamie Bernstein recalled that her mother "pointedly did not invite any press to the fund-raiser." Jamie Bernstein, *Famous Father Girl: A Memoir of Growing Up Bernstein* (Harper, 2018), 110. Yet there were journalists there, and in their capacity as journalists.
99. Earl Caldwell, "Declining Black Panthers Gather New Support from Repeated Clashes with Police, *NYT*, December 14, 1969, 64.
100. Dan Wakefield, "Open Journal," review of the Commentary Reader," *NYT*, August 7, 1966. Conservative critic Roger Kimball, writing in the *New Criterion*, denounced the "hypocrisy" of the *NYRB*. See Kimball, "Nostalgia for Molotovs: 'The New York Review,'" April 1998.
101. James Wolcott, "Thirty-Five Years of Fireworks," *NYRB*, October 4, 1998.
102. See Nathan Miller, "Some in 'In Group' Counterattack Radical Chic," *Baltimore Sun*, December 20, 1970.

CHAPTER TEN

1. Author's interview with Domna Stanton.
2. Harry Belafonte is sometimes listed as a guest, but one imagines Wolfe would have mentioned his presence there, since Wolfe wrote a fair amount about his wife.
3. Richard Feigen is the brother of pioneering feminist lawyer Brenda Feigen-Fasteau. Jean Stein had earlier gone by her married name, vanden Heuvel.
4. I have relied on the accounts of other attendees, including those of journalists other than Tom Wolfe who were present. I have interviewed three other attendees: Domna Stanton, who was an invited guest; and defense committee members, Lisa Weinstein and Martin Kenner. However, Wolfe's account of the evening is the most complete, and I have relied on parts of his account of that evening, particularly the exchanges between Don Cox, the guests, and Leonard Bernstein. In her appearance on the *David Susskind Show*, Curtis said that Wolfe's account of the dialogue was mostly accurate. Transcript of the *David Susskind Show*, Box 232, F 1, 12, 1970, TWP/NYPL, 16.
5. Interview with Kenner, CUBPP, 80.
6. Cox, *Just Another*, 134. Heyday Press decided to change the book's title after Black bookstores refused to stock the book. The press changed it to the less controversial *Making Revolution*. The original title was a reference to W. E. B. Du Bois, who said in a speech broadcast on Radio Peking in 1959 that "in my country for nearly a century I have been nothing but a nigger." Cox used it as the epigraph of his memoir.
7. Cox, *Just Another*, 134.
8. Cox, *Just Another*, 46.
9. Cox, *Just Another*, 120–21.
10. Claudia Dreyfus interview with Gerry Lefcourt in *Our Time: An Anthology of Interviews from the East Village Other*, ed. Allen Katzman (Dial Press, 1972), 147.
11. David Burnham, "Off-Duty Police Here Join in Beating Black Panthers," *NYT*, September 5, 1968.
12. Jan Hoffman, "Public Lives: A Witness to the Revolution Recalls Abbie," *NYT*, August 24, 2000, Sec B.
13. Author's Interview with Kenner; transcript of *Susskind Show*; author's Interview with Stanton.
14. John Gruen, *The Private World of Leonard Bernstein* (Viking Press, 1968), 147.

15. Jamie Bernstein interviewed by SFist, 2008, quoted by Bonanos, "The Making of Tom Wolfe's 'Radical Chic.'"
16. Ned Rorem, "Many Lives, Many Deaths," Leonard Bernstein Remembered, *NYT*, October 21, 1990; author's Interview with Stanton.
17. Author's Interview with Kenner.
18. Grace Lichtenstein, "Famous Father Girl: a Memoir," NYCitywoman, January 4, 2024.
19. Karl Meyer letter to the Bernsteins, "Material Related to the Black Panther Fundraiser," LBC-LOC.
20. See Lardner, *I'd Hate Myself*, 142–47.
21. Bayard Rustin, "Black Panthers and Their Policy," *New York Amsterdam News*, January 17, 1970.
22. Bernstein's Letter to the Editor, "Material Related to Black Panther Benefit," LBC-LOC, 3.
23. John Rockwell, "Bernstein Triumphant," *The NYT Magazine*, August 31, 1986.
24. Bernstein's Letter to the Editor, "Material Related to Black Panther Benefit," LBC-LOC, 3.
25. Rorem, "Many Lives, Many Deaths."
26. Doug Ireland, "A Party of Beautiful People Raises 10G for Panthers," *New York Post*, January 15, 1970.
27. Berry quoted in Trip Gabriel, "Lee Berry, Black Panther in a 'Radical Chic' Time, Dies at 78," *NYT*, March 26, 2024.
28. Charlotte Curtis, "The Bernsteins' Party for Black Panther Legal Defense Stirs Talk and More Parties," *NYT*, January 24, 1970.
29. Bernstein's Letter to the Editor, "Material Related to Black Panther Benefit," LBC-LOC, 4.
30. Bernstein, *Famous Father Girl*, 110.
31. Some have said that the benefit resulted in the state finally allowing the male prisoners to be incarcerated in one facility, in Queens. But according to Murray Kempton, that change was forced on the state by a federal judge in his December 1969 ruling. Kempton, *The Briar Patch*, 38.
32. Author's interview, Domna Stanton, September 13, 2019.
33. David Denby, "Leonard Bernstein Through His Daughter's Eyes," *The New Yorker*, June 18, 2018.
34. Roger Wilkins quoted in Greenwald, *A Woman of the Times: Journalism, Feminism, and the Career of Charlotte Curtis* (Ohio University Press, 1999), 213.
35. "When Leonard Bernstein Partied with the Black Panthers," March 29, 2018, BBC, accessed December 8, 2024: https://www.bbc.co.uk/programmes/articles/3dWyNLc1rMqSnXytbgwhjnh/when-leonard-bernstein-partied-with-the-black-panthers
36. Ireland, "A Party of Beautiful People."
37. Charlotte Curtis, "Mrs. Leonard Bernstein Helps Raise Funds for the Panthers," *NYT*, January 14, 1970.
38. Charlotte Curtis, "Black Panther Philosophy Debated at the Bernsteins," *NYT*, January 15, 1970.
39. This was his daughter Jaime's observation. Bernstein, *Famous Father*, 112.
40. Morris Kaplan, "Bomb Plot Is Laid to 21 Panthers," *NYT*, April 3, 1969.

41. Cole Interview with Kenner, CUBPP, 82.
42. *New York Times* Editorial, "False Note on Black Panthers," January 16, 1970.
43. Author's Interview with David Bright Burnham, December 29, 2020.
44. For *Times* reporter Julie Baumgold on Curtis's stories never being cut and Robertson on Curtis being the "little woman," see Greenwald, *A Woman of the Times*, 89.
45. Robin Morgan, *Saturday's Child: A Memoir* (Norton, 2001), 262.
46. It was Janet Malcom who likened the biographer to a "professional burglar, breaking into a house, rifling through certain drawers that he has good reason to think contain jewelry and money, and triumphantly bearing his loot away." Janet Malcolm, "The Silent Woman," *The New Yorker*, August 23, 1993.
47. Transcript of the *Susskind Show*.
48. I contacted Marilyn Greenwald, Curtis's biographer and several people who worked at the *Times* during Curtis's tenure there. No one seems to know the full story. I did find in Wolfe's archive an undated note in his Radical Chic file, a reminder to call Charlotte Curtis. He later said that they spoke about the hors d'oeuvres. Wolfe claimed in "Radical Chic" that Curtis stood by her reporting in the second article she filed. Perhaps she did in the days immediately following its publication, but she came to regret what she had written. Wolfe, *Radical Chic*, 81; Bonanos, "The Making of Tom Wolfe's Radical Chic."
49. The *Susskind Show* devoted a whole evening to a discussion of "Radical Chic," to which Wolfe was invited. He declined the invitation, but those who accepted included Charlotte Curtis, John Simon, Wyatt Cooper, Richard Feigen, and Marya Mannes. The transcript of the show can be found in Box 232, F1, p. 3, TWP/NYPL.
50. Sydney Gruson quoted in Greenwald, *A Woman of the Times*, xi.
51. Curtis, "The Bernsteins' Party," 21.
52. Cox recalls the wholesale cancellation of Panther fundraisers. Cox, *Just Another*, 135. This is confirmed by Kenner in his interview by Lewis Cole, CUBPP, 87.
53. Charlotte Curtis, *The Rich and Other Atrocities* (Harper & Row, 1976), 107.
54. Felicia Bernstein, "Panthers' Legal Aid," Op-Ed, *NYT*, January 21, 1970.
55. Karl Meyer, letter to Felicia Bernstein, January 26, 1970. See "Materials Related to the Black Panther Fundraiser," 1970, LBC-LOC.
56. "Races: Upper East Side Story," *Time*, January 26, 1970, Box 95 F 6, TWP/NYPL.
57. "The Panther and The Law," *Newsweek* 75, no. 8 (February 23, 1970), Box 95 F 6, TWP/NYPL. See also Gordon Mantler, "'The Press Did You In': The Poor People's Campaign and the Mass Media," *The Sixties: A Journal of History, Politics, and Culture* 3, no. 1 (June 2010): 39.
58. James Weschler, "That Party," the *New York Post*, undated clipping, "Radical Chic," 1970, Box 95.6, TWP/NYPL.
59. The letters of support—and a few letters criticizing the Bernsteins—are in "Materials Related to the Black Panther Fundraiser," 1970, Leonard Bernstein Collection, LOC.
60. Mary Connelly, "Bernstein: It Wasn't a Party at All," *New York Post*, January 23, 1970.
61. Henry J. Taylor, "Bernstein Said in Trouble," newspaper clipping, January 30, 1970, "Radical Chic," 1970, Box 95.6, TWP/NYPL.
62. Paul Hofmann, "Protests from U.S. Jews Stir Controversy in Israel," *NYT*, June 21, 1979.

63. For another source on the FBI's efforts to fracture working relations between Jews and Blacks, see Paul Krassner, *Confessions of a Raving, Unconfined Nut: Misadventures in the Counter-Culture* (Simon & Schuster, 1993), 171–72.
64. Jamie Bernstein says that the FBI files showed that most of the protestors were "FBI plants." Bernstein, *Famous Father*, 112; Curtis Gentry, *J. Edgar Hoover: The Man and the Secrets* (Norton, 1991), 647; Barry Seldes, *Leonard Bernstein*, 116–17; "Leonard Bernstein Asserts F.B.I. Used 'Dirty Tricks' Against Him," *NYT*, Oct. 22, 1980.
65. McEneaney, *Tom Wolfe's America*, 59.
66. Eye Too, "Woe Is Lenny," *Women's Wear Daily*, February 18, 1970, "Radical Chic", 1970, Box 95.6, TWP/NYPL.
67. Author's interview with Domna Stanton, September 13, 2019. Goldsmith had considerable clout at *New York*. It was her money that enabled the magazine to become independent. When she told Wolfe he was all wrong about Stanton's necklace, he did cut it.
68. Robert Fizdale, letter to the Bernsteins, January 31, 1970, LBC-LOC.
69. Notes of Wolfe's researcher, "Radical Chic," Box 95.6, 1970, TWP/NYPL.
70. Burton, *Leonard Bernstein*, 392.
71. John M. Lee, "Bernstein Denies Shift on the Panthers," *NYT*, February 22, 1970.
72. Cox, *Just Another*, 133. Cole Interview with Kenner, 83–84.
73. Gruen reports that Felicia Bernstein practically accused him of writing the essay. "You can't have it both ways, John," she snarled at him. Yet she may have known that he, too, spoke to Wolfe's assistant. Gruen, *Callas Kissed Me . . . Lenny Too! A Critic's Memoir* (Powerhouse Books, 2008), 215–16.
74. Aryeh Neier of the New York Civil Liberties Union January 23, 1970, press release in "Materials Related to the Black Panther Fundraiser," 1970, Leonard Bernstein Collection, LOC.
75. Leon Quat, Letter to the Editor, *NYT*, unpublished, "Materials Related to the Black Panther Fundraiser," 1970, Leonard Bernstein Collection, LOC.
76. Tevi Troy, *Intellectuals and the American Presidency: Philosophers, Jesters, Or Technicians?* (Rowman & Littlefield, 2003), 106; Alex Ross, "The Legend of Lenny," *The New Yorker*, December 7, 2008.
77. Bruce Oudes, ed., *From the President: Richard Nixon's Secret Files* (Harper & Row, 1989), 106.
78. Cox, *Just Another*, 135.
79. The writer was Martin Niemöller.
80. Murray Kempton, "Free at Last," *New York Review of Books*, June 17, 1971.

CHAPTER ELEVEN

1. David Greenberg argues that in the 1950s the *Times* and other respected newspapers were seen as "sober voices of the political center," and not as organs of the left. This idea that the Times was liberal originated with white Southern segregationists who were angry about the paper's coverage of the civil rights movement. The *Times* remained a centrist newspaper through the sixties. David Greenberg, "'The Idea of 'the Liberal Media' and Its Roots in the Civil Rights Movement," *The Sixties: A Journal of History, Politics, and Culture* 1, no. 2 (Dec. 2008): 171.
2. Pete Hamill quoted in Seymour Krim, "The Newspaper as Literature/Literature as Leadership," in Krim, *What's This Cat's Story?* (Paragon House, 1991), 126.

3. Curiously, in early drafts of "Radical Chic," Wolfe did include first-person narration. TWP/NYPL, Box 96, F 2. Marc Weingarten, *The Gang That Wouldn't Write Straight* (Crown, 2006), 124. Wolfe later listed other new journalists who did not write in the first person, such as Gay Talese and Jimmy Breslin, at least at first. See James Kaplan, "Tom Wolfe on How to Write New Journalism," in *Rolling Stone*, November 5, 1987.
4. Wolfe said one reason he spent so much time in those white suits was because it was "fun" seeing the annoyed reactions of New Yorkers. See his 1987 appearance on the *Late Show with David Letterman*, accessed May 31, 2024: https://www.youtube.com/watch?v=yPcvm-gNXV4
5. Daniel Horowitz, *Consuming Pleasures: Intellectuals and Popular Culture in the Postwar World* (University of Pennsylvania Press, 2012), 272.
6. As a city desk reporter at the *Washington Post*, he covered Southern segregationists' filibuster of the Civil Rights Act of 1960. Doug Cumming, "Tom Wolfe, Reporter: His Relationship to Old New Journalism and to New New Journalism," *Journal of Magazine Media* 9, no. 1 (Fall 2006): 11.
7. Daniel Horowitz believes Wolfe was influenced by the work of Bolshevik-turned-Soviet-dissident Yevgeny Zamyatin. See Horowitz, *Consuming Pleasures*, 277.
8. Thomas Kennerly Wolfe Jr., "The League of American Writers: Communist Organizational Activity Among American Writers, 1929–1942," PhD diss. (Yale University, 1956).
9. Wolfe describes his beat as the "American statusphere" in 1969. See Gregg J. Kilday, "Tom Wolfe," *The Harvard Crimson*," May 8, 1969.
10. For the relevant quoted material, see Wolfe, "The League," 67, 339, 335, 270, 272. For a useful account of what animated certain writers, see Maurice Isserman, *Reds: The Tragedy of American Communism* (Basic Books, 2024), 140–41; Murray Kempton, *Part of Our Time: Some Ruins and Monuments of the Thirties* (NYRB, 1998).
11. David Potter letter to Tom Wolfe, Box 1, F 3, TWP/NYPL.
12. Michael Holzman, "The Ideological Origins of American Studies at Yale," *American Studies* 40, no. 2 (Summer 1999): 87.
13. His committee members' comments on the department's evaluation form can be found in Box 1, F 3, TWP/NYPL.
14. Potter letter to Tom Wolfe, May 19, 1956, Box 1, F 3, TWP/NYPL.
15. Letter to Chaz, June 9, 1956, June 9, 1956, Box 1, F 3, TWP/NYPL.
16. An influential booster of modernist writers, Pearson played a key role during World War II in the creation of the X-2 counterespionage program in the Office of Strategic Services, the forerunner of the CIA. See Greg Barnhisel, *Code Name Puritan: Norman Holmes Pearson at the Nexus of Poetry, Espionage, and American Power* (University of Chicago, 2024), 311.
17. Wolfe letter to Marshall Fishwick, undated, Box 1, F 2, TWP/NYPL.
18. Wolfe sets up the scene in "Foreword: Murderous Gutter Journalism," in Wolfe, *Hooking Up* (Picador, 2000). See also Ben Yagoda, *About Town: The New Yorker and the World It Made* (Scribner, 2000), 335.
19. Part Two of Wolfe's takedown was called "Lost in the Whichy Thickets: *The New Yorker*."
20. Wolfe, "Foreword," in *Hooking Up*, 252. Yagoda, *About Town*, 337. Wolfe said he did speak to Charlayne Hunter-Gault, the wife of one of his colleagues at the *Tribune*. Hunter-Gault was one of two Black students who had integrated the University of

Georgia and had begun working at *The New Yorker*. Wolfe never explained why he was interested in her place of employment, and she freely shared stories with him. Weingarten, *The Gang*, 2.
21. Yagoda, *About Town*, 337.
22. Wolfe, "Tiny Mummies!" in *Hooking Up*, 262.
23. Wolfe, "Lost in the Whichy," in *Hooking Up*, 277.
24. White and Salinger quoted in Yagoda, *About Town*, 339–40.
25. Renata Adler, *Gone: The Last Days of The New Yorker* (Simon & Schuster, 1999), 86.
26. Renata Adler and Gerald Jonas, "The Letter," *Columbia Journalism Review*, January 1, 1966; Leonard C. Lewin, "Is Fact Necessary?" *Columbia Journalism Review* 4, no. 4 (Jan. 1, 1966).
27. Adler, *Gone*, 89–90.
28. Lewin, "Is Fact Necessary?" 32. Felker shared Wolfe's privileging of narrative flow over the factual. Years later, Felker was the editor on Gail Sheehy's award-winning *New York* article about Times Square prostitution. When it later came out that one especially compelling figure in Sheehy's account, a prostitute she called Redpants, was a composite figure, Felker said that Sheehy's draft had noted she was a composite figure. He explained that, as her editor, he had removed that admission because it disrupted the narrative. See Harrison Smith, "Gail Sheehy . . . Dies at 83," *Washington Post*, August 25, 2020.
29. Dwight Macdonald published two articles about Wolfe's methods. "Parajournalism, or Tom Wolfe and His Magic Writing Machine," *NYRB*, August 26, 1965, and "Parajournalism II: Wolfe and The New Yorker," *NYRB*, February 3, 1966.
30. Macdonald, "Parajournalism."
31. Macdonald, "Parajournalism II."
32. Wolfe, "Afterword: High in the Saddle," in *Hooking Up*, 291.
33. Wolfe letter to parents, July 27, 1957 or 1958, Box 1, F 4, 1957–61, TWP/NYPL.
34. Weingarten, *The Gang*, 100. Felker quoted in Gabriel Snyder, "Tom Wolfe Disinters 'Tiny Mummies!' After 35 Years," *Observer*, February 14, 2000, https://observer.com/2000/02/tom-wolfe-disinters-tiny-mummies-after-35-years/
35. Richard Kluger, *The Paper*, 337, Kindle edition.
36. Carol Iannone, "A Critic in Full: A Conversation with Tom Wolfe," *Academic Questions* 21, no. 2, August 11, 2008, https://www.nas.org/blogs/article/a_critic_in_full_a_conversation_with_tom_wolfe
37. Tom Wolfe, "The New Journalism," in Tom Wolfe and Edward Warren Johnson, *The New Journalism* (Harper & Row, 1973), 24.
38. Wolfe's uncritical recounting of Kesey's remarks that day, which included an attack on Paul Jacobs, was telling. Kesey mocked Jacobs, a well-known leftist who addressed the crowd that day, as a latter-day Mussolini, because, it seems, he was bald and gesticulated as he spoke. Berkeley journalist Robert Scheer described Jacobs as anticommunist, hardly an admirer of authoritarians. Wolfe often spoke of his "saturation reporting," as Krim noted. (See Krim, *What's This Cat's Story*, 128.) But if Wolfe had bothered to ask just a few questions the day of the march, he would have learned that, as Scheer put it, he got Jacobs "all wrong. He picked on exactly the wrong person." Wolfe's reporting of that day's protest, Scheer said, "was just lousy." Author's Interview with Robert Scheer, July 30, 2020. The quotes from Kesey's speech appear in Tom Wolfe, *Electric Kool-Aid Acid Test* (New York: Bantam, 1999), 221–25. Parts of

several chapters of *Acid Test* first appeared in early 1967 in the *New York Herald Tribune*. The book was published in August 1968. Wolfe did cover the occasional protest as a working reporter. See Kluger, *The Paper*, 306.
39. Wolfe, *Acid Test*, 356–57.
40. Wolfe, *Acid Test*, 26, 238–39.
41. In a January 18, 1963, letter to his son, the senior Wolfe suggested that before criticizing the welfare system he might want to consider the conditions that led to its adoption. In a May 1, 1962, letter to his parents about John F. Kennedy, Wolfe Jr. ventured that the president might want the first manned space flight to fail so he could "manipulate the country behind the scenes to cause a depression and thereby justify wholesale nationalization of industry." Box 1, F 7; Box 1, F 4, Box 1 F 5, TWP/NYPL.
42. Wolfe letters from New Haven to Hoffman and Taft, Box 1, F 3, TWP/NYPL.
43. Wolfe letter to Helen, December 4, 1955, Box 1, F 2, TWP/NYPL.
44. Christopher Lehmann-Haupt, Books of the Times: "Tom Wolfe at the Crossroad," *NYT*, November 25, 1970, 34.
45. Wolfe, *Radical Chic*, 3–4.
46. Wolfe, *Radical Chic*, 113.
47. The quotations about Bernstein's notes are from John Gruen, *The Private World of Leonard Bernstein* (Viking Press, 1968), 100–101.
48. Seldes, *Leonard Bernstein*, 21–22.
49. Letter from Bernstein to Helen Coates, November 11, 1940, Box/Folder 13, LBC-LOC, accessed November 26, 2024: https://www.loc.gov/resource/music.muslbcorr-00429/?sp=2&st=image&r=-0.243,-0.043,1.55,0.61,0
50. Bernstein counted among his friends the white writer William Styron whose 1967 book, *The Confessions of Nat Turner*, generated precisely this reaction from many Black critics. See Gruen, *The Private World*, 102.
51. Humphrey Burton, *Leonard Bernstein* (Faber & Faber, 1995), 387–88.
52. Wolfe, "Lost in the Whichy," in *Hooking Up*, 277.
53. Here, Wolfe is paraphrasing Buckley, *Radical Chic*, 98.
54. Wolfe, "The Man Who Invented New York," *New York* Magazine, July 3, 2008, accessed June 26, 2024: https://nymag.com/news/media/48341/
55. Justin Vaisse, *Neoconservatism: The Biography of a Movement* (Harvard University Press, 2010), 61.
56. In "Radical Chic," Wolfe notes that Bernstein had defended himself and his wife against the *Times*' charge that they were jetsetters or masochists. It was all "nauseating," he reported Bernstein saying. However, this conversation appears in shorthand in Wolfe's notes. It's unclear if Wolfe himself made that call but chose to not identify himself in the text or if another reporter made the call on his behalf. See Wolfe, *Radical Chic*, 104; Radical Chic Notes, page 21, Box 95.6, TWP/NYPL.
57. Seldes, *Leonard Bernstein*, 105–6.
58. It is possible that Wolfe learned of Bernstein's past as a fellow traveler when he was researching his dissertation.
59. Gruen, *The Private World*, 151–53.
60. Moore, *A Special Rage*, 268.
61. Wolfe, *Radical Chic*, 77.
62. Wolfe, *Radical Chic*, 38, 49.
63. Wolfe, *Radical Chic*, 11.

64. Bernstein, *Famous Father Girl*, 6–7. Felicia Bernstein explained in a letter to her husband that their life in New York felt so "Bernstein." Undated Letter from Felicia Bernstein to Leonard Bernstein, Box 60A/F 16–18, LBC, LOC.
65. In earlier drafts of "Radical Chic" the scene in which Leonard Bernstein offers a mint to Panther Don Cox—a key scene in the text—happens at different moments, suggesting that his account likely misrepresents the order in which things unfolded that night. See drafts of "Radical Chic" in Box 96, f 2, TWP/NYPL.
66. See Elon Green, "Annotation Tuesday! Tom Wolfe and Radical Chic," May 13, 2014, https://niemanstoryboard.org/stories/annotation-tuesday-tom-wolfe-and-radical-chic/
67. Green, "Annotation Tuesday!" Even an editor as seasoned as Jason Epstein of the *New York Review of Books* appears to have misunderstood certain views as Wolfe's, not those of his offstage narrator. Jason Epstein, "Journal du Voyeur," *NYRB*, December 17, 1970, accessed June 27, 2024: https://www-nybooks-com.libproxy2.usc.edu/articles/1970/12/17/journal-du-voyeur/
68. Wolfe, *Radical Chic*, 8, 47, 65.
69. Box 96, F 2, TWP/NYPL.
70. Tom Wolfe on William F. Buckley's "Firing Line," December 17, 1970. See also Tom Wolfe, "The Birth of 'The New Journalism': Eyewitness Report," *New York* Magazine, February 14, 1972.
71. Tom Wolfe, "The New Journalism," in Wolfe and Johnson, *The New Journalism*, 32.
72. For their friends, Wolfe's claim that the benefit grew out of their desire to be chic seemed especially ludicrous. Wyatt Cooper, *David Susskind Show* Transcript, 15, Box 232, F 1, TWP/NYPL.
73. Leonard Bernstein quoted in Jean Stein papers, Box 90, FF 14.
74. Alex Ross, "The Legend of Lenny," *The New Yorker*, December 7, 2008.
75. Note from Wolfe's researcher at *New York*, to Tom Wolfe, Box 95 F 6, 1970, TWP/NYPL.
76. Gruen, *The Private World*, 97.
77. The description of the Bernsteins' suppers appears in Wolfe, *Radical Chic*, 6.
78. Research notes, 95.5, 1970, TWP/NYPL.
79. Wolfe wants to know how Stanton made his money and who his new wife is. Research notes, 95.5, 1970, TWP/NYPL.
80. Wolfe, *Radical Chic*, 103; author's Interview with Stanton.
81. Wolfe, *Radical Chic*, 104–8; author's Interview with Stanton.
82. Rowland Evans and Robert Novak, "Red Panthers?" clipping, January 14, 1970, Box 95 F 6, TWP/NYPL. It is true that Cleaver traveled from Algiers to North Korea, where he spent a month. He hoped to get weapons and money from the government there. See Elaine Mokhtefi, *Algiers, Third World Capital* (Verso Press, 2018), 101.
83. "A Panther Admits," *NYT*, January 17, 1970.
84. Kathleen Rout, *Eldridge Cleaver* (Twayne, 1991), 144.
85. For scholarly treatment of the media's treatment of the Panthers, see Rhodes, *Framing the Black Panthers*; Edward P. Morgan, "Media Culture and the Public Memory of the Black Panther Party," in *In Search of the Black Panther Party: New Perspectives on a Revolutionary Movement*, ed. Jama Lazerow and Yohuru Williams (Duke University Press, 2006).
86. Wolfe, *Radical Chic*, 108.

87. Several people who wrote him admiring letters regarded Wolfe as a believer in the Movement.
88. Lehmann-Haupt, "Tom Wolfe."
89. Wolfe, *Radical Chic*, 7.
90. Green, "Annotation Tuesday!"
91. Brant Mewborn's interview with Tom Wolfe in *Rolling Stone*, November 10–December 1987.
92. Hunter S. Thompson, *Proud Highway: Saga of a Desperate Southern Gentleman, 1955–1967* (Ballantine, 1997), 640.
93. Tom Wolfe's book editor, Henry Robbins, wrote to Richard Kluger, who was then the editor of the *New York Herald Tribune*'s Book Week supplement. Robbins wrote to complain about the bad review. Box 4, F 3, TWP/NYPL.
94. Bonanos, "The Making of Tom Wolfe's 'Radical Chic.'"
95. Joyce Haber, *San Francisco Chronicle*, August 28, 1970, about a benefit for the Los Angeles 18, the Panthers who were arrested last year in Los Angeles during the raid.
96. Research notes on the virility gap, Box 95.6 (1970), TWP/NYPL.
97. Wilda Williams, "Radical Wolfe," *Film Forward*, September 16, 2023, accessed June 17, 2024: https://film-forward.com/documentary/radical-wolfe
98. Perhaps another reason that many Old Leftists seemed favorably inclined to Wolfe's "Radical Chic" is that they were Trotskyists and knew that Hannah Weinstein and Leon Quat had been a part of the Communist Party's orbit.
99. Tom Hayden, *Reunion: A Memoir* (Random House, 1988), 417.
100. Alpert, *Growing Up Underground*, 237.
101. Jamal Joseph, *Panther Baby: A Life of Rebellion and Reinvention* (Chapel Hill: Algonquin Books, 2012), 138. The Black press seems to have refrained from attacking Bernstein. The *Chicago Defender* noted that Bernstein called Beethoven's "Fidelio," which he was conducting for the New York Philharmonic Young People's Concerts on CBS, "a celebration of human rights." See "Bernstein to Conduct *Fidelio*," *Chicago Defender*, March 28, 1970.
102. Epstein, "Journal," *The New York Review*.
103. It was the leftist Michael Harrington who in 1973 labeled them "neo-conservatives." They did not reject the label. See Anthony Elghossain, "The Enduring Power of Neoconservatism," *The New Republic*, April 3, 2019.
104. Advocates of this approach have argued that its deployment has lowered crime, but without racial bias. They sometimes claim that stop-and-frisk policies introduced racist bias. For a critique of broken windows theory, see Bench Ansfield, "How a 50-Year-Old Study Was Misconstrued," *Washington Post*, December 27, 2019.
105. Douglas Martin, "Raymond K. Price Jr., 88, a Key Nixon Speechwriter Is Dead," *NYT*, February 14, 2019.
106. Raymond K. Price letter to Wolfe, Box 10, F 1, TWP/NYPL.
107. Nathan Miller, "Some in 'In Group' Counterattack Radical Chic," *Baltimore Sun*, December 20, 1970.
108. Bruce Oudes, ed., *From the President: Richard Nixon's Secret Files* (Harper & Row, 1989), 466.
109. Rev. Lester Kinsolving, "Another Case of 'Radical Chic': Cited," *Raleigh News and Observer*, May 8, 1971.

110. Christopher Lehmann-Haupt, Books of the Times, "A Tumble into the Void," *NYT*, May 14, 1971, 39. He was reviewing an intriguing new book about the Panthers, *A Special Rage* by Gilbert Moore.
111. Chapin quoted in John M. Lee, "Bernstein Denies Shift on Panthers," *NYT*, February 22, 1970.
112. She made this comment in 2008. She is quoted in Bonanos, "The Making of Tom Wolfe's 'Radical Chic.'"
113. For the Bernsteins' benefit, see Charlotte Curtis, "Bernsteins Raise $35,000 for the Berrigan Defense," *NYT*, May 12, 1971. Francis X. Clines, "F.B.I. Head Scored by Ramsey Clark," *NYT*, November 18, 1970. Clark announced the formation of the Committee for Public Justice on November 17, 1970. Alice Kessler-Harris, "Lillian Hellman's Convictions," *The Chronicle of Higher Education*, April 22, 2012.
114. Jonathan Cott, *Dinner with Lenny: The Last Long Interview with Leonard Bernstein* (University of California Press, 2013), 85.
115. Donal Henahan, "Leonard Bernstein, 72, Music's Monarch, Dies," *NYT*, October 15, 1990.
116. Cott, *Dinner with Lenny*, 84–85.
117. Nigel Simeone, ed., *Letters of Leonard Bernstein* (Yale University Press, 2013), 301; Seldes, *Leonard Bernstein*, 127.
118. 1983 Interview with Ron Reagan from GEO 5 (October 1983), reprinted in Scura, *Conversations*, 192.
119. Sidney Blumenthal, *The Rise of the Counter-Establishment* (Union Square Press, 2008), 5.
120. Christopher Hitchens, "A Wolfe in Chic Clothing," *Mother Jones*, January 1983.
121. Green, "Annotation Tuesday!"
122. Here, my views align with those of Michael E. Staub in his important piece, "Black Panthers, New Journalism, and the Rewriting of the Sixties," *Representations* 57 (Winter 1997): 52–72, which I read in the final stages of writing. Staub draws attention to Wolfe's many coded references to Bernstein's queerness and the not-so coded references to the Jewishness of Bernstein and many of the guests.
123. One exception is Devin Fergus's pioneering book *Liberalism, Black Power, and the Making of American Politics, 1965–1980* (University of Georgia Press, 2009).
124. Andrew Ferguson, "The Right Wolfe," *Commentary*, November 2012.
125. Joseph Epstein, "The Statustician!" *Weekly Standard*, May 24, 2018.
126. See the incisive essay by Alice O'Connor, "Financing the Counterrevolution," in Bruce J. Schulman and Julian E. Zelizer, *Rightward Bound* (Harvard University Press, 2008), 153–54, 168.
127. Paul Jacobs, "Return of the Native," *Mother Jones*, August 1976. T. D. Allman, "The 'Rebirth' of Eldridge Cleaver," *NYT* magazine, January 16, 1977.
128. Lewis Lapham letter to Tom Wolfe, February 2, 1973, TWP/NYPL, Box 12, F 6.
129. As recently as 2019. Gail Lumet found the whole episode too painful to discuss with her ex-husband Sidney's biographer. See Maura Spiegel, *Sidney Lumet: A Life* (St. Martin's, 2019), 249.
130. Sally Quinn, "Viva La Causa! Radical Chic Revisited," *Washington Post*, May 3, 1975.
131. Green, "Annotation Tuesday!"
132. Ash Blonde, letter to Wolfe, Box 9, F 5, TWP/NYPL. She signed it Ash Blonde.
133. Jane Fonda, *My Life So Far* (Random House, 2005), 165.

134. "Jane Fonda in Five Acts," Susan Lacy, producer, HBO Documentary Films, 2018.
135. Author's Interview with Steve Wasserman, August 21, 2020.
136. Author's Interview with Kate Coleman, August 9, 2020.
137. Author's Interview with Steve Wasserman.
138. Brown, *A Taste of Power*, 209–10.

PART FIVE

1. Author's interview with Gloria Steinem, July 30, 2020.
2. Hilliard, *This Side*, 284.

CHAPTER TWELVE

1. My emphasis on the support that left liberals gave to the Panthers breaks with most histories of the Panthers, but particularly with the argument put forward by Waldo Martin and Joshua Bloom in their award-winning history of the Black Panther Party, *Black Against Empire*. They attribute the party's (and the larger Movement's) decline to liberals, either for turning against the party or for trying to neutralize it through co-optive reforms. In their view, conservatives were not the biggest threat to the Panthers. Instead, they argue that "concessions to blacks and opponents of the war reestablished the credibility of liberalism to key constituencies." With the Democratic Party pushing to end the war, they argue that the Nixon administration "rolled back the draft and created affirmative action programs, the United States normalized relations with revolutionary governments abroad, and black electoral representation ballooned." In those changed circumstances, they contend that the "politics of armed self-defense became impossible to sustain." However, those "concessions" were made by the Nixon administration, which may not have been in all ways reactionary, but surely cannot be described as liberal. As for liberalism's credibility, did it fully regain credibility in the early '70s? Nixon won in a landslide against the Democratic candidate, the liberal George McGovern, in 1972. Apart from the Carter years of 1976–80, the Democratic Party had a solid record of defeat from 1968 until 1992. Something else worth mentioning is that the Panthers had gone far beyond advocating armed self-defense, and the losses from their battles with the police, and their own internal strife, with crucial assistance provided by the FBI, damaged the party badly. Their argument also rests on their claim that liberals went "on the attack" as the Panthers' ranks grew, and here their evidence is Wolfe's "Radical Chic" and Edward Jay Epstein's "The Black Panthers and the Police." While the magazines that published these consequential pieces were more liberal than conservative, their authors were not liberal. See Bloom and Martin, *Black Against Empire*, 393–94, 351–52.
2. Several months earlier, MCAR had called for an investigation of the police department's treatment of the party. The ensuing investigation, conducted by the department, brushed off any concerns about harassment. See University of Michigan's Policing and Social Justice HistoryLab, "Detroit Under Fire," 2021, https://policing.umhistorylabs.lsa.umich.edu/s/detroitunderfire/page/black-panther-party
3. Joseph B. Treaster, "Brewster Doubts Fair Black Trials," *NYT* April 25, 1970. It was a page-one story in the *Times*. See also Bass and Rae, *Murder*, 139–40.
4. Francis X. Clines, "F.B.I. Head Scored by Ramsey Clark," *NYT*, November 18, 1970. Clark announced the formation of this organization on November 17, 1970, at a

news conference. He described it as a group of prominent private citizens, who were concerned that the United States was entering a "period of political repression." The historian Alice Kessler-Harris, and biographer of Lillian Hellman, has written about Hellman's pivotal role in the formation of this group. In the face of Nixon's attack on the protest movements of the late 1960s, Hellman "drew on her celebrity to organize friends of every political persuasion into a group called the Committee for Public Justice." Alice Kessler-Harris, "Lillian Hellman's Convictions," *The Chronicle of Higher Education*, April 22, 2012.
5. Clines, "F.B.I. Head Scored."
6. John Kifner, "New Study Asked in Blacks' Deaths," *NYT*, November 8, 1973.
7. Lewis Cole interview with Martin Kenner, CUBPP.
8. Fergus, *Liberalism, Black Power, and the Making of American Politics*, 116–25. Even though the party had once discouraged taking money from the state or foundations, by the early 1970s it had grown more receptive. The Menil Foundation provided $4,000 to the Houston Panthers' Breakfast for School Children Program and California gave $90,000 a year to the Panthers' Oakland Community School. For the Panthers' policy on taking this sort of money, see Austin, *Up Against the Wall*, 357 and 394n53.
9. See Hilliard, *This Side*, 248–49.
10. For the Baltimore arrests, see "Baltimore Police Hold 10 Panthers," *NYT*, May 1, 1970; "Student Linked to a Killing Linked to Panthers," *NYT*, December 13, 1970.
11. Edward Jay Epstein, "The Black Panthers and the Police: A Pattern of Genocide?" *The New Yorker*, February 13, 1971. For more on the ongoing conflict, including the discussion between Garry and Epstein and David Frost on the latter's TV show, see Julia Reed, "Debate over Panther Deaths Continues," *The Harvard Crimson*, March 3, 1971.
12. Andrew Holter, "A Homecoming for Murray Kempton," *Lapham's Quarterly*, December 12, 2017; Cox, *Just Another*, 123.
13. One well-positioned centrist Republican with ties to Yale passed this on to Yale's top leaders. See Bass and Rae, *Murder*, 150.
14. The numbers vary widely. According to Bloom and Martin, 10,000 were there. See their book, *Black Against Empire*, 353. By contrast, Earl Caldwell, who reliably covered the Oakland Panthers for the *New York Times* noted that Newton was mobbed by his supporters but put the number of his supporters in the hundreds, not the thousands. Earl Caldwell, "Newton Is Freed on $50,000 Bail," *NYT*, August 6, 1970.
15. Caldwell, "Newton Is Freed," 24.
16. Newton quoted in Richard Goldstein, "Angela Davis on Trial in Marin," *Village Voice*, May 6, 1971, https://www.villagevoice.com/angela-davis-on-trial-in-marin/
17. Interview with Elsa Knight Thompson, Oral History of the Black Panther Party, BAP, Box 1.B, Box 2, F 25, 12. According to Congressional investigators, Bishop Moore made a $20,000 donation to the Panthers' Free Breakfast for Schoolchildren Program, but it was used toward meeting the $50,000 bond for Newton's release. See Committee on Internal Security, U.S. House of Representatives, *Gun Barrel Politics*, August 1971, 66, https://babel.hathitrust.org/cgi/pt?id=mdp.39015081808514&seq=78
18. Falciola, *Up Against the Law*, 180–83. Nearly two weeks after Jackson's death, the *NYT* tried to piece together what had happened that day in San Quentin Prison. Wallace Turner, "Two Desperate Hours: How George Jackson Died," *NYT*, September

3, 1971. For one book-length treatment of George Jackson and the Panthers, see Jo Durden-Smith, *Who Killed George Jackson?* (Knopf, 1976).
19. Earl Caldwell, "Black Panther Leader Eulogizes Jackson as Hero," *NYT*, August 29, 1971, 53.
20. Cleaver quoted in Gifford, *Revolution or Death*, 130. This quote is from the paper "The New National Black Leadership," n.d., in Kathleen Cleaver's archive.
21. Sources cite wildly different numbers of participants at the RPCC. Hilliard says 15,000 and the *New York Times* says 6,000. Hilliard, *This Side*, 313; Paul Delaney, "Panthers Weigh New Constitution," *NYT* September 7, 1970.
22. See Anonymous, "The Days Belonged to the Panthers," and "lesbian testimony," *off our backs* 1, no. 11 (Sept. 30, 1970): 4–5; Martha Shelley, "subversion in the women's movement: what is to be done," *off our backs* 1, no. 13 (Nov. 8, 1970): 5–7.
23. Paul Alkebulan, *Survival Pending Revolution: The History of the Black Panther Party* (University of Alabama Press, 2007), 68; Delaney, "Panthers Weigh New Constitution"; Paul Delaney, "Panthers to Reconvene in Capital to Ratify Their Constitution," *NYT*, September 8, 1970. Many observers note that Huey Newton's speech at the first convention was a disaster. See Mumia Abu-Jamal, *We Want Freedom: A Life in the Black Panther Party* (Common Notions, 2016), 72–77.
24. Barbara, Karen, and Sally, "Revolutionary People's Constitutional Convention 'We Never Got Together," *Liberation News Service*, December 5, 1970, 14.
25. Unnamed author, response to LNS's RPCC coverage, *Liberation News Service*, December 23, 1970, 5–6.
26. Hilliard quoted in Bass and Rae, *Murder*, 116.
27. According to revolutionary intercommunalism, capitalism now transcended the nation-state; it called for connecting poor U.S. communities with those around the globe. Few party members understood it. See Spencer, *The Revolution Has Come*, 102; Bloom and Martin, *Black Against Empire*, 312. For Albert's quote, see Hilliard, *This Side*, 321.
28. Hilliard, *This Side*, 303–6.
29. See the discussion of FBI documents in the coverage of Dhoruba bin Wahad's lawsuit against the government. John Kifner, "Ex-Panther in Prison Says Evidence Was Concealed," *NYT*, April 3, 1989, https://www.nytimes.com/1989/04/03/nyregion/ex-panther-in-prison-says-evidence-was-concealed.html?searchResultPosition=12
30. Caldwell, "Black Panther Leader Eulogizes," 53. George Jackson had called for a people's army that would shove "a blade in the throat of fascism." See George Jackson, "George Jackson on Withdrawal," *The Black Panther*, August 28, 1971. The entire issue of the *Black Panther* was devoted to the slain Jackson, and politically he expressed views much closer to those of Cleaver than Newton. It is quite possible that Newton spoke as he did in his eulogy because he had reason to fear that the prison gang/political group that George Jackson had formed, the Black Guerrilla Family (BGF), might kill him. The reasons that George Jackson and the BGF turned on Huey Newton and the Oakland Central Committee are detailed in Hilliard, *This Side*, 378–81; Pearlman, *Call Me Phaedra*, 268, 362. Six months after Newton was released on bail, in a January 1971 interview, Newton said that the Panther program was "armed struggle." See Newton, "Repression Breeds Resistance," January 16, 1971, in Newton, *To Die*. Note the 1970 date given in this collection is incorrect.

31. Kenner quoted in Don Cox, "The Split in the Party," in Kathleen Cleaver and George Katsiaficas, *Liberation, Imagination, and the Black Panther Party* (Routledge, 2001), 121.
32. Afeni Shakur quoted in Kempton, *The Briar Patch*, 189. There was speculation at the time that Sam Napier was the father of Tupac Shakur, but that seems to have not been the case. However, she was close to Napier.
33. The best account of her life is Pearlman's *Call Me Phaedra*.
34. Newton's new positions on the Black church and Black capitalism were announced in the *Black Panther* newspaper. Huey P. Newton, "Black Capitalism Re-Analyzed," *Black Panther Intercommunal News Service*, June 5, 1971. At least in the Bay Area, it also grabbed the attention of the mainstream press. Tom Findley, "The Church and the Panthers," *San Francisco Chronicle*, May 24, 1971.
35. Huey P. Newton, "On the Defection of Eldridge Cleaver from the Black Panther Party and the Defection of the Black Panther Party from the Black Community," *Black Panther*, April 17, 1971. It is reprinted in David Hilliard and Donald Weise, eds., *The Huey P. Newton Reader* (Seven Stories, 2002), 206.
36. Huey P. Newton, "Eldridge Cleaver," *Revolutionary Suicide* (Penguin Books, 1973), 143.
37. Michael Koncewicz, "Tom Hayden and Jane Fonda, Capitol Hill Antiwar Lobbyists," in *Jacobin*, March 11, 2024, https://jacobin.com/2024/03/hayden-fonda-vietnam-antiwar-lobbyists
38. Author's Interview with Roxanne Dunbar-Ortiz, May 4, 2021.
39. That same day of the New York townhouse explosion, the Detroit Weatherman collective reportedly planned to carry out two bombings of the Detroit police to protest their racist violence. Had an informant not deactivated the bombs, they would have killed police officers and ordinary people. Eckstein, *Bad Moon*, 31–32.
40. Rudd, *Underground*, 215–16, 192.
41. Rudd, *Underground*, 254.
42. See Daniel S. Chard, *Nixon's War at Home: The FBI, Leftist Guerrillas, and the Origins of Counterterrorism* (University of North Carolina Press, 2021), 100.
43. Hayden, *Reunion*, 417.
44. Lawrence Roberts, *Mayday 1971* (Mariner, 2020), 333.
45. Waskow quoted in Farber, *Chicago '68*, 207. To give credit where it is due, Waskow, who was a seasoned Movement veteran and more moderate than some, advised this course of action as early as 1968. Readers will remember he preached a conciliatory course of action four years earlier with Bob Moses after the Democratic Convention.
46. Bill Zimmerman, *Troublemaker: A Memoir from the Front Lines of the Sixties* (Doubleday, 2011), 389.
47. Zimmerman, *Troublemaker*, 368–69.
48. For an examination of grassroots political activism across the ideological spectrum, see Michael Foley, *Front-Porch Politics: The Forgotten Heyday of American Activism in the 1970s and 1980s* (Hill and Wang, 2013).
49. Earl Caldwell, "Huey Is Free at Last," *NYT*, December 19, 1971. Although many believed the party was paying for the penthouse, which it justified because of security concerns, others contend that wealthy white supporters were footing the bill. Jamal Joseph is just one of the Panthers who criticized Newton's lifestyle, but he was hardly alone. Martin Kenner and Donald Freed maintain that others—Bert Schneider and

or Stanley Sheinbaum—and not the party, were paying the rent on his penthouse. So did David Hilliard in *Huey*, 178. For the Cetewayo quote, see C. Gerald Fraser, "Black Panther Fugitive in Algiers Charges . . ." *NYT*, March 12, 1971, 43.
50. Brown, *A Taste of Power*, 276–77.
51. Email correspondence with Martin Kenner, April 10, 2022.
52. Brown's October 26 speech was reprinted in the *Black Panther*, November 9, 1972.
53. Jean Stein's Interview with Anne Weills, JSP/NYPL, Box 161, F4.
54. Author Interview with Martin Kenner, September 23, 2020.
55. Patrick Goldstein, "Man, What a Trip That Was," *Los Angeles Times*, August 15, 1999; on the New Hollywood, see Peter Biskind's incisive, *Easy Riders, Raging Bulls* (Simon & Schuster, 1998).
56. Author Interview with Martin Kenner, September 23, 2020.
57. Brown, *A Taste of Power*, 262–63.
58. Schneider told Daniel Ellsberg about Newton's brilliance. The Bay Area journalist Kate Coleman claims that Newton and Schneider were more than friends. Their bond was "enormous—and ultimately romantic and sexual, as well as fraternal and comradely." Coleman, "True Hollywood Story: The Producer and the Black Panther," *Salon*, June 9, 2012. Two decades earlier, the topic of Schneider's relationship with Newton came up in Jean Stein's unpublished September 29, 1991, interview of the activist Anne Weills. Stein, whose parents had been Hollywood royalty, had been around Schneider, but had not seen him for some years, until they were guests at a 1989 wedding party for Dennis Hopper. Stein said she was struck by the change in Schneider's appearance. He looked a lot older and the way he moved made her wonder if he might now be gay. Given Schneider's well-documented heterosexual relationships, it seems unlikely he was gay. Possibly, he was bisexual, but the evidence appears to be slim to nonexistent. There is also extensive evidence of Newton's heterosexuality. Weills was friendly with Newton's last wife, Fredrika, but Weills seemed not to know anything about Newton's sexuality. She did mention his time in prison, which was at the California Men's Colony in San Luis Obispo, where, as Newton later noted, a high percentage—he claimed 80 percent—of the prisoners were homosexual. Although Newton publicly declared the Panthers' support for gay men and lesbians shortly after his release in 1970, Weills noted that while he was incarcerated at the Men's Colony, he made a tape in which he spoke about his extreme discomfort, even disgust, with the male homosexuality he witnessed. Jean Stein Interview with Anne Weills, JSP/NYPL, Box 188, F 4. For Newton's belief that homosexual sex in prison was a "pseudosexuality," see his book, *Revolutionary Suicide*, 270–1. For an incisive discussion of prison sex, see Regina Kunzel, "Situating Sex: Prison Sexual Culture in the Mid-Twentieth United States," *GLQ* 8, no. 3 (2002): 253–70.
59. Elaine Woo, "Bert Schneider Dies at 78," *Los Angeles Times*, December 14, 2011.
60. Peter Biskind, "Remembering Producer Bert Schneider: Father of the New Hollywood Movement," *Vanity Fair*, December 16, 2011.
61. Coleman, "True Hollywood Story." The two men freebased cocaine, reportedly sometimes with the actor Richard Pryor, who was slated to play Newton in a Hollywood movie in the early stages of development. Those movie plans were upended in the summer of 1980, when Pryor accidentally set himself on fire after freebasing coke.
62. Hilliard, *This Side*, 277.

63. Lewis Cole Interview with Alex Hoffmann, Columbia University Black Panther Project, hereafter referred to as CUBPP.
64. No scholar has done more to uncover the story of the Panthers' publishing and finances than Andrew Fearnley. His groundbreaking article is "The Black Panther Party's Publishing Strategies," 205–9.
65. The trip was made financially possible by the death of Communist Anna Louise Strong, who left money in her will to the Panthers. Author's interview with Kenner.
66. Cole interview with Kenner, CUBPP. Kenner says Newton wanted him to become the group's consigliere.
67. Roz B. Payne, "Movement Lawyers," in "What We Want, What We Believe," Newsreel Films, 2006. Payne's Interview with Gerald Lefcourt accessed November 25, 2024; no longer accessible. https://video-alexanderstreet-com.libproxy1.usc.edu/watch/movement-lawyers/transcript
68. Stephen George Chaberski, "The Strategy of Defense in a Political Trial: The Trial of the 'Panther 21,'" PhD diss. (Columbia University, 1975), 201.
69. Payne interview with Lefcourt, "Movement Lawyers." Lee Berry was transferred from the Tombs to Bellevue Hospital in November 1969. His bail was lowered to $15,000 in April 1970, and then all charges against him were dropped. Gabriel, "Lee Berry."
70. Donald Freed, *Agony in New Haven: The Trial of Bobby Seale, Erika Higgins, and the Black Panther Party* (Figueroa Press, 2008), 194. Freed's book was originally published by Simon and Shuster in 1973.
71. Ann Fagan Ginger, "Doris Bin Walker Discusses the Angela Davis Case," *Human Rights* 2, no. 2 (Fall 1972): 143.
72. Moore, *A Special Rage*, 262.
73. Moore, *A Special Rage*, 262. Kathleen Cleaver quoted in the documentary, *American Justice on Trial: People v. Newton*, Andre Abrahams and Herb Ferrette, dirs., 2022.
74. Bob Blauner, *Still the Big News: Racial Oppression in America* (Temple University Press, 2001), 149. Garry questioned six expert witnesses, including Blauner, who explained why it was so vital that the jury be unbiased. In his testimony, Blauner defined Black Americans as an internal colony in America. For more on Garry, see Falciola, *Up Against the Law*, 92–94.
75. C. J. Hirschfield, "New Film Examines Black Panther Huey Newton's 1968 Trial," *The Oaklandside*, April 21, 2022, https://oaklandside.org/2022/04/21/new-film-examines-black-panther-huey-newtons-1968-trial/
76. Chaberski, "The Strategy," 208–9.
77. Hill, *Men, Mobs, and Law*, 284.
78. Moore, *A Special Rage*, 238.
79. Moore, *A Special Rage*, 240.
80. The juror is quoted in Moore, *A Special Rage*, 234.
81. Falciola, *Up Against the Law*, 91–92.
82. Bass and Rae, *Murder*, 171.
83. The original indictment included 21 Panthers. However, by the time of the trial's start, the number of Panthers in the courtroom was 13 because two could not be found, and others were in jail elsewhere on other charges or had been severed from the case because they were too sick or too young.
84. Lee Berry may have been in court at the very beginning, but by April 1970 his bail was reduced and the charges against him were shortly dropped.

85. Chaberski, "The Strategy," 211, 226, 216.
86. The alternates were two white men, one Black woman, and one Black man. See Edward Kennebeck, *Juror Number Four: The Trial of Thirteen Black Panthers as Seen from the Jury Box* (Norton, 1973), 13. See also Stephen George Chaberski, "The Strategy," 218.
87. Kennebeck, *Juror*, 94.
88. Catherine Breslin, "One Year Later: The Radicalization of the Panther 13 Jury," *New York Magazine*, May 29, 1972, 59; Chaberski, "The Strategy," 333.
89. Chaberski, "The Strategy," 134; the lawyers were given access in December 1969.
90. Judge Murtagh repeatedly warned the 21's lawyers that they needed to get their clients to abide by courtroom conventions. Edith Evans Asbury, "Panther Counsel Pressed by Judge," *NYT*, March 25, 1970.
91. Interview with Gerald Lefcourt, Roz Payne Movement Lawyers, accessed May 6, 2021, no longer accessible.
92. Adrienne Rooney, "*The Battle of Algiers* and Colonial Analogy in the Panther 21," *Journal of African American Studies* 23, no. 4 (Dec. 2019): 461–64.
93. Rooney, "*The Battle of Algiers*," 455.
94. Kennebeck, *Juror*, 136–37.
95. Kempton, *The Briar Patch*, 272.
96. Chaberski, "The Strategy," 104–5, 187.
97. Kennebeck, *Juror Number Four*, 133.
98. Gerrie Traum, "The Panther 21 Acquitted," Liberation News Service (LNS), May 19, 1971, 9.
99. Chaberski, "The Strategy," 249, 252.
100. Kennebeck, *Juror Number Four*, 80.
101. Chaberski, "The Strategy," 286.
102. Chaberski, "The Strategy," 232.
103. Kempton, *The Briar Patch*, 266.
104. Chaberski, "The Strategy," 26.
105. Chaberski, "The Strategy," 198.
106. Chaberski, "The Strategy," 196.
107. Payne Interview with Lefcourt.
108. Rooney, "*The Battle of Algiers*," 466.
109. Chaberski, "The Strategy," 191–96.
110. Kempton, *The Briar Patch*, 240.
111. Kennebeck, *Juror Number Four*, 197.
112. Kempton, *The Briar Patch*, 268.
113. Breslin, "One Year Later," 54; Chaberski, "The Strategy," 414.
114. This point had been emphasized by the only Black lawyer of the defense team, Charles T. McKinney. Edith Evans Asbury, "Black Panther Party Members Freed After Being Cleared of Charges," *NYT*, May 14, 1971.
115. Chaberski, "The Strategy," 326–27.
116. Chaberski, "The Strategy," 333–35.
117. Kennebeck, *Juror Number Four*, 226.
118. Chaberski, "The Strategy," 337.
119. Kempton, *The Briar Patch*, 279.
120. Chaberski, "The Strategy," 338.

121. Breslin, "One Year Later," 60.
122. Kennebeck, *Juror Number Four*, 235.
123. Chaberski, "The Strategy," 338.
124. Interview with Gerald Lefcourt, Roz Payne Movement Lawyers. Link accessed May 6, 2021, no longer live.
125. Interview with Gerald Lefcourt.
126. Breslin, "One Year Later," 60.
127. Breslin, "One Year Later," 62.
128. Breslin, "One Year Later," 60–63.
129. Author's Interview with Martin Kenner, November 30, 2020. It is worth mentioning that relations between some of the defendants had frayed also. Of her involvement in the 1971 Panther 21-authored book, *Look for Me in the Whirlwind*, published by Random House, Afeni Shakur revealed to Jasmine Guy that the letter to Judge Murtagh attributed to the 21 was one she had no hand in writing. "They wouldn't let me participate," she said. See Guy, *Afeni Shakur*, 90.
130. Chaberski, "The Strategy," 341.
131. "The Panther Acquittal," *NYT*, May 15, 1971.
132. Kunstler quoted in Chaberski, "The Strategy," 344–45.
133. Lefcourt quoted in Chaberski, "The Strategy," 347.
134. Freed, *Agony*, 323–29.
135. Bass and Rae, *Murder*, 202–6; Freed, *Agony*, 333–39.
136. Freed, *Agony*, 336.
137. "Bobby Seale Goes to Trial," UPI: The African American Experience, accessed March 15, 2025: https://digitalcommons.chapman.edu/upi_african_american/263/
138. Stephen Shames and Bobby Seale, *Power to the People: The World of the Black Panthers* (Abrams, 2016), 349.
139. David A. Andelman, "4 of 'Harlem 5' Guilty on Arms Counts," *NYT*, May 14, 1971; "Twelve Detroit Panthers Cleared in Slaying," *NYT*, July 1, 1971.
140. Healey and Isserman, *Dorothy Healey*, 220.
141. "Remarks on Signing the Crime Control Act," the American Presidency Project, accessed March 15, 2025: https://www.presidency.ucsb.edu/documents/remarks-signing-the-organized-crime-control-act-1970;
"The Angela Davis Tragedy," *NYT*, October 16, 1970.
142. One of the CP comrades with whom Davis was closest was Dorothy Healey. Her account is thorough and gives somewhat more detail here. Healey and Isserman, *Dorothy Healey*, 217.
143. Dina Hampton, *Little Red: Three Passionate Lives Through the Sixties and Beyond* (Public Affairs, 2013), 53.
144. Bettina Aptheker, *The Morning Breaks: The Trial of Angela Davis* (Cornell University Press, 2014), xvi. Aptheker revealed this detail only in 2014, a detail she had omitted when she wrote the book in 1975.
145. Sol Stern, "The Campaign to Free Angela Davis . . . and Mitchell Magee," *NYT*, June 27, 1971.
146. Isserman, "Where Have All the Convict Heroes Gone," 113–17.
147. Daniel Rosenberg, "The Free Angela Movement in Global Context, 1970–72," *American Communist History* 19, no. 3–4 (2020): 191–261.

148. "Farmer Who Aided Angela in Hiding," *Pomona News*, March 2, 1972, 13. "Notes on People," *NYT*, March 25, 1972.
149. Ann Fagan Ginger, "Doris Bin Walker Discusses the Angela Davis Case," *Human Rights* 2, no. 2 (Fall 1972): 142–43.
150. Ginger, "Doris Bin Walker," 142–43. However, it is worth noting that the jury forewoman, Mary Timothy, who wrote a book about the trial, did not fault the District Attorney for his conduct toward the potential juror.
151. Ginger, "Doris Bin Walker," 143.
152. For a rundown of the votes, see the book by the jury's foreperson, Mary Timothy, *Jury Woman* (Glide Publications, 1975), 238–54.
153. Aptheker, *The Morning Breaks*, 274–75.
154. Earl Caldwell, "Angela Davis Acquitted on All Charges," *NYT*, June 5, 1972.
155. Healey and Isserman, *Dorothy Healey*, 220.
156. Williams, "No Haven."
157. Chaberski, "The Strategy," 424.
158. Janes Baldwin, "An Open Letter to My Sister, Miss Angela Davis," *NYRB*, January 7, 1971.
159. Aptheker, *The Morning Breaks*, 165.

CONCLUSION

1. Les Ledbetter, "15,000 Exhorted by Angela Davis," *NYT*, June 30, 1972. The crowd was reportedly multiracial. "Notes on People," *NYT*, June 7, 1972.
2. Isserman, *Reds*, 300–302. The group that Davis and leaders of her defense committee formed was the CP-aligned National Alliance Against Racism and Political Repression. See Angela Davis, *Angela Davis: An Autobiography* (Random House, 1974), 397-99.
3. Nelson George, "Angela Davis," *NYT*, October 19, 2020.
4. I am quoting Murray Kempton's description of what happened to 1930s radical unionists in his 1955 book about the '30s. Kempton, *Part of Our Time*, 293.
5. Author's Interview with Roxanne Dunbar-Ortiz, May 4, 2021.
6. Rubin's fellow ex-Yippie Abbie Hoffman did commit suicide in 1989. Three years earlier, Rubin had partnered up with him on the lecture circuit, with Rubin advocating for the establishment and Hoffman for the Movement. "Sixties Activist Jerry Rubin Dies," *LAT*, November 29, 1994. "Remembering Jerry Rubin," *Agenda*, January 1995, accessed March 22, 2025: https://aadl.org/node/249482
7. After his death, his widow, Fredrika Newton, began working as a nurse in addiction medicine. She believes he suffered from undiagnosed bipolar condition. See her remarks in Hilliard, *Huey*, 280. Jennie Rothenberg Gritz, "The Misunderstood Visionary Behind the Black Panther Party," *Smithsonian Magazine*, August 22, 2023, https://www.smithsonianmag.com/history/the-misunderstood-visionary-behind-the-black-panther-party-180982740/
8. Cox, *Just Another*, 207; Author Interview with Kenner; Katy Butler, "Huey Newton Talks of Booze and Boredom," *San Francisco Chronicle*, November 5, 1984.
9. Carmichael, *Ready*, 672–79.
10. T. D. Altman, "The 'Rebirth' of Eldridge Cleaver," *NYT Magazine*, January 16, 1977.
11. Gifford, *Revolution or Death*, 250.

12. Many of Cleaver's friends were deeply skeptical about the sincerity of his makeover. See Altman, "The 'Rebirth' of Eldridge Cleaver."
13. The first article by a leftist to reveal the underside of the Black Panther Party was written by the journalist and former UC-Berkeley SLATE activist Kate Coleman. Her piece, coauthored with Paul Avery, "The Party's Over," appeared in *New Times*, July 10, 1978. Horowitz, who was questioning his leftist beliefs, but was not yet antileft, was a primary source for their piece, which was commissioned by the Center for Investigative Reporting (CIR). Following its publication, Coleman, Avery, and the CIR staff received so many death threats that they had to go into hiding and temporarily close the office. Coleman's investigative work focused on the left, which has led many to wrongly dismiss her work as that of a conservative. In 1995, she placed the article, "A Death in Berkeley," about the murder of Van Patter, in *Heterodoxy*, a right-leaning journal started in 1992 by Horowitz and his colleague Peter Collier. Coleman later regretted publishing it there. "I was tarnished by Horowitz, which was hard." Fellow leftist Steve Wasserman wanted Coleman to write a book about the Panthers for Heyday Books, his publishing house. She declined because by that point she knew that few former Panthers would cooperate with someone who was a critic of the party. Author's Interview with Kate Coleman, August 9, 2020. For Horowitz's account of switching sides, see *Radical Son: A Journey Through Our Times* (The Free Press, 1997). Also useful is Scott Sherman, "David Horowitz's Long March," *The Nation*, June 15, 2000 and Steve Wasserman, "The Curious Case of David Horowitz," Scheerpost, April 30, 2025: https://scheerpost.com/2025/04/30/the-curious-case-of-the-late-david-horowitz. For more on Coleman, see Clay Risen, "Kate Coleman, Who Documented the Bay Area Counterculture, Dies at 81," *NYT*, April 6, 2024.
14. One-time Panther supporter Bob Blauner admitted years later that Panther supporters like himself "didn't want to know" what was happening inside the party. Sociologist Blauner had testified for the defense in Huey Newton's first trial. Blauner's indictment of the left (and himself) appeared in his review of Hugh Pearson's book about the Panthers, *The Shadow of the Panther*, in the *NYT*, July 10, 1994.
15. Author's Interview with Robert Scheer.
16. The term was used by Nancy Cott in her book, *The Grounding of Modern Feminism* (Yale University Press, 1987).
17. Breines, *The Trouble Between Us*, 156–57.
18. Breines, *The Trouble Between Us*, 157–62.
19. In connecting the dots between the Rainbow Coalition and Obama's election in 2008, I have drawn primarily upon Peniel E. Joseph, *Dark Days, Bright Nights: From Black Power to Barack Obama* (Basic Books, 2010), 164–88; Williams, *From the Bullet to the Ballot*; Clarence Lusane, "To Fight for the People: The Black Panther Party and Black Politics in the 1960s," in *The Black Panther Party Reconsidered*, ed. Charles E. Jones (Black Classic Press, 1998), 454.
20. Jakobi E. Williams, "The Original Rainbow Coalition: An Example of Universal Identity Politics," *Tikkun*, November 12, 2013.
21. Newton quoted in Butler, "Huey Newton Talks of Booze and Boredom."
22. Rubin paraphrased in Gumbo, *Yippie Girl*, 104.
23. This interview is not dated, and it is not clear who is conducting it. Interview with Jerry Rubin, Box 6, F13, SAJGAP/UMSCRC.
24. Interview with Jerry Rubin.

25. Roxanne Dunbar-Ortiz, "Outlaw Woman: Chapters from a Feminist Memoir-in-Progress," in Rachel Blau DuPlessis and Ann Snitow, *The Feminist Memoir Project* (Three Rivers Press, 1998), 114.

AFTERWORD

1. "Leonard Bernstein Asserts F.B.I. Used 'Dirty Tricks' Against Him," *NYT*, October 22, 1980.
2. Bernice Johnson Reagon, "Coalition Politics: Turning the Century," in Barbara Smith, ed., *Home Girls: A Black Feminist Anthology* (Rutgers University Press, 1983), 356–57.

Interviews

David Burnham, December 29, 2020
Clayborne Carson, September 12, 2022
Kate Coleman, August 9, 2020
Peter Davis, March 13, 2021
Roxanne Dunbar-Ortiz, May 4, 2021
Gay Falk, May 10, 2021
Bill Fletcher Jr., April 12, 2023
Stefan Forbes, July 3, 2024
Ann Froines, November 23, 2023
Judy Gumbo, December 23, 2021
Wesley Hogan, May 21, 2021
Melanie Kask, April 16, 2021
Martin Kenner, September 23, 2020 and November 20, 2020
James Lafferty, March 25, 2023
Jeremy Larner, September 4, 2020
Grace Lichtenstein, July 28, 2020
Mike Miller, July 9, 2021
Donna Murch, December 20, 2021
Matthew Penn, May 10, 2021
Vivian Rothstein, March 7, 2021
Mark Rudd, email correspondence, April 4 and April 6, 2022
Robert Scheer, July 30, 2020.
Domna Stanton, September 13, 2019
Gloria Steinem, July 30, 2020
Paul Stetzer, October 7, 2022
Margery Tabankin, September 4, 2019
Katrina vanden Heuvel, March 13, 2021
Elijah Wald, October 22, 2021
Steve Wasserman, August 21, 2020
Anne Weills, November 4 and December 9, 2021
Lisa Weinstein, December 2, 2020
Cathy Wilkerson, March 30, 2022
Narda Zacchino, January 22, 2021

Index

For the benefit of digital users, indexed terms that span two pages (e.g., 52–53) may, on occasion, appear on only one of those pages.

Images are indicated by an italic *i*.

Abu-Jamal, Mumia, 174–175
Adams, Emmie Schrader, 76–77, 87, 99–100, 101n101
Adler, Renata, 267
Adventures of Robin Hood, The, 237–238, 237n87
Afro-American Association (AAA), 141–142
Agnew, Spiro, 274
Ahmad, Akbar Muhammad (Maxwell Stanford), 78, 101n100, 104n118, 143
Albert, Judith (Gumbo), 129, 187, 197
Albert, Stew, 157, 161–162, 185n16, 187, 196–197, 303
Al Fatah, 279–280
Ali, Muhammad, 122n46
Allen, Donna, 148n34
Allen, Ernest Jr., 139
Allen, Louis, 28–29, 39
Allen, Pam (Chude) Parker, 51–52, 56n151, 78, 106n134
Alpert, Jane, 284
American Civil Liberties Union (ACLU), 260, 298
American Federation of Labor and Congress of Industrial Organizations (AFL-CIO), 75
Americans for Democratic Action (ADA), 60
Anthony, Earl, 172–173
anticommunism, 66, 220–221, 264–265. *See also* House Un-American Activities Committee (HUAC)
anti-Semitism, 43–45, 51–52, 107, 241–242, 353–354
antiwar movement
  Bernstein's involvement in, 230
  and civil rights activists, 122n46, 123n53
  growth of, 127, 306–309
  radical whites' involvement in, 122–124
  SNCC's involvement in, 106–107, 106n134, 117
Aoki, Richard, 144
Aptheker, Bettina, 342
Arnesen, Eric, 3n2
Assembly of Unrepresented People, 122
Atlanta Project (Vine City Project), 100–104
Atlantic City, 59. *See also* Democratic National Convention (Atlantic City, 1964)
  challenging of Mississippi regulars at, 59–62
  context of liberal views at, 66–67
  Democratic Party's view on MFDP challenge at, 62–65
  fears about backlash over compromise at, 67–69
Avery, Annie Pearl, 7n1
Axelrod, Beverly, 148*i*
  as alleged communist, 164n6
  background of, 147–151, 148n34, 153–154
  and Black Panther Party, 155–162
  and MFDP challenge at Atlantic City, 60
  and Panthers' cross-racial collaborations, 138
  relationship with Cleaver, 150–154, 159–160, 159n73, 159n80
  relationship with Garry, 163
Ayers, Bill, 204–206

bail money, 23, 71
Baker, Elaine DeLott, 67–77
Baker, Ella Jo, 14*i*
  and divisions in SNCC, 18

Baker, Ella Jo (*Continued*)
 drifted away from SNCC, 105
 and Freedom Vote, 32
 for Hayden, a model of womanism and integrationism, 89
 influence on SNCC, 13–16, 13n39
 and MFDP challenge at Atlantic City, 60, 62n17
Balagoon, Kuwasi (Donald Weems), 324
Baldwin, James, 17*i*, 139, 224–225, 225n48, 342
Ballis, George, 60
Baraka, Amiri (LeRoi Jones), 43, 157, 157n67, 159, 171, 225n48
Barry, Marion, 54, 346
Battle, Randy, 11*i*
Battle of Algiers, The, 322, 325
Bay, Robert, 280–281
Bay Area exceptionalism, 144–145
Beal, Frances, 55n143
Belafonte, Harry, 32, 70–71, 243n2
Belafonte, Julie Robinson, 278
Belfrage, Sally, 48, 48n104
Berland, Jim, 177–178
Berman, Marshall, 133
Bernard, Sidney, 225n46
Bernstein, Burton, 259
Bernstein, Felicia Montealegre. *See also* "Radical Chic: That Party at Lenny's" (Wolfe)
 activism of, 230, 287
 blowback from benefit held at home of, 214, 230, 256–262
 with Don Cox, 252*i*
 events of Panther 21 benefit held at home of, 243–249
 and impact of "Radical Chic," 287
 New York Times' coverage of benefit held at home of, 250–256
 throws benefit for Panther 21, 239–242
Bernstein, Jamie, 247–248, 250, 257–258, 276, 287
Bernstein, Judith Braun, 238–239
Bernstein, Leonard. *See also* "Radical Chic: That Party at Lenny's" (Wolfe)
 and antiwar movement, 127
 blowback from benefit held at home of, 214, 256–262
 conspiracy against, 353–354
 depiction of, in "Radical Chic," 263–271, 274–276
 with Don Cox, 252*i*
 events of Panther 21 benefit held at home of, 243–249
 fame of, 239
 homosexuality of, 258, 287
 and impact of "Radical Chic," 287–288
 New York Times' coverage of benefit held at home of, 250–256
 persecuted by FBI, 215, 227–230, 258, 353–354
 political views of, 227–230, 271–275
 Prelude, 271–273
Bernstein, Shirley, 282–283
Bernstein, Walter, 238–239
Berry, Lee, 240, 316n69, 320n84
Berry, Marva, 240, 243, 249
bin Wahad, Dhoruba (Richard Moore), 175, 230–231, 324–325, 327*i*, 328
Bird, Joan, 330
Biskind, Peter, 313
Black consciousness, 92, 96–97
Black Guerrilla Family (BGF), 303n30, 304
Black identity, 96, 96n71
Black nationalism, xix, xx–xxi, 85, 91, 91n39, 101–103, 129, 141–146, 147, 157, 172–173, 174–175, 176–177, 190–191, 214, 349–350
Black Panther, 139n13, 179n80, 189, 200–201, 314
Black Panther Party. *See also* Panther 21
 alliance between Peace and Freedom Party and, 167–168, 174
 attempted merger with SNCC, 168–172
 authorship of books allegedly written by members of, 139n12
 benefits and backlash from working with white radicals, 172–181, 305
 and Black nationalism in Oakland, 143–144
 challenges facing, 213
 Cleaver and Axelrod and, 155–162
 cross-racial collaborations of, 138–139, 157, 161–162, 165–166, 167–168, 177–181, 190–191, 196–210, 315–319
 depiction of, in "Radical Chic," 280–281
 dualism, 139, 189–191, 314–315
 early membership of, 146n27

Easter Plot, 192–193, 231, 324–325
financial support for, 179–181, 298n8, 310–315
formation of, 94–95
growth of, 190–196
historiography of, 139, 139n13
left liberals' alleged role in decline of, 297n1
and New Left, 165–166
Newton on, 350
partners with Communist Party, 196–202, 209, 209n111
protest at California State Assembly, 137–138
relations with liberals and radicals, 297–310
reported agreement with Al Fatah, 279–280
Stronghold Productions, 313–315
support for, 213–214
survival programs, 188n23, 188n24, 188–190, 200, 246–247, 279
trials of Panther 21 and Seale/Huggins, 320–332
violent clashes with police, 159, 176–177, 183–187
and Weatherman, 203–210
Black Power
as deployed by white radicals, 121–123, 124–126
elasticity of, 91
fallout from, 106–109
and National Conference for New Politics, 132
rise of, 90–91, 92–94
SNCC's turn to, 91–97, 101–106, 105n132
transformative reframing, 92
Black separatism, 97–98, 100–106, 138–139, 143–144, 146, 154, 170
relationship to Black nationalism, 91n39
Blake, J. Herman, 139n12, 319
Blauner, Bob, 318, 318n74, 345n14
Block, Luke (Bob), 99–100
Bloom, Joshua, 297n1
Bond, Julian, 7n4, 4, 49, 78, 104–105, 346
Borinski, Ernst, 32–33
Boudin, Kathy, 207*i*
Braden, Anne, 13, 13n37, 19, 99–100

Braden, Carl, 13, 13n37, 99–100
Branch, Taylor, 54n138
Brando, Marlon, 180
Brandt, Barbara, 77n93
Breines, Wini, 129
Brent, Bill, 156*i*
Brewster, Kingman, 297–298
Brogan, D. W., 66n30
Brotherhood of Sleeping Car Porters, 145
Brown, Cecil, 161
Brown, Ed, 73
Brown, Elaine, 292, 310–312
Brown, H. Rap, 107–108, 122n49, 132, 168–169, 170–171
Brown, James, 92
Brown, John, 204–205, 208
Browning, Frank, 149
Bryant, C. C., 8n15
Buchanan, Patrick, 285
Buckley, William F., 222, 273–274, 284–285
Bullins, Ed, 157, 157n67
Burnham, David Bright, 246, 254–255
Burns, Nathaniel (Sekou Odinga), 324

Cade, Cathy, 25–26, 56n151
Caldwell, Earl, 195
California Democratic Council, 60
California State Assembly, 137–138
Calvert, Greg, 121, 127, 130, 134
Campbell, James T., 174
campus-based student activism, 127–129. *See also* Students for a Democratic Society (SDS)
carceral state, 284–285
Carmichael, Stokely (Kwame Ture), 29*i*, 88*i*
and antiwar movement, 122
on Atlanta Project separatists, 103–104
criticism of white radicals, 170, 195n57
embraces Black Power, 105–106, 105n132, 142–143
on female volunteers, 53
and Freedom Vote, 34
on impact of Summer Project, 78
on importance of Freedom Schools, 51–52
on interracial organizing, 98
on MFDP challenge at Atlantic City, 65
moves to Africa, 344–345
news coverage of, 107–108

Carmichael, Stokely (Kwame Ture) (*Continued*)
  opposes expulsion of white SNCC staffers, 102
  organizes in Lowndes County, 94–95
  on Panthers' relationship with lawyers, 198
  on Panthers' violence and cross-racial politics, 175–176
  on post-Atlantic City malaise, 70
  and racial conflict in SNCC, 96–97
  on RAM separatists, 104n118
  and regional friction in SNCC, 54–55
  replaces Lewis as SNCC chairman, 98
  resigns from Black Panthers, 195
  Rustin's influence on, 16–18
  on SNCC, 5
  and SNCC–Panther Party partnership, 169–172
  and SNCC's repudiation of Rustin, 74
  on *Times*' article on Black Power, 101–102
  and Waveland retreat, 86–87, 87n23
  on white activists of SNCC, 20, 49–50
  on white-on-white organizing, 99–100
Carson, Clayborne, 15, 17–18, 93–94, 96, 108, 131
Carter, Bunchy, 173, 190
cause parties, 217–222. *See also* Panther 21
Center for Investigative Reporting (CIR), 345n13
Cetewayo (Michael Tabor), 309–310, 325, 328, 345
Chaberski, Stephen, 321–324, 331
Chaney, James, 44–45, 45n91, 46i, 52, 62, 69
Chapin, Schuyler, 259
Chávez, César, 221
Che-Lumumba Club, 333–334, 335–336
Chessman, Caryl, 147
Chicago Eight, 185–187, 196, 200–201
Chicago police, 193
Child Development Group of Mississippi (CDGM), 77–78
Chisholm, Shirley, 213–214
Christianity
  radical, 12–13
  SNCC's sidelining of, 105

civil disobedience, 12–13, 18, 20–21, 92–93, 146
Civil Rights Act (1964), 52, 66–67
Civil Rights Congress (CRC), 145, 145n22
Clark, Judith, 207i
Clark, Katie, 41–42
Clark, Mark, 193, 239–240
Clark, Ramsey, 213–214, 297–298, 297n4
class. *See also* radical chic; "Radical Chic: That Party at Lenny's" (Wolfe)
  and Black Power, 105
  and Economic and Research Action Project, 113n1, 118–121, 118n16, 125, 205
  new working-class theory, 124
  SNCC's assumptions regarding, 72–73
Cleaver, Eldridge, 156i
  and alliance between Black Panthers and PFP, 167–168
  and attacks on cops, 184–187
  background of, 146–148, 153–154
  and Black Panther Party, 155–162
  on Black Panthers' militarism, 184
  on Black Panthers' survival programs, 188–189
  on Communist Party, 199–200
  on Kim Il Sung, 201
  as Lovdjieff's student, 147n30
  moves to Algiers, 187, 345
  and New Left, 165–166
  and Panthers' partnerships, 196–197, 199–200, 207–209, 300
  and Panthers' partnerships with left-wing activists, 196
  on police aggression, 194
  post-Movement life of, 345
  relationship between Newton and, 303–304
  relationships with white radicals, 163
  relationship with Axelrod, 150–154, 159–160, 159n73, 159n80
  returns to America, 289–290
  and Revolutionary People's Constitutional Convention, 300, 303
  and SNCC–Panther Party partnership, 168, 170–171
  speaks at University of California, Irvine, 164i

on Weatherman, 207–209
on white allyship, 166, 200, 204–205
on Yippie, 185n16
Cleaver, Kathleen Neal, 159, 164–165, 165*i*, 167, 174, 188–189, 317
Cobb, Charles, 50–51, 61–62, 104
Cohen, Stonewall, 44
COINTELPRO, 101n101, 107–108, 189, 194, 295
Cold War, 66
Coleman, Kate, 312–313, 312n58, 345n13
Coles, Robert, 70n50
Collier, Robert, 253–254
Commentary, 285
Committee for Public Justice (CPJ), 287, 297–298, 297n4
Communist Party. *See also* anticommunism; House Un-American Activities Committee (HUAC)
    Axelrod on, 149
    Bay Area progressives' involvement with, 145
    Braden's alleged involvement with, 13n37
    and civil rights movement, 3n2
    Davis trial, 332–342
    and Du Bois Clubs, 146n25
    New Leftists' views on, 165–166
    partners with Black Panther Party, 196–202, 209, 209n111
    rich radicals' involvement in, 219
Congress for Racial Equality (CORE), 7, 91, 154, 245
Congress of Industrial Organizations (CIO), 236
conservative foundations, 289
Conyers, John, 148, 297
"Cotton Curtain," 7–8
Council of Federated Organizations (COFO), 31, 39, 83
Countryman, Peter, 119
Cox, Courtland, 23–24, 71n60, 94–95, 347
Cox, Don, 156*i*, 252*i*
    and benefit for Panther 21, 243, 244–245, 247–249, 253, 259–261, 275
    on Black nationalism of New York Black Panthers, 174–175
    on Black Panther membership numbers, 146n27
    cosmopolitanism, 245
    on Huey Newton, 344
    Kempton's support for, 299
    moves to Africa, 345
    and Newton prison break plot, 160
    on some Panthers' misunderstanding of Black Panther Party, 174
Crain, William, 243
Cruse, Harold, 105
Cultural and Scientific Conference for World Peace, 236–237
cultural nationalism, 172–173, 174–177
Currier, Audrey, 40
Currier, Stephen, 40
Curry, Constance, 20–21, 70
Curtis, Charlotte, 222, 222n28, 223*i*, 250–256, 255n48, 257–258

Daniels, Carolyn, 72
Davis, Angela, 139n16, 139, 199, 209n111, 332–343, 338*i*, 341*i*, 347–348
Davis, Rennie, 291–292, 296*i*, 316
Days of Rage, 205–206
Dellinger, David, 122, 296*i*
Del Pozzo, Theresa, 99–100
Democratic National Convention (Atlantic City, 1964). *See* Atlantic City
Democratic Party. *See also* Atlantic City
    and MFDP challenge at Atlantic City, 62–63
    realignment of, 61, 67
Dennis, Dave, 45n91, 347
Dennis, Eugene, 17–18
Dennis, Peggy, 17–18
Didion, Joan, 198
Diggers, 188, 188n23
Dimitrov, Georgi, 200–201
Dittmer, John, 40n66, 52, 73n71
Dixon, Aaron, 188n23
Doar, John, 23
Dodge, Mabel, 217–218
Dohrn, Bernadine, 206, 207*i*
Donaldson, Ivanhoe
    on being defined by locals, 74
    and Freedom Vote, 34–35
    on increased whites in SNCC, 38
    on MFDP challenge at Atlantic City, 61–62
    post-Movement life of, 346
    on white-on-white organizing, 113n1, 100

draft/draft resistance, 122, 122n46, 123–124, 124n58, 125–127, 309
Draper, Alan, 73n71
Du Bois, W. E. B., 16–17, 244n6
Du Bois Clubs, 120–121, 146, 146n25
Dunbar-Ortiz, Roxanne, 305, 343–344, 351
Durr, Virginia, 68n42, 77–78, 226–227
Dylan, Bob, 144

Easter Plot, 192–193, 231, 324–325. *See also* Panther 21
Eastland, James, 77–78
Economic and Research Action Project (ERAP) of SDS, 113n1, 118–121, 118n16, 125, 205
Ehrlichman, John, 191n43
Electric Kool-Aid Acid Test, The (Wolfe), 268–271
Epstein, Edward Jay, 299
Epstein, Jason, 284
Epstein, Joseph, 215, 285, 289
Evans, Linda, 207*i*
Evans, Rowland, 279–280

Fanon, Frantz, 93
Farmer, James, 31–32
fascism, 201–202
Federal Bureau of Investigation (FBI). *See also* Hoover, J. Edgar
  actions against Black Panthers, 189, 194–195
  and Axelrod's alleged involvement with Communist Party, 149
  COINTELPRO, 101n101, 107–108, 189, 194, 295
  Davis wanted by, 334–335
  and Panthers' partnership with Communist Party, 202
  surveils Bernstein, 227–229, 258, 287–288
  tracks SNCC, 35, 104, 107–108
Feingold, Mimi, 125–126
Felker, Clay, 266–267, 267n28, 268
feminism, 129–130
Fenton, David, 235*i*
Fergus, Devin, 298
Ferguson, Andrew, 289
Fizdale, Robert, 259
Flacks, Richard, 115n2, 118
Fonda, Jane, 290–291

Forcade, Tom, 235*i*
Ford, Joudon, 192
Forman, James, 21*i*, 24*i*, 41*i*
  and Black Power, 94
  criticizes cross-racial coalitions, 107
  denounces Israel, 107
  on FOS contributions, 86
  on future of SNCC, 83
  at National Conference for New Politics, 132
  news coverage of, 107–108
  Newton on separatist speech of, 168–169
  and northerners in SNCC leadership positions, 54
  as original Black Panther, 95
  post-Movement life of, 347
  and record-keeping of SNCC, 139
  on SNCC clothing, 25
  and SNCC finances, 20, 40–41, 40n67
  and SNCC–Panther Party partnership, 170–172
  and Summer Project, 40
  and transcending race at Waveland, 89
  and white-on-white organizing, 100
Forman, Mildred, 26*i*
Fox, Ingram, 321, 327–330
Fraser, Steve, 223
Free Breakfast for School Children Program, 188–189, 200
Freed, Donald, 139n12, 299, 332
Freedom Budget, 75
Freedom Rides, 7
Freedom Schools, 50–52, 77–78
Freedom Summer. *See* Mississippi Summer Project
Freedom Vote, 31–36
Free Huey! campaign, 163n1, 166, 167–168, 170–171, 173
Free Speech Movement (FSM), 116n5, 116–118
Frey, Dick, 37–38
Frey, John, 34, 159, 166, 176, 187
Friends of SNCC (FOS), 23, 34, 40–41, 71, 85–86
fundraising
  for Black Panthers, 179–181, 298n8, 310–315

for SNCC, 20, 20n68, 23, 40–41, 71,
    86, 91–92, 102, 106–107, 106n134,
    107n138, 108n142, 116, 311

Ganz, Marshall, 347
Garman, Betty, 23, 69n45, 71n60
Garrett, Jimmy, 98–99, 106, 199
Garrett-Forte, Janice, 173–174
Garrow, David, 139n12
Garry, Charles
    Axelrod and, 149
    background of, 163–164
    Cleaver and, 150
    on conducting a political trial, 318
    and Newton's defense, 34, 153, 164–166,
        165*i*, 197–198, 199*i*, 317–319
    and Panthers' partnership with
        Communist Party, 202
    on police killings of Panthers, 299
    on Seale/Huggins trial, 331
Gary, James, 323
Genet, Jean, 314–315
Giles, Ben, 323
Gitlin, Todd, 34, 34n21, 119, 346
Glazer, Nathan, 285
Gold, Arthur, 259
Goldberg, Art, 139n12, 200n72
Goldman, Emma, 217–219
Goldsmith, Barbara, 258–259, 258n67
Goldwater, Barry, 66
Goodlett, Carlton Benjamin, 145, 145n21
Goodman, Andrew, 44–45, 46*i*, 52, 62, 69,
    220
Gornick, Vivian, 224
Gorton, Doy, 96
Gottlieb, Bob, 126
Gray, Victoria, 75–76
Great Society programs, 67, 73
Greenberg, David, 263n1
Grizzard, Vernon, 128*i*
Grogan, Emmett, 188, 188n23
Gruen, John, 260, 271–273, 274–275, 277
Guggenheimer, Ellie, 278
Guinea, 70–71
gun ownership, 92–93
Guyot, Lawrence, 35, 78, 105, 346

Haber, Joyce, 282
Haldeman, H. R., 261
Hall, Bill, 103

Hall, Gus, 199–200
Hall, Jacqueline Dowd, 3n2
Hamer, Fannie Lou, 56–57, 62–63, 64*i*, 65,
    102–103
Hamlett, Ed, 13n37
Hampton, Fred, 191*i*
    assassination of, 193, 239–240, 298–299
    criticism of Weatherman, 205–208
    Rainbow Coalition, 190–191
    Wolfe's silence on growing evidence of
        police hit job on, 280–281
Hansen, Bill, 101n101
Hanson, Bruce, 41*i*
Harding, Vincent, 42–43
Harper, David B., 318–319
Harrington, Michael, 61, 118, 241, 283
Harris, Albert, 335, 338–339
Harris, David, 72n64, 124n58
Harris, Donald, 93
Harrisburg Seven, 287
Hartford, Bruce, 99n89
Hayden, Casey, 22*i*
    disputes accusations of Carmichael's
        sexism, 87n24
    and Economic and Research Action
        Project, 113n1, 118n16, 120
    and expulsion of white SNCC
        staffers, 113, 113n1
    on MFDP challenge at Atlantic City, 62
    on office work, 25–26
    on post-Atlantic City malaise, 70
    post-Movement life of, 346
    on retention of white volunteers, 81–82
    "Sex and Caste," 126, 129, 129n83
    and Summer Project, 38–39
    and ubiquity of race at Waveland, 89–90
    and white terror, 29
    on working interracially, 20, 24–25, 82
    and work of white SNCC staffers, 20–23
Hayden, Tom, 59n3, 116, 118, 120, 128*i*,
    241, 296*i*, 346
Head Start Program, 77–78
Healey, Dorothy, 68–69, 183, 199–200, 341
Heanes, Herbert, 159
Hecksher, August, 253–254
Hecksher, Mrs. August, 253–254
Hellman, Lillian, 228, 235, 238, 297n4
Helms, Richard, 307
Hemphill, Janie L., 338–339

Hewitt, Ray "Masai," 190, 240
Hilliard, David, 296i
  advice to white radicals, 303
  on Black Panther membership, 146n27
  Black student unions' resistance to Panthers' cross-racial work, 173
  charges against, 185n17
  on Cleaver's plan to seize Merritt College, 196–197
  differing views in party of militarism, 183–184
  FBI and police thwart Panthers' aims, 295
  on Free Breakfast for School Children Program, 188
  Kenner and, 313–314
  on New York Panthers' cultural nationalism, 174–175
  and partnership between Black Panthers and PFP, 167–168
  and Stronghold Productions, 314
  and support for Panthers of Winston-Salem, 298
  on Yippie, 197
Hills, Fred, 328
Hinckle, Warren, 151
Hine, Darlene Clark, 109
hippies, 124–125, 129, 144, 305–306
Hoffman, Abbie, 124–125, 125n63, 129, 197, 233i, 235i, 296i, 306, 311–312, 344n6
Hoffman, Anita, 235i
Hoffman, Julius, 196
Hoffmann, Alex (Sascha), 158, 178–179, 188n29, 300, 313–314, 317
Hogan, Frank, 192–193
Hogan, Wesley, 34–35, 36n43
Hollis Springs project, 71
Holt, Len, 31, 31n4, 59–60, 61n11
Hoover, J. Edgar, 62–63, 107–108, 180, 189, 191–192, 191n43, 194, 230, 258. *See also* Federal Bureau of Investigation (FBI)
Horne, Gerald, 145n21, 163n1
Horowitz, David, 133, 345, 345n13, 346
Horton, Myles, 13
Hottelet, Richard, 279–280
House Un-American Activities Committee (HUAC), 220, 228, 228n57. *See also* anticommunism

Howard, Elbert, 296i
Howard, Ruth, 40–41, 77, 94–95, 94n61, 108–109
Howe, Irving, 225n45, 226, 241, 283
Huerta, Delores, 290
Huggins, Ericka, 167, 194–195, 316, 319, 331–332, 333i, 346
Huggins, John, 173
Humphrey, Hubert, 62–63, 150
Hunter-Gault, Charlayne, 266n20
Hurst, Claude, 60
Hurst, E. H., 27–28
Hutton, Bobby, 184–185, 184n7

Independent Citizens Committee for the Arts, Sciences and Professions (ICCASP), 236–237
Indochinese Peace Campaign (IPC), 308–309
informants, 191i, 193–195
Innis, Roy, 131–132, 132n90
Institute for Policy Studies (IPS), 68, 132, 307–308
integration, 93, 98
International Longshoremen's and Warehousemen's Union (ILWU), 145
interracialism
  of East Bay Branch of Civil Rights Congress, 145
  Lewis on, 209
  and Mississippi Summer Project, 36–42
  and SNCC–Panther Party partnership, 168–169, 170–172
  of Student Nonviolent Coordinating Committee, 4–5, 10, 19–27, 36n43, 55–56, 76–77
  and white-on-white organizing, 98
Ireland, Doug, 251
"Is Fact Necessary" (Lewin), 267
Israel, 107
Isserman, Maurice, 336

Jackson, George, 152–153, 300, 303n30, 304, 334–335, 339–340
Jackson, Jesse, 348–349
Jackson, Jonathan, 334–335, 339–340
Jacobs, John, 203
Jacobs, Paul, 268n38
Jaglom, Henry, 311
Jeffries, Hasan, 94–95, 108n143

INDEX

Jenkins, Timothy, 8n9, 32–33
Jensen, Lowell, 317
Jewish Defense League (JDL), 258, 353–354
Jews
    collaborations between Blacks and, 16–18, 18nn55–56
    idea of parallel experiences of Blacks and, 43–45
    and Mississippi Summer Project, 43–45
    unraveling of coalition between Black radicals and, 241–242
Joel, Super, 235*i*
Johnson, Lyndon Baines, 45, 61, 61n10, 62–65, 66–67, 107–108, 127. *See also* Great Society programs
Jonas, Gerald, 267
Jones, Barbara, 40n64
Jones, Charles, 32
Jones, Hettie, 159
Jones, Jeff, 203
Jones, LeRoi (Amiri Baraka), 43, 157, 157n67, 159, 171, 225n48
Joseph, Jamal, 309n49
Joseph, Peniel E., 138n11

Kahane, Meir, 258
Kahn, Tom, 17n51
Karenga, Maulana, 141–142, 173, 177, 347–348
Kask, Melanie, 152, 160
Katz, Sanford M., 243
Kaufman, Jonathan, 43–44
Kazin, Michael, 226
Keating, Edward, 151
Kempton, Murray, 140, 166, 230–231, 261–262, 299, 322–324, 326, 327*i*
Kennebeck, Edward, 321–323, 328–329
Kennedy, Ethel, 222
Kennedy, John F., 27n95, 61, 229, 269n41
Kennedy, Robert F., 31–32, 65
Kenner, Martin, 235*i*
    on attack on Napier, 304
    and benefit for Panther 21, 238–239, 243
    and blowback from Panther 21 benefit, 259–260
    and defense of Panther 21, 232–234
    on Felicia Bernstein, 244
    and impact of "Radical Chic," 287
    leftist activism of, 133–134

    and *New York Times'* coverage of benefit for Panther 21, 250–251, 254
    and Panther 21 trial, 330
    and Panther finances, 313–315
    post-Movement life of, 347
    on Schneider, 311–312
Kesey, Ken, 268–270, 268n38
Kessler-Harris, Alice, 297n4
Khachigian, Ken, 285
Kim Il Sung, 201
King, Martin Luther Jr., 47*i*. *See also* Southern Christian Leadership Conference (SCLC)
    assassination of, 184
    criticizes Vietnam War, 106–107
    and MFDP challenge at Atlantic City, 63–64
    nonviolence of, 92–93
    on parallel experiences of Blacks and Jews, 44
    Rustin and, 16
    on SNCC workers, 7n1
King, Mary
    on COFO, 39
    and expulsion of white SNCC staffers, 113n2
    on inclusiveness of SNCC, 90
    on insurgency in white communities, 99n89
    post-Movement life of, 346
    "Sex and Caste," 126, 129
    on SNCC budget, 71n62
    on SNCC community, 4–5
    and Summer Project, 49
    and Waveland retreat, 87, 89–90
King, Mel, 348
Kinsolving, Lester, 286
Kluger, Richard, 268
Koch, Edward I, 240
Kopkind, Andrew, 130, 208
Krim, Seymour, 224–226, 225n48
Kristol, Irving, 284–285
Krogh, Egil, 261
Ku Klux Klan (KKK), 45, 97–98
Kunstler, William, 246, 330–331
Kurshan, Nancy, 235*i*

Ladner, Dorie, 26*i*, 36
Ladner, Joyce, 17n51, 26*i*, 54–55, 346
Lane, Mary, 77

Lapham, Lewis, 289–290
Lardner, Ring Jr., 236–238
Lawson, James, 12–13, 12n30
Lawson, Steven F., 61
League of American Writers, 264
Lee, Bobby, 190–191
Lee, Herbert, 27–29
Lefcourt, Gerald
 and attorney for Abbie Hoffman, 233*i*
 and benefit for Panther 21, 243, 246, 249
 and defense of Panther 21, 232–233, 315–316
 and Panther 21 trial, 321–322, 324–325, 329
 on Seale/Huggins trial, 331
left-wing politics and mentors, as influencing SNCC activists, 11–18
Lehmann-Haupt, Christopher, 270–271, 280, 286
Lester, Julius, 96n76, 98–99, 103, 121–122
Levison, Stanley, 16
Lewin, Leonard C., 267
Lewis, John
 on Black Power, 90–92
 Carmichael replaces, as SNCC chairman, 98
 commitment to Black revolutions in Africa, 91n38
 and Freedom Vote, 34
 on impact of Summer Project, 78
 on interracialism, 209
 liberal cocktail party circuit, 91–92
 and Malcolm X, 93
 on MFDP challenge at Atlantic City, 61–62
 post-Movement life of, 346
 on racial conflict in SNCC, 96–97
 on racially motivated murders, 45
 on sex during Summer Project, 56
 sidelined by Forman, 54
 on SNCC donations, 108n142
 speeches of, 17n51
 on white-on-white organizing, 100
Lewis, Michael, 283
liberal foundations, 40–41, 107, 289
liberalism
 Cold War, xxiii, 66, 220
 conservatives' attacks on, as elitist, 220, 285, 353

historiography, xxiii, 297n1
limousine and linoleum liberals, 222–223
New Left's relation to, xxiii, 120–121, 224–226, 290
Panthers' relations with liberals, 210, 297–300, 297n1
SNCC's growing skepticism about, 43, 68–69, 89, 93
liberal masochism, 273–274
liberal paternalism, 42–43, 115–116, 131–132
Lichtenstein, Nelson, 67
limousine liberals, 222–223
Lindsay, John, 222–223
linoleum liberals, 223
Little, Joanne (Joan), 347–348
Los Angeles Police Department, 193–194
Lovdjieff, Chris, 147n30
Love, Ken, 204*i*
Lowenstein, Allard, 33, 33nn16–17, 63–64, 113n2
Lowndes County, Alabama, 94–95
Lowndes County Freedom Organization (LCFO), 94–95, 94n61, 108, 108n143, 143
Lubell, David, 314
Lumet, Gail, 238–240, 251, 259, 290
Lumet, Sidney, 228
lumpenproletariat, 155–156, 190
Lynd, Staughton, 49–50, 72n69, 122, 124
Lyon, Danny, 103

Macdonald, Dwight, 267–268, 270–271
Machtinger, Howard, 207*i*
MacLeish, Archibald, 219–220
Mailer, Norman, 115
Major, Reginald, 172–173
Makeba, Miriam, 344–345
Malcolm X, 93, 138, 142
Malcom, Janet, 255n46
Marcuse, Herbert, 336, 337*i*
Marine Cooks and Stewards Union (MCSU), 145
Markfield, Wallace, 281
Marshall, Burke, 23
Marshall, Thurgood, 7n5
Martin, Waldo, 297n1
Martínez, Elizabeth "Betita" Sutherland, 87*i*
 Axelrod collaborates with, 160

and collaborations between Jews and
   Blacks, 18n56
post-Movement life of, 347
on problems facing SNCC, 88–89
salary of, 86
on SNCC's move to Black
   Power, 104–105
and Summer Project, 38–39
on treatment of whites in SNCC, 96
on white-on-white organizing, 100
Marvin X, 157, 157n67
Marxism, 134
McAdam, Doug, 43–44, 49n107, 56n157
McAfee, Rodger, 336–337, 338*i*
McComb, Mississippi, 69
McDew, Charles, 15–16
McGovern, George, 285
McGrath, Alice, 219–220
Meacham, Stewart, 128*i*
Medical Committee for Human Rights, 52
Merritt College, 196–197
Meyer, Karl, 213n2, 248, 256
Michigan Committee Against Repression
   (MCAR), 297, 297n2
Miller, Loren, 91
Miller, Merle, 226n51
Miller, Mike, 12*i*, 34–35, 37–38, 41–42,
   91n38, 113, 347
Miller, Nathan, 285
Mills, C. Wright, 115–116, 115n2, 121,
   128–129
ministers, involvement in SNCC, 13
Minnis, Jack
   and Black Panther Party, 95
   and Carmichael's unseating of Lewis, 98
   and challenging of Mississippi regulars at
      Atlantic City, 59–60
   discovers law enabling formation of
      LCFO, 94–95
   and SNCC's research department, 23–24
   and Waveland retreat, 82*i*
   and white-on-white organizing, 100
   and work of white SNCC staffers, 20–21
Minor, Ethel, 103n109, 171
Mississippi Freedom Democratic Party
   (MFDP). *See also* Democratic National
   Convention (Atlantic City, 1964)
   Congressional Challenge of, 75–76

divide between SNCC and, 72–73,
   73n71
jams entrance to Atlantic City's
   Convention Hall, 63*i*
launching of, 59–60
opposes Vietnam War, 122n46
registration in, 49–50, 53
support for, 60
Mississippi Summer Project
   backlash against, 53–54
   canvassing, 50
   community centers, 50–51
   confrontation of problems related
      to, 71–72
   and criticism over interracialism in
      SNCC, 36–42
   federal protection of civil rights workers
      during, 69
   freedom schools, 50–52, 77–78
   impact of, 75–79
   as potential path toward achieving Black
      voting rights, 35–36
   and redefinition of solidarity in
      SNCC, 42–45
   tensions and accomplishments of, 52–57
Mitchell, Henry, 243, 253
Mitford, Jessica, 69n42, 145, 148, 226–227
Moore, Amzie, 8–9, 8n15, 31–32
Moore, Gilbert, 316, 318–319
Moore, Honor, 326
Moore, Iris, 238–239, 243, 249, 327*i*
Moore, Paul, 300
Moore, Richard (Dhoruba bin Wahad), 175,
   230–231, 324–325, 327*i*, 328
Moratoriums to End the War in
   Vietnam, 127, 230
Morgan, Jo-Ann, 158
Morrison, Toni, 96n71, 178, 349
Moses, Robert (Bob) Parris, 12*i*, 41*i*
   and antiwar movement, 122
   beginnings in SNCC, 8n9, 4
   and Black Power, 94–95
   emulation of, 49, 84
   on folding of CDGM, 77–78
   on Freedom Rides, 7
   and Freedom Schools, 51–52
   and Freedom Vote, 33, 35
   and Free Speech Movement, 117–118
   on future of SNCC, 82–83

Moses, Robert (Bob) Parris (*Continued*)
   on gaining community trust, 8n15
   on impact of Summer Project, 78
   influence of, 84–85, 116n5
   on intragroup divides in SNCC, 90
   on mass meetings, 13
   and MFDP challenge at Atlantic City, 59–61
   on Moore, 8–9
   moves to Africa, 344–345
   NAACP on, 27
   on nonviolence, 92–93
   parts ways with SNCC, 105
   on post-Atlantic City objectives, 72
   post-Movement life of, 347
   and redefinition of solidarity in SNCC, 42
   and regional friction in SNCC, 54–55
   Rustin's influence on, 17–18
   and SNCC approach and strategy, 10–12
   on SNCC finances, 107
   on SNCC growth and success, 76–77
   on SNCC's approach to economic issues, 89
   on SNCC's interracialism, 19
   and Summer Project, 35–36, 37–39, 41–42, 48–49
   on Sweeney, 113n2
   voter registration efforts of, 8
   Waskow's correspondence with, 68
   at Waveland conference, 84*i*
   on white-on-white organizing, 99–100
   and white terror, 27–29
   and work-study project, 39
Mostel, Zero, 228n57
Mount Olive Baptist Church, 10
movement-building, xviii, 14–15, 68–69, 132–133, 307–310
   organizing against one's own unfreedom, 115–116, 120–130, 133–134
Moynihan, Daniel Patrick, 261
Mulford Act, 137
Mulvey, Harold, 331–332
Murch, Donna, 161, 188n24
Murray, Pauli, 3n3
Murtagh, John J., 208, 231–232, 321–323, 327–329
Muste, A. J., 122

Napier, Sam, 37n32, 304
National Association for the Advancement of Colored People (NAACP), 8–9, 27–28, 31–32, 77, 91–93, 149, 190–191, 220, 249, 279, 297
National Committees to Combat Fascism (NCCFs), 201
National Conference for New Politics (NCNP), 107, 131–132
National Council of American-Soviet Friendship (NCASF), 234–236
National Council of Churches, 20, 52, 68–69
nationalism, 91n39, 100–106. *See also* Black nationalism
National Lawyers Guild, 18, 53, 149, 178–179, 314, 318–319
National Mobilization to End the War in Vietnam, 291–292
National Student Association (NSA), 20–21, 101n102
National United Committee to Free Angela Davis (NUCFAD), 334–336, 339
Nation of Islam (NOI), 91, 141–142, 147
Nazi analogy, 44, 246–247
Nazi Germany, 44, 51–52, 66, 242
Neier, Aryeh, 260
neoconservatism, xxii–xxiii, 274, 284–285
Nesbit, Lynn, 225
Newfield, Jack, 146n25
New Haven chapter of Black Panthers, 194–195
new journalism, 224, 263, 267–268, 277
New Left, 34, 115n2, 115–120, 121, 133–134, 165–166
Newson, Jerry, 145
Newton, Fredrika, 344n7
Newton, Huey P.
   on all Americans as colonized, 200
   and alliance between Black Panthers and PFP, 167
   authorship of books ostensibly written by, 139n12
   on Axelrod, 158
   and Black nationalism in Oakland, 141–142, 143–144, 146
   on Black Panther membership, 146n27
   and Black Panther Party, 138, 155–156

on Black Panthers' militarism, 183–184
and Black Panthers' relationship with Communist Party, 209n111
and Black Panthers' survival programs, 188–189
defense of, 164–168, 197–198, 199*i*, 317–319
dismissed of manslaughter charges, 309–310
duality of, 139
and end of Panthers, 344
espouses repression, 183, 185
on Forman's separatist speech, 168–169
Free Huey! campaign, 163n1, 166, 167–168, 170–171, 173
Garry and, 153
image in rattan chair, 158, 186*i*
and Kenner's split from Panthers, 314–315
lifestyle of, 309–310, 309n49
opposes Panthers battling Oakland police, 184–185
post-Movement life of, 344n7, 350
relationship between Cleaver and, 303–304
released on bail, 34
and Revolutionary People's Constitutional Convention, 301, 301*i*, 303
Schneider and, 311–313, 312n58, 313n61
and SNCC–Panther Party partnership, 169, 172
and Stronghold Productions, 313–314
on Treuhaft, 145
turn toward electoral politics, 310
verdict in first trial, 187, 317–319
violent clash with Oakland police, 159–160
and white radicals, 178–179, 305
Williams's influence on, 141
on working cross-racially, 173
Newton, Melvin, 139n12
new working-class theory, 124
New Yorker, The, 224–225, 266–268
New York magazine, 266–268, 281–282
New York Police Department (NYPD), 191–193
New York Review of Books, The, 241, 267–268
New York Times, 101–102, 257–258, 263n1
Nixon, Richard
and antiwar movement, 127
and blowback from Panther 21 benefit, 261
on capture of Angela Davis, 335
and decline of Black Panther Party, 297n1
and draft resistance, 127
and impact of "Radical Chic," 285
and police violence, 191–192
War on Drugs to attack "perceived enemies," 191n43
nonviolence, 12–13, 18, 20–21, 92–93, 146
Nonviolent Action Committee (N-VAC), 93–94
Noonan, Martha Prescod Norman, 12*i*, 54–55
Norman, Silas Jr., 97n77
North Carolina Civil Liberties Union (NCCLU), 298
Northern Student Movement, 22–23, 34, 41–42
Norton, Eleanor Holmes, 87n23
Novak, Robert, 279–280

Oakland, California, Black nationalism in, 141–146
Obama, Barack, 349
O'Connor, Alice, 289
Odinga, Sekou (Nathaniel Burns), 324
O'Donnell, Sheila, 152
Office of Economic Opportunity (OEO), 77–78
office work, 23, 25–26, 37–38
Oglesby, Carl, 122n46, 134
Old Left, 115–116, 165–166, 199–200, 226, 228, 283–284, 291, 333
O'Neal, William, 191*i*, 193
On the Town (Bernstein), 227–228
Oppenheimer, Robert, 237
Other America, The (Harrington), 118

Palestine, 107
Panther 21. *See also* "Radical Chic: That Party at Lenny's" (Wolfe)
benefits for, 214
blowback from benefit for, 256–262
defense of, 232–238, 315–316

Panther (*Continued*)
　Easter Plot, 192–193, 231, 324–325. *See also* Panther 21
　events of benefit for, 243–249
　New York Times' coverage of benefit for, 250–256
　radical chic and Bernsteins' benefit for, 227, 238–242
　trial of, 208, 230–232, 320–331
Patterson, William, 145n21, 163n1, 166–167, 197–198, 197n67, 199–202
Patton, Gwen, 54
Payne, Charles, 25, 32n8, 36n43, 73–74, 96, 107–108
Payne, Roz, 139n12
Peace and Freedom Party (PFP), 132, 167–168, 174, 189, 196
Peacock, Willie, 78
Pearlman, Lise, 318
Pearson, Norman Holmes, 265
Peck, Abe, 235*i*
Pell, Eve, 152–153
People of New York Against Lumumba Abdul Shakur et al., The. See Panther 21
Phillips, Joseph A., 321, 322–323, 328–329
Phillips, Mickey, 314
Phipps, Cynthia, 253
Piercy, Marge, 126
Plimpton, Freddie, 221
Plimpton, George, 221
Podhoretz, Norman, 241, 274, 282, 289–290
police. *See also* Panther 21
　assassination of Hampton, 193, 298
　campaign of repression against Black Panthers, 190–196
　shoot-outs with Black Panthers, 159, 176–177, 183–187
　Weatherman's attacks on, 208
Pontecorvo, Gillo, 322
Poole, Cecil F., 213–214
"Port Authority Statement," 124
Port Huron Statement, 115–116
Potter, David, 265
Potter, Paul, 34, 118, 118n16, 119–121, 121n44
Poussaint, Alvin, 70
Prelude (Bernstein), 271–273
Preminger, Otto, 248–249, 257

Price, Leontyne, 244
Price, Raymond K., 285–286
Prinz, Joachim, 44, 44n86
prisoners' rights movement, 152–153
Private World of Leonard Bernstein, The (Gruen), 271–272
Procaccino, Mario, 222–223
Proctor, Roscoe, 197–198
Progressive Labor (PL) Party, 120–121, 203
Project 2025, xx
Pryor, Richard, 313n61

Quat, Leon, 243–244, 247, 260–261
Quotations from Chairman Mao Zedong, 144

Rabinowitz, Dorothy, 286
Rabinowitz, Joni, 18n55
Rabinowitz, Victor, 18n55
Rackley, Alex, 194–195, 299
radical chic, 215. *See also* "Radical Chic: That Party at Lenny's" (Wolfe)
　and benefit for Panther 21, 238–242
　and cause parties, 217–222
　coinage of term by Seymour Krim, 224–226, 226n51
　and defense of Panther 21, 232–238
　and limousine liberals and linoleum liberals, 222–223
　and politics of Bernsteins, 227–230
　ubiquity of trope, 282
Radical Chic and Mau-Mauing the Flak Catchers (Wolfe), 282, 286, 288–289
"Radical Chic: That Party at Lenny's" (Wolfe), 214–215
　"general mindset" of, 277–281
　impact of, 281–292, 295, 353
　narration in, 276–277
　and Wolfe journalistic credibility, 267–268, 270–278
radical Christianity, 12–13
Rafelson, Bob, 311, 313
Rahv, Philip, 283
Rainato, Joe, 329–330
Rainbow Coalition, 190–191, 348–349
Ramparts, 132, 146, 151–152, 153–154, 157, 172–173, 178
Randolph, A. Philip, 16–17, 75
Rangel, Charles, 213–214
Raskin, Marcus, 68

Rauh, Joseph, 63–64
Reagon, Bernice Johnson, 5, 8, 57, 347–348, 354
Red Scare, 219–221, 228
Reed, Ishmael, 225–226
religion, as influencing SNCC activists, 11–13, 18. *See also* Christianity
repression
  against Black Panthers, 137, 184–185, 192–196, 295
  Black Panthers' survival programs, 188–190
  and growth of Black Panther Party, 190–196
  against SNCC, 62–63
research, 23–24
Retherford, Jim, 235*i*
Reuther, Walter, 61, 63–64
Revolutionary Action Movement (RAM), 78–79, 101nn100–101, 104, 104n118, 142
Revolutionary People's Constitutional Convention (RPCC), 300–303, 309
Rhodes, Jane, 179n80
Richards, Dona, 37, 39, 51–52
Richardson, Judy, 23–24, 81, 102–103
Robbins, Jerome, 228, 228n57, 229, 273
Robbins, Terry, 203
Roberts, Gene, 323–324
Robertson, Nan, 254–255
Robeson, Paul, 197–198, 220, 220n17, 228
Robin Hood. See *Adventures of Robin Hood, The*
Robinson, Jackie, 66
Robinson, Mrs. T, 223*i*
Robinson, Ruby Doris Smith, 61–62, 90, 105–106, 108
romanticizing the poor, 25, 72–74, 118–120, 143
Roraback, Catherine, 333*i*
Rorem, Ned, 247–249
Ross, Alex, 277
Roth, Robert, 207*i*
Rothstein, Vivian, 125
Rubin, Jerry, 161, 185n16, 235*i*, 344, 350
Rudd, Mark, 203, 209, 231, 305–306
Rush, Bobby, 346, 348–349
Rustin, Bayard, 17*i*
  aims for Democratic realignment, 61
  disagreements with SNCC, 74–75
  early influence on SNCC activists, 13, 16–18
  and Freedom Vote, 34
  on government attacks against Black Panthers, 213–214
  homosexuality, 16, 16n46
  and MFDP challenge at Atlantic City, 61n11, 62–64
  on New Deal coalition, 67, 67n36
  Panthers' alleged threat against, 248
  promotes Freedom Budget, 75
  on SNCC's repudiation of Atlantic City compromise, 67
  on white activism, 97, 97n78
  on white backlash, 66
Ryon, Stephanie, 341*i*

Salmieri, Steve, 250–251
Sams, George, 195n57, 299
Samstein, Mendy, 38, 44, 64–65, 69, 90, 123, 124, 125n63, 347
  draft resistance, 124, 125n63
Sanders, Ed, 235*i*
Sanger, Margaret, 218
Savio, Mario, 3n6, 49, 115n2, 116–118, 117*i*, 116n5, 116n9
Scheer, Robert, 68–69, 132, 146, 164*i*, 177–178, 227, 230, 268n38, 315, 346
Schneider, Bert, 291–292, 311–313, 312*i*, 312n58, 313n61
Schwerner, Michael, 19n63, 20, 44–45, 45n91, 46*i*, 52, 56n151, 62, 69
Seale, Bobby
  and Black nationalism in Oakland, 141–142, 143–144, 146
  and Black Panther partnerships, 167–168, 170, 202
  and Black Panthers' pivot to survival programs, 188
  charged in torture and killing of Rackley, 194–195
  defense of, 316, 319
  on early Black Panther adherents, 155–156
  on interracial organizing, 204–205
  and Newton's defense, 165*i*

Seale, Bobby (*Continued*)
　on New York Black Panthers, 175
　on police aggression, 185–187
　political activism of, 344
　receives large donation for the
　　party, 179–180
　runs for office, 310
　Seize the Time, 139n12, 200, 200n72
　trial of, 196, 331–332
　on white reaction to Black Panthers, 138
Seale, John, 231
Search and Destroy report, 298
Seize the Time (Seale), 139n12, 200, 200n72
Seldes, Barry, 229
Self, Robert, 145
Sellers, Cleveland
　and Black staffers recruited by SNCC, 82
　on closing of Hollis Springs project, 71
　and MFDP challenge at Atlantic City, 61
　on Moses, 49
　on post-Atlantic City objectives, 72
　and SNCC–Panther Party
　　partnership, 169
　on SNCC staffers, 48–49
　on white backlash against Mississippi
　　Summer Project, 53–54
　on white-on-white organizing, 100
sex, 56–57, 56n157
"Sex and Caste" (Hayden and King), 126, 129, 129n83
sexism, 87, 87nn23–24, 90, 125–126
Sexual Freedom League (SFL), 144
Shabazz, Betty, 157
Shakur, Afeni, 153, 231, 299, 304, 326, 327*i*, 329–330, 330n129
Shakur, Lumumba, 176–177, 329–330
Shakur, Tupac, 37n32, 330
Shawn, William, 266–267
Sheean, Jimmy, 33n15
Sherrod, Charles, 11*i*
　on growth of right-wing white citizens
　　councils, 69
　and importance of staff confronting race
　　at Waveland, 89
　on moving of SNCC's goalposts, 88
　parts ways with SNCC, 104
　post-Movement life of, 346
　and SNCC approach and strategy, 8–12
　and SNCC's "as if" philosophy, 8
　and Summer Project, 37
Shirah, Sam, 97–98
Siegel, Dan, 176–178
Silver, Robert, 241
Simon, John, 240
Sims, Tracy (Taman Tracy Moncur), 146
sit-ins, 3, 31–32
Slaughter, Arlene, 180, 314
Sleepy Lagoon Defense Committee
　(SLDC), 219–220
Slesinger, Tess, 219, 313
Smith, Barbara, 348
Smith, Jean Wheeler, 10, 56, 82*i*
Snellings, Roland (Askia Touré), 51n125
Soledad Brothers, 334, 339–340
Soledad Brothers Defense Committee
　(SBDC), 334
solidarity, redefinition of, 42–45
Soul on Ice (Cleaver), 160
Soul Students Advisory Council
　(SSAC), 142
Southern Christian Leadership Conference
　(SCLC), 8n9, 9–10, 14–16
Southern Conference Educational Fund
　(SCEF), 13, 13n37, 26–27, 105
Southern Student Organizing Committee
　(SSOC), 97–98
Southwest Georgia Project, 104
Soviet Union, 60
Spencer, Robyn C., 173–174
Spiegel, Michael, 207*i*
Stalinism, 188–189, 188n29
Stanford, Maxwell (Akbar Muhammad
　Ahmad), 78, 101n100, 104n118, 143
Stansell, Christine, 218
Stanton, Domna, 247–248, 250, 258–259, 278
Stanton, Frank, 247–248, 278
Stapp, Blair, 158
Staub, Michael E., 44n85, 220n17
Stein, Andrew, 221
Stein, Jean, 257, 312n58
Steinem, Gloria, 126, 221, 221n25, 225n45, 257, 295
Stembridge, Jane, 15*i*, 15–16, 19–20, 39, 45n94
Stender, Fay, 152, 178–179, 304, 317, 334–335
Stennis, John, 77–78

Stern, Sol, 138n9
Stone, I. F., 67–69, 220
Strickland, William, 41–42, 67n36
Stronghold Consolidated/Stronghold Productions, 139n12, 313–315
Student Interracial Ministry (SIM), 104
Student Nonviolent Coordinating Committee (SNCC). *See also* Mississippi Summer Project
  and antiwar movement, 122n46
  approaches and strategies of, 8–18
  assumptions about class held by, 72–73
  Atlanta Project (Vine City Project), 100–104
  Black Panther Party's attempted merger with, 168–172
  divide between MFDP and, 72–73, 73n71
  expulsion of white staffers from, 102–104, 103n109
  "The Fairy Tale," 86
  fallout from adoption of Black Power, 106–109
  "floaters" *versus* "hardliners," 83–85
  formation of, 3–4
  and Freedom Summer, 47–52
  and Freedom Vote, 31–36
  fundraising for, 20, 20n68, 23, 40–41, 71, 86, 91–92, 102, 106–107, 106n134, 107n138, 108n142, 116, 311
  gender relations, 87, 87nn23–24, 90
  Hoffman's criticism of, 125n63
  impact of, 7–8, 7n1
  internal strife in, 81–89, 95–106
  interracialism of, 4–5, 10, 19–27, 36n43, 55–56, 76–77
  locals' doubts concerning, 72–74
  Lowndes County Freedom Organization (LCFO), 94–95, 94n61, 108, 108n143, 143
  mass meetings, 13
  Mississippi Summer Project and criticism over interracialism in, 36–42
  moving of goalposts of, 60, 88–89
  nationalist minority in, 100–106
  payroll costs of, 71–72, 71n60
  Peg Leg Bates meeting, 102–104
  position paper of, 101–102, 101n102
  post-Atlantic City challenges of, 71–72
  post-Atlantic City malaise in, 70–71
  post-Atlantic City objectives of, 72
  public perception of, 53
  racial conflict in, 89–91, 95–96
  recruitment of white students into, 40, 40n64
  redefinition of solidarity in, 42–45
  regional friction in, 54–55, 86
  research department, 23–24
  Southwest Georgia Project, 37–38, 55, 104
  staff numbers of, 36n43, 49n107
  turns away from coalitions with liberals, 69–75
  turn to Black Power, 91–97, 101–106, 105n132
  Waveland retreat, 81–91
  and white-on-white organizing, 97–100
  and white terror, 27–29, 69–70
Students for a Democratic Society (SDS), 34, 115–121, 122n46, 123n53, 124, 127, 133–134, 203
Subversive Activities Control Board, 261
Sullivan, Claudette, 329–330
Sullivan, Ed, 228
survival programs of Black Panther Party, 188n23, 188n24, 188–190
Sweeney, Dennis, 43, 113n2, 123

Tabor, Michael (Cetewayo), 309–310, 325, 328, 345
Taconic Foundation, 40–41
Tappis, Steve, 205–206
Tepperman, Jean, 125
Thalberg, Irving G. Jr., 181
Thelwell, Michael, 84–85, 102–104, 104n118, 107, 346
Third World Women's Alliance, 55n143
Thompson, Elsa Knight, 178, 300
Thompson, Hunter, 263–264, 281
Thompson, Kathleen, 109
Thorne, Richard, 144
Tillinghast, Muriel, 24–25, 50, 346
Till-Mobley, Mamie, 166–167
Time, 257
"Tiny Mummies!" (Wolfe), 266–268
Touré, Askia (Roland Snellings), 51n125
Treuhaft, Robert, 145
Truman, Harry, 60, 220–221
Trusty, Karen Haberman, 56n151

United Automobile Workers (UAF), xxii, 60–61, 63–64
United Farm Workers (UFW), 221, 290
United Front Against Fascism (UFAF), 201–202, 205, 295, 309
University of California–Berkeley, 116–117, 142–144
Unpossessed, The (Slesinger), 219
US, 173, 177

Vaisse, Justin, 274
Varela, Maria, 38–39, 346
Vega, Julia, 276
Vietnam War, xxii, 100–101, 122n46, 123n53, 127–129, 226, 309. *See also* antiwar movement
Vine City Project (Atlanta Project), 100–104
Visser-Maessen, Laura, 81n3
Voter Education Project, 40n66
voter registration, 27, 27n91, 101–102. *See also* Freedom Vote; Mississippi Summer Project
Voting Rights Act (1965), 53, 76

Wakefield, Dan, 224
Walker, Doris Bin, 316, 339
Walker, Pamela, 226n51
Wallace, George, 66–67
Wallace, Mike, 195
Walters, Barbara, 243–244, 248, 250–251
Warden, Donald, 92n44
Ware, Bill, 78
War Powers Act (1973), 308–309
Washington, Harold, 348–349
Washington Post, 248, 256, 269–270, 281
Waskow, Arthur, 68, 132, 307–308, 307n45
Wasserman, Steve, 144–145, 291–292, 345n13
Watts uprising (1965), 93–94, 106
Waveland retreat, 81–91
Weatherman, 203–210, 238, 305–306
Weems, Donald (Kuwasi Balagoon), 324
Weills, Anne, 128i, 149, 177–178, 214, 214n6, 303–304, 310–311, 312n58, 347
Weiner, Lee, 296i
Weinstein, Hannah, 234–239, 243, 250–251
Weinstein, Lisa, 243, 244n4

Weschler, James, 257
West, Cornel, 105
Whitaker, Mark, 101–102, 101n102
White, Ralph, 324, 326
White, Walter, 33n15
White Citizens' Councils, 97–98
White Folks Project, 97–99
white guilt, 56, 56n151, 126, 302
white-on-white organizing, xxv, 37, 97–100, 103, 121, 125, 132
white radicals. *See also* Progressive Labor (PL) Party; Students for a Democratic Society (SDS); Weatherman
  benefits and backlash from working with, 172–181
  and Black Panther Party, 161–162, 166, 300–310, 315–319
  Cleaver and, 157, 163
  and explosion of Movement, 124–130
  and National Conference for New Politics, 131–132
  and New Left, 115–120
  and organizing against one's own unfreedom, 113–114, 115–116, 120–130, 133–134
white terror, 27–29, 69–70
Wicker, Tom, 251
Wilkerson, Cathy, 203, 207i
Wilkins, Roger, 239, 249–250, 257, 297–298
Wilkins, Roy, 213–214
Williams, Robert F., 92–93, 141, 169
Willner, Phyllis, 188n23
Wilson, James Q., 284–285
Wilson, Joel, 164n6
Wilson, Wes, 150
Wittman, Carl, 118n18
Wolcott, James, 241
Wolfe, Tom, 269i. *See also* "Radical Chic: That Party at Lenny's" (Wolfe)
  appropriation of term "radical chic," 225–227, 226n51
  and benefit for Panther 21, 217, 248
  The Electric Kool-Aid Acid Test, 268–271
  and hostility to the left, 263–266, 268–270, 288
  and impact of "Radical Chic," 288
  and *New York Times*' coverage of benefit for Panther 21, 250–251, 255

Radical Chic and Mau-Mauing the Flak Catchers, 282, 286, 288–289
   representations of his relations with people of color, 268–270
   "Tiny Mummies!" 266–268
women's liberation, 55n143, 129–130, 301
Women's Trade Union League (WTUL), 218
Woodard, Komozi, 91n39
working-class theory, new 134
Wretched of the Earth (Fanon), 93
Wynn, Prathia Hall, 55

X, Malcolm, 93, 138, 142
X, Marvin, 157, 157n67

Yagoda, Ben, 266–267
Young, Andrew, 47*i*, 257
Young, Coleman, 297
Young Patriots, 190–191
Youth International Party (Yippie), 129, 185n16, 196–197

Zellner, Bob, 24*i*
   and Black Power, 95
   and expulsion of white SNCC staffers, 103n109, 103
   on infiltration of SNCC, 101n101
   and interracialism of SNCC, 26–27
   on Moses, 11
   post-Movement life of, 347
   SNCC's impact on, 5
   and white-on-white organizing, 97, 99–100
   and work of white SNCC staffers, 20–21
Zellner, Dottie, 24*i*
   and Black Power, 95
   and expulsion of white SNCC staffers, 103, 113
   on female volunteers, 53
   on information available to FOS, 85–86
   and LCFO emblem, 95
   post-Movement life of, 346
   and Summer Project, 41–42
   and work of white SNCC staffers, 24
Zimmerman, Bill, 307–309
Zinn, Howard, 13, 19, 83